OFFICERS WHO DIED
IN THE SERVICE OF
BRITISH COMMONWEALTH
AND COLONIAL NAVIES,
REGIMENTS AND CORPS
AND AIR FORCES
1914 - 1919

S.D. & D.B. Jarvis

The Naval & Military Press Ltd

Published by

The Naval & Military Press Ltd
Unit 10 Ridgewood Industrial Park,
Uckfield, East Sussex,
TN22 5QE England

Tel: +44 (0) 1825 749494
Fax: +44 (0) 1825 765701

www.naval-military-press.com
www.military-genealogy.com
www.militarymaproom.com

In reprinting in facsimile from the original, any imperfections are inevitably reproduced and the quality may fall short of modern type and cartographic standards.

Went the day well ? We died and never knew,
But, well or ill, Freedom, we died for you.

ANON.

INTRODUCTION

Volumes 1 and 11 of The Cross of Sacrifice Series have been acknowledged as the most significant contribution to expanding knowledge of the First World War to be published for a great number of years. The compilers have received tributes from all serious students of the conflict for their diligence and accuracy.

In this Volume Mr S.D. Jarvis and his Father, Mr D.B. Jarvis, have tackled the Commonwealth and Colonial contribution to the conflict. British Officers seconded to Colonial regiments are listed in Volume 1 of this series. The Commonwealth and Colonies made a substantial effort to support the cause often far beyond their size and capacity. Listed in this volume are the officers of Australia, Canada, New Zealand, South Africa, Newfoundland, Southern and Northern Rhodesia, The West Indies, Nyasaland, Seychelles, Malta, Honduras, Nigeria and East Africa. As in Volumes 1 and 11 detail is given from the War Graves Commission registers.

It must be appreciated that the conflict was so great, the numbers of deaths so enormous that no reference book on the subject of the Great War can be perfect. The information given at the time was subject to mis-spelling and of course mis-recording. For those who wish to research further, many opportunities exist.

Though small in number, the compilers have included in this volume the Officers of the fledgling Commonwealth Navies and Mercantile Marine plus those of their Air Forces.

Trevor J. Davies December 1994

How to Interpret the Information Given

Examples

ABBEY, Edgar George,	Lt Aust 38Inf kia 17.7.17. CR Belgium 42
SURNAME:	ABBEY
FIRST NAMES:	Edgar George
RANK:	Lieutenant
DECORATIONS:	None identified
CAUSE OF DEATH:	Killed in Action
DATE:	17.7.1917
UNIT:	Australian 38th Infantry
REGISTER:	CR Belgium 42 (see Appendix 1)

AITKIN, Andrew,	2Lt SA 4SAInf B'Coy kia 20.9.17. MR29 AITKEN
SURNAME:	AITKIN
FIRST NAMES:	Andrew
RANK:	2nd Lieutenant
DECORATIONS:	None
CAUSE OF DEATH:	Killed in Action
DATE:	20.9.1917
UNIT:	South African 4th Infantry B. Company
REGISTER:	MR 29 (see Appendix 1)
INFORMATION TAKEN FROM ALTERNATIVE SOURCES	Possible spelling AITKEN

CAMPBELL, Frederick William,	V.C. Capt Can 1Bn dow 19.6.15 CR France 102
SURNAME:	CAMPBELL
FIRST NAMES:	Frederick William
RANK:	Captain
DECORATIONS:	Victoria Cross
CAUSE OF DEATH:	Died of Wounds
DATE:	19.6.1915
UNIT:	Canadian 1st Battalion
REGISTER:	CR France 102 (see Appendix 1)

A

ABBEY,Edgar George — Lt Aust 38Inf kia 17-7-17 CR Belgium 42
ABBEY,Edwin Austin — Lt Can 4CMR kia 10-4-17 CR France 522
ABBOTT,C.F. — Lt SA 1CapeCps kia 6-11-17 CR Tanzania 1 &EAfrica 11
ABBOTT,Cecil James — Lt Can 78Bn 21-5-17CR France 81
ABBOTT,Edward Lyman.MC&Bar. — Capt Can52Bn kia 14-8-18 CR France 987
ABEL,Arthur Howard — 2Lt NZ 22519 2AIR kia 1-9-18 CR France 307
ABELL,Murray C. — Capt Can CAMC 5-3-20 CR Canada 1100
ABENDANA,Eric Montague — Lt Can 2BnCE ded 16-10-18 CR France 113
ABERNETHY,Kenneth Shorland — 2Lt NZ 14182 1/3NZRB dow 16-8-17 CR Belgium 339
ABERNETHY,Reginald McClure — 2Lt Aust AFA 5Bde kia 22-5-18 CR France 885
ACHESON,Dudley Alan Herbert — Lt Can 54Bn (BCR)5-11-16MR 23
ACKERMAN,Arthur Ross.MC. — Lt Can1LTMB dow 11-10-16 CR Canada 1380
ACKHURST,George — 2Lt NZ 18207 1WIR kia 4-10-17 MR 30
ADAIR,Hamilton John — HMaj Can CAMC 3GenHosp 13-12-18 CR France 34
ADAM,James — Lt Aust 44Inf kia 26-8-18 CR France 626
ADAMS,Alfred Roy — Lt Can CFA 3Bde dow 17-10-18 CR Surrey 1
ADAMS,Athol Gladwyn — Lt Aust 5Inf attAFC 67Sqn dedacc 19-2-17 CR Egypt 1
ADAMS,Bramwell George — Lt Aust 9Bn 25-2-17MR 26
ADAMS,Cedric Gilbert.MID — Lt NZ 2/180 NZFA dow 11-10-16 CR Hamps 30
ADAMS,Charles Cecil Ogden Macfee — Lt Can 16Bn 13-6-16MR 29
ADAMS,Coleman Boyd — Lt Can 1Bn kia 15-8-17 CR France 161
ADAMS,Dorney — Lt Can 38Bn dow 2-9-18 CR France 95
ADAMS,Edward.MC. — Capt Aust 30Inf kia 18-3-18 CR Belgium 48
ADAMS,Francis Charles Somerset — Capt Aust AIF AAMC 29-4-21CR Aust 85
ADAMS,Joseph Dorney — Lt Can 38Bn 1918
ADAMS,Joseph Francis — 2Lt Aust 35Inf kia 12-10-17 CR Belgium 125
ADAMS,Loring Brooks — Lt Can 5ATCoy (Rnfcement pool Can Engrs) 22-6-18 CR France 792
ADAMS,Raymond — 2Lt Aust 12Bn 6-5-17 MR 26
ADAMS,William Affleck.DSO.MID — Maj Aust 3Pnrs kia 15-10-17 CR Belgium 84
ADAMS,William Holloway — Capt Can7Bn 15-4-18CR Sussex 200
ADDIS-BLACK,Thomas Charles — Lt Aust RAN Bridging Train ded 7-4-16 MR 41
ADDISON,Alphonse Colenbrander — 2Lt SA 2SAInf kia 12-10-16 MR 21
ADDISON,Ernest Colenbrander — 2Lt SA 2SAInf kia 4-5-18 MR 29
ADDISON,William Emmott — 2Lt Aust 18Inf kia 22-8-15 MR 6
ADDY,Edward — Lt Aust 9Inf ded 18-8-15 CR Europe 1
ADES,S.A. — Lt Aust 35Inf 22-8-18CR France 642
ADIE,John McClelland — Lt Can 1MMGBde 3-11-18CR France 1196
ADLER,Gustave — Capt SA SAMC ded 14-2-18 CR SAfrica 52
ADOLPH,Victor Emiel.MC. — 2Lt NZ 13/225 ICC NZ'Coy dow 31-3-18 CR Syrias 2
AGAR,Egan Zinkan — Capt Can 9RBn &RAF 54Sqn kia 13-4-18 CR France 346
AGAR,Harold Edward — Lt Can PPCLI A'Coy kia 13-10-17 MR 29
AGER,George Samuel — Lt Can 16Bn 22-4-15MR 29
AGGETT,William — Lt Aust 9Bn 23-7-16MR 26
AGGETT,William Harvey — Lt Can 4Bn (1COR) kia 6-11-17 MR 29
AGNEW,Augustus Wateous — Maj Can 3PnrBn 17-9-16CR France 59
AHERN,Timothy Patrick — Lt Aust 54Inf kia 19/20-7-16CR France 255
AHNALL,Karl.DCM. — 2Lt Aust 28-Inf ded PoW 2-3-17 CR France 927
AIRD,William Douglas — Lt Can 44Bn 26-10-17 CR Belgium 123 10Bn
AIREY,Frederick Arthur — Lt NZ 30102 OIR 2 OtagoR dow 30-9-17 CR Belgium 11
AISTON,Colin James — Lt Aust AFA 6Bde dow 22-9-17 CR France 102
AITCHISON,Alexander William.MC. — Lt Can 13Bn dow 13-5-16 CR Belgium 11
AITKEN,James Murray.MC. — Lt Aust 11Bn 10-8-18MR 26
AITKEN,Robert Frederick — Lt Can 78Bn 9-4-17 CR France 549
AITKEN,Robert James — Capt Can 1Bn (MR) 13-6-16MR 29
AITKIN,Andrew — 2Lt SA 4SAInf B'Coy kia 20-9-17 MR 29 AITKEN
ALBRIGHT,Solon — Lt Can 15Bn dow 9-8-18 CR France 29

ALCOCK,Augustus	2Lt Can RNewfndlandR kia 14-4-17 MR 10
ALCOCK,Frank	2Lt SA RhodR att3/2KAR 3-9-17 CR EAfrica 8
ALDERSON,G.L.MC.	Lt SA 12Inf ded 11-8-16 CR EAfrica 1
ALDRIDGE,Arthur George	Lt NZ 12/1875 AIR 6Coy dow 10-8-15 MR 6
ALDRIDGE,Joseph George	Rev SA YMCA attSA Bde 8-10-18 CR France 844
ALEXANDER,Charles Henry	Lt Aust 9LtTMB kia 8-6-17 CR Belgium 110
ALEXANDER,Gavin Douglas.DCM.MIDx	2Lt NZ 4/513 NZE dow 15-9-16 CR France 188
ALEXANDER,John	Lt Can 25NSR 1-10-16 MR 23
ALFORD,Gordon Beresford	2Lt Aust1Inf dow 12-8-16 CR London 26
ALGIE,Colvin Stewart	Capt NZ 12/294 2AIR kia 21-7-16 CR France 922 20-7-16
ALGIE,Wallace Lloyd.VC.	Lt Can 20Bn kia 11-10-18 CR France 761
ALKENBRACK,Ibri Burton	Lt Can 75Bn 2-9-18 CR France 426
ALLAN,Andrew Robert	Lt Aust 40Inf dow 10-1-17 CR France 285
ALLAN,Charles Victor	Lt Can CFA 8ABde 31-8-18 CR France 1195
ALLAN,Edward Blake	Lt Can 16Bn 3-6-16 CR Belgium 127
ALLAN,George Ernest	2Lt Aust 53Inf kia 19-7-16 MR 7
ALLAN,Gerald Archbold	Lt Aust19Inf kia 5-6-18 CR France 209
ALLAN,James Robert	HCapt Can 8Bn att3DivSigCoy 20-9-16 CR France 430
ALLAN,Myrton Trangmar	Lt Aust 20Inf dow 27-7-16 CR France 515
ALLAN,William Donald.DSO.	LtCol Can 3Bn ded 1-10-16 CR Canada 1688
ALLAN,John	2Lt NZ 6/14461 AIR kia 27-3-18 CR France 156
ALLAN,Morton McLeod	Lt Aust 12Inf 20-9-17 MR 29
ALLAN,Robert James.MC.MM.	Lt Can 14Bn 11-8-18 CR France 693
ALLAN,Thoburn Stephen .MC.	Capt Can RCR 26-8-18 CR France 1189 Stephens
ALLAN,Thomas A.	Lt Can 19Bn 8-8-18 CR France 424
ALLARDYCE,George Gilmour	Lt Aust4Inf dow 18-5-18 CR Eire 24
ALLEN,Alexander	Chpn4Cl NZ48144 Chpns attNZRB 4Bn 3Bde kia 8-5-18 CR France 63
ALLEN,Angus Sutherland.MC.	Capt Aust 4Inf dow 21.7.18 CR France 134
ALLEN,Arthur Spencer.MC.	Capt Can 18Bn &RFC 9Sqn 30-4-17 MR 20
ALLEN,Bertram Kerr	Lt Can 21Bn 15-9-16 CR France 1505
ALLEN,Geoffrey Dunster	Lt AustAFC dedacc 3-7-18 CR Glouc 172
ALLEN,Harold Gordon	2Lt NZ12/686 AIR 16Coy kia 25-4-15 CR Gallipoli 10
ALLEN,Henry	2Lt Aust 3Inf dow 7-8-15 CR Gallipoli 30
ALLEN,Hilton Bede	Lt Aust 45Inf kia 7-6-17 CR Belgium 168
ALLEN,John	2Lt Aust 13Bn 29-8-16 MR 26
ALLEN,John Candish	Lt NZ 24304 AIR 2AuklandR dow 19-10-17 CR Belgium 16
ALLEN,Lionel Arthur Singleton	Lt Can 38Bn 30-9-18 CR France 113
ALLEN,Reginald Arthur Sinclair	CaptCan 5Bn dow 30-4-15 CR France 102
ALLEN,Reginald Harold	2Lt NZ 6/941 2CIR kia 2-10-16 CR France 385
ALLEN,Samuel Hall	Lt Can 212Bn &RFC 12-10-17 CR Belgium 383
ALLEN,T.M.	Cdt Aust 1313 AFC 27-4-17 CR Surrey 80
ALLEN,Victor William.MC.MM.	2Lt SA 4SAInf &RAF 103Sqn mbk 9-6-18 CR France 360
ALLEN,William Alexander	Lt Can 58Bn 18-4-17 CR France 68
ALLEN,William Robert	Lt Aust 57Inf kia 1-2-17 CR France 400
ALLEY,Eric Buckingham.MID.	Capt NZ 9/239 2OIR dow 17-6-16 CR France 285
ALLIN,Elton Culbert	Lt Can 44Bn 9-5-17 CR France 81
ALLISON,Cecil Howarth Malbon.MID.	Lt NZ 11/489 WMR dow 9-12-17 CR Palest 9
ALLISON,Ernecliffe Paley	2Lt Aust 18Bn 4-8-16 MR 26
ALLISON,John Oliver.MC.	Lt Can 4RBn (WOR) &RAF 30Sqn 15-5-18 MR 38
ALLWORTH,Parker Roy	Lt Aust AFA 8Bde kia 5-6-17 CR France 262
ALMAS,Ernest Norval	Lt Can 38Bn dow 31-10-17 CR Belgium 11
ALMON,John E.	Lt Can PPCLI 30-10-17 CR Belgium 123
ALPAUGH,Agnes Estelle	Nurse Can CAMC ded 12-10-18 CR Canada 342
ALPORT,Jean Ogilvie	Nurse Can 4GenHosp 1918
ALTHOUSE,E.	Lt Aust 53Inf 30-9-18 CR France 446
AMBERY,C.L.F.	Capt Can 3Bn(1COR) 20-9-16 CR France 1505
AMBERY,George Edward	Lt Can 50Bn kia 3-6-17 CR France 58
AMBROSE,Kenneth Duncan	2Lt NZ 23/1302 3MGC kia 15-9-16 CR France 389
AMPHLETT,Frank	Capt Aust 35Inf 12-10-17 MR 29
AMSDEN,William George	Lt Can 4Bn 8-8-18 CR France 652
ANCELL,Eric Guest	2Lt NZ14349 2AIR kia 19-10-16 CR France 922
ANDERSON,Albert Mendelssohn	2Lt AustAFC 71Sqn kia 6-1-18 CR France 258

ANDERSON,Albert Naples	Lt Aust ALH dow 25-4-17 CR Egypt 2
ANDERSON,Alfred William	Lt Can 38Bn 29-9-18CR France 715
ANDERSON,Andrew	Lt Aust 7AMGC 20-9-17MR 29
ANDERSON,Charles Alexander	2Lt SA 3SAInf dow 19-7-18 CR France 25
ANDERSON,David Stewart	Lt Can 20Bn 28-6-16CR Belgium 11
ANDERSON,Edward Handfield	2Lt Aust57Inf kia 20-7-16 MR 7
ANDERSON,Enderby Gordon	Capt Aust AASC 12Coydow 29-7-15 MR 6
ANDERSON,Frederick Andrew	Lt NZ 15445 2CIR kia 1-10-16 MR 9 7-6-17
ANDERSON,Frederick John	Lt Can85Bn (NSR)28-10-17 MR 29
ANDERSON,G.L.MC.	Lt SA12SAInf dow 12-8-16
ANDERSON,Hugh Caldwell	Lt/Capt Can 2CRT 11-8-17CR Belgium 5
ANDERSON, Hugh Graham	Lt Can 7Bn dow 22-10-18 CR France 13 Hew
ANDERSON,John	Lt Can 116Bn 8-8-18 CR France 485
ANDERSON,John Gibson.MC.MID	Maj Can5Bn (SR) kia 10-11-17 MR 29
ANDERSON,Kenneth Henry	2Lt Aust 15Inf kia 9-5-15 CR Gallipoli 31
ANDERSON,Kieran Leopold	Lt Aust 16Inf kia 2-5-15 MR 6
ANDERSON,Leo William Hall	Lt Aust kia kia 7-8-15 CR Gallipoli 29
ANDERSON,Lou Donald Miller	Lt Can 15Bn ded 18-10-18 CR Canada1 690
ANDERSON,Patrick Sinclair.MID	2LtAust 4Infdow 30-4-15 CR Egypt 3
ANDERSON,Percival William.MC.	Maj Can 85Bn (NSR) kia 28-10-17 MR 29
ANDERSON,Ralph	Capt Aust 52Inf dow 8-6-17 CR Belgium 90
ANDERSON,Renwick William Hunter	Lt Can 10Bn kia 27-9-18 CR France 147
ANDERSON,Roy	Lt Aust AIF 7Inf 14-1-19CR Aust 322
ANDERSON,Thomas	Lt SA 3SAH kia 8-9-16 CR EAfrica 39
ANDERSON,Tully Wallace.DCM.	Lt Can 44Bn dow 4-6-17 CR France 12
ANDERSON,W.	Lt SA 6SAInf kia 10-8-16 CR Tanzania 1 &EAfrica 9
ANDERSON,William Kay.MC.	Lt Can RTC EORD 1918
ANDERTON,Edward	Lt EA EA CensorDept ded 30-11-18 CR EAfrica 19
ANDREW,Patrick John Alexander	Capt Can 5Bn 15-8-18CR France 361
ANDREW, Wilfred Bissell	Lt Can 1CORD SecdRFC 12-2-18CR France 1678
ANDREWS,Gordon Stewart	Lt Can CFA 18-11-15 CR Canada 1694
ANGOVE,Edward Lawrence	Lt Aust 10Inf kia 23-8-18 CR France 526
ANGWIN,B.MC.	Lt Aust 28Inf 5-12-19CR Aust 456
ANNEAR,Harold Norman	Capt Aust 6Inf dow 5-10-17 Belgium 5
ANNEAR,William Richard	Capt Aust 11Inf kia 25-4-15 MR 6
ANNIS,Wilbur Fawcett	Lt Can RAF 58Bn 1918
ANNONI,Joseph	2Lt Aust 13Inf kia 27-8-15 MR 6
ANQUETIL,Henry Stewart.MM&Bar	2Lt Aust MGC 2Coy kia 4-10-17 CR Belgium 22
ANSELL,Herbert Abraham	2Lt Aust 8AMGC kia 23-10-16 CR France 744
ANSLEY,Alfred James	Maj Can 15Bn 14-10-16 MR 23
ANSLOW,Roy	Lt Aust 53Inf kia 1-9-18 CR France 511
ANTILL,A.E.J.	2Lt SA 1CapeCps dow 21-9-18 CR Palest 3
APJOHN,Frank James	Lt Can CGA 8Bty3Bde dow 6-8-18 CR France 29
APPELBE,Ernest Francis	Capt Can 198Bn ded 4-4-16 CR Canada 1517
APPLEBY,Arthur Harold	Capt Aust 12Bn 6-5-17 MR 26
APPLEBY,Norman.MM&Bar.	Lt Can 31Bn 29-3-17MR 23
APPLEBY,Wilfred Lawson	Capt Aust 18Inf kia 20-9-17 CR Belgium 115
APPLEGARTH,Gordon Henry.MC.	Capt Can 19Bn 27-8-18CR France 162
APPLETON,Frederick William	Lt Aust 14Inf kia 8-8-18 CR France 699
APPLETON,William Trail	2Lt Aust 7Inf kia 24-7-16 CR France 699
APPS,Charles	Lt Can 2CMR 2-1-18 CR France 223
ARAM,John Thomas Hamilton	Capt Aust 57Inf 25-9-17MR 29
ARBLASTER,Charles	Capt Aust 53Inf ded 24-7-16 CR France 1276
ARBUCKLE,John Farafee	Lt Can 31Bn 26-9-16MR 23
ARCHBALD,Frederick F.	Lt Can 60Bn dow 17-10-16 CR Canada 256
ARCHER,Howard Allen	Capt Can 8Bn 24-1-18CR France 223
ARCHIBALD,John Arnold	Lt Aust 11Inf dow 24-9-18 CR France 446
ARCUS,William Norton.MID.	Lt NZ 4/520 Engrs kia 11-10-17 CR Belgium 35
ARDAGH,Arthur Halford	Capt Can 20Bn kia 10-5-17 CR France 557
ARDEN,Neville Henry.MID.	Capt NZ 23/1288 3OIR kia 4-10-17 CR Belgium 125
ARDIFF,James Henry	Lt Can 26Bn ded 26-2-21 CR Canada 1054
ARMITAGE,Harold Edwin Salisbury.MID.	Capt Aust 50Infkia 3-4-17 CR France 1488

ARMITAGE,Reginald Montague	2Lt Aust 47Bn 11-4-17MR 26
ARMOUR,John Douglas.OBE.MID	Maj CanCFA 2Bde 21-2-19CR Surrey 1
ARMSTRONG,Athol Langford	Lt SA 8Horse 25-11-18 CR Bedfordshire 71
ARMSTRONG,Donald Goldsmith	2Lt Aust 21Inf kia 9-10-17 CR Belgium 126
ARMSTRONG,Francis Leofric.MID.	Lt Aust 15Inf kia 10-5-15 CR Gallipoli 8
ARMSTRONG,Geoffrey Clifford Wilson	Capt NZ 12/3216 2AIR 3Coy kia 15-9-16 CR France 389
ARMSTRONG,George	Lt Aust 2Pnrs kia 18-12-17 CR France 297
ARMSTRONG,Hutton Perkins	Lt Aust 15Inf kia 10-5-15 MR 6
ARMSTRONG,John Douglas	Lt Can Engrs 11FCkia 9-4-17 CR France 81
ARMSTRONG,Paul Lindon	Lt Can 73Bn 29-10-16 CR France 430
ARMSTRONG,Purvis Ford	Lt Can 26Bn B'Coy (NBR) dow 6-11-17 MR 29
ARMSTRONG,Thomas.MM.	Lt Can FA 2Bde 18-2-18CR France12
ARMSTRONG,Thomas Acheson	Lt Aust 33Inf 12-10-17 MR 29
ARMSTRONG,William Robinson	Lt Can 78Bn kia 8-8-18 CR France 652
ARNALL,Harry Frood	Maj Aust AIF 2Pnrs 14-8-20CR Aust 112
ARNOLD Arthur James	2Lt NZ 40744 1CIR dow 27-8-18 CR France 84
ARNOLD,Ralph Irving	2Lt Aust15Bn AIF 8-8-16 MR 26 &CR France 390
ARNOLD,William Henry.MID	2Lt Aust 21Inf dow 17-11-16 CR France 385
ARNOLDI,Ernest Clifton	LtCol Can CFA 2ArtyBdeHQ ded 11-6-18 CR Canada 1245
ARNOTT,Alexander Montgomery Wilson	Lt Can 8CRT 6-8-17 CR France 285
ARNOTT,Bruce Hardy	Capt Aust 52Inf kia 18-8-17 CR Belgium 17
ARUNDEL,Henry.MM.	2Lt Aust 16Inf kia 26-9-17 CR Belgium 125
ASCHE,Frithoy Harold	Lt Aust 41Inf kia 31-1-17 CR France 922
ASHCROFT,Lancelot Edgar	Lt Can 54Bn kia 9-4-17 CR France 81
ASHER,John Henry	Lt Aust AFA 11Bde kia 2-9-17 CR France 285
ASHMEAD,Cyril Garfield John.MC.	Lt Aust 37Bn 30-8-18MR 26
ASHPLANT,William Norman	Maj Can 1Bn 22-9-16MR 23
ASHTON,Sidney Charles	Capt NZ 13283 AMR kia 31-10-17 CR Palest 1
ASPINALL,William Robert.MC.	Capt Aust AMC 1FA kia 20-7-17 CR Belgium 15
ASTBURY,Neville Ayrton	Lt Can 49Bn 16-9-16MR 23
ATCHISON,George Milton	HCapt Can DR CMR 15-4-18CR Canada 1245
ATHERTON,William Joseph.MC.	Capt Can 5CMR 26-8-18CR France 419
ATKIN,John Percy Hume	Lt Can CFA 4Bde 4-2-19 CR Belgium 267
ATKINS,Harold Augustus Randolph	2Lt Aust 1Bn 23-7-16MR 26
ATKINSON,Bertram	Lt Aust 23Inf kia 21-9-15 CR Gallipoli 7
ATKINSON,Charles Herbert	Lt Can 110Bn 1922
ATKINSON,Clifford Bowen	2Lt Aust 21Bn 5-5-17 MR 26
ATKINSON,Edward Huon	2Lt Aust AIF 12ALH 23-7-18CR Aust 262
ATKINSON,Ernest Andrew Campbell	2Lt Aust 9AMGC 13-10-17 MR 29
ATKINSON,James Victor.MID	Capt Aust 49Inf kia 5-4-18 CR France 177
ATKINSON,Joseph Henry	Lt Can CFA 3Bde CHA 22-10-16 CR India 97A
ATKINSON,Samuel Arnold	Lt/TCapt NZ 14714 RB 2Bn 3Bde D'Coykia 5-6-17 CR Belgium 48
ATTWOOD,Henry	2Lt Aust 7Inf kia 20-9-17 CR Belgium 115
ATWILL,Joseph	Lt NZ 14901 2OIR kia 1-10-16 MR 11
AUBRY,Joseph Eugene	Lt Can 22Bn ded 1-11-19 CR Canada 254 H.
AUCHTERLONIE,Archibald Vivian	Lt Aust 25Inf kia 20-10-15 CR Gallipoli 18
AUCHTERLONIE,Cecil Arthur.MC&Bar.	Lt Aust 25Inf kia 10-8-18 CR France 526
AUDY,Prosper John Theodore	Lt Can 2CMR kia 28-7-16 CR Belgium 5
AUGER,Albert Raymond.OBE.	HCapt Can 11DistCFC 1919
AULD,Ernest William	Lt CanCE 3DivSigCoy kia 7-8-18 CR France 303
AULD,F.A.	2Lt SA 2SAInf kia 8-1-18 CR France 439
AUSTIN,Colin Douglas	Maj Aust 3Inf kia 6/8-8-15 CR Gallipoli 7
AVARD,David Henry.MC.	2Lt Aust19Bn 3-5-17 MR 26
AVERY,Wifred Perceval	Capt Aust 1TC kia 25-4-17 CR Belgium 5
AWREY,Le Roy Eaton	Lt Can 1BnCMGC kia 30-8-18 CR France 532
AYERS,Sydney Winton	Lt Aust AFC dow 24-11-17 CR France 245
AYLEN,Cyril Keith	Lt Can FA 7Bde kia 19-4-16 CR Belgium 28
AYLING,Arthur Bernard	2Lt NZ 23/58 1/3NZRB B'Coy dow 4-11-18 CR France 206
AYRE,Eric S.	Capt Can 1RNewfndlandR kia 1-7-16 CR France 339
AYRE,Gerald W	2Lt Can RNewfndlandR kia 1-7-16 MR 10
AYRE,Wilfrid D.	2Lt Can 1RNewfndlandRkia 1-7-16 CR France 220
AYTOUN,Frederic Ernest	Maj Can 1Bn 22-9-16CR France 430

B

BABCOCK,Andrew Enos   Lt   Can   18Bn   1922
BACKHUS, Reginald John   Lt   Can   29Bn   9-8-18 CR France 649 BACKHOUSE
BACKMAN,Percival Stanley   Lt   Aust 6Inf 4-10-17MR 29
BADDELEY,Herman Stuart   Lt NZ12/688 AIR 16Coy   kia 25-4-15 MR 6
BADDILEY,Augustus George   2Lt NZ 12/17   AuklandR   ded   19-11-18 CR NZ 257
BADGER,Archibald James Robert Lt Can 5Bn   kia 1-9-18   CR France 688
BAENSCH,Herbert Ernest   Lt Aust 58Inf kia 22-6-18 CR France 195
BAGE,Edward Frederick Robert Capt   Aust Engrs 3FC   kia 7-5-15   CR Gallipoli 30
BAIGENT,Cyril Victor   Maj NZ 3/314   NZMC   ded 9-1-23
BAIGENT,Ivanhoe Edward   2Lt NZ22618   WMR dow 14-11-17 CR Palest 9
BAILEY,Basil Wilberforce   Lt Can   72Bn 9-2-18 CR France 81
BAILEY,Daniel McGuinness W.   Lt   Aust 9Inf   3-11-17MR 29
BAILEY,Francis William Samuel Lt   Aust   51Bn3-9-16 MR 26
BAILEY,Guy Brooke.MID.   Capt Aust52Inf kia 28-3-17 CR France 1484
BAILEY,Henry   LtCol   Aust   9Inf   8-5-16 CR Aust 146
BAILEY,Joseph Panet MM.   Lt Can 38Bn kia 2-9-18   CR France 426 Paget
BAILEY,Roy.MC.   Capt   Can 3Bn   8-8-18 CR France 488
BAILEY,Walter Leslie   Lt   Aust5Pnrs   dow 10-5-18 CR France 71
BAILLIE,George Irvine   Lt Can 5CMR   8-8-18 CR France 485
BAILLIE,William Sharpe   Lt Can 87Bn 13-5-18CR France 95
BAIN,Archibald Cockburn.MC.   Lt Can 75Bn   kia 2-9-18 CR France 426
BAIN,J.T.   Capt   SA 1SAInf   kia 20-9-17 MR 29
BAIN,John   Lt   Can 3MGC dow 11-11-17 CR Belgium 16
BAIN,John Scott.MID   Lt Can 13Bn ded   3-2-19   CR France 34
BAIN,John Sinclair   Lt   NZ 10/1730   WIR   kia 8-8-15   MR 5
BAIN,William Alexander   2Lt   NZ 8/2251   4\1OIR   dow 28-9-16 CR France 833
BAINES,Egerton Bancks   Lt Can4Bn (1COR) kia 27-7-16 MR 29
BAIRD,Alexander Watson.MC&Bar. Capt   Can 116Bn 8-8-18 CR France 485
BAIRD,Andrew Stuart   Lt   Can 14Bn   kia 8-8-18   CR France 488
BAIRD,James.MC.   Lt Can   87Bn   dow 23-11-18 CR France 146
BAKER,Basil Rupert   HCapt&QM Can CAMC 22Bn 7-5-17 CR Kent 28
BAKER,Charles Talbot   Lt Can 49Bn   29-9-18CR France 481
BAKER,Charles William   Capt   Can CAVC   10-1-17CR London 2
BAKER,Edith Agnes   SNurse   SASAMNS 1SAGHded   6-11-18 CR France 52
BAKER,Franklin Colin   Lt Can 20Bn 9-8-17 CR France 480
BAKER,George Harold   LtCol   Can5CMR   kia 2-6-16   CR Belgium 5
BAKER,Harry Charles   Capt   Can16Bn 26-9-16MR 23
BAKER,Henry Aylesworth   Lt Can 31Bn (AR)6-11-17MR 29
BAKER,Horace Greely   Maj Can 46Bn   20-8-17CR France 81
BAKER,Horace Morgan   Capt   Aust AFA 1Bde ded   11-4-16 CR France 1571
BAKER,Margaret Elisa   Sister   Can   CAMC   ded 30-5-19 CR Canada 1208
BAKER,Miriam Eastman   Nurse Can CAMC 15GenHosp 17-10-18 CR Bucks 54
BAKER,Spencer   Lt Can   46Bn   26-10-17 CR Belgium 123
BAKER,Thomas Charles Richmond.DFC. Capt MM&Bar Aust AFC 4Sqn   kia 4-11-18 CR Belgium 367
BAKER,Thomas Massey   Lt   Can 10Bn C'Coykia 15-11-16 CR France 81
BAKER,William James   Capt   SARhodNatR dow 29-3-17   CR EAfrica 40
BAKER,Wallace Westerfield   2Lt   Aust 10Inf AIF22-8-16MR26 CR France 390
BAKER,William Alton.MM.   Lt   Can 5Bn   17-2-19CR France 40
BALCOM,Harold Cecil   Lt Can69Regt   dedacc 12-12-17 CR Canada 622
BALDIE,William David   2Lt   Aust 24Inf   kia 5-10-18 CR France 443
BALDWIN,Dorothy Mary Yarwood Nurse   Can CANS 3StatHosp   30-5-18CR France 84
BALFE,Joseph Rupert   Lt Aust 6Inf kia 25-4-15   MR 6
BALL,Albert Ransome   Lt   Can 10Bn   dow 29-4-15 CR Canada 360
BALL,Ernest Smyth   Lt Can   7CRT   dow 31-7-17 CR Belgium 7
BALL,George Beverly   WTO   Can `Seagull' 1918
BALL,Sidney Haskell   Lt Can HQCFC   ded   17-9-18 CR France 40
BALLACHEY,Panayoly Percy   Maj   Can 58Bn   14-6-16CR Belgium 5 Panayoty

5

BALLARD,Albert Edward	2Lt Aust 42Inf dow 19-10-17 CR Belgium 11
BANCROFT,Thomas	Lt SA 2SAInf kia 21-3-18 MR 27 &MR 29
BANFIELD,Leonard John	Capt Aust 18Inf kia 22-8-15 MR 6
BANFIELD,Thomas Henry	Lt Can 54Bn 9-4-17 CR France 81
BANKIER,Samuel	Lt Aust 4Bn 16-4-18MR 26
BANKS,Harry.MC.	Lt Can 102Bn 2COR 17-10-18 CR France 34
BANKS,Henry Dunbar	Lt NZ 33098 2WIR kia 4-11-18 CR France 1077
BANKS,Kenneth George	Lt Aust 7Inf ded 3-3-19 CR Belgium 330
BANKS,Robert James	Lt Can 43Bn (MR) 26-10-17 MR 29
BANNER,Albert	2Lt Aust 60Inf 27-9-17MR 29
BANNERMAN,James William Hugh	Lt NZ 46912 WIR 2 OtagoR dow 23-12-17 CR Belgium 11 kia
BANNISTER,Herbert Stanley	Lt Can 50B n &RAF 21-6-18CR France 102 10Bn
BARBER,Percy Louis	Lt Can 21Bn kia 3-11-17 CR Belgium 125
BARBER,Ralph Evan	2Lt Aust 28Bn 18-11-16 MR 26
BARCLAY,Clifford Clapcott	2Lt NZ 6/404 CIR kia 25-4-15 MR 6 Lt
BARCLAY,Lindsay Trail	Lt Can 58Bn 8-10-16MR 23
BARDER,Rothwell Oliver	Lt Aust 20Inf dow 18-9-16 CR Belgium 11
BARKER,Arthur Richard	Lt Aust 22Inf kia 24-4-18 CR France 199
BARKER,David Jellett	Lt Can 87Bn kia 27-9-17 CR France 81
BARKER,Rollo William	2Lt Aust AHA 36HAG dow 27-2-18 CR France 297
BARLOW,Arthur Eldred Dight	Lt Aust FA 6Bde kia 28-5-17 CR Belgium 136
BARLOW,John Edgar	Lt Aust 3Inf kia 6/8-8-15 CR Gallipoli 7
BARLOW,Sydney William	LtCol Aust 11ALH 15-12-19 CR Aust 206
BARLOW,Wilfred Griffith	Lt Aust 58Bn 12-5-17MR 26
BARNARD,Gilbert Richard	Lt SA 1CapeCps ded 22-7-16 CR Palest 3
BARNARD,L.C.	Maj SA CapeAuxHorseTrCps ded 10-1-18
BARNARD,Norman Francis Watts	Lt Aust 1Pnrs kia 11-8-17 CR Belgium 15
BARNES,Charles Albert.MID	Capt Aust 11Inf kia 28-4-15 MR 6
BARNES,Ethel	Sister NZ 22/101 ANS ded 27-7-23
BARNES,Frank Eugene	2Lt Aust 15Bn 11-4-17MR 26
BARNES,Jack Harry Frogley	2Lt Aust 46Inf dow 8-5-17 CR France 145
BARNES,John Henry.MC&Bar.	Lt Can 44Bn 2-11-18CR France 146
BARNES,Reginald Brooke	Lt Can 18Bn 15-9-16MR 23
BARNES,Rennie Hamilton	Lt Can 31Bn 11-10-18 CR France 761
BARNES,Robert William Otty	Lt Can 26Bn 16-1-17MR 23
BARNES,Vincent Samuel	2Lt Aust 33Inf kia 3-2-18 CR Belgium 42
BARNES,Wilfred Robert.MC.	Lt Can 31Bn 3-5-17 CR France 557
BARNES,William Edward	Lt Can NewfndlandR dow 13-4-18 CR France 40
BARNETT,Frederick George	Capt Aust 17Inf kia 2-8-18 CR France 1170
BARNETT,Lionel Tom	Lt Aust 9Inf dow 25-2-17 CR France 744
BARNFATHER,Andrew Ernest Ralph	2Lt Aust 58Inf kia 19-7-16 MR 7
BARR,James Stevenson	Lt Can 52Bn 21-10-16 CR France 40
BARR,John Haddin.MID.	Lt NZ 6/3525 2OIR dow 15/16-9-16CR France 188
BARRATT,Reginald Frank	Lt Aust FA 1Bde dow 22-8-17 CR Belgium 165
BARRETT,H.G.MM.	2Lt Can 1NewfndlandR 16-8-17MR 30
BARRETT,Joseph Frank.DCM.	2Lt Aust 51Bn 24-4-18MR 26
BARRETT,Rupert Sunderland	Lt Aust 8Inf kia 25-4-15 CR Gallipoli 7
BARRIE,Thomas Brown.MC&Bar.	Capt Can72Bn att3InfBdeHQ 2-10-18CR France 214
BARRON,Joseph	Lt Aust FA 53Bty 14Bde kia 31-7-17 CR Belgium 11
BARRY,Charles Lucien Maurice	Lt Can 22Bn 1919
BARRY,Owen Cressy	Lt Aust RFC 4Sqn 11-5-18MR 26
BARTER,Henry	Lt Aust 45Inf kia 23-11-16 CR France 277
BARTLE,Deane Stanley	Lt Can75Bn 24-8-16CR Belgium 37
BARTLE,Leonard Hamilton	Lt Aust 19Inf dow 1-11-17 CR France 40
BARTLE,Thomas William	2Lt Aust AFC 69Sqn dedacc 15-6-17 CR Lancs 308
BARTLETT,Albert Therburn	Lt Aust AIF 57Inf17-9-19CR Aust 325
BARTLETT,Bertha	Nurse Can Newfndland VAD ded 3-12-18 CR London 1
BARTLETT,James Stanley Forbes	Lt Aust 3Bn 25-7-16MR 26
BARTLETT,Rupert W.MC&Bar	Capt Can RNewfndlandR kia 30-11-17 MR 10
BARTLETT,Walter Harry	Lt Can 27Bn 14-9-16MR 23
BARTLEY,R.V.	2Lt Aust AFC 3-7-18 CR Hamps 4

BARTLEY,Thomas James	2Lt Aust 42Inf kia 10-6-17 CR Belgium 108
BARTON,Alfred Richard	2Lt SA 3SAInf kia 20-7-16 MR 21 18-7-16
BARTON,Francis Maxwell	Capt Aust 13Inf kia 11-8-16 CR France 742
BARTON,Harold Pryor	Lt Aust 2Inf kia 23-5-15 CR Gallipoli 7
BARTON,Irvine Julius.MC.	Lt Aust 52Inf dow 5-4-18 CR France 44
BARTON,Robert Anthony	Lt Aust 45Inf 9-6-17 MR 29
BASEDOW,Fritz Newton.MC.	Lt Aust31Inf dow 25-4-18 CR France 145
BASSON,C.C.	Lt SA 4Horse ded 23-2-16 CR EAfrica 58
BASTEDO,Alfred A.	Lt Can 1Bn (WOR) 23-4-15MR 29 Carburt
BATCHELOR,Ferdinand Campion	LtCol NZ 3/313 NZMC ded 31-8-15 CR NZ 77
BATCHELOR,Walter John	Lt Can 87Bn 29-10-18 CR France 40
BATE,Newell Holland	Lt Can 7Bn 13-3-18CR France 480
BATEMAN,Charles Arthur	Lt Can 31Bn kia 6-6-16 CR Belgium 84
BATEMAN,George Simpson	Lt Can 39Bn attRFC Ex2Bn dedacc 18-5-16 CR Hamps 4
BATEMAN,Herbert Pearson	Lt Aust 28Inf kia 5-8-16 CR France 832
BATEMAN,Reginald John Godfrey.MID	Capt Can 46Bn 3-9-18 MR 23
BATES,Albert Edward	Chpn4Cl Aust 3AustAuxHosp ded 9-2-19 CR Surrey 1
BATES,Bernard John	Lt Can 18Bn 15-9-16CR France 239
BATES,Charles Joseph	Capt Aust 10Inf kia 19-5-16 CR France 254
BATES,George Ronald.DCM.	2Lt NZ 24/345 2/3NZRB kia 4-11-18 CR France 1077
BATES,William	Maj Can 25Bn dow 23-3-16 CR Belgium 182
BATH,Edward Osler	Capt Can 15Bn ded 23-11-18 CR Canada 1517
BATSON,Arthur Richard.MC&Bar.	Capt Can 50Bn C'Coy kia 2-9-18 CR France 427
BATTERSBY,William Falconer.MC.	Maj Can 1MMGBde 25-3-18MR 23
BATTYE,Eric Charles	Capt Aust 1ALH kia 16-7-18 CR Palest 3
BATTYE,Ernest Joseph	Lt Aust AFA 11Bde kia 29-9-18 CR France 528
BATY,Edward	Lt Can 8Bn kia 9-8-18 CR France 693
BAUCHOP,Arthur.CMG.	LtCol NZ Cmdg OMR dow 10-8-15 MR 6
BAUSET,Maurice Edouard	Capt Can 22Bn kia 16-9-16 CR France 150
BAWDEN,Alexander Reginald	Maj Can8Bn kia 15-8-17 CR France 224
BAWDEN,Richard Philip	Capt Can CFA 9Bde 10-8-18CR France 589
BAXENDALE,W.	MajSA BrSAPol 22-10-16 CR EAfrica 40 J.W.
BAXTER,Cecil William.MC.DCM.	LtAust 3FA kia 13-8-17 CR Belgium 24
BAXTER,David Russell.MC.	Capt&QM Aust 25Inf dow 13-6-18 CR France 71
BAXTER,Edwy Sutherland	LtCol Can 114Bn ded 15-2-16 CR Canada 1497
BAXTER,Erasmus.MC.	Lt NZ 23290 1/3NZRB dow 12-10-18 CR France 560 Capt
BAXTER,Frederick James.MC&Bar	Lt Aust AIF 38Inf 19-6-21CR Aust 328
BAXTER,Rowland Thomas	2Lt NZ 12/703 2AIR kia 30-7-17 MR 9
BAY,William Bradley	Lt Can 5Bn dow 8-6-17 CR Surrey 1
BAYLES,Stanley Swithin.MM.	Lt Can 1CMR 13-9-18MR 23
BAYLISS,William Alfred	Lt Aust 60Bn 27-4-18MR 26
BAYLY,Robert Horatio Roy	Maj NZ 12/26 AIR kia 20-5-15 MR 6
BAYLY. Z.B.	Lt SA 4SAInf ded 17-4-19 CR SAfrica 81 BAYBY
BAYNE,Charles MacVicar	Lt Can 1CMR (SR) kia 26-10-17 MR 29
BAYNTUN,A.R.	Lt Aust 7Inf 30-6-16CR France 285
BEADEL,Geoffrey Pitt	2Lt NZ 36305 2CIR kia 4-9-18 CR France 756
BEAGLEY,Thomas George	Capt Can 14Bn 9-8-18 CR France 693
BEALER,Harold Van Allen.DCM.MM.MID	Lt Can 42Bn 7-1-18 CR Surrey 1
BEAN,H.K.	LtCol Aust AAMC 3LtHorseFA ded 25-9-16 MR 41
BEANLAND,Charles Henri	2Lt Aust 25Inf dow 4-7-18 CR France 29
BEARUP,Harry	Lt Aust 1Pnrs kia 14-9-17 CR Belgium 34
BEATON,William Evan.MC.	Capt Can 14Bn 1916
BEATTIE,James Ogston	Lt Can 1BCR RBn attRFC 24-1-18CR Belgium 140
BEATON,William Evens.MC.	Lt Can 14QuebecR 26-9-16MR 23
BEATTIE,Percival Moore	2Lt NZ 38797 3/3NZRB kia 4-11-18 CR France 521
BEATTY,Alexander	2Lt Aust 21Inf kia 26-8-16 CR France 832
BEAUBIEN,Louis Antonio	Lt Can 22Bn C'Coy kia 4-6-16 CR Belgium 15
BEAUDRY,Abel P.	Lt Can 22Bn 15-9-16CR France 1505
BEAUFORT,K.	Nurse SA SAMNS 21-10-18 CR SAfrica 144
BEAVER,Wilfred Norman	Lt Aust 60Inf dow 26-9-17 CR Belgium 11
BEAVIS,James Sutherland	Lt Aust 39Inf dow 13-7-18 CR France 300

BECHER,Archibald Victor	Maj Can CAMC att33Bn	25-12-15 CR Canada 1178
BECHER,Henry Campbell	Maj Can 1Bn kia 15-6-15 CR France 571	
BECHRAFT,Thomas C.	Lt Can 21Bn kia 9-4-17 CR France 68	
BECK,Guy Armstrong	Lt Can RCR kia 9-4-17 CR France 68	
BECKETT,Austin Arlington	Lt Can 20Bn kia 15-8-17 CR France 480	
BECKETT,John Maxwell	Lt Can 3DivSigCoy kld 21-10-17 CR Belgium101	
BECKETT,Samuel Gustavus.MID	LtCol Can 75Bn 1-3-17 CR France 81	
BEDDY,Norman Wilhelm	2Lt SA 2SAInf kia 12-4-17 CR France 604	
BEDELL,Willet V.	FltCadet Can RCNAS 1918	
BEECHEY,Frederick James	Lt NZ 22695 2.OIR NZEF kia 25-7-18 CR France 576	
BEECROFT,Harvey Taylor	Lt Can 7MGC 8-10-16MR 23	
BEEHAN,Anselm Jerome	2Lt NZ 22909 3/3NZRB kia 27-3-18 MR 12	
BEEKEN,William Christian	Lt Aust 3Inf kia 6-8-15 CR Gallipoli 7	
BEEKMAN,Antonie	Capt NZ 4/646 NZE kldacc 15-6-16 CR NZ 79	
BEERS,Francis Charles Cole-Bowen	LtCan 4Bn kia 8-10-16 MR 23	
BEGG,Charles Mackie.CB.CMG.MIDx3	Col NZ 3/306 NZMC DMS ded 2-2-19 CR Surrey 156	
BEGG,Colin Erle	Lt Aust AFA 11Bde kia 5-10-18 CR France 375	
BELCHER,Charles Stuart.MC.	Maj Can 44Bn kia 11-5-17 CR France 81	
BELCHER,Leslie Kenneth.MC.	Capt Can 8Bn kia 29-9-18 CR France 597	
BELCHER,Percy James	Capt Can 49Bn D'Coy kia 30-10-17 CR Belgium 11	
BELCHER,Robert	LtCol Can 138Bn ded 10-2-19 CR Canada 547	
BELFORD,George Percival St.John	LtCan 1Bn kia 30-8-18 CR France 688	
BELL,Alexander Herbert	Capt Can 25Bn 16-3-16CR Belgium 182 2CMR att5InfBde	
BELL,Andrew Leslie	Lt Can 10Bn (AR) kia 22-4-15 MR 29	
BELL,Arthur Egbert	Lt Can2BnCMGC dow 26-8-18 CR France 581	
BELL,Bert Adams	2Lt Aust 28Inf 29-7-16MR 26	
BELL,C.S.	Lt SA 4SAInf kia 20-7-16	
BELL,Charles Arthur	Lt Can 58Bn kia 8-10-16 CR France 239	
BELL,Charles Haskel	Lt Can2DAC TMB 29-10-16 CR France 41	
BELL,David Hunter.MC.	Capt Can 16Bn 8-10-16CR France 239	
BELL,Henry	Lt Can 1Bn 28-9-18CR France 34	
BELL,Irving Duncan Peter	Lt Can 2FldCoy 1915	
BELL,James Alexander Terras	Capt NZ 3/156A NZMC MFA ded 29-12-14 CR Egypt 9	
BELL,John	Capt Aust 68Sqn dow 27-12-17 CR France 446	
BELL,Kenneth Allan	2Lt Aust 19Inf kia 26-7-16 CR France 832	
BELL,Patrick Thomas Clark	Lt Aust 28Inf 29-7-17MR 26	
BELL,Ralph William	Capt Can18Bn &RAF 98Sqn 17-5-18MR 20	
BELL,Reginald Wilberforce	Lt Can 28Bn 26-1-16CR Wales 168	
BELL,Robert Fleming	Lt Can25Bn 28-4-17MR 23	
BELL,Sydney Garnett	Lt Aust AFA 2Bde kia 19-9-18 CR France 446	
BELL,Sydney William	Lt Can8Bn (MR) 14-6-16MR 29	
BELL,Thomas.MM.	2Lt NZ 6/1464 1CIR kia 23-10-18 CR France 206	
BELL,Trevor S.	Lt Can 27Bn kia 15-9-16 CR France 280	
BELL,William Douglas	Lt Can 4MGC kia 15-9-16 MR 23	
BELL-IRVING,Duncan Peter	Lt Can Engrs 2FC kia 26-2-15 CR Belgium 451	
BELL-IRVING,Roderick Ogle.DSO.MC.	MajCan 16Bn 1-10-18CR France 422	
BELT,James Edwin Devey	Lt Can 20Bn kia 28-6-16 CR Belgium 11	
BELYEA,Warren Herbert	Maj Can 26Bn 20-3-16CR Belgium 182	
BELZILE,Charles Eugene	Lt Can 22Bn 29-9-16CR France 102	
BENNETT,Carl Norwood	Lt Can 8MGC &RAF ded 24-6-18 CR Surrey 1	
BENNETT,Edwin Bolton	2Lt NZ 24326 2/3NZRB kia 12-10-17 MR 30	
BENNETT,Francis Reginald	Lt Aust 19Inf 9-10-17MR 29	
BENNETT,George W.	Capt Can 2Bn 23-4-15CR Belgium 96 Maj	
BENNETT,Harry James	Lt Can 21Bn attRAF 49Sqn kia 24-9-18 CR France 924	
BENNETT,James Norman	Lt Aust 1Inf 4-10-17CR Belgium 125	
BENNETT,Joseph Llewellyn	2Lt NZ 21142 2/3NZRB kia 12-10-17 MR 30	
BENNETT,Robert Avenel.MC.	Lt Aust FA 13Bde kia 4-10-17 CR Belgium 19	
BENNETT,Robert Burton.MC.	Lt Aust 4Inf kia 4-10-17 CR Belgium 125	
BENNETT,William Henry David	Capt Can 13Bn 15-8-17CR France 223	
BENNIE,Stanley James	Lt Aust 21Inf kia 5-10-18 CR France 446	
BENNY,William Whitford	Lt Can 1BnCMGC dow 30-10-18 CR Germany 3	

BENSON,Claude Elmhurst.DCM.	Capt Aust 9Inf kia 2-7-16 CR France 348
BENSON,Ernest Charles	2Lt Aust56Inf kia 4-2-17 CR France 374
BENSON,Henry	2Lt NZ 7/1545CMR dow 31-3-18 CR Syria 2
BENSON,James.DCM.	2Lt Aust 32Inf kia 20-7-16 MR 7
BENSON,Percy	Lt Can 4ResBn 24-9-17CR Sussex 111 1CanInf
BENSON,Samuel Percy	Lt Can 78Bn 9-4-17 CR France 1896
BENTLEY,David Benjamin	Maj Can CAMC 2FA ded 5-4-17 CR Kent 28
BENTLEY,George Alfred	Lt Aust13Inf kia 4-2-17 CR France 374
BENTLEY,Lloyd Owen	Capt Can CFA ConSecGHQ ded 23-11-19 CR Canada 694
BERGIN,M.MC.	Chpn3Cl Aust AAChpns 12-10-17 CR Belgium 82
BERGLUND,Charles Bertram	Lt Aust AASC 29Coy ded 4-11-18 CR France 52
BERKINSHAW,Edwin Lyle	Capt Can 2CMR 3-6-16 CR Belgium 127
BERMINGHAM,William Martin.MC.	Lt Aust AMGC 24Coy dow 17-2-18 CR France 193
BERNARD,Victor Raymond	2Lt NZ21/42 4/3NZRB kia 4-11-18 CR France 521
BERNSTEIN,Dora	SNurse SASAMNS ded 6-11-18 CR Mddx 40
BERRY,Albert James Frederick	2Lt NZ 23/362 4/3NZRB kia 12-10-17 CR Belgium 123
BERRY,Roy Morley	Lt Aust 25Inf kia 7-2-17 CR France 239
BERRYMAN,Stanley	Lt NZ 7/166 CMR kia 30-3-18 CR Syria 2
BERTRAM,Aimers Stirling	Lt Can 58Bn dow 10-7-17 CR Surrey 1
BERTRAM,James Knowles	Capt Can 20Bn att1InfBdeHQ 22-9-16CR France 430
BERTRAM,Rolf Guillaume	Lt Can 8Bn dow 6-9-16 CR London 8
BERTRAND,Lancelot Joseph.MC.	Lt Can 7Bn 15-8-17MR 23
BEST,Frederick Webster	Lt Can CMGC att RFC dedacc 12-11-17 CR France 40
BEST,George William	Lt Aust AFC 3Sqn kia 12-4-18 CR France 71
BEST,John Frederick Charles	Lt Aust AIF Engrs 13FC 21-12-19 CR Aust 112
BETTLE,Hilda Maude	Sister SA SANS 7-2-19 CR EAfrica 86
BEVAN,Charles Stanley.MM.	Lt Can 16Bn dow 9-4-17 CR France 573
BEVAN,John William Maurice	Lt Can 124Bn att RFC dow 26-9-17 CR France 769
BEVAN,Maurice	Lt Can see BEVAN,J W M
BEVAN,Thomas Harold Hill	Capt Can 4BnCMGC 18-2-19CR France 40
BEVERIDGE,Frederick Richard	2Lt Aust 5Bn 25-7-16MR 26
BEVISS,Meller	2Lt SA2SAInf mbk 24-3-18 MR 27
BEWICKE,Sydney John Fleming	Lt Aust4Inf kia 2-5-15 CR Gallipoli 23
BIBBY,Arthur Hilgrove	Capt Can 7Bn 15-8-17CR France 550
BICE,Edward John.MC.	Lt Aust AFC kia 8-8-18 CR France 526
BICKLE,George Berry	Lt Can Corps CycBn ded 3-10-20 CR Canada 1691 15Bn
BICKNELL,Cyril Alfred	2Lt NZ 10/132 1WIR dedacc 23-6-16 CR France 922
BICKNELL,Louisa Annie	SNurse AustAANS 1GH ded 25-6-15 CR Egypt 9
BIDDLECOMBE,T.W.	Cmdr Aust RAN lent to RN HMS Q27 kia 13-3-17 MR 2
BIDDULPH,Cyril	Lt Can PPCLI 26-8-18CR France 421
BIDDLE,Fred Leslie.DSO.	Maj Aust FA 2Bde dow 17-8-17 CR Belgium 8
BIDEN,Noel Ernest	Capt Aust Engrs 3FC ded 21-12-15 CR Greece 11
BIDSTRUP,Wilfred Vivian Hubert Luther	Lt Aust 50Inf kia 3-4-17 CR France 1488
BIGGAR,Edward James	Lt Can 78Bn kia 5-3-18 CR France 161 16Bn
BIGGAR,Roy Warren	Lt Can 116Bn kia 3-3-18 CR France 522
BIGGSLEY,Herbert Alexander	Lt Aust 6Inf kia 18-7-15 CR Gallipoli 31
BIGNELL,Leslie Hugh	Lt Aust 19Bn 7-4-18 MR 26
BIGWOOD,Paul Herrick	Lt Can162Bn attRFC 57Sqn kia 21-6-17 CR Belgium 5
BILLOT,Herbert Edward	Lt Can28Bn dow 11-5-18 CR France 95
BILLS,Arthur Philip	Lt Aust 50Inf kia 11-8-18 CR France 329
BILSLAND,William	Lt Can 10Bn 21-7-17CR France 161
BILTON,,Norman Creighton	Lt Can 3BdeCGA 1919
BINET,Louis Joseph	Lt Can 22Bn 16-9-16MR 23
BING,Edward Charles Cameron	Lt Can25Bn 11-6-18CR France 174
BINGAY,Lloyd Woolsey	Capt Can 8Bn 30-1-16CR France 40
BINGLE,Ronald Rayden	Capt Aust 4Pnrs dow 8-8-18 CR France 1172
BINKLEY,Basil Ward	Lt Can 15RBn attRFC 12-7-17CR France 285
BINMORE,Reginald Eric (Rex)	Lt Can 87Bn B'Coy kia 8-8-18 CR France 652
BINNIE,George Webster	Lt Aust 13Inf kia 3-5-15 MR 6
BINNS,P.MC.	Capt Aust 6Bn 8-7-17 MR 26
BINNS,Percy	Lt Aust 2Bn 13-8-18MR 26

BINNS,Percy Vere.MC.	Capt CanHQ1BdeCE kia 28-8-18 CR France 54
BIRCH,Charles William	Maj CanCFA 10Bde dow 25-5-17 CR France 64
BIRCHALL,Arthur Percival	LtCol Can 4Bn (1COR) 23-4-15MR 29
BIRD,Alfred Thomas	Lt Can 8Bn 31-8-18CR France 421
BIRD,Francis William	Lt Can 29Bn kia 10-8-16 CR Belgium 15
BIRD,Montagu Herbert	Lt Can 134Bn attRAF 9-7-18 CR France 71
BIRDLING,Arthur John Ware.MID	Lt NZ 7/1195 2CIR kia 20-9-16 MR 11
BIRKS,Frederick.VC.MM.	2Lt Aust 6Inf kia 21-9-17 CR Belgium 115
BIRMINGHAM,Herbert Frederick	Lt Can 54Bn dow 10-8-18 CR France 29
BIRNS,Cyril Garnet	Lt Can16Bn kia 2-9-18 CR France 687
BIRSS,Alexander Cecil	2Lt NZ 26/52 2/3NZRB kia 12-10-17 MR 30
BIRT,James Coombe.MC.	Lt Aust 28Inf kia 3-10-18 CR France 234
BISHOP,Harold Mackay	2Lt Aust 3Inf kia 5-11-16 CR France 307
BISHOP,Arthur Leonard	Lt Can 2Bn 10-9-16CR France 74
BISHOP,John	Capt NZ 25/1222 NZRB ded 15-1-17 CR Surrey 1
BISHOP,John Joseph.MID.	2Lt NZ 23294 1OIR 4Coy kia 12-10-17 MR 30
BISHOPRIC,John Lloyd	Lt Can49Bn (AR) 29-10-17 MR 29
BISSETT,Ian McGowan	Lt SA 8SAInf ded 13-2-17 CR Tanzania 1 &EAfrica 35
BLACK,Alexander	Lt Can 10Bn kia 9-4-17 CR France 68
BLACK,Angus Nathan	Lt Can COC 1915
BLACK,Cyril Lloyd Phipps	2Lt NZ 45031 2/3NZRB kia 30-7-18 CR France 576
BLACK,David Christie.MC.MID	Lt Can 10Bn 28-4-17MR 23
BLACK,E.E.	ProbNurse SASAMNS ded at sea
above is prob:- Black,Eleanor Eileen	VAD,BRCS ded at sea on Kenilworth Castle 4-6-18 MR 40
BLACK,Edgar Pattyson	Lt Can CFA 8Bde 9-6-17 CR France 68
BLACK,Fergus N.	Lt Can 9Bn ded 7-2-15 CR Canada 1245
BLACK,George Harry	2Lt NZ 11/2392 1OIR kia 14-7-16 CR France 922
BLACK,Mathew David	2Lt Aust 11Inf kia 23-6-18 CR France 526
BLACK,Percy Charles Herbert.DSO.DCM.	Maj Aust 16Bn 11-4-17MR 26
BLACK,Reginald.MC.	Lt Aust 6ALH dow 17-8-17 CR Egypt 2
BLACK,Reginald Stellwagon	Lt Can 27Bn (MR) dow 6-11-17 MR 29
BLACK,Robert John	Maj Can 54Bn dow 12-4-17 CR France 12
BLACKADER,Gordon Home	Capt Can 42Bn 1916
BLACKBURN,Charles Frederick	Lt Can 44Bn kia 28-9-18 CR France 714
BLACKBURN,Reginald Vernon.DSO.MC.MID	Maj Can 28Bn dow 29-8-18 CR France 95
BLACKET,Alan Russell	Lt Aust 19Inf dow 16-8-16 CR France 102
BLACKET,John Wesley.MID	Capt Aust 27Inf kia 4-7-16 CR Belgium 48
BLACKET,Joseph Arnold	Lt Aust27Inf kia 10-6-18 CR France 209
BLACKLEY,Thomas Albert	Lt Aust 31Inf 27-9-17MR 29
BLACKLOW,Mervyn William	Lt Aust 12Inf kia 12-8-18 CR France 526
BLACKMAN,Arthur Ross.MM.	2Lt NZ23/968 2/3NZRB kia 9-9-18 CR France 415
BLACKMORE,Colin Alexander	Lt Aust AIF AFA 8Bde 28-6-20CR Aust 112
BLACKMORE,Lewis Gordon	2Lt Aust 1Bn 23-7-16MR 26
BLACKWOOD,James	Lt Can 3CanRlyTrps 23-1-19CR France 40
BLAIR,Andrew Paterson	2Lt Aust 9Inf dow 24-7-16 CR France 44
BLAIR,Harold.MC.	Lt Can 46Bn 28-9-18CR France 147 Capt
BLAIR,James Kent	Lt Can 28Bn 2-10-16MR 23
BLAIR,John Riggall	Lt Aust AFC kia 26-1-18 CR France 285
BLAIR,Mathew	Lt Aust 7 LtTMB 7-4-18 MR 26
BLAIR,Ormond Thomas	Lt Can 72Bn kia 12-11-16 CR France 430
BLAIR,Thomas Herbert	2Lt Aust 38Inf dow 28-5-17 CR Belgium 451
BLAKE,Herbert Raymond	2Lt NZ 11/736 WMR ded 28-11-18 CR Egypt 15
BLAKE,Leslie Russell.MC.MID	Capt Aust AFA 5Bde dow 3-10-18 CR France 446
BLAKE,Valentine	2Lt NZ6/2832 2CIR kia 9-12-15 CR Gallipoli 18
BLAKELY,Thomas Nelson	Capt Can CAMC 11GenHosp ded 29-12-20 CR Canada 115
BLAKENEY,Cyril	Lt NZ 7/1568 CMR kia 9-8-16
BLANCHARD,William James	2Lt SA 3SAInf kia 20-9-17 MR 29
BLANCHARD,Robert	Lt Aust 22Inf 4-10-16MR 29
BLANCHARD,William Hutchison	Capt Can CAVC ded 8-10-17 CR Canada 1688
BLASHKI,Roy Hector.MID	Capt Aust FA 14Bde kia 3-8-17 CR Belgium 11
BLASKETT,William George	2Lt Aust 48Bn 11-4-17MR 26

BLATCHFORD,Thomas Lewis	Capt	Can 36 att1Bn 26-4-16 CR Belgium 453
BLATHERWICK,James K.	Capt	SA BrSAPol 26-10-18 CR EAfrica 101
BLAYDES,Andrew Murvell DelmÇ	2Lt	Aust 3Inf kia 6/8-8-15 CR Gallipoli 7
BLEE,Horace Edgar.MID	2Lt	Aust 16Inf dow 4-7-18 CR France 119
BLENNERHASSETT,Arthur Reginald.MID.	Capt&Adjt	NZ 23070 1WIR kia 4-11-18 CR France 1077
BLICK,Leslie Colin	Lt	Aust7Inf kia 25/30-4-15 MR 6
BLISS,A.H.J.	2Lt	SA 3SAInf kia 26-2-16 CR Egypt 1
BLOIS,Harry Morris	Lt	Can50Bn 10-4-17 CR France 1896
BLOOMFIELD,Albert Cecil Cutting	Lt Can	1CMR B'Coy kia 8-4-18 CR France 522
BLOTT,William McGregor	Lt	Can RCR B'Coy 13-5-17 CR Germany 3
BLUCK,Alfred Charles	Capt	NZ 13/281 AMR kia 22-5-15 CR Gallipoli 11 18-5-15
BLUETT,C.W.C.MC.	Lt	Aust 9Inf 3-11-17 CR Belgium 125
BLUNDEN,Denis Alfred	Lt	Can 3BnCMGC 10-9-18 CR France 421
BLYTH,Edward Pearson.DCM.	Lt	Aust 20Inf dow 8-4-18 CR France 37
BLYTHE,Percy.MM.	Lt	Aust 28Inf kia 10-6-18 CR France 209
BODDINGTON,Frederick Eckersley	Capt	Aust 46Bn 11-4-17 MR 26
BODEN,H.MC.	2Lt	Aust 40Inf 29-9-18 CR France 446
BODWELL,Howard Lionel.CMG.DSO.	LtCol	Can CE 2PnrBn ded 15-1-19 CR Canada 180
BOGER,William Otway.DFC.	Capt	Can LSH &RAF 56Sqn 10-8-18 MR 20
BOGGS,Herbert Beaumont	Lt	Can 7Bn 26-2-15 CR Belgium 69
BOGLE,Gilbert Vere.MID	Capt	NZ 3/534 NZMC kia 17-9-16 CR France 399
BOLE,James Gordon	Lt	Can 2BnCMGC kia 28-8-18 CR France 310
BOLE,Lawrence Francis Gartner C.	Lt	Can RCR kia 9-4-17 CR France 68 Gartney
BOLE,Warner.MC.MM.	Lt	Can 44Bn (NBR) 28-10-17 MR 29
BOLLINGER,George Wallace	2Lt	NZ 10/1024 2WIR dow 10-6-17 CR France 285
BOLLINGHAM,Benjamin	Lt	Aust 21Inf 9-10-17 MR 29
BOLSTER,Herbert George	Maj	Can2Bn (EOR) 24-4-15 MR 29
BOLTE,Felix Oliver	Lt	Can 3Bn kia 2-9-18 CR France 687 Olivier
BOLTON,Grace Errol	Nurse	CanBRCS 16-2-19 CR Canada 256
BOLTON-WOOD,Albert Raymond.MC.	Capt	Aust20Inf dow 5-11-17 CR France 145
BOLUS,D.K.	ProbNurse	SA SAMNS ded at sea
above is prob:- Bolus,Dorothea Kathleen Mary Miss VAD drd 4-6-18 CR Devon 2		
BOND,Alfred Herbert	Lt	Aust44Inf dow 12-10-17 CR Francc 102
BOND,Francis Spencer	Capt	Aust AIF 6AAMC 1-4-16 CR Aust 304
BOND,Frederick George.MC.	Capt	Can CFA 6Bde kia 29-10-17 CR Belgium 11
BOND,Hedleigh St.George	Lt	Can CE 2FC 15-8-17 CR France 573
BOND,Sydney Stanna	Capt	Aust 25Inf 9-10-17 MR 29
BONE,Thomas Henry	Capt	Aust 44Inf kia 5-10-17 CR Belgium 125
BONES, A.	Lt	SA SAMR att1KAR kia 28-10-16 CR Eafrica 40
BONNILY,John	Lt	Aust 52Inf dow 4-5-18 CR France 145
BONNYCASTLE,Richard Henry	Maj	Can CAMC ded 7-10-17 CR Canada 1357
BOONE,Claude Arthur	2Lt	Aust 54Inf kia 19/20-7-16 CR France 255
BOORN,Reginald Henry	Lt	Aust 27Inf dow 19-8-16 CR France 40
BOOTH,Eric Robert	Capt	Aust29Inf kia 23-3-17 CR France 756
BOOTH,John Lionel Calvert	Lt	Aust 12Inf dow 1-5-15 MR 6
BOOTH,Norman Waterhouse	2Lt	Aust 18Inf kia 6-11-16 CR France 744
BOOTH,Stephen	Lt	Can RCD 8-8-18 MR 23
BORROWMAN,Andrew	Lt	Can 19Bn 16-8-17 CR France 705
BORTHWICK,David Scott	Lt	Can 1CMR (SR) 2-6-16 MR 29
BORTHWICK,George Bruce	Lt	Can 19Bn 16-4-18 CR France 504
BORTHWICK,Keith	Lt	Aust 8ALH kia 7-8-15 MR 6
BORTHWICK,Peter	Lt	Can 43Bn (MR) 26-10-17 MR 29
BOSCAWEN,Hugh Townshend.MID	Capt	NZ 13/11 2WIR kia 4-10-17 CR Belgium 125 5/11A
BOSTOCK,Alexander Hewitt	Lt	Can LSH att4MtdRif kia 26-7-16 CR Belgium 5
BOSWELL,Leonard C.MM.	Lt	Can 21Bn 28-8-18 CR France 14
BOTHAMLEY,James Powell	Lt	SA 2SARif ded 28-12-16 CR EAfrica 40
BOTHWELL,George Edwin	Lt	Can 1CMR 15-9-16 MR 23
BOTHWELL,Samuel James.DCM.	Maj	Can 1CMR kia 9/12-4-17 CR France 522
BOTTEN,Robert Hillman	Lt	Aust 27Inf kia 2-3-17 CR France 385
BOTTERELL,Edward Simpson	Capt	Can15Bn 26-6-16 CR Belgium 11
BOUCHER,Cyril Jephson	2Lt	SA 2SAInf B'Coy dow 8-9-16 CR France 81

BOUCHER,Edgar Allen	Capt Can31Bn 15-9-16MR 23
BOUCHER,William Robert	Lt Can 46Bn 26-3-17CR France 81
BOUCHETTE,Edward Errol	Lt Can 87Bn 30-9-18CR France 148 Edouard
BOULLY,Leslie.DCM.	2Lt Aust 16Inf kia 5-8-17 CR Belgium 168
BOULTER,Harry Stewart	Capt Can 124PnrBn B'Coy kia 4-4-17 CR France 81
BOULTON,Rusell Heath	Lt Can 3BnCE kia 14-8-18 CR France 881
BOULTON,Stephen Philip	Lt Aust AFA 2Bde dow 3-10-18 CR France 528
BOURGEOIS,Georges	LtCol Can8GenHosp 1919
BOURGEOIS,Rene	Lt Can 14Bn 17-8-17CR France 223
BOURKE,John Joseph	Lt Aust 2AMGC 20-9-17MR 29
BOURNE,Herbert Hallowell	Lt Can 54 Bn 3-6-16 MR 29 4CMR (1COR)
BOUTCHER,Henry William J.	2Lt Aust 44Inf21-4-18CR France 71
BOVELL,Vernon Llewellyn	2Lt Aust12Inf 15-9-17MR 29
BOWD,Henry William	Lt Aust AFC kia 25-10-17 CR Egypt 9
BOWDEN,Charles Maxwell	2Lt Aust 22Bn 19-5-18MR 26
BOWDEN,John Tom	Lt SA 8SAInf dow 7-6-16 CR Tanzania 1 &EAfrica 5
BOWDEN,John Charles	2Lt Aust 59Inf kia 19-7-16 MR 7
BOWDEN,John Desborough	2Lt NZ 23924 1\2CIR dow 10-10-16 CR France 833
BOWEN,Clarence Edward	Lt Aust 60Bn 27-4-18MR 26
BOWEN,Cyril John	2Lt Aust 34Inf ded 15-9-16 MR 40
BOWEN,Harold Thomas	Lt Can 2CMR dow 2-1-18 CR France 223
BOWER,W.C.E.	Lt Can RAMC att1RNewfndlandR 19-10-16 CR France 374
BOWER-BINNS,John S.	Lt Can RAF 21Bn 1918
BOWIE,George Pigrum	Capt Can 5Bn A'Coy kia 7-7-15 CR Belgium 339
BOWIE,Robert Ross	Maj NZ 7/920 CMR ded 10-7-15 CR Egypt 9
BOWKER,Alan Duthie	Lt SA 4SAInf mbk 24-3-18 CR France 624 dow
BOWKER,Osborne Henry Paget	Lt Can 29Bn kia 9-4-17 CR France 68
BOWLBY,George Herbert	Capt Can CAMC 1916
BOWLBY,Robert Archer	Lt Can 212Bn 1918
BOWLER,Daniel Cornelius.MC.	Capt NZ 14025 2/3NZRB kia 12-10-17 MR 30
BOWRA,Fredk Douglas Atlee	Lt Aust Engrs 4FC kia 29-10-15 CR Gallipoli 31
BOWRAN,John 2	Lt Aust 54Inf 25-9-17MR 29
BOWRING,Charles Thurston	Lt Can 44Bn att10MGC 29-12-16 CR France 81
BOWRING,William Alfred.MID	Capt NZ 24/9 2/3NZRB kia 24-9-16 MR 11
BOWRON,Henry Allan	Lt NZ 7/1196 CMR kia 23-12-16 CR Egypt 2
BOYCE,William Ernest	Capt Can CADC 1918 ded 8-11-18 CR Canada 302
BOYD,James Tennant Whitworth	Capt Can CAMC 7GH 16-6-18CR Sussex 111
BOYD,James William	Lt Can RFC 3DivCyc 4-2-17 CR France 95
BOYD,Mascall Brooks Hamilton	Lt Can 4CMR 1CanTankBn 20-6-18MR 24
BOYD,Mossom Richard	Lt Can 50Bn 18-11-16 MR 23
BOYD,T.H.MC.	Lt Aust 6Inf 4-10-17CR Belgium 123
BOYES,Andrew Colquhoun	Lt NZ 8/1092 2OIR kia 16-5-16 CR France 922
BOYES,David Alexander	Lt Can 102Bn B'Coy 9-4-17 CR France 81
BOYLE,Eben Archibald.MC&Bar.	Capt Can 8Bn 1-10-18CR France 214
BOYLE,Mahlon Lambert.MC.	Maj Can 49Bn kia 23-8-17 CR France 223
BOYLE,Niel Stuart	Lt Aust 26Inf dow 5-9-18 CR France 145
BOYLE,Russell Lambert.MID	LtCol Can 10Bn 25-4-15CR Belgium 151
BOYS,Herbert James	Lt Can 27Bn 10-5-18CR France 63
BOYS,Walter Granluse	Capt Aust 25Inf dow 5-8-16 CR France 44
BRACEWELL,A.	2Lt SA 1SAInf dow 28-3-18 CR France 145
BRACKIN,Garnet Garfield	Lt Can 18Bn 26-8-18CR France 162
BRADBURN,Cornelius Patrick	Lt Aust MGC 23Coy dow 4-10-17 CR Belgium 3
BRADEN,W.MC.	Lt Aust 29Inf 9-8-18 CR France 526
BRADFORD,Frederick William	Lt Can 44Bn 23-8-17MR 23
BRADLEY,William Ferguson.MID	Maj Can 1Bn 3-5-17 CR France 1059
BRADSHAW,William Frederick Whittle	Lt Can 195Bn ded 29-8-16 CR Canada 487
BRAITHWAITE,William McCarthy.MC.	Capt Aust 22Inf kia 3-10-18 CR France 234
BRAIM,Henry S.	2Lt Aust AFC 26-10-20 CR Aust 35
BRAMBLEY,Percy Richard	2Lt NZ18214 1AIR 16Coy dow 28-2-17 CR France 285
BRAMLEY,Edward	Lt SA CapeAuxHorseTrans ded 8-1-21 CR SAfrica 69
BRANT,Cameron Donald	Lt Can 4Bn (1COR) kia 24-4-15 MR 29

BRASELL,Jack Stanley	Lt Aust AFA 1Sqd 25-6-17MR 34
BRASHAW,Joseph Arthur	Capt Aust 16Inf kia 7-8-15 MR 6
BRASSEY,William Leslie.MM.	Lt Can 2Bn 27-9-18CR France 481
BRAUND,George Frederick.VD.	LtCol Aust 2Inf kia 4-5-15 CR Gallipoli 30
BRAY,William Marks	Lt Aust AIF 25Inf 14-7-15CR Aust 112
BREACH,Sydney Frederick.MID	2Lt NZ 25/945 2/3NZRB kia 8-10-18 CR France 611
BRECKENRIDGE,Hugh	2Lt Aust 19Inf kia 3-5-17 CR France 646
BREDIN,Chas Edgar Atheling.DSO.MID	Capt Can 28Bn 18-11-17 CR France 8
BREEN,Gordon.MM.	2Lt Aust 23Inf kia 4-7-18 CR France 1170
BREMNER,Alastair Bruce	Capt SA NRhodPol 1-1-18 CR EAfrica 73
BREMNER,Andrew Douglas	2Lt NZ 10270 2AIR kia 15-9-16 MR 11
BRENNAN,K.A.	Nurse Aust AANS 24-11-18 CR Leics 63
BRENNAN,Peter Austin	Lt Can 54B n dow 7-6-17 CR France 81 75Bn
BRENNAN,William Keating	Lt Aust 12ALH dow 20-4-17 CR Palest 8
BRETHERTON,Arnold Romsey	Capt Aust 18Inf kia 26-12-16 CR France 374
BREW,Thomas.DCM.	2Lt Aust 2Inf kia 4-10-17 CR Belgium 22
BREWER,Robert.MID	Lt Aust 41Inf kia 29-9-18 CR France 212
BREWER,Thomas	Lt NZ 11153MGR dow 3-10-17 CR Belgium 11
BREWSTER,Arthur Clarence.MC.	Lt Aust 23Inf 4-10-17CR Belgium 453 &MR29
BREWSTER,Frank Edward2	Lt Aust AMGC 5Coy dedacc 11-4-16 CR France 285
BREWSTER,Harold Staples	Lt Can RFC RCR ded 6-12-16 CR Canada 1464
BRICHTA,Geoffrey Joseph Ogilvie	LtCan 2CMR att16RFCkia 6-3-17 CR France 12
BRICKER,George Gilbert	Capt Can HQCFC ded 27-10-18 CR France 1822
BRIDGE,F.W.	Lt SA 8SAInf ded 27-11-16 CR EAfrica 40
BRIDGEMAN,Guy Clive.MC.	2Lt NZ 9/15 NZFA ded 14-11-18 CR NZ 243
BRIDGES,Eric Forster	Lt SA RhodNatR dow 1-2-17 CR EAfrica 40
BRIDGES,William Throsby.KCB.CMG.MID Sir	MajGen Aust AIF 1DivHQ18-5-15CR Aust 481
BRIDGEWATER,Harold Ernest	PaymstrSub Lt Can RNCVR `Rainbow' ded 22-10-19 CR Canada 154
BRIDGMAN,Francis Harvey	Capt Aust49Inf 7-6-17 MR 29
BRIGGS,Henry Francis	2Lt AustMGC 14Coy20-7-16MR 26
BRIGHT,Albert Edward	Lt CanCFA 5Bde 9-4-17 CR France 68
BRIGHT,Clarence	Lt Can CASC 1DivMTCoy 18-11-18 CR France 1142
BRIGHT,Harold Wheeler	Lt Can 153Bn 8-7-16 CR Canada 1232
BRIGHTON,Andrew Melville	Lt Can 102Bn 27-9-18CR France 715
BRILLANT,John.VC.MC.	Lt Can 22Bn 10-8-18CR France 1170
BRIND,Eric Thomas	Maj Aust 23Bn 28-7-16MR 26
BRINSMEAD,Reginald William.MC.	2Lt Aust 8Inf 17-12-17 MR 29
BRISCOE,Ross Dickenson	Lt Can9Bn 6-1-15 CR Wilts 2
BRISTED,Edward Griffith	2Lt NZ 6/1786 1CIR kia 3-12-17 MR 8
BRITT,William	Lt Aust 51Inf kia 10-6-18 CR France 1170
BRITTAN,Harold Rolleston	2Lt NZ 41213 1/3NZRB kia 5-4-18 CR France 156
BRITTAN,Stanley Victor	Lt Can 13Bn kia 13-60-16 CR Belgium 11
BRITTON,Russell Hubert.DSO.	LtCol Can CFA 5Bde 2-5-17 CR France 268
BRITTON,Thomas Henry.MC.	Lt Aust 34Inf dow 21-6-18 CR France 145
BROAD,Thomas Harold	Capt Can 116Bn 17-9-18CR France 154
BROAD,William Edward Lee	Lt Can5Bn kia 9-4-17 CR France 68
BROADBRIDGE,Norman Leslie	2Lt Aust 3Pnrs dow 7-9-18 CR France 526
BROADFOOT,Daniel James	Lt Can44Bn 23-8-17MR 23
BROADGATE,Frederick King	Lt NZ 26360 NZE kia 30-9-18 MR 12
BROCK,Halcombe Ferrier	Lt Aust 3ALH kia 2-6-15 CR Gallipoli 31
BROCK,John Daniel	Lt Can 26Bn 17-9-16MR 23
BROCKETT,Archibald Geoffrey	2Lt NZ 10/3151 1OIR kia 15-7-16 CR France 922
BROCKLEBANK,Stanley Howson.MC.MID	Capt Can 46Bn dow 20-9-18 CR France 13
BRODIE,Benjamin Greenup	Capt Aust 34Inf kia 5-3-18 CR Belgium 339
BRODIE,John Grey	Lt Aust 31Inf 26-9-17MR 29
BRODIE,Thomas Gregor	Capt Can CAMC 20-8-16CR London 12
BRODZIAK,Cedric Errol Meyer.DSO.	Maj Aust 3AMGC kia 31-8-18 CR France 511
BROKENSHA,Hawtrey Vivien	Lt SA NatalLHorse kia 27-4-15 CR SAfrica 3
BROMILOW,Ivon Carlston	Lt Aust AFA 1Bde dow 7-11-16 CR France 400
BROMLEY,Herbert Asheton	Lt Can 7Bn (BCR) kia 24-4-15 MR 29 Assheton
BROOK,Arthur O'Connor	Lt Aust AFC 3Sqn kia 27-6-18 CR France 71

BROOK,E.J.	Lt SA 2SAInf kia 17-10-18 CR France 940
BROOK,Frank Richard.MID	Lt Aust 43Inf kia 4-7-18 CR France 1170
BROOK,Julian Cornelius	Lt NZ 12/600 1/3NZRB dow 2-9-18 CR France 239
BROOKES,Ewen McLean	2Lt NZ 2/403 NZFA kia 4-10-16 CR France 453
BROOKFIELD,George Leonard Purchas	2Lt NZ 13/657A AMR kia 8-8-15 MR 5
BROOKS,Ernest John	Maj Can 25Bn kia 15-9-16 MR 23
BROOKS,Robert Elsmer	Lt Can CFA &RAF 8-4-18 CR Scot 503 Elesmere
BROOKS,William Abercombie	2Lt Aust 15Inf ded 2-3-16 CR Egypt 9
BROOKS,William Charles	2Lt Aust51Bn 30-3-18MR 26
BROSSEAU,Jacques	Lt Can 22Bn 18-6-16CR Belgium 11
BROTHERHOOD,Wilfred Cashel	Lt Can 14Bn (QR)24-4-15MR 29
BROTHERTON,Thomas.DCM.	Capt Can1MMGBde 29-10-17 MR 29
BROUGH,Herbert William	2Lt Aust AFA 5Bde dow 1-5-17 CR France 565
BROWN,Arthur Ernest	2Lt SA1SAInf kia 16-7-16 MR 21
BROWN,Allan	Capt Aust 49Inf kia 20-7-19 MR 70
BROWN,Arthur Henry	Lt SA 1SAInf kia 19-10-16 CR France 385 18-10-16
BROWN,A.H.	Lt SA 4SAInf kia 20-7-16 CR France 402
BROWN,Alasdair Norman	Lt Can 4CMR 26-8-18CR France 1189
BROWN,Allan	Capt Aust 49Inf kia 20-7-19 CR Europe 179
BROWN,Anthony	2Lt NZ 2/2364 NZFA 5Bty kia 24-8-18 CR France 518
BROWN,Carl Oscar	2Lt Aust 9Inf dow 28-5-18 CR France 180
BROWN,Charles Dane	Lt Aust 16Inf 26-9-17MR 29
BROWN,Charles Henry	Lt Can 27Bn dow 10-11-17 CR Belgium 11
BROWN,Chas.Henry Jeffries.DSO.MIDx3	LtColTBrigGen NZ 15/14 AIR Cmdg1InfBde kia 8-6-17 CR France 285
BROWN,Cyril George	Lt Aust AFA 13Bdekia 28-12-16 CR France 307
BROWN,Cyril Ivan	Lt NZ 36251 NZFA dow 13-12-17 CR Surrey 1
BROWN,David.MC.	Lt Aust 41Inf dow 17-8-18 CR France 145
BROWN,Douglas Lambert	Lt Aust 30Inf kia 18-10-17 CR Belgium 115
BROWN,Edmund Gordon	Lt Can CFA 11Bde 3-4-17 CR France 12
BROWN,Ernest Samuel	LtCol Aust 3Inf kia 6/8-8-15 CR Gallipoli 30
BROWN,Ewart Cudemore	Lt Can 7RBn &RFC ExPPCLI dedacc 14-8-17 CR Lincs 181
BROWN,Felix Ballard	Maj NZ6/1104 CIR 2CanterburyR kldacc 7-3-17 CR Belgium 54
BROWN,Frederick Ruyter.MM.	Lt Can 29Bn dow 10-4-17 CR France 12
BROWN,Frederick Vincent	Capt NZ 35376 NZFA kia 1-9-18 CR France 745
BROWN,G.S.	Lt SA HArty 25-7-19CR SAfrica 121
BROWN,Garnet Wollesley	Capt Aust 2Inf kia 6/8-8-15 CR Gallipoli 7
BROWN,George Thomas.MC.	Lt Can 27Bn dow 23-4-17 CR France 95
BROWN,Harold	2Lt Aust 5 LtTMB kia 7-2-17 CR France 385
BROWN,Henry Jesse Trimmer	2Lt Aust 7Bn 25-7-16MR 26
BROWN,Horace Parker.MID	Capt Aust 9LtTMB kia 12-5-17 CR Belgium 137
BROWN,James Monteagle	2Lt Aust 25Inf kia 29-7-16 CR France 280
BROWN,John Ranby	Lt Can 102Bn kia 27-9-18 CR France 715
BROWN,Marion SinclairS	Nurse NZ 22/104 ANS drd 23-10-15 MR 35
BROWN,Ralph Russell James	Maj Can 44Bn att9 LtTMB dow 31-10-17 CR Belgium 3
BROWN,Richard Austin.MC.	Capt Can 15Bn 14-11-17 CR Belgium 11
BROWN,Richard Thomas	Capt Aust 2Inf kia 2-5-15 MR 6
BROWN,Robert	Lt Can CE 3DivSigCoy 5-9-19 CR Wales 673
BROWN,Robert Elliott.MC.	Lt Can 28Bn dow 1-10-18 CR France 147
BROWN,Russell Stanley	2Lt Aust 34Bn 8-5-18 MR 26
BROWN,Thomas.MC.	Lt NZ 10951 1/3NZRBkia 23-8-18 CR France 514
BROWN,William Nimms	Lt SA 1SAInf kia 7-7-16 MR 21
BROWN,William.MM.	2Lt Aust 51Bn 3-9-16 MR 26
BROWN,William Ebert	Lt Can 58Bn kia 28-9-18 CR France 714 Eberts
BROWN,William Ormiston	Lt Can 18Bn 8-8-16 CR Belgium 15
BROWNE,Albert Edward	Lt Can 16Bn 9-4-17 CR France 68
BROWNE,Gordon Minto	2Lt Aust 42Inf dow 2-10-18 CR France 446
BROWNE,Harry Dalzell	Lt Can9MGC kia 10-7-16 CR Belgium 15
BROWNE,Norman John.MC.	Lt Aust 12Inf dow 22-3-18 CR Belgium 90
BROWNELL,Lauriston	Lt Aust 27Inf dow 3-10-17 CR Belgium 11
BROWNLEE,William Fisher.MID	Lt Can 21Bn 16-9-16MR 23
BROWNLOW,Leonard Rockley	2Lt Aust 33Inf 12-10-17 MR 29

BROWNRIDGE,William James	Lt Can 2TankBn 13-10-18 MR 24
BRUCE,Arthur Ernest	Lt Aust39Inf dow 9-5-18 CR France 116
BRUCE,Charles Tupper	Lt CanCFA attRFC kia 13/14-4-17 CR France 98
BRUCE,George B.	Capt Can 15CLH ded 12-11-18 CR Canada 543
BRUCE,George William	LtCol Can Cmdg181Bn dedacc 22-4-16 CR Canada 1688
BRUCE,James.MC.DCM.	Lt Aust 34Inf kia 17-7-18 CR France 1170
BRUCE,John Kemp	Chpn4Cl Aust att3AustHospded 9-2-18 MR 40
BRUCE,Thomas Fraser	2Lt Aust 36Inf 12-10-17 MR 29
BRUCE,William	Lt Can 210Bn SaskatchR &RAF 25-5-18CR France 1658
BRUDEWOLD,Thorkell Nathan	2Lt SA 2SAInf kia 15-7-16 MR 21
BRUFORD,Harry Russell Beamish	Lt Aust 26Bn 3-10-18MR 26
BRUMBY,Harold Robert	2Lt NZ 12/2618 1AIR kia 28-9-16 MR 11
BRUNDRIT,Thomas Joseph	Capt Aust 5ALH kia 8-11-15 CR Gallipoli 22
BRUNS,Ernest Otto Alfred	Lt Aust 16Inf kia 2-5-15 MR 6
BRUNTON,Lawrence.MC.	Lt Aust AFA 10Bdekkia 4-7-18 CR France 1170
BRUNTON,Reginald Ruston.MC.	Lt Can 75Bn 3-10-17CR Belgium 84
BRYAN,William Thomas	Capt Aust 44Inf kia 8-6-17 CR Belgium 108
BRYAN-BROWN,Guy Spencer	Chpn4Cl NZ41286 Chpns kia 4-10-17 MR 30
BRYANT,Edmund Cosentine	Capt SA2SAInf kia 8-12-17 CR France 439
BRYCE,Colin.MID.	Capt NZ 22664 OIR kia 3-12-17 CR Belgium 112
BRYDON,Kenneth Mackenzie	Lt Aust Engrs 14FCkia 12-10-17 CR Belgium 112
BRYDON,Robert George Howie	Maj Can 102Bn 9-4-17 CR France 81
BRYDON,Robert Oliver.MID	Capt NZ 23/18 2/3NZRB kia 16-9-16 CR France 277
BRYDON,Walter.DSO.	Maj SAHArty kia 12-4-18 CR France 179
BRYSON,Elmer Clark	Lt Can 13Bn 8-10-16CR France 239
BRYSON,Joseph Hutcheson	Lt Aust 9Inf dow 16-3-18 CR France 193
BUCHANAN,Charles Franklin.MC.	Lt Can 7Bn kia 12-10-18 CR France 421
BUCHANAN,Fitz-Herbert Price	Capt Can 13Bn kia 28-6-16 CR Belgium 11
BUCHANAN,John Bruce.MID	Maj Aust 36Inf kia 12-10-17 CR Belgium 125
BUCHANAN,Joseph David	Capt Aust AAMC 2 LtHFA dow 21-12-15 CR Egypt 9
BUCHANAN,Leo	Lt Can 3MGCoy kia 19-4-16 CR Belgium 120
BUCHANAN,Leslie	Lt Aust 31Inf dedacc 5-9-18 CR France 13
BUCHANAN,Reginald Heber Bancroft	Lt Can 24Bn 18-1-16CR Belgium 60
BUCHANAN,Roy Workman Pendrie	Lt Can 31Bn kia 25-8-18 CR France 174
BUCHANAN,Victor Carl.DSO.	LtCol Can 13Bn kia 26-9-16 CR France 430
BUCHLER,Frederick Lancelot.MID	LtT Capt NZ 23/1575 3/3NZRB C'Coy kia 6-4-18 MR 12
BUCKLAND,Reginald John 2	Lt Aust 8ALH dow 9-8-16 CR Egypt 2
BUCKLAND,William Alexander John	Lt Aust AFC 3Sqn kia 6-5-18 CR France 71
BUCKLEY,Hugh Cornelius	Capt Aust22Inf dedacc 27-4-16 CR France 347
BUDDELL,William Henry.DCM.	Lt Can 26Bn ded 2-2-19 CR Belgium 306
BUGBY,Francis Eli Cromwell	Lt Aust AIF 1DivATMB 21-6-20CR Aust 112
BUKES,R.	Lt SA 11MtdRif kia 27-3-15 CR SAfrica 54
BULKELEY,Richard Farley.MC.	Lt Aust 3Inf kia 17-8-16 CR France 280
BULL,Jeffrey Harper.DSO.	Maj Can 75Bn 8-8-18 CR France 589
BULL,Leopold.MC.	Lt Aust 46Inf dow 7-4-18 CR France 62
BULL,Lewis Marsden	Lt Aust 1Inf kia 18-9-18 CR France 528
BULLEN,Norman John	Maj Aust AMC 15FA dow 16-10-17 CR Belgium 19
BULLER,Herbert Ceceil.DSO.	LtCol Can PPCLI 1916
BULLOCK-WEBSTER,Frank	Lt Can 11MGC attRFC 23Sqn 20-9-17CR Belgium 72
BUMPUS,Leslie Rider	Lt AustFA 6Bty 2Bdekia 22-7-17 CR Belgium 15
BUNCOMBE,Walter Harry	Lt Aust 47Inf kia 12-10-17 CR Belgium 125
BURDEN,Clive Britten	Capt Aust AAMC dedacc 8-5-17 CR Surrey 1
BURDETT,A.F.	Capt SA SASC MechTrsnptded 4-11-18 CR SAfrica 69
BURDETT,Charles Grant.Sir	LtNZ 66607 NZDC ded 21-11-18 CR NZ 242
BUREN,N.	2Lt SA 3SAInf ded 7-5-20 CR SAfrica 69
BURGE,Clifford Charles	Lt Aust 24Inf kia 14-8-18 CR France 1170
BURGE,Joseph	Lt Aust 2ALH kia 7-8-15 CR Gallipoli 8
BURGER,Frederick Max	Lt Can 3Bn kia 14-10-18 CR France 273
BURGES,Edward Travers	Maj SA 1SAInf Ex SAMRkia 18-7-16 MR 21
BURGES,James Clement	Lt Aust 34Inf 12-10-17 MR 29
BURGESS,Edward Francis	Lt Can 1Bn 1-10-18CR France 597

BURGESS,Rosswell Morris	Capt Can CADC ded 5-1-18 CR Canada 1694
BURGESS,Stewart Salmond	2Lt Aust 20Inf kia 6-4-18 CR France 1170
BURGESS,Walter Hartley.DSO.	LtCan 50Bn 10-8-18CR France 692
BURGIN,John Robert	Capt NZ 18/29 ChpnsDept2-12-20CR NZ 194
BURKE,Frank James	Capt Can 38Bn 11-10-18 CR France 113
BURKE,Frank M.	Lt Can 1NewfndlandR kia 14-10-18 CR Belgium 405
BURKE,Harold.MC.	Capt Aust 5Inf kia 23-8-18 CR France 699
BURKE,Richard Joseph	Lt Can 79CoyCFC 8-9-18 MR 24
BURLEY,Leslie James	2Lt Aust 3Inf dow 20-5-15 MR 6
BURLEY,M.F.	2Lt SA 2SAInf kia 25-12-16 CR France 1182
BURN,Harold Thomas	2Lt Aust 58Inf dow 23-12-16 CR France 145
BURNARD,Alfred Thomas Evan	2Lt NZ 27214 1CIR kia 2-9-18 CR France 307
BURNARD,Eric Mountjoy	2Lt NZ6/1085 CIR dow 10-5-15 CR Gallipoli 1
BURNE,Basil Ernest	Capt SA 2SAInf kia 12-10-16 MR 21
BURNHAM,Sidney Smith.DSO.	Maj Can 19Bn B'Coy att2DivHQ kia 9-8-18 CR France 652
BURNS,George Herbert.MM&Bar.	Lt Can 43Bn 28-8-18MR 23
BURNS,Robert David	Lt Aust MGC 14Coy 20-7-16MR 26
BURNS,Ronald	Capt Aust 3Inf kia 25-4-15 MR 6
BURNS,Vincent Alexander	Lt Aust 36Inf dow 11-6-17 CR France 297
BURNS,William James Gordon.DSO.	Maj Can CFA 32Bty 8ABde kia 28-9-18 CR France 481
BURR,Joseph Martin	Lt Aust 21Inf dow 17-3-18 CR Belgium 339
BURRIDGE,Herbert William	Chpn NZ 18/8 Chpns ded 26-12-22
BURRIN,David James	Lt Aust 1Inf kia 23-8-18 CR France 526
BURROWS,Bruce Hosmer Acton	Lt Can CE 12FC kia 25-11-16 CR France 150
BURROWS,Charles Stuart.MC.	Capt Can 58Bn kia 1-10-18 CR France 611
BURROWS,Edward.MID	Lt NZ 25/16 3/3NZRB kia 22-9-16 MR 11
BURROWS,Martin	2Lt SA 3SAInf kia 9-4-17 CR France 452
BURROWS,Mark Kenneth	Lt Can 44Bn 27-9-18CR France 714
BURSTAL,Richard Stewart	2Lt Aust1Bn 25-7-16MR 26
BURT,Francis Sinclair	Lt Aust AMGC 4Bn kia 24-4-18 CR France 144
BURTENSHAW,Francis J.MC.	Lt Aust 41Inf kia 15-5-18 CR France 116
BURTON,Clerke Colqhoun	Capt Aust ImpForceHQ TransSect ded 14-12-18 CR Wilts 129
BURTON,Ernest Wilfred	Lt Aust AFC dedacc 4-4-18 CR Scot 398
BURTON,Francis James	2Lt Aust 4ALH kia 31-10-17 CR Palest 1
BURTON,Harry James	Lt Aust 16Inf kia 2-5-15 MR 6
BURTON,James Lindsay	Lt Can 19Bn 8-8-18 CR France 1170
BUSCOMBE,Robert Frederick Edwin	Lt Can 7Bn 21-6-15CR France 571
BUSH,Walter Clarence	Lt Can3Bn 29-4-17CR France 95
BUSHELLE,John Edward Wallace	Capt Aust36Inf kia 6-4-18 CR France 889
BUSKIN,Alexander Frank	2Lt Aust 6ALH kia 17-9-15 CR Gallipoli 22
BUSSELL,Alfred Joseph.MC.	Lt Aust 10Inf kia 13-10-18 CR France 340
BUTCHER,William Patrick	LtCol Can SchMktry 1921
BUTLER,Brian Nairn	2Lt Aust 12Inf kia 18-9-18 CR France 366
BUTLER,Edward Lionel Austin	2Lt Aust 12Inf dow 23-8-16 CR France 74
BUTLER,Howard Richard Henry	2Lt AustAFC kldacc 2-6-18 CR Scot 520
BUTLER,William Amos Norris	2Lt Can RAF 10TrgDepotStn Ex PPCLI kld 2-8-18 CR Norfolk 259
BUTLER,William F.	Master Can MercMar SS`PortDalhousie' 19-3-16MR 24
BUTSON,William George	Lt Can 4CMR dow 10-4-17 CR France 32
BUTTERCASE,Robert Dingwall	Lt Aust AFA 41Bty 4DAC kia 5-4-18 CR France 885
BUTTERWORTH,Alfred Francis	Capt Can 162Bn 1916
BUTTERWORTH,Frank Alexander.MM.	Lt Aust AFC 4Sqn kia 16-10-18 CR France 31
BYDDER,Charles	1stEngr CanMercMar SS`PortDalhousie'19-3-16MR 24
BYRD,Alfred Thomas	Lt Can 8Bn 1918
BYRNE,Albert John	Lt Aust 10Inf kia 25-4-15 CR Gallipoli 30
BYRNE,Leslie.MC.	Lt Aust 46Inf kia 18-9-18 CR France 375

C

CADDEN,John James — Lt Aust AnzacProvostCpsded 31-10-18 CR Surrey 1
CADDEN,Robert Labertouche — Lt AustAIF 30Inf 28-12-17 CR Aust 112
CADDY,James.DCM.MM.MID — 2Lt Aust 7Inf kia 9-8-18 CR France 526
CADELL,Henry Charles Dight.MC. — Capt Aust 35Inf 12-10-17 MR 29
CADELL,Thomas Leonard — Lt Aust 3Inf dow 22-6-15 MR 6
CADLE,Lawrence Miles — Capt Aust 18Inf kia 14-5-18 CR France 833
CADOLLE, Albert — Lt Can 22Bn 10-8-18 CR France 1170 CADOTTE
CADUSCH,James John — 2Lt Aust 38Inf kia 7/9-6-17 CR Belgium 168
CAFFREY,Lawrence — Lt Can CFA 8ABde 7-3-18 CR France 68
CAHILL,Thomas Kevin — Lt Aust 39Inf kia 30-8-18 CR France 624
CAIRNS-PENNY,Desmond Ferguson — Lt AustAFA 8Bde kia 5-6-17 CR France 262
CALDER,H.MM. — 2Lt SA 2SAInf kia 12-10-16
CALDER,William John Kekewich.MM. — 2Lt SA 2SAInf 12-10-16 MR 21
CALDER,William McLureH — Capt&QM Can att5HQCFC Ex PPCLI kldacc 1917 CR France 1830 1-11-18
CALDERWOOD,David Millar — 2Lt Can RAF 20Sqn Ex Pte106121 1CMR 20-9-18 MR 20
CALDWELL,David Wallace — Lt Aust 27Inf kia 2-3-17 CR France 385
CALESS,Francis Burleigh — Capt Aust 26Inf 5-8-16 CR France 1890
CALL,George Walter — Lt Can 1Bn 2-5-17 MR 23
CALLAGHAN,Stanley Robert — 2Lt Aust 34Inf 1-10-17 MR 29
CALLAGHAN,Thomas Hugh.DCM. — Maj Can 72Bn kia 9-4-17 CR France 81
CALLAN,Charles James — Lt Aust 38Inf kia 29-9-18 CR France 1495
CALLARY,Philip Ignatius — Capt Aust 9ALH kia 29-8-15 MR 6
CALLAWAY,Frederick William Berni — 2Lt Aust 2Inf kia 5-9-16 CR Belgium 127
CALLEN,Vincent Charles.MM. — Lt Aust 34Inf kia 20-8-18 CR France 247
CALLINAN,Frank Paul — 2Lt Aust AFA 3Bde dow 6-5-17 CR France 512
CALLINAN,Laurence Hurley — Capt Aust AFA 12Bde dow 9-9-18 CR France 145
CAMERON,Alexander Douglas — Lt Aust36Inf kia 4-4-18 CR France 424
CAMERON,Arthur Archibald — 2Lt Aust9Inf kia 26-2-17 CR France 744
CAMERON,Charles Ross — Capt Can 2Bn 30-8-18 MR 23
CAMERON,Colin Campbell — Lt Aust AFC 1Sqn ded 18-11-18 CR Egypt 7
CAMERON,David Todd — Capt Can HQCFC ded 30-8-20 CR Canada 132
CAMERON,Donald — 2Lt Aust 1 2LtTMB 10-6-17 MR 29
CAMERON,Donald Ewan — Lt Can PPCLI kia 15-3-15 CR Belgium 111
CAMERON,Douglas Upton — Maj Can 2CMR kia 30-10-17 CR Belgium 5
CAMERON,Ian MacKenzie — Lt Can 15Bn kia 9-4-17 CR France 523
CAMERON,James Duncan McIntyre — Lt Can 72Bn 11-8-18 CR France 586
CAMERON,John Angus.DSO. — Lt Can 31Bn 17-2-18 CR France 522
CAMERON,John David — 2Lt NZ 9/908 Pnrs kia 7-8-17 CR Belgium 50 Donald
CAMERON,John Scott — Lt Can 27Bn 8-11-18 CR Sussex 200
CAMERON,McRae Cumberland — 2Lt NZ 13689 1/3NZRB A'Coy kia 10-9-17 CR Belgium 113
CAMERON,Norman Donald — Lt NZ 11/216 WMR kia 30-5-15 MR 6
CAMERON,Oliver Lorne — Lt Can 54Bn 10-8-18 CR France 29
CAMERON,W.M. — Lt SA 8Inf kia 26-4-15 CR SAfrica 18
CAMERON,William — 2Lt Aust 9ALH kia 4-9-15 CR Gallipoli 17
CAMERON,William Alexander — HMaj Can77Bn &43CanMilitia ded 24-2-17 CR Canada1 245
CAMERON,William McIlwraith — Capt Aust26Inf kia 8-8-18 CR France 144
CAMPBELL,Alexander — Capt Can CE 2FC 19-10-14 CR Canada 1245
CAMPBELL,C.K.D. — 2Lt Aust 58Inf 30-9-18 CR France 446
CAMPBELL,Charles Vincent.OBE. — LtCol Can 52DistCFC 97CanR ded 6-5-21 CR Canada 1456
CAMPBELL,Christina — NSister Can CAMC 5GenHosp drd 27-6-18 MR 24
CAMPBELL,Colin Stanley — Lt Can 38Bn 22-2-17 CR France 81
CAMPBELL,Daniel Gordon — Capt Can16Bn 9-4-17 CR France 68
CAMPBELL,Donald Gordon — 2Lt Aust 51Bn 3-9-16 MR 26
CAMPBELL,Douglas Gordon — Capt Aust FA 5Bde kia 21-10-17 CR Belgium 34
CAMPBELL,Duncan.MC. — Capt Can FGH 20-11-17 CR France 1483
CAMPBELL,Duncan Gordon — Lt Can Artly attRFC 20Sqn 2CORD kia 19-2-18 CR Belgium 11

CAMPBELL,Duncan John McLeod	Lt Can 31Bn kia 11-7-16 CR Belgium 15
CAMPBELL,Frederick Fincastle	Lt Aust 47Inf 7-6-17 MR 29
CAMPBELL,Frederick William.VC.	Capt Can 1Bn dow 19-6-15 CR France 102
CAMPBELL,George Henderson	Lt Can 1PnrBn C'Coy kia 16-5-16 CR Belgium 5
CAMPBELL.Gerald	Lt Aust 11Inf dow 1-4-18 CR France 139
CAMPBELL,Glen.DSO.	LtCol Can 107PnrBn 1917
CAMPBELL,Harrison McDowell.MC.	Lt Aust 27Inf dow 23-11-16 CR France 833
CAMPBELL,Harry Davies.MID	H Capt Can 24Bn dow 30-7-17 CR France 178
CAMPBELL,Irvine Fleming	Capt Aust 2Inf dow 2-6-15 MR 6
CAMPBELL,J.A.	Lt Aust 12Inf 28-12-17 CR Aust 456
CAMPBELL,John	3rdEngr Can MercMar SS`Togona' 16-5-18MR 24
CAMPBELL,John Donald	Lt Aust 6AMGC 9-10-17MR 29
CAMPBELL,John Duncan	Lt Can 4CMR 26-10-17 CR Belgium 101
CAMPBELL,John Alex	Lt Aust 12Inf kia 28-12-17 CR Belgium 42
CAMPBELL,John James.MC.	Lt Can FA 3Bde 26-10-17 CR Belgium 35
CAMPBELL,Kenneth Archibald	Lt Can 42Bn kia 23-1-17 CR France 68
CAMPBELL,Kenneth Claude	Lt Can 60Bn 6-6-16 CR Belgium 15
CAMPBELL,Kenneth Leon Taylor.MC.	Maj Can 5Bn 28-4-17CR France 68
CAMPBELL,Kenneth Preston	Lt Can RAF 196Bn 28-11-18 CR Middx 34
CAMPBELL,Lorne Douglas.MC.	Lt Can 49Bn C'Coy dow 5-10-18 CR France 40
CAMPBELL,Neil	Lt Aust 3TC 10-4-18MR 26
CAMPBELL,Norman Gordon	Lt Can CFA 10Bde 10-11-17 CR Belgium 10
CAMPBELL,O.J.	Lt Aust 20Inf 7-2-17 CR Dorset 110
CAMPBELL,Robert Bailey	Capt Can26Bn 8-8-18 CR France 1170
CAMPBELL,Roland Playfair	LtCol Can CAMC 6FA kia 16-9-16 CR France 430
CAMPBELL,Sydney James	Capt Aust 8ALH dow 14-7-15 MR 6
CAMPBELL,Walter Victor	Capt AustADC ded 7-11-19 CR Surrey 1
CAMPBELL,Warren Knight	Lt Can CASC 2DAC attRFC 7-9-16 CR Canada 1203
CAMPBELL,William Alexander	Capt Can 194Bn ded 27-12-17 CR Canada 183
CAMPBELL,William Archibald	Lt Can 16Bn att RFC 225Bn 26-4-17CR France 777
CAMPBELL-JOHNSTON,Alexander C.	Lt Can 16Bn 2-9-18 CR France 687
CAMPKIN,Reginald	Lt Can 116Bn dow 27-8-18 CR France 14
CAMPLING,Albert Edward	Lt Aust 20Inf kia 14-6-16 CR France 83
CANN,Gilbert Franklin	Lt Can 85Bn dow 16-1-18 CR France 266
CANNAN,Douglas Herman	Capt Aust 15Inf kia 8-8-15 MR 6
CANT,James	2Lt Aust 19Bn 3-5-17 MR 26
CANTLON,Frederick Henry.MC.	Lt Can 19Bn (1COR) &RFC 11Sqn 18-3-18MR 20
CARBERT,Charles Molyneaux.MC.	Capt Can 20Bn attRFC 1-2-17 CR Belgium 158
CAREY,Alfred Blake.CMG.DSO.	LtCol Can 54Bn 1922
CAREY,Conrad George	Lt Can 43Bn 21-9-16CR France 280
CAREY,Cyril Fuller	2Lt NZ 6/3959 WIR dedacc 7-11-16 CR Wilts 115 CIR
CAREY,Joseph Martin	Lt Can 78Bn dow 18-4-18 CR Canada 183
CAREY,Tomas Joseph	2Lt Aust 25Inf kia 29-7-16 CR France 280
CAREY,William Vincent	Lt Can 19Bn att4CanTMB kia 30-9-16 CR France 1505
CARGO,James Roy	2Lt NZ 10/740WIR kia 3-6-15 CR Gallipoli 29
CARLILE,Edward Keith	Lt Aust 7Inf dow 28-2-17 CR France 177
CARLING,Gordon Burleigh	Capt Can CASC ded 18-6-18 CR Canada 1245
CARLISLE,Randil Hugh Frederick	2Lt Aust 20Inf kia 15-11-16 CR France 389
CARMICHAEL,Chalmers	2Lt SA 1/8N&DR att2SAInf 15-7-16MR 21
CARMICHAEL,John	Capt Can CAMC 8FA dow 5-4-18 CR France 95
CARMICHAEL,Kenneth Miller	Lt Can 13Bn 8-10-16MR 23
CARMICHAEL,Thomas McLeod	Lt Aust 7Inf 8-5-15 MR 4
CARMICHAEL,Wilmore Lorne	Lt Can 4Bn 17-8-17CR France 223
CARNCROSS,Cyril Cutten	2Lt NZ 39724 1/3NZRB kia 12-10-17 MR 30
CARNE,Philip Spencer.MSM.MID	Lt Aust 24Inf ded 25-10-18 CR Surrey 1
CARPENTER,David Reid	2Lt NZ 12/8 AIR kia 6/10-5-15 MR 13
CARR,Elwyne Albert	Lt Aust 42Inf kia 27-4-18 CR France 210
CARR,Eric Thomas	Lt Aust 59Inf kia 19-7-16 MR 7
CARR,H.G.	2Lt Aust AFC 11-5-18CR Hamps 192
CARR,Howard Bevan	Lt Aust 50Inf 26-9-17MR 29
CARR,Robert James	Lt SA 1MilConst ded 29-10-18 CR SAfrica 8

CARRICK,Lawrence Stanley	Lt Can49Bn 15-9-16MR 23
CARRIGAN,Andrew Hugh.MC.	Lt Aust FA 113Bty 13Bdekia 2-11-17 CR Belgium 10
CARRINGTON,Christopher	Capt NZ 2/773 NZFA dow 8-10-16 CR France 374
CARRODUS,Percy John	2Lt Aust 49Inf kia 3-9-16 CR France 280
CARROL,James William	Lt Can 22LH ded 13-3-15 CR Canada 392 9CMR
CARROLL,Horace Yeomans	Lt Can 87Bn 21-10-16 MR 23
CARRUTHERS,Kenneth B.MID	Maj Can CFA 5Bde 28-10-17 CR Belgium 10
CARRUTHERS,Thomas Frederick	Lt Can 78Bn 9-4-17 MR 23
CARRUTHERS,Walter.MM&Bar.	2Lt NZ 3/85 2WIR kia 29-9-18 CR France 379
CARSE,Arthur Edward.MID	Lt Aust16Inf dow 2-5-15 CR Egypt 3
CARSE,Franc Samuel	Capt Aust AFA 12Bde dow 2-5-17 CR France 512
CARSON,Cecil Frank	2Lt Aust 44Inf kia 4-4-18 CR France 210
CARSON,George Moffatt.MM.	Lt Aust 33Inf Ex36Bn kia 31-8-18 CR France 511
CARSON,James Henry.MC.	Lt Can 31Bn 1-7-18 CR France 95
CARSON,John Clontarf Kelvyn.MC.	Capt Can 14Bn 11-8-18CR France 693
CARSS,Adair	Lt Can 102Bn 21-10-16 CR France 430
CARTER,Albert Desbrisay.DSO&Bar	Maj Can RAF 1TrgGrp ExCanInfkld 22-5-19 CR Sussex 55
CARTER,Charles Raymond.MM.	2Lt NZ 12/1911 2AIR dow 18-9-18 CR France 84
CARTER,Duncan Campbell	Lt Aust RFC 5-9-18 MR 26
CARTER,Edgar Alfred	Lt Aust 26Inf kia 3-10-18 CR France 234
CARTER,Francis Bird	Maj Aust 16Inf kia 27-4-15 MR 6
CARTER,Harry	Lt Can 7Bn (BCR) kia 11-11-17 MR 29
CARTER,Henry Alfred	Lt Can29Bn B'Coy 21-8-17MR 23
CARTER,Hugh Baker	Lt Can 6MGCoy 1921
CARTER,Ralph Barr	Lt Can 31Bn &RFC 22Sqn 19-8-17MR 20
CARTER,Raymond Stuart	Lt Can 16Bn 1916
CARTER,Robert Ernest H	Lt CanCADC 22-2-17CR Canada 1245
CARTER,Walter Earl	Lt CanLSH &RFC 22-3-18CR Wilts 28
CARTHEW,Charles	Lt Aust 8ALH kia 7-8-15 MR 6
CARTHEW,William Morden	Lt Can 49Bn kia 3-6-16 CR Belgium 92
CARTWRIGHT,James Hattill.MC.	Capt Aust Engrs 2Div dow 2-9-18 CR France 119
CARVICK,J.B.N.MC.	Lt Aust 24Inf 7-8-16 CR France 515
CASCADEN,John Bryson	Lt Can 49Bn (AR) kia 3-6-16 MR 29
CASEY,Charles Frederick.MC	Lt Can 1CMR kia 15-9-16 MR 23
CASEY,Robert.MC.	Lt Aust 44Inf dow 7-4-18 CR France 40
CASEY,William Archer	Maj Can7Bn 8-9-16 CR France 430
CASH,James Norman	2Lt Aust AFC kia 6-1-18 CR France 258
CASH,Wilfred Arthur	Lt Can 18Bn kia 10-10-18 CR France 761 Wilfrid
CASKEY,Thomas Edward	Maj Can 29Bn 9-9-17 CR Sussex 200
CASSIDY,Arthur Ardagh	Lt SA 8SAInf mbk 19-7-17 MR 52 dow
CASSIDY,Alfred Robert	2Lt Aust1Inf kia 9-4-17 CR France 530
CASTLE,Arthur Penfold	Lt NZ 24/22 2/3NZRB kia 15-9-16 CR France 432
CATANI,Enrico Ferdinando	Lt Aust 21Inf kia 29-7-16 CR France 1890 & CR France 832
CATER,Albert Desbrisay.DSO.	Maj Can RAF 26Bn 1919
CATES,Athol	Lt Aust FA 11Bde kia 11-9-17 CR Belgium 19
CATRON,William George	Lt Aust8Inf kia 3-3-17 CR France 277
CATTELL,Reginald Percy.MC.	Lt Can 46Bn 6-5-17 CR France 81
CAVANAGH,Harry	Lt Can CE 1ATCoy dow 4-9-16 CR London 8
CAVE,Edmund Jasper Shalcrass	2Lt Can RAF 8Sqn Ex CanInf kia 14-8-18 CR France 526
CAZALET,Clement Marshall	2Lt NZ 15/16 InfBdeHQ dow 8-8-15 MR 6
CHABREL,Francis George	Capt Aust 16Inf kia 7-8-15 MR 6
CHADWICK,Frederick William	Lt Can 26Bn kia 6-1-16 CR Belgium 60
CHADWICK,Reginald Matin	Lt SA RhodR att2KARded 16-10-16 CR EAfrica 19
CHALK,William Joseph	Lt Can 100Bn &RFC 59Sqn14-4-17MR 20
CHALMERS,Adam Peden	Capt Can CAMC 16-5-17CR WIndies 33
CHALMERS,Colin Edmund Alleyne	2Lt Aust 52Inf kia 7-6-17 CR Belgium 75
CHALMERS,Hector L.	Lt Can 43Bn 12-9-20CR Canada 116
CHAMBERLAIN,Horace	Lt Aust 40Inf dow 30-3-18 CR France 62
CHAMBERS,Arthur Frank	Maj Aust 2ALH dow 20-4-17 CR Palest 8
CHAMBERS,James Alexander	Lt Can 72Bn 2-9-18 CR France 95
CHAMBERS,John Cyril.MM.	2Lt Aust 25Inf dow 31-1-17 CR London 8

CHAMBERS,Leslie Keith	Capt Aust17Inf kia 29-7-16 CR France 267
CHAMBERS,Robert William Laws	Capt Aust 9Inf kia 21-8-16 CR France 314
CHAMBERS,Samuel Wallace Graham	Lt Can16Bn 6-7-15 CR France 922
CHAMBERS,Selwyn	Maj NZ 11/672 WMR C'Sqn kia 7-8-15 MR 5
CHAMPAGNE,Ernestine	Nurse Can CAMC 8GH ded 24-3-19 CR Canada 372
CHAMPION,Christopher Henry Duncan.MID.	Lt Aust 3Bn 14-4-18 MR 26
CHAMPION,Geoffrey Servante	Lt Aust 4Inf kia 25-7-16 CR France 832
CHAMPION,Leonard John	Lt SA BrSAPol dow 4-10-18 CR EAfrica 15
CHANT,Earle Marion	Lt Can 67Bn &RAF 16Sqn 4-4-18 CR France 403
CHANT,Gordon Leslie	Capt Aust 2Inf kia 5-9-16 CR Belgium 127
CHAPLIN,Arthur	Lt Can CFA 4Bde 3-5-17 CR France 268
CHAPMAN,Alick Atkinson Hon	Lt & QMAust 12Fld Amb Aust AMC dow 27-1-17 CR France 833
CHAPMAN,Duncan	Maj Aust 45Inf kia 6-8-16 CR France 832
CHAPMAN,Edward Laurie Elliot	Lt Aust 33Inf kia 12-7-17 CR Belgium 42
CHAPMAN,Earl Haddon Simpson	2Lt Aust 7Inf dow 27-4-15 MR 6
CHAPMAN,Eric Burton Elliott	2Lt Aust 35Inf 7-6-17 MR 29
CHAPMAN,Frank.MID.	Maj NZ 13/634 AMR kia 8-8-15 MR 5
CHAPMAN,Frederick Edward	2Lt Aust AFA 10Bde dow 11-8-18 CR France 71
CHAPMAN,Harley Waldron	Lt Aust 36Inf kia 16-7-17 CR Belgium 42
CHAPMAN,Henry Stanley	Lt Aust 3Bn 25-7-16 MR 26
CHAPMAN,Jackson Alexander Fletcher	Lt Can CFA 1Bde 3-6-16 MR 29
CHAPMAN,John Ernest	Lt Aust AFC kia 8-8-18 CR France 526
CHAPMAN,Percy Wellesley.MC.	Capt Aust 55Inf kia 12-3-17 CR France 400
CHAPMAN,William John.MC.	Lt Can2Bn dow 10-9-18 CR France 52
CHAPPELL,Allan Charles	Capt Aust 56Inf dow 28-9-17 CR Belgium 11
CHAPUT,Joseph Donat	Lt Can CAMC 4StatHosp ded 19-3-20 CR Canada 254
CHARLTON,Arthur Henry	Lt NZ45312 2/3NZRB kia 3-2-18 CR Belgium 307
CHASE,Allen Autliores	Lt SA 4SAInf kia 17-4-18 MR 29
CHASELING,Issiah	LtCol Aust AIF AASC 8-4-19 CR Aust 94
CHATTERTON,Willoughby E.	Lt Can 3Bn 8-10-16 CR France 239
CHAUNCY,Clement Lamothe	Lt Aust 56Inf dow 2-4-17 CR France 832
CHAUVIN,Edward Henry.MID	Lt Can 5CMR 1-10-16 MR 23
CHEADLE,Francis Bowman	Lt Aust 18Inf dow 12-5-16 CR France 275
CHEDZEY,Henry Charles	Lt CanCFA 2Bde ded 26-1-19 CR Canada 1691
CHENEY,Edward.MC.	Lt Aust 50Inf dow 12-3-18 CR France 139
CHERRY,Herbert Meade	LtCol Can 8Bn ded 6-7-21 CR Canada 119
CHERRY,Percy Herbert.VC.MC.	Capt Aust 26Inf kia 27-3-17 CR France 646
CHESTER,R.S.	2Lt SA HArty 73SB dow 12-4-18 CR France 88
CHILDS,Arthur James	Maj NZ 24/2 2/3NZRB kia 15-9-16 CR France 277
CHILVERS,Oscar Mackeknie	2Lt Aust51Inf kia 15-8-16 CR France 280
CHINNER,Eric harding	Lt Aust32Inf dow PoW 20-7-16 MR 7
CHIPMAN,Leverett De Veber	Capt Can13Bn ded 16-12-18 CR Canada 793
CHIPMAN,Nathan Lewis	Lt Can 85Bn kia 16-6-17 CR France 924
CHIRNSIDE,William	2Lt NZ 24965 FA dow 11-10-17 CR Belgium 20
CHISHOLM.George Phillip	Lt Can 5Bn kia 27-9-18 CR France 147
CHISNALL,Charles Alain	Lt Can RAF 9RBn 28-5-19 CR Yorks 294
CHOAT,Joseph Cyril	2Lt SA 4SAInf dow 24-4-18 CR France 134
CHOATE,Frederick Henry	Lt Can ARD (LSH) &RAF 4-6-18 CR Wilts 116
CHRISTENSEN,Christian Peder	Lt Aust 39Inf kia 29-7-17 CR Belgium 42
CHRISTIANSEN,Godfrey Charles	Capt Aust 56Inf ded 24-9-17 CR WAfrica 30
CHRISTIAN,Andrew George	Capt Aust 1Inf kia 1-5-15 CR Gallipoli 31
CHRISTIANSON,Richard Francis	Lt Aust 2Inf dow 4-10-17 CR Belgium 72
CHRISTIE,Allan Leslie	Capt NZ 3/2915 NZMC ded 10-11-18 CR NZ 239 9-11-18
CHRISTIE,Andrew Fleming	Lt Can27Bn 26-8-18 CR France 162
CHRISTIE,Herbert Alfred	Lt NZ 2/615 FA kia 2-6-17 CR Belgium 43
CHRISTIE,Howard Thomas	Lt Can 6CGR 66CanMilitia ded 5-11-19 CR Canada 731
CHRISTIE,John Hatchell Halliday	Lt Can 2CMR 10-4-17 CR France 58
CHRISTIE,Norman Cahill	Lt Can 85Bn 28-10-17 CR Belgium 125
CHRISTIE,Robert William Ewart	Lt Can CE 2DivSigCoy kia 21-9-18 CR France 309
CHRISTIE,Wm Davidson Carns.DSO.	Lt Capt Can 13Bn dow 17-9-18 CR France 34
CHRISTMAS,Frederic John	2Lt Aust 3Pnrs kia 27-6-17 CR Belgium 42

CHRISTOPHERS,Herbert Henry	Capt NZ 24/7 2/3NZRB	kia 2-6-16 CR France 922
CHRISTOPHERS,Reginald Gillon	2LtNZ 60286 10OIR	dow 13-10-18 CR France 560
CHURCH,Arthur.MC.	Lt EA EAIC ded	14-2-18 CR EAfrica 11
CHURCHILL,Alfred Snow	Lt Can RCR kia 9-4-17	CR France 68
CHURCHILL,Arthur Norton Hickling	Lt Can 1Bn dow 7-9-15	CR Belgium 138
CHURCHILL,Burpee Clair	Lt Can 52Bn 15-8-18	CR France 987
CHURCHUS,Walter.DSO.	Lt Col Aust 7FA kia 1-4-18	CR France 833
CHUTE,Claude Henry	Lt Aust 31Inf 26-9-17	MR 29
CHUTE,Frederick Russell	Lt Can 17MGCoy 14-8-17	CR Surrey 144
CLAPPERTON,George	Lt Can 58Bn 13-6-16	CR Belgium 127
CLARE,Emily	Sister Aust AANS 17-10-18	MR 65
CLAREBROUGH,Charles Alfred Walter	LtAust 21Inf kia 26-8-16	CR France 832
CLARIDGE,Ralph Elsmere	Lt Aust 50Bn 25-4-18	MR 26
CLARK,Alexander James	Lt NZ 10/2367 WIR kia 13-8-15	MR 5
CLARK,C.H.B. or CLARKE,C.H.B.	Capt SA MtdRif attKARkia 28-10-16	CR EAfrica 40
CLARK,Charles Loaring	Lt Can 3Bn dow 17-6-15	CR France 571
CLARK,David Goodlet	2Lt Aust RFC 22-11-17	MR 26
CLARK,Edward	Lt Aust 3Inf dow 3-10-17	CR Belgium 11
CLARK,Edward Denison	Lt Aust 43Inf dow 8-6-17	CR France 285
CLARK,Ernest James	2Lt Aust 21Inf dow 24-8-16	CR France 44
CLARK,Harold Ross	Lt Aust 8Inf kia 16-9-17	CR Belgium 19
CLARK,Herbert Cameron Russell.MC&Bar.	Lt Capt Can 7Bn dow 20-11-18	CR France 40
CLARK,Isobel	SNurse NZ 22/108 ANS drd 23-10-15	MR 35
CLARK,John Ross	Lt Aust 24Inf kia 4-8-16	CR France 832
CLARK,Lewis Emerson	Capt Can CAMC att87Bn 8-6-17	CR France 81
CLARK,Paul Graham	2Lt NZ 46224 2/3NZRB kia 26-8-18	CR France 518
CLARK,Percy John.MID.	2Lt NZ 23/36 5MGC kia 11-10-17	MR 30
CLARK,Ralph Bradford	Lt Can 26Bn 17-9-16	MR 23
CLARK,Reginald Crago	2Lt NZ25/17 3/3NZRB kia 4-10-16	MR 11
CLARK,Thomas Archibald	Lt NZ 8/24 OtagoR 10Reinf ded 25-11-18	CR NZ 243
CLARK,William Frederick.MC.	Lt Aust 55Inf kia 17-4-18	CR France 1173
CLARKE,Clarence Victor	2Lt Can RAF Ex 1CanInf ded 16-2-19	CR Derbyshire 117
CLARKE,Emil John Hamilton	Lt Aust AFA 11Bde kia 15-4-17	CR France 565
CLARKE,Ernest	2Lt NZ 28616 1WIR kia 24-8-18	CR France 239
CLARKE,Guther Robert Carlisle	Maj Aust 34Inf kia 12-10-17	CR Belgium 308
CLARKE,Ivor John	Lt Can 28Bn 20-5-17	CR France 68
CLARKE,Lancelot Fox.DSO.	LtCol Aust 12Inf kia 25-4-15	CR Gallipoli 30
CLARKE,Lionel Esmonde	Lt Can 4CMR (1COR) 3-6-16	MR 29
CLARKE,M.	Lt SA 5SAInf kia 16-11-17	CR Tanzania 1
CLARKE,Paul Brooks	Lt Can 124PnrBn 27-10-17	CR Belgium 101
CLARKE,Warring Kennedy	Capt Can CFA 8ABde 7-3-18	CR France 68
CLARKE,William Robinson Henry	2Lt NZ 4/2170 NZE WirelessCoy ded 8-7-16	CR Iraq 6
CLARKSON,David Birrell	Lt Can 47Bn 5-5-17	CR France 81
CLARKSON,David William.MC.	Maj Can 14Bn kia 9-8-18	CR France 29
CLARKSON,Maurice Arundel	Lt Can FA 8Bde 21-4-17	CR France 12
CLASPER,Walter James.MC.	Lt Aust AustMGC 4Coy dow 30-4-18	CR France 71
CLASPER,William Urwin	Lt Aust 13Inf dow 21-4-17	CR France 145
CLAYDEN,Walter James	Lt Aust 23Inf kia 1-9-18	CR France 624
CLAYDON,Arthur.DFC.	Capt Can RAF 32Sqdn CFA kia 8-7-18	CR France 924
CLAYTON,Edward Reginald.MC.	Capt Can 85Bn (NSR) kia 30-10-17	MR 29
CLAYTON,G.J.G.MC.	Lt Aust 18Inf 30-7-18	CR France 1170
CLAYTON,Harry	Lt Aust 1Pnrs 25-7-16	MR 26
CLEARY,Cecil	2Lt Aust 18Inf 20-9-17	MR 29
CLEEVES,Alfred Christian	Lt Can CFA 4Bde ded 21-5-19	CR Canada 166
CLEGHORN,Allen MacKenzie	Capt CanCAMC ded 20-3-16	CR Hamps 80
CLEMENGER,William Percy	Lt Aust 4Inf kia 10-3-18	CR Belgium 131
CLEMENT,Sydney Reynold	Capt Aust 5Inf kia 26-4-15	CR Gallipoli 7
CLEMENTS,Charles Edward	Maj Aust 31Inf dow 22-7-16	CR France 102
CLEMENTS,Ernest	WTO Can `Grilse' 1916	
CLEMENTS,John Herbert	Lt Can 6BnCE 1921	
CLEVEN,Endre Johannesen H	Capt Can197Bn kldacc 3-7-16	CR Canada 116

CLEVERLY,Henry	Lt Aust 28Inf dow 11-10-17 CR Belgium 3
CLIBBORN,John Barclay	Lt Can 3CMR 26-11-15 CR Belgium 138
CLIFF,Norman Victor.MC&Bar.	Capt Can 3Bn kia 30-8-18 CR France 313
CLIFFORD,Albert George.MC.	Lt Aust 51Bn 3-9-16 MR 26
CLIFFORD,Herbert Edward	Capt SA 2SAInf dow 19-7-16 CR France 145
CLIFT,Cecil Bayly	Lt Can RNewfndlandR kia 12-10-16 MR 20
CLIFTON,William Powell	Lt Can 11MGCoy 21-8-17 CR France 81
CLINKSKILL,James Thomas	Capt Can 10Bn 26-9-16 MR 23
CLIPPERTON,William Henry	Lt Can 8Bn 17-8-17 CR France 88
CLONAN,J.P.S.	Lt Aust 36Inf 10-11-17 CR France 276
CLOSE,Arthur.MC.DCM.	Lt Can14Bn 1-10-18 CR France 148
CLOSE,Stanley Robert	2Lt Aust 8Inf dow 28-4-15 MR 6
CLOSS,William Osborne	2Lt NZ 22670 2OIR kia 22-7-17 CR France 262
CLOUSTON,Edgar Boyd	Lt Aust MGC 4Coy dow 26-9-17 CR Belgium 11
CLUETT,Vincent	2Lt Can NewfndlandR dow 26-11-17 CR France 40
CLUFF,Francis Nicholas	Lt Can 49Bn kia 28-8-18 CR France 732
COATES,Eric Albert	2Lt NZ 11/643 MGSqn ded 14-11-18 CR NZ 194
COATES,Randolph Edward Oswald	Lt NZ 12/59 1AIR dow 7-6-17 CR Belgium 50
COATES,William Henry	Lt NZ 13/991 AMR attRFC kia 22-7-17 MR 20
COATMAN,Arthur Sindel Mehrtens	2Lt NZ 8/25 2OIR kia 12-10-17 MR 30
COBB,John Wesley	Lt NZ 10/35 1AIR kia 7-6-17 MR 9
COBB,T.W.	2Lt Egypt EgyptLabCps 15-12-20 CR Hamps 8
COBBE,Ernest	2Lt NZ 25/262 4/3NZRB kia 12-10-17 MR 30
COBBOLD,Walter Frederick	Lt Aust 28Inf kia 10-6-18 CR France 209
COBDEN,Cecil Melton	2Lt Aust 39Inf kia 10-8-18 CR France 526
COBOURNE,Clarence Taylor	Capt NZ 13/39 1AIR 1-10-18 MR 12
COCHRAN,Frank Eardley.DSO.	Maj SA 2SAInf kia 24-3-18 MR 27
COCHRAN,Frederick John	Lt Aust 24MGC Ex 35Sqn 13ALH kia 17-10-17 CR Belgiu 310
COCHRAN,Robert Harvey.MC.	Lt Can 38Bn 29-10-18 CR France 1252
COCKBURN,George Angus	Lt Can 1Bn dow 19-5-16 CR Belgium 11
COCKBURN,Gordon Allan	Lt Can CFA attRFC kia 8-11-17 CR Belgium 123
COCKRILL,Culmer Hurst	Lt Aust 26Inf kia 8-8-18 CR France 1170
COCKSHUTT,Harvey Watt	Lt Can 4CMR 2-6-16 CR Belgium 116
CODE,John Edmund	Capt Can 122Bn ded 19-9-16 CR Canada 1536
CODE,William Wellis	Lt Can 5Bn kia 9-8-18 CR France 586 Willis
CODRINGTON-FORSYTH,Guy Percy	Lt Aust 48Bn 11-4-17 MR 26
COEN,Francis	Capt Aust 18Bn 28-7-16 MR 26
COETZEE,J.J.R.	Capt SA MilMagistrate 31-10-18 CR SAfrica 19
COFFEE,Frank Mathew	Lt Aust 24Inf kia 18-11-15 CR Gallipoli 7
COGHLAN,George Houghton	Lt Can 19Bn 8-8-18 CR France 1170
COHEN,Myer Tutzer.MC.	Lt Can 42Bn 3-11-17 CR Belgium 126
COLE,Charles Edward	Lt Can 19Bn dow 21-5-17 CR France 12
COLE,Frederick Minden.DSO.	LtCol Can Cmdg 1BdeCGA ded 7-7-20 CR Canada 256
COLE,Montague Henry	2Lt SA 3SAInf attRAF kia 30-6-18 CR France 1632
COLE,Samuel B.	2Lt Can 1NewfndlandR kia 9-10-17 CR Belgium 126
COLE,Walter Frank	Lt Can 18Bn 28-8-18 CR France 421
COLEGRAVE,Arthur Philip	Lt Can 3Bn 27-9-18 CR France 481
COLEMAN,Edward Longden.MM.MID	Lt Aust AFA 1Bde dow 29-4-18 CR France 180
COLEMAN,Herbert Napier	2Lt NZ 36739 1CIR kia 13-4-18 CR France 1013
COLEMAN,Spencer William	Lt Aust 29Inf kia 9-8-18 CR France 526
COLLESS,Stanley.MC.DCM.	Lt Aust 55Inf kia 1-9-18 CR France 627
COLLIE,Alan.MC.	Lt Can 44Bn 28-9-18 CR France 714
COLLIER,Bertram Henry Frank	2Lt Aust 1Bn 23-7-16 MR 26
COLLIER,Clarence Timbrell	2Lt Aust 53Inf kia 20-7-16 MR 7
COLLIN,Charles Louis	Lt Aust 42Inf kia 1-9-18 CR France 216
COLLIN,George Rowland	Lt Can 3Bn 30-8-18 CR France 313
COLLIN,Leslie Norman	Lt Aust 15Inf kia 9-5-15 MR 6
COLLINS,Arthur Joseph	Lt Aust 55Inf kia 16-4-18 CR France 1173
COLLINS,Eric Arthur	Capt AustAFA 12Bde dow 4-5-17 CR France 512
COLLINS,Frank Erskine Hobbs	Lt Aust 47Inf 12-10-17 MR 29
COLLINS,Frank Peter	Lt Can 2PnrBn dow 23-7-17 CR France 480

COLLINS,Frederick Bissett	Lt Aust 21Inf 4-10-17MR 29
COLLINS,George Donald	Lt CanCE ded 23-7-19 CR Canada 465
COLLINS,Harold.DCM.	Lt Aust 6Inf kia 10-8-18 CR France 526
COLLINS,Hubert Percival	Lt Can 9MGCoy 30-10-17 MR 29
COLLINS,John Arnold	Lt Can 49Bn C'Coy kia 29-9-18 CR France 481
COLLINS,Thomas	Lt Can 1BnCMGC kia 2-10-18 CR France 240
COLLINS,William Edward	2Lt NZ 23109 4/3NZRB kia 9-6-17 MR 9
COLLINS-MORGAN,Charles Edward.MC.	2Lt NZ 10/1295 1AuklandR dow 5-10-17 CR Belgium 3
COLLISON,Herbert Youngman,	Lt Aust 10Inf kia 25-2-17 CR France 744
COLLIVER,William Gordon	Lt Aust43Inf kia 1-9-18 CR France 511
COLLUM,William Henry P.MC.	Maj Can 22Bn att11InfBdeHQ dow 14-8-17 CR France 178
COLMAN,Douglas Allen	Lt Can 47Bn 28-9-18CR France 715
COLMAN,Frederick	Lt Aust 43Inf kia 4-6-17 CR Belgium 451
COLQUHOUN,Frederick Gibson.MID	Lt Can 72Bn 1-3-17 CR France 81
COLQUHOUN,Wyndham John	Lt Can 15Bn ded 8-11-18 CR Canada 1464
COLTMAN,Charles Stanley.MC.MID	Maj Aust 4Inf ded 6-1-16 CR Egypt 9
COLUMB,David Sutherland	Maj NZ24302 WIR 5-2-21 CR NZ 79
COLVIN,James.MM.	2Lt Aust 5Inf kia 9-8-18 CR France 526
COLVIN,William	2Lt Aust 8Bn 25-7-16MR 26
COLYER,Henry Maxwell	Lt Aust 36Bn 12-4-18MR 26
COMBE,Robert Grierson.VC.	Lt Can 27Bn kia 3-5-17 MR 23
COMINS,Percival Richards.VD.	Capt Aust 6Inf ded 30-11-15 CR Greece 11
COMMINS,Chester Francis.MC&Bar.	Capt Can 1Bn 1-10-18CR France 597
COMMINS,William Kennedy.MC.	Capt Can 75Bn 9-8-18 CR France 589
COMPTON,John Sleight	Lt Can 78Bn 27-9-18CR France 714
CONCANON,George Lewis Blake.MID	Capt Aust2Inf kia 27-4-15 MR 6
CONDON,Richard Merrick (Will)	2Lt Aust 22Inf kia 5-8-16 CR France 832
CONNELL,Eric McIntyre	Lt Can 15Bn 13-6-16CR Belgium 15
CONNELL,William Anderson.DCM.	Capt Aust 12Inf dow 28-12-17 CR Belgium 42
CONNELLY,Clive Emerson	Capt Aust14Inf kia 28-8-15 MR 6
CONNELLY,Eric Winfield.DSO.	Maj Aust 3DivHQ dow 9-9-18 CR France 526
CONNELLY,Kenneth Gastrelle	Lt Aust 18Inf 3-11-17MR 29
CONNERS,Allan De Vere.MC.	Maj Can10Bn dow 25-9-16 CR France 44
CONNOCK,Joseph George	2Lt SA 2SAInf kia 20-7-16 CR France 402 19-7-16
CONNOR,John Wright.MID.	Lt Aust20Inf dow 6-5-16 CR France 768
CONNOR,William Joseph Sanderson	Lt Can CFA 4Bty 3Bde 1Bde dow 5-7-16 CR Belgium 4
CONRAD,Ervin Simeon	Lt Can 31Bn 15-9-16MR 23
CONRAD,Harold Victor	Lt Aust 42Inf kia 8-8-18 CR France 526
CONROY,William Matthew.MC.MM.	Lt Aust28Inf dow 2-10-17 CR Belgium 84
CONVERY,Joseph A.	Lt Can RFC LSH 11-3-18CR France 1277
CONWAY,Neil John	2Lt Aust 10ALH 3-5-18 MR 34
COOK,Alfred Edward	Maj Aust 9ALH dow 4-7-15 CR Europe 1
COOK,Charles Fred Denman.DSO.MIDx2	LtCol NZ 10/543 1WIR ded 2-5-18 CR Berks 86
COOK,George Thornhill Chpn/	Capt SA 3SAInf kia 11-7-16 MR 21
COOK,George Alfred	Lt Can 1CMR 13-11-17 CR France 40
COOK,Herbert	Lt Can 152Bn &RFC 70Sqn kld 17-10-17 CR Belgium 18
COOK,John	Lt Can 2CMR 29-9-18CR France 715
COOK,Samuel Yardley	Lt Can 72Bn drd 3-7-19 CR Wales 571
COOK,Sydney	2Lt Aust 36Inf 12-10-17 MR 29
COOK,William Ernest	Lt Aust28Inf kia 26-3-17 CR France 646
COOK,William Lea	Lt Can 50Bn 3-2-17 MR 23
COOKE,Clive Ernest Alexander	Capt Aust 51Inf kia 24-4-18 CR France 144
COOKE,Frederick Eli Hitchon	Capt NZ 2/835 NZFA Cmdg 5Bty kia 14-10-16 CR France 188
COOKE,Gerald Charles Northcott	Lt Can 50Bn 28-7-17CR Oxford 69
COOKE,Henry	Capt Can CAPC 10Bn 3-2-15 CR Surrey 152
COOKE,J.A.E.	Lt SASAFA StokesMortars kia 19-7-17 CR Tanzania 1 &EAfrica 38
COOKE,John Soden	Lt Can 27Bn 19-11-16 CR France 557
COOKE,Joseph Henry	2Lt Aust 11Inf kia 2-5-15 MR 6
COOKE,LeonardCharles.MC.	Lt Aust 11Inf 7-10-17MR 29
COOKSLEY,William John Farmer	2Lt Aust 47Bn 5-4-18 MR 26
COOLAHAN,J.S.MC.	Lt Aust AMGC 5Coy 3-5-18 CR France 1142

COOMBE,Ewart Henry	Lt Can 2Bn 3-5-17 MR 23
COOMBE,Harry Heywood	2Lt Aust 10Bn 23-8-18 MR 26
COOMBS,Charles Vesta Victoria	Lt Can 116Bn 27-12-19 CR Surrey 1
COOMER,Francis John	2Lt Aust 4 LtTMB dedacc 23-9-16 CR France 200
COOPER,Arthur Bernard	2Lt SA 2SAInf kia 20-9-17 CR Belgium 453 &MR 29
COOPER,Arthur Edward	Lt SA 2SAInf kia 26-3-18 MR 27
COOPER,Arthur Lionel Keith	Lt Aust 11GenServAustReinf ded 14-11-18 CR Wilts 115
COOPER,Albert Edward	2Lt Aust 53Inf kia 29-3-17 CR France 245
COOPER,Allen Claude.MC.	Lt NZ 12/321 2AIR 6Coy kia 7-6-17 MR 9
COOPER,Arthur Edward Hamilton	2Lt Aust 33Inf kia 16-7-17 CR Belgium 42
COOPER,Charles Edwin.MC.	Maj Can 3Bn 28-4-17 CR France 68
COOPER,Charles Theodore	Lt Can 1MMGBde dow 8-1-19 CR Surrey 1
COOPER,Hubert Lloyd	Lt Aust 3Inf dow 28-7-16 CR France 44
COOPER,K.J.	Lt Aust 2Inf 9-4-17 CR France 564
COOPER,Sydney Baker.MM.	Lt Can 19Bn 27-8-18 CR France 310
COOPER,Walter John	Lt Can CFA 2DAC kia 20-5-17 CR France 68
COOPER,William Stanley	Lt AustFA 7Bde dow 22-9-17 CR Belgium 11
COPE,Anthony Dennis	Lt Can 8Bn kia 28-9-18 CR France 214
COPE,Arthur Lindsay	Lt Aust21Inf kia 1-9-18 CR France 511
COPELAND,William Wilfred	Lt Can 19Bn dow 23-12-18 CR France 40
COPP,Harold William Walter	Lt Can 3Bn `Toronto'Coy kia 30-8-18 CR France 688
COPP,Thomas Pearson	Lt Can 102Bn kia 23-10-16 CR France 430
CORBETT,Archibald Gladstone	Capt Aust AMC drd 25/26-6-20 MR 26
CORBETT,Edgar Charles	Lt Can 29Bn kia 21-8-17 MR 23
CORBETT,Raymond	Lt Can 21Bn 3/4-11-17 CR Belgium 125
CORBETT,John Mainer	2Lt NZ12/1600 AIR kia 8-6-15 MR 6
CORBETT,Thomas	2Lt NZ 8/336 OtagoR ded 10-3-20 CR NZ 88
CORCORAN,George Francis	2Lt Aust 31Inf dow 30-10-16 CR France 833
CORCORAN,Thomas Leo.MC.	Lt Aust 10Inf dow 30-5-18 CR France 28
CORDINER,Richard Charles	Lt Can 50Bn 12-4-17 CR France 1896
CORDINGLY,Robert Cecil	Lt Can 9MGC 4-6-16 CR Belgium 127
COREY,James Wallace	Lt Can 69124 26Bn kia 28-8-18 CR France 309
CORLEY,Anthony Purdon Hegarty	Capt Aust 11Inf kia 17-9-15 CR Gallipoli 22
CORMACK,Alexander Gair	Capt Aust 3Inf kia 23-8-18 CR France 526
CORMIER,Alfred Sylvany	Lt Can25Bn 29-8-18 CR France 14
CORMODY,Alexander Ford	Lt NZ 6/3212 1CIR kia 8-7-16 CR France 922
CORNE,William	Lt Aust 22Bn 26-2-17 MR 26
CORNELL,Archibald Clayton	Lt Can 16Bn 9-4-17 CR France 68
CORNELL,Harold Gordon	2Lt AustAFC 68Sqn kia 11-12-17 CR France 177
CORNELL,Stanley Anderson.MID	Lt Can CFA 8Bde 4-1-19 CR Surrey 1
CORNER,Fred Williams	2Lt Aust 26Inf kia 26-3-17 CR France 646
CORNEY,Hubert Hume.MM.	Lt Aust 21Inf kia 9-10-17 CR Belgium 123
CORNFORD,Ernest Stanford	2Lt NZ 6/2099 CIR 2CanterburyR kia 7-7-17 CR Belgium 31
CORNISH,Philip Victor	Capt Can PPCLI dow 4-6-16 CR Belgium 11
CORNISH,Richard.DCM.	Lt Aust 29Inf dow 29-4-18 CR France 71
CORNWITH,George Cameron	Lt Can 2BdeCGA 5-11-18 CR France 1196
CORR,Frank Joseph	Lt Can 20Bn 28-6-16 CR Belgium 11
CORREY,Allan Obed.	Lt Aust 53Inf dow 26-9-17 CR Belgium 11
CORRIGAN,Leo James	2Lt Aust 18Inf 20-9-17 MR 29
COSSON,John George.DCM.MID	2Lt Aust 48Bn 7-8-16 MR 26
COSTER,Albert Frederick	Lt SA 1SARif dow 3-10-17 CR EAfrica 40 kia
COSTIGAN,Charles Telford.DSO.MC.	CaptCan 10Bn (AR) 11-11-17 MR 29
COSTIGAN,John Francis	Maj Can50Bn kia 21-3-17 CR France 81
COSTIN,Eric Balfour.MM.	Lt Aust 4Inf dow 8-5-17 CR France 512
COSTIN,Joseph William	Lt Aust9Inf kia 25/28-4-15 MR 6
COTE,Paul Emile.MC.	Capt Can 22Bn 6-3-18 CR France 12
COTGRAVE,Montague Lewis Farmar	Lt Can 2Bn (EOR) 6-11-17 MR 29
COTTAM,Bartholomew	Lt Can 21Bn 1-12-16 MR 23
COTTER,Henry Francis	2Lt NZ 17594 NZFA Z'TMB dow 11-6-17 CR France 285
COTTERELL,Fred James.MC.	Capt Aust55Inf kia 2-9-18 CR France 627
COTTERELL,George Edward	Lt Aust28Inf kia 3-10-18 CR France 1461

COTTERILL,Eric Roland	2Lt Aust 13Inf	kia 9-5-15 CR Gallipoli 8
COTTON,Charles Penner	Lt Can CFA 2Bde	kia 2-6-16 CR Belgium 11
COTTON,Malcolm John Bernard	Capt Aust 2Bn	24-7-16 MR 26
COTTON,Ross Penner	Capt Can 16Bn att 3InfBdeHQ	kia 13-6-16 CR Belgium 11
COTTRIL,W.S.	Maj SA SAMC	14-4-18 CR SAfrica 62
COULSON,Byard John	Lt Can 75Bn	kia 2-9-18 CR France 426
COULTER,Leslie Jack.DSO.	Maj Aust 3ATC	kia 28-6-17 CR France 224
COULTER,Reginald Bruce	Lt Aust 27Inf	dow 16-10-17 CR Belgium 11
COULTON,Stanley Gordon	2Lt Aust 2Pnrs	dow 16-11-16 CR France 399
COUPAR,Simon James Stuart	Lt NZ16/200 Pnrs	kia 29-6-16
COURTNEY,John Classon	Lt Aust RFC 4Sqn	7-4-18 MR 26
COUSINS,Frank Leicester	2Lt Aust 59Inf	kia 19-7-16 MR 7
COUTTS,Charles Clifford	Lt Aust 31Inf	kia 27-9-17 CR Belgium 112
COUVE,Alan Crawford	Lt Aust 8Inf	dow 26-4-15 CR Gallipoli 30
COUVE,Henry Thomas Ludson	2Lt Aust 8Inf	8-5-15 MR 4
COWAN,Alan William Russell	Lt Can 73Bn	20-8-16 CR Belgium 11
COWAN,Charles Davenport	2Lt Aust 7Bn	6-11-16 MR 26
COWAN,Gerard Henderson	Lt Aust AFC 2 Sqn	ded 22.2.19 CR France 134
COWAN,Henry Rawlings	Lt NZ 10/116 WIR D'Coy	dow 13-5-15 CR Egypt 6
COWAN,James George.MID.	Lt NZ 8/28 OIR	kia 7-5-15
COWAN,John	Lt Can 16Bn	9-4-17 CR France 68
COWAN,Stewart	Lt Can 24Bn	kia 1-10-16 MR 23
COWAN,Thomas Conolly	Maj Can CAMC	5-5-18 CR Canada 1178
COWARD,William Aubrey	Lt Aust 24Bn	22-8-16 MR 26
COWELL,W.R.DSO.	Maj SA 1CapeCps	dow 21-9-18 CR Palest 3 20-9-18
COWEN,Edwin.MC.DCM.MID	Capt Can 14Bn	12-7-17 CR France 12
COWIE,Alfred Cranstone	2Lt NZ 10/3809 2WIR	kia 2-10-16 CR France 385
COWIE,Graham Robertson	Capt SA SAMC attRGA 50Bde	dow 3-9-18 CR France 14
COWIE,William Warden	Maj SA 3Horse	dow 9-9-16 CR EAfrica 39 kia
COWLES,John Richmond.MC.MID.	Maj NZ23/9 Cmdg 4/3RB	kia 25-11-17 CR Belgium 19
COX,Albert Charles	Lt Aust AMGC 14Coy	kia 20-7-16 CR France 348
COX,Alan Birchenall	Lt Aust6Inf	kia 8-5-15 CR Gallipoli 2
COX,Ernest Herbert	Lt Can 8Bn	22-5-18 CR France 46
COX,Frederick John	2Lt Aust 1Inf	kia 6/8-8-15 CR Gallipoli 7
COX,Harold	Lt Aust 31Inf	kia 20-7-16 CR France 525
COX,Herbert William	2Lt NZ 2/2391 FA 4HB	dow 23-9-18 CR France 512
COX,James Paul Gee	Lt Aust 10ALH	19-9-18 MR 34
COX,Norman Davidson	2Lt NZ 41430 2WIR	kia 31-8-18 CR France 512
COX,Percy Travers	Lt Can 2BnCE	kia 27-9-18 CR France 688
COX,Wallace	Capt Aust 1ALH	dow 7-8-15 MR 6
COX,Wilfred James	Lt NZ 41180 2AIR	kia 27-3-18 MR 12
COXEN,Charles Frederick	2Lt SA 3SAInf	kia 20-9-17 MR 29
COXWEL,W.S.G.	Lt SA RhodR att1KAR	18-10-17 CR EAfrica 11
COZENS,Thomas Evan	Lt Aust 21Inf	kia 24-2-17 CR France 385
CRABBE,Keith George Wallace	Lt Aust 14Inf	kia 22-8-15 MR 6
CRADDICK,William Rupert	2Lt Aust 2Inf	kia 6/8-8-15 CR Gallipoli 7
CRAGG,Gerald Edwin	Lt Can 3Bn	kia 3-6-16 CR Belgium 11
CRAIES,William Alexander.MID	Maj Aust 52Inf	kia 25-4-18 CR France 1170
CRAIG,Alexander Fraser	Lt Can 25Bn	16-9-16 MR 23
CRAIG,Edward Arthur	2Lt NZ 25988 AIR 2AuklandR	dow 5-10-17 CR Belgium 11
CRAIG,Lorne Bean.MM.	Lt Can 58Bn	30-9-18 CR France 714
CRAIG,Thomas Harold	Lt Can 52Bn	kia 14-8-18 CR France 987
CRAMER,Augustus Henry Marmaduke	Lt SASANatLab	ded 29-9-19 CR SAfrica 144
CRANE,John Wilbur	Capt Can 216Bn (1COR) &RAF 19Sqn	30-10-18 MR 20
CRANE,Stanley Combermere.MID	Lt Aust FA 5Bde	dow 30-9-17 CR Belgium 19
CRANSWICK,John Stewart	2Lt Aust 40Inf	kia 13-1-17 CR France 922
CRANSWICK,Thurston George.MC.DCM.	Lt Aust AIF 40Inf	18-11-20 CR Aust 252
CRAVEN,Leslie Alic.MC.	Lt NZ 7/511 MGS	ded 4-10-18 CR NZ 8 CMR
CRAWFORD,Arthur Grant Ross.MC.	Lt NZ 16282 ICC NZBn	dow 9-6-18 CR Egypt 9
CRAWFORD,James Phillip	Capt Can3Bn	kia 27-9-18 CR France 274
CRAWFORD,Richard Gilpin	Lt Can PPCLI	dow 9-5-15 CR France 284

CRAWFORD Roy Bruce.MM.   Lt Can   1Bn   kia 1-10-18 CR France 597 Royal
CRAWLEY,Aubrey Clarence   Lt Aust 44Inf   kia 17-2-18 CR Belgium 68
CRAWLEY,William Asheton   Lt Can64Bn (2CORD) attRFC   drd 30-12-17 MR 41
CREASY,Walter.MC.   Lt Can CFA 6Bde 8-11-16CR France 515 4Bde
CREED,Harold Elvey Frederick   Capt SA   2SAInf15-7-16MR 21
CREIGHTON,Ernest   Lt Can 13Bn   8-8-18 CR France 489
CREIGHTON,Frank Albro   LtCol Can 1Bn   dow 16-6-16 CR Belgium 11
CREIGHTON,George Gillespie   Lt Can   43Bn   drd 18-7-17 CR Canada 119
CRESWELL,Randolph William.MID   Capt Aust   3AustBn ImpCamCps kia 6-11-17 CR Palest 1
CREW,Joseph Edward   Capt Aust FA 2Bde kia 20-10-17 CR Belgium 19
CRIBB,Charles William Edward   Maj NZ 6/1110 CIR   dow 9-8-15   MR 6
CRICK,Oswald William   Lt Aust 43Inf dow 4-10-17 CR Belgium 3
CRINNION,John Francis   Lt Can1Bn   30-8-18CR France 310
CRITCHLEY,John Asheton.MC.   Maj   Can LSH   dow 5-4-17   CR France 164
CROCHETIERE,Georges Etienne Rosario Chpn4Cl Can   ChpnServs att22Bn   kia 2-4-18   CR France 748
CROCKER,Frederick Talbot   Lt Aust AIF Depot 9-5-15 CR Aust 430
CROCKER,Robert Clive   Capt   Aust AFA 6Bty   kia 12-7-15 CR Gallipoli 3
CROCKETT,Arthur Raymond   Lt Can 8Bn   9-8-18 CR France 693
CROCKFORD,Edward Clifford Howson   Lt Aust 58Inf   dow 11-8-18 CR France 71
CROMBIE,Charles Stuart Grenville   Lt   Can   5Bn   9-7-17 CR Surrey 1
CROMBIE,Vincent Robert Alexdr.MC.   LtCan   19Bn   dow 26-10-18 CR France 40
CROMM,Alfred   Lt Can 54Bn   27-9-18CR France 715
CRONIN,Alfred.DCM.   Lt Aust 58Inf   dow 24-2-18 CR France 297
CROOKS,David Robert   Capt   Aust AIF Depot 8-4-20 CR Aust 375
CROSHAW,Oswald Mosley.DSO.   LtCol Aust GlasgowYco att53AustInf   dow 26-9-17   CR Belgium 165
CROSSKILL,James Henry   Lt   Can RCR att7TMB23-10-18 MR 23
CROSSLAND,Roy Charles   2Lt   Aust Engrs 1FC 18-8-16MR 26
CROW,Gordon Wilson.MC.   Lt Can CFA 7Bty 2Bde   17-9-16CR France 1505
CROW,Robert Harold   Lt Aust   13Inf kia 3-5-15   CR Gallipoli 8
CROWDY,Charles Hutton   Capt   Can 13Bn   19-10-15 CR France 922
CROWE,William Gordon Hamilton   Lt Aust 37Inf   kia 10-2-18 CR France 705
CROWL,Joseph Terrell   Capt Aust 8ALH   kia 27-6-15 CR Gallipoli 29
CROWLE,Herbert Walter   2Lt Aust 10Inf   dow 25-8-16 CR France 74
CROWLEY,Clive Stanley.DCM.   Lt Aust 33Inf   dow 25-6-18 CR France 303
CROWTHER,William   Lt Can   176Bn (2COR) &RFC 10Sqn 31-10-17 MR 20
CROWTHER,William Beverley.MC.   Maj   Can 3Bn   kia 3-5-17   CR France 68
CROZIER,Thomas Edwin   Lt Can   8Bn kia 9-8-18   CR France 693
CRUDDAS,Norman   2Lt SA   3SAInf kia 20-9-17 CR Belgium 92 &MR 29
CRUICKSHANK,Errol   Lt Aust 101Inf kia 25-12-17 CR Belgium 42
CRUMB,Eric Leander   Lt Can 1CMR att3EntrchBn 12-10-16 MR 23
CUDDY,Wilson MacWilliam   Lt Can 1Bn   dow 24-9-16 CR France 44
CULLUM,John Arthur.MC&Bar   Capt   Can28Bn 10-11-16 CR France 32
CULHAM,Hubert Anthony   Capt   Can CAMC attCFA 1Bde kld 4-10-18 CR France 147
CULLEN,Hedley Elbert   2Lt   Aust 10Inf   dow 10-8-15   MR 6
CULLING,Evelyn Claude   Capt   Can2Bn (EOR) 24-4-15MR 29
CULTON,William James   Lt Aust   40Inf   kia 12-2-17 CR France 705
CUMMING,Dewar Goring Charles.MC&Bar Capt   Aust 48Bn 3-5-18 MR 26
CUMMING,Isobel Katherine   Nurse   Can CAMC 1GH ded 4-2-21 CR Canada 832
CUMMING,James Douglas   Lt Can   5Bn   28-4-17MR 23
CUMMINGS,Roy Lytton   2Lt   Aust AFC dedacc 28-8-18 CR Glouc 172
CUNLIFFE,George Alexander   Capt   Can 31Bn D'Coy   kia 9-8-18   CR France 652
CUNNINGHAM,Alexander   2Lt NZ 9/265 OMR dow 7-6-18 CR Lancs 7
CUNNINGHAM,E.S.   Midmn Aust RAN HM S/M K17 drd 31-1-18 MR 2
CUNNINGHAM,Harold Sherratt   Lt Can 47Bn attRAF dow 17-8-18 CR France 1170
CUNNINGHAM,Herbert David.MC   Lt CanRCD 26-3-18MR 23
CUNNINGHAM,Robert Alexander   Lt Can46Bn   27-9-18CR France 482
CUNNINGHAM,Royston Kingsborough   Lt Aust1Inf   kia 19-5-15 CR Gallipoli 31
CUNNINGHAM,Stanley Lovell.MC.   Capt   Can 21Bn 27-8-18CR France 581
CUNNINGHAM,Trevor Russell.MID   Maj Aust27Inf AIF 4- 8-16 MR 26 &CR France 390 2-8-16
CURLEWIS,Gordon Levason   Capt   Aust 16Inf   kia 9-5-15   CR Gallipoli 30
CURLEWIS,Kenneth   Lt Aust 14Inf   kia 8-8-15   MR 6

CURNOW,Herbert Franklin	Capt	Aust 22Inf kia 5-8-16 CR France 280
CURRIE,Archibald.MM.	Lt	Aust5ALH 25-9-18MR 34
CURRIE,James Maxwell	Lt	Can 5Bn 25-5-15CR France 727
CURRIER,Everett Dyson	Lt	CanCMGC BordenMG 26-9-16CR France 430
CURRY,Leon Hall	Capt	Can 42Bn 19-10-15 CR France 922
CURRY,Matthew Goodwin	2Lt	NZ 41429 NZInf 40Reinf ded 5-9-18 CR NZ 318A
CURRY,Walter Eyre	Maj	Can 3Bn 9-4-17 CR France 68
CURRY,Walter Howard	Lt	Can 19Bn kia 27-8-18 CR France 419
CURTIS,Richard Haddon	2Lt	Aust AFC kia 6-1-18 CR France 258
CURWEN-WALKER,Arthur Herbert	Lt	Aust 14Inf dow 3-5-15 MR 6
CURWEN-WALKER,Jack Keith	Lt	Aust AFC 2Sqd kia 3-5-18 CR Palest 9
CUTHBERT,Niven	Lt	Aust 2Inf dow 2-11-16 CR France 105
CUTHBERTSON,Douglas Macpherson.MID.	Capt	NZ 2/1384 NZFA 6HB dow 30-3-18 CR France 64
CUTHBERTSON,Frank	2Lt	NZ 13885 OtagoR ded 4-9-21
CUTHBERTSON,George Isaac.MM.	2Lt	NZ 13886 2OIR kia 9-10-18 CR France 658
CUTLER,Cecil James Kelly	2Lt	NZ 19088 2AIR ded 4-11-16 CR France 297
CUTTEN,Leslie Raymond	Capt	Can2Bn 5-6-16 CR Belgium 11
CUTTS,Ernest Lionel Shaw	2Lt	Aust 32Inf dow 3-6-18 CR France 29

D

DABB,Reginald Henry	2Lt	Aust 8Inf dow 26-9-16 CR Germany 1
DABBS,John Wilfred.MM.	2Lt	Aust 2Inf kia 5-9-16 CR Belgium 127
DADSON,Frederick Horace	Lt	Aust 14Bn 11-4-17MR 26
DAFFARN,Maurice	Lt	SA NRhodPol 24-4-15CR EAfrica 73
DAGG,Ainslie St.Clair	Sister	Can CAMC 15GH ded 29-11-18 CR Bucks 54
DAGG,John Stewart	2Lt	NZ 12/2620 2AIR kia 15-9-16 MR 11 &CR France 1891
DAKERS,F.C.	Master	Can MercMar SS"Tagona' 16-5-18MR 24
DAKIN,Clarence Herbert	Lt	AustMGC 5Coy 15-4-17MR 26
DALE,Charles Coning	Lt	Aust8ALH kia 7-8-15 MR 6
DALE,Clarence Russell	Capt	Can 5Bn 2-8-17 CR France 223
DALE-TAYLOR,Thomas	2Lt	NZ 13/2981 AMR dow 15-8-16 CR Egypt 9
DALGLEISH,Norman.DSO.	Lt	Aust 58Inf dow 9-10-18 CR France 146
DALKEITH-SCOTT,Charles	Lt	Can 15Bn (1COR) &RFC 70Sqn30-9-17MR 20
DALLINGER,James Type	Capt	NZ 10/162 WellingtonR ded 22-6-20 CR NZ 253
D'ALPUGET,Jacques Montague	2Lt	Aust 54Inf kia 17-7-16 CR France 348
DALTON,James	Lt	Aust 7ALH ded 19-12-18 CR Asia 52
D'ALTON,William Denholm	Lt	Aust29Inf kia 29-4-18 CR France 23
DALY,Clarence Wells Didier.DSO.MID	LtCol	Aust 6Inf kia 13-4-18 CR France 200
DALY,Frederick.MID.	Lt	NZ 2/190 NZFA 4Bde kia 25-9-16 CR France 399
DALZELL,George Alden	Lt	Can 121CoyCFC ded 24-3-20 CR Canada 954
DANAHER,James	Lt	Aust 31Inf 27-9-17MR 29
DANAHER,Michael Timothy.MM.	2Lt	Aust 58Inf dedacc 11-4-19 CR Belgium 336
DANARD,Avera V.	Lt	Can 20Bn B'Coy dow 5-6-16 CR Belgium 11
DANCEY,Reginald William	Lt	NZ 2/211 NZFA ded 12-6-19 CR NZ 79
DANE,Thomas	Lt	Can 46Bn 14-8-18CR France 881
DANGAR,Clive Collingwood.MC.MID	Maj	Aust GL attAIF HQ Ex 13Huss 4-7-18 CR Aust 112
DANGERFIELD,Joseph Garnet	Lt	Aust 6Inf 8-5-15 MR 4
DANIEL,Fleetwood Earnscliffe	2Lt	Can RFC Ex CFA 9Bty kldacc 20-12-17 CR Wilts 115
DANIEL,Vivian Belton	2Lt	Aust11Inf kia 6-5-17 CR France 646
DANIELL,Groves Edward.MC.MID.	Capt	NZ 2/256 NZFA kia 4-10-16 CR France 453
DANIELS,Albert Murdock	Capt	Can15Bn (1COR) 24-4-15MR 29 Murdoch
DANN,Eyre Frederick Morton	Lt	Can 72Bn D'Coy dow 3-11-16 CR France 59
DANNEFAERD,William Jacob	2Lt	Aust 2Inf kia 6/8-8-15 CR Gallipoli 7
DARBYSHIRE,Jack	Lt	Aust Engrs 2FC kia 20-9-17 CR Belgium 112
DARBYSHIRE,Lionel Charles	Lt	Can 54Bn 31-7-17CR France 81

DARCHE,Auguste Raoul	Capt Can 4Bn dow 28-5-15 CR France 202
D'ARCY,Alfred John Keith	Lt Can 21Bn dow 16-4-16 CR France 64
D'ARCY-IRVINE,Carol	Capt Aust 13Inf kia 20-6-18 CR France 119
DARDEL,Aurel Louis	Lt AustAFA 12Bde dow 8-5-17 CR France 512
DARE,Norman Douglas	Capt SA 7SAInf 3-5-17 CR Tanzania 1 &CR EAfrica 16
DARLING,Charles	2Lt NZ 14191 4/3NZRB kia 26-8-18 CR France 1484
DARLING,Robert Clifford	Capt Can 15Bn dow 19-4-15 CR Canada 1688
DARNELL,Aubrey Hugh.DSO.MID	Maj Aust 11Inf dow 24-9-18 CR France 446
DARO,N.D.	Capt SA 7SAInf ded 3-5-17
DARTNALL,Clement Arthur.MM.	2Lt NZ 6/2590 CIR ded 15-11-18 CR NZ 243
DASHWOOD,John Lovell.MC.	Maj Can58Bn 13-4-17CR France 1321
DAUPHINEE,Owen Gates	Lt Can 25Bn 20-8-17MR 23
DAVENPORT,Harry	Lt Aust See SWENDSON True name MR 29
DAVENPORT,Guy Kennedy.MC.	Lt Aust AFA 4Bde kia 10-4-17 CR France 1484
DAVEY,Charles Basil Trevor	2Lt Aust 7Inf dow 27-4-15 MR 6
DAVIDSON,Alfred James	Lt Aust AFA 4Bde dow 30-9-18 CR France 446
DAVIDSON,David Grant	Lt Can 23RBn attRFC 11Sqn 23-8-17CR France 120
DAVIDSON,Edgar Robert	2Lt Aust 43Inf dow 4-7-18 CR France 1170
DAVIDSON,Eric Sinclair	2Lt Aust Engrs 4FC kia 4-7-18 CR France 1170
DAVIDSON,Frank Bennett	Lt Aust 39Inf dow 14-8-18 CR France 119
DAVIDSON,Frank Stanley	Capt AustEngrs 2FC kia 15-9-18 CR France 446
DAVIDSON,John Charles	Lt Aust 1Inf dedacc 3-6-16 CR France 200
DAVIDSON,John Robert	Capt Aust 8Inf 4-10-17MR 29
DAVIDSON,Lawrence Lowell	Lt Can 12FA 5Bn 25-11-17 CR France 64
DAVIDSON,Peers	LtCol Can 73Bn 5CanMilitia ded 19-7-20 CR Canada 256
DAVIDSON,Robert Francis	Capt Can CAMC ded 12-12-18 CR Canada 1691
DAVIDSON,Thomas Alan	2Lt NZ 10/1124 WIR 9Coy kia 8-8-15 MR 5
DAVIDSON,William	Maj Aust 1Inf dow 19-8-15 MR 6
DAVIDSON,William Robert.MC.	Capt&Adjt Aust 46Inf16-8-17MR 29
DAVIE,Hugh Scott	Lt Can 44Bn 17-2-18CR France 547
DAVIE,Harry Percy Claude.MM.	2Lt NZ 11/243 FA kia 23-4-18 CR Belgium 11
DAVIE,James	Capt Aust AMC 1FA dow 6-10-17 CR Belgium 11
DAVIES,Alan Cathcart	Lt Aust59Inf att15Aust LtTMB dow 25-4-18 CR France 71
DAVIES,Bert Oliver.DCM.	Lt Aust 30Inf kia 22-6-18 CR France 207
DAVIES,Claude William	Lt Aust 19Bn 3-5-17 MR 26
DAVIES,Eowyn Hugh.MC.	Capt Aust AIF Emgrs 6FC 14-11-20 CR Aust 307
DAVIES,Ernest Langford	Lt Can 87Bn kia 21-10-16 MR 23
DAVIES,Frederick Harry	Lt Can 10Bn 1-5-17 CR France 68
DAVIES,H.W.	Lt SA SAVC 21-12-19 CR SAfrica 53
DAVIES,Henry Arthur.MID.	Capt NZ 2/408A NZFA 3Bde dow 15-9-16 CR France 399
DAVIES,Leslie	Lt Aust 53Inf kia 1-9-18 CR France 624
DAVIES,Norman StanleyEngr	Lt Aust RAN HMAS`Barambah' ded 19-10-18 MR 2
DAVIES,Reginald Owen	2Lt NZ33103 OIR 1 OtagoR kia 18-2-18 CR Belgium 19
DAVIES,William Evan	Lt Can10Bn attRFC 11-5-17CR France 528
DAVIN,Henry Arthur	Lt Can 14Bn 13-6-16CR Belgium 127
DAVIS,A.	Capt SA SASC AnimalTrnspt ded 3-12-18 CR SAfrica 24
DAVIS,Arthur	Lt Aust 57Inf ded 27-2-19 CR France 931
DAVIS,Donald Chester	Capt Can LSH ded 2-9-16 CR Canada 562
DAVIS,Edward Frank	Lt Can RCR dow 9-6-17 CR France 88
DAVIS,Eric Radford Maxwell.MC.	Capt Can 4Bn 27-9-18CR France 481
DAVIS,F.M.	Capt SA 2SAInf kia 20-9-17
DAVIS,Frank Watts	2Lt Aust 50Inf kia 2-2-17 CR France 400
DAVIS,Gustavus Mitchell	Maj Can CAMC HS drd 27-6-18 MR 24
DAVIS,Harry Alfred	Lt Can 2BnCMGC dow 7-9-18 CR Surrey 91
DAVIS,Henry Bartlett.MC.	Lt Aust 13Inf kia 2-10-18 CR France 212
DAVIS,Henry Stanley	Capt Aust46Bn 11-4-17MR 26
DAVIS,Herbert.MID	Lt Aust AIF AASC 22-6-19CR Aust 112
DAVIS,Herbert Stanley	Lt Aust 5Bn 16-6-18MR 26
DAVIS,Irwin	Lt Can RCR 4.12.16 CR Essex 41
DAVIS,J.	2ndEngr Can MercMar SS`PortDalhousie' 19-3-16MR 24
DAVIS,Lena A.	Nurse Can CANS 4GH 21-2-18CR Hamps 118 2SH

DAVIS,Reginald Neville Craig	Lt Can 3Bn 24-5-15MR 23
DAVIS,Reginald William	Maj Can 75Bn dow 2-7-17 CR France 81
DAVIS,William Edwin	2Lt Aust6Inf 8-5-15 MR 4
DAVIS,William Henry.MC.	Chpn4Cl Can ChpnServs att4CMR 9-8-18 CR France 584
DAVIS,William Mahlan	LtCol Can 2Pnrs ded 8-10-18 CR Canada 1245 54Bn
DAVIS,William Robert Berry	Lt Aust 8Inf2-4-18 MR 29
DAVISON,Arthur	2Lt Aust 56Inf kia 8-3-17 CR France 374
DAVISON,Edward.MM.	Lt Can 4CMR 6-6-17 CR France 269
DAVISON,Francis	Lt NZ 7/639 CMR kia 7-8-15 CR Gallipoli 18
DAVY,Edmund Bromley	2Lt NZ 18900 2Bn 3RB dow 12-10-17 CR Belgium 3
DAVY,Francis Lempriere	Capt Aust 47Inf 7-6-17 MR 29
DAVY,John Harper	Lt Can 14Bn kia 8-8-18 CR France 424
DAW,Herbert Bethune	Lt Can 58Bn 26-4-16CR Belgium 115
DAWKINS,Charles Stanley	Capt Aust51Bn 3-9-16 MR 26
DAWKINS,William Henry	Lt Aust Engrs 2FC DivHQkia 20-5-15 CR Gallipoli 30
DAWSETT,Percy John	2Lt Aust 22Inf kia 4-10-18 CR France 234
DAWSON,Alan Douglas Gibb	Lt Aust2Inf kia 25-4-15 MR 6
DAWSON,Edward	Capt Aust 3Inf kia 6/8-8-15 CR Gallipoli 7
DAWSON,Ernest Charles	Lt Can 8Bn 9-8-18 CR France 693
DAWSON,Erskine William Douglas Hamilton	Lt Aust 3AustBn ImpCamCps 11Coy dow 6-11-17 CR Palest 1
DAWSON,Herbert Benjamin	Maj Can 50Bn 4-6-17 CR France 12
DAWSON,Howard Charles	Lt Can 26Bn kia 12-1-17 CR France 547
DAWSON,Irvin Harrison.MC.	Lt Can CFA 1Bde dow 1-9-18 CR France 95
DAWSON,John Allison	Lt Can 26Bn kia 8-8-18 CR France 424
DAWSON,John Kenneth	Lt Can 102Bn C'Coy kia 8-8-18 CR France 589
DAWSON,Thomas Howard	Lt NZ 2/2602 NZFA 3DAC dow 11-6-18 CR France 84 acckld
DAY,Calvin Wellington	Lt Can 2Bn (EOR) 1Coy 23-4-15MR 29
DAY,Kenneth Maitland	2Lt Aust 35Inf kia 12-10-17 CR Belgium 125
DAY,Norman Frank	Lt Aust 8Inf dow 21-9-18 CR Surrey 1
DAYTON,Ernest Perdue	Lt Can 54Bn dow 22-6-17 CR France 32
De CENT,Kenneth Owen	Capt NZ 23471 2OIR dow 12-4-18 CR France 62
De GRUCHY,Charles Southwell.MC.	Lt Can CFA 3Bde dow 18-7-17 CR France 12
DE LA COUR,P.V.	2Lt SA 4SAInf kia 15-5-18
De MEILLON,Copernicus Kepler	Capt SA SAIC &5MR kia 22-2-15 CR SAfrica 1
De QUETTEVILLE,Stanley Nelson	Engr Lt Can RCN HMS`Indefatigable' 13-5-16MR 24
De SALIS,Frank Robert Lawson	Lt Can RCR 1916
De VINE,Clayton Howard	Lt Can 50AR kia 3-6-17 MR 23
De WINTON,Cyril Peel	Lt Aust 2Inf kia 12-10-16 CR Belgium 167
De YOUNG,Arthur Granville.MC.	LtCan RFC 25Bn 12-1-18CR France 113
DEACON,Lester Jerome	Lt Can CASC 5DivCavBdeSupCol ded 28-7-17 CR France 225
DEAN,Archibald Robert.MC.	Lt Aust 14Inf 2-12-16CR London 23
DEAN,Ernest	Lt Aust AIF 13AICC 27-10-20 CR Aust 94
DEAN,Leonard Widlake	Lt NZ 2/438 NZFA kia 2-9-18 CR France 512
DEAN,Roy Chester	Lt Can 26Bn B'Coy 25-9-18CR France 481
DEANE,Edward Wilkinson	Capt AustAAMC 1AustGH ded 4-4-16 CR Egypt 9
DEANS,Alexander	2Lt NZ 27693 3CIR kia 4-10-17 MR 30
DEANS,John Harold	Lt Can CORD &RFC 84Sqn 8-11-17MR 20
DEASE,Joseph Victor	Lt Aust 20Inf dow 10-12-17 CR Surrey 1
DeCHENE,Arthur Miville	Capt Can 22Bn 1916
DECK,Robin Howell	2Lt NZ 7/797 CMR kia 29-8-15 MR 14
DEE,George Keith.MID.	Capt NZ 24/11 3/3NZRB dow 8-6-17 CR France 285
DEER,Herbert Edward	Lt Can 75Bn 7-2-19 CR Hamps 2
DE FRAGA,Cecil	Capt Aust AASC 1DivSupplyCol dedacc 23-10-17 CR France 139
DEGENHARDT,Francis Evan	2Lt Aust 27Inf dow 11-8-18 CR France 71
DELANCEY,James Arnold.MC.	Maj Can25Bn 9-4-17 CR France 68
DELANY,Norman Joseph	Lt Aust AFA 2Bde dow 19-9-18 CR France 836
DELMAGE,Richard Barber	Lt Can 43Bn kia 27-9-18 CR France 256
DEMPERS,Herbert Johann N.	Lt SA MtdCmdos kia 8-4-15 CR SAfrica 17
DEMPSEY,James Daniel	Lt Can 58Bn dow 14-4-17 CR France 1276
DEMPSEY,John	Rev Aust AAChpnsded 13-6-17 CR Egypt 9
DENCH,Harold	Capt Aust 38Inf kia 24-8-18 CR France 396

DENHAM,Norman Eden	Lt Can 44Bn 27-9-18CR France 714
DENISON,George H.	Maj Can 19Bn kia 8-5-17 CR France 68 Taylor
DENISON,Walter Thompson	Lt Can 28Bn dow 3-10-18 CR France 214
DENNE,Victor Edward.MM.	Lt Aust 52Inf dow 26-5-18 CR Surrey 1
DENNIS,Eric Reginald.MC.	Capt Can 2Bn kia 5-4-17 CR France 68
DENNIS,Hugh Oliver	Lt Can 21Bn 1918
DENNISON,Harry Stuart	Capt CanPPCLI(EOR) kia 8-5-15 MR 29
DENNISON,John	2Lt Aust 2Pnrs 13-6-17MR 26
DENNISTOUN,John Rodeyn MID	Lt Can 1DivCycCoy attRFC kia 4-5-16 CR France 1031
DENNY,Arnold Lorimer	2Lt Aust 56Inf dow 26-7-16 CR France 768
DENSEM,John.DCM.	2Lt NZ 24/736 4/3NZRB kia 26-8-18 CR France 1484
DENT,James Harrison	Lt Can 1Bn (WOR) 6-11-17MR 29
DENT YOUNG,William	Lt Aust 11Inf kia 5-5-17 CR France 1488
DENTON-CLARKE,Thomas Henry	2Lt Aust 35Inf kia 7-6-17 CR Belgium 51
DENTRY,Norman Hugh St.Omer	Lt Aust 1Pnrs kia 31-10-17 CR Belgium 34
DERAVIN,Francis Arthur	Capt Aust AAMC ded 8-7-17 CR Dorset 110
DERBYSHIRE,Wilfred.MC.	Lt Can 78Bn 20-5-19CR Lancs 164
DeROSSITER,Walter W.	Lt Can87Bn 1917
DERRICK,Cecil Reginald	Maj Aust 22Inf kia 8-8-15 MR 6
DE SALIS,F.R.L.	Lt Can RCR 2-6-16 CR Belgium 72
DES BRISAY,Arthur St.Croix	Lt Can 5CMR ded 5-5-20 CR Canada 742
DESLAURIERS,Alexander. MC	Lt Can 22Bn 4-2-19 CR Belgium 294 Alexandre
DESMOND.Robert Dennis	Lt Aust MGC 6Coy 3-5-17 MR 26
DETHIER,Edouard Myers	Lt SAHQRecs&CampStaff ExCMR 29-9-18CR SAfrica 62
DETLAR John Arnold	Lt Can 1SiegeBty ded 17-4-21 CR Canada1 298 DETLOR
DETTLING,Francis Charles	Capt SA MilConst PolTrngDepot 27-10-18 CR SAfrica 23
DeVARENNES,Henri	Lt Can 22Bn 16-8-17CR France 550
DEVEREUX,Geoffrey De Bohun.MC.	Maj NZ 12/1190 1AIR kia 1-10-18 CR France 1483
DEVINE,Clayton Howard	Lt Can 50Bn 1917
DEVINE,Patrick	Lt Aust 9Inf 3-11-17MR 29
DEVINE,William Melville.MM.	Lt Aust 49Inf dow 6-4-18 CR France 169
DEVITT,William George	2Lt Aust 17Inf kia 9-11-16 CR France 744
DEVLIN,Francis Cecil Cochran	LtCan RCanMil attRWAFFGambiaCoy 16-10-17 CR Tanzania1 &EAfrica 11
DEVLIN,Henry Lyman	Lt Can 75Bn (1COR)kia 9-9-16 MR 29
DEWSON,Richard William.MC.DCM.	Capt Aust AASC 3DivTrn 27-5-18CR France 303
DEY,George Roy McGregor	2Lt Aust 10Bn 23-8-16MR 26
DIBBLE,Harry.MM.	Lt Can 19Bn 8-8-18 CR France 424
DIBBS,Owen Burton	Capt Aust 45Inf kia 1-4-18 CR France 197
DICK,Charles Henry	Lt SA 3SAInf kia 20-7-16 MR 21
DICK,George MacDonald	Lt Can 78Bn &RFC 5Sqn 29-5-17MR 20
DICK,William Thomas	Capt Aust MGC 14Coy kia 28-9-17 CR Belgium 11
DICKENS,Glen Mervyn	Lt Aust 17Inf 9-10-17MR 29
DICKERSON,V.S.	2Lt SA2SAInf kia 8-12-17 CR France 439
DICKESON,Colin Addison.MC.	Lt A Capt NZ 24/2128 CycBn kia 26-4-18 CR Belgium 11
DICKEY,Cecil Vernon	2Lt NZ 26/26 3/3NZRB kia 12-10-17 MR 30
DICKEY,Horace Arthur	Capt Can25Bn dow 15-9-16 CR France 430
DICKIE,Adam	Lt Aust 41Inf kia 10-6-17 CR Belgium 168
DICKINSON,Herbert Spencer	Capt Aust57Inf kia 25-9-17 CR Belgium 19
DICKINSON,Ruby S	Nurse Aust AANS 23-6-18CR Middx 82
DICKINSON,Sydney Harvey	Lt Can 7Bn att 2LtTMB 27-9-18CR France 147
DICKSON,A.	Maj SA PofWVltrs
DICKSON,Norman	Lt Aust 15Inf dow 27-4-15 MR 6
DICKSON,Selwyn Ray	Lt Aust 21Inf kia 1-9-18 CR France 511
DIETZE,J.H.	2Lt See SANDOE,J.H. true name CR France 375
DIFFORD,A.N.	Lt SA 1CapeCps kia 20-9-18 CR Palest 3
DIFFORD,William Membry	Lt Can 8Bn attRAF 8Sqnkia 3-10-18 CR France 240
DIGGES-LA-TOUCHE,Everard	2Lt Aust 2Inf kia 6/8-8-15 CR Gallipoli 7
DIGGORY,Reginald William	Lt Can CAPC ded 20-6-18 CR Canada 323A W.R.
DILLON,William Pearson	Maj CanCAMC 2GH 4-5-15 CR France 1
DILLOW,William	Lt Aust 55Inf kia 1-10-18 CR France 528
DILWORTH,Edward Erskine.MC.	Lt Aust Engrs 2FC dow 6-5-18 CR France 180

DIMSEY,Lyle Sanderson	Lt Aust 37Inf dow 5-10-17 CR Belgium 3
DINGLE,Henry.MM.	2Lt Aust 1Inf dedacc 20-2-17 CR France 177
DINGWALL,Frederick James	LtCol Can 1Ent Bn ded 13-2-18 CR Canada 112 60Bn
DINNEEN,James Dalton.MID.	Capt NZ 66239 1AIR dow 1-10-16 CR France 833
DITZELL,Fred	Lt Aust 35Inf kia 12-10-17 CR Belgium 125
DIVER,Frederick George	Lt Can 87Bn 21-10-16 CR France 239
DIXON,Elijah March	Capt Can CAVC 27-9-18CR France 65 Marsh
DIXON,John Warren	Lt Can 12BnCE 10-2-19CR Surrey 1
DIXON,Norman Edward	Lt Aust 37Bn 10-2-18MR 26
DIXON,Thomas William Eric.MC.MM.	Capt Can 4CMR kia 3-8-18 CR Belgium 11
DOAK,Johnstone Freeman	Lt Can 28Bn (SR) kia 6-11-17 MR 29
DOANE,William Edward Everett	Lt Can 25Bn 1-10-16CR France 832
DOBBIE,Henry Stewart.MC.	Lt Aust 14Inf dow 7-8-16 CR France 44
DOBBIN,Graham Leonard	Lt Can 14Bn att1InfBdeDepot 15-3-19CR France 146
DOBIE,John Milton	Capt Can 4CMR 28-8-18CR France 421
DOBIE,Meldrum Boyd	2Lt Aust 1Pnrs ded PoW 28-5-16 CR France 924
DOBLE,Frank Edward	2Lt SA 7SAInf kia 19-7-17 CR Tanzania 1 &EAfrica 38
DOBLE,John James	Lt Can 116Bn kia 11-4-17 CR France 68
DOBSON,Robert Ambrose	Lt Aust 44Inf kia 24-4-18 CR France 210
DOBSON,William James	Maj Can 1Bn 9-7-16 CR Belgium 112
DOCHERTY,Malcolm.DSO	LtCol Can HQ CavBde LSH 1-12-17CR France 417
DODD,Albert William.MC.	Lt Can 8Bn 5-9-18 CR France 14
DODDS,George Sidney	Lt Aust 41Inf dow 29-9-18 CR France 446
DODDS,Philo Epps	WTO Can `Addah' 1917
DODGE,George Tomlinson.MC.	HCapt&QM Can 87Bn 27-11-18 CR France 1142
DODSON,Frederick Hugh	Lt NZ12/683 AIR 6Coy kia 25/29-4-15 MR 6
DODSON,Reginald Henry	Lt NZ10/3807 1WIR kia 18-9-16 MR 11
DODSON,W.F.L.	Lt Aust 10Inf 19/20-9-17 CR Belgium 112
DODWELL,George Worsley Magor	Lt Can 87Bn kia 15-8-17 MR 23
DODWORTH,Cecil Grayson	Lt Can 28Bn kia 18-11-16 CR France 742 54Bn
DOHENY,John Edward	Lt Can 20Bn 29-4-16CR Belgium 11
DOHERTY,James.MC&Bar.	Maj Aust AFA 7Bde ded 26-2-19 CR Surrey 1
DOIDGE,Ernest Lancelot	Lt Can RAF 99Sqdn ManitobaR31-7-18CR France 1675
DOIG,Allan Torrance.MC.	Lt Aust 17Inf ded PoW 27-6-18 CR France 1076
DOIG,Charles John.MC.	Capt Aust 33Inf kia 1-10-18 CR France 212
DOIG,David MacNair	Lt Aust 47Inf dow 29-3-18 CR France 185
DOLMAN,Garnet Victor	Lt Can 3Bn kia 30-7-17 CR France 570
DOLMAN,Harold Edward.MID	Lt Can 19Bn 14-11-17 CR Belgium 11
DOLTON,Stanley Vincent	Lt Aust45Inf kia 20-11-16 CR France 277
DON,George Marshall	Lt NZ 57317 1.OIR dow 25-8-18 CR France 579
DONAHAY,Clarence	2Lt Aust AFC kia 26-1-18 CR France 285
DONALD,John	Lt Can 24Bn 5BdeHQ 3-7-17 CR France 178
DONALD,William James	Lt Can 47Bn 28-9-18CR France 714
DONALDSON,Frederick	Capt Aust 9Inf ded 23-10-18 CR France 52
DONALDSON,Gertrude	Nurse Can CAMC 1GH 29-7-19CR Canada 1134
DONALDSON,John Ebenezer	Capt Aust 19Inf dow 11-8-16 CR France 40
DONALDSON,Joseph Kenneth	Lt Aust 18Inf kia 22-8-15 MR 6
DONISCH,William Frederick	Capt Aust 25Inf kia 14-11-16 CR France 385
DONN,John Murray	2Lt NZ 2CIR kia 2-10-16 MR 11
DONNAN,Arthur Victor	2Lt NZ 23929 4/3NZRB dow 10-6-17 CR France 297
DONNE,Stanley Ernest	2Lt NZ 33100 Engrs 5ROS dow 22-10-17 CR Belgium 5
DONNELLY,James John.MC.	Capt Can 1RNewfndlandR kia 12-10-16 CR France 307
DOOLAN,William Richard	2Lt Aust8Inf 8-8-16 CR France 832
DORAN,Victor Frederick	2Lt Aust 16Inf 11-6-17MR 29
DORE,Patrick	CaptChpn NZ13/655 ChpnsDept ded 15-7-18 CR NZ 245
DORE,William Henry	Capt Can SRD &RAF 107Sqn kld 9-8-18 MR 20
DORNEY,William Michael	Lt Aust33Inf kia 30-8-18 CR France 511
DORNONVILLE de la COUR,Paul Victor	Lt SA SAInf &RAF 11Sqn 15-5-18 CR France 63
DORON,Frank Beecher	Lt Can 20Bn attRFC 9Sqn kia 13-8-17 CR Belgium 18
DORWOOD,William	2Lt SA 4SAInf kia 9-4-17 CR France 728 DORWARD
DOTHIER,E.M.	Lt SA CampCmdtStaff ded 29-9-18

DOUBLEDAY,Jack Lindsay	Lt Aust ADCps ded 30-10-18 MR 41	
DOUCET,Joseph Theophilis	Lt Can 26Bn 9-8-18 CR France 29	
DOUGALL,Norman.MC.	Lt Aust 10Inf kia 6-5-17 CR France 1485	
DOUGALL,Thomas.MC.	Lt Can 18Bn 19-8-17 CR France 12	
DOUGALL,Walter Keith	Lt NZ8/185 2OIR dow 15-9-16 CR France 197	
DOUGALL,William see DOUGLAS,W.		
DOUGAN,William Alexander	Lt Can 29Bn 27-9-16 CR France 280	
DOUGHTY,James Davidson	Lt Can 1Bn 1922	
DOUGHTY,Ralph Dorschel.MC.	Lt Aust 3FA dow 25-7-17 CR Belgium 24	
DOUGHTY,William Trenton	2Lt NZ 24353 WIR 1WellingtonR kia 31-7-17 CR Belgium 51	
DOUGLAS,Allan Ritchie	2Lt NZ 30110 OIR 2 OtagoR kia 11-8-17 CR Belgium 52	
DOUGLAS,Carola Josephine	NSister Can CAMC HS drd 27-6-18 MR 24	
DOUGLAS,Francis	2Lt SA 4SAInf kia 19-7-18 CR France 324	
DOUGLAS,Hugh Maxwell	Lt Aust 47Inf dow 8-4-18 CR France 40	
DOUGLAS,John Sholto.MM.	Lt Can 50Bn 30-11-18 CR Oxford 83	
DOUGLAS,Robert Fargher	Lt Can 47Bn 3-9-18 CR France 427 Farqher	
DOUGLAS,Roger.MC.DCM.	Lt Aust AFC dedacc 13-11-19 CR Surrey 1	
DOUGLAS,Thomas Birtwistle	Lt Can 10Bn 28-4-17 MR 23	
DOUGLAS,William.MC.	Lt Can SRD 46Bn attRAF kia 21-7-18 CR France 1332 DOUGALL	
DOUGLAS,William Bowman	Capt Aust 3Inf dow 5-5-15 MR 6	
DOUGLASS,Charles Irving	Lt Can 25Bn dow 11-4-16 CR France 1031 DOUGLAS	
DOUGLASS,George Percival.MC.	Lt Aust RFA 157Bde Ex 5AustInf dow 25-8-18 CR France 100	
DOULL,John	LtCol Can RCR ded 1-7-16 CR Canada 256	
DOUST,Frederick Herbert.MC.	Lt Aust 13Inf 26-9-17 MR 29	
DOUST,Harold.MC.	Lt Aust 30Inf kia 30-9-18 CR France 375	
DOVEY,Reginald Walter	Lt Aust AMGC 4Bn kia 4-7-18 CR France 1170	
DOW,Robert John Gunn	Lt Can 49Bn (AR) 30-10-17 MR 29	
DOWDING,Albert	Lt Aust 34Inf dow 5-6-18 CR France 29	
DOWDING,Isaac William	Capt CanCAPC ded 15-2-19 CR Surrey 1	
DOWER,Alexander	Lt Can 10Bn dow 11-4-17 CR France 12	
DOWLER,John Wilton Douglas	Lt Can 47Bn dow 11-4-17 CR France 12	
DOWLER,William Herbert	Capt Can CAMC 1919	
DOWLING,Eric Sheen	2Lt Aust 1ALH dow 18-11-17 CR Palest 9	
DOWLING,I.	CaptSA SAMC 19-10-18 CR SAfrica 81 J.	
DOWLING,Max Russell Laidley	Lt Aust 4Inf dow 30-7-16 CR France 145	
DOWN,Edgar Gordon	Lt Aust 8ALH kia 23-12-16 CR Egypt 2	
DOWNE,Cyril Lester Gordon.MSM.	Aust AFC 1Sqn dedacc 3-3-19 CR Egypt 9	
DOWNTON,John Gibson.MM.	Lt Can 49Bn D'Coy 9-6-17 MR 23	
DOWSETT,David	Lt Aust FA 1DAC kia 8-8-17 CR Belgium 15	
DOXEE,William John	Lt Can 2Bn (EOR) 26-4-15 MR 29 DOXSEE	
DOYLE,Henry Thomas	2Lt NZ 25/21 WIR drd 10-10-18 CR Eire 14	
DOYLE,James Justin	2Lt NZ 8/365 1OtagoR ded 15-11-18 CR NZ 243	
DOYLE,Richard Henry	Lt Aust 36Inf kia 10-6-17 CR Belgium 451	
DRACUP,George Franklin	Lt Can 128Bn att RFC 42Sqn 28-7-17 CR France 285	
DRADER,Robert Eugene	Lt Can 49Bn 16-9-16 MR 23	
DRAKES,Percy William.MM.	Lt Can 4CMR 16-9-16 CR France 59	
DRAPER,Charles McKenny	2Lt Aust 45Inf kia 6-8-16 CR France 832	
DREHER,Charles Frederick William	Lt Can CFA 5Bde ded 7-1-20 CR Canada 1245	
DREW,William George.MM.	2Lt Aust 47Inf kia 24-1-17 CR France 277	
DREWERY,Elgin Cyrus	Lt Can 2Bn kia 8-12-17 CR France 81	
DREYER,J.S.	2Lt SA 1CapeCps kia 20-9-18 CR Palest 3	
DREYER,Norman Lockhart.DSO.	Maj Aust AFA 114HB dow 6-8-18 CR France 303	
DRIDAN,Victor Gillard	Lt Aust 50Inf dow 16-8-16 CR France 44	
DRINKWATER,Leo Sidney	Capt Aust 45Inf kia 7-8-16 CR France 832	
DRIVER,G.E.MID	Lt SA 8Horse kia 7-9-16 CR EAfrica 39	
DRON,Douglas Alexander	Maj NZ6/1517 2CIR kia 8-10-18 CR France 660	
DRUMMOND,Gregor Stuart	Lt Can 52Bn kia 16-9-16 CR France 280	
DRUMMOND,Guy Melfort	Lt Can 13Bn kia 22-4-15 CR Belgium 125	
DRUMMOND HAY,Eric	Lt Can 16Bn kia 2-9-18 CR France 687	
DRUMMOND HAY,Leonard Vivian.MC.Maj	CanPPCLI kia 14-8-18 CR France 360	
DRUMMOND,John	Lt Aust 44Inf 10-10-17 MR 29	

DRUMMOND,Kevin Stewart.MC.	Lt Can 24Bn kia 8-8-18 CR France 1015
DRUMMOND,Lindsay	Lt Can CE 1FC &RFC 1Sqn 18-5-17MR 20
DRUMMOND,Morris Cook	Lt Aust 18Bn 3-5-17 MR 26
DRUMMOND,William Colenso	Capt NZ35/3 NZRB ded 20-11-18 CR NZ 265
DRURY,Edmund Hazen	Maj Can MHQCE CanMilitia 31-1-17CR Canada 354
DRYSDALE,Thomas John Hirst	2Lt NZ 4/95A 3/3NZRB dow 6-4-18 CR France 169
DU PREEZ,C.J.	Lt SA MtdRif18
DUCHARME,Louis Joseph Ovide	LtCol Can CFA 76Bty ded 12-3-17 CR Canada 109
DUCHESNAY,Frank Alexander	Lt Can CASC att2CanDivTMB dow 25-3-19 CR Surrey 1
DUCHESNE,William Sydney	Lt Aust 1Inf kia 25-4-15 CR Gallipoli 10
DUDLEY,John Charles Amphlett	Lt NZ 2/2344 NZFA 2BdeAC ded 22-2-19 CR Germany 1
DUDSON,Louis Chanel.MID.	2Lt NZ 25/20 3/3NZRB kia 28-10-18 CR France 521
DUFF,Calvin Fraser Wallace	Lt Can 54Bn 8-8-18 MR 23
DUFF,Hew Ramsay.MID	LtCol Can CAMC 7GH ded 8-2-16 CR Egypt 9 5SH
DUFF,James Robertson	Lt Can 43Bn 8-10-16MR 23
DUFFIELD,Frank	2Lt Aust 14Inf kia 22-8-15 MR 6
DUFFY,Desmond Gavan	2Lt Aust 20Inf kia 15-11-16 CR France 399
DUGGAN,George Wilfred.MC.	Lt Can RAF & FGH 12-11-18 CR Wilts 115
DUGGAN,Kenneth L.	Maj Can 5CMR 1917
DUGIT,Robert Louis	Maj Can 2Bn 3-3-17 MR 3
Du HAMEL,Henri Masson	Maj Can CAMC 6GH ded 3-2-18 CR Canada 254
DULEY,Lionel Thomas	2Lt Can 1NewfndlandR kia 29-9-18 CR Belgium 125
DUMONTIER,Alfred Emery	Lt Can 56Bn ded 10-9-20 CR Canada 542
DUNBAR,Frederick	2Lt Aust 20Inf dow 15-11-16 CR France 399
DUNBAR,William James	Chpn4Cl Aust att11ALH kia 7-11-17 CR Palest 8
DUNCAN,Alan Barrie.MC.	Capt Can 75Bn 29-9-18CR France 148
DUNCAN,Andrew Warwick.MC.	Lt Can 38Bn 9-4-17 CR France 81
DUNCAN,Arthur Jackson	Capt Can 19Bn 11-10-18 MR 23
DUNCAN,Charles Andrew	Lt Can 46Bn 28-9-18CR France 714
DUNCAN,Charles F.	Lt Can 104Regt CanMilitia ded 5-10-18 CR Canada 171
DUNCAN,George Gordon	Capt Can 10Bn 22-5-15CR France 260
DUNCAN,George Harry	Lt Aust 18Inf dow 9-8-18 CR France 1170
DUNCAN,Henry Aulus	Lt Can 16Bn 9-10-16MR 23
DUNCAN,William Munro.MID.	Lt NZ 3/667 NZMC ded 15-7-18 CR Hamps 30
DUNDAS,Frederick Charles	Lt Aust 29Inf ded 20-7-18 CR Wilts 135
DUNK,Stephen	Lt Can 2CMR 1-10-16MR 23
DUNKLEY,Andrew Robert	2Lt Aust 51Bn 3-9-16 MR 26
DUNLOP, George Fraser	Lt Can 192Bn ded 17-3-18 CR Canada 559 Charles
DUNLOP,Harry.MC.	Capt Can CAMC att102Bn dow 2-11-18 CR France 1253
DUNLOP,Robert.MC.	Capt Can 75Bn 7-9-18 CR France 34
DUNN,Francis Henry.MC.	Capt&Adjt Aust 23Bn 3-5-17 MR 26
DUNN,Gertrude Eliza	Sister SA SAMNS ded 14-12-18 CR SAfrica 30
DUNN,Joseph Donald	Lt Can 7Bn (BCR)3-6-16 MR 29
DUNN,Robert Alexander	2Lt Aust AFC kldacc 13-8-18 CR Glouc 172
DUNN,St.Clair	Capt Can CAMC attPPCLI 9-3-18 CR France 522
DUNNET,John Clouston	Capt NZ2/214 NZFA 12Bty 3Bde dow 5-4-18 CR France 62
DUNSDON,Charles Edward	Lt Aust Engrs 4FC 9-8-16 MR 26
DUNSFORD,Leonard	Lt Can 4CMR kia 17-12-16 CR France 157
DUPLISSIE,Roy	Lt Can RCR 28-9-18CR France 243
DuPREEZ,Gideon Joubert	Lt SA 18MtdRif kia 25-1-15 CR SAfrica 165
DUPUY,Romeo	Lt Can 22Bn 29-8-18CR France 14
DURACK,N.J.	2Lt Aust AIF 10ALH28-11-20 CR Aust 459
DURANT,William Macliesh	Lt NZ 4/1223 NZE dow 14-9-16 CR France 452
DURHAM,Percy Neil	Lt Aust 51Inf ded 22-4-17 CR Surrey 1
DURIE,William Arthur Peel	Capt Can 58Bn A'Coy kia 29-12-17 CR Canada 1694
DURMAN,Arthur.MC.	Lt Can 24Bn 15-10-17 CR France 68
DURRANT,C.M.	Lt SA RhodNatR 2CapeCps 25-7-18CR EAfrica 90
DURSTON,Norman Henry	Lt Aust 16Inf dow 9-5-15 MR 6
DUSSAULT,Alexina	NSister Can CAMC HS 27-6-18MR 24
DUTHIE,David Keith	2Lt NZ 24/121 1/3RB kia 7-8-17 CR Belgium 52
DUTHIE,Robert Leiper Martin	Lt NZ 8/162 OIR dow 12-5-15 CR Gallipoli 3

DUTHIE,Wilfred Alexander   Lt   Can   CMGC 5Coy 15-9-16CR France 1505
DUTTON,George Arthur   Lt   Aust 38Inf   kia 29-8-18   CR France 624
DU VAL,Edward William   Lt   Can PPCLI   kia 2-7-18   CR France 504
DUVAL,Josias Louis   Maj Can CAMC 1FA lostatsea 26-8-15   MR 40
DUXBURY,Leslie Varley   2Lt Aust32Inf   dow 6-9-18   CR France 526
DWYER,Albert Valentine   Lt   Aust 23Inf   dow 3-12-15   MR 6
DWYER,Edward Joseph   Lt   Can 25Bn   drd 10-12-17   MR 40
DYER,Harold Charles.MM.   Lt   Aust 8Inf   kia 9-8-18   CR France 526
DYER,Herbert Francis   2Lt NZ 6/2605 CIR 1CanterburyR kia 8-1-18   CR Belgium 72
DYER,R.C.DCM.MM&Bar.   Capt   Can 8Bn   30-12-18 CR Europe 179 &MR 70
DYKE,George Connock   Lt   Aust 48Bn   6-8-16 MR 26
DYKEMAN,Charles Edgar   Lt   Can 43Bn   8-10-16MR 23
DYKES,Samuel McPherson   2Lt Aust 56Inf   kia 1-11-16   CR France 385
DYSON,Alfred Noel   Lt   Aust   AFA 8Bde   dow 8-6-17   CR France 285

E

EADE,Henry Arthur   Capt   Aust   35Inf   dow 5-4-18   CR France 45
EADES,Alfred Bailey   Lt   AustAFA 12Bde   ded   12-11-18 CR Surrey 1
EADIE,Shaver   Lt   CaptCan   8Bn   2-3-16 CR France 85
EAKIN,Albert Graham   Lt   Can 1CMR kia 1-1-18   CR France 51 EAKINS
EALES,Thomas Whiteway.DCM.   Lt   Aust 21Inf   kia 19-5-18   CR France 207
EAMER-GOULT,Harry George Howard   Lt   Can 7Bn   kia 13-6-16   CR Belgium 27
EARDLEY-WILMOT,Frederick Lawrence Lt Can   PPCLI 19-3-15CR Belgium 11
EARLE,Arthur Percy   Lt   Aust AMGC 6Coydow 24-7-17   CR Surrey 1
EARLE,Wallace Sinclair   2Lt Can   GL &RFC Ex CanEngrs 16-4-16MR 20
EARLY,Frank Douglas   Capt   Can CAVC LSH   ded 15-5-18   CR Canada 1595
EARNSHAW,Sidney Peter   Lt   Can 42Bn   13-8-18CR France 360
EAST,Joseph Thomas.MID   2Lt Aust 12AMGC 12-10-17 MR 29
EAST,Walter Henry.MM&Bar.MID   Capt   Aust FA 1Bde   kia 5-10-17   CR Belgium 15
EASTMAN,Harold Sydney   Lt   Can 28Bn   9-8-18 CR France 649
EASTWOOD,P.B.   Capt   SA SASC   17-11-17 CR SAfrica 62
EATON,Edward Carter   Lt   Can 60Bn RAF 65Sqnkia 26-6-18 CR France 516
EATON,Daniel Isaac Vernon   LtCol   Can CFA 8Bde   dow 11-4-17   CR France 12
EATON,Jaffray   Lt   Can   4CMR (1COR) kia 26-10-17 MR 29
EATON,John Norris   Lt   Can 43Bn   kia 5-4-17   CR France 68
EATON,Leonard Carl   Capt   Can 5CMR (QR) 29-10-17 MR 29
EATON,Rupert William.MC.   Lt   Can 54Bn   kia 27-91-8 CR France 714
EATON,Thomas Alden   Lt   Can   3Bn   30-7-17CR France 570
EBELING,Claude Roy   Lt   Aust   AFC 2Sqn   dedacc 23-8-18 CR France 34
EBSARY,Samuel Joseph   2Lt   Can 1RNewfndlandR dow 15-10-16 CR France 145
ECCLES,Vernon John Lamont   Capt   Can31Bn   27-9-16CR France 280
EDDIE,Maxwell Hardwicke   Lt   Aust RFC 5-9-18 MR 26
EDDIS,Arthur George   Lt   Can3Bn 27-5-15MR 23
EDDY,Jack Rylot   Capt   Aust FA 1DAC   kia 4-10-17   CR Belgium 15
EDENS,John Francis   Lt   Can 1RNewfndlandRdow 20-11-17 CR France 667
EDENS,Leonard A.   Lt   Can 1NewfndlandR attRFC dow 18-3-18 CR Belgium 140
EDGAR,Charles Le Gallais   2Lt Can 1NewfndlandR kia 26-2-17   CR France 786
EDGAR,Francis   Lt   Can 2MGCoy kia 26-9-16   CR France 832
EDGECUMBE,Henry Francis   Lt   NZ 27691   MGC   ded   15-11-18 CR NZ 209
EDGERTON,Eric Henry Drummond.DSO.MM&Bar   Lt Aust 24Inf kia 11-8-18 CR France 1170
EDGETT,Louis Stanley   Lt   Can 60Bn   dow 10-5-17   CR France 88
EDGINGTON,Frederick Sydney   2Lt Aust 20Inf   kia 20-9-17   CR Belgium 115
EDMEADES,Constance Alexandra   Sister   SA   SAMNS 17-10-18 CR SAfrica 62
EDMONSON,Edwin   Lt   Aust 28Inf   kia 2-9-18   CR France 624

EDMONSTON-FEARN,Alfred Jesse	Lt Aust FA 8Bde kia 6-7-17 CR Belgium 42
EDRIDGE,Albert	2Lt NZ7/512 MMGS dow 30-3-18 MR 34
EDSON,Charles Robert	2Lt Aust 27Inf dow 17-8-17 CR Belgium 16
EDWARDS,Benjamin Noel William	2Lt Aust 7Inf kia 8/9-8-15 CR Gallipoli 7
EDWARDS,Charles Crichton.MM&Bar	2Lt Aust 20Inf 9-10-17 MR 29
EDWARDS,Chas Joseph Knight,DCM.MID.	Lt NZ 2/444 FA dow 4-10-17 CR Belgium 18
EDWARDS,Frederick Curtain H/	Lt&QM SA 4SAInf drd 13-9-18 MR 40 12-9-18
EDWARDS,George Peacock	Lt Aust 1ALH ded 20-11-16 CR Egypt 9
EDWARDS,Gilbert.MC.	Lt Can2Bn 11-9-17 CR France 179
EDWARDS,Herbert Hamilton	Capt Can 21Bn 11-5-18 CR France 84
EDWARDS,Joseph Plimsoll	Lt Can CE 1FC kia 28-4-17 CR France 68
EDWARDS,Norman Allen	Lt Can PPCLI (EOR) kia 8-5-15 MR 29
EDWARDS,Rupert Henry Adams	Lt Aust AFA 10Bde kia 28-4-17 CR France 565
EDWARDS,William James Munro	Lt Aust 1ALH kia 3-11-17 CR Palest 1
EGAN,Edward Roland	2Lt Aust 2Inf dow 14-8-15 CR Egypt 3
EGAN,William Joseph	Capt Can 7CRT 4-5-17 CR Belgium 4
EGGLESTONE,Richard Ewen	Lt NZ 8/1070 OIR kia 2/3-5-15 MR 6
EGGLESTONE,Valentine Joseph	Capt NZ 8/1147 OIR kia 6-6-15 CR Gallipoli 31
EIBEL,Henry Alfred	2Lt Aust 15Bn 11-4-17 MR 26
EINARSON,John	Lt Can 1CMR (SR)7-11-17 MR 29
EITELBERG,Louis Henry	Lt Aust 23Inf 6-11-17 MR 29
EKERS,Archer	Lt Can 87Bn dow 16-9-16 CR Belgium 15
EKIN SMYTH,Ralph Ratnevelo Raymond	Capt Aust 52Inf kia 3-9-16 CR France 516
ELAND,Reginald George Walton	Lt Can 31Bn 3-5-17 MR 23
ELDER,Howard Thomas	Lt Aust 5Inf dow 9-5-15 MR 6
ELDER,John Andrew Dow.MC.	Lt Can 38Bn 1918
ELDING,Charles	Lt Can 46Bn 10-8-18 MR 23
ELIOT,Lionel Hyman	Lt Can 75Bn 9-4-17 CR France 1896
ELL,Alfred Henry Waldock	2Lt NZ 11635 1CIR kia 23-10-18 CR France 206
ELLENDER,William Alfred	Lt Can CFA 3Bde Ex RHA Y'Bty kia 2-9-18 CR France 421
ELLIOT,Charles Clifton	Lt Aust AFA 3DAC ded 8-11-18 CR France 146
ELLIOT,Charles Sinclair	Capt Aust RAN 30-3-15 CR Aust 234
ELLIOT,Dudley Sinclair	Lt Aust 35Inf 12-10-17 MR 29
ELLIOT,Henry George	Lt SA 3SAInf mbk 20-7-16 MR 21 18-7-16
ELLIOT,John George	2Lt Aust AustReinf ded 1-11-18 CR Wilts 115
ELLIOT,Thomas Hampton	Capt Aust 48Inf kia 28-3-18 CR France 196
ELLIOTT,Claude E.	2Lt Can RAF 4TrngDepotStn Ex CanAMC kld 5-9-18 CR Cheshire 192
ELLIOTT,Dudley Marwood	2Lt Aust 11Inf dow 18-9-18 CR France 446
ELLIOTT,Edward Patrick	Lt Can CE 2Bn kia 1-9-18 CR France 309
ELLIOTT,Frank H.	Capt Can 26Bn ded 2-7-18 CR Canada 1028
ELLIOTT,Frederick Fletcher	Lt Can 7Bn (BCR) kia 3-6-19 MR 29
ELLIOTT,George Stephenson.MC.	Capt Aust AMC kia 25-9-17 CR Belgium 19
ELLIOTT,John	Lt Can 16Bn 2-9-18 CR France 687
ELLIOTT,John McCreary	Lt CanLSH &RFC 60Sqn 16-4-17 MR 20
ELLIOTT,Joseph	Chpn Can ChpnServs 12-12-19 CR Canada 1178
ELLIOTT,Leslie Shaw	2Lt Aust 3Inf kia 3-5-16 CR France 707
ELLIOTT,Lorne Burton	Lt Can 46Bn 17-11-17 CR Surrey 1
ELLIOTT,Thomas Ninian	Maj Can2CRT A'Coy 28-9-17 CR Belgium 5
ELLIOTT,Thomas Patrick	Maj Aust60Inf kia 19-7-16 MR 7
ELLIOTT,William Nixon	Lt NZ 11572 CIR 1CanterburyR kia 3-12-17 CR Belgium 72
ELLIS,Alfred Thomas	2Lt Aust 26Inf 21-9-17 MR 29
ELLIS,Arthur William F.	Maj Can 19Bn 13-4-17 CR France 102
ELLIS,Douglas Quirk	Lt Can RFC CRT ded 8-2-18 CR Canada 1667
ELLIS,Edwin George	2Lt NZ25992 2AIR kia 4-10-17 MR 30
ELLIS,Frederick Walter	2Lt Aust 28Inf dow 30-7-16 CR France 74
ELLIS,Henry	Lt Aust 17Inf dow 16-4-17 CR France 512
ELLIS,John Reginald Mitchinson	LtCan 16Bn9-8-16 CR France 200
ELLIS,Oliver Hiram	Capt SA SAPC CampCmdtStaff ded 20-6-18 CR SAfrica 31
ELLIS,Walter Whyte	Maj Aust 13Inf kia 3-5-15 CR Gallipoli 30
ELLISDON,Fredk Joseph Herring.MID.	Lt NZ 12/2281 1AIRkia 26-9-16 MR 11
ELMSLEY,Remy Basil	Lt Can 5BnCE kia 4-10-18 CR France 715 Bazil

ELMSLIE,James McGregor.MID	Maj NZ 11/629 WMR kia 9-8-15 MR 5	
ELSLEY,Lloyd	Lt Can 124Bn attRFC 23Sqn 5-4-17 CR France 403	
ELTHAM,William Keith	Lt Aust AFA 1Bde kia 31-12-16 CR France 374	
ELTIS,Robert Harry Mervyn.MM.	2Lt Aust Engrs 6FC kia 26-7-18 CR France 1170	
ELTON,H.See SKELTON true name		
ELY,Percy Alfred	Lt NZ1KEdwHorse attNZEF ded 17-11-18 CR London 8	
EMERSON,Percy Tivy	Lt NZ 11/701 WMR 9Sqn kia 30-5-15 MR 6	
EMINSON,H.L.	Lt SA 8SAInf kia 19-7-17 CR Tanzania 1 &EAfrica 38	
EMPSON,Lancelot William	Lt Can 58Bn kia 1-1-17 CR France 68	
EMSLEY,William Henry H	LtCol Can ChpnServs ded 15-10-19 CR Canada 1582	
EMSLIE,S.	Lt SA 5NatLab C'Coy drd 21-2-17 MR 40	
ENGELBRECHT,Jacobus Paulus.MID	Capt SA MilLabCps8-12-18CR EAfrica 8	
ENRIGHT,William James	Capt CanCAMC HS drd 27-6-18 CR France 65	
EPPS,James Hubert	Lt Aust 41Inf kia 18-2-17 CR France 922	
ERREY,Leonard Geo Prentice.DSO.MC.	Lt Aust 8Inf dow 4-10-17 CR Belgium 72	
ERSKINE,Marguerite M.StJ.	Nurse SA SAVAD attBRCS 14-11-18 CR Devon 72	
ESAM,Stanley Owen	2Lt NZ 23751 1WIR kia 16-9-16 MR 11	
ESPIE,Alexander	Lt Aust AIF 43Inf 3-12-17CR Aust 212	
ESSLEMONT,John	Lt Can 54Bn dow 21-11-16 CR France 145	
ETHELL,John Oliver	2Lt Aust 23Inf 4-10-17MR 29	
EVANS,Alexander Easson	Lt Can7Bn 5-1-16 CR Belgium 339	
EVANS,Alfred James Lawrence.MID	Lt Can 3Bn dow 7-12-15 CR France 285	
EVANS,Charles Herbert	Lt Can 4CRT ded 7-2-19 CR Scot 235	
EVANS,Cyril Ansell	Lt Can 85Bn dow 4-8-18 CR France 14	
EVANS,David Gerald.MC.	Capt Aust8Inf dow 20-9-17 CR Belgium 11	
EVANS,David Stanley	Lt Aust 23Inf kia 20-3-17 CR France 1484	
EVANS,Edward Cassils	Capt Can42Bn dow 24-3-19 CR Canada 256	
EVANS,Ernest Andrew	Capt Aust 60Inf kia 19-7-16 MR 7	
EVANS,Francis Meredith	2Lt NZ 26/67 4/3NZRB kia 4-11-18 CR France 206	
EVANS,G.F.	Capt Aust 48Inf 14-8-16CR France 1505	
EVANS,Glyndwr David	2Lt Aust 1TC kia 25-4-17 CR Belgium 127	
EVANS,Herbert Howell	Lt CanRFC 2CMR 5-4-17 CR France 95	
EVANS,James Lloyd	Capt Can 5Bn kia 1-9-18 CR France 309	
EVANS,John Llewellyn	Lt Can54Bn D'Coy kia 1-3-17 CR France 81	
EVANS,John Lovell	Lt Can 52Bn 10-8-18CR France 29	
EVANS,Thomas Hatfield	2Lt Aust 3Inf kia 26-4-15 CR Gallipoli 31	
EVANS,William David	Lt Can46Bn &RAF kld 11-6-18 CR Wales 551	
EVATT,Raymond Scott.MC.	Lt Aust 20Inf 20-9-17MR 29	
EVE,Frank Arshure	Lt Can 28Bn 27-9-16CR France 102	
EVELEIGH,Albert Winthrop	Lt Can 52Bn dow 23-12-20 CR Canada 993	
EVERETT,Alfred Frank	Lt Aust25Inf 19-2-17CR London 1	
EVERETT,W.F.	LtCol Aust6ALH 17-8-15CR Hamps 64	
EVERITT,Frank Edward	2Lt Aust 1Inf dow 20-7-16 CR France 430	
EVERITT,George	Lt Can 29Bn 25-9-16CR France 1505	
EWART,Douglas Marsden.MC.	Lt Can7BnCE kia 26-8-18 CR France 1182	
EWENS,George Arthur	Lt Can 58Bn 22-10-17 CR Belgium 22	

F

FACEY,Stephen George.DCM.	2Lt Aust 59Inf kia 4-7-18 CR France 207
FADDY,Francis Horatio.MID	Lt Aust 13Inf kia 3-5-15 MR 6
FAHEY,Ernest Edward	Lt Can 78Bn 27-9-18CR France 714
FAIR,Robert McCamus	Capt Can 24Bn att5 LtTMB kia 16-9-16 MR 23
FAIRBAIRN,William	2Lt NZ2/121 NZFA 10Bty kia 21-10-16 CR France 513
FAIRCLOUGH,Robert Twentyman	2Lt Aust6Inf kia 7-8-15 MR 6
FAIRLIE,John Raymond	2Lt Aust 25Inf ded 13-2-16 CR Egypt 8

FAIRWEATHER,Francis Edward.MC&Bar.	Capt Aust 38Inf kia 29-9-18 CR France 1495
FAIRWEATHER,Frank Russell	Capt Can 26Bn kia 17-9-16 MR 23
FAIRWEATHER,J.McI.DSO.	LtCol SA SAMCycCps kia 18-2-17 CR EAfrica 40
FAIRWEATHER,Warren Hatheway	Lt Can 26Bn 8-8-18 CR France 425
FAITHFULL,Gordon Chamberlain	Lt Can 75Bn 9-4-17 CR France 1896
FALCONER,James Alan.MC.	Lt Aust 57Inf kia 25-4-18 CR France 119
FALCONER-STEWART,Peter Douglas	Lt Can 16Bn att3LTMB 1-9-18 CR France 687
FALLIS,Everett Boyd Jackson	Lt Can 102Bn 9-4-17 CR France 81
FANNING,Frederick.MIDx3	Capt Aust 56Inf dow 1-11-16 CR France 188
FARISH,George Colhns	Capt Can25Bn ded 28-10-18 CR Canada 887
FARLEIGH,Alfred Gordon.MC.	Lt Aust 33Inf kia 22-8-18 CR France 396
FARLOW,Colin Herbert	2Lt Aust 13Inf dow 15-8-16 CR France 74
FARLOW,F.G.MC.	Lt Aust 11ALH 25-9-18CR Palest 11
FARMER,Melville Orchard	Lt Aust9ALH 30-4-18MR 34
FARMER,Paul Douglas	Lt SA1SAInf kia 24-3-18 MR 27
FARMER,Reginald William Bartlett	Lt Aust RANR HMAS`Torrens' ded 9-10-18 CR Italy 42
FARNSWORTH,Edward Ernest.MM.	2Lt NZ 3/1699 1/3NZRB kia 12-9-18 CR France 415
FARQUHAR,Allan.MC.	2Lt NZ 6/452 2CIR kia 24-8-18 CR France 512
FARQUHAR,Arthur Wallace Kemmis	Lt Aust AFC Ex 6ALH kia 26-6-18 CR Palest 9
FARQUHAR,Francis Douglas.DSO.	LtCol Can PPCLI 21-3-15CR Belgium 111
FARR,Cecil Jardine	Lt Can 46Bn 12-4-17CR France 81
FARRAR,George Herbert.Sir.DSO.	Col SA HQRecs&CampStaff 20-5-15CR SAfrica 41
FARRIER,Charles Percy	Lt Aust10Inf kia 9-5-15 CR Gallipoli 7
FARRY,Charles	2Lt Aust 1Inf 4-10-17MR 29
FATT,William Maberly	Lt Can CCycBn attRFC 4-1-17 CR Surrey 15
FAULKNER,Albert Edward	Lt Can 29Bn 28-5-19CR Canada 543
FAULKNER,William George	Lt Aust 44Inf kia 31-8-18 CR France 624
FAWCETT,James Howard	Lt Can 4Bn 11-4-17CR France 95
FAY,George	Capt Aust 8ALH kia 1-12-17 CR Palest 9
FAY,J.E.	4thEngr Can MercMar SS`Miniota' 31-8-17MR 24
FEINDEL,John H.	Lt Can 25Bn 9-4-17 CR France 68
FEINHOLS,H.	Lt SA HQRecs&CampStaff 8-10-18CR SAfrica 120
FELL,Gerald Horton	Lt NZ 10/2816 1WIR kia 7-6-17 CR Belgium 89
FELSTEAD,Theo.	2Lt Aust AFC 16-1-18MR 26 &CR Aust 307
FELTON,Arthur Alfred	Lt Aust4Bn 17-4-18MR 26
FELTON,Edgar Dean	2Lt Aust 20Inf dow 9-8-16 CR France 74
FENDER,William Martin	Lt Aust1AICC 19-4-17MR 34
FENIX,Norman George	2Lt SA 2SAInf dow 17-10-16 CR France 177
FENNELL,Thomas Harold	Lt Can 2CMR kia 17-5-16 CR Belgium 5
FENTON,Hubert Jefferson	Lt Can 54BN 17-10-16 MR 23
FENTON,John Wilfred.MM.	Lt Aust AFA 15Bty dow 19-6-18 CR France 102
FENWICK,George Paget Owen	Lt Can 7MGCoy kia 30-10-17 MR 29
FERGUSON,A.B. Sub	Lt Aust RAN 14-7-20CR Aust 449A
FERGUSON,Adam	Lt Aust AMGC 2Coy dow 1-9-18 CR France 119
FERGUSON,Angus Salier	Lt Aust48Inf kia 3-5-18 CR France 144
FERGUSON,Arthur Gardre	Capt Aust 20Inf kia 14-6-16 CR France 83
FERGUSON,Douglas Abbott	2Lt AustAFC dedacc 18-8-18 CR Surrey 1
FERGUSON,Ewan Cameron	2Lt NZ 23/972 3/3NZRB kia 2-10-16 MR 11
FERGUSON,Harry Wensley	Lt Can 26Bn kia 15-3-16 CR Belgium 60
FERGUSON,Hector James Abbott.MC&Bar	Lt Aust Engrs 1DivSigs kia 21-10-17 CR Belgium 15
FERGUSON,J.Roy	2Lt Can RNewfndlandR kia 1-7-16 MR 10
FERGUSON,John Ferrier	Lt Can 43Wing RAF 1PnrBn ded 16-10-18 CR Canada 487
FERGUSON,John Stephen	Lt Aust Engrs 14FC dow 27-7-16 CR London 9
FERGUSON,Kenneth	Lt SA NRhodPol ded 19-10-18 CR EAfrica 73
FERGUSON,Thomas Karl	Lt Aust 47Inf kia 11-10-16 CR Belgium 37
FERGUSON,William Bruce.MC.	Lt Can RAF 9CRT 7-7-18 CR Essex 45
FERGUSON,William Frederick	Lt Can 2Bn kia 3-9-18 CR France 688
FERGUSSON,Herbert Hilton	Lt Aust 3Inf kia 9-8-18 CR France 1170
FERNE,Gordon Bent	Lt Can 1MMGBde 10-10-18 CR France 147
FERRIER,William Forbes.MM.	Lt Can 21Bn kia 11-10-18 CR France 761
FERRIS,Ernest Lyon	Capt Can49Bn 16-9-16MR 23

FERRIS,James Robinson	Capt Can 49Bn ded 11-10-18 CR France 34
FETHERS,Erle Finlayson Denton	Maj Aust 5Inf kia 25-4-15 CR Gallipoli 7
FETHERS,Percival George Denton	Lt Aust 24Bn 3-5-17 MR 26
FEWSTER,George Edward	Lt Aust 15Inf kia 4-7-18 CR France 424
FFITCH,Harry Herbert	Lt NZ 6/954 CIR A'Coy kia 26-4-15 MR 6
FIDGE,Ronald Lacey.MM.	2Lt Aust 18Inf dow 21-9-17 CR Belgium 11
FIELD,Charles Valentine Geary	Lt Can 4Bn attRFC 16Sqn 12-1-16 CR France 924
FIELDER,Bertram Hayes	Lt Can 7Bn 1918
FIELDING,William Stevens	Capt Can 7Bn (BCR) 27-9-17 CR France 274 &MR 29 10-11-17
FIFE,Gordon Stanley	Lt Can PPCLI 2-9-16 CR Belgium 309
FILMER,Walter Stephen	2Lt Aust 22Bn 3-5-17 MR 26
FINCH-DAVIES,Claude Gibney	Lt SA 1MR 3-8-20 CR SAfrica 171
FINDLAY,Charles	Lt Aust 8Inf kia 23-8-18 CR France 526
FINDLAY,Ernest Brainerd	Lt Can 54Bn dow 3-9-18 CR France 14
FINK,George Paul	Lt Can CASC 28-9-17 CR Canada 1219
FINLAY,George Lush.MC.	Capt Aust 5Inf ded 9-2-19 CR France 40
FINLAY,William Seymour	Lt Aust 24Inf kia 29-11-15 CR Gallipoli 7
FINLAYSON,Robert John Stanley	2Lt Aust 1TC dedacc 25-6-17 CR Belgium 97
FINLAYSON,Roderick Hamilton	Lt Can 7Bn 20-4-17 CR France 40
FINLAYSON,Ronald Berry	Lt Aust 1Inf kia 5-11-16 CR France 307
FINLEY,Charles Arthur	Lt Can 58Bn (2COR) 26-10-17 MR 29
FINN,Edward Arthur	Lt Can 31Bn 9-8-18 CR France 652
FINN,William Clifford	Lt Can 4BnCMGC 30-9-18 CR France 147
FINNEY,Sylvester Webster	Lt Can 58Bn 1919
FINNIE,Alexander	Lt Aust AFC kia 22-5-18 CR France 705
FISCHER,Frank Reinhardt	Lt Aust 6Inf kia 10-8-18 CR France 526
FISHER,Bruce Fitzgerald	Lt Can CFA 30Bty 8ABde kia 8-8-18 CR France 424
FISHER,Edwin Maurice	Capt Can 10Bn (AR) 3-6-16 MR 29
FISHER,Frederick James	Lt Can 7Bn (BCR) 10-11-17 MR 29
FISHER,George	Lt Can 75Bn dow 20-12-16 CR London 8
FISHER,Harold Laurence	Lt Can 8Bn 22-7-16 CR Belgium 127
FISHER,Harry Waterman	Lt Can 4Bn 7-5-16 CR Belgium 15
FISHER,Herbert Courteney	Lt Can 5CMR 2-10-16 CR France 59 Henry
FISHER,Herbert John	Lt Aust AFA 2Bde dow 3-10-18 CR France 528
FISHER,John Thompson	Lt Can 43Bn kia 30-8-17 CR France 480
FISHER,Sidney John	Lt Can 29Bn BRCD attRAF kldacc 30-9-18 CR France 1844
FISHER,Walde Gerald	Lt Aust 42Inf kia 5-4-18 CR France 833
FISHER,William Graham Duncan	Lt Aust 18Inf dow 24-3-17 CR France 40
FISK,Stanley Howells	2Lt Aust 30Inf kia 11-10-17 CR Belgium 128
FITCH,Richard Dallington	2Lt NZ 22186 2CIR dow 6-5-18 CR France 84
FITZGERALD,Frederick	Capt Can PPCLI 1915
FITZGERALD,Leslie Emmet James	Lt Aust 5Inf kia 25-7-16 CR France 402
FITZGERALD,Richard McGuinness	2Lt Aust 18Bn 4-8-16 MR 26
FITZGERALD,R.G.R.	Capt Can PPCLI kia 26-1-15 CR Belgium 111 real name MANSFIELD
FITZHENRY,D.A.	Sister SA SAMNS ded 1-12-18 CR EAfrica 1
FITZPATRICK,Frank Bertie	Lt Aust 13Inf 28-9-16 MR 29
FITZPATRICK,N.	2Lt Aust AFC 16-1-19 CR Europe 23
FITZPATRICK,P.N.G.	Maj SA HArty 71SB kia 14-12-17 CR France 381
FITZPATRICK,Walter Vincent.MID	2Lt Aust 51Inf kia 5-4-18 CR France 177
FITZPATRICK,Wilfred	Lt Can 5Bn (SR) 24-4-15 MR 29
FITZPATRICK,William Sydney.MM.	2Lt Aust 13Inf kia 11-6-17 CR Belgium 88
FITZ-ROY,Charles Henry.MC&Bar.	Lt Can 10Bn kia 28-9-18 CR France 147
FJELDSTED,Asgeir H	Capt&QM Can 223Bn ded 30-8-16 CR Canada 78
FLACK,Basil John Ingleby	2Lt SA 2SAInf kia 12-10-16 MR 21
FLANAGAN,H.	S Nurse SA SAMNS ded 30-3-20
FLANAGAN,James.MC.	Lt NZ 23325 MGC ded 13-12-18 CR Lincs 61
FLASHMAN,James Froude	LtCol Aust AAMC 1AustHosp ded 12-2-17 CR France 64
FLEMING,Alan Seed	Lt Can 101CoyCFC 10-9-18 CR Surrey 78
FLEMING,Arthur Gordon Slane.MID	Lt Can 26Bn kia 15-8-17 CR France 480 Garnet
FLEMING,Hamilton Maxwell	Capt Can 16Bn (MR) 24-4-15 MR 29
FLEMING,John Forbes Menzies	Lt NZ 11/1616 1OIR dow 30-9-16 CR France 40

FLEMING,Richard Lucien Gilbert	LtNZ 25/7 2/3NZRB kia 7-6-17 CR Belgium 168
FLEMMER,Wilfred Hopley	2Lt or Lt SA 2SAInf dow 18-7-16 CR France 23
FLETCHER,Basil George Wellard	Capt Aust 13Bn 11-4-17MR 26
FLETCHER,John Harry	Capt Aust 24Inf kia 5-10-18 CR France 444
FLETT,Irving Russell	Lt Aust 23Bn 28-7-16MR 26
FLINT,Clarence Kells.MC.	Lt Can 49Bn kia 28-9-18 CR France 481
FLOCKART,Robert Pearce	Maj Aust 5Inf dow 15-7-15 MR 6
FLOOD,John William	2Lt NZ5/244A 2WIR dow 8-11-18 CR France 658
FLOOK,Albert James John.MM.	Lt Can44Bn 27-9-18CR France 714
FLOWER,William Evelyn Francise	2Lt NZ 12/296 AIR 6Coy kia 25/29-4-15 MR 6
FLOWERDEW,Gordon Muriel.VC.	Lt Can LSH dow 31-3-18 CR France 185
FLOWERS,Walter Henry	Lt Aust 49Inf ded 25-10-18 CR Hunts 96
FLYNN,A.R.	Lt SA 3Horse kia 8-9-16 CR EAfrica 39
FLYNN,Hugh Michael.DCM.MID.	2Lt Aust 9Inf 20-9-17MR 29
FODEN,William Roy	2Lt NZ 23/1047 2CIR 12Coy kia 12-10-17 MR 30
FOERS,Frank Everest	2Lt Aust7Inf kia 20-9-17 CR Belgium 115
FOGARTY,Andrew Christopher	Lt Aust24Inf kia 7/12-8-15 CR Gallipoli 7
FOGARTY,Gerald Saunders	Lt Can 87Bn kia 2-9-18 CR France 310
FOLEY,Frederick David	Lt Can 26Bn 30-9-16MR 23
FOLEY,Raymond George.MC.	Lt Can 2Bn attRFC 27Sqn 8-3-18 CR France 1061
FOLKINS,Harry Allison	Maj Can 38Bn 1917
FOLLETTE,Minnie Asenath NSister	Can CAMC HS drd 27-6-18 MR 24
FOLLEY,Edwin Powell	2Lt Aust 28Inf kia 3-9-18 CR France 624
FOORD,Edward Alec	Lt Can 78Bn attRAFkia 27-6-18 CR France 1170
FOORD,James.MC.	Maj Can 2CMR 28-10-17 CR Belgium 5
FOOTE,Oliver Cecil Hardwick	2Lt Aust 25Inf kia 11-1-18 CR Belgium 50
FORBES,Arthur John	Lt SA 1LovatScts att1/3KAR kia 21-10-17 CR EAfrica 11
FORBES,Donald Brotchie	Lt Can 31Bn kia 9-4-17 CR France 68
FORBES,Louis Herbert.MC.	2Lt SA 1SAInf mbk 23-3-18 MR 27
FORBES,Muirton Warrand	Lt Aust 2Inf kia 24-5-18 CR France 28
FORBES,Joseph William.MID	Lt Aust 6Inf kia 20-9-17 CR Belgium 115
FORBES,Muirton Warrand	Lt Aust 2Inf kia 24-5-18 CR France 28
FORBES,Sydney Trovorrwo	Lt Aust 11Bn 22/25-7-16 MR 26
FORBES,William George	Lt Aust 26Inf 21-9-17MR 29
FORD,Angus MacDonald	Capt Can CAMC dedatsea 16-1-20 MR 40
FORD,Francis Walter	Lt Can 19ResBn (1CMR) 25-9-17CR Hamps 1
FORD,James Patrick.MID	Lt AustFA 6Bde kia 2-8-17 CR Belgium 15
FORD,Leonard James	TMaj NZ 6/2027 2CIR kia 12-10-17 CR Belgium 126
FORD,Robert Bertram	Lt Can CE 2TC kia 2-6-16 MR 29
FORD,Rufus Philip	Lt Aust 10Inf 7-10-17MR 29
FORD,Sydney Kelso	Lt Aust 9Bn 23-7-16MR 26
FORDE,Walter Patrick	2Lt NZ 8/1735 1OIR dow 13-8-16 CR France 285
FORDER,William George Symons	2Lt SA 4SAInf dow 22-9-17 CR Belgium 3
FORDHAM,Eric Surrey Wynter	2Lt Aust 11Inf 20-9-17MR 29
FORDHAM,Roy Ogilvie	2Lt Aust 10Inf kia 8-4-17 CR France 1484
FORMBY,William Kenneth	WTO Can `Shearwater' 1917
FORNERI,Agnes Florien	NSister Can CAMC 8GH 24-4-18CR Hamps 2
FORNERI,David Alwyn	Lt Can 73Bn 1-3-17 MR 23
FORREST,Hugh Alexander	Lt NZ 30104 2/3NZRB kia 12-10-17 CR Belgium 96
FORRESTER,John Matheson	Lt SA2SAInf C'Coykia 12-10-16 CR France 285
FORRESTER,Joshua Alexander	Lt Aust 2Inf kia 2-5-18 CR France 28
FORSTER,James Herbert	Capt Can1CMR dow 15-10-16 CR France 145
FORSTER,William	Lt Aust 21Bn 3-5-17 MR 26
FORSYTH,James Cobban	Capt Can CAMC 1GH dow 8-9-18 CR Wales 389
FORSYTH,Norman Leslie	Lt NZ 6/3319 1OIR kia 7-6-17 CR Belgium 89
FORSYTH,Reginald James Thomas	2Lt AustAFC dow 16-2-18 CR Shrop 145
FORSYTH,William Fraser	Lt Can 28Bn dow 4-10-18 CR France 214
FORSYTH-INGRAM,J.L.	2Lt SA 2SAInf
FORSYTHE,Alexander Elder	2Lt NZ 6/228 CIR `Nelson'Coykia 6/10-5-15 MR 13
FORTESCUE,Margaret Jane	NSister Can CAMC HS drd 27-6-18 MR 24
FORTH,W.V.	2Lt SA 2SAInf kia 12-4-17 CR France 604

FORWOOD,Reginald Ernest	Lt Aust 27Inf dow 20-11-16 CR France 833
FOSS,Cecil Maitland.MC.	Capt Aust 28Inf dow 11-8-16 CR France 74
FOSS,Henry Clinton.MID	2Lt Aust 28Inf 3-5-17 MR 26
FOSS,Samuel James Beart	2Lt NZ10/338 2AIR dow 24-9-16 CR France 177
FOSTER,Frederick Rathbone	TCapt NZ 12/2601 2AIR kia 8-6-17 MR 9
FOSTER,John	Lt Can 1CMR kia 9-4-17 CR France 523
FOSTER,John Askin.MID	Maj Aust 12Inf kia 23-8-18 CR France 526
FOSTER,John Grierson	2Lt NZ 9/989 OMR dow 24-8-15
FOSTER,John Grierson	2Lt NZ 11151 2OMR kia 2-10-16 MR 11
FOSTER,Reginald William	Lt Aust 15Inf kia 8-8-15 MR 6
FOSTER,Robert George	Lt Can8Bn 9-8-18 CR France 693
FOSTER,William Gare	Lt Can 44Bn kia 18-11-16 CR France 239 Gore
FOSTER,William Garland.MC.	Capt&Adjt Can 54Bn dow 14-10-18 CR France 214
FOTHERGILL,Albert Edgar	Lt Aust 9Inf kia 20-4-16 CR France 707
FOTHERGILL,John Charles.DCM.	2Lt NZ 13286 2OIR kia 23-10-18 CR France 206
FOTHERINGHAM,John Beveridge	Lt Can 20RBn (QR) &RFC 45Sqn 7-7-17 MR 20
FOURIE,William Hendrik Boshoff	LtSA 5Horse kia 7-9-16 CR EAfrica 39
FOWLER,A.G.	Capt SA SAR OverseasDom
FOWLER,Cyril Douglas Gilroy	Lt NZ 13690 MGC kia 26-5-18 CR France 5
FOWLER,Percival Leonard	Lt Aust 29Inf 8-8-18 CR France 23
FOWLIE,Alexander James H	Capt Can RCR 1914
FOX,A.F	Capt Aust AMC 1AustGenHosp ded 24-8-18 MR 26
FOX,Catherine Anne	S Nurse NZ22/118 ANS drd 23-10-15 MR 35
FOX,William Harold	Lt Can 1Bn 1-10-18CR France 147
FOXEN,William E.MC.	Lt Can 50Bn 13-11-18 CR France 40
FRAME,Robert Steele	Lt Can 110Bn 13-1-18CR Canada 1207 28Regt
FRAME,William Layton	Lt Can 102Bn dow 11-6-17 CR Surrey 1
FRANCIS,Albert	Lt Can 2CMR 29-9-18CR France 148
FRANCIS,J.L.	2Lt SA2SAInf dow 26-10-18
FRANCIS,John Walter.MID	Lt Aust 59Inf 26-9-17MR 29
FRANCIS,Trevor.MC.	Capt Aust 53Inf kia 14-3-17 CR France 374
FRANCIS,Vincent	Lt Aust AIF 42Inf 24-5-19CR Aust 307
FRANCK,Alexander	2Lt SA 7SAInf mbk 12-2-16 CR EAfrica 56 dow
FRANCKLYN,George Edward	Capt Can CASC 1DivTr 7-12-15CR Kent 180
FRANDI,Ateo	Capt NZ 10/1169 WIR 2Reinf kia 6/10-5-15 MR 13
FRANKLIN,Reginald Norris.DSO.	Maj Aust AIF 2ALH 6-7-19 CR Aust 112
FRANKLYN,Cyril Clyde	Lt Aust FA 6Bty 2Bdekia 22-8-17 CR Belgium 15
FRANKLYN,John William	2Lt Aust 11Inf dow 6-8-15 MR 6
FRASER,Alexander Daniel	Lt Can 85Bn kia 7-11-17 CR France 40
FRASER,Alexander Gordon	Lt Can21Bn dow 18-9-16 CR France 74
FRASER,Archibald Brydone	Lt Can 72Bn 1-11-16CR France 430
FRASER,Arthur Milton	Lt Can RCR 26-8-18CR France 1189
FRASER,Basil Earle	Lt Can 25Bn 8-4-18 CR France 169
FRASER,David	Capt Can 50Bn 27-9-18CR France 714
FRASER,Douglas Playfair.MID.	Capt NZ 6/408 2CIR kia 20-9-16 MR 11
FRASER,Finlay	2Lt Aust MGC 5Coy 3-5-17 MR 26
FRASER,Finlay David	Capt Can 4Bn 12-8-16CR France 64
FRASER,George Christian	2Lt Aust 33Inf 15-10-17 MR 29
FRASER,Hubert Percy	Lt Aust 22Bn 3-5-17 MR 26
FRASER,Hugh.DCM.	Lt Aust Engrs 3FC dow 31-5-18 CR France 180
FRASER,James.MC.	Lt Aust 15Inf kia 4-7-18 CR France 424
FRASER,James George	Lt Aust 33Inf dow 28-4-18 CR France 145
FRASER,James Gibson Laurier	Lt Can 16Bn kia 4-3-18 CR France 161
FRASER,John Bruce	Capt Can 3BnCMGC kia 4-9-18 CR France 427
FRASER,Magnus	2Lt NZ 45318 RB dow 9-1-18 CR Belgium 11
FRASER,Margaret Marjory	Matron CanCAMC HS drd 27-6-18 MR 24
FRASER,Simon.MID	2Lt Aust 58Bn 12-5-17MR 26
FRATER,Robert Andrew	2Lt NZ 12/1026 AIR MG Sect dow 30-4-15 MR 6
FRAYNE,William Stanley	Capt Aust 10Inf kia 6-8-15 CR Gallipoli 7
FRAZIER,F.V.	Lt USA AmericanArmy 24-3-18CR France 1063
FREADMAN,Zavel Ephraim	2Lt Aust AFC 4Sqn dedacc 9-9-17 CR Middx 40

40

FREDERICK,Charles Clarence	Cadet2695 Aust AFC 5TrgSqn dedacc 4-2-19 CR Glouc 172
FREDRICKSON,Christine	Nurse Can CAMC ded 28-10-18 CR Canada 25
FREED,Edward Victor.MC.	Capt NZ 24308 1OIR dow 25-8-18 CR France 518
FREEMAN,Aubrey Harold	2Lt Aust Engrs 6FC kia 8-11-16 CR France 744
FREEMAN,Douglas	Lt Aust 16Inf kia 26-9-17 CR Belgium 88
FREEMAN,Douglas Stephen	Lt Aust 15Inf kia 3-5-15 MR 6
FREEMAN,Harry Percival	Lt Can RFC 134Bn 21-1-18CR Middx 26
FREEMAN,Harvey.MC.	Lt Aust 11MGC kia 15-10-17 CR Belgium 125
FREEMAN,Nelson Porter	Capt Can CAMC 1920
FREEMAN,Norman David	Lt Aust 42Inf 31-7-17CR Belgium 453 &MR29
FREEMAN,William Ellis.MC.	Capt Aust 15 LtTMB dow 14-12-17 CR France 297
FREEME,George	Lt NZ 3/109ANZDC ded 12-11-23
FRENCH,Cecil John.MC.	Lt Can 4BnCMGC 28-9-18CR France 256
FRENCH,George Timothy	Lt Aust 26Inf dow 5-10-17 CR Belgium 11
FRENCH,Gordon Rae.MID	Lt Can 87Bn att11 LtTMB dow 6-10-18 CR France 146
FRENCH,William Alexander	Lt NZ 9/141 1OIR kia 12-10-17 CR Belgium 125
FREW,Reginald Lansell	Lt Aust FA 8Bde kia 17-9-17 CR Belgium 19
FREWIN,Victor Joseph	Lt Aust 18Bn 15-4-18MR 26
FRIEDRICHS,Karl Richard	Maj Aust27Inf kia 21-4-18 CR France 177
FRIZELLE,Thomas James	Maj Aust AAMC 1FA dow 2-12-17 CR France 13
FROST,William Osmond	Lt Aust 23Inf kia 2-10-17 CR Belgium 308
FROUDE,W.G.F.	Lt SA 5MR 25-11-14 CR SAfrica 154
FRY,Henry Philip	Capt Aust10ALH kia 29-8-15 MR 6
FRY,John Samuel	2Lt SA 4SAInf kia 13-7-16 MR 21
FRY,Sydney Charles	2Lt Aust AFC 8TrgSqndedacc 24-8-18 CR Glouc 172
FRYER,Hal Charles.MC.MID	Maj Can 52Bn 4-9-17 CR France 480
FULLARTON,James Macbeth.MM.	2Lt Aust 54Inf kia 19-10-17 CR Belgium 112
FULLER,Howard	Lt Can 15Bn 3-6-16 CR Belgium 127
FULTON,Alexander Roy	2Lt Aust 8Inf kia 20-9-17 CR Belgium 96
FULTON,Arthur Leeman	Maj Aust 47Bn 7-8-16 MR 26
FULTON,Harry Townsend.CMG.DSO.MIDx2	TBrigGen NZ 23/1 NZRB dow 29-3-18 CR France 62
FULTON,David Roger	2Lt Aust 20Inf 6-11-17MR 29
FULTON,Parker Alonzo	Lt Can26Bn 17-8-17CR France 480
FURNELL,Gilbert James.MID	Lt Aust 2Pnrs dow 19-9-17 CR Belgium 19
FURZE,Walter Laighton Mason	Lt Can CFA 2DAC kia 13-8-18 CR France 652
FYFE,Alexander Howard Parker	2Lt Aust 8MGC kia 26-9-17 CR Belgium 112
FYSHE,Francis	Lt Can CFA 2Bde 27-11-15 CR Belgium 138

G

GABITES,Cyril Douglas	Lt NZ 8/1988 OIR kia 3-12-17 MR 8
GABY,Alfred Edward.VC.	Lt Aust 28Inf kia 11-8-18 CR France 526
GAETZ,Harold Leonard	Maj Can 5Bn kia 26-9-16 MR 23
GAIR,Ivan Noble	Lt Aust 31Inf dow 30-9-18 CR France 446
GALAGHER,Frederick Alfred	Lt Aust 6Inf 8-5-15 MR 4
GALAUGHER,William Nelson	Lt Can 1Bn 20-3-15CR France 276
GALBRAITH,Alexander Norman	Capt Ceylon CeylonPlantersRifCps 16-2-15CR Eire 541
GALE,Withall Piddington	Capt Can CAMC ded 20-10-18 CR Canada 323A
GALLAHER,Minnie Katherine	NSister Can CAMC HS drd 27-6-18 MR 24
GALLEN,Harold	Lt Can 60Bn C'Coy dow 4-6-16 CR Belgium 11
GALLOWAY,Albert Hugh	2Lt Aust 32Inf dow 16-2-17 CR France 400
GALT,Gerald,	Lt Can Engrs 3TC kia 25-12-16 CR Belgium 53
GALT,James Henry	Lt Can 1LTMB ded 23-2-19 CR Surrey 115 4Bn
GALT,John	Lt Can LSH kia 9-12-15 MR 29
GALWAY,John Campbell	Maj Can 2PnrBn C'Coy kia 18-4-17 CR France 68

GAMBLE,John Scott	Lt Aust 31Inf 27-9-17MR 29	
GAMMELL,Norman Frederick	Lt Can PPCLI 26-8-18CR France 421	
GAMMON,Richard Thomas.MM.MID	Lt Aust FA 14Bde kia 31-7-17 CR Belgium 10	
GANE,Francis Egmont	Capt Can 13Bn 1916	
GANNON,William Robert	Lt Aust 60Inf dow 6-9-18 CR France 145	
GARATY,John Francis	2Lt Aust35Inf kia 20-12-17 CR France 922	
GARBUTT,Sarah Ellen	Nurse Can CANS OntMilHosp 20-8-17CR Surrey 1	
GARD,Joseph Henry	Capt Aust 11BdeHQ dow 31-7-18 CR France 29	
GARDINER,John.MC.	Lt Aust AFA 6MedTMBkia 1-9-18 CR France 511	
GARDINER,Julian Reginald Gladstone	2Lt Aust 20Bn 11-8-18MR 26	
GARDNER,Archibald Ramsay	Capt Aust 55Inf kia 9-5-17 CR France 1488	
GARDNER,Cyril.DCM&Bar.	2Lt Can RNewfndlandR kia 1-7-16 MR 20	
GARDNER,Stanley Douglas.CMG.MC.	LtCol Can 7 att38Bn dow 30-9-18 CR France 113	
GARLAND,Hugh Gordon.DCM.	Lt Aust 48Inf kia 3-5-18 CR France 144	
GARLICK,Harry William	Lt Aust5Inf kia 11-7-18 CR France 25	
GARLING,Leslie.MID	Lt Aust 45Inf 7-6-17 MR 29	
GARLING,Terence Ward	Maj Aust AFA 37Bty 10Bde dow 5-4-18 CR France 44	
GARNER,Vivian Gilbert	2Lt Aust 14Inf 8-8-17 MR 29	
GARNETT,Wade Shenton	Maj Aust AAMC att2AGH dow 15-4-18 CR France 145	
GARNHAM,Stanley Milwood	2Lt Aust 3Inf kia 8-8-15 MR 6	
GARRARD,Clifford Edgar	Lt Aust 39Inf kia 31-8-18 CR France 526	
GARRATT,Charles Clement.DCM&Bar	2Lt Aust 16Inf ded 9-11-18 CR France 52	
GARRETT,Richard Daryl	Lt Can 3Bn kia 5-11-17 CR Belgium 10 Ralph	
GARRETT,William Gibbs	Lt Can CFA 6Bde dow 9-11-17 CR France 145	
GARROW,John Ure	Lt Can 74Bn att4CMR dow 12-9-16 CR France 74	
GARTELL,Albert Reginald Stanley	Capt Aust AIF Engrs 3SigTrps 26-3-16CR Aust 212	
GARTRELL,William Henry	Capt Aust26Inf dow 18-11-16 CR France 927	
GARTSIDE,Joseph Arthur	Lt Can 78Bn dow 23-5-17 CR France 12	
GARTSIDE,Robert	LtCol Aust 8Inf kia 8-5-15 CR Gallipoli 2	
GARY,Franklin Jude.MC&Bar.	Maj Can 102Bn 2-9-18 CR France 14	
GASKELL,Richard Pennington	Lt Aust 30Inf kia 25-2-17 CR France 307	
GASS,Laurence Henderson	Lt CanCGA 5SB dow 8-4-17 CR France 12	
GASTON,Thomas William.MSM.	2Lt Aust 6Inf kia 23-8-18 CR France 526	
GATCUM,Leslie Harold	2Lt AustFA 8Bde kia 12-9-17 CR Belgium 19	
GATIEN,Charles Emile Joseph Antoine Guillaume	Lt Can 22Bn kia 15-8-17 CR France 1723	
GATLIFF,Frank Edward	Capt Aust FA 14Bde kia 6-8-17 CR Belgium 10	
GAUVREAU,Leo	Lt Can 85Bn att16MGC29-10-17 CR Belgium 128	
GAY,Harry Gillon	2Lt Aust 6Inf kia 26-10-17 CR Belgium 123	
GEACH,Samuel Stanley	2Lt SA 1SAInf B'Coy kia 16-10-18 CR France 716	
GEAR,John Foster.MC.	Lt Aust24Inf kia 5-10-18 CR France 235	
GEARING,Harry Alan Cheshire	Lt Aust AASC ded 16-3-17 CR Hamps 8	
GEARY,J.G.	Capt Aust 13Inf 8-8-18 CR France 1170	
GEDDES,Cyril Arthur	Lt Aust16Inf kia 2/3-5-15 MR 6	
GEDDES,John	Capt Can 16Bn (MR) dow 24-4-15 MR 29	
GEDDES,John Rowland	Lt Can Depot 36Bn attRFC 23Sqn 3-11-17CR Belgium 16	
GEDDES,Richard Luther	Lt Can 54Bn 7-9-17 MR 23	
GEE,H.J.MC.	Capt Aust 11ALH 25-9-18CR Palest 11	
GEE,Harry Herbert Allan	Maj SA 3SA Inf kia 19-7-16 CR France 402 2SAInf	
GEERNAERT,Theodore John	Lt Can CFA 23Bty 5Bde kia 12-5-18 CR France 504	
GELL,Ewan Victor	Lt Can 27Bn 3-5-17 MR 23	
GEM,William	Capt SA SAMC att10SAInfded 29-2-16 CR EAfrica 58	
GEMMELL,David	Capt SA 4SAInf D'Coy 22-9-17MR 29	
GEMMELL,Gordon Stewart	Lt Aust 11Inf kia 10-8-18 CR France 526	
GEORGE,Keith Harrison	Lt Aust AFA 1Bde 7-11-17MR 29	
GEORGE,Leslie	Lt Aust AFC 12-5-18CR Hamps 167	
GEPP,Arthur Edward Carl	Lt Aust 28Bn 5-8-16 MR 26	
GERMAIN,Russell Langworth	Lt Can 20Bn kia 10-11-18 CR Belgium 241 Longworth	
GERMAN,Harry Edgar or GERMAIN	Lt Can 75Bn dow 1-7-17 CR France 8	
GERVAIS,Joseph Arthur	Lt Can 14Bn 26-9-16MR 23	
GETTY,Andrew	Lt Aust 28Inf dow 6-6-18 CR France 71	
GHENT,Lloyd	Capt Aust 3MGC kia 20-9-17 CR Belgium 310	

GIBAUT,Alfred Philip	Lt Can 10Bn 8-4-17 CR France 1896	
GIBBINGS,Cecil Theodore	Capt Aust 28Inf kia 28-7-16 CR France 402	
GIBBINS,Norman	Capt Aust 55Inf Ex3Bnkia 20-7-16 CR France 255	
GIBBS,Richard Horace Maconchie.MC.	LtAust 59Inf kia 19-7-16 MR 7	
GIBBS,Stanley Gordon.MID	LtCol Aust ASC 2DivTrn kia 20-9-17 CR Belgium 11	
GIBBS,Walter George	Lt NZ11767 WIR 2WellingtonR dow/kia 26-9-18 CR France 13	
GIBLIN,Leonard	Lt Aust 3Pnrs kia 31-12-16 CR France 922	
GIBSON,Alexander James	Lt Aust 37Inf kia 30-9-18 CR France 212	
GIBSON,Benjamin Digby	Capt Aust 9ALH drd 14-1-17 CR Egypt 2	
GIBSON,David.MC.MM&Bar.	Lt Can 5Bn 9-8-18 CR France 585	
GIBSON,Donald	Lt Can 4Bn 27-9-18CR France 214	
GIBSON,Francis Malloch	Lt Can 15Bn kia 19-8-15 CR France 922	
GIBSON,Gregory James	Capt Aust 47Inf dow 28-3-18 CR France 62	
GIBSON,Harold Alexander Frater	Lt Can 58Bn 8-10-16MR 23	
GIBSON,John Alexander	Lt Can 116Bn dow 3-4-18 CR France 95	
GIBSON,Lawrence Percival Kennedy	Lt Can 19Bn dow 7-3-16 CR France 285	
GIBSON,McKenzie	Lt NZ 6/635 1CIR kia 12-10-17 MR 30	
GIBSON,Peter	Lt Aust 15Inf kia 8-8-15 MR 6	
GIDONY,Francesco	Lt Can 14Bn dow 17-4-17 CR France 12	
GILBERT,Anson Elliott	Lt Can CFA attRAF ded 5-11-18 CR Canada 1667	
GILBERT HAWKEN,Ada	SNurse NZ NZANS ded 28-10-15 CR Egypt 6	
GILCHRIST,Albert George	2Lt Aust 24Inf kia 1-9-18 CR France 1472	
GILCHRIST,Harold	Lt Aust 6Inf 4-10-17MR 29	
GILCHRIST,Horace William	Lt Aust 7ALH dow 29-6-15 MR 6	
GILCHRIST,Walter Richard.MC.	Capt Aust Engrs 6FC 3-5-17 MR 26	
GILCHRIST,William	2Lt Aust42Inf 31-7-17MR 29	
GILES,Arthur McKillar	Lt Aust 4Inf kia 6/8-8-15 MR 6	
GILES,Charles Innis.MM.	Lt Can 20Bn kia 11-10-18 CR France 241	
GILES,George M.	LtCol Can CAMC 1916	
GILKER,John Samuel	Maj Can 31Bn 27-9-16MR 23	
GILL,Lloyd Hassell	2Lt Aust14Inf kia 28-9-17 CR Belgium 88	
GILL,Reginald Henry.MC.	Capt Aust 28Inf kia 28-9-17 CR Belgium 11	
GILL,William James Nelson.MSM.	Lt Can 4BnCMGC kia 2-9-18 CR France 421	
GILLESPIE,Alex C.	Lt CanEngrs 12Bn ded 6-12-20 CR Canada 1380	
GILLESPIE,John Wilfred	Lt Can 16Bn 12-9-17CR France 570	
GILLESPIE,Robert	Lt NZ13/312 AMR ded 29-10-20 CR NZ 194	
GILLESPIE,Roy Carman	Lt Can 72Bn (BCR)31-10-17 MR 29 Cairman	
GILLETT,Lawrence Henry	Capt NZ 12/1416 3AIR kia 3-10-17 MR 30 2-10-17	
GILLIAT,Edward Norman.MC.	Maj Can 16Bn 12-8-18CR France 1170	
GILLIES,David Martin	2Lt Aust 15Inf kia 7-8-15 MR 6	
GILLIES,William Keith	2Lt Aust Engrs 8FC kia 19-10-17 CR Belgium 34	
GILLISON,Andrew.MID	Chpn4Cl Austatt14Inf dow 22-8-15 CR Gallipoli 18	
GILLISSIE,Harold G.	Capt Can CAMC ded 21-2-18 CR Canada 180	
GILLMAN,Thomas	Lt NZ 8/1741 1OIR kia 14-7-16 CR France 922	
GILMOUR,Arthur Clair	Lt Can 11CRT &RFC 82Sqn 6-3-18 MR 20	
GILMOUR,Douglas Bracewell	Lt Can 42Bn 29-9-18CR France 481	
GILMOUR,Robert Noble	Lt Can 125CoyCFC (RCR) 19-2-18CR Surrey 1	
GILROY,Sidney Wellington	Maj Can 13Bn 8-10-16CR France 239	
GILSON,William	Capt Can 1Bn (WOR) kia 6-11-17 MR 29	
GIRLING,Theodore Augustus	Capt Can CAVC att2DivHQ 1-3-19 CR Belgium 265	
GIRLING-BUTCHER,Walter Lancelot	LtNZ 8/4064 2OIR kia 31-3-18 CR France 220	
GIVEEN,Butler M.	Lt Can 13Bn kia 13-6-16 CR Belgium 112	
GLANFIELD,William D.	Lt Aust 8ALH ded 15-10-18 CR Syria 2	
GLANVILLE,Roland Belfield.MC.	Lt Aust 8Inf kia 4-10-17 CR Belgium 128	
GLASFURD,Duncan John	Brig Gen Aust Cmdg 12Bde Aust Inf dow 12-11-16 CR France 833	
GLASGOW,Ernest John	Lt Can 21Bn 9-5-18 CR France 63	
GLASGOW,Ira Hyde	Lt Can 78Bn kia 9-4-17 CR France 548	
GLASSON,Alfred Bertram	Lt Aust 8Inf kia 8-8-15 CR Gallipoli 30	
GLEASON,Ernest Leslie McLeod	Lt Can 102Bn 9-8-17 CR France 81	
GLENDINNING,Alfred John	Capt AustFA 2Bde kia 2-8-17 CR Belgium 15	
GLIDDON,George Clarence	Capt Can CAMC MO 10Bn 11-5-15CR France 284	

GLOSSOP,Walter Herbert Newland	Maj Can 225Bn (BCRD) 1-4-18 CR Surrey 1	
GLOSSOP,William Henry.MM.	2Lt Aust 35Inf kia 6-5-18 CR France 833	
GLOVER,Frank Wesley	Lt Can CE 3TC 29-3-19CR Surrey 1	
GLOVER,John	2Lt Aust 51Bn 3-9-16 MR 26	
GLOVER,John Donald.MID	Capt&Adjt Can 4Bn (1COR) kia 23-4-15 MR 29	
GLOVER,Leonard Charles	2Lt Aust28Bn 29-7-16MR 26	
GLOWREY,Lindsay Gordon	2Lt Aust 16Bn 11-4-17MR 26	
GOBLE,Norman Francis	2Lt Aust 33Inf dow 14-10-17 CR Belgium 3	
GOCHER,William Whitley.MM&Bar	2Lt Aust 45Inf kia 7-6-17 CR Belgium 168	
GODDARD,Archibald Spencer	Capt Can 5Bn 26-9-16MR 23	
GODFREY,Alexander Taylor	Capt Can CAMC ded 21-8-18 CR Canada 835	
GODFREY,Charles Norman	2Lt SA2SAInf kia 22-3-18 MR 27	
GODFREY,Henry Melville	2Lt SA 3SAInf kia 9-4-17 CR France 729	
GODFREY,Thomas Charles Edward,MC.	Capt Aust 24Inf 4-10-17MR 29	
GODLEE,John	2Lt Aust RFC 32Sqn &ALH kia 19-7-16 CR France 80	
GODWIN,Charles Richard Magrath	Lt Can CFA 1Bde kia 4-4-16 CR Belgium 15	
GODWIN,John Lockhart	Lt Can FA 1DAC attZIC TMB 8-7-16 CR Belgium 15	
GODWIN,Thomas Ernest	Lt Can RFC BCRD 21-8-17CR Belgium 140	
GOFFIN,Reginald George	Lt Can 29Bn D'Coy9-8-18 CR France 649	
GOGAY,Archibald Wilfred	Capt Can CASC 2-11-18CR France 40	
GOING,Charles Henry Bernard	Lt SA 2RhodR C'Coy attKAR kia 18-8-17 CR EAfrica 11	
GOLD,William Ernest	Lt SA 10SAInf ded 6-4-17 CR Tanzania 1 &EAfrica 35	
GOLLER,Alfred Ernest	Chpn4Cl Aust ChpnsServs kia 29-9-18 CR France 1495	
GOM,W.	Capt SA 10SAInf ded 29-2-16	
GOMBERT,France	2Lt Aust 17Inf kia 28-8-15 MR 6	
GOMMELL,D. A	Capt SA 4SAInf kia 21-9-17	
GOOCH,Frederick John	Lt CanCFA 2Bde kia 15-8-17 CR France 161	
GOODALE,Walter Henry	Lt Can SRD 46Bn attRAF 104Sqn 1-8-18 CR France 1667	
GOODALL,A.Morton	Lt SA 6SAInf kia 21-3-16 CR EAfrica 13	
GOODALL,Sydney Herbert	Maj Can 16Bn 8-10-16CR France 239	
GOODCHILD,Thomas A.	Capt Can CAMC ded 12-10-20 CR Canada 119	
GOODE,George Noakes Macaulay	Lt Aust 47Inf dow 12.6.17 CR France 134	
GOODE,Herbert James	Lt Can 2PnrBn 16-9-16CR France 1505	
GOODEVE,Arthur Erskine	Lt Can PPCLI 17-9-16MR 23	
GOODEVE,Stewart Marcon	Lt Can 21RFC 13BdeCFA 20-11-17 CR Belgiun 16	
GOODHUGH,P.H.	2Lt Can RAF 46Sqn Ex CMGC dow 29-9-18 CR France 658	
GOODING,Samuel Jewell	2Lt NZ16354 ICC dow 11-12-17 CR Egypt 9	
GOODMAN,Ambrose Harold	Lt Can 116Bn dow 15-8-18 CR France 145	
GOODSON,Arthur Godfrey	2Lt Aust 24Inf kia 3-8-16 CR France 832	
GOODWIN,B.W.MC.	Lt SA 3SAInf kia 30-4-18	
GOODWIN,Erdington	Lt NZ 16/1326 MGBde dow 28-8-18 CR France 798	
GOODWIN,Ernest Leslie	Lt Aust 19Inf ded 10-3-17 CR Wilts 3	
GOODWIN,Francis Willie.MC&Bar	Lt Aust 8Inf kia 4-10-17 CR Belgium 112	
GOODWIN,Leo Francis.MC.MID	Capt Can 38Bn 27-9-18CR France 714	
GOODWIN,Robert	2Lt NZ 12/2610 2AIR kia 1-10-16 MR 11	
GOODYEAR,Hedley John.MC.	Lt Can102Bn kia 22-8-18 CR France 586	
GOODYEAR,Stanley C.MC.	2Lt Can RNewfndlandR kia 10-10-17 MR 10	
GOOSSENS,Frank William	Capt Can 78Bn dow 14-4-17 CR France 102	
GORDON,Aldwyn Remington	2Lt NZ 8/2924 1/3NZRB dow 26-8-18 CR France 84	
GORDON,Charles	Lt Can 31Bn 26-9-16MR 23	
GORDON,Charles George	Maj Aust 2Inf kia 25-4-15 MR 6	
GORDON,Charles Haughton McKay	Maj Can 5Bn ded 5-4-19 CR Canada 487 68Bn	
GORDON,Erskine W.	Lt Can EORD PPCLI &RAF 98Sqn 31-7-18CR France 1429	
GORDON,Henry Russell	Lt Can3Bn (1COR) kia 13-6-16 MR 29	
GORDON,John Aaron	Lt Can BCRD 12-8-18CR France 1472	
GORDON,John Alexander	Lt Can 4Bn kia 4-4-18 CR France 57	
GORDON,Leslie Farries.MC.	Lt Can 50Bn kia 15-8-18 CR Hamps 64	
GORDON,MacLaren	Lt Can 102Bn kia 21-10-16 CR France 239	
GORDON,Robert Hunter	Lt Aust 20Inf kia 12-11-16 CR France 389	
GORDON,Thomas Fowler.MM.	Lt Aust 56Inf dow 30-11-17 CR France 297	
GORDON,Walter Hetherington	Lt Can CFA 2DAC 30-10-16 CR France 133	

GORDON,Walter Leslie Lockhart	Capt Can 2Bn (EOR) kia 23-4-15 MR 29
GORMAN,Elwood Hazen	Lt Can 4CMR kia 20-9-18 CR France 686 25Bn
GORMAN,Mary	S NurseNZ 22/73 ANS drd 23-10-15 MR 35
GORMAN,Thomas Clarence	Lt Can Engrs 2TC18-3-18CR Belgium 15
GORRELL,Charles Willson Farran	Col Can CAMC 24-1-17CR Canada 1337
GOSSIP,James	Lt Aust 1Pnrs dow 25-8-18 CR France 526
GOUGH,Geoffrey Charles	Lt Can 1Bn 17-8-15CR Belgium 138
GOUICK,John Alexander	Lt Can CFA 1Bde dow 15-4-18 CR France 95
GOULD,Elwyn Samuel	Capt Aust 27Inf kia 9-10-17 CR Belgium 123
GOULD,George Darling.VD.	Maj Aust AIF Depot 8-6-15 CR Aust 252
GOULD,Herbert Valentine	Maj Aust Engrs 1Div dow 8-5-18 CR France 180
GOULD,John Barker	Capt Can 44Bn 21-10-18 CR France 1297
GOULD,Leslie Henry	Lt CanBCRD &RFC 20Sqn 15-10-17 MR 20
GOULD-TAYLOR,John.DFC.	Lt AustAFC kia 3-10-18 CR France 234
GOULDEN,Frederick Charles	Capt Nig Cmdg RlyDetachment NigForce drd 28-3-15 CR Eire 58
GOULDING,John Hannington	Capt NZ 6/1542 CIR kia 6-6-15 CR Gallipoli 31
GOULDSMITH,Leonard Frank.MM&Bar.	Lt Can 3Bn 11-8-18CR France 699
GOULLEE,Frederick Charles	Lt Aust 28Inf kia 11-6-18 CR France 209
GOULT,Harry George	Lt Can 7Bn 1916
GOURLIE,James Howard Keith	Lt Can 75Bn kia 3-4-17 CR France 81
GOVAN,Walter Tait	Lt Can 21Bn C'Coydow 28-8-17 CR France 88
GOVE,Hugh Wilfred	2Lt SA3SAInf mbk 21-7-16 MR 21
GOW,John Eckford	2Lt Can FA attRAF 204Sqn dow 10-8-18 CR Belgium 140
GOWDY,Harold	2Lt NZ 6/39622CIR kia 20-9-16 MR 11
GOWENLOCK,Ernest Stanley	2Lt Aust 57Inf dow 10-4-18 CR France 185
GOWING,Archie Lanchester	2Lt Aust 13Bn 11-4-17MR 26
GRACE,Thomas Marshall Percy.MID.	2Lt NZ 10/127 WIR kia 8-8-15 MR 5
GRADY,Ernest Edgar Daniel.MID	Capt SA 4SAInf A'Coy kia 12-4-17 CR France 604
GRAHAM,Dugald Maxwell Lockwood	Maj Aust 2ALH kia 13/14-5-15 CR Gallipoli 8
GRAHAM,Edward William	Lt Can RAF 56Sqn Ex CASC 3-1-19 CR France 658
GRAHAM,James Graham	Maj Can 50Bn ded 30-7-19 CR Canada 562
GRAHAM,John	Capt NZ 39730 CIR dow 4-10-17 CR France 40
GRAHAM,Robert Wishart	Lt Aust 2LtTMB 4-10-17MR 29
GRAHAM,Stuart Millard	Capt AustAAMC 1FA dow 22-8-16 CR France169
GRAHAM,Thomas Donald	Capt Aust 4Pnrs kia 2-10-17 CR Belgium 19
GRAHAM,Thomas Fleck	Capt Can CAMC 3SH Ex 8CMGC dow 20-9-18 CR France 145 3GH
GRAHAM,William Field	Capt Can8RlyTrps ded 28-9-19 CR Canada 1663
GRAHAM,William Nelson.MC.	Capt Can 31Bn dow 22-5-18 CR France 84
GRANDY,Frederick Norman	Lt Can 20Bn 28-8-18CR France 421
GRANGER,Wilfred Bert	Lt Aust8Inf dow 22-8-15 CR Gallipoli 30
GRANT,Alexander Robert.MM.	Lt Can 87Bn kia 18-10-18 CR France 924
GRANT,Alexander.DSO.	Maj Can 78Bn kia 11-8-18 CR France 692
GRANT,Allan Herbert	2Lt Aust40Inf 12-10-17 MR 29
GRANT,Arthur Marden	Lt Aust 29Inf 26-9-17MR 29
GRANT,Charles Arnold	Lt CanPPCLI dow 2-9-18 CR France 14
GRANT,David	Maj NZ 6/409CIR kia 25/29-4-15 CR Gallipoli 11
GRANT,E.D.	Lt Aust AFC 4-4-18 CR London 25
GRANT,George Gordon.MID	Lt Aust AAMC ded 31-8-18 CR Palest 8
GRANT,George Muir	Lt Aust 8ALH kia 7-8-15 MR 6
GRANT,Grace Mabel	Nurse Can CAMC ded 12-9-19 CR Canada 745A
GRANT,HervÇ Murray.MC.	Capt Can 52Bn dow 28-10-17 CR Belgium 11
GRANT,Horace Belford	Lt Can27Bn 21-8-17MR 23
GRANT,James Alfred	Lt Aust AIF 46Inf 21-12-18 CR Aust 376
GRANT,James Henry	Lt Can 102Bn 20-12-16 CR France 40
GRANT,John	Lt Can 75Bn 2-9-18 CR France 426
GRANT,John.MM.	Lt Aust 15Inf dow 23-5-18 CR France 71
GRANT,Lionel Edwin	Lt Aust 39Inf 4-10-17MR 29
GRANT,Oswald Wetherald.MC.	Lt Can 1Bn (WOR) kia 13-6-16 MR 29
GRANT,Russell Walker	Lt Aust 25Bn 15-11-16 MR 26
GRANT,Samuel Alexander	Maj NZ 15/131 AIR dow 11-8-15 MR 6
GRANT,Thomas Roy	Lt Aust 7Inf kia 11-8-18 CR France 526

GRANT,Thomas Smaile	2Lt NZ 11/1877 FA kia 8-11-17 CR Belgium 24
GRANT,W.	2Lt Aust 8Inf 24-5-16CR France 276
GRANT,Walter	Lt Can 5Bn 16-8-17MR 23
GRANT,William.MID.	Chpn NZ 11/86 ChpnsServs attWIR kia 28-8-15 MR 14
GRANT,William Henry	Maj Can 44Bn 25-10-16 CR France 239
GRANT,William Hoyes	2Lt Can 1NewfndlandR kia 16-7-16 CR France 35
GRAPES,John Wellington	2Lt Aust 8Inf dedacc 24-7-17 CR France 251
GRASETT,Hugh Alexander MacKay	Lt Can 3Bn B'Coy (1COR)kia 13-6-16 MR 29
GRATION,Harold Victor Godfrey	2Lt Aust 58Bn 18-9-16MR 26
GRAVE,Howard Burton.MM.	2Lt NZ 2/2951 NZFA ded 19-9-18 CR Sussex 111
GRAVES,Charles Leo	Capt Can 25Bn attRFC kia 24-4-17 CR France 238 Lee
GRAVES,Geoffrey Austin Joseph	Lt Can 1CMR kia 18-3-16 CR Belgium 72
GRAY,Alfred Edgar	2Lt Aust 3AustReinfs ded 28-10-18 CR Wilts 190
GRAY,Allan	Capt Can 72Bn kia 29-9-18 CR France 714
GRAY,Angus Douglas.MC.	Lt Can4MGCoy ded 25-10-18 CR Canada 1597
GRAY,Benjamin Bell	Lt Can 29Bn A'Coy 10-4-17MR 23
GRAY,Clark Maxwell	2Lt Aust 58Inf kia 19-7-16 MR 7
GRAY,F.L.	Lt Aust 8Inf 18-4-18CR France 353
GRAY,Harold	Lt Aust 5Bn 25-7-16MR 26
GRAY,Harold Seward	Capt Can GHQ 58Bn 16-8-18CR France 40
GRAY,James Hawthorne	2Lt NZ 10/357 WIR A'Coydow 9-5-15 MR 6
GRAY,John	Lt Can 13Bn 9-10-16CR France 239
GRAY,Linton Valentine	Lt Can 1CMR &RFC 7Sqn 16-8-17MR 20
GRAY,Robert Murray McCheyne.MC.	Lt Can 46Bn 30-9-18CR France 113
GRAY,W.J.	Capt SA 2SAInf kia 15-7-16
GREATBATCH,Edwin Percy	2Lt NZ 26/787 2\3NZRB dow 20-10-16 CR France 768
GREEN,Carleton Carroll	Capt Can 13Bn 26-9-16CR France 430
GREEN,Caroline Graham	Nurse CanCAMC HS 1922
GREEN,Charles.MC.	Lt Can 20Bn kia 1-10-16 CR France 1505
GREEN,Donald Benjamin T	Capt NZ 3/324 2CIR kia 5-4-18 CR France 742
GREEN,Frank	Mr Aust YMCA Rep att3InfBde ded 27-10-18 CR France 52
GREEN,Frederick Douglas Leach	Lt Can CFA 6Bty 2Bdekia 2-6-15 CR France 260
GREEN,Garnet George.MC&Bar.	Capt SA 2SAInf kia 22-3-18 MR 27
GREEN,Harry Franklyn	Capt Aust AAMC dow 29-11-15 CR Gallipoli 7
GREEN,James Leslie	2Lt NZ6/239 2CIR dow 12-10-17 MR 30
GREEN,John Henry Stanley	2Lt Can RNewfndlandR att RFA 57 Sqn kia 7.7.17 CR France 134
GREEN,Keith Eddowes	Capt Aust 10Inf kia 25-4-15 CR Gallipoli 30
GREEN,Lionel John	2Lt Aust 11Inf kia 21-3-18 CR Belgium 131
GREEN,Matilda Ethel	Nurse Can CANS 7GH ded 9-10-18 CR France 40
GREEN,William Robert	Maj Can 44Bn A'Coykia 3-6-17 CR France 81
GREEN,William Thomas Raymond	Lt Aust 54Inf dow 8-4-18 CR France 1173
GREENE,Robert Eric	Lt Can38Bn A'Coy kia 18-11-16 CR France 314
GREENE,Walter,DCM.	Lt Can 1RNewfndlandR kia 20-11-17 CR France 911
GREENEWALD,Albert.MC.	Capt SA SAMC 11-11-16 CR SAfrica 53
GREENSHIELDS,George Jerrard.MID.	Capt Aust 7FA kia 1-4-18 CR France 833
GREENSHIELDS,Melville	Capt Can 13Bn dow 3-6-16 CR Belgium 11
GREER,George Arque	Lt Can CASC 3DivTr 28-9-16CR France 430
GREER,Thomas Boles	Lt Can 38Bn dow 21-7-17 CR France 40
GREGG,Albert Thomas	Lt Can 47Bn 27-9-18CR France 714
GREGOR,Mark	Lt Aust 44Inf kia 20-6-18 CR France 1170
GREGORY,Ernest Albert Edward	Maj Aust 8ALH kia 27-6-15 CR Gallipoli 29
GREGORY,William Henderson	Lt Can 4Bn 9-4-17 CR France 68
GREIG,G.O.	Lt Aust 8Inf kia 4-10-17 CR Belgium 112
GREIG,Norman James.MID	2Lt Aust 7Inf kia 12-7-15 MR 6
GREIG,William Cuthbertson	Lt Aust 22Inf dow 30-4-17 CR France 512
GRESTOCK,Howard	Lt Can 73Bn 5-2-17 CR France 924
GREWAR,Gertrude Agnes	Sister Aust AIF AANS 24-5-21CR Aust 421
GREWAR,S.G.	Lt SA SthnRif ded 14-5-15 CR SAfrica 17
GRIEVE,David Clark	Lt Can13Bn kia 9-4-17 CR France 68
GRIFFEN,Reginald Theodore	2Lt Aust 32Inf kia 20-7-16 MR 7
GRIFFIN,Arthur Lionel	H Capt Can CAPC 23-3-16CR Hamps 80 CASC 3DivTrn

GRIFFIN,James Richard	2Lt Aust22Bn 3-5-17 MR 26
GRIFFITH,Donald Clive	2Lt NZ 11583 2EntBn kia 23-7-18 CR France 622
GRIFFITH,George Whitehouse	Capt Aust AustRedCross ded 22-3-18 CR Warwick 5
GRIFFITH,Henry Hunter	Maj Aust AAMC 3TransptSect ded 23-3-19 CR Middx 39
GRIFFITHS,C.J.C.	Lt SA 1SAInf dow 10-4-18 MR 29
GRIFFITHS,George Henry	Lt Can 2CMR 8-8-18 CR France 652
GRIFFITHS,Graham	2Lt NZ 6/3229 CIR doi 13-2-16 CR Egypt 8
GRIFFITHS,Harold Maurice.MC.	Capt Aust 5Inf kia 8-5-17 CR France 512
GRIFFITHS,Joseph.MC.	Lt Can 73Bn dow 2-3-17 CR France 12
GRIFFITHS,Percy Ormond	Lt Aust19Inf kia 8-8-18 CR France 1170
GRIGGS,Albert	Lt Aust RFC 23-11-17 MR 26
GRIMSON,George Manthorpe	Lt Aust 36Inf dow 7-6-17 CR France 297
GRIMSTONE,Lionel Edward	Lt NZ 11/473 1/1NZFA kia 8-10-18 CR France 611
GRIMWADE,Edward Norman	2Lt NZ 189052AIR dow 1-8-17 CR France 297
GRINLINGTON,Dudley	Lt Aust 48Inf dow 17-10-17 CR Belgium 3
GRISDALE,Arnold	Capt Can CAMC ded 12-10-18 CR Canada 1650
GRITTEN,Stanley William.MC.	LtAust 5AMGC 10-10-17 MR 29
GROENEWALD,A.	Capt SA SAMC ded 11-11-16
GRONDIN,Maurice Marcel	Lt Can 14Bn 3-6-16 CR Belgium 127
GROOM,William Edward	Capt Aust 14Inf kia 7-8-15 MR 6
GROSVENOR,Burnett Buckingham	Lt Can 3Bn kia 30-8-18 CR France 313
GROUND,Harry Oscar	Capt Aust 60Inf dow 22-7-16 CR France 285
GROVE,Leander de Lorme	Lt Aust 49Inf kia 3-9-16 CR France 280
GROVE,Raymond Hinton	2Lt Aust AFC dedacc 19-8-18 CR Scot 520
GROVES,Harold Morton	Lt Can 58Bn kia 25-10-17 CR Belgium 3
GRUAR,Frederick William	2Lt NZ 18188 WellingtonR ded 14-6-23
GRUBB,William Edward Kemp	Lt Aust 40Inf kia 28-3-18 CR France 833
GRUNSELL,Alexander John.MM.	Lt Aust 34Inf kia 31-8-18 CR France 526
GUAN,Charles Henry	Lt Aust 4Inf kia 23-8-18 CR France 526
GUAY,Pierre EugÇne.MC.	Lt Can 22Bn 1-5-18 CR France 174
GUBBINS,Launcelot Russell	2Lt NZ 2/746 FA kia 23-4-18 CR Belgium 11
GUEST,Ivor Arthur Melville	LtSA 1CapeCps kia 6-11-17 CR Tanzania 1 &EAfrica 11
GUEST,Ralph	Lt Can 46Bn 18-11-16 MR 23
GUILD,William Forbes.MID	Capt Can 52Bn att12BnHQ dow 10-4-17 CR France 12
GUILFOYLE,Thomas Reginald	Capt Can CAMC 1SH 28-10-18 CR Hamps 2
GUINESS,Arthur Grattan	2Lt NZ 5/166 2/3NZRB kia 12-10-17 MR 30
GUINESS,Francis Benjamin Hart	2Lt NZ 7/921 CMR dow 25-8-15 MR 6
GUINESS,William John Pritchard	Capt NZ 24/1267 NZRB dow 12-10-17
GUINEY,Edward Castray	Capt SA 2SARif drd 12-2-16 MR 46 12-2-18
GUNN,Alexander McKay	Lt Can 44Bn 23-8-17MR 23 Andrew
GUNNER,Harold.MM.	2Lt Aust 48Inf kia 30-9-16 CR Belgium 37
GUNNING,Roy Henry	Maj Can 46Bn 21-8-17CR France 81
GURNER,Leonard	Lt Aust 60Inf kia 14-7-18 CR France 247
GURNEY,Albert Newton	Lt Can 4Bn dow 12-9-18 CR France 34
GURR,Albert Jackson	2Lt Aust 19Bn 14-11-16 MR 26
GUTHRIE,Frederick Alexander	Lt Aust 1ALH kia 3-11-17 CR Palest 1
GUTHRIE,Richard Hampden	Lt Aust 27Inf dow 6-11-16 CR France 188
GUTHRIE,Robert Storrie	Lt Aust 48Inf 12-10-17 MR 29
GUTHRIE,Thomas Errol	Capt NZ 3/1735 NZMC kia 3-7-16 CR France 922
GUY,Lionel Claude	2Lt Aust FA 1/1Bde dow 3-11-17 CR Belgium 11
GWILLIM,Frank Llewellyn	Lt Can 29Bn ded 27-11-16 CR Heref&Worc 96
GWYN,Charles Campbell	Capt Can 18Bn kia 9-4-17 CR France 68
GWYN,Donald Stodart.MC.	Lt Can RCD drd 10-10-18 CR Eire 14
GWYNNE,L.H.	Lt EA ULEA 10-3-18CR EAfrica 10
GYSIN,Leonard Samuel	Maj Can 8Bn 26-9-16MR 23

H

HAAHOF,Allan Christie	2Lt SA 1SAInf kia 17-7-16 MR 21
HACKETT,William Thomas	Capt CanCADC 25-2-19CR France 40
HADDOCK,Geoffrey	Lt Can 24Bn D'Coy 17-9-16MR 23
HAFFNER,Henry John A.	Lt Can Engrs 8FC 30-5-16CR Belgium 6
HAGAN,Thomas Percival	Lt Aust 32Inf kia 19-7-16 MR 7
HAGARTY,Daniel Galer	Lt Can PPCLI 2-6-16 CR Belgium 112
HAGGAR,Eric Newman	Lt Aust 21Bn 20-3-17MR 26
HAGGARD,Rider Lancelot	Capt Can PPCLI 3Coy kia 30-10-17 CR Belgium 123
HAGUE,Owen Carsley Frederick	Lt Can CFA 7Bty 2Bde 2-5-15 CR France 200
HAHN,E.A.L.	2Lt SA1SAInf kia 16-7-16
HAIG,George	Lt Aust 30Inf kia 8-8-18 CR France 1173
HAIG,William Richard.MC.	Lt Aust 17Inf dow 26-11-18 CR Surrey 1
HAINS,Clarence Cecil	Capt Aust AAMC dedacc 14-4-19 CR Belgium 336
HAINS,Redvers Seymour	Lt SA 1SAMR kia 5-11-14 CR SAfrica 43
HAIR,Harold Gilbert	Lt NZ 26/1549 1AIR kia 26-3-18 CR France 344
HALBERT,Samuel Frederick Taylor	LtCan CAVC ded 25-2-21 CR Canada 1488
HALDANE,Ewen McGregor	Lt Can 15Bn 18-8-17CR France 223
HALE,Walter Horace Elgar	Lt Aust 12Inf kia 5-10-17 CR Belgium 125
HALE,William Fraser	Capt Can CAMC 1GH 8-6-18 CR France 95
HALES,Albert Charles	2Lt Aust 18Inf 9-10-17MR 29
HALES,Colin	Lt Aust 1ACycCps kia 20-12-16 CR France 188
HALIDAY,Frederick Arthur	2Lt NZ 13/77 AMR ded 4-5-21 CR NZ 184
HALL,Abraham,MC.MID.	Lt NZ 15/47 WMR kia 1-4-18 MR 34
HALL,Alexander MacRae	Lt Can 67PnrBn 4-9-16 CR Belgium 15
HALL,Arthur James.MM.	2Lt Aust 13Bn 4-7-18 MR 26
HALL,Edward Alan	Lt Aust 13Inf dow 21-8-18 CR France 119
HALL,Franklin Edward	Maj Can 87Bn 18-11-16 CR France 150
HALL,Frederick Averill	Lt Can 44Bn 18-10-16 CR France 430
HALL,George Osborne	Capt Can 1Bn 16-6-17CR France 40
HALL,Gerald,Stevenson	2Lt NZ 12/3342 2AIR kia 30-8-18 CR France 307
HALL,Harry Frederick	2Lt NZ 12/3343 2AIR kia 9-6-17 MR 9
HALL,Harry John.MC.	Maj Can 43Bn dow 8-10-16 CR France 59 16Bn
HALL,Henry John	2Lt Aust 54Inf kia 19/20-7-16 CR France 82
HALL,Henry Johnson	2Lt NZ 30111 3AIR A'Coy kia 4-10-17
HALL,John Kenworthy	Lt Aust 46Inf kia 8-8-18 CR France 526
HALL,Norman	2Lt NZ 8/2501 1OIR dow 13-6-16 CR France 285
HALL,Russell McKay	Lt Can 5CMR &RAF 98Sqn 28-5-18CR Belgium 385
HALL,Sydney Gordon Leslie	2Lt Aust 11Inf kia 8-8-15 MR 6
HALL,Sydney Raymond	Capt Aust 10Inf kia 25-4-15 CR Gallipoli 30
HALL,Terence Smythe	Lt Can 5CMR (QR) 30-10-17 MR 29
HALL,Victor Ernest	2Lt Aust 14Inf kia 29-3-18 CR France 798
HALL,William Henry	Lt SA SASpServ ded 31-12-18 CR Tanzania 1 &EAfrica 15
HALL,William Titus	Lt Can 75Bn 27-9-18CR France 715
HALLAHAN,Walter Rewi.MC.MM.	Capt Aust 11Inf kia 18-9-18 CR France 446
HALLAM,Ernest Walter	Capt Can 18Bn 29-9-15CR France 285
HALLAM,Frank Harold	Lt Can 24Bn 12-10-17 CR France 68
HALLENSTEIN,Dalbert Isaac	Lt Aust 5AMGC kia 2-9-18 CR France 511
HALLIDAY,Francis	Lt Aust AFA 4Bde dedacc 28-11-18 CR France 446
HALLIFAX,Leslie John	2Lt Aust 16Inf 12-8-16CR France 1890
HALLIGAN,John	Lt Aust 59Inf dedacc 31-5-17 CR France 177
HALLISEY,John Francis	Lt Can 25Bn 8-4-17 CR France 68
HALLSMITH,Ewart Martin	Lt Can 1CMR 4-11-18CR France 1142
HALLY,Colin.MC.	Lt NZ23935 MGC kia 6-4-18 CR France 156
HALSEY,James Charles	Maj Can 102Bn ded 22-8-18 CR Canada 146
HALSTEAD,Albert Edward.MC.	Capt Aust 42Inf kia 16-4-18 CR France 210
HALSTEAD,Chester William.MC.	Lt Can 1Bn1-10-18CR France 597

HAM,Alfred Edward	Lt SA 2SARifs attSASpServ dow 6-5-18 MR 52
HAMBER,Harold Balleny	HCapt CanCAPC &RFC kld 22-6-17 CR Surrey 1 &London8
HAMBLETT,John Hamilton	Lt Aust 7Bn 9-8-18 MR 26
HAMILTON,Charles B.	2Lt Aust 5Inf 18-5-15CR Egypt 3
HAMILTON,Clarence Dickenson	Capt Can CAMC 2CCS 141FA ded 9-10-18 MR 24
HAMILTON,David James	2Lt Aust 12MGC kia 7-6-17 CR Belgium 451
HAMILTON,Donald	Lt Can 4BnCMGC 8-8-18 CR France 652
HAMILTON,Douglas Kipp	Lt Can 54Bn kia 8-8-18 CR France 589
HAMILTON,Frank Gordon.MM&Bar.	2Lt AustMGC 2Bn 5-10-18MR 26
HAMILTON,Frederick Samuel	Lt Can CASC 1ResPkded 12-11-17 CR Canada 256
HAMILTON,George Henry	Lt Can 13Bn dow 29-9-17 CR France 113
HAMILTON,Henry Edward Redmond	Capt Can 3CRT 19-5-17CR France 81
HAMILTON,Herbert Henry Parke	Lt Aust 26Inf dow 14-8-18 CR France 71
HAMILTON,Hubert Arthur	2Lt NZ 7/592 CMR kia 22-8-15 MR 14
HAMILTON,James Arlow C.	Lt Can 27Bn dow 18-9-16 CR France 74 Arlon
HAMILTON,John William	Maj Aust 6Inf kia 25-4-15 MR 6
HAMILTON,William Hugh	Lt Aust 14Inf kia 18-5-15 CR Gallipoli 31
HAMLIN,Herbert Bowen.DSO.	Maj Aust 10ALH ded 30-5-19 CR Egypt 8
HAMLIN,William Latham Blacker	Lt Can 87Bn dow 25-9-17 CR France 12
HAMMAND,Kendall	Capt Aust 25Inf dedacc 30-1-16 CR Egypt 16
HAMMELL,Henry Eric	Lt Aust Engrs 2FC dow 22-5-18 CR France 102
HAMMOND,Ernest Leonard	Capt NZ 25/8 4/3NZRB kia 31-7-16 CR France 82
HAMMOND,G.Meysey.MC.MM.	Capt Aust 28Inf 14-6-18CR France 71
HAMMOND,Herbert Harold	Maj NZ 7/590 CMR kia 9-8-16 CR Egypt 2
HAMMOND,Herbert James	2Lt Aust 48Inf kia 11-4-17 CR France 646
HAMMOND,Themetre James	Lt Aust RFC 2Sqn12-6-18MR 26
HAMPSHIRE,J. served as HAMSHERE,J.	
HAMPSON,James Thomas.MC.	2Lt Aust 19Inf dow 6-10-18 CR France 446
HAMSHERE,John.DCM.	Lt Can CFA 3Bde dow 12-7-17 CR France 68 real name HAMPSHIRE
HANCOCK,Frank Herbert.MID	Capt Aust50Inf kia 24-4-18 CR France 144
HANDLEY,WilliamJohn	Capt Aust 2ALH kia 16-7-18 CR Palest 3
HANDS,Reginald Harry Myburgh	Capt SA HArty attRGA dow 20-4-18 CR France 102
HANKINSON,Elmore Leslie	Lt Can 18Bn 6-10-18CR France 147
HANKS,Alfred Charles	2Lt SA 3SAInf kia 15-7- 16 MR 21 16-7-16
HANLAN,Edward Gordon	Lt Can RFC 12ResBndedacc 9-8-17 CR Canada 1689
HANLEY,George Tyndall	Lt Can27Bn 8-1-17 CR France 224
HAMLEY,John Matthew	Lt Aust 5ALH kia 6-6-15 MR 6
HANNA,Bessie Maud	Nurse Can 3StatHosp 1921
HANNA,Donald Bertram	Lt Can 2CMR C'Coy 10-8-18CR France 360 Bertrand
HANNA,Harold Leander	Lt Can 3Trng Depot RAF CFA 23-4-18CR Wilts 115
HANNAFORD,Alfred Crawford.MC&Bar.Capt Can 87Bn dow 3-10-18 CR France 214	
HANNAFORD,Charles Richard	Lt Aust17Inf 20-9-17CR Belgium 310
HANNAFORD,John Haines	Lt Can 20Bn 10-5-17CR France 557
HANNAH,Robert.DCM.	Lt Aust 13 LtTMB Ex 49Inf 12-10-17 MR 29
HANNAN,Sylvester Francis.MC.	Lt Can 3Bn dow 7-2-17 CR Warwick 7
HANSEN,Stewart Murray.MC.	Capt Aust 14Inf dow 7-2-17 CR France 44
HANSON,John Clarence	Lt Can 104CanInf att RFC 55Sqn14.7.17 CR France 134
HARCUS,James Logie	Maj Aust 20Inf kia 11-12-15 MR 6
HARDIMAN,William Leech	Lt Can 31Bn 6MGCoyded 16-1-20 CR Canada 576
HARDING,Francis	Lt Can 78Bn 28-9-18CR France 214
HARDING,Herbert George	Lt Aust AFA 4Bde kia 10-4-17 MR 26 &CR France 1484
HARDING,Maurice Alfred	Lt NZ 11/1875 WMR kia 23-12-16 CR Egypt 2
HARDWICH,R.E.S.MM.	2Lt SA 2SAInf dow 9-4-17 CR France 96
HARDWICK,William Emlyn.MC&Bar.	Lt Aust 21Inf kia 5-10-18 CR France 446
HARDY,David.MM.	Lt Aust 11Inf dedacc 31-10-17 CR Belgium 11
HARDY,Dudley Freeman	Capt Aust 8Inf kia 18-8-16 CR France 832
HARE,Frank	2Lt NZ 8/14953AIR dow 2-8-17 CR Belgium 136
HARE,Herbert Patrick	Lt Aust AFA 3Bde dow 8-8-16 CR France 74
HARKER-THOMAS,Francis Rowlands	Lt Can 102Bn 27-9-18CR France 714
HARKNESS,Edward	Capt Aust AIF AAMC 2-8-17 CR Aust 307
HARKNESS,Edward John George	Lt Aust 2Inf kia 6/8-8-15 CR Gallipoli 7

HARKNESS,Norman John	Lt Can 1Bn (WOR) 6-11-17MR 29
HARLE,Douglas Allan	2Lt NZ 24365 WIR kia 4-10-17 CR Belgium 128
HARLEY,Hubert Satchell.MC.	Capt NZ 7/2019 2CIR `Nelson'Coy kia 2-10-16 MR 11
HARLING,Thomas Leslie	Lt Can5CMR 3-6-16 CR Belgium 127
HARMON,Burdette William.MC.DCM.	Lt Can 52Bn &RAF 56Sqn 10-5-18CR France 1170
HARPER,Albert Edward	2Lt Aust 4Pnrs kia 31-12-16 CR France 400
HARPER,Arthur Henry Sedgwick	2Lt NZ 14545 1WIR ded 9-12-16 CR France 64
HARPER,Bertram	2Lt SA Rho dNatR 26-10-18 CR EAfrica 101 NRhodPol
HARPER,Gordon Gerald.DCM MID.	2Lt NZ 7/516 CMR dow 12-8-16 CR Egypt 9
HARPER,Harold William	2Lt Aust 21Inf kia 4-10-17 CR Belgium 128
HARPER,John Arthur	Lt Can 29Bn 27-9-16MR 23
HARPER,Norman Robert.MC.	2Lt NZ6/645 EntBn 3CanterburyR dow 15-4-18 CR Belgium 38
HARPER,Norman Stuart	Lt Can 99Sqdn RAF 1RBn 25-6-18CR Germany 3
HARRINGTON,Reginald.DCM.	Lt Aust 59Inf Ex 4ALHdow 10-6-18 CR Hamps 64
HARRIOTT,George	Capt Aust 24Inf 4-10-17MR 29
HARRIS,Augustine John	2Lt Aust 14Inf dow 12-4-17 CR France 564
HARRIS,Claude Llewellyn	Capt Can 7Bn kia 9-4-17 CR France 1059
HARRIS,Dermot Alan	Lt Can 4Bn D'Coy 9-8-18 CR France 360
HARRIS,Edward.MID.	Capt NZ7/2018 AMR 2MaoriPnrBnkia 14-11-17 CR France 177 18-9-16
HARRIS,Ernest William	2Lt Aust MGC 3Coy 5-5-17 MR 26
HARRIS,Francis William	Lt Can 2CMR kia 29-9-18 CR France 715
HARRIS,Frank Walter	Capt Aust 57Inf kia 19-8-16 CR France 348
HARRIS,Harold Robert	Lt Aust 14Inf kia 8-8-15 MR 6
HARRIS,Hubert Jennings Imrie	LtCol Aust 5ALH kia 31-7-15 CR Gallipoli 22
HARRIS,J.J.F.OBE.	Maj SA 1SAInf ded 21-1-20
HARRIS,J.V.MC.	Capt SA CapeCps 1SAInf kia 20-9-18 CR Palest 3
HARRIS,John	Lt Aust 24Bn 3-5-17 MR 26
HARRIS,John James Fitzgerald.OBE.	Maj SA 1SAInf20-1-20CR Eire 144
HARRIS,Norman Chambers	Lt NZ 11/602 WMR dow 9-8-15 MR 5
HARRIS,Philip Vernon	2Lt Aust42Inf dow 11-6-17 CR France 297
HARRIS,Roy	Capt NZ 3/3071NZMC kia 5-4-18 CR France 220
HARRIS,Thomas Victor	Lt Aust 7Inf dow 9-8-18 CR France 526
HARRIS,Wallace Cranmer	Lt SA SASC AnimalTrnspt ded 27-9-17 CR Tanzania 1 &EAfrica 38
HARRIS,Webster Henry Fanning	H CaptChpn4Cl Can ChpnsServs att6BdeHQdow 4-5-17 CR Surrey 1
HARRIS,William.MM	Lt Aust 18Bn 7-3-17 MR 26
HARRISON,Fred	Capt SA 7Inf (2KimberleyR) C'Coy dow 26-4-15 CR SAfrica 18
HARRISON,Harvey Edward.MC&Bar.	Lt Can 78Bn dow 15-9-18 CR France 52
HARRISON,J.H.H. Surg	Capt Honduras BrHondTerForce 26-4-16CR CentAmerica 1
HARRISON,James Vincent	Lt Can 50Bn kia 16-4-18 CR France 184
HARRISON,John Henry	2Lt Aust 3Inf dow 21-9-15 CR Greece 11
HARRISON,John Louis.MID	Lt Aust Engrs 4DivSigCoy kia 5-4-18 CR France 885
HARRISON,Raymond Hill	Lt Aust 12Inf dow 16-5-17 CR Lancs 155
HARRISON,Roy	Maj Aust 54Inf kia 20-7-16 CR France 525
HARRISON,Samuel Leonard Tilley	Lt Can 38Bn 29-9-18CR France 715
HARRISON,William	Lt Can 54Bn 11-4-17CR France 81
HARRISS,Hutton Allen	Capt Can 82Bn 1922
HARRY,Samuel William	Capt Aust 15Inf kia 10-5-15 MR 6
HART,Albert Leonard Donald	Lt Aust 4Inf dow 21-9-17 CR Belgium 11
HART,Alfred Joseph	2Lt Aust 22Bn 27-7-16MR 26
HART,Athol	2Lt NZ 41976 3/3NZRB A'Coy kia 21-8-18 CR France 1327
HART,Francis.DCM.	Lt Can CavBdeMGSqdn 1-4-18 MR 23
HART,George Hope Campbell	Lt Aust12Inf dow 25-4-18 CR France 180
HART,Morris	2Lt Aust 42Inf 4-10-17MR 29
HART-McHARG,William Fredk Richard	LtCol Can 7Bn 24-4-15CR Belgium 151
HARTLAND,Leslie Richard	Lt Aust 8Inf kia 26-7-15 CR Gallipoli 31
HARTLEY,John William Murray	2Lt Aust 12MGC dow 9-1-17 CR France 833
HARTLEY,Thomas Dallwood	Lt NZ2/1258A FA kia 28-1-18 CR Belgium 35
HARTLEY,William Garfield	Capt Aust 48Inf dow 9-8-16 CR France 74
HARTMAN,Robert Ross	Lt Can 11LTMB 2-9-18 CR France 426
HARTNELL-SINCLAIR,Hubert	Lt Aust 13Inf dow 9-8-15 CR Gallipoli 18
HARTNEY,James Cuthbert	Lt Can 11RBn attRFC 1917 CR France 98

HARVEY,Archibald John.MM.	Lt Can 29Bn dow 12-11-17 CR Belgium 11
HARVEY,Arthur Allan	Lt Can3Bn 13-5-17CR Glouc 9
HARVEY,Edward Charles.DCM.MM.	Lt Can 3Bn 8-9-16 CR France 430
HARVEY,Frederick	Lt Aust AFC 67Sqn kia 12-11-17 CR Palest 2
HARVEY,Gerald Wallace	2Lt Aust 41Inf kia 14-4-17 CR Belgium 54
HARVEY,John Irvine	Lt Can 52Bn 16-9-16CR France 280
HARVEY,Robert Valentine	Capt Can 7Bn dow 8-5-15 CR Germany 3
HARVEY,William George.MC.	Capt Aust 1Pnrs kia 14-9-17 CR Belgium 34
HARVIE,Robert.MID	Lt Can 72Bn 31-8-18CR France 419
HARWOOD,Victor Albert	Lt Aust 51Inf kia 12-10-17 CR Belgium 123
HASELDEN,Cyril Gerrard	Capt Aust RE attAustCpsHQ 27-11-18 CR France 931
HASSAM,Oscar Donald.MID	Lt Aust AustProvostCps dow 20-5-18 CR France 895
HASSALL,Raymond Langley	Lt Aust 5Pnrs dow 30-9-18 CR France 446
HASTINGS,Melville Alfred	Lt Can 52Bn dow 3-10-18 CR France 40
HASTINGS,Norman Frederick.DSO.MID.	Maj NZ 11/61 WMR dow 9-8-15 CR Gallipoli 18
HASTINGS,Warren Oswald	Lt NZ45314 1CIR kia 5-4-18 CR France 220
HASTINGS,William George	2Lt Aust 11Bn22/25-7-16 MR 26
HASTINGS,William Roy	Lt Can 16Bn 8-10-16 MR 23 Roy
HASTWELL,Hugh Norman	2Lt Aust 10Inf kia 30-6-18 CR France 193
HATRICK,James Grierson	Capt NZ 12/3672 2AIR kia 2-10-16 MR 11
HATTON,Angelo Talbot.MID	Maj Aust FA 5Bde kia 9-11-17 CR Belgium 34
HATTON,Thomas	Lt Can 52Bn 4-4-16 CR Belgium 309
HAUGHTON,Thomas Henry Eric	2Lt Aust 23Bn 4-8-16 MR 26
HAUSER,Edwin Wesley	2Lt Aust 21Bn 7-5-17 MR 26
HAWKE,Samuel Stephen	2Lt Aust 48Bn 5-8-1 MR 26
HAWKE,Stanley	2Lt Aust AFC ded 13-7-18 CR Cornwall 122
HAWKE,Watkin Williams.MM.	2Lt Aust 4Inf dow 6-11-17 CR Belgium 125
HAWKEN,Ada Gibert	SNurse NZ 22/123 ANS ded 28-10-15
HAWKES,Francis Danby Tolmby	Lt Can42Bn 29-9-18CR France 481
HAWKES,Waldemar Robert	Lt Aust 21AMGC 29-10-17 MR 29
HAWKES,Walter James.MC.MM.	Lt Can 43Bn dow 5-9-18 CR France 34
HAWKINS,F.C.	Lt SA 1SAH att1/2KAR 15-11-17 CR Tanzania 1 &EAfrica 11
HAWKINS,Kenneth Belmont	Lt Can 24Bn kia 9-3-17 CR France 68
HAWKINS,Percival George	Lt Can 73Bn 1-3-17 MR 23
HAWORTH,Ashley Aston	Lt NZ 3/3102 MC att1AuklandR kia 1-2-18 CR Belgium 72
HAY,Archibald Walter	LtCol Can 52Bn (MR) 3-6-16 MR 29
HAY,Bruce Somerville.MID.	Capt NZ 9/530 OMR kia 7-8-15 MR 5
HAY,Charles William	Lt Aust RFC drd 8-4-18 MR 26
HAY,John Gilmour	Lt Can 47Bn dow 12-11-16 CR France 44
HAY,John Reginald Begg	Lt NZ18436 2OIR dow 29-9-18 CR France 379
HAYLEN,Francis Henry	Lt Aust2Inf 21-9-17MR 29
HAYMEN,Frank Granville	Lt Aust9Inf kia 25/28-4-15 MR 6
HAYNE,Arthur Adrian Nevill	Capt Can 9Bn 24-4-20CR Hamps 64
HAYS,Francis Reginald	2Lt Aust 24Bn 5-8-16 MR 26
HAYTER,Cyril.MID.	Lt NZ 7/63 CMR kia 28-8-15 MR 14
HAYWARD,John J.W.	Lt Can CFA 3Bde 19-10-17 CR Belgium 35
HAZEN,James Murray	Lt Can CFA 7Bde19-4-16CR Belgium 11
HAZLETT,William George.MC.	Lt Can 21Bn ded 24-10-18 CR Canada 1270
HEAL,Frank Henry	LtCol SA 1SAInf kia 24-3-18 MR 27
HEAL,John Thomas	Lt Aust 43Inf 31-7-17MR 29
HEALY,Cecil	2Lt Aust 19Inf kia 29-8-18 CR France 1472
HEALY,Michael Damien	Lt Aust 25Inf 20-9-17MR 29
HEALY,William Patrick.MC.	2Lt Aust 25Inf kia 14-11-16 CR France 385
HEARN,R.J.R.	Capt&Adjt SA 2SA Inf kia 24-7-16 CR EAfrica 40 Rifs
HEARNE,William Weston.DSO.MID	Col Aust AMC 5DivHQ kia 17-10-17 CR Belgium 19
HEARNS,BeatriceS	Nurse SA SAMNS 20-10-18 CR SAfrica 144
HEARPS,Alfred John	2Lt Aust 12Bn 19/22-8-16 MR 26
HEATH,Bernard Stanley.MC.	Lt Can 1MGCoy 11-11-17 CR Belgium 101
HEATH,Charles Thomas McIntosh	Lt Aust AFA 5Bde 26-9-17MR 29
HEATH,Clendon Charles	Lt Can 28Bn 15-9-16MR 23
HEATH,F.T.	Lt SA MtdCmmdo 23-1-15CR SAfrica 171

HEATHER,Frederick Amblec.MC.MM.   Lt Can 2CMR   9-4-17 CR France 68
HEATON,George   Lt Aust 7Inf   4-10-17MR 29
HEAVINGHAM,E.MID   Capt SA 2Horse dow 11-9-16 CR EAfrica 39
HEBB,Gordon Maurice   Lt Can 78Bn   14-10-16 CR France 280
HEDGECOCK,Alfred Homewood   Lt Aust 57Inf 31-8-18CR France 627
äHEDGES,William.MC.   Lt Can 10Bn   27-9-18CR France 147
HEIGHINGTON,Geoffrey.MC.   Lt Can 4CMR 2-11-18CR Devon 258
HEITHERSAY,Austin James   Lt AustEngrs 1FldSqndow 12-1-17 CR Egypt 2
HELLER,Thomas James   Lt Aust 10ALH   kia 7-8-15   MR 6
HELLIWELL,Henry John   Lt Can CASC   ded   5-11-18 CR Canada 547
HELLIWELL,Joseph Grant   Capt   Can 1Bn C'Coy   kia 15-6-15 MR 23
HELMER,Alexis Hannum   Lt Can CFA 1Bde kia 2-5-15   MR 29
HELMER,Richard Alexis.CMG.   BrigGen   Can   MHQ GS   ded   1-2-20   CR Canada 1245
HELMS,Jacob.DCM.   2Lt Aust 19Bn   14-11-16 MR 26
HEMING,Leslie Duncan   Capt   Aust 16Inf kia 8-8-15 MR 6
HEMMING,Thos Davies Robertson.CMG. MajGen   Can   HQ MD3   1919
HEMSLEY,Francis Henry   Lt Can16Bn   16-8-17MR 23
HENDERSON,Alan Dudley   Lt Aust 7Inf   dow 27/30-4-15 MR 6
HENDERSON,Archibald Gordon.DCM.MID. Capt NZ   8/872   2EntBn acckld 8-9-18   CR France 512
HENDERSON,C.W.   Capt   SA SALabCps 14-12-18 CR EAfrica 36
HENDERSON,Clifford Crozier   Lt Can   75Bn   kia 2-9-18   CR France 426
HENDERSON,Ernest Brian   Lt Can 3Bn attRAF3-11-18CR Canada 1121
HENDERSON,George Wyndham   Lt NZ 10/23691WIR dow 24-6-16 CR France 285
HENDERSON,James   Lt NZ   13/277AMR   kia 8-8-15   MR 5
HENDERSON,John Keith   Capt   Aust   13Bn   14-8-16MR 26
HENDERSON,Lachlan MacAlister   Lt Aust   AIF 12ALH9-4-15 CR Aust 47
HENDERSON,Maurice Russell   Lt Can 58Bn 13-6-16CR Belgium 5
HENDERSON,Norman   Lt Can 10Bn   kia 14-4-18 CR France 184
HENDERSON,P.D.   LtCmdr   Nig NigeriaMarine &RNR28-3-15CR Cornwall 23
HENDERSON,Richard Arthur   Lt   Can 54Bn attCE 11FCkia   11-4-17   CR France 81
HENDERSON,Robert   Lt Can   21Bn   9-4-17 CR France 522
HENDERSON,Robert James.MC&Bar   Capt   Aust 13Inf   dow 13-5-18   CR France 40
HENDERSON,Robert Oswald.DSO.   LtCol   Aust   39Inf   kia 29-9-18 CR France 1495
HENDERSON,Ronald Grahame.MC.   Lt Aust18Inf kia 9-4-18   CR France 144
HENDERSON,Ronald Lennox.MC.   Capt   AustAAMC   31-7-17CR Surrey 1
HENDERSON,Rupert Howard   Capt   Aust 7Inf   kia 8/12-5-15 CR Gallipoli 2
HENDERSON,William   2Lt Aust   49Bn   5-4-18 MR 26
HENDERSON SMITH,George Holt   2Lt   Aust 11Inf   kia 25-5-15 CR Gallipoli 7
HENDRY,Norman Thomas   2Lt   SA 3SAInf kia 20-9-17   MR 29
HENEY,John Bower Lewis.MC.   Lt CanCFA 9Bde &RFC 9-3-18 CR France 98
HENLEY,Alfred William   Lt Aust 51Inf   dow 4-4-17   CR France 832
HENLEY,Harold Leslie   Capt   Aust 13Bn 15-8-16MR 26
HENNAN,Victoria Belle   NSister   Can   CAMC 9GH 23-10-18 CR Kent 180
HENNESSEY,Wynnum Groom McDonald   2Lt Aust   6Inf   kia 10-2-17 CR France 385
HENNESSY,May   SNurse Aust   AIF AANS9-4-19 CR Aust 296
HENNING,William.MC   2Lt NZ11376 1/3NZRB   dow 13-9-18   CR France 512
HENRY,Clarence   2Lt   Aust   AIF 2ALH 7-7-16 CR Aust 146
HENRY,Hugh Donald   Lt   Can   7Bn   15-8-17MR 23
HENRY,Lewis Brock   Capt   Can   58Bn   kia 30-8-17   CR France 480
HENRY,William   Lt Can   102Bn   27-9-18CR France 715
HENSLEY,John Manuel   Capt   Can 85Bn A'Coy kia   30-10-17 CR Belgium 125
HENTY,Edward Ellis   Lt Aust 8ALH   kia 7-8-15   CR Gallipoli 29
HENWOOD,Horace Norman.MID   Maj   Aust 10Inf kia 1-3-18   CR Belgium 131
HEPBURN,Dennis Peter   Lt Can 47Bn dow 3-11-18 CR France 40
HEPWORTH,Oswald Horatio.MC&Bar.   Capt   Can 29Bn   dow 11-8-18 CR France 1170
HERAUD,Thomas Frank.DCM.   2Lt Aust21Inf   4-10-17MR 29
HERBERT,Charles Lloyd   Lt Aust 43Inf   4-10-17MR 29
HERBERT,Claude H.   Lt Aust RAN HMAS`Huon' 6-11-18CR Italy 12
HERBERT,James Edward.MC.   Capt   Aust 26Inf   dow 17-4-18 CR France 44
HERBERT,James Laidlaw.MID.   Lt   Capt NZ 9/2350 1OIR kia 30-9-16 MR 11
HERBERTSON,Robert Charles   Capt   Aust Engrs 1FC 23-7-16MR 26

52

HERD,Rupert Holton	Lt Aust AFC dedacc 16-6-17 CR Sussex 144
HERDER,Arthur J.	2Lt Can RNewfndlandR dow 1-12-17 CR France 446
HERDER,Hubert Clinton	Lt Can 1RNewfndlandR kia 1-7-16 CR France 1490
HERERON,Charles.MM.	Lt Can 2CMR 16-11-18 CR Belgium 203
HERITAGE,Felix Hereward Gordon Norfolk.MID	Lt Aust 10Inf 20-9-17MR 29
HERITAGE,Keith.MC.	Capt Aust 19Inf kia 26-7-16 CR France 832
HERMAN,Roy Percival	2Lt NZ 6/65 1CIR kia 8-7-16 CR France 922
HERON,Cuthbert Victor	Lt Aust 60Inf dow 27-6-18 CR Kent 137
HERON,Gordon Ruthven	Maj Can 78Bn kia 9-4-17 CR France 548
HERPS,Claude Herbert S.	Lt Aust 36Inf D'Coy dow 17-9-17 CR France 145
HERRICK,Arthur Desmond.MC.MIDx2	Capt NZ 11/271 WMR kia 14-11-17 CR Palest 9
HERRON,Arthur Stuart	Lt Can 2Bn kia 30-8-18 CR France 688
HERRON,William Arthur	Lt Can RCR dow 21-3-19 CR NIreland 106
HERZOG,Joseph James Charlton	2Lt NZ 23/345 3AIR dow 17-12-18 CR France 40
HESSON,Frederick Leopold	Capt Can 78Bn 24-8-18CR France 586
HETHERINGTON,Francis Martin	Lt Can 52Bn 18-8-16CR Belgium 127
HETHERINGTON,Hugh	Lt Can 8Bn 15-4-17CR France 68
HETHERINGTON,John Edgar	Lt Can 2MGCoy 22-7-16CR Belgium 127
HEUGH,David McNeil	Lt Aust 2Inf dow 29-4-15 MR 6
HEUSTON,Francis Robert	Lt Can 14Bn 7-4-16 CR Belgium 11
HEWAT,John Paterson	Capt NZ 6/2485 1OIR kia 8-10-18 CR France 911
HEWETSON,Samuel Wilkinson	LtCol Can CAMC 8FA 6-3-17 CR Scot 741
HEWISH,Arthur Leslie	Capt Aust 3Inf kia 5-10-17 CR Belgium 88
HEWITT,Arthur Lifford Oliver	2LtNZ 11/1395 WMR dow 9-2-16 CR Egypt 9
HEWITT,Clarence Frederick	Lt Can CADC ded 16-3-17 CR Canada 254
HEWITT,James Thomas	Lt Can 7Bn (BCR) 11-11-17 MR 29
HEWITT,Thomas Cotgrave	Capt Aust 26Bn 29-7-16MR 26
HEWSON,Charles Douglas	Lt Can75Bn 9-4-17 CR France 1896
HEWSON,Thomas	2Lt Aust RFC 7-7-17 MR 26
HEXT,Avenal Pickering	Capt Aust 30Inf dow 20-6-18 CR France 71
HEXTALL,Leonard John	Lt Can 50Bn 21-11-16 CR France 59
HIBBERD,John Swallow	Lt Can 47Bn 1918
HIBBS,Reginald Kenneth	Capt Aust31Inf 26-9-17MR 29
HICKINBOTHAM,Claude Walker	2Lt Aust 46Inf dow 15-6-17 CR France 285
HICKLING,Reginald	2Lt Aust 51Inf 12-10-17 MR 29
HICKMAN,Cuthbert	2Lt NZ 12/19842AIR ded 12-11-18 CR France 40
HICKMOTT,Rupert George	2Lt NZ6/3961 2CIR kia 16-9-16 MR 11
HICKS,Oswald Austin	Lt Can CMGC 17-12-18 CR Canada 1178
HIGGINBOTHAM,George M.MVO	Maj Can 3Bn 11-3-15CR Kent 202
HIGGINBOTHAM,Lindon Howard Russell	Capt Aust 3Inf dow 21-6-18 CR France 28
HIGGINS,Mervyn Bournes.MID	Capt&Adjt Aust 8ALH HQ kia 23-12-16 CR Egypt 2
HIGGINS,Omar Leonard	Lt Can 1CMR 12ResBn ded 23-1-19 CR Canada 183
HIGGINSON,John Lucas	Capt Can 4Bn kia 15-11-15 CR Belgium 43
HIGHAM,Ernest Augustus	Lt Aust 51Inf dow 27-4-18 CR France 29
HILDYARD,Nora MildredS	Nurse NZ 22/125 ANS drd 23-10-15 MR 35
HILL,A.MC.	Lt Aust 10Inf 30-5-18CR France 25
HILL,Harold Frederick	Capt Can 38Bn kia 9-4-17 CR France 81
HILL,Harold Rowland	Lt Aust 25Inf kia 4-10-17 CR Belgium 308
HILL,Phillip Geoffrey Porvys	Maj Aust 1Inf dow 9-6-15 CR Europe 5
HILL,R.	Lt SA 4SAInf kia 9-10-15
HILL,Roland Justice.MC.MID.	Capt NZ 8/1506 OIR kldacc 3-3-18 CR France 860
HILL,Roy Mortimer	Lt SA 4SAInf 9-10-18CR France 1391
HILL,Samuel John.MM.	Lt Aust 45Inf kia 18-9-18 CR France 366
HILL,Thomas Ninian Wardrop	Lt Aust14Inf kia 8-8-15 MR 6
HILL,Walter James.MID	Lt SA2SAInf kia 20-7 -16 MR 21 17-7-16
HILL,William John Rusden.MC.	2Lt NZ 12/2567 2AIR dow 5-9-18 CR France 52
HILLIARD,Geoffrey Crosier	Lt Can RCD dow 11-12-17 CR France 40
HILLIER,Robert James Bradley	Lt Aust 10Bn 25-7-16MR 26
HILLIS,Charles Russell	Lt Can 116Bn dow 25.2.18 CR France 134
HILLMAN,Eric Montague	Lt Aust 2Inf kia 18-9-18 CR France 528
HILTON,Harry Eltham	Lt Can 42Bn kia 9-4-17 CR France 81

HILTON,Joseph Finian	Lt Aust9Bn 25-2-17MR 26
HINCKESMAN,John William	Lt Can 47Bn (WOR)kia 27-10-17 MR 29
HINDE,Kenneth John	2Lt Aust 3Inf kia 5-5-15 MR 6
HINDLESMITH,Arthur	2Lt NZ28046 2WIR dow 1-10-18 CR France 512
HINDS,Frank Eugene	Lt Can 38Bn 12-4-171 CR France 64
HINDSON,William Ernest.Rev	H Capt Can ChpnServs 153Bn 18-9-18CR Canada 1175
HINES,Hubert Thomas	Lt Aust 45Inf kia 18-9-18 CR France 366
HINES,Walter John	Lt Aust 15Inf kia 6-8-18 CR France 23
HINGSTON,Reginald Basil	Lt Can 24Bn kia 8-8-18 CR France 1170
HINMAN,Arthur Gurr	Lt Aust 15Inf dow 10-5-15 CR Gallipoli 8
HINSON,Heber Basil	Capt NZ18221 CMR dow 30-3-18 CR Syria 2
HINTON,Charles John Morton	2Lt SA 4SAInf dow 15-2-17 CR France 95
HINTON,Herbert Gerald	Lt Aust2ALH kia 7-8-15 CR Gallipoli 31
HINTON,Wilfrid Frank	Capt Aust33Inf kia 13-10-17 CR Belgium 125
HIPWELL,John Basil	Lt Can CFA 2Bde dow 17-6-16 CR Belgium 11
HIRST,Joseph Mark	Lt Aust FA 10Bde kia 21-9-17 CR Belgium 113
HITCHCOCK,Frank Norman Spurrell	Capt NZ 3/1242 NZMC kia 21-10-16 CR France 188
HOARE,Charles Walter	Lt Can19Bn 14-8-16CR France 285
HOBBS,R.A.	Surg Lt Aust RAN HMAS`Melbourne' 13-2-19CR Hamps 7
HOBBS,Ronald Stanley.MC.	Lt Aust 36Inf dow 5-4-18 CR France 144
HOBDAY,Stephen G.DCM.	Lt Can 3Bn 1916
HOBKIRK,Charles Hamilton	Lt Can 25Bn kia 17-9-16 CR France 280
HOBSON,N.S.	Lt SA MtdCmdos kia 25-11-14 CR SAfrica 102
HOCKEN,Richard Henry	Lt Can CLH kia 10-10-18 CR France 404
HOCKEY,J.O.	SNurse SA SAMNS
HOCKIN,Frederick	Lt Can 1Bn kia 27-7-17 CR France 550
HOCKIN,John Treverne	2Lt Aust 25Bn 29-7-16MR 26
HOCKING,Edward	2Lt Aust 44Inf 9-6-17 MR 29
HOCKLEY,Albert Chalmers	Lt SA SASC ded 16-8-16 CR Tanzania 1 &EAfrica 5
HOCKLEY,Rupert Reginald.DSO.	Maj Aust 2Pnrs dow 20-9-17 CR Belgium 11
HODDLE-WRIGLEY,Theodore	2Lt AustMGC 14Coy 20-7-16MR 26
HODGKINSON,Samuel Charles Lindsey	Lt Aust RAN HMAS `Australia' ded 1-8-15 CR Derbyshire 23
HODGKINSON,W.O.	Maj Aust AIF 5DivBaseDepot 5-1-18 CR Aust 146
HODGSON,John Eastwood	Lt Can PPCLI 5-11-18CR Surrey 1
HODGSON,Walter	2Lt Aust 19Inf dow 6-8-16 CR France 74
HOFFE,Thomas Mitchell	Capt&Adjt SA CapeCps ded 23-9-17 CR EAfrica 1
HOFMEYR,Nicholas Jacobus	Capt SA SAMC 1MtdBdeFA 25-6-16CR Tanzania 1 &EAfrica 5
HOGAN,Arthur Douglas	Lt Aust 21Inf 9-10-17MR 29
HOGARTH,E.C.	Lt Aust 21Inf 9-10-17MR 29
HOGARTH,Eric Gordon	Capt Aust22Bn 3-5-17 MR 26
HOGG,Alexander William	2Lt SA 1SAInf kia 18-4-18 CR Belgium 11
HOGG,James Scholes	Lt Aust 42Inf dow 1-8-17 CR France 297
HOGG,Norman Hugh	Lt NZ 136823OIR dow 15-12-17 CR France 64
HOGG,William Thomas	Lt Aust 29Inf dow 27-9-17 CR Belgium 11
HOGGART,William Ross	Capt Aust 14Inf kia 27-4-15 CR Gallipoli 8
HOGGARTH,William Paton	Lt Aust 50Inf kia 2-4-17 CR France1 488
HOGUE,Oliver	Maj Aust 14ALH ded 3-3-19 CR Surrey 1
HOLBEN,Robert Ernest	2Lt NZ 2/1401 NZFA dow 3-11-16 CR France 52
HOLCROFT,Herbert Spencer	Lt Can CE 2TC 8-7-16 CR Sussex 133
HOLDER,Frank Phillip	Lt Aust 54Inf kia 1-9-18 CR France 627
HOLDSWORTH,Thomas Wendell	Lt Can 27Bn 1916
HOLGATE,Edward Spencer	Lt Aust 60Bn 27-4-18MR 26
HOLDEN,Hugh Cyprian	Lt Aust 7ALH kia 23-11-15 CR Gallipoli 22
HOLDSWORTH,Thomas Wendell	Lt Can 27MR 15-9-16MR 23
HOLLAND,Ernest Hudson.MC.	Capt Can 1MMGBde B'Bty 24-3-18MR 23
HOLLAND,George Henry.MC.MID.	Maj NZ 12/373 1AIR R15Coy kia 15-5-18 CR France 156
HOLLAND,George Kilvert	Lt Can 3Bn kia 6-11-17 CR Belgium 10
HOLLAND,Hickson Rains	Maj Can 7CMR dow 10-9-16 CR France 74
HOLLAND,James Albert	Lt Can 85Bn 1912-9-18 CR France 421
HOLLAND,Walter Cluny Stewart	Lt Can 1Bn kia 4-5-17 CR France 68
HOLLAND,Walter Percival	Lt Aust 25Inf kia 9-6-18 CR France 196

HOLLIDAY,William Jeffrey.MC.	Maj Can 14Bn 16-4-17CR France 102
HOLLIDGE,Robert C.DCM.MM.	Lt Can19Bn drd 23-6-19 CR Canada 1679
HOLLINGSWORTH,F.	Lt SA 1RhodR MGSect kia 26-4-15 CR SAfrica 18
HOLLINGWORTH,Albert	Lt Can QRD attRAF 8Sqn 25-6-18CR France 1564
HOLLINGWORTH,John Manson	2Lt SA 1SAInf A'Coy mbk 20-7-16 CR France 402 kia
HOLLINS,John Lewis	Lt SA 1CapeCps(EEF) ded 15-10-18 CR Egypt 1
HOLLIS,Norman Silvester	Capt Aust AFA 2Bde dow 3-10-18 CR France 528
HOLLIS,Oscar Harold	Lt Can43Bn 23-10-17 CR Belgium 125
HOLLIS,William Joseph.MIDx3.	Lt NZ 11/760A WMR 3Reinf ded 13-11-18 CR NZ 243
HOLLOWAY,Robert Palfrey.MID	Lt Can RNewfndlandR kia 14-4-17 MR 10
HOLLY,James Walter	Lt Can 25Bn B'Coy kia 8-8-18 CR France 1015
HOLMES,Carleton Colquhoun	Lt Can 7Bn (BCR) 24-4-15MR 29
HOLMES,Ernest Randal	Lt Aust AFA 1DivArtlyBdedow 30-10-16 CR France 389
HOLMES,K.W.	Lt Aust AFC 11-8-17CR France 1314
HOLMES,Louis Gordon	Capt Aust 3BdeHQ dow 23-6-15 MR 6
HOLMES,Mathew.MID	LtCol NZ 3/1 NZMC ded 15-11-18 CR NZ 258
HOLMES,Richard Dewey	2Lt SA 4SAInf C'Coy kia 9-4-18 MR 29
HOLMES,Victor Napoleon William	Lt Can 26Bn dow 4-10-16 CR France 59
HOLMES,William.CMG.DSO.VD.	MajGen Aust 4DivHQ kia 2-7-17 CR France 297
HOLMES,William Dumbleton.DSO.MC.MID	Capt Can 7Bn 13-6-16CR Belgium 127
HOLT,Gordon Cyril	2Lt Aust 1Inf dow 9-10-17 CR Belgium 11
HOLT,Norman Richard	Lt Aust 21Inf 1-9-18 CR France 624
HOME,James	2Lt Aust 4Inf dow 13-5-15 CR Egypt 6
HOMER,Herbert William	2Lt Aust 26Inf dow 1-6-17 CR Surrey 1
HONEY,Samuel Lewis.VC.DCM.MM.	Lt Can 78Bn dow 30-9-18 CR France 686
HOOD,James S.	Lt Can 3Bn 1917
HOOKE,Frank Morton	Capt Aust 6Inf dow 3-6-15 CR Egypt 6
HOOPER,Charles William	Capt Aust 10Bn 25-7-16MR 26
HOOPER,Robert James Mansfield	Lt Aust10Inf kia 27-5-15 CR Gallipoli 24
HOOPER,Robert Murdoch Finlayson	Capt Aust 5Inf kia 9/10-8-15 CR Gallipoli 7
HOOPER,Thomas Alfred	Lt Aust 5Bn 18-8-16MR 26
HOOPER,Walter Thomas	Maj Can 78Bn 9-4-17 CR France 548
HOPE,John William Jacob	Lt Can26Bn kia 17-5-16 CR Belgium 4
HOPGOOD,Edward William Frank	Lt Can QRD (87Bn) attRAF 14-10-18 CR Kent 216
HOPGOOD,Lionel Raymond	2Lt SA 1SAInf dow 10-4-18 MR 29
HOPKINS,Clive Boyer.MID	Capt Aust 14BdeHQ kia 20-7-16 CR France 348
HOPKINS,Fred Holmes	LtCol Can17Bn dcdacc 30-1-16 CR Canada1 430
HOPKINS,Herbert Horace	Lt SA SASpServ dcd 27-7-18 CR EAfrica 90 25-7-18
HOPKINS,Vernon Newland	2Lt Aust 17Inf dow 21-9-17 CR Belgium 11
HOPKINS,Vivian Phelps	2Lt NZ 23/785 1/3RB kia 21-3-18 CR Belgium 19
HOPKIRK,William Spottiswoode	2Lt NZ 10/2508 1WIR kia 1-6-16 CR France 922
HOPPER,Joseph Stewart	Lt Aust FA 14Bde kia 6-8-17 CR Belgium 10
HOPTROFF,Wallace Frank	Capt SA 2SAInf kia 18-7-16 CR France 1890 &MR21
HORAN,Henry James	Capt Can 52Bn 16-9-16MR 23
HORAN,James Ambrose	Lt Can 46Bn 25-10-16 MR 23
HORE,Robert William.DSO.	Maj Aust AFA 4Bde dow 9-10-18 CR France 146
HORNBY,Geoffrey	Lt Can 7Bn 24-5-15MR 23
HORNBY,Leslie Laurence	Capt Aust 59Bn 29-9-18MR 26
HORNE,William John	Lt Aust 45Inf kia 18-9-18 CR France 366
HORNER,Archibald Herbert	Lt Can PPCLI 13-4-16CR Belgium 72
HORNER,Asa Milton	Lt Can 4CMR 16-9-16CR France 44
HORNIMAN,Lancelot Vicary	Lt Aust55Inf kia 1-9-18 CR France 511
HORNSBY,Charles Cooper	Capt SA NRhodPol ded 12-5-17 CR EAfrica 40
HORROCKS,John Ainsworth	2Lt Aust 27Inf dow 23-5-18 CR France 71
HORSEY,Clifton Manbank	Lt Can13Bn kia 22-4-16 CR Belgium 4
HORTON,Andrew Allison	Lt Can 1Bn A'Coy kia 1-10-18 CR France 597
HORTON,John Robert	Lt Can RCR dow 7-10-16 CR France 145
HORTON,Tom Whittaker	Lt Aust 2Inf 4-10-17MR 29
HORWOOD,Alfred Ernest.MC.	Maj NZ 2/582 NZFA 7Bty kia 1-8-17 CR France 262
HOSACK,J.C.	Lt SA GL CaprCps 20-7-16CR Tanzania 1 &EAfrica 2
HOSFORD,George Ernest	Lt Can18Bn kia 17-10-18 CR France 241

HOSFORD,Samuel Richard	Lt Can5Bn	kia 1-9-18 CR France 688
HOSIE,Arthur David	Lt Can43Bn	9-10-16MR 23
HOSIE,Robert James.MC.	Lt Can54Bn	22-3-17CR France 12
HOSKING,Arnold Kingsley.MC.	Maj Aust 20Inf	kia 20-9-17 CR Belgium 125
HOSKING,Thomas	2Lt Aust RFC 2Sqn28-3-18MR 26	
HOSKING,Walter Willoughby	Lt Aust 27Inf	kia 4-7-16 CR Belgium 48
HOSKINS,Ronald	Lt Can 10Bn (AR)kia 22-4-15 MR 29	
HOST,Walter Joseph.MM MID	Lt Aust 2Inf	dow 24-7-16 CR France 44
HOUGH,George	2Lt Aust 16Inf	kia 6-12-16 CR France 277
HOULDSWORTH,Edgar	Lt Can 3PnrBn 4Coy 15-4-17CR France 68	
HOULIHAN,John Vincent	Capt Aust29Inf	26-9-17MR 29
HOULKER,James	Maj NZ 6/1572 CIR dow 10-8-15 MR 6	
HOUSTON,Alexander McLean.MBE.	LtCol Can 10Bn MilHQ ded 16-10-18 CR Canada 1282A	
HOUSTON,Colin	2Lt Aust 17Bn	3-5-17 MR 26
HOUSTON,William	Lt Can 16Bn	kia 16-8-18 CR France 699
HOWARD,Charles Matthew.MC.	Lt Can 58Bn	kia 8-10-16 CR France 239
HOWARD,Francis	Lt Aust RFC 2Sqn 27-10-18 MR 26	
HOWARD,Francis Carl	Lt Can 75Bn A'Coy 9-9-16 CR France 705	
HOWARD,Frederick	2Lt NZ 1/384 1WIR kia 8-6-17 CR Belgium 89	
HOWARD,Hubert Charles	Lt Aust 59Inf	kia 19-7-16 CR Belgium 96
HOWARD,Murray Leo	Lt Can WORD &64RAF 25-7-18CR France 10	
HOWARD,Richard Watson.MC.	Lt Aust RFC	22-3-18MR 26
HOWARD,Rupert	Lt Can 16Bn	kia 4-9-16 CR France 393
HOWARD,Thomas Spencer	Lt Aust 8ALH	kia 7-8-15 MR 6
HOWARD,William Jesse Edward.MC.	Capt Can 44Bn att10TMB 22-7-17CR France 12	
HOWAT,G.	Capt SA 4SAInf kia 12-10-16	
HOWDEN,Harold Charles.MC&Bar.	Maj Aust48Inf	dow 5-7-17 CR France 297
HOWDEN,Peter	2Lt NZ 22564MGC dow 21-10-17 CR France 64	
HOWDEN,Thomas Henry	2Lt Aust 43Inf	4-10-17MR 29
HOWDEN,William.MID.	2Lt NZ8/1263 1OIR kia 30-9-16 MR 11	
HOWE,Gilbert	2Lt NZ 2/96 NZFA 9Bty kia 10-1-17 CR France 922	
HOWE,Harold	Lt Can 66Regt ded 27-11-15 CR Canada 742	
HOWE,John	Lt Can 14Bn	25-4-16CR Belgium 11
HOWELL-PRICE,Owen Glendower.DSO.MC.	Lt Col Aust Cmdg 3Inf dow 4-11-16 CR France 833	
HOWELL-PRICE,Philip Llewellyn.DSO.MC	Maj Aust 1Inf 4-10-17MR 29	
HOWELL-PRICE,Richmond Gordon.MC.	2Lt Aust 1Inf dow 4-5-17 CR France 1486	
HOWES,David Edwin	Capt Can CAMC 1GH19-5-18CR France 40	
HOWIE,William Gladstone	2Lt NZ 9/557 OMR ded 30-9-15 CR Europe 23	
HOWLEY,Francis John	Lt Can 7SH dedacc 6-12-17 CR Canada 745A 26ResBn	
HOWSON,Charles Edwin	Lt Can 25Bn	1-10-16MR 23
HOYLES,Hugh Lewis	Lt Can 42Bn	12-8-18CR France 360
HUBBARD,Arthur Charles.MC.	Capt NZ 14347 2AIR 16Coy kia 4-10-17 MR 30	
HUBBARD,John Randolph	Lt Can 42Bn A'Coykia 29-9-18 CR France 481	
HUBBE,Hermann Fritz	Capt Aust 1Pnrs kia 23-7-16 CR France 430	
HUBER,Herbert William	Lt Malta KOMaltaR att1RInnisFus7-1-16 MR 4	
HUDSON,Arthur	2Lt Aust 31Inf	kia 19-7-16 MR 7
HUDSON,Athol	2Lt NZ 24/15471/3NZRB kia 14-7-16 CR France 82	
HUDSON,Cecil Arthur Henry.DCM.MM&Bar	Lt Can 8Bn dedacc 26-9-18 CR France 646	
HUDSON,Ernest Alfred Knight.DSO.	Maj Aust AnzacMtdDivHQded 27-10-18 CR Palest 3	
HUDSON,Evan Gibb	2Lt NZ 61946 WIR kia 16-9-16 CR France 415 3/3RB A'Coy 9-9-16	
HUDSON,J.L.	Lt Honduras BrHondTerForce 8-5-20 CR CentAmerica 1	
HUDSON,Joseph Omirei	Lt Can 22Bn kia 3-11-16 CR France 559 HUDON Omeril	
HUDSON,William Henry	Capt Can2Bn 8-10-16CR France 430	
HUET,Frank Pearce Y.	Lt AustADC ded 3-2-19 CR Wilts 167	
HUGGINS,Cyril George	Lt Can102Bn	kia 14-5-17 CR France 81
HUGHES,George Henry	2Lt Aust 44Inf	8-6-17 MR 29
HUGHES,James Chester	Lt Can CE 6FC	15-11-15 CR Belgium 182
HUGHES,Leslie Richard	Lt Aust 45Inf	dow 1-10-18 CR France 146
HUGHES,Lionel Murray	2Lt NZ 44935 3/3NZRB kia 27-3-18 CR France 156	
HUGHES,Melville Rule	Capt Aust AAMC 5Div dow 2-4-17 CR France 564	
HUGHES,Roger Forrest	Capt Aust AAMC 1Fld Ambdow 11-12-16 CR France 833	

HUGHES,Roland Llewellyn	Lt Aust26Inf kia 21-2-17 CR France 385
HUGO,Laurence William Albert	Lt NZ 10/7 WIR kia 27-4-15 CR Gallipoli 11
HULBERT,Leslie Victor	Capt NZ 2/1018 NZFA kia 21-10-16 CR France 188
HULKS,Frederick	Lt Aust 32Inf kia 19-7-16 MR 7
HULL,Arthur Vincent Leopold	Lt Aust 18Inf kia 9-10-17 CR Belgium 128
äHULL,Claude William	Lt Can CFA 1Bde ded 20-2-19 CR Canada 1245
HULL,Harold Louis	Lt CanCFA 1DivTMB 3-6-16 MR 29
HULSE,L.R.	Capt Honduras BrHondTerForce 28-4-18CR CentAmerica 1
HUME,Arthur Grenville	Maj NZ 10/1853 AIR kia 8-8-15 MR 5 WIR
HUME,Earle Walter	Lt Can 27Bn 28-4-18CR France 63
HUME,Peter Gulland	Capt NZ3/446A NZDC ded 31-5-16 CR NZ 40
HUME-STORER,John Cameron	Capt Can CASC &RFC mbk 17-2-17 MR 40
HUMPHREY,Humphrey Charles.VD.	Maj SA 11SAInf kia 9/11-5-16 CR Tanzania 1 &EAfrica 5
HUMPHREYS,Robert George.MM.	Lt Aust 1Inf kia 16-4-18 CR France 19
HUMPHREYS,W.	Lt SA 6SAInf ded 19-10-18
HUMPHRYS,Thomas Sydney	Lt Aust 26Bn 26-3-17MR 26
HUNMAN,Andrew Victor.MID	Maj Aust AAMC 9FA dow 20-5-17 CR France 922
HUNT,Francis William	Capt Aust 54Inf kia 1-10-18 CR France 375
HUNT,Gladstone Montague.MC.	Maj Aust AAMC 1FA 4-10-17MR 29
HUNT,Herbert John.MC.	Lt Aust 4AMGC kia 10-8-18 CR France 699
HUNT,Leonard Walter	Lt Can CE1TramCoy 7-11-18CR France 1196
HUNT,Myrtle Margaret	Nurse Can CAMC ded 16-1-18 CR Canada 777
HUNT,Sinclair Edward	2Lt Aust 55Inf kia 1-9-18 CR France 511
HUNT,Victor Alfred	2Lt SA 4SAInf kia 9-4-17 CR France 452
HUNTER,David de Venny	Chpn4Cl Austatt55Inf kia 28-9-17 CR Belgium 112
HUNTER,Frederick Charles	Lt Can 4ResBn 1922
HUNTER,Herbert Humphreys	Capt Aust7Inf 8/12-5-15 MR 4
HUNTER,James	Lt Can 20Bn dow 8-4-17 CR Surrey 1
HUNTER,Joseph Fleming Keith	Capt NZ 12/2337 2AIR kia 15-9-16 MR 11
HUNTER,Reginald John	Lt Aust 19Inf dow 5-6-18 CR France 71
HUNTER,Reginald Verden.MC.	Aust AFA 12Bde ded 13-11-18 CR Surrey 1
HUNTER,Robert	Capt SA 8SAInf 27-6-17CR SAfrica 53
HUNTER,Robert Clive	Lt Aust 2Inf kia 13-6-16 CR France 276
HUNTER,Robert William	2Lt Aust 37Inf kia 23-4-17 CR France 922
HUNTER,William Yeates	Maj Can WarOff Ex18RBn19AC kia 28-9-18 CR Belgium 15
HUNTINGTON,Stanley Hustler	2Lt NZ 44550 1/3NZRB dow 6-4-18 CR France 169
HUNTLEY,Clive Neilson Reynolds	LtAust Engrs 1FC dow 4-5-15 MR 6
HUOT,Lucien Roger	Lt Can 22Bn dow 16-8-17 CR France 80
HURLEY,Francis Joseph.DCM.	Lt Can 14Bn kia 1-9-18 CR France 687
HURRY,George	Lt Aust 15Inf 18-10-17 MR 29
HUSBANDS,William T.MIDx2	Capt SA BrSAPol (NRhodPol) 14-12-18 CR EAfrica 73
HUTCHINS,Horace	Maj Can 21Bn 9-4-17 MR 23
HUTCHINSON,Arthur Justin Sanford	Maj Aust 58Inf kia 19-7-16 MR 7
HUTCHINSON,Frank Oliver	Lt Can 85Bn (NSR) kia 30-10-17 MR 29
HUTCHINSON,Frederick Mellor	Capt Can CE 11FC 1-3-17 CR France 68
HUTCHINSON,Percy Lynn	Lt SA 2SARif ded 5-12-17 CR EAfrica 77
HUTCHINSON,Samuel Arthur.MC.	Lt Can 7BnCE ded 13-1-21 CR Canada 256
HUTCHINSON,Sydney Ormond	Lt Aust 19Inf dedacc 15-4-18 CR France 85
HUTCHINSON,Thomas Wilson	Lt Can116Bn dow 25-7-17 CR France 68
HUTCHISON,Henry(Harry).DSO.MC.MID	Maj Can 3Bn dow 5-11-17 CR Belgium 11
HUTTON,John	2Lt Aust 16Inf kia 30-8-16 CR France 314
HUTTON,Lincoln George	Lt Can 1Bn 13-12-16 CR France 81
HUXHAM,William Spencer	Lt Can 5Bn 15-8-17CR France 149
HUXTABLE,Geoffrey	2Lt SAMilLabCps 10-12-18 CR EAfrica 36
HUXTABLE,Robert Beveridge.CMC.DSO.VD.ColAust	AIF AAMC 11-5-20CR Aust 112
HUYCKE,Frederick Arthur	2Lt Can RAF Ex CanFA drd 3-9-18 MR 40
HYAM,William Raymond	Lt Aust 13ALH attAFCdow 30-3-17 CR Egypt 2
HYDE,Albert John	Lt Aust 6Inf 4-10-17MR 29
HYDE,Charles Edward	Lt Can 13Bn 7-8-18 CR France 489
HYETT,Alan Newcombe	Lt Aust 38Inf kia 2-6-17 CR Belgium 451
HYMAN,Eugene McMahon	Lt Can 14Bn kia 26-9-16 MR 23
HYNDMAN,Thomas Macauley	HCapt Can 10CMR ded 22-7-15 CR Canada 487 H.

I

IEVERS,Hugh Frank	Lt SA 1MR kld 30-10-15 CR SAfrica 20
IKIN,Harry	Lt Aust 36Bn 3-3-18 MR 26
INCE,William Campbell	Lt Can 8MGCoy kia 2-6-16 CR Belgium 106
INESON,Dick.MC.MM.	Lt Can 58Bn kia 27-8-18 CR France 421
INGHAM,Frank Milton	2Lt Aust AFA 5Bde dow 20-10-17 CR France 139
INGLES,George Leycester	HCapt Chpn4Cl Can ChpnServs att3Bn 1-1-15 CR Wilts 2
INGLIS,Archibald John	Lt Aust55Inf kia 2-9-18 CR France 511
INGLIS,Charles Meldrum.MC.	Lt Can 72Bn 27-9-18CR France 714
INGLIS,Herbert McClelland	LtCol NZ NZMC 17-9-17CR NZ 194
INGLIS,Thomas Bell	Capt Can47Bn 18-10-18 CR France 273
INGPEN,Edward Lucian	Lt SANRhodPol dow 10-6-16 CR EAfrica 73
INGRAM,Harold Aubrey Thomas	Lt Aust 25Inf dow 13-8-18 CR France 71
INKSETTER,George Addison	LtCol Can CE 4DivHQ 15-10-16 CR France 59
INNES-HOPKINS,James Randolph	Capt Can 5Bn 25-5-15CR France 727
INNES-JONES,Evan Scott	2Lt NZ 13/374 AIR ded 7-11-18 CR Staffs 114
ION,John	Lt Aust 32Inf dow 25-7-16 CR France 102
IRELAND,Frederick Ernest William	Lt Aust Engrs 2DivSigsdow 17-19-17 CR Belgium 11
IRELAND,Richard Alfred	Capt Can CAMC att5CMR(QR) kia 30-10-17 MR 29
IRVINE,Andrew Balfour	Lt Can 29 Bn kia 7-4-16 CR Belgium 11 27Bn
IRVINE,Chester Hamilton	Lt Can 31Bn 25-6-18CR France 174
IRVINE,Francis Duncan	Maj Aust 1Bde HQ kia 25/28-4-15 MR 6
IRVINE,Joseph	2Lt Aust 4Inf kia 4-10-17 CR Belgium 125
IRVINE,Norman Ramsay	Lt Aust FA 4Bde dow 9-10-17 CR Belgium 11
IRVINE,Stannus Charles Edward.MID	Lt SA NRhodRifs18-4-15CR EAfrica 73
IRVINE,Wesley William	Lt Can43Bn 28-9-18CR France 243
IRVING,Arthur Beaufin	Lt Can 16MR 8-10-16MR 23
IRVING,Thomas Craik.DSO.	LtCol Can Engrs2FC Cmdg4DivHQ 29-10-17 CR Belgium 8
IRVING,William Alexander	Maj Can CFA 10Bde 11-10-16 CR France 430
IRVING,Willie	2Lt Aust 11Inf 2-11-17MR 29
IRWIN,De Witt Oscar	HCapt Can YMCA att10Bn(AR) 28-4-15MR 29
IRWIN,Thomas Robert	Lt Aust AMGC 3Bnkia 8-8-18 CR France 1170
ISAACS,Herbert Cyril	2Lt NZ 12/2185 1AIR kia 4-10-17 MR 30
ISAACSON,Colin de Stuteville.MC.	CaptSA EA GL &Staff dow 11-6-17 CR EAfrica 10 UL
ISDELL,Helena Kathleen	SNurse NZ 22/130 ANS drd 23-10-15 MR 35
ISGAR,Percy Hawkes	Maj SA SAFldTelCps 5-12-18CR Hamps 13
IVERS,H.F.	Lt SA MtdRif kld 30-10-16
IZDEBSKI,Charles Victor	2Lt Aust 25Inf 2-9-18 CR France 511

J

JACK,Alexander Douglas	Lt NZ 12/2339 AuklandR ded 15-11-18 CR NZ 257
JACK,Benjamin Douglas	Maj Aust 54Inf kia 9-4-18 CR France 490
JACK,George Edmund	Capt Can 1Wks Bn ded 14-12-18 CR Belgium 287 3CanInf
JACK,Thomas.MC.	Capt Aust 42Bn 12-8-18MR 26
JACKA,Frederick Clifton	2Lt NZ 12/3526 1AIR kia 30-8-18 CR France 560
JACKSON,Alban Brittain	2Lt NZ 12/2613 1AIR kia 29-8-18 CR France 307
JACKSON,Albert Heyward.MM.	Lt Aust10Inf kia 24-4-18 CR France 324
JACKSON,Alfred Charles Harrop	2Lt Aust 6Inf dow 9-8-15 CR Greece 10

JACKSON,Allan Raymond	2Lt Aust 55Inf kia 30-9-18 CR France 526
JACKSON,Arthur Bangay	Lt Can 54Bn kia 1-3-17 CR France 81
JACKSON,Aubrey	Capt NZ 13681 1/3NZRB kia 5-9-18 CR France 307
JACKSON,David Alexander	Lt Aust 10ALH kia 7-8-15 MR 6
JACKSON,George Olaf John Ceada	Lt Can 10Bn dow 28-4-17 CR France 95
JACKSON,Hector J.R.MC.	Capt Can 10Bn dedacc 25-1-20 CR Canada 180
JACKSON,Hugo Anthony L.C.	Lt Can 10Bn kia 28-4-17 CR France 68
JACKSON,John William	Capt SA 3SAInf kia 20-7-16 MR 21 Maj
JACKSON,John Kenneth Edward.MID.	Lt NZ 10/395 2WIR dow 28-3-18 CR France 1013
JACKSON,Norman Leslie	Lt Aust 29Inf kia 23-7-18 CR France 207
JACKSON,Percy Edward	Capt Aust 28Inf kia 31-5-16 CR France 285
JACKSON,Percy John.MM.	Lt Can 87Bn kia 15-8-17 MR 23
JACKSON,Thomas Gilbert	2Lt NZ 2/167 NZFA kia 8-10-18 CR France 611
JACKSON,Walter Bentley	2Lt Aust 28Inf dow 3-5-17 CR France 512
JACOB,Kenneth Grant	Lt Aust 12Inf kia 30-5-18 CR France 28
JAFFRAY,Alfred John	Capt Aust9ALH kia 29-8-15 CR Gallipoli 16
JAGGARD,Jessie Brown	Matron Can CAMC 3SH 25-9-15CR Greece 11
JAMES,Cecil Arthur	Lt Can1Bn 15-6-15CR France 571
JAMES,George Everett	Capt Aust 8Inf dow 24-7-16 CR France 515
JAMES,Robert Francis	2Lt Aust 51Inf dow 21-10-17 CR Belgium 84
JAMES,Thomas Parry	Capt NZ 11/488 WMR 2Sqn dow 12-8-15 MR 6
JAMESON,Charles Chalmers	2Lt Aust 42Inf kia 4-4-17 CR Belgium 54
JAMESON,Charles Inglis	Lt Can 43Bn attRFC 21-8-16CR France 200
JAMESON,George Willis	Capt Can 16Bn 23-4-15CR Belgium 96
JAMESON,William	Lt Can 27Bn 15-9-16MR 23
JAMIESON,Douglas Dunbar.MC.	Maj Aust 8ALH dedacc 29-7-18 CR Egypt 7
JAMIESON,Mabel Elizabeth	SNurse NZ 22/133 ANS drd 23-10-15 MR 34
JAMIESON,Walter Hyatt	Lt Can 1st Army HQ Ex1CORD attRAF ded 28-10-18 CR Surrey 1
JAMIESON,William Francis.DSO.	Capt Can 52Bn 28-9-18CR France 714
JANIN,Georges Alex Francis Romain	Maj Can 5FC drd 17-11-15 MR 40 HQ 2Div
JAPHET,A.	Intptr Aust CofG &Intptrs att3AustInf24-7-15CR Greece 10
JAQUES,Maurice Alexander	Lt Can 13Bn 3-9-16 MR 23
JARDINE,Lewis	2Lt NZ 9/45 NZFA kia 25-9-16 CR France 399
JARRETT,Frank Harold	Capt Aust 35Inf dow 5-7-17 CR France 285
JARRETT,Owen George	2Lt NZ 24/474 2/3NZRB dow 8-10-18 CR France 1483
JARVIS,Jessie Agnes	Nurse Can CAMC ded 23-5-18 CR Canada 674
JARVIS,Leonard Charles	Lt Can 18Bn C'Coy kia 20-7-17 CR France 570
JARVIS,William Dummer Powell	Lt Can 3Bn C'Coy(1COR) kia 24-4-15 MR 29
JASSINOWSKY,Abraham	Capt SA SAMC ded 23-10-18 CR SAfrica 22
JAY,Frederick William	Capt Can 1Bn 9-7-16 CR Belgium 112
JEFFERS,John Patrick	Lt Aust RFC 3Sqn 19-9-18MR 26
JEFFERS,W.C.	Capt Can CAMC ded 15-7-17 CR Canada 1430
JEFFERSON,Joseph Mathews	Lt Aust 53Bn 10-5-17MR 26
JEFFERY,Edward	Lt Can 16Bn dow 28-7-18 CR France 14
JEFFERYS,Ernest Howard	Cadet747 Aust AFC 6Sqn dedacc 28-8-18 CR Glouc 172
JEFFRESON,Clarence	Lt Can2CMR att3EntrchBn 30-9-16MR 23
JEFFREY,Charles Lucas	Lt Can 44Bn (NBR) kia 27-10-17 MR 29
JEFFRIES,Clarence Smith.VC.	Capt Aust 34Inf kia 12-10-17 CR Belgium 125
JEKILL,Henry Edgar	Lt Can 29Bn 9-8-18 CR France 649
JELLETT,Laurence Gray	Lt Can 49Bn dow 28-1-17 CR France 95
JENKIN,William	2Lt Aust 7Bn 19-8-16MR 26
JENKINS,Edward William	Capt AustAFA 6Bde kia 21-12-16 CR France 188
JENKINS,Elvas,Elliott	LtAust 1Pnrs dow 19-7-16 CR France 397
JENKINS,Richard Lewis Hay Blake	Maj Aust20Inf kia 11-12-15 MR 6
JENNER,Lenna Mae	Nurse Can CAMC 12-12-18 CR Surrey 1
JENNINGS,John Edgar	Lt Aust 21Bn 3-5-17 MR 26
JENNINGS,Lancelot Shadwell.MID.	Capt NZ 8/2502 2OIR kia15-9-16MR 11 &CR France 390
JENNINGS,William Cornelius	Lt Aust 53Inf kia 25-9-17 CR Belgium 125
JENNINGS,William Harold	Lt Aust 46Inf kia 3-4-18 CR France 197
JENSEN,Ernest Peter Carl	Lt Can 58Bn 8-10-16MR 23

JENSEN,Francis Ernest	2Lt Aust 28Inf dow 13-9-15 MR 6
JEPSON,Henry Rothwell	Lt Can47Bn dow 5-8-17 CR France 102
JERRY,Arthur S.MM.	2Lt Aust 28Inf dow 26-3-17 CR France 646
JESSOP,John Reginald	Lt Can 52Bn 6-10-16MR 23
JESSOP,Napier Arnott	Lt Can 7Bn kia 29-4-15 CR Belgium 152
JEWKES,Wallace Gordon	Lt Aust 39Inf dow 10-1-17 CR France 200
JICKELL,Hugh Nelson	Lt NZ11/65 AIR 3AuklandR dow 19-10-17 CR Belgium 3
JILLEY,Oscar.MID	Capt Aust 48Inf dow 6-8-16 CR France 74
JOHANSEN,George Frederick	Lt Aust8Inf 4-10-17MR 29
JOHNS,Frederick Noel.MC.	Capt T Maj NZ 3/1113 NZMC 3FA kia 25-8-18 CR France 518
JOHNS,William Henwood	Lt NZ 13/368 AMR kia 31-10-17 CR Palest 1
JOHNSON,Albert Lewis Brightmare	Capt Can 31Bn 1-10-16CR France 40
JOHNSON, Allan Barrie.MC.	Lt Can 45RFC 44Bnkld 27-1-18 CR Lincs 181 Alan
JOHNSON,Ambrose	Capt Can 38Bn 29-9-18CR France 715
JOHNSON,Arthur Edward	FltCadet Can RAF Ex CAMC drd 28-10-18 MR 40
JOHNSON,Charles Aubrey.MC.	Capt Aust 53Inf dow 2-10-18 CR France 446
JOHNSON,Christian Martin	Capt Aust 25Bn 15-11-16 MR 26
JOHNSON,Edwin Campbell	Lt Aust 32Inf kia 30-9-17 CR Belgium 113
JOHNSON,Francis Rupert	Lt Aust58Inf kia 29-9-18 CR France 375
JOHNSON,Frederick Miller	Maj Aust AAMC 6FA kia 29-11-15 CR Gallipoli 7
JOHNSON,Frederick Richard	Lt Aust 1ATC dow 30-9-18 CR France 446
JOHNSON,Hugh Stanley	Lt Can 24Bn 3-10-18CR France 147
JOHNSON,J.L.O.	Lt SA
JOHNSON,John Edward	2Lt Aust 16Bn 30-8-16MR 26
JOHNSON,John Heber.MC&Bar.	Lt Aust 14Inf kia 2-5-18 CR France 424
JOHNSON,Lacey Arthur	Lt Can CFA 2DAC dow 16-1-16 CR Canada 256
JOHNSON,Melvin Ohio	Capt Can 5CMR (QR) 30-11-17 MR 29
JOHNSON,Norman Lloyd	Capt Aust 29Inf dow 18-12-17 CR France 297
JOHNSON,Olaf Percival	Capt NZ 13/152 AMR kia 9-8-16 CR Egypt 2
JOHNSON,Percy Edward	Lt Can 38Bn kia 28-6-17 CR France 81
JOHNSON,Reginald Lorraine	Lt Can 54Bn A'Coy kia 9-4-17 CR France 58
JOHNSON,Thomas William.MM.	Lt Can 8Bn kia 29-9-18 CR France 147
JOHNSTON,Alexander Thomas	2Lt NZ 24/480 4/3NZRB kia 3-8-18 CR France 281
JOHNSTON,Arthur Thomas	Maj Can 102Bn kia 2-9-16 CR Belgium 15
JOHNSTON,Cameron Gordon	2Lt NZ 4/120 3RB kia 7-6-17 CR Belgium 42
JOHNSTON,Edwin Lavergne	HCapt Can2CRT ded 10-11-17 CR Canada 1688
JOHNSTON,Eric Franklin	HCapt Can ChpnServs att2CanDiv ded 18-11-18 CR France 40
JOHNSTON,Francis Earl.CB.MIDx4.	MajTBrGen NZ 10/512A NZRB kia 7-8-17
JOHNSTON,George Ernest	Capt Aust 8Inf kia 23-8-18 CR France 526
JOHNSTON,George Robinson	Cadet2704 Aust AFC dedacc 24-3-18 CR Hamps 202
JOHNSTON,James Alexander Kerr	Lt Aust 7Inf dow 19-5-15 CR Egypt 9
JOHNSTON,Jonathan Locke	HCapt&QM Can CAMC 9SH ded 3-11-18 CR Surrey 91
JOHNSTON,Lyell Carson	Lt Can 4CMR D'Coy11-4-17CR France 522 Corson
JOHNSTON,Russell Kerfoot	Maj Can 72Bn 1-3-17 CR France 81
JOHNSTON,William Eli	2Lt NZ 10069 AuklandR ded 21-1-18 CR NZ 226 20-1-18
JOHNSTONE,G.O	2Lt TransvaalScot
JOHNSTONE,Gordon Simpson	Lt Can38Bn 4-11-18CR Derbyshire 57
JOHNSTONE,Lawrence	Maj Can 50Bn 1917
JOHNSTONE,Lewis Howard	Capt Can 25Bn kia 1-10-16 MR 23
JOHNSTONE,Lawrence	Maj Can 50Bn 20-5-17CR Derbyshire 20
JOHNSTONE,W.J.	Capt TransvaalScot
JOHNSTONE,William.MC&Bar.	Lt Can 52Bn 15-8-18CR France 987
JOLLIFFE,Reginald Heber Manning	Lt Can 38Bn kia 9-4-17 CR France 81
JOLLY,Sidney	2Lt SA 1SAInf dow 5-11-18 CR France 146
JOLLY,William David.MID.	Capt NZ 8/2798 1OIR kia 14-7-16 CR France 922
JOLLY,William James	Lt Can 49Bn 9-10-16CR France 314
JONES,Adolphus William Percy.DCM.	LtAust 15Inf 24-9-17MR 29
JONES,Albert Edward Mills	Maj NZ 16/538 WIR 3WellingtonR dow 11-10-17 CR Belgium 3
JONES,Alfred Selwyn Basil	Lt Can 9CRT ded 9-2-19 CR Wales 598
JONES,Arthur	2Lt NZ 2/593 13/3NZFA kia 12-11-16 CR France 1092

JONES,Denis Robert.MM.	2Lt Aust 50Bn 3-9-16 MR 26
JONES,Elmer Watson.DSO.	LtCol Can 21Bn kia 8-8-18 CR France 303
JONES,Frank	2Lt NZ 8/2508 1OIR dow 23-9-16 CR France 177
JONES,Frank Aubrey.CMG.DSO.	LtCol SA 4SAInf Ex WelshR kia 11-7-16 CR France 630
JONES,Frank Russell.DCM.	2Lt Aust 25Inf dow 10-10-17 CR Belgium 11
JONES,Frederick Caverhill	Maj Can 13Res Bn ded 28-7-17 CR Canada 1028 115Bn
JONES,George Edwin Allen	Col Can HQ MDS ded 3-2-18 CR Canada 323A 13Bn
JONES,Henry Charles	Lt Can 3Bn 31-12-15 CR Wilts 20
JONES,Herbert	Maj Can CAMC 5FA 5-3-17 CR France 95
JONES,John Tillson	2Lt SA 1SAInf kia 18-10-16 MR 21
JONES,John Ellington	Lt Can 1Bn kia 9-4-17 CR France 68
JONES,Lynus Delbert	Maj Can 2InfBD 1920
JONES,McCulloch Hill	Lt Can 1Bn 15-6-15 MR 23
JONES,Mervyn Campbell Allen	Lt Can 2341412 CFA 60Bty 14Bde kia 30-9-18 CR France 481
JONES,Oscar Anglesey	Capt Aust21Inf dow 4-5-17 CR France 512
JONES,Ralph Egerton Norris	Lt Can 27Bn (MR) kia 6-4-16 MR 29
JONES,Richard William Fisher	Maj Can 124PnrBn 15-4-17 CR France 81
JONES,Roy Victor	Lt Can 75Bn 9-4-17 CR France 1896
JONES,Rupert Charles.MC.	Lt Aust 33Inf dow 3-5-18 CR France 145
JONES,Samuel Emlyn	2Lt Aust 48Bn 11-4-17 MR 26
JONES,Stanley Livingstone	Maj Can PPCLI 8-6-16 CR Belgium 158
JONES,Sydney	2Lt Aust AFC 3Sqn kia 15-6-18 CR France 71
JONES,Trafford	Lt Can CASC attRFC 16-5-16 CR Belgium 15
JONES,Wyn Rowland Rhys	Lt Can 46Bn 10-8-18 CR France 692
JONSSON,Hallgrimur.MC.	Lt Can BCRD &RAF 12Sqn 3-9-18 MR 20
JORDAN,Benjamin Stevens	Maj NZ 6/1109 CIR kldacc 24-5-18 CR Wilts 160
JOSE,Wilfrid Oswald	Lt Aust50Inf kia 3-4-17 CR France 1488
JOSEPH,Herbert Allen	2Lt SA 3SAInf dow 8-6-17 2Regt
JOSLYN,Harold Waddell	Lt Can SRD &RFC 20Sqn 17-8-17 MR 20
JOUBERT,Sydney Herbert.MC.	2Lt Aust 15Inf dow 29-9-17 CR Belgium 11
JOWETT,Percy John	Capt SA 1SAInf mbk 20-7-16 CR France 1890
JOY,Edward Ware	Maj Can 87Bn 9-4-17 CR France 81
JOYCE,Neville Stanley	Lt NZ 6/2901 2CIR dow 8-6-16 CR France 285
JOYNT,Gerald Victor Woolcott	Lt Aust 57Inf kia 25-9-17 CR Belgium 19
JUBB,John Thomas	2Lt NZ 22692 NZRB ded 11-2-23
JUDD,James Martin.MM.	Lt Aust 35Inf kia 22-8-18 CR France 642
JULIAN,Robert David	Lt Aust 14Bn 2-7-16 MR 26
JULL,George Frederick	Lt Can 28Bn 5-5-17 CR France 68
JUNGE,Walter Harold	2Lt NZ 8/830 1OIR 4Coy kia 5-9-18 CR France 905
JUNOR,Kenneth William.MC.	Lt Can 11MGCoy ARAF 56Sqn 23-4-18 MR 20
JUPP,Clifford Henry Oliver	2Lt Can RNewfndlandR kia 1-7-16 MR 10
JURD,Ernest Albert	2Lt NZ 13/369 AMR kia 8-8-15 MR 5
JURY,James	2Lt Aust 27Inf kia 9-10-17 CR Belgium 125

K

KAA,Pekama	Capt NZ 16/620 Pnrs kia 14-8-17 CR Belgium 42
KAIPARA,Autini Pitara	2Lt NZ 16/10 Pnrs kia 4-8-17 CR Belgium 52
KALER,Charles	Lt Aust 13Inf kia 11-4-17 CR France 581
KALMER,Paul Douglas	Lt Aust AIF 6Inf 26-5-20 CR Aust 377
KANN,Roy Joseph	ChpnH Capt Can ChpnServs 17-10-18 CR Canada 1095
KAPPELE,Ernest Reece	Lt Can 75Bn 9-4-17 CR France 1896
KAVANAGH,Joseph John.MC.	Lt Can 24Bn 8-8-18 CR France 1170
KAY,Francis Bert	Capt Aust 49Inf 7-6-17 MR 29
KAY,G.W.P.	Lt Aust 5Inf 6-6-18 CR France 25
KAY,Henry	Lt Aust 50Bn 24-4-18 MR 26

KAY,J.R.	2Lt Aust 25Inf 27-3-17CR France 565
KAY,James	Lt Can CGA 5SB 28-7-17CR France 924
KAY,John.MC.	Maj Can 1BnCMGC ded 15-12-18 CR Canada 1688
KAYSER,Julius August William	Maj Aust 12Inf kia 16-2-17 CR France 385
KEALY,Ida Lilian	NSister Can CAMC 1GH ded 12-3-18 CR Hamps 2
KEAM,Frank Finley	Lt Aust 3Pnrs kia 17-6-17 CR Belgium 42
KEANE,Hermann Theodore D'Hoche.DSO.	Lt SA 1SAInf ded 30-10-18 CR SAfrica 62
KEANE,John Michael	2Lt Aust 58Inf kia 29-9-18 CR France 375
KEARNEY,James Hugh O'Neill	Lt Aust 25Inf kia 5-6-18 CR France 210
KEARSLEY,George Cecil.MM.	Lt Can 75Bn kia 30-9-18 CR France 240
KEATING,Percy Firmin	Capt CanCASC 1917
KEATS,William Vivian	Lt Aust 52Inf 10-6-17MR 29
KEAY,Seawood Peter	2Lt Aust AFC 4Sqn dow 22-8-18 CR France 31
KEELEY,Ernest James	2Lt SA4SAInf kia 23-7-18 MR 32
KEEN,Thomas Llewellyn.MC.	Cadet210 Aust AFC dedacc 12-3-19 CR Glouc 172
KEENE,Roy Oscar Claude	Lt Aust FA 2Bde kia 16-11-17 CR Belgium 19
KEEPING,Kimball Fletcher	Lt Can 8SBty Garrison Art dow 6-9-17 CR France 769
KEID,Leonard	Lt Aust 49Bn 3-9-16 MR 26
KEILLOR,Thomas Balfour.MC&Bar.	Lt Aust 28Inf kia 3-10-18 CR France 1461
KEIR,John.MC.	Capt NZ 30100 1WIR 1Coy kia 23-10-17 MR 30
KEIRAN,Richard Clement	Lt Aust6Inf dow 9-5-15 CR Gallipoli 1
KELIGHER,Patrick James	Capt NZ 33102 OIR 2 OtagoR kia 11-8-17 CR Belgium 52
KELL,Bertram Thomas	Lt Aust 28Inf dow 8-8-18 CR France 71
KELLAWAY,Frank Gerald.MC.	Lt Aust 22Inf 4-10-17MR 29
KELLETT,Frederick	Lt Can 8Bn ded 18-9-14 CR Canada 323A
KELLY,Cecil Byron	2Lt Aust 47Bn 11-4-17MR 26
KELLY,Edward Thomas	Maj Can 4Bn (1COR)kia 22-4-15 MR 29
KELLY,Ernest Tilton Sumpter	Lt Can 1Sqdn RAF EORD 19-6-18CR France 924
KELLY,George Edward Eccleston	2Lt Aust 2Inf kia 25-4-15 MR 6
KELLY,J.P.	2Lt Aust 1Inf 23-8-18CR France 526
KELLY,James Francis	Lt Can 27Bn 10-4-17CR France 68
KELLY,Leo Patrick	Lt Aust 7Inf dow 11-8-18 CR France 119
KELLY.Magus Sigurdur	Lt Can ManitobaR &RAF 15-5-18CR France 180
KELLY,Martin,G.	Capt Can96Bn dcd 29-8-17 CR Canada 1448
KELLY,Robert George Campbell	LtCol Can 149Bn 12-12-15 CR Canada 1164
KELLY,William Archibald	2Lt Aust 6Inf kia 20-9-17 CR Belgium 115
KELLY,William Charles	Lt Aust3ALH kia 14-7-18 CR Palest 3
KELLY-HEALY,James Patrick	2Lt Aust42Inf 4-10-17MR 29
KELMAN,George	Lt Can 16Bn 8-11-17CR Belgium 125
KELSALL,Charles Proctor	Lt Aust 17Inf kia 14-5-18 CR France 209
KELSALL,Victor Albert.MID.	Capt NZ 11/674 WMR kia 8-8-15 MR 5
KEMBALL,Arnold Henry GrantCB.DSO.	LtCol Can 54Bn 1-3-17 CR France 81
KEMBER,Richard Henry.MM.	2Lt NZ6/836 2CIR kia 20-9-16 MR 11
KEMKEMIAN,A.	Intptr Aust 2ALH 17-4-17CR Palest 1
KEMMIS,Ernest Henry George	Capt Aust 4DivHQ dedacc 22-7-18 CR France 300
KEMMIS,William Scott	2Lt Aust 19Bn 27-7-16MR 26
KEMP,Albert Cheesman	Lt Aust 1ALH MGSqd dow 14-4-18 CR Palest 3
KEMP,Alexander Robert	Lt Aust 41Inf kia 3-4-17 CR France 922
KEMP,Frederick.MM.	Lt Can 54Bn dow 2-9-18 CR France 1182
KEMP,Goldwin Otter	Lt Can 38Bn ded 31-7-20 CR Canada 1245
KEMP,Sam	Lt Can 58Bn 7-12-18CR Germany 3
KENDALL,Ernest	Capt Can 1CMR 30-9-16MR 23
KENNEDY,Alexander	Lt Can 7Bn 15-8-17MR 23
KENNEDY,Arthur Herbert.MID	Capt Aust 23Inf ded 26-8-16 CR Germany 3
KENNEDY,C.J.	Capt SA SASpServ
KENNEDY,Harry Alexander	Lt CanRFC 3MGCoy & GL 22-8-17CR France 924
KENNEDY,Hugh Angus	Lt Can 7Bn 15-11-17 CR France 64
KENNEDY,James Mark	Lt Aust 26Bn 5-11-16MR 26
KENNEDY,John Henry Mitchell	Lt Can 250Bn dcd 13-10-18 CR Canada 116 5Bn
KENNEDY,John Keefer	Lt Can 7Bn dow 14-8-16 CR Belgium 11

KENNEDY,Malcolm Stuart	Capt Aust 1DivHQ Ex52Inf dow 2-1-18 CR Belgium 97	
KENNEDY,Thomas	Capt Can 101Bn ded 8-8-21 CR Canada 116	
KENNEDY,Thomas Henry.MC.	Lt Aust 38Inf kia 15-4-18 CR France 196	
KENNEDY,William Smith	Lt Can1CMR 26-10-17 CR Belgium 126	
KENNETT,Claude	2Lt Aust 22Inf ded 17-8-16 CR France 40	
KENNY,David Alexander.MID.	Capt NZ 11/2277 MGC ded 6-4-18 CR Surrey 1	
KENNY,Nelson Clarke	Lt Can 54Bn kia 18-5-17 CR France 81	
KENNY,William Aimer	Lt Can 1CMR ded 24-2-19 CR Scot 387	
KENT,Edgar	2Lt Aust 10Bn 22-8-16MR 26	
KENT,N.A.	2Lt Aust 14Inf 12-4-17CR France 563	
KENT,Stanley Hornsby.MC&Bar.	Capt Can 10Bn 29-4-17CR France 95	
KENT,Victor John	Maj Can CFA 13Bde4-3-18 CR France 480	
KENWORTHY,John Gibson	Lt Can 16Bn (MR) 24-4-15MR 29	
KER,Henry George	2Lt Aust 9Inf dow 16-7-15 CR Gallipoli 22	
KER,Robert Rev.H	Maj Can 19Regt attHQ WellandCanalForce ded 21-2-17 CR Canada 1531	
KERNAGHAN,Arthur.MM.	Lt Aust Engrs 7FC dow 1-9-18 CR France 626	
KERNAN,Edward Joseph	2Lt Aust 5Inf dow 20-9-17 CR Belgium 11	
KERNICK,Reginald George.MID	2Lt SA 3SAInf dow 5-10-17 CR Belgium 3	
KERR,Alan James	Lt Aust 24Inf kia 27-7-16 CR France 832	
KERR,Alexander	Lt Can 10Bn dow 16-11-17 CR Belgium 11	
KERR,Eric John	Capt Aust AAMC kia 4-10-17 CR Belgium 84	
KERR,Herbert Gladstone	Lt Can 3Bn 25-5-15MR 23	
KERR,Hyndman Henry	Capt Can CADC ded 7-10-19 CR Canada 256	
KERR,James	2Lt Aust 55Inf kia 18-5-17 CR France 1488	
KERR,James Duncan	Lt Can 43Bn 16-8-18MR 23	
KERR,John Wilson	2Lt Aust 5Inf dow 26-4-18 CR France 27	
KERR,Robert John Leslie	2Lt Aust57Inf kia 23-4-18 CR France 119	
KERR,William Buchanan	Lt Aust 16Inf kia 2-5-15 MR 6	
KERR,William Gordon	Lt Can CGA 131SBkia 25-10-16 CR France 5	
KERSE,Charles Allanton.MID.	2Lt NZ 8/240 2OIR kia 25-7-18 CR France 204	
KERSHAW,John.MID	Lt Aust 37Inf kia 12-8-18 CR France 526	
KERSHAW,Robert	Lt Can 1NewfoundlandRdow 9-3-18 CR Belgium 84	
KERSLAKE,George Knight	Lt Aust Engrs 1FC kia 15-9-18 CR France 446	
KESHAN,Malcolm McLeod	Lt Aust 3Inf kia 23-8-18 CR France 526	
KESSELL,Harry	Lt Aust 15Inf dow 3-7-15 CR Egypt 9	
KESSLER,Victor Emanual	2Lt SA 1SAInf kia 18-10-16 MR 21	
KESTEVEN,Douglas Leighton	Lt NZ 44189 CIR dow 24-8-18 CR France 1512	
KETCHFORD,C.T.K.	Lt SA 2SAInf kia 20-7-16	
KETTLE,Desmond Fosbery	2Lt NZ13/876 AMR kia 28-8-15 MR 14	
KEYES,Arthur Francis	Lt Can 31Bn 16-9-16MR 23	
KIBBLEWHITE,Edward Henry Turner.MC	Lt NZ 10/960 AIR 1MGCoy dow 11-5-15MR 11 kia 16-9-16	
KIBURZ,Leo Albert	Lt Can 5CRT ded 24-11-18 CR Bucks 64	
KIDD,Clarence Errol.MC.	Capt Can 3Bn 1918	
KIDD,Robert	Lt Aust 58Inf 25-10-17 MR 29	
KIDSON,Alfred DeVere	Lt Aust 56Inf 26-9-17MR 29	
KIELLY,Leroy Bell	Lt Can4Bn 1916	
KIFT,William Kitchener	Lt Can 116Bn dow 29-4-17 CR France 40	
KILBORN,Arthur R.DSO.MC.MM.	Lt Can 78Bn 27-9-18CR France 714	
KILL,Albert Edward	Lt Can MMG Borden Bty 10-11-17 MR 29	
KILLINGSWORTH,Harry Leslie	2Lt Aust 38Bn 28-5-17MR 26	
KILPATRICK,Albert George	2Lt Aust 33Inf 12-10-17 MR 29	
KIMBALL,Merrill Paul	Lt Can 10Bn (AR) 3-6-16 MR 29	
KIMMINS,Albert Edward	Maj Can 1Bn (WOR) 24-4-15MR 29	
KING,Arthur Miles	Lt Can 60Bn kia 12-8-16 CR Belgium 15	
KING,C.	Lt SA 11SAInf kia 11-5-16 CR Tanzania 1 &EAfrica 5	
KING,Claude Napier	Lt Aust MGC 4Bn 8-8-18 MR 26	
KING,Edmund Bromley	Lt Aust 12Inf dow 17-4-18 CR France 180	
KING,Francis.MID	2Lt SA1SAInf kia 12-4-17 MR 20	
KING,George Augustus.DSO&Bar.MIDx5.LtCol NZ 11/680 1CIRkia 12-10-17 CR Belgium 84		
KING,Gerald Lawrence	Lt Can CE 7FC kia 28-3-18 CR France 68	

KING,Gilbert Lennox	2Lt NZ 16307 AMR dow 15-11-17 CR Palest 9
KING,Herbert William	Capt NZ 22513 2AIR kia 21-2-17 CR France 276
KING,Horace Chamberlain.MC.	Capt Aust 28Inf dow 7-4-18 CR France 62
KING,James Bruce	Lt Aust 22Inf dow 5-5-16 CR France 275
KING,Jessie Nelson	Sister Can CAMC 1GH 4-4-19 CR France 34 3GH
KING,Joseph Henry	Capt Can 54Bn 18-11-16 MR 23
KING,Lancel Lytton	2Lt NZ27696 3WIR kia 4-10-17 MR 30
KING,Mervyn Douglas	2Lt Aust 5Bn 18-8-16MR 26
KING,Walter de Mayhew.MC.	Capt&Adjt CanCLH 30-9-18CR France 274
KING,William Keith.MC.	Lt Aust 2ALH kia 14-7-18 CR Palest 3
KING-MASON,Charles	Capt Can 24Bn 1921
KING-MASON,Charles George Dalegarth	Lt Can 5Bn (SR) kia 24-4-15 MR 29
KINGSMILL,Henry Ardagh	Capt Can CAMC 11-2-20CR Canada 1178
KINGSMILL,Horace Frederick.DSO.	Maj Aust FA 1Bde kia 8-8-17 CR Belgium 15
KINGSMITH,Percival Edward	Lt Can 31Bn 4-5-17 CR France 1314
KINLOCH,Watson.MC.	Lt Can 7Bn 4-10-18CR France 40
KINNEAR,D.	ChOff Can MercMar SS`Carthaginian' 4-9-15 MR 24
KINNISH,Henry Arthur	Lt Aust 10Bn 21-8-16MR 26
KINSMAN,Harley Stanley	2Lt Aust23Bn 3-5-17 MR 26
KINTON,Clarence Edward	Lt Can NSRD RCR attRAF 57Sqn 5-9-18 CR France 1307
KINVIG,James Gordon	2Lt NZ 11774 WIR 2WellingtonR kia 31-7-17 CR Belgium 51
KIPPEN,Arnold A.	Lt Can 75Bn kia 2-9-18 CR France 426
KIRBY,Charles Parker	2Lt Aust 33Inf dow 18-2-17 CR France 102
KIRBY,Owen Bruce	Lt Aust 36Bn 4-4-18 MR 26
KIRKBRIDE,Roland John Herbert	Lt Aust 38Inf dow 15-10-17 CR Belgium 8
KIRKBY,Hartley	2Lt SA 4SAInf kia 24-3-18 MR 27
KIRKCONNELL,Walter Allison	Lt Can 14Bn kia 8-8-18 CR France 488
KIRKE,Errol Wharton.MID	Capt Aust 18Bn 4-8-16 MR 26
KIRKE,Gilbert Shuttleworth	2Lt Aust 25Bn 5-8-16 MR 26
KIRKER,Douglas Russell	Capt NZ 12/3214 AuklandR ded 1-12-18 CR NZ 194
KIRKHAM,Malcolm	Lt Aust 59Inf kia 2-9-18 CR France 511
KIRKLAND,George	Lt Aust AMGC 4Coy 13-4-17CR France 1293
KIRKLAND,Hugh Edward.MC.	Capt Aust AAMC att2FldArtlyBde kia 3-10-18 CR France 528
KIRKLAND,William Duncan.MC.	Maj Aust AMC 2FA kia 22-7-17 CR Belgium 15
KIRKLEY,Wilfred	2Lt NZ 8/4435 1WIR kia 17-9-16 MR 11
KIRKPATRICK,Alexander Douglas	Lt Can 3Bn C'Coy (1COR) kia 23-4-15 MR 29
KIRKWOOD,William Russell Barton	Lt Aust 19Bn3-5-17 MR 26
KIRSCH,Rudolph Norman Clive	Capt Aust8Inf 4-10-17MR 29
KIRSTEN,Peter Andrew	Capt SA SASpServ ded 6-12-18 CR EAfrica 75 A.P.
KISSEL,Gustav Hermann	Lt USA AvnSecSigResCps attRAF 43Sqnkia 12-4-18 CR France 705
KITCHEN,Frank Glanfield	Capt Aust 7Inf dow 10-8-18 CR France 71
KITCHEN,Jack Zadkiel	Lt Aust 51Inf kia 26-4-18 CR France 144
KITSON,Harold Strachan	2Lt AustAFC dedacc 15-6-17 CR Lincs 181
KITTO,Alexander John	Lt CanCFA 12Bde kia 16-9-16 CR France 150
KLOTZ,Hubert Norman	Lt Can 2Bn B'Coy (EOR)kia 23-4-15 MR 29
KLUG,George Eric	Lt Aust AFA 8Bde 108HB dow 12-5-18 CR France 71
KLUG,Lewis Conrad.MM.	2Lt Aust 29Inf kia 9-8-18 CR France 526
KNAPP,William Harold	Lt CanPPCLI 1922
KNIGHT,David	2Lt Aust 36Inf dow 8-5-18 CR France 69
KNIGHT,Edward Lewin Eaton	Maj Can MMG CmdgEatonsMotorBty 26-9-16CR France 150
KNIGHT,George Bernard	2Lt NZ8/1532 2OIR kia 12-10-17 MR 30
KNIGHT,George William	Lt Can FGH kia 3-8-16 CR France 397
KNIGHT,Mervyn Digby.MC.	Lt Aust 60Inf kia 6-7-18 CR France 207
KNIGHT,Norman Godwin	Lt Can FGH 5-7-17 CR London 12
KNIGHT,William Charles	2Lt Aust 5Bn 25-7-16MR 26
KNOWLES,John	Lt NZ 11/783 MGC ded 16-12-18 CR Belgium 265
KNOWLES,Reginald Marshall	Lt Can 7BnCE 9-8-18 CR France 485
KNOWLING,Albert James	Lt Can PPCLI kia 28-9-18 CR France 481
KNOX,Hilda Mary	Sister Aust AANS ded 17-2-17 CR France 145
KNOX,John Henry	Lt Can 2CRT 30-3-18CR France 1024 Harry

KNOX,William Johnstone.MC.MID	Capt Aust FA 13Bde dow 20-8-17 CR Belgium 10
KNOX-KNIGHT,Ernest	LtCol Aust 37Inf kia 10-8-18 CR France 526
KOHERE,Henare Mokena	2Lt NZ 16/1018 Maori (Pnr)Bn dow 16-9-16 CR France 833 Mokeua
KOKIRI,Tango	2Lt NZ 20598 Maori Pnrs ded 21-4-17 CR NZ 238A
KOZMINSKY,Maurice Edward	2Lt Aust 7Inf dow 19-8-16 CR France 44
KRENCHEL,Otto Bertel.MC.DCM.	Lt Can 13Bn kia 2-9-18 CR France 687
KRETCHMAR,Edmund Herman	Lt Aust 16Inf kia 6-5-15 MR 6
KRIEG,Louis Paul	Lt Aust AFC kia 19-8-18 CR Palest 9
KYLES,Lloyd Butler	Lt Can 15Bn 2-10-18CR France 113
KYLIE,Edward Joseph	Capt Can 147Bn 14-5-16CR Canada 1430

L

LABATT,Robert Hodgetts	LtCol Can 4Bn ded 6-2-19 CR Canada 1668A
LABEREE,Carl Gordon	Lt Can87Bn dow 28-11-18 CR Surrey 1
LACE,William Northey	Capt NZ 5/638A ASC dow 30-4-18 CR Surrey 1
LACEY,Leonard John	2Lt Aust 3Inf dow 10-7-16 CR France 64
LACY,Frank Archer	Lt Can 50Bn ded 6-9-19 CR Canada 543
LADE,Stephen.MID	Lt Aust 13LH dow 25-9-17 CR Belgium 11
LADLER,John	Lt Can 50Bn 26-4-17CR France 924
LaDUKE,Harold Edgar	Lt Can 54Bn 10-8-18CR Hamps 2
La FAND,RenÇ Darche.MM.	LtCan 75Bn30-9-18CR France 148 La FOND
LAFFERTY,Francis Delmar	BrigGen Can RCA ded 29-11-19 CR Canada 323A
LAGDEN,Richard	Lt Aust 45Inf 12-10-17 MR 29
LAIDLAW,Arthur Frederick	2Lt NZ 35642 2AIR kia 27-3-18 CR France 643
LAIDLAW,William John Scott.MM.	Lt Can 5Bn 27-11-17 CR France 781
LAIDLEY,William Shepheard.MC.	Capt Aust AFA 1Div dow 22-8-18 CR France 119
LAING,Elmer Winfred Drake.MC.	Lt Aust 12Inf kia 8-5-18 CR France 28
LAING,John Gordon.MID	Lt Can 2MGCoy 10-11-17 MR 29
LAING,Murdoch	Lt Can 24Bn dow 18-9-16 CR France 102
LAING,Patrick James Stevenson.DCM.	Lt Can 19Bn C'Coy 18-8-17CR France 570
LAING,Wilbert Stuart	Lt Can CE 2FC 27-11-16 CR France 81
LAIRD,John Hewitt	Lt Can 24Bn 15-8-17CR France 480
LAKE,Geoffrey	Lt Can RNCVR HMCS`Lansdowne' 25-10-18 CR Canada 658
LALONDE,Ruric Harold	Lt Can CAMC ded 6-10-18 MR 40 LALANDE
LALOR,Joseph Peter	Capt Aust 12Inf kia 25-4-15 CR Gallipoli 10
LAMB,John	2Lt SA RE 179Coy dow 17-10-17 CR Belgium 16
LAMB,Joseph	Lt NZ 4/511NZE dow 20-6-16 CR France 922
LAMBART,Charles Edward Kilcoursie	LtCan 1CMR B'Coy (SR) 5-6-16 MR 29
LAMBDEN,Albert Wheeler	2Lt Aust 42Inf dow 4-10-17 CR Belgium 19
LAMBKIN,James Benjamin	Capt Can CASC 1917
LAMERTON,George Arthur.MC.	Lt Aust 11Inf kia 10-8-18 CR France 526
LAMERTON,Walter Leslie	Lt Aust53Inf kia 1-9-18 CR France 624
LAMONTAGNE,Charles Horace	Maj Can 16MR 29-4-17MR 23
LAMPARD,Victor Walter.MC.	Lt Aust 27Inf kia 2-9-18 CR France 511
LA NAUZE,Charles Andrew	Capt Aust 11Inf kia 28-6-15 CR Gallipoli 22
LANDELS,Bertram Howard	Lt Can 15/1COR 26-9-16MR 23
LANE,Charles Henry Chepmell	Lt Can 10Bn kia 15-8-17 CR France 149
LANE,Clement Frederick Wills	Lt Aust 6Inf kia 25-4-15 MR 6
LANE,Cyril Herbert Dodson	Maj Aust18Inf kia 29-8-15 MR 6
LANE,Eric Stannage Hamilton	Lt Can 85Bn D'Coy kia 2-9-18 CR France 421

LANE,Frederick William	Lt Aust 47Inf kia 28-3-18 CR France 196
LANE,Lionel William	Lt Aust 53Inf kia 21-11-17 CR Belgium 76
LANE,Lisle Mervyn	Lt Aust 4Inf kia 2-3-17 CR France 385
LANE,Maitland Percival	Lt Can 29Bn 27-9-16CR France 1505
LANE,Percy E.	Lt Can PPCLI 1915
LANG,Frank Harold	Lt Aust Engrs 5FC26-7-16MR 26
LANG,Horace	2Lt NZ 24/1544 4/3NZRB kia 20-7-16 CR France 82
LANG,Sidney Albert	Lt CanCERD ded 6-10-18 CR Canada 1691
LANG,Thomas John	Lt NZ 15/118NZAPC ded 18-7-18 CR Egypt 9
LANG,William	Capt Aust 6ALH dow 13-8-15 MR 6
LANGFORD,Everett Alexander	Lt Can 52MR 8-8-18 MR 23
LANGFORD,Horace A.	Capt Can 30BCHorse CanMilitia ded 27-5-20 CR Canada 180
LANGHORNE,Francis Harold	Lt Can 2CMR 29-9-18CR France 715
LANGMEAD,George	Lt Can 1RNewfndlandR dow 8-12-17 CR France 398
LANGMUIR,Gavin Ince	Lt Can 15Bn (1COR) 22-4-15MR 29
LANGSTAFF,James Miles.MID	Maj Can75Bn kia 1-3-17 CR France 81
LANSER,Henry Miller	2Lt Aust 1Inf kia 5-11-16 CR France 512
LANTZ,Orrin Lincoln.MC.	Lt Can 85Bn 6-11-18CR France 1142
LANTZKE,Herbert John	Lt Aust AIF AMGC 8-1-20 CR Aust 471
LANYON,Robert Jordan	2Lt Aust 28Bn 3-5-17 MR 26
LAPAGE,Edward	2ndEngr Can MercMar SS`Dunelm' drd 17-10-15 MR 24
LARACY,Francis Patrick.MC	Lt Aust 1Inf lostatsea 10-10-18 MR 40
LARDNER-BURKE,E.C.	Capt SA 5SAInf kia 10-8-16 CR Tanzania 1 &EAfrica 9
LARDNER-BURKE,H.D.	Lt SA 5SAInf kia 20-6-16 CR Tanzania 1 &EAfrica 3
LARKIN,George William	2Lt Aust 28Inf dow 7-8-16 CR France 102
LARKIN,John	2Lt Aust 41Inf kia 5-10-17 CR Belgium 125
LARKIN,John Vernon	2Lt Aust 8Inf kia 9-8-18 CR France 649
LARKINS,Frank Lockwood Sub	Lt Aust RAN HMAS`Platypus'(S/M J2) 20-6-19MR 2
LARNACH,Leslie Norman.MC.	Lt Aust 31Inf dow 10-8-18 CR France 71
LARTENELL,Arthur Joseph	Lt Can 4CRT 18-11-17 CR France 1361
LATTA,Charles Harold	Lt Aust58Inf dow 23-7-16 CR France 8
LATTA,Robert Peter	Lt Can7Bn (BCR) 29-4-15MR 29
LATTER,Ernest Henry.MC.	Capt Can 5Bn 11-12-18 CR Belgium 265
LAURIE,James Gordon	Lt Can 19Bn 9-5-17 CR France 777 10Bn
LAURIE,Leonard Buxton	Lt Aust 10Inf dow 27-4-18 CR France 27
LAURIE,Stuart M.	Lt Can 4MGCoy 2-11-17CR Belgium 84
LAVAIE,Louis Rosario.MM.	Lt Can 22Bn 15-9-16CR France 1505 LAVOIE
LAVIE,George Sissmore	Lt NZ 6/2895 2CIR kia 11-6-16 CR France 922
La VIOLETTE,Joseph Rodolphe Alexander Dumont	Lt Can 42Bn 9-4-17 MR 23 Alexandre
LaVIOLETTE,Lambert Dumont.MC.	Maj Can 22Bn dow 28-8-17 CR Canada 254
LAW,Francis Andrew	Lt Can 24Bn 19-3-19CR Surrey 1
LAW,John Crawford	Capt Can 2SSCoy 28-5-19CR Canada 1687
LAW,Oswald Ross	Lt Aust 48Inf kia 14-8-16 CR France 1505
LAWLOR,Edward James	Capt SA HArty 73Bty ded 8-12-21 CR Europe 51 dow
LAWLOR,Francis John	Lt Can 87Bn dow 7-4-18 CR France 184
LAWRENCE,Alfred John	Lt Can COC 25-5-20CR Canada 1245
LAWRENCE,Alfred William	Capt AustEngrs 1Div ded 27-2-18 CR France 1359
LAWRENCE,Clarence Victor	Lt Can CASC 3DivTr 1-11-18CR Canada 1104
LAWRENCE,Ernest Wilkinson.MC.	Capt Can 4Bn kia 1-10-18 CR France 597
LAWRENCE,Henry Ruthven	Capt SA SAMC 1FAded 14-12-18 CR Belgium 330 7-12-18
LAWS,Harold Augustus	Lt Can 8MGCoy &RFC 23-2-18CR Norfolk 247
LAWSON,A.J.	2Lt SA SL attRoadCps 17-12-18 CR EAfrica 52
LAWSON,Charles Murray	Lt Can 26Bn 26-11-15 CR France 285
LAWSON,Douglas McKinnon	Lt Can 85Bn dow 7-9-18 CR France 13
LAWSON,Frank	Lt Can 18Bn dow 12-4-16 CR Belgium 11
LAWSON,George William	Lt Can 8MR 28-4-17MR 23
LAWSON,John Betts.MC.	Lt Aust 41Bn 29-9-18MR 26
LAWSON,Percy Harold	2Lt Aust AFC kia 6-1-18 CR France 88
LAWSON,Wilfred Edwin	Maj Can CFA 5Bde 29-8-18CR France 14
LAYCOCK,John Scatcherd	Capt Can15Bn kia 11-6-17 CR France 523

LAYTON,Edward Charles Morris	Capt SA 11SAInf kia 3-9-16 CR Tanzania 1 &EAfrica4
LAYTON,Francis Paul Hamilton	Lt Can 4CMR 24-7-16CR Belgium 127
LAYTON,William	Lt Aust 33Inf dow 17-10-17 CR Belgium 11
LAZER,Henry Joseph	Lt Aust 33Inf kia 24-3-17 CR France 922
Le'CREN,Hubert Ernest	2Lt NZ 1/691 4/3NZRB kia 26-8-18 CR France 563
LEA,Clarence.MC	Capt Can4CMR ded 24-9-19 CR Canada 1688
LEACH,Harold Oakley.MC.	Lt Can 4CMGC kia 2-9-18 MR 23
LEACH,Robert Onebye.MC.	Lt Can 5Bn kia 28-9-18 CR France 147
LEADLEY,Percival George	Lt Can 50Bn kia 3-6-17 CR France 58
LEADBEATER,John	Capt Aust 5Bn 25-7-16MR 26
LEAK,Llewellyn Weston Claude	Lt Aust 27Inf dow 4-9-18 CR France 526
LEAKE,George Arthur	2Lt Aust 10ALH kia 29-8-15 MR 6
LEAN,Harry Gladstone,	Lt Can 5MtdRif QuebecR 15-9-16MR 23
LEANE,Allan Edwin	Capt Aust 48Bn 2-5-17 MR 26
LEANE,Allan William	LtCol Aust 28Inf dow 4-1-17 CR France 176
LEANE,Benjamin Bennett	Maj Aust 48Inf kia 10-4-17 CR France 646
LEARMOUTH,Okill Massey.VC.MC.	Maj Can 2Bn dow 19-8-17 CR France 178
LEAVER,Graham Holland	Lt Aust 10Inf kia 20-9-17 CR Belgium 112
LECKIE,Norman Ewing	Maj Can 58Bn kia 23-4-16 CR Belgium 115
LEDINGHAM,James Allan	Capt Can RNewfndlandRkia 9-10-17 MR 10
LEDWARD,Charles Hubert	2Lt Aust23Inf dow 4-9-18 CR France 119
LEE,Charles John Nairne	Lt Can 54Bn 27-9-18CR France 715
LEE,Clarence Eli.MC.	Lt NZ 30114 2WIR kia 26-8-18 CR France 239
LEE,Frederick Charles	2Lt SA 3SAInf dow 9-4-17 CR France 97
LEE,Gordon D'Arcy	Maj Can 46Bn 3-5-17 CR France 81
LEE,Harry William	Maj Aust 25Inf kia 21-3-17 CR France 518
LEE,Joseph Caldwell	Lt SA 1SAInf attSAPC ded 15-10-18 CR SAfrica 121
LEECH,Hart	Lt Can 1MtdRif SasR kia 15-9-16 MR 23
LEER,Charles Edward.MID	Capt Aust3Inf kia 25-4-15 MR 6
LEES,Gerald Oscar	Capt Can13Bn (QR) kia 25-4-15 MR 29
LEES,John Stanley Havelock.MID	2Lt Aust 30Inf kia 19-7-16 MR 7
LEES,Wilfred Robert	2Lt SA 4SAInf kia 12-4-17 MR 20
LEESE,Victor.MM.	Lt Can16Bn kia 1-10-18 CR France 240
LEFEBVRE,RenÇ	CaptCan 22Bn kia 16-9-16 CR France 280
LeFEVRE,Stanley.MC.	Lt Aust39Inf kia 30-8-18 CR France 624
LEGERE,AimÇ Antoine	Lt Can CFC attRFC 3TrngSqn kld 11-9-17 CR Sussex 55 LEGER
LEGGO,Ayton Richey	Lt Can RFC CLH kia 24-3-17 CR France 95
LEHMANN,Benno Carl.MC	Lt Aust 3AMGC 21-9-17MR 29
LEICESTER,John Charles	Capt Can CAMC 1stTD 6-8-18 CR Canada 1178
LEIGH,Henry Godfrey Thomas	2Lt SA LabCps &SAFA 11-11-18 CR France 34
LeLIEVRE,Roger Horace	Lt CanRAF QRD 31-8-18CR Middx 66
LEMARCHAND,F.L.J.	Lt SeychellesCarrierCps6-1-19 MR 65
LeMESURIER,George Stuart	Lt Can 24Bn 11-6-16CR Belgium 453
LeMESURIER,Henry Vernon.MC&Bar.	Lt Can RCD dow 18-4-18 CR France 145
LEMIEUX,Louis Jules Rodolphe.MC	LtCan 22Bn dow 29-8-18 CR France 14
LE MOTTEE,Jack Beaumont.MID	Maj NZ6/820 NZEF CIR 13Coy 8-7-19 CR London 12
LE NAY,Louis Leon.MID	Capt Aust 11Inf kia 10-8-18 CR France 526
LENEHAM,Robert Eric	Lt Aust AFA 1Bde 10-5-16CR Aust 40
LENNON,John	Lt Aust 22Inf kia 9-6-18 CR France 196
LENNOX,Charles Simpson	Lt Can116Bn 24-7-17CR France 924
LeNOEL,Noel Edwin	2Lt NZ 12/581 AuklandR ded 14-2-22
LEONARD,Arthur Vincent	Capt Can CAMC drd 27-6-18 MR 24
LEONARD,Edwin Woodman.DSO.MID	LtCol Can CFA 3Bde dow 9-4-17 CR France 88
LEONARD,John.MC.	Lt Can 75/1COR 13-7-18MR 23
LEPPER,Basil Ray	Lt Can CFA 13Bde kia 27-9-18 CR France 274
LeQUESNE,Robert	Lt NZ 15/204 TrpshpsStaff `Mokoia' ded 4-12-19 CR NZ 251
Le-ROY,Osmond Edgar	Capt Can 46Bn 28-10-17 CR Belgium 3
LESLIE,Alexander Henry	Lt Aust 18Inf 20-9-17MR 29
LESLIE,Charles Austin	2Lt Aust 60Bn 12-5-17MR 26
LESLIE,Edwin Thornton	Lt Can 38Bn dow 30-11-16 CR France 145

LESLIE,Ernest Hodgson	Capt Can 47Bn ded 16-3-19 CR Cheshire 142
LESLIE,Francis Aylwin	Capt&Adjt Aust 15Bn 11-4-17MR 26
LESLIE,Gordon Franklin	Lt Can 46Bn 26-10-17 CR Belgium 308
LESLIE,Ronald Douglas.MID	Lt Aust 26Inf dow 5-11-16 CR France 744
LESLIE,Walter Aland	Capt AustAFA 3Bde dow 6-5-15 CR Gallipoli 22
LESLIE,William Brown	Lt Can 44Bn 28-9-18CR France 714
LESLIE,William Leichhardt	Lt Aust 18Inf kia 22-8-15 MR 6
LESTER,Edward Gabriel	Lt Can 102Bn 25-6-17CR France 102
LESTER,John William	Lt Can73QuebecR 1-3-17 MR 23
LETCH,Harold Alexander.MC.	Lt Aust AFC 1Sqn kia 22-8-18 CR Palest 9
LETCHFORD,Charles Thomas Kenneth	2Lt SA 2SAInf kia 20-7-16 CR France 402
LETOURNEAU,Adjutor	Lt Can 22QuebecR9-8-18 MR 23
LETTE,Alfred D.	Lt Aust AIF 3ALH 3-9-19 CR Aust 410
LEUNIG,James Henry.DCM.	2Lt Aust 16Inf ded 10-9-18 CR France 52
LEVETUS,Arthur	Lt Aust 28Bn 29-7-16MR 26
LEVI,Keith Maurice.MID	Capt Aust AAMC 1GH kia 7-8-15 CR Gallipoli 6
LEVIN,William Fitz Gerald	Maj NZ 11/787 DHQ dow 25-12-15 CR Egypt 6
LEVINGSTON,Alfred	HCapt&QM Aust 11ALH ded 17-11-17 CR Palest 2
LEVY,Hilton Sydney	Lt Aust 35Inf 12-10-17 MR 29
LEWINGTON,Ronald Walter	Lt Can19Bn 27-8-18CR France 419
LEWIS,Cecil Charles	2Lt Aust AFC dedacc 14-8-18 CR Glouc 172
LEWIS,David Llewellyn	Capt Can 18CMR ded 12-11-18 CR Canada 17
LEWIS,E.S.DCM.	2Lt Aust 10Inf 2-10-17CR Belgium 113
LEWIS,Frederick George	Lt Aust42Inf kia 1-9-18 CR France 624
LEWIS,George Lloyd	Lt Can RCR kia 16-9-16 MR 23
LEWIS,Henry Francis	Lt Can44Bn 12-4-17CR France 924
LEWIS,John Simon	Maj Can 87Bn kia 18-11-16 CR France 150
LEWIS,Leslie Forbes	Lt Aust AFA 12Bde dow 5-5-17 CR France 512
LEWIS,Owen Gower	Lt Aust AFC 3Sqn kia 12-4-18 CR France 71
LEWIS,Robert James	Capt Aust 25Inf kia 18-6-16 CR Belgium 48
LEWIS,Samuel Eldridge	Lt NZ 22906 4/3NZRB G'Coy kia 5-4-18 MR 12
LEWIS,Spencer Herbert	Capt Can 1CMR (SR) kia 5-6-16 MR 29
LEWIS,Stanley Edward	Lt Can 10AR 24-5-15MR 23
LEWTAS,Frank Gordon	Lt Can BCRD &RAF kldacc 21-4-18 CR Lancs 368 102Bn(2COR)
LEYS,James Robert Ruxton.MC.	TCapt NZ 15/557A EntBn 3 OtagoR dow 17-4-18 CR Belgium 38
LEYSHON,T.St.L.	Capt SA SAMC ded 22-5-18 CR EAfrica 77
LIARDET,Leonard Maughan	Capt NZ24/10 3/3NZRB dow 3-10-16 CR France 40
LICK,Vernon Cuthbert	Lt Can 116Bn kia 23-7-17 CR France 68
LIDDELOW,Aubrey	Capt Aust 59Inf kia 19-7-16 MR 7
LIEBSEN,S.MC.	Capt SA SAMC kia 22-3-18
LIGHTBODY,Cluny James	Lt Can PPCLI 1-1-17 CR Belgium 11
LILBURNE,Arthur Melville.MC.	LtAust AFA 6Bde ded 11-7-18 CR Surrey 1
LIMA,Bertram Lewis.KBE.Sir	Capt Can ExpedForce 24-2-19CR London 12
LIMB,Arthur.MIDx2	Lt Aust AIF 10Inf 7-5-20 CR Aust 245
LIMERICK,St.Ian	Lt SA10SAInf dow 17-8-16
LINDEMAN,Frank William	Maj Aust 1Inf dow 23-7-16 CR France 515
LINDSAY,Arthur Lodge	Lt Can 16Bn (MR) 22-4-15MR 29
LINDSAY,Thomas James Edwin	Lt Aust 45Inf kia 5-4-18 CR France 197
LINDUS,Leonard Tasker	Lt Aust26Bn 29-7-16MR 26
LINEHAM,Albert	Lt Can 102Bn dow 10-4-17 CR France 12
LINES,Roland Walter	Lt CanCE 1FC kia 9-9-16 CR France 430
LINFORD,Harry Alfred James.MID	2Lt Aust ImpCamelCps AustBn kia 9-1-17 CR Egypt 2
LINFORTH,Arthur Tippins	Lt Can 52MR 16-9-16MR 23
LINKLATER,Charles Henry.MC.	Capt Aust 33Inf 11-6-17MR 29
LINNELL,Henry Rupert.DSO.MID	Maj Can 78MR 11-8-18MR 23
LINSLEY,Gordon.MC.	Lt Aust AFA 10Bde dow 7-4-18 CR France 62
LINTON,Lloyd Clarke	Lt Can RCR ded 14-11-19 CR Canada 116
LINTON,Richard	Col Aust Cmdg6Inf ded 2-9-15 CR Greece 10
LINTOTT,Arthur Newton	Lt AustAFA 10Bde dow 9-8-18 CR France 71
LISTER,Charles Roy	Capt Aust AAMC 2GH ded 21-11-18 CR France 34

LISTER,William Roberts.MC.	Lt Can 1Bn dow 3-5-17 CR France 95
LITTLE,James Hector	Lt Can20Bn kia 9-4-17 CR France 68
LITTLE,Leonard William	Lt Can 8Bn 9-8-18 CR France 693
LITTLE,Neville Hall	Capt Can CAMC 13FA dow 29-10-18 CR France 113
LITTLE,Nevill Montague	2Lt Aust 49Bn 3-9-16 MR 26
LITTLER,Charles Augustus.DSO.	Capt Aust 52Bn 3-9-16 MR 26
LIVINGSTON,Daniel Archibald.MM.	Lt Can 25Bn kia 7-4-18 CR France 174
LIVINGSTON,Hugh D'Alton	Lt Can 116Bn 27-8-18CR France 154
LIVINGSTONE,Alexander Renel	Lt NZ 12553 CMR kia 25-11-17 MR 34
LIVINGSTONE,Charles Donald	Maj Can 1CMR 12-10-16 CR France 832
LIVINGSTONE,David	Lt Can 1MMGBde 10-10-18 CR France 147
LIVINGSTONE,Harry Montague	Capt Can 18Bn 1922
LIVINGSTONE,Hugh Douglas	Lt Can 2Bn kia 27-7-18 CR France 174
LLOYD,Albert.MC.	Lt Can87Bn 3-9-18 CR France 310
LLOYD,Arthur Stephen Kenyon	Lt Can 28SasR kia 7-5-17 MR 23
LLOYD,Charlewood Derwent.MC.	Capt Can 13QuebecR 1-10-18MR 23
LLOYD,John Lewis	Lt Can 102Bn kia 8-8-18 CR France 589
LLOYD,Lionel Bertie Eld	Lt Can CMR &RAF CR Dorset 109
LLOYD,Robert Boutillier.DCM.	Lt Can 26Bn 25-9-18CR France 481
LLOYD,William Thomas	Capt NZ14/144 NZSC ded 26-11-19 CR NZ 1
LOCKE,John Henry Thomas	Capt SA8SAInf D'Coy dow 28-3-16 CR EAfrica 56
LOCKHART,Frank Edwin	Lt Can 26Bn (NBR) 6-4-16 MR 29
LOCKHART,Henry William E.	Capt Can CAMC 7SH 11-10-18 CR Canada 360
LOCKHART,Herbert Franklin	Lt Can 85Bn 10-8-18CR France 586
LOCKHART,Thomas Downie	Lt Can 1Bn (WOR) 23-4-15MR 29 Downey
LOCKHART,William Eric	Lt CanCE 2DivSigCoy &RFC12-6-17CR France 31
LOCKLEY,Alexander Hamilton	Lt Aust AFC 4Sqn kia 5-9-18 CR France 924
LOFT,Arthur	Lt Can 44Bn (NBR) kia 28-10-17 MR 29
LOGAN,Preston	Lt NZ 13/155 AMR dow 22-5-15 MR 6
LOGAN,Thomas Edgar	Lt Can RAF NSRDdedacc 22-11-18 CR Canada 818
LOGAN,Thomas James	Maj Aust 2ALH kia 7-8-15 CR Gallipoli 8
LONGLEY,Lloyd Ernest	Lt Can RCR kia 26-8-18 CR France 427
LOGHRIN Samuel Monteith	Maj Can 18WOR 15-9-16MR 23
LONGMAN,John Miller	Lt Can 87QuebecR 21-10-16 MR 23
LONGSTREET,Selby Brittan	Lt Can 19Bn 9-4-17 CR France 68
LONGWORTH,Frederick John.MC.	Lt Can CFA 9Bde dow 10-11-18 CR Belgium 214
LONGWORTH,J.A.	2Lt Aust 34Inf 12-10-17 CR Belgium 125
LONSDALE,Frank Leslie	Capt Aust17Inf dow 28-9-15 CR Europe 1
LONSDALE,Walter	2Lt NZ 23/814 NZRB 3Bde dow 19-9-16 CR France 52
LOPTSON,Svienbjorn.MC.MM.	Lt Can PPCLI 29-9-18CR France 481
LORAM,Stanley Arthur	2Lt Aust AFC 3Sqn kia 15-6-18 CR France 71
LORD,John Stone W.	2Lt Aust AFC dedacc 12-5-18 CR Hamps 167
LORIE,Arnold.MID.	2Lt NZ 12/2556 3AIR 6Coy kia 28-12-17 MR 8
LORIMER,Kenneth	Lt Can 4BnCMGC 8-8-18 CR France 589
LORY,J.J.	Capt SA MilLabCps12-12-18 CR EAfrica 36
LOUDON,Brian Melville	Lt Can 15Bn kia 1-9-18 CR France 687
LOUDON,Walter John	Capt Can 102Bn 23-1-21CR WIndies 10
LOUIS,Reginald Hinton	Lt Can 49Bn 13-4-17CR France 12
LOUW,M.H.H.	Lt SA MtdCmdos ded 27-3-15 CR SAfrica 44
LOVE,Hugh Thomas Mercer	Lt Can 102Bn ded 15-5-20 CR Canada 180
LOVEDAY,Arthur Collins	Lt Aust 28Inf dow 12-8-18 CR France 119
LOVELAND,Henry	Lt Can 78Bn attRFCkld 2-4-17 CR France 407
LOVETT,G.T.	Capt Aust 8Inf 1-8-18 CR France 25
LOVETT,Norman Beresford.MC&Bar.	Capt Aust 54Inf kia 9-4-18 CR France 1173
LOWDEN,Cedric Lloyd Charles	2Lt Aust 36Inf19-7-17MR 29
LOWDEN,J.H.	Lt SA 7SAInf kia 11-3-16 CR EAfrica 56
LOWE,James Watt.MC.	Capt Can 46Bn 21-8-17CR France 81
LOWE,Margaret	Nurse Can CANS 1GH dow 28-5-18 CR France 40
LOWES,John Wasdale	Lt Can 28Bn kia 11-10-18 CR France 761
LOWIE,J.B.	ChOff Can MercMar SS`Pomeranian' 15-4-18MR 24

LOWRIE,George	Lt Can 102Bn kia 8-6-17 CR France 81
LOWTHER,Eric Lionel	2Lt Aust 17Bn 27-7-16MR 26
LUCAS,Alfred	Lt Aust AIF 2DAC 20-2-19CR Aust 323
LUCAS,Arthur	2Lt Aust 27Inf kia 2-3-17 CR France 385
LUCAS,Charles Daniel	Lt Aust 12Inf kia 25-7-16 CR France 832
LUCAS,David Elmer	Lt SA2SAInf kia 21-9-17 MR 29
LUCAS,Frederick Travers	Maj Can 54Bn 1-3-17 CR France 81
LUETCHFORD,Donovan Frank.MM.	2Lt Aust 48Inf kia 3-5-18 CR France 144
LUMB,Edward Frank	Lt Aust 20Inf 9-10-17MR 29
LUMLEY,Corale	Nurse NZ VAD 25-11-18 NZ 243
LUMSDEN,Walter Gerald	Lt Can 38Bn 18-11-16 CR France 150
LUNN,Geoffrey Cyril	Lt Can29Bn 30-5-18CR France 504
LURY,George Henry	2Lt NZ 12/2021 1AIR kia 29-8-18 CR France 512
LUSCOMBE,Claud Leslie	Lt Aust 13Inf kia 1-3-18 CR Belgium 131
LUTHER,John Fitzmaurice Guy	Capt Aust 15Inf dow 25-8-15 CR Gallipoli 19
LUTON,William Franklin	Capt Can CAMC 20-10-18 CR Glouc 9
LUTZ,Roy Courtney	Lt Can 10Bn 10-9-16CR France 430
LUXFORD,John Aldred.CMG.MIDx2	Chpn LtCol NZ 8/307A Chpns ded 28-1-21 CR NZ 224
LUXTON,Clarence James	Capt Aust 6Inf kia 26-4-15 CR Gallipoli 18
LUXTON,Robert Jackson	Lt Aust 15Bn 11-4-17MR 26
LYDDON,F.C.	Lt IA IAUL att4LpoolRkia 26-4-15 CR Belgium 4
LYDDON,Hugh Edmund	Lt Aust Engrs 1FC4-10-17MR 29
LYDON,Frederick Luke	LtCol Can 51CanMilitia ded 10-9-17 CR Canada 256
LYE,Alfred Edward Hilton	Lt Can FGH 26-2-18CR France 446
LYE,George Thomas	Lt Can 85Bn C'Coy kld 25-9-18 CR France 1182
LYLE,Haydon Stratton.MC.	Capt Can 2CMR kia 6-11-18 CR Belgium 203
LYNCH,Cecil Audley	Lt NZ 27689 1AIR dow 1-8-17 CR France 102
LYNCH,George David	Maj Can 16MR 8-10-16MR 23
LYNCH,William Henry	2Lt 226 Aust 4Inf dow 14-8-15 CR Europe 4
LYNE,Claude Hume	Lt&QM Aust 12Inf ded 7-4-16 CR France 1571
LYON,A.R.	Lt Aust AIF 49Inf8-7-20 CR Aust 146
LYON,Allan Herbert Donald	Lt Can MGC 14Coy 10-11-17 MR 29
LYON,Charles Herbert Scott	2Lt Aust 15Inf dow 27-9-17 CR Belgium 11
LYON,Charles Hugh	Lt Aust 3AustBn ImpCamCps kia 7-11-17 CR Palest 1
LYON,Donald	Lt Can 14MGCoy 1917
LYON,Lawrence Gordon	Lt Can RCR 11-9-18CR France 421
LYONS,Howard Maitland	2Lt Aust 42Inf kia 26-2-17 CR France 922
LYONS,John Mahler.MC.MM.MSM.	Lt Aust 17Inf 9-10-17MR 29
LYTTLE,David John Albert	Lt NZ 8/1107 OIR kia 3-5-15 MR 6

M

MAASDORP,A.MC.	2Lt SA HArty 73SB dow 18-4-18 CR France 10
MABEN,Keppoch Macdonald	TCapt NZ 18913 2/3NZRB kia 26-8-18 CR France 518
MACARTHUR,Guy Darcy Davney	Lt Aust 13Inf ded 25-12-15 CR Egypt 9
MACARTHUR,James McPherson	Lt Can 24Bn 9-4-17 CR France 68
MACARTNEY,Donald Halliday	Lt Can PPCLI kia 26-8-18 CR France 421
MACARTNEY,Ernest Eldred	Lt Can2WksBn 28-3-18CR France 81
MACASKILL,William Ross	Lt Can26RBn attRFC 19-6-17CR France 200

MacBEAN,Colin Hendrie.MID	2Lt Aust 10ALH kia 29-8-15 MR 6
MACCALLUM,John Thomson.DCM.	Lt Can 50Bn 10-4-17CR France 1896 McCALLUM
MacCARTHY,Henry Harold	Lt Aust 4Inf kia 23-7-16 CR France 832
MacCOLL,Allan Evan	Maj Can CAMC 5-5-19 CR Canada 1300
MacCUISH,Kenneth Angus	Capt Can CAMC 9FA att5CMR dow 31-10-17 CR Belgium 11
MacDERMOT,Arthur George Cecil	Maj Can 13Bn kia 1-10-18 CR France 597
MACDIARMID,Allan Montrose	Lt Aust 45Bn 5-4-18 MR 26
MACDIARMID,John Campbell	Capt NZ 35940 NZMC ded 18-3-17 CR NZ 258
MacDIARMID,John James	Lt Aust 17Bn 3-5-17 MR 26
MACDONALD,A.W.H.MC.	Capt&QM SA 3SAInf see McDonald,A.W.
MACDONALD,Alexander Farquhar	Lt Can 10Bn 8-4-17 CR France 68
MACDONALD,Alexander Gilmour	Lt Can 102Bn ded 18-5-18 CR Canada 180
MACDONALD,Alexander Warren	Capt Aust 34Inf kia 30-8-18 CR France 511
MACDONALD,Angus Donald	Lt Can 85Bn (NSR) 30-10-17 MR 29
MacDONALD,Archibald Walter	Lt Can 19Bn 15-9-16CR France 1505
MACDONALD,Arthur Robert	2Lt NZ8/2070 2OIR kia 23-1-18 CR Belgium 88
MACDONALD,Clarence Vivian	Lt Capt Can 49Bn Ex56Bnded 28-3-18 CR Canada 543
MacDONALD,Donald.MM.	2Lt SA 4SAInf kia 21-10-17 MR 29 22-10-17
MACDONALD,David Henderson	Lt Aust 11Inf kia 28-6-15 CR Gallipoli 22
MACDONALD,Donald Randolph	Lt Can 29Bn 3-6-18 CR France 504
MACDONALD,Donald Ryerson	Lt Can 18Bn B'Coy kia 16-8-17 CR France 480
MacDONALD,Donald W.	Lt Can 15Bn see McDonald,D.W.
MACDONALD,Frederick Vernon	2Lt SA 1SAInf kia 18-10-16 MR 21
MACDONALD,George Fraser	Lt Can 50Bn 18-11-16 CR France 430
MACDONALD,George Oxley	2Lt Can 63Bn trans toRAF No1SchAero 1-5-18 CR Berks 86
MACDONALD,Graham Bremner	Lt Can 7Bn 12-4-17CR France 64 Brymner
MACDONALD,Hugh John.MM.	Lt Can 16Bn 12-2-19CR Sussex 200
MacDONALD,James Shaw Rose	Capt Aust FA kia 31-7-17 CR Belgium 29
MacDONALD,John Angus.MC.	Lt Can 47Bn 11-11-16 CR France 430
MacDONALD,John Robert	Lt Can 10AR Ex56Bnkia 28-4-17 MR 23
MacDONALD,John William	Lt Can 1WOR 15-6-15MR 23
MacDONALD,Katherine Maud	Nurse Can CANS 1GH kia 19-5-18 CR France 40
MACDONALD,Modo Daniel	Lt Can 3Bn 1915
MACDONALD,Neil	Lt Aust 23Inf dow 29-7-16 CR France 44
MACDONALD,Norman	Capt Aust 13Inf kia 4-2-17 CR France 44
MACDONALD,Norman Macleod	Lt Can 5CMR kia 19-5-16 CR Belgium 5
MACDONALD,Ronald Alexander Leslie	Lt Aust 1ALH kia 9-8-16 CR Egypt 2
MACDONALD,Ronald JohnH	Capt&QM Can 9ResBn 27-7-17CR Surrey 1 202Bn
MACDONALD,Stanley Kenneth Leighton	Lt Can CFA 7Bde 30-9-17CR France 150
MacDONALD,Temple William Faber	Maj Can CGA 2Bde 5SB 2-4-18 CR France 95
MACDONALD,Thomas Howard	LtCol Can CAMC HS drd 27-6-18 MR 24
MACDONALD,Wilfred Charles	Lt Can 16Bn ded 25-6-21 CR Canada 177
MACDONALD,William Campbell	Col Can 1InfBde kldacc 21-1-17 CR Canada 1686
MACDONELL,Ian Cameron	Lt Can LSH RFC 9Sqn 2-7-16 MR 20
MACDONELL,James Alexander.DSO.	LtCol Can 1PnrBn ded 15-6-18 CR Canada 180
MACDONELL,Winfred Smythe	Maj Can CAMC ADMS 15-11-18 CR Surrey 1
MacDONNELL,Leonard Francis	2Lt Aust 26Inf 4-10-17MR 29
MacDONNELL,Wm. Hildige Armstrong	Capt Aust 42Inf kia 3-7-18 CR France 119
MACDOUGALL,Alan Robert Thomas	Lt NZ 8/3132 2OIR kia 15-9-16 MR 11 &CR France 390
MacDOUGALL,Andrew	Lt Can 1CMR (SR) 3-6-16 MR 29
MacDOUGALL,Ewan Alan	Maj Can CFA 3Bde8-5-16 MR 29
MACE,Arthur Bell Esterford	Lt Can 7Bn kia 12-10-16 CR France 430
MACE,William Ralph	Lt Aust 19Inf kia 29-9-15 CR Gallipoli 31
MacEACHEN,Rebecca Helen	Sister Can CAMC ded 16-11-18 CR Canada1 325 McEACHEN R.E.
MacEWAN,John	2Lt SA 4SAInf kia 17-4-18 MR 29
MACFARLANE,Alexander S.MC&Bar.	Lt Can 4DivTMB 27-9-18CR France 482
MACFARLANE,Archibald Henry.MID	Capt Aust 11Bn 22-7-16MR 26
MACFARLANE,Bruce Campbell	Lt Can 60Bn kia 3-6-16 MR 29
MacFARLANE,Duncan Buchanan	Capt NZ23/7 3/3NZRB kia 7-6-17 MR 9
MACFARLANE,Edward MacFarlane	Capt Aust 3Inf dow 2-8-15 MR 6

MACFARLANE,James Edward	2Lt Aust AFA 10Bdedow 30-7-18 CR France 71	
MACFARLANE,James Lennox real name WHITE,Eric Edward	Lt Can BCR attRFC 17-8-17CR Belgium 140	
MacFARLANE,John Reginald Norman	Capt Can HQ CFC Ex CanCpsCycBn ded 22-2-19 CR Middx 42	
MACGREGOR,Alexander	Capt Can 28Bn 9-8-18 CR France 649	
MacGREGOR,Archibald Robert	Capt Can 15Bn 24-4-15CR Belgium 115	
MacGREGOR,George Everett	Lt Can87QuebecR18-11-16 MR 23	
MacGREGOR,Harold Philip.MC.	Lt Can 73QuebecR 1-3-17 MR 23	
MacGROTTY,Francis Alexander	Lt Can 116Bn 25-12-17 CR France 223	
MACHATTIE,Daniel Hay	Capt NZ 17/250 NZVC doi 20-12-16 CR Egypt 9	
MACHIN,Roland Frank Charles	2Lt AustAFC dow 18-9-18 CR France 327	
MACHUM,Ronald Sutherland	Lt Can 52Bn dow 28-8-18 CR France 14	
MACINTOSH,A.	Maj Can 16Bn 28-4-17CR France 68	
MACINTOSH,John Fullarton.MC.	Capt Can 28Bn kia 1-10-18 CR France 715	
MacINTOSH,William Alexander	2Lt Aust 26Bn 14-11-16 MR 26	
MACK,Brian Hamilton	Capt Aust AAMC 7FA kia 10-4-17 CR France 1484	
MACK,Ernest Harold	Lt Aust 8ALH dow 23-12-16 CR Egypt 2	
MACK,Joseph Sub	Lt Aust RANattDport Div HMS`Defence'kia 31-5-16 MR 2	
MACK JOST,Norman Roy	Lt Can 9ResBn att49Bn (AR) dow 3-6-16 MR 29	
MACKAY,Adam Bruce.MC.	2Lt Aust 42Inf dow 4-4-18 CR France 71	
MacKAY,Alexander Henry	Lt Can 5Bn 22-5-15MR 23	
MacKAY,Alexander Herbert R.MC.	Capt Can 5Bn kia 12-4-17 CR France 570	
MacKAY,Arthur Gordon	Lt Can 20RBn attRFCkia 18-5-17 CR France 1182	
MacKAY,Atwood Talbot.DSO.	Maj CanCFA 2Bde 26-10-18 CR France 34	
MACKAY,David Glen	Lt Aust 39Inf dow 5-10-17 CR France 285	
MacKAY,Donald Aylmer	Maj Can 87Bnm 1920	
MacKAY,Donald Roy	Capt Can 4CMR 5-12-15CR Belgium 339	
MACKAY,Francis Edward Maxwell.MM.	2Lt Aust 10MGC 12-10-17 MR 29	
MacKAY,John	Lt Can PPCLI 3-10-18CR France 214	
MacKAY,MacKay	Lt Can PPCLI dow 27-8-18 CR France 14	
MACKAY,Murdoch Nish.MID.	Maj Aust 22Inf kia 4-8-16 CR France 832	
MACKAY,Peter	2Lt NZ 9/305OMR kia 7-8-15 MR 5	
MACKAY,Reay	Capt Can 26NBR 27-8-18MR 23	
MACKEDIE,Alan Reginald	Capt Can18Bn kia 28-8-18 CR France 421	
MacKENDRICK,Gordon King	Lt Can 58/2COR 8-10-16MR 23	
MACKENZIE,A.R.	Capt SA 8SAInf ded 16-11-17 CR SAfrica 53	
MACKENZIE,Arthur Cobcroft	Capt Aust 1Inf kia 23-7-16 CR France 832	
MacKENZIE,C.M.	Capt SA SASC 20-7-15CR SAfrica 171	
MACKENZIE,Donald Alvin.MM.	Lt Can CFA attRAF 10Sqn kia 28-10-18 CR Belgium 159	
MacKENZIE,George Lawrence Bisset	Lt Can 3Bn kia 7-6-16 CR Belgium 11	
MacKENZIE,Gordon Alexander Gordon	Lt Can 16MR kia 22-5-15 MR 23	
MacKENZIE,Harry Stuart	Lt Can78Bn kia 24-8-18 CR France 586	
MacKENZIE,Hector	Lt Can 50Bn dow 21-8-17 CR France 12	
MacKENZIE,Ian Russell.DSO.	Lt SA 2CapeCps ded 13-9-17 CR EAfrica 75 dow	
MACKENZIE,John.MID.	Lt NZ 12/160 2AIR dow 22-2-17 CR France 768	
MACKENZIE,John Gladstone	Capt Aust AAMC 6FA kia 21-5-16 CR France 275	
MacKENZIE,Kenneth Gordon	Maj Can 102Bn 20-11-16 CR France 430	
MACKENZIE,Ronald	2Lt Aust 20Inf kia 30-7-16 CR France 832	
MacKENZIE,Ross MacAulay	Capt Can 85Bn (NSR) 28-10-17 MR 29	
MacKENZIE,Ulric Knut	Capt SA 10SAInf A'Coy dow 8-9-16 CR Tanzania 1 &EAfrica 4	
MacKENZIE,Wallace Alexander	Lt Can 8Bn (MR) 25-4-15MR 29	
MacKENZIE,William Arthur	Lt Can 1Bn kia 6-11-17 CR Belgium 125	
MacKEOWN,W.J.F.	Capt SA BrSAPol	
MACKESY,Henry Frederick Ernest	2Lt NZ 13/254 AMR 4Coy kia 7-8-15 CR Gallipoli 20	
MACKEY,William Herbert	Lt Can21Bn 5-10-18CR France 34	
MACKIE,Arthur George	Lt Can 72BCR 9-4-17 MR 23	
MACKIE,Douglas Cecil.MC.MID	2Lt SA 1SAInf kia 19-7-18 CR France 25	
MACKIE,James Matthew.DCM.	Lt Can 27Bn &RAF 25Sqn 16-7-18MR 20	
MacKINLAY,Thomas Hart	Lt Can 29Bn dow 26-10-16 CR France 102	
MacKINNON,Aubrey	Lt Can 85Bn 21-3-18CR France 547	

MacKINNON,Ian.MID	Capt Can 43MR attMGC 9Coy 8-10-16MR 23
MacKINNON,John Younger	Lt Aust 4Inf kia 6-8-15 CR Gallipoli 7
MACKINTOSH,Arthur	Maj Can 16Bn 1917
MacKINTOSH,Charles Alexander	2Lt SA 1SAInf kia 10-4-18 MR 29
MacKINTOSH,Peter McLeod	Lt Can 67PnrBn dow 10-9-16 CR Belgium 11
MACKINTOSH,W.A.	Lt SA 8SA Inf dow 21-3-18 CR EAfrica 13 12Reg
MACKY,Thomas Roy Bayntun	2Lt NZ 25/73 1OIR kia 11-10-17 MR 30
MacLACHLAN,James S.	Lt Can 5CMR 14-10-16 CR France 832 Gill
MacLACHLAN,Ninian	2Lt NZ 40155 2WIR kia 27-8-18 CR France 239
MacLAURIN,Henry Normand.MID	Col Aust 1BdeHQ kia 27-4-15 CR Gallipoli 24
MacLAURIN,Howard James	Lt Can 16Bn 14-6-16CR Belgium 11
MACLEAN,Alan Pratt	Capt Can 20Bn &RFC 11Sqn18-3-18MR 20
MacLEAN,Arthur Smith	Lt Can 13Bn dow 15-8-17 CR France 178 McLEAN
MacLEAN,Charles Alexander	Lt Can 46Bn ded 14-9-20 CR Canada 457
MACLEAN,Donald.MID	Lt Can PPCLI kia 5-7-17 CR France 81
MACLEAN,Ewen Lawrence B.	Lt Can 5Bn see McLean,E.L.B.
MACLEAN,Henry Sorley	2Lt NZ 11152 2OIR kia 1-10-16 CR France 385
MACLEAN,John Clark.MC&Bar.	Capt NZ 9/663OIR attRE 235LtRlyCoy dow23-1-19 CR France 1029 acckld
MacLEAN,Norman MacLeod	Capt Can 13Bn kia 8-8-18 CR France 489
MacLEAN,Reginald Leopold	Lt Aust19Inf ded 2-11-18 CR NIreland 33
MACLEAN,Walter Leonard	Maj Can CAMC 1CCS kld 10-11-17 CR France 1361
MACLEAN,William Norman.MC&Bar.	Maj Can 29Bn dow 7-3-19 CR Scot 756 Capt
MacLENNAN,William	2Lt NZ 2/200 FA kia 28-5-17 CR Belgium 43
MacLEOD,David Douglas	Capt Can 49Bn A'Coy dow 8-6-16 CR France 40
MACLEOD,Kenneth Alexander	Lt Aust 13Inf kia 3-5-15 MR 6
MACLEOD,Margaret Christine	Nurse Can CAMC 2GH ded 20-12-19 CR Canada 644
MACLEOD,Murdoch Keith	2Lt NZ 22439 CIR 2CanterburyR dow 13-10-17 CR Belgium 3
MACLEOD,Norwood	Lt Can CFA attRFC14-10-17 CR Belgium 16
MACLEOD,Talisker Donald	Lt Aust3Inf kia 6/8-8-15 MR 6
MacMILLAN,Alexander Pearson.MC.	Lt Can 1CMR kia 26-8-18 CR France 1189
MacMILLAN,Michael Allan	Lt Can1CMR 9-4-17 CR France 523
MacMILLAN,Thomas Muir	2Lt SA 4SAInf kia 19-8-17 CR France 662
MACMORRAN,James	Capt NZ 10/2371 1WIR kia 30-8-18 CR France 512
MacMULLEN,E.R.	Lt EA UL EA 30-6-16CR EAfrica 2
MACNAMARA,Brian.MC.	Lt Aust FA 10Bty 4Bde kia 8-10-17 CR Belgium 5
MacNAMARA,William James	Capt Can 3Bn kia 14-6-16 CR Belgium 11
MACNAUGHTON,Ian Robert R.	Lt Can 24Bn 26-4-16CR Belgium 28
MACNEE,Thomas Rodger	Capt Aust 36Inf kia 12-4-18 CR France 526
MACNEIL,Charles Herman	Lt Can MRD &RFC kld 27-10-17 CR Norfolk 255 Flt Lt
MacNEIL L,James Grant.MC.	Capt Can CAMC 6FA kia 12-10-18 CR France 241
MacNEVIN,William Gordon	Capt CanCADC 3-2-18 CR Canada 1132
MACOSO,P.D.	Lt SA 2SARif ded 6-7-20
MacPHAIL,Donald George	ChpnH Capt CanChpnServs att72Bn drd 27-6-18 CR France 1809
MACPHERSON,Agnes.RRC.	Nurse Can CANS 3SH 30-5-18CR France 84
MACPHERSON,Allister Ewen	Lt NZ 41211 2/3NZRB dow 26-8-18 CR France 518
MACPHERSON,Charles Kenneth	Lt Can42Bn 25-10-17 CR Belgium 10
MACPHERSON,Christopher Salmon	Lt Can RCR attRAF 18-9-18CR Cambs 16
MacPHERSON,Huntley Wilson.MC.MID	Maj Can RCHA kia 10-10-18 CR France 441
MACPHERSON,John Ross.DSO.MID	Capt Can PPCLI kia 26-8-18 CR France 421
MacPH ERSON,Joseph Louis	Lt Can 31Bn 15-9-16CR France 832 MACPHERSON
MACQUEEN,James.MC.MID	Capt SA 2RhodR ded 14-12-17 CR EAfrica 1
MacRAE,Malcolm.MC.	Lt Can 1CMR dow 29-9-18 CR France 243
MACRAE,Norman	Maj Aust 4Pnrs kia 2-10-17 CR Belgium 19
MACRAE,Norman Farquhar	Capt Aust 28Bn 29-7-16MR 26
MADDEN,Norman John.MC.	Lt Aust 22Inf kia 18-8-18 CR France 526
MADDOCK,John.MM.	2Lt Aust 9Inf kia 18-9-18 CR France 375
MADELL,Edward Rupert	2Lt Aust FA 1Bde dow 22-8-17 CR Belgium 11
MADILL,Ralph Mackenzie	Lt Can 9ResBn attRFC 21-7-17CR France 285
MAGNAN,Joseph A.	Capt Can CAMC ded 12-11-19 CR Canada 274
MAGNUSSON,Oscar	2Lt NZ 14026 3WIR kia 4-10-17 CR Belgium 128

MAGUIRE,Gordian Francis(Frank)	Capt Can 2Bn 2Coy kia 21-9-16 CR France 430
MAGUIRE,John Timothy.MC.	Lt Aust8Inf 4-10-17MR 29
MAHAN,Adam George	Maj NZ 13/2001 1AIR kia 4-10-17 MR 30
MAHARG,Ivan Clark	Lt Can 1CMR 29-9-18CR France 405
MAHONEY,Christopher Richard	2Lt Aust 43Bn 1-9-18 MR 26
MAHONEY,Daniel	Capt Can CAMC ded 1-1-19 CR Canada 180
MAHONEY,Timothy	Lt Aust 40Bn 30-8-18MR 26
MAHONY,John Austin.MC.	Capt Aust 24Inf dow 9-10-18 CR France 446
MAIN,Charles Teesdale	2Lt Aust 35Inf 12-10-17 MR 29
MAIN,Eric Claude	2Lt Aust 52Bn 3-9-16 MR 26
MAINARD,T.J.	2Lt Aust 8Inf 25-10-17 CR Belgium 125
MAINSTONE,Arthur.MM.	Lt Aust 19Inf 15-3-18MR 29
MAIONI,Louis Robert.MC.	Lt Can 2BnCE dow 29-9-18 CR France 214
MAIR,Edward Hugh	Capt Aust 58Inf kia 15-7-16 CR France 525
MAIR,James Knox	Lt Can 52Bn kia 28-8-18 CR France 421
MAISEY,Frederick Thomas	Lt Aust3Inf 2-9-18 CR France 145
MAITLAND-DOUGALL,William McKinstry	Lt Can `Dolphin' HMSub D3 kia 15-3-18 MR 25
MAJOR,Albert Frederick	Lt Can 14Bn 3-6-16 CR Belgium 127
MAJOR,Henry Lawrence	Lt Can 116Bn 15-6-17CR Glouc 9
MAKEHAM,Charles Edgar	2Lt NZ 23/818 4/3NZRB kia 12-9-18 CR France 662
MAKIN,George Leslie	Lt Aust 5Inf dow 8-9-18 CR France 145
MAKIN,Joseph	2Lt NZ 10/2497 1WIR kia 30-9-18 CR France 1483
MALCOLM,Alexander	Lt Can 43Bn 5-4-17 CR France 1321
MALCOLM,George	2Lt NZ 419814/3NZRBkia 28-3-18 CR France 156
MALCOLMSON,George	Lt SA 8Horse kia 9-8-16 MR 50
MALE,Eric Charles	2Lt SA 4SAInf kia 20-7-18 MR 323
MALLETT,Cecil Alfred	Chpn NZ 7/779 Chpns doi 30-9-18 CR France 40 70779
MALLETT,Stanley.MID	Lt SA 3SAInf dow 17-10-16 CR France 515 kia
MALLOCH,William John Ogilvie	LtCol Can 4GH ded 18-2-19 CR Canada 1688 2DistDepot
MALONE,Edmond Leo.MC.	Lt NZ 11/699 WIR dow 6-4-18 CR France 64 1/3NZRB
MALONE,John Thomas	HCapt Can 185Bn ded 9-12-16 CR Canada 745
MALONE,Maurice Edward	Lt Can 15Bn dow 3-6-16 CR Belgium 11
MALONE,William George.MIDx2.	LtCol NZ 10/1039 WIR kia 8-8-15 MR 5
MALONEY,John Francis	Lt Can 21Bn (EOR) 9-11-17MR 29
MALPAS,Harold Egerton	Lt Aust MGC 7Coy 7-8-16 MR 26
MANDERS,Frank Arnold	2Lt Aust 3Pnrs kia 4-3-17 CR France 922
MANDERS,Neville	Col NZ DDMS(Anzac) AMS kia 9-8-15 CR Gallipoli 20
MANDY,G.J.S	2Lt SA 2SAInf kia 8-12-17 CR France 439
MANGAN,Robert Russell	Lt Can 2Bn 2-4-17 CR France 68
MANGER,W.D.S.	Capt Aust 5Inf 21-7-15CR London 1
MANLEY,John Fitzpayne	Lt Can 72Bn 9-4-17 CR France 548
MANNING,Charles Edge.MID	Maj Aust 24Inf kia 7-8-16 CR France 515
MANNING,Frederick Charles	Lt Can 85Bn dow 15-4-17 CR France 64
MANNING,Gerry Owen	Capt Aust AIF 1TropicalForce 18-6-15CR PNG 1
MANNING,Godfrey George	Capt Aust 4Pnrs kia 8-8-18 CR France 526
MANNING,Leslie Ivan.MC.MID.	Lt NZ 24/1906 2/3NZRB kia 26-8-18 CR France 518
MANSFIELD,C.G.C.	2Lt SA 4SAInf kia 20-12-17 CR France 439
MANSFIELD,Herbert Alfred	Capt Aust 11Bn 22/25-7-16 MR 26
MANSFIELD,R.G.R.	Capt CanPPCLI kia 26-1-15 CR Belgium 111 served as FITZGERALD
MANSFIELD,William Henry	2Lt NZ 6/868 MGC 2Coy dow 7-6-17 CR France 285
MANTLE,Alfred Frank	Maj Can 28SasR ded 11-7-19 CR Canada 256
MANUEL,Samuel	2Lt Can 1RNewfndlandR dow 4-3-17 CR France 105
MANVILLE,Alfred John	Capt Can 15ResBn 1919
MARCHANT,Frederic Norman	Capt&QM NZ 7/89 CMR dow 31-12-16 CR Egypt 2
MARCHBANK,Ogilvie James	Lt Can CE attRAF2-6-18 CR Wilts 3
MARCOSO,P.D.	Lt SA 2SARif 6-7-20 CR SAfrica 52
MARDON,A.W.L.	Lt SA 2CapeCpskia 22-5-18 CR EAfrica 77
MARê,Benjamin Paulus Bernardo	Lt SA ProtGarR ded 21-10-18 CR SAfrica 1
MARGETTS,Ivor Stephen.MID	Capt Aust 12Bn 24-7-16MR 26
MARJASON,Leonard	Lt Aust 18Inf kia 27-8-15 CR Gallipoli 17

Name	Rank	Force	Unit	Date	Location
MARKHAM,Ralph Farrar	Capt	Can	16Bn	19-8-15	CR France 922
MARKHAM-MILLS,Frederic Charles	Lt	Aust	AFC 2Sqn	ded 18-12-18	CR France 457
MARKWELL,William Ernest.DSO.MID	Maj	Aust	2ALH	kia 31-10-17	CR Palest 1
MARPLE,Sydney	Lt	Can	52Bn	28-6-17	CR France 32
MARPOLE,Clarence Mawson	Capt	Can	3CRT	ded 16-7-18	CR Canada 180 239Bn
MARRIOTT,Thomas.MC	Maj	SA	2SARif	ded 3-5-20	CR Nhants 30 4-5-20
MARRIOTT,William John	Lt	NZ	6/3214 2CIR	kia 20-9-16	MR 11
MARSDEN,Harry Oswald Furlong	2Lt	NZ	24387 3WIR	kia 4-10-17	CR Belgium 125
MARSDEN,John Burley	Lt	Aust	33Bn	30-3-18	MR 26
MARSDEN,Joseph Stanley	2Lt	NZ	18580 3WIR	kia 4-10-17	MR 30
MARSH,Cyril Godfrey	2Lt	Aust	8ALH	kia 7-8-15	MR 6
MARSHALL,Albert Frederick	HCapt&QM	Can	2GenHosp	26-8-18	CR France 13
MARSHALL,Clarence Beaumont.MID	Lt	Aust	52Inf	kia 25-4-18	CR France 1170
MARSHALL,Francis MacGregor	2Lt	NZ	9/309 1OIR	kia 3-12-17	CR Belgium 84
MARSHALL,Guy L.	Lt	Can	2BnCMGC	1922	
MARSHALL,Harold John	Lt	SA	2SARif	kia 7-9-16	CR EAfrica 40
MARSHALL,John Edmund	2Lt	Aust	6Inf	kia 7-8-15	MR 6
MARSHALL,John James	Capt	Aust	55Inf	kia 27-4-18	CR France 119
MARSHALL,Kenneth Edward Dix	Lt	Aust	38Inf	12-10-17	MR 29
MARSHALL,Roland G.	Capt	Can	28Bn	ded 24-2-20	CR Canada 506
MARSHALL,Walter Sydney	Lt	Can	3PnrBn	4-10-16	CR France 44
MARSHALL,William Renwick.DSO.MID	LtCol	Can	15Bn	kia 19-5-16	CR Belgium 11
MARTELL,Walter Urban.MM.	Lt	Can	85Bn (NSR)	28-10-17	MR 29
MARTELL,William R.	CaptRev	Can	75Bn	14-12-18	CR Canada 811
MARTIN,Alexander Morrison	2Lt	NZ	13/404 AMR	dow 10-9-16	CR Egypt 9
MARTIN,Alick Gregory.MC.	Capt	Can	PPCLI att9RB	23-3-18	CR France 1893
MARTIN,Archibald Farquhar	Capt	Aust	AFA 11Bde	kia 5-4-18	CR France 885
MARTIN,Arthur Anderson.MID.	Maj	NZ	3/1737 NZMC	dow 17-9-16	CR France 300
MARTIN,Charles Henry	Lt	Aust	RFC 4Sqn	17-2-18	MR 26
MARTIN,Charles Stuart.MC.	Capt	Can	42Bn	kia 29-9-18	CR France 481
MARTIN,Ernest Milton	Lt	Aust	24Inf	kia 31-8-18	CR France 511
MARTIN,Frederick John Strange	Lt	Can	58Bn	dow 30-8-18	CR France 14
MARTIN,Frederick William Scott.MM.	Lt	Aust	10Inf	20-9-17	MR 29
MARTIN,John Joseph	Lt	Can	2CMR (1COR)	30-10-17	MR 29
MARTIN,Norman.MC.	Lt	Aust	21AMGC	29-10-17	MR 29
MARTIN,Stanley Frederick Aylwin	Maj	Can	PPCLI	EOR 15-9-16	MR 23
MARTIN,Thomas Henry	2Lt	Aust	21Bn	26-8-16	MR 26
MARTIN,William Stanley	2Lt	Aust	AFC 4Sqn	kia 12-6-18	CR France 180
MARTINEAU,Horace Robert.VC.	Lt	NZ	8/1074 OtagoR	ded 7-4-16	CR NZ 78
MARTYN,Edgar Meath	Lt	Can	RAF	19Bn1918	
MARTYN,Paul Maxwell.MC&Bar.	Lt	Aust	1Pnrs	ded 10-5-18	CR Surrey 1
MARTYR,Frederick	2Lt	Aust	15Bn	8-8-16	MR 26
MARXSEN,Robert	Lt	Aust	57Inf	kia 3-9-18	CR France 1472
MASCHMEDT,Lawrence Phillip	2Lt	Aust	MGC 12Coy	dow 2-10-17	CR Belgium 11
MASON,Eric Wier	Lt	SA	HArty 75SB	dow 12-8-17	CR France 102
MASON,Frederick Ward	2Lt	Aust	19Bn	3-5-17	MR 26
MASON,George Francis	Capt	Can	16Bn 3Coy	kia 1-10-18	CR France 597
MASON,Harry Denver	Lt	Can	67PnrBn	28-4-17	CR France 32
MASON, Morton Joseph.MC.	Capt	Can	16Bn	2-9-18	CR France 687 Morten
MASSEY,Charles Constantine	Lt	NZ	6/969 1CIR	ded 24-11-18	CR NZ 258
MASSEY,Harry Edward Moncrieff	Capt	Aust	52Bn	3-9-16	MR 26
MASSIE,Frank Raymond	Lt	Aust	12ALH	ded 15-10-18	CR Syria 2
MASSIE,Hugh Vaughan.MM.	2Lt	Aust	22Inf	dow PoW 8-3-17	CR France 927
MASSON,Robert Geoffrey	Lt	Can	156Bn &RFC	kia 24-5-17	CR France 705
MASTERS,George.MID.	2Lt	NZ	4/112A Pnrs attRAF	kia 3-4-17	MR 20
MASTERS,Herbert Victor	Lt	AustEngrs	1AnzacWirelessSect	dedacc 15-4-18	CR France 882
MATHER,Elphinstone Forrest S.	Capt	Can	8Bn	kia 9-4-18	CR France 68
MATHER,Leslie Francis Strong.DSO.	LtCol	Aust	Engrs 5Div	23.1.19	CR France 1223
MATHESON,Alexander	Lt	Can	3Bn CMGC	29-9-18	CR France 686 2Bn
MATHESON,Gordon McMichael	Lt	Can	44Bn	kia 10-8-18	CR France 649

MATHESON,R.T.	Lt SA NatalLHorse kia 27-4-15 CR SAfrica 3
MATHISON,Gordon Clunco Mackay	Capt Aust AAMC dow 18-5-15 CR Egypt 3
MATTHEW,Robert Theodore	Lt Can 60Bn 12-8-16CR Belgium 15
MATTHEWS,Alfred James.MC.	Lt Can 1Bn dow 13-6-17 CR France 40
MATTHEWS,Alfred Joseph	Capt Can27Bn 26-2-16CR Belgium 182
MATTHEWS,Charles	Lt Aust 38Inf 12-10-17 MR 29
MATTHEWS,Frederick Wm.Horden.DCM	2Lt Aust 6AMGC kia 8-11-16 CR France 744
MATTHEWS,Harold Stratton	Lt Can CFA 2B de 3-6-16 MR 29 1Bde
MATTHEWS,Henry Edward.MC.	Lt Can CE 3TC 1920
MATTHEWS,John Hilbert	2Lt Aust 14Inf kia 8-8-15 MR 6
MATTHEWS,Robert	Lt Can 60Bn drd 7-5-15 CR Eire 14 &Eire77
MATTHEWS,Walter Fenwick	Lt Aust AFA 13Bde kia 27-5-17 CR France 307
MATTHEWS,William Montague	Lt Can 38Bn 29-9-18CR France 715
MAUDE,Cornwallis Charles Wyndham	2Lt Aust 9ALH kia 13-8-15 CR Gallipoli 11
MAUDE,Edward Andomas	Lt NZ 30106 3/3NZRB kia 17-8-17 CR Belgium 109 Andamas 18-8-17
MAUDSLEY,Arthur James Aloysius.MIDx	2Lt Aust 38Inf kia 31-8-18 CR France 624
MAUGHAN,David Landale	2Lt Aust MGC 14Coy kia 26-9-17 CR Belgium 34
MAUND, Frederick Charles Garland	Lt Can 18Bn 15-9-16MR 23 Frederic
MAUNDER,Darcy Silvester	2Lt Aust 49Bn 5-4-17 MR 26
MAUNSELL,John William	Lt Aust 5Inf kia 9-8-18 CR France 526
MAURICE,Francis Dennison	Lt NZ 6/410 CIR dow 10-5-15 MR 6
MAWDESLEY,Sam	Lt SA 2SAInfded 27-7-19 MR 40
MAWHINNEY,William Lee	Lt Can 54Bn kia 2-3-17 CR France 12
MAWLEY,Gerald	Lt NZ 26/35 4/3NZRBkia 12-10-17 MR 30
MAXFIELD,Gordon Loris.MC.	Capt Aust 24Bn 3-5-17 MR 26
MAXFIELD,Hugh	Lt SA MilLabCps 8-12-18CR EAfrica 36
MAXTED,Spencer Edward	Chpn4Cl Aust att54Inf kia 19/20-7-16 CR France 525
MAXWELL,A.	Cmdr Can MercMar SS`Pomeranian' 15-4-18MR 24
MAXWELL,George Herbert	Maj Can CGA 5SiegeBty 18-2-17CR France 95
MAXWELL,William	Lt Aust 38Inf 12-10-17 MR 29
MAY,George Geoffrey	Lt Can 75Bn 9-4-17 CR France 1896
MAY,Richard William	Lt Aust 42Inf dow 12-2-17 CR France 922
MAY,Royston Kennilworth Sydney	Lt Aust 1Inf ded 16-5-15 CR Egypt 9
MAYERSBETH,Joseph William	Capt Aust 48Inf 12-6-17MR 29
MAYGAR,Leslie Cecil.VC.DSO.VD.	LtColAust 8ALH dow 1-11-17 CR Palest 1
MAYNARD,Charles Henry	2Lt Aust Engrs 2DivSigs ded 25-10-18 CR France 52
MAYNARD,Herbert Harold.MM.	Lt Aust 48Bn 5-4-18 MR 26
MAYNE,George Cuthbert	Lt NZ 7/179 CMR kia 8-8-15 MR 5
MAYNE,Joseph Henry Edwin	Maj SA MilMagistrate 18-2-18CR SAfrica 4
MAYO,George Dyer	Lt NZ 11/104WMR dow 7-8-15 MR 5 kia
McAFEE,Louis Corbin	Lt Can28Bn dow 23-10-18 CR France 214
McALISTER,Douglas William	Lt NZ 22667 1AIR dow 5-4-18 CR France 1013
McALLAN,G.H.	Lt&QM SA SAMC ded 14-12-18 CR SAfrica 69
McALLISTER,Adam	Maj Aust 8ALH dow 7-5-17 CR Egypt 9
McALLISTER,Alexander B.	Lt Can 9CRT 23-9-17CR Belgium 5
McALPINE,Frank.MM.	Lt Can CMGC 18-4-19CR Canada 1386
McALPINE,John Edward	Lt Aust 21Inf dow 10-6-18 CR France 40
McANDIE,David.MC.DCM.MM.MID	Capt Can 10Bn kia 15-8-18 CR France 699
McARTHUR,Arthur Keirley	Capt NZ 12/26232AIR dow 30-3-18 CR France 40 Keirby
McARTHUR,D.MC.	Lt Aust 54Inf 1-9-18 CR France 627
McBANE,Dugald	Capt Can CAMC 1-11-18CR Canada 1104
McBEAN,Herbert William	Lt Aust 40Inf kia 9-5-18 CR France 885
McBEATH,Arthur Groat.MM.	Lt Can78Bn C'Coy dow 4-2-18 CR France 570
McBRADY,Robert W.	Lt Can 141Bn kldacc 2-10-17 CR Canada 1448
McBRIDE,Claude Archibald	Capt Can 2GH 10-10-19 CR Canada 1255 CADC
McBRIDE,James.MID	Lt Aust Engrs 1FCkia 13-9-16 CR Belgium 127
McBRIDE,Norman Harold	Lt Aust 3ALH kia 22-12-17 CR Palest 9
McCABE,David Watson McDonald	Lt Can 5Bn 12-4-17CR France 12
McCALL,Lyman Clark	Lt Can 87Bn 1916
McCALLUM,Daniel	Capt Aust 51Inf kia 3-9-16 CR France 516

McCALLUM,Earle Carman	Lt Can 78Bn (MR) 30-10-17 MR 29 MacCALLUM
McCALLUM,G.P.	Lt SA 1MilConst 11-9-20CR SAfrica 81
McCALLUM,James.MM&Bar.	Lt Can 3BnCMGC 5-10-18CR France 214
McCALLUM,John Gordon	Capt NZ 7/796 ICC dow 11-1-17 CR Egypt 2
McCARTER,Arthur William Adair	2Lt SA 3SAInf kia 12-10-16 CR France 385 dow
McCARTER,Douglas Sherwood	Lt Can CFA9Bde 29-9-18CR France 715
McCARTER,Ronald George Adair	2Lt SA 2SAInf 8-10-18CR France 843
McCARTHY,James Charles	Capt NZ 33097 1AIR dow 4-11-18 CR France 206
McCARTHY,Rae Brydon	Lt Can 78Bn 9-4-17 CR France 548
McCARTHY,William Offley	Capt SA 2RhodR dow 26-8-16 CR EAfrica 9
McCARTIN,Leo Aloysius.MC.	Lt Aust 22Bn 18-8-18MR 26
McCARTY,Patrick Thomas	2Lt Aust 24Inf kia 1-9-18 CR France 511
McCLATCHEY,Thomas	Lt Can 102Bn 27-9-18CR France 715
McCLEAVE,Harry Austin	Lt Can13Bn dow 10-10-16 CR France 59
McCLEERY,Edgar Percy Everard	Lt AustAFC 4Sqn kia 17-8-18 CR France 82
McCLINTOCK,James Donaldson	Lt Can 27Bn 10-4-17CR France 68
McCLURE,E.R.	Lt SA MilLabCps27-6-19CR EAfrica 51
McCLURE,Henry	Lt Can 44MR 23-8-17MR 23
McCLURE,J.	WTMech Aust RAN HMAS`Sydney' 1-2-19 CR Kent 46
McCLURE,James Hannay Stewart	Capt Can 16Bn 17-6-16CR Wilts 129
McCLURE,Joseph Andrew Bright	Lt Can27MR 21-8-17MR 23
McCOLL,Alexander Bastin .MID.	Capt NZ10/18 1WIR kia 2-7-16 CR France 922 Baston
McCOLL,Douglas Chambers	Lt Can 10Bn (AR) 22-4-15MR 29
McCOLL,Hugh	Lt Aust 38Inf kia 12-8-18 CR France 1170
McCOLL,L.C.	Lt Can 87Bn att11 LtTMB kia 15-9-16 CR Belgum 15
McCOMB,Harold Ashley	Capt Can 4Bn 21-10-19 CR Canada 1691
McCONAGHY,David McFie.CMG.DSO.	LtCol Aust 55Inf dow 9-4-18 CR France 185
McCONE,John	Lt Can CE &RFC 41Sqn 24-3-18MR 20
McCONECHY,Archibald William	Lt Can 16Bn 8-8-18 CR France 487
McCONKEY,Benjamin Bertram.MC.	Capt CanCFA 15Bty 6Bde 30-5-18CR France 63
McCONNELL,Clifford	Lt Can5Bn 18-8-17CR France 1724
McCONNELL,James	Lt Aust 3Pnrs kia 22-8-18 CR France 247
McCONVILLE,Clarence Edward	2Lt Aust 8Bn 25-7-16MR 26
McCONVILLE,Don.MM.	2Lt Aust FA 102Bty 2Bdekia 20-10-17 CR Belgium 19
McCONVILLE,Victor Hugh	2Lt Aust AFA 14Bde dow 5-10-17 CR France 40
McCORD,George Rankin	Lt Can 58Bn 9TMB ded 1-2-19 CR Canada 1060
McCORKELL,James Ignatius J.	Lt Can 116Bn 12-8-18CR France 360
McCORMACK,Andrew Campbell	Capt Can CAMC 3SH ded 27-7-20 CR Canada 1409
McCORMICK,Alexander.MM.	Lt Can 31Bn 9-8-18 CR France 652
McCORMICK,Arthur Beamer.MC.	Capt Can 3/1COR 10-4-17MR 23
McCORMICK,Norman William	2Lt Aust 22Inf kia 7-11-16 CR France 744
McCORMICK,William Raymond	2Lt/ Lt NZ12/4305 AIR 1AuklandR kia 7-6-17 CR Belgium 48
McCOY,John Henry	Lt Can 16Bn 7-6-16 CR Belgium 127
McCRAE,Geoffrey Gordon.MID	Maj Aust 60Inf kia 19-7-16 CR France 348
McCRAE,John	LtCol Can CAMC 3GH 28-1-18CR France 64
McCREA,Frank DobrÇe	Capt Can RCR kia 28-9-18 CR France 243
McCREANOR,Joseph.DCM.	2Lt NZ 12/4045 AIR kia 1-9-18 CR France 307
McCUAIG,Robert Ernest	Capt CanCMGC 1 or2TankBn 14-10-18 MR 24
McCULLOCH,Colin Vernon	Lt Aust 2Inf kia 11-4-18 CR France 300
McCULLOUGH,David	Capt Can 38EOR 10-8-18MR 23
McCULLOUGH,William Charteris	Lt Aust 25Inf dow 11-8-18 CR France 71
McCURDIE,Archibald	Lt Aust Engrs 6FC dow 10-12-16 CR France 145
McDAVITT,James	Lt Can 14Bn 1918
McDERMID,George Duncan.MC.	Lt Can 2CMR kia 7-11-18 CR Belgium 203
McDERMOTT,Alfred George	2Lt Aust44Bn 29-9-18MR 26
McDERMOTT,James Patrick	Lt Aust 51Inf dow 7-2-18 CR Belgium 17
McDIARMAID,Benjamin.MC.MID	Maj Can 54Bn 30-9-18CR France 148
McDIARMID,Jessie Mabel	NSister Can CAMC 5GenHospdrd 27-6-18 MR 24
McDIARMID,John Heron	Capt Can 4Bn ded 15-9-16 CR Canada 1287
McDONALD,Albert William.MC.MID	Capt SA 3Inf dow 21-9-17 CR Belgium 3

McDONALD,Alexander Duncan	Lt Can 4CMR	9-8-18 CR France 584
McDONALD,Archibald Kerby	2Lt Aust 45Bn	5-4-18 MR 26
McDONALD,Cecil Jack.MC.	Lt Aust3Inf	dow 19-9-18 CR France 194
McDONALD,Donald Wallace	Lt Can 15/1COR	15-8-17MR 23
McDONALD,Duncan Buchanan	Lt NZ 11/555 WMR	dow 6-6-15 MR 6
McDONALD,Geo.StJohn Fancourt.DSO.	Maj Aust AHAG 36th	dow 22-3-18 CR France 139
McDONALD,Herbert Daniel.MC.	Lt Can CGA 6SB	28-4-17CR France 268
McDONALD,James.MC.	Lt Can 72Bn	kia 2-9-18 CR France 532
McDONALD,John Duncan Campbell	2Lt NZ 26/121 4/3NZRB	ded 25-10-18 CR France 40
McDONALD,James Glen	Lt Aust 19Bn	7-4-18 MR 26
McDONALD,William Joseph.MM	2Lt Aust 51Inf	26-9-17MR29
McDONALD,William Thomas.MID	Capt Aust 4Inf	kia 16-8-16 CR France 280
McDOUGAL,Agnes	Nurse Can 10StatHosp	18-7-19CR Canada 1097
McDOUGALL,Charles Reynolds	2Lt Aust2Inf	ded 16-8-15 CR Europe 1
McDOUGALL,Clarence Hobart	Capt Can 7CRT	dow 4-5-17 CR Belgium 11
McDOWELL,Alexander Robert	2Lt Aust17Inf	9-10-17MR 29
McDOWELL,John William	Lt Can CGA 1SB	13-12-17 MR 29
McELLISTER,John Thomas	Lt Aust 1AMGC	dow 25-5-18 CR France 28
McELROY,Victor Henry.DFC.	Lt Can CE &RAF 3Sqn	2-9-18 CR France 687
McEWEN,Cuthbert Finnie.DSO.	Maj Can CLH	kia 21-10-18 CR France 1292
McFADDEN,George Adam Gordon	Lt Aust 1MGC	dow 21-9-18 CR France 13
McFARLANE,Cecil Charles James	2Lt Aust 36Inf	kia 20-12-17 CR France 922
McFARLANE,John Ratcliffe	Lt Can 85Bn (NSR)	kia 30-10-17 MR 29 Ratcliff
McFARLANE,Peter	Lt Aust 34Inf	kia 2-6-18 CR France 144
McFAUL,Wesley Clarence	Lt Can 19Bn	10-11-18 CR Belgium 241
McGEE,Charles Edward	Capt Can 5SasR	kia 26-5-15 MR 23
McGEE,Francis Clarence	Lt Can 21EOR	kia 16-9-16 MR 23
McGIBBON,Gilbert Donald	Capt Can 13Bn	dow 20-4-16 CR Belgium 4
McGIBBON,Hugh Maxwell	Lt Can 29BCR	21-8-17MR 23
McGIBBON,John Walter	Lt Can 28Bn	kia 15-9-16 CR France 280
McGIFFIN,George Allan	Capt Can24Bn	kia 27-8-18 CR France 309
McGILL,Florence McCarthy	2Lt Aust19Inf	dow 29-6-16 CR France 285
McGILP,Clyde.DSO.MIDx2	Maj NZ2/280 NZFA AuklandBty	ded 14-11-18 CR NZ 243
McGINNES,John	Lt Aust 35Inf	dow 22-8-18 CR France 119
McGINNIS,Mary Geraldine	Sister Can CAMC	10-2-20CR Canada 1177
McGINNIS,William Clark	Lt Can CETD	11-12-16 CR Canada 1300
McGOVERN,Arthur Lawrence	Capt Can 28Bn	kia 7-6-16 CR Belgium 15
McGOVERN,Joseph	2Lt NZ 5/519 1AIR	kia 1-10-18 CR France 712
McGOWAN,Charles	Lt Can 5CMR	3-6-16 Cr Belgium 15 25Bn
McGOWAN,J.C.	ChEngr Can MercMar SS`LakeMichigan'	15-4-18MR 24
McGOWAN,Thomas Edward	2Lt Aust 3Inf	dow 19-10-15 CR Greece 11
McGOWEN,Frank Fernie	Lt Can 16Bn	kia 9-4-17 CR France 68
McGRATH,James John	Lt Aust 36Inf	kia 21-1-17 CR France 922
McGREGOR,A.M.MC.	Maj SA HArty	ded 7-12-18
McGREGOR,Duncan Alexander	Lt Can 8Bn	8-9-16 CR France 150
McGREGOR,James Herrick H	Capt Can 16Bn	(MR)24-4-15MR 29
McGREGOR,John	2Lt NZ 39400OIR	kia 16-4-18 MR 9
McGREGOR,Matthew MacKay	Lt Aust 50Inf	dow 3-5-18 CR France 145
McGREGOR,Ross	2Lt or Lt SA 1SAInf	dow 19-10-18 CR France 611
McGREGOR,William Clarence.MC.	Lt Aust 49Inf	kia 16-9-18 CR France 366 served as MURRAY
McGUIRE,Albert George	Capt Aust1Inf	dow 7-5-15 CR Egypt 6
McGUIRE,Harry Boulton	Lt Can4Bn	dow 24-4-15 CR Belgium 151
McGUIRE,Martin Augustus	Lt Aust 11Inf	kia 19-7-18 CR France 28
McGUIRE,Norman James.MC.MM.	Lt Aust 13Inf	kia 18-9-18 CR France 366
McHARDY,John	Lt Can 18Bn	26-8-18CR France 581
McHARDIE,Cyril James	2Lt NZ3/700 1WIR	kia 22-5-18 MR 12
McHATTIE,Donald Gordon.MID	Capt Aust ASC 3DivTrn	dow 17-7-17 CR Belgium 42
McHUGH,Anthony Lavelle	Maj Can 3CRT	kia 19-5-17 CR France 81 Larelle
McILQUHAM,James Maxwell.MC.	Lt Can CFA 9Bde	6-11-17CR Belgium 3
McILROY,George Thomas	Lt NZ 24311 1/3NZRB	kia 12-10-17 MR 30

78

McILVEEN,Wesley	Lt Can 52Bn 27-8-18CR France 421
McINERNEY,George Valentine	Lt Can CFA 53Bty 13Bde kia 27-9-18 CR France 647
McINERNEY,J.M.	Lt Aust 10Inf 28-6-18CR France 25
McINNES,Samuel Alexander	Lt Aust 40Inf kia 1-2-17 CR France 922
McINTOSH,Rebecca	NSisterCan CAMC 9GH ded 7-3-19 CR Wales 673
McINTOSH,Frederick Richard	Lt Aust 59Inf dow 28-9-17 CR Belgium 11
McINTOSH,Harold	LtCol Aust 12ALH dow 24-4-17 CR Egypt 2
McINTYRE,Aaron	2Lt Aust 25Inf 29-7-16MR 26 &CR France 1890
McINTYRE,Douglas Neil	Lt Can16Bn 8-11-17CR Belgium 125
McINTYRE,Ernest Stewart	Capt NZ 9/323 1OIR dow 28-7-17 CR France 297
McINTYRE,Hector	Maj Aust 1LH kia 1-10-17 CR Belgium 19
McINTYRE,John.MC.	Capt Aust 28Inf kia 28-2-17 CR France 385
McINTYRE,John Albert	2Lt Aust 22Inf 4-10-17MR 29
McINTYRE,John Harold	2Lt Aust 1Bn 5-11-16MR 26
McINTYRE,Peter	Lt NZ 6/684 2MGC kia 12-10-17 MR 30
McINTYRE,Robert.MC.MM.	Lt Can 42Bn dow 3-11-17 CR Belgium 3
McINTYRE,Thomas Alexander	Lt Aust 45Inf 10-6-17MR 29
McINTYRE,William George	Lt Can29Bn kia 9-4-17 CR France 68
McISAAC,William Fielding	Capt Can CAMC 9SH dow 3-6-18 CR France 40
McIVOR,Donald Alexander	Lt Can16Bn dow 2-9-17 CR Surrey 1
McIVOR,Joseph Hartley	Lt Can 25Bn 10-8-18CR France 1170 MacIVOR
McKAY,Eric Brodie	Lt Aust 22Inf dow 10-8-16 CR France 145
McKAY,Evelyn Verrall	Nurse Can CAMC 3GH 4-11-18CR France 34
McKAY,George	Lt Aust 4Inf dow 6-5-17 CR France 512
McKAY,J.G.	Lt Aust AMGC 19-8-16CR France 1890
McKAY,William Stewart	Lt Aust 50Bn 24-4-18MR 26
McKECHNIE,Malcolm Archibald.MC.	Capt Can CAMC 6FA dow 8-8-18 CR France 71
McKEE,Frederick George	2Lt NZ 6/308 2CIR kia 20-9-16 MR 11
McKEE,William Carey	Lt Can 1MtdRif SasR 26-8-18MR 23
McKEEFRY,Michael Joseph Augustine	Lt NZ 39725 2OIR kia 5-11-18 CR France 521
McKEEVER,James Campbell	Lt Can RAF 58Bn 16-3-21CR Canada 1200
McKELL,Victor Cleveland	Lt Aust 1Inf 4-10-17MR 29
McKELLOP,A.	1stOffr Can MercMar SS`Pomeranian' 15-4-18MR 24
McKENNA,Edward Albert	Capt Aust 7Inf kia 25/30-4-15 CR Gallipoli 7
McKENZIE,Archbd.Ern.Graham.DSO&Bar	LtCol Can 26Bn 28-8-18CR France 162
McKENZIE,Arthur Francis Murray	Lt Aust 46Inf dow 26-8-18 CR France 145
McKENZIE,Bruce Gray	Lt Aust 30Inf kia 12-10-17 CR Belgium 125
McKENZIE,Charles Haddon	S.Spurgeon Lt Can CFA 1Bde kia 7-5-17 CR France 68
McKENZIE,Donald Brace	Maj NZ 9/325 OtagoR ded 19-11-18 CR NZ 257
McKENZIE,Duncan	2Lt Aust 38Inf 13-10-17 MR 29
McKENZIE,Hugh McDonald.VC.DCM.	Lt Can 7MGCoy kia 30-10-17 MR 29
McKENZIE,Ian Ross	Lt Can 21Bn kia 11-10-18 CR France 761
McKENZIE,Mary Agnes	NSister Can CAMC HS drd 27-6-18 MR 24
McKENZIE,Norman	2Lt Aust AIF 14Inf16-1-18CR Aust 94
McKENZIE,Robert McNeil Crawford	Lt Aust 9Inf dow 21-9-17 CR Belgium 11
McKENZIE,Samuel Aubrey	2Lt Aust 9Inf kia 21-8-16 CR France 832
McKENZIE,Seaforth William	Lt NZ 19087 2WIR attRFC 101Sqn kldacc 26-1-18 CR France 200 kia
McKENZIE,Theodore Cuyler	Lt Can CGA 3Bde 8SB 19-2-19CR Surrey 1
McKENZIE,U.K.	Capt SA 10SAInf see Mackenzie,U.K.
McKENZIE ,Walter Michael	Lt NZ 8/80 OIR kia 9-8-15 MR 5 MacKENZIE
McKENZIE,Walter Wake	Capt Can CAMC ded 19-2-17 CR Kent 180
McKENZIE,Ian R.	Lt Can 21Bn 1918
McKEOUGH,William Stewart	Maj Can 18WOR 15-9-16MR 23
McKEOWN,John Alexander Hunter	Lt Aust AFC kia 14-10-18 CR France 1887
McKERIHAN,Harold George	Lt Aust 2Inf dow 16-8-15 CR Egypt 3
McKIE,Kenneth Clinton	2Lt Aust49Inf dow 9-6-17 CR France 297
McKILLOP,John Charles	Capt NZ53841 NZRB ded 24-7-20 CR NZ 271
McKINLAY,Archibald Franklin	Lt Can 2Bn kia 8-8-18 CR France 425
McKINLEY,H.R.	Lt Aust 14Inf 11-4-17CR France 564
McKINLEY,William Henry	Capt Can87Bn 2-9-18 CR France 531

McKINNEY,Daniel Joseph	Capt Can 1Bn A'Coy (WOR) kia 13-6-16 MR 29
McKINNON,Andrew Charles	2Lt Aust 60Inf kia 19-7-16 MR 7
McKINNON,Chester Neil	Lt Can 29BCR 21-8-17MR 23
McKINNON,Hugh Edgar.MC&Bar.MID.	Maj NZ10/135 2WIR kia 4-11-18 CR France 1077
McKINNON,Ian Laughlin	Lt Can PPCLI 27-8-18CR France 421 MacKINNON
McKINNON,Leo	Lt Can 7Bn 9-4-17 CR France 523
McKINNON,Martin William	Capt Can 85Bn 10-8-18CR France 586 MacKINNON
McKINTOSH,C.A.	2Lt SA 1SAInf see MacKintosh,C.A.
McKISSOCK,Wilfred Earl	Lt Can 1CORD attRFC 16Sqn kia 1-6-17 CR France 58
McKNIGHT,Augustus W.	Lt Can Engrs4FC 11-8-16CR Belgium 15
McKNIGHT,Locksley	Lt Can 49AR 16-9-16MR 23
McLACHLAN,Donald Ronald	Capt SA 3SAInf kia 18-7-16 MR 21 MacLachlan 16-7-16
McLACHLAN,Neil.MC.	Lt Aust 6Inf kia 10-8-18 CR France 649
McLACHLIN,Ewen	Lt Can CFR RBde Artly 19-8-17CR Kent 180 2Bde
McLAGAN,Patrick Douglas Maclure.MID	Lt Can 4LabCps kia 15-10-17 CR Belgium 35
McLAREN,Frederick Gates	Lt Can4Bn ded 7-2-16 CR France 85
McLAREN,John Ferguson	Lt Can 58Bn dow 20-4-17 CR France 32
McLAREN,Joseph.MID	Maj Can 10Bn kia 23-4-15 CR Belgium 4
McLAREN,William Humphrey	Maj Can 19Bn kia 15-9-16 MR 23 &CR France 393
McLAUGHLIN,Arthur Edward	Maj Can 2Bn 11-9-16CR France 44
McLAUGHLIN,Geoffrey.MC.	Maj Aust FA 1Bde dow 4-11-17 CR Belgium 11
McLAURIN,Archibald McGibbon	LtCol Aust 8ALH ded 23-11-18 CR Lebanon 1
McLAY,Stanley Gordon	2Lt Aust 7Inf dedacc 15-4-15 MR 41
McLEA,Kenneth Wetzlar	Lt Can FA 3DAC 28-10-17 CR Belgium 8
McLEAN,Albert	Lt Can 18Bn 15-8-17MR 23
McLEAN,C.C.	2Lt SA 2SAInf dow 13-4-17 CR France 95
McLEAN,Archibald Liddell.MC.DCM.	Lt Can 14Bn 2-9-18 CR France 687
McLEAN,Cecil Gower	Lt Can CMGC 7Bn9-4-18 CR France 68
McLEAN,Daniel Herschell.DCM.	Lt Can 72Bn ded 22-6-21 CR Canada 180
McLEAN,Duncan.MM.MIDx2.	2Lt NZ 9/383 2OIR kldacc 3-3-18 CR France 860
McLEAN,Edward Byron	Lt Can 50Bn 18-11-16 MR 23
McLEAN,Ewen Lawrence Bedson	Lt Can 5Bn kia 9-4-17 CR France 68
McLEAN,John	2Lt NZ 30108OIR 2OtagoR 14Coy ded 15-10-17 CR Belgium 3
McLEAN,John Lackey	Lt Aust 45Inf 27-9-17MR 29
McLEAN,Rena Maud.RRC.	NSister CanCAMC 2StatHospdrd 27-6-18 MR 24
McLEAN,Robert John	Lt Can 24Bn 4-4-19 CR France 1142
McLEAN,Ronald Douglas	2Lt NZ12/3759 2AIR 6Coy kia 15-9-16 MR 11
McLEAN,Stewart Smith.MC.	Lt Can87Bn kia 30-9-18 CR France 597
McLEAN,Terence Patrick	Maj Can 46Bn 18-11-16 MR 23
McLEAN,Thomas Malcolm	Capt Can 85Bn B'Coy dow 10-8-18 CR France 360
McLEAN,William John	Lt Can 18Bn 9-4-17 CR France 68
McLEARN,James Alexander	Lt Can 460267 43Bn dow 8-8-18 CR France 303
McLEISH,Stuart	Lt Can 58Bn 2-9-17 CR France 480
McLELLAN,Lawrence Herbert	Lt Can19Bn 26-5-18CR France 504
McLENNAN,Bartlett.DSO.	LtCol Can 42Bn kia 3-8-18 CR France 303
McLENNAN,James George	Lt SA SASC 20-4-19CR EAfrica 47 MACLENNAN
McLENNAN,John Donald	Lt Can 72Bn kia 9-4-17 CR France 548
McLENNAN,William Norman	Lt Can 16Bn kia 13-6-16 CR Belgium 11
McLEOD,Albert	Capt Aust 16Inf kldacc 5-12-16 CR Scot 653
McLEOD,Harvey Garfield	Maj CanCFA 2Bde 4-12-15CR Belgium 138
McLEOD,James	2Lt Aust 13Inf kia 10-8-15 CR Gallipoli 17
McLEOD,John Owen	Lt Can 85Bn 2-9-18 CR France 426 MacLEOD
McLEOD,Maurice Leslie	2Lt Aust 8Inf kia 25-4-15 CR Gallipol 22
McLEOD,Norman George Morrison.MC.	Maj MID Can 8MR 26-9-16MR 23
McLEOD,Roderick Campbell	LtCol Can CAMC 9SH 4-1-17 CR Hamps 3
McLEOD,William Harold	2Lt Aust5Inf 8-5-15 MR 4
McLEOD,William McLaren	Lt Can CAMC 10-10-18 MR 24
McLERNON,Leslie Somers	Capt NZ10/1079 9WIR kia 8-8-15 MR 5
McMAHON,J.T.	2Lt Aust Engrs 3FC 9-4-17 CR France 437
McMAHON,Randolph George Finlay.MC.	Lt Aust 4Inf ded 23-2-19 CR Belgium 316

McMANAMEY,James Whiteside Fraser	Maj Aust 19Inf kia 5-9-15 CR Gallipoli 16	
McMASTER,Allen Stewart	2Lt Aust 3Inf kia 9-4-17 CR France 756	
McMASTERS,Robert Thompson	Capt Aust 10ALH kia 7-8-15 MR 6	
McMEANS,Ernest D'Harcourt	Capt Can 8Bn kia 22-5-15 CR France 279	
McMENAMIN,James Joseph	Chpn NZ 6/1215 Chpns att2CIR kia 9-6-17 CR France 264	
McMICHAEL,James Albert	2Lt Aust 37Inf 12-10-17 MR 29	
McMICHAEL,John Edward	Lt EA UL EA att4/3KAR ded 12-5-17 CR EAfrica 35	
McMILLAN,Ronald Malcolm	2Lt Aust 6Inf kia 21-9-17 CR Belgium 112	
McMILLAN,Donald Gordon.MC.	2Lt NZ 2/59 NZFA 6HB kia 28-9-18 CR France 597	
McMILLAN,Robert Drummond.MC.	Lt Can CFA 2Bde 13-10-18 CR France 155	
McMULLEN,Sidney Walter	2Lt Aust 5Bn 25-7-16MR 26	
McMULLEN,William Harold.DCM.	2Lt Aust 25Inf kia 5-11-16 CR France 385	
McMULLIN,Walter John.MC.	Lt Aust FA 1Bde kia 4-10-17 CR Belgium 10	
McMURDIE,Edward Aphonsus	Lt Can 49Bn kia 29-9-18 CR France 481	
McMURTRY,Eric Ogilvie	Maj Can24Bn attRFC 16Sqn 28-4-17CR France 32	
McNAB,Peter	Capt NZ 3/1246A NZMC ded 15-11-18 CR NZ 194	
McNAIR,George Orme	Capt Can 58Bn 1-5-16 CR Belgium 309	
McNALLY,Percy Byron	Lt Can ARD 50Bn attRFC 55Sqn 13-8-17CR Belgium 365	
McNALLY,Stanley Melville	Lt Can 31Bn 8-11-17CR Belgium 72	
McNAMARA,James	Capt Aust 52Inf kia 3-9-16 CR France 742	
McNAUGHTON,James	ChEngr Can MercMar SS`Tagona' 16-5-18MR 24	
McNAUGHTON,Peter	Capt Can 49Bn (AR) kia 5-6-16 MR 29	
McNEIL,Angus John	Capt Can 6CGR ded 7-10-18 CR Canada 869	
McNEIL,John Zuill	2Lt SA 1CapeCps dow 7-11-17 CR Tanzania 1 &EAfrica 11	
McNEILL,James	Capt Can 1CMR 16-9-16MR 23	
McNICOL,Duncan Bannatyne	2Lt NZ 16/809 Pnrs dow 4-8-17 CR France 297	
McNICOL,Reginald Hugh	Lt Aust 1DivSigs att2BdcHQ dow 29-4-18 CR France 27	
McNIVEN,Harold George	Lt NZ 24384 2CIR kia 24-10-18 CR France 741	
McPHAIL,Irene	SNurse Aust AIF AANS 4-8-20 CR Aust 307	
McPHEE,Murdock Neil.MC.	Capt Can CE 4FC drd 17-4-17 MR 40	
McPHERSON,H.A.	Maj Aust 12Bn 24-12-18 MR 26	
McPHERSON,James Joseph	Capt Aust 46Inf 12-6-17MR 29	
McPHERSON,Thomas Roy	Maj Aust 18Inf kia 22-8-15 MR 6	
McQUAIG,Norman	3rdEngr Can MercMar SS`PortDalhousie' 19-3-16 MR 24	
McQUARRIE,Donald Archibald.MC.MID	Capt Can 54Bn kia 30-9-18 CR France 148	
McQUEEN,George William	Lt Aust 14Bn 29-3-17MR 26	
McQUEEN,J.MC.	Capt SA 2RhodR see MacQueen,J.	
McQUEEN,John Alexander.MC.	Lt NZ 8/602 CIR 1CanterburyRkia 11-12-17 CR Belgium 72	
McQUIGGIN,William	Lt Aust 1ALH kia 4-8-16 CR Egypt 2	
McRAE,Duncan John	Lt Can 50Bn attRFC 2-2-17 CR France 1321	
McRAE,Philip Felton	Capt NZ 24/15 2/3NZRB kia 12-10-17 CR Belgium 125	
McROBERTS,Evan Oswald	2Lt NZ 22550 1AIR 15Coy kia 4-10-17 MR 30	
McSHANE,Noel Edmund	Lt Aust 1Bn 25-7-16MR 26	
McSHANE,William Stephen	Lt Aust6Bn 9-8-18 MR 26	
McSHARRY,Terence Patrick.CMG.DSO&Bar.MC.	LtCol Aust 15Inf dow 6-8-18 CR France 23	
McSPADDEN,William	Maj Can CMPC ded 19-12-18 CR USA 19	
McTAGGART,George Stewart.DCM.	Capt Aust 28Inf dow 9-8-18 CR France 1170	
McTAGGART,Harry James	Lt Can 20Bn 15-9-16MR 23	
McTAGGART,William Broder.DSO.	Maj Can CFA 3Bde 2-9-18 CR France 1182	
McTAVISH,R.A.	Lt SA SA Post&TelCps 21-2-17CR Hamps 8	
McTAVISH,Stewart Allen	Lt Can 8Bn 26-9-16MR 23	
McWHIRTER,Clifford John.MM.	Lt Aust 10ALH dow 6-10-18 CR Palest 9	
McWILLIAM,C.N.	Capt SA 6SAInf Ex 1DurbanLI kia 17-8-16 CR EAfrica 39	
McWILLIAM,Stirling Alexander	Lt Aust 9ALH dow 30-5-15 CR Gallipoli 11	
MEAD,Clement Gordon .MC.	Capt Can 49Bn A'Coy 18-1-18CR France 570	
MEADER,Thomas Aubrey	Lt Aust 38Inf ded 16-11-18 CR France 52	
MEAGER,Hubert Richard William	Lt Aust 3Inf kia 6/8-8-15 MR 6	
MEAGHER,Norman Richard Thomas	Lt Aust 40Inf kia 4-10-17 CR Belgium 125	
MEARES,Douglas Seymour	Lt Aust 43Inf ded 14-10-18 CR Surrey 1	
MEASDAY,Frederick Taylor	2Lt Aust 27Bn 5-11-16MR 26	

MEDDINGS,Walter Harry	Maj NZ 48142 2CIR kia 11-10-17 MR 30
MEDLAND,Frederick Ross	Lt Can3Bn (1COR) kia 24-4-15 MR 29
MEDLICOTT,George Herbert	2Lt SA 2SA Inf kia 15-10-16 MR 21 3Reg
MEE,John Norman	Lt Can 31Bn kia 25-6-18 CR France 174
MEEK,Ethelbert Eldridge	Capt Can CAMC 3SH kld 30-5-18 CR France 84
MEETLING,J.M.J.	Lt SA SASC kia 4-2-15
MEGAN,Gerald Wallace	Lt Can 13Bn 27-9-18CR France 274
MEGGITT,William Thomas	Lt Aust45Bn 21-2-17MR 26
MEHAN,Alfred.MM.	2Lt Aust AFA 2DAC 2-9-18 CR France 624
MEIGH,James	Lt Aust 42Bn 25-8-18MR 26
MEIKLE,David	Lt Can 5Bn kia 25-5-15 MR 23
MEIKLE,John	Lt Can RCD 8-8-18 MR 23
MELANSON,Albert Joseph	Lt Can CFC &RAF 2Sqn 9-5-18 MR 20
MELLETT,Henrietta	Sister Can CAMC att15GHdrd 10-10-18 CR Eire 24
MELLOR,Frederick Courtney	Lt Can 1RNewfndlandR kia 1-7-16 CR France 220
MELVILLE,James Alexander	2Lt NZ 12/413 AuklandR 6HaurakiCoy ded 15-11-18 CR NZ 243
MELVILLE,Robert James Gordon	2Lt Aust4Inf dedacc 27-9-16 CR Belgium 11
MENARY,Arthur Aubrey	Lt Aust 18Inf dow 4-5-17 CR France 512
MENDELSOHN,Berrol Lazar	Lt Aust55Inf kia 20-7-16 MR 7
MENDOZA,Howard Kingsley	Lt Aust 52Inf 11-6-17MR 29
MENGERSEN,Herman Edgar	Lt Aust 25Inf dow 22-9-17 CR Belgium 72
MENNIE,Edward Thomas.MC.	Capt Can 38Bn dow 7-11-18 CR France 1196 F.T.
MENTEATH,Charles Bruce Stuart	Lt NZ 10/1082 WIR kia 6/10-5-15 MR 13
MENZ,Henry Berhold	Capt Aust 28Inf ded 27-11-15 CR Egypt 6
MENZIES,Cecil William	Lt Aust2Inf 22-9-17MR 29
MENZIES,James Arthur	Lt Can 76Bn (1CORD) attRFC 33Sqn kia 25-9-17 CR Lincs 136
MENZIES,William Barnet	2Lt NZ 7/92 CMR kia 9-8-16 CR Egypt 2
MERCER,Andrew Robert	Lt Can 49Bn 9-4-17 CR France 573
MERCER,Arthur Edward	Capt Can 2Bn 11-10-15 CR France 285
MERCER,Malcolm Smith.CB.MID	MajGen CanGOC 3Div HQkia 3-6-16 CR Belgium 11
MERCER,Mervyn Louis Emerson	Lt SA SAIC dow 7-8-17 CR Tanzania 1 &EAfrica 10
MERCER,William Joseph	2ndEngr CanMercMar SS`Armonia' 15-3-18MR 24
MEREDITH,Benjamin Peter George	Lt Aust 4ALH kia 31-10-17 CR Palest 1
MEREDITH,John Redmond	Maj Can GL 95 att23Bn ded 25-11-16 CR Canada 1694
MEREDITH,Robert Ellaby	Lt Can 1RBn &RAF 25-7-18CR France 1107
MEREDITH,Stanley Price	2Lt Aust MGC 25Coy dow 2-10-17 CR Belgium 11
MERKLEY,Myles Earl	Lt Can 31Bn (AR)kia 6-11-17 MR 29
MERRETT,Charles Darrell	Lt Aust AFC dedacc 16-5-16 CR Kent 7
MERRICK,Albert Sydney Joseph	2Lt NZ 38197 NZRB ded 24-3-21 CR NZ 275
MERRITT,Cecil Mack	Capt Can 16Bn (MR) 23-4-15MR 29
MERRITT,William Hamilton	Col Can CAMC ded 6-10-18 CR Canada 1688
MERIVALE,John Laidley	2Lt Aust 4Inf kia 6/9-8-15 CR Gallipoli 7
MERSEREAU,Charles James S.	Lt Can 26Bn 8-8-18 CR France 1170
MERZ,George Pinnock.MID	Lt Aust AFC 30Sqn attRFC 30-7-15MR 38
METCALFE,Alva Elmer.MC.	Lt Can 31Bn kld 8-11-17 CR Belgium 72
METCALFE,Francis Bramall	Capt Aust AAMC 10FA att38Inf dow 6-10-17 CR Surrey 1
METCALFE,George Andrew.MID	Lt Can 1Bn 15-6-15MR 23
METCALFE,Henry.DCM.	Lt Can 85Bn kia 29-9-18 CR France 715
METCALFE,Henry Ernest	Lt NZ4/1225 NZE kia 13-4-17 CR France 1182
METCALFE,James Beverley.DSO.MC.	Maj Aust AAMC 10FA dow 25-4-18 CR France 71
METELERKAMP,G.	Lt SA 2RoadCps 8-12-17CR Tanzania 1 &EAfrica 38
METHERAL,Thomas Arthur	Lt Can 19RBn &RFC 45Sqn 5-6-17 MR 20
METHERALL,George Tennyson	Lt Can26Bn 7-6-18 CR France 504
METTAM,A.F.	2Lt Aust 7Inf 15-5-18CR France 28
METTERS,Alfred	Chpn1Cl AustAIF ChpnsDept 1-3-18 CR Aust 212
MEUDELL,Colin Grant	2Lt Aust RFC 43Sqn Ex AustImpForce 10-8-17 CR France 88
MEULI,Lorenz Wilfred	2Lt NZ 6/4577 1WIR kia 16-9-16 MR 11
MEWBURN,John Chilton	Lt Can 18Bn 15-9-16CR France 280
MEYER,Arthur Percival Fitzmaurice	Lt Aust 7Infkia 16-4-18 CR France 200
MICHAEL,Duncan	Maj Can 43Bn 8-10-16MR 23

MICHAELSON,Richard Gibson	Lt Can 2Bn (EOR) &RAF ded 9-2-19 CR Lancs 71
MICHELL,Sydney	Lt Can CFA 1Bde dow 3-10-16 CR France 40
MICHENER,Leo St.Orban	Lt Can CETD &RFC kld 2-8-17 CR Suffolk 173 CAMC 5FA
MIDDLETON,Arthur Z	Lt Can 27Bn 27-9-16MR 23
MIDDLETON,Roy Oswald	Capt Aust 3Inf kia 25-7-16 CR France 832
MIELL,Albert.MID	LtCol Aust9ALH kia 7-8-15 CR Gallipoli 29
MILBURN,George Noble	Lt Can 1Bn kia 5-4-17 CR France 68
MILES,Charles.DCM.	Lt Can49Bn 26-10-18 CR Derbyshire 74
MILES,Herbert Frederic	Lt Aust 39Inf kia 8-5-18 CR France 207
MILES,J.A.W.D.	Capt SA KAR
MILES,Robert Stevens.MC.	Lt Aust 8Inf dow 22-4-17 CR France 512
MILES,Thomas Francis	Capt Aust 5DivTMB ded 26-2-17 CR France 74
MILFORD,Thayer Vincent	Lt Can 18Bn 20-10-18 CR France 214
MILK,Archibald Payne.MM.	Lt Can 52Bn 8-8-18 CR France 485
MILLAR,Arthur Graemesty	Lt Can 3Bn 14-11-16 CR France 81 Graemesley
MILLAR,B.H.C.	Lt Aust 1AMGC 25-4-18CR France 27
MILLAR,John	2Lt NZ 180184/3NZRB kia 12-10-17 MR 30
MILLAR,John William.MID	Capt Aust47Inf 7-6-17 MR 29
MILLARD,Leonard	Lt NZ 9/55 1OIR kia 14-7-16 CR France 922
MILLER,Albert Leslie	Capt Aust 51Bn 14-8-16MR 26
MILLER,Alexander Henderson	Lt Aust 57Inf kia 25-9-17 CR Belgium 112
MILLER,Alexander Lorimer	Lt Aust 10Inf dow 8-5-17 CR France 512
MILLER,Armour Adamson	Maj Can 19Bn 21-6-18CR France 169
MILLER,Arnold Fraser	Lt Can 5CMR 15-9-16MR 23
MILLER,Arthur William	2Lt Aust 27Inf kldacc 18-7-171 CR France 251
MILLER,Clive Lancelot	Lt AustFA 8Bdc kia 4-7-17 CR Belgium 42
MILLER,Crawford T.	Lt Can 36Rcs Bn &RFC kld 8-12-16 CR Hertfd 87 76Bn
MILLER,F.J.	2Lt Aust AIF Aust Naval&MilForces26-4-18CR PNG 5
MILLER,George John	Capt SA 1SAInf kia 16-7-16 MR 21
MILLER,George Charles Stewart	Lt Aust AFA 2Bde dow 4-3-17 CR France 453
MILLER,Howard Billou	Maj Can CFA 8Bdc dow 18-11-17 CR Belgium 10
MILLER,James	Capt Aust 16Inf kia 2-5-15 MR 6
MILLER,Patrick Theodore	Lt Aust 12Inf kia 28-12-17 CR Belgium 42
MILLER,Robert Gibb	2Lt SA 2SAInf A'Coykia 20-7-16 MR 21 15-7-16
MILLER,Randolph	2Lt Aust 7Inf dow 19-5-15 MR 6
MILLER-STERLING,H.J.G.S.	LtSA NigR
MILLIGAN,Alexander Wilson.MID	Lt Can 7Bn 2-9-18 CR France 688
MILLIKEN,Morris James	2Lt NZ 13/279 AMR dow 8-8-15 CR Gallipoli 18
MILLS,Alvah Cressman	Lt Can RCR kia 28-9-18 CR France 214
MILLS,Cecil Beaumont	Lt Aust 23Bn 4-8-16 MR 26
MILLS,Frank Elton.MID	2Lt SA 2SAInf dow 5-4-18 CR France 40
MILLS,Gordon Wallace Markham.MC.	Lt Aust 13Inf kia 6-7-17 CR France 297
MILLS,Harris McClure	Lt Can 4CMR kia 1-10-16 CR France 314
MILLS,John	Lt Can 14Bn 27-6-16CR Belgium 127
MILLS,John Brier	Maj Aust AFA 2Bdc dow 30-5-15 CR Gallipoli 3
MILLS,Robert Sydney	Lt Can CASC TD 25-3-16CR Kent 180
MILLS,Samuel Ernest Goold.MC.	Capt Aust 32Inf kia 25-10-17 CR Belgium 19
MILLS,Sydney Sylvanus.MC	Lt Aust10Inf 20-9-17MR 29
MILLYARD,Reuben De Lemme	Lt Can PPCLI 30-9-18CR France 240
MILN,Alexander	Maj Can 75Bn 18-11-16 CR France 239
MILNE,Arthur James	Capt SA SAMC dcd 7-12-18 CR EAfrica 77
MILNE,David.MC.	Lt Can 10Bn 2-9-18 CR France 688
MILNE,Edward Ramsay.MC.DCM&Bar.	Capt Can10Bn 10-10-18 CR Eire 301
MILNE,George Eric.MC.	Capt Aust46Inf dow 5-4-18 CR France 169
MILNE,John Alexander.DSO.	LtCol Aust 36Inf kia 12-4-18 CR France 526
MILNE,John Clarence	Capt Can 28Bn (SR) 6-6-16 MR 29
MILNER,J.T.	Maj Aust AIF AFA 25Bde 14-6-21CR Aust 469
MILNES,Herbert Albert Edwin	2Lt NZ 22525 3AIR kia 4-10-17 CR Belgium 125
MILSON,Stewart.MID	Capt Aust 4Inf kia 6/8-8-15 CR Gallipoli 7
MINARD,Asa Raymond	Lt Can 38Bn C'Coy dow 30-6-17 CR France 81

MINCHIN,Joseph Henry	2Lt Aust 51Inf kia 2-4-17 CR France 568
MINCHINTON,Gordon Edward	Lt Can 27Bn 9-4-17 CR France 68
MINERDS,Henry Ernest Clifford	Lt Aust 50Inf kia 18-10-17 CR Belgium 101
MINIFIE,Percival Carl	Lt Aust 2AMGC 4-10-17MR 29
MINNAAR, M.L.V.	Lt SA MtdCmdos kia 23-12-14 CR SAfrica 107 W.L.V.
MINNS,Alan Gurney	Lt Can 3Bn dow 6-11-17 CR Belgium 3
MINSTER,William Arnold	Lt Aust 6Inf dow 5-10-17 CR Belgium 11
MIRAMS,James Herbert.MC.	Maj Aust Engrs 13FC dow 19-8-16 CR France 74
MISSEN,Wilfred	Lt Can 47Bn kia 5-5-17 CR France 81
MITCHELL,Alan	Lt Aust 30Inf kia 20-7-16 MR 7
MITCHELL,Albert	Capt Aust 4MGC dow 18-5-18 CR France 29
MITCHELL,Charles Leslie	2Lt Aust 9ALH 19-4-17MR 34
MITCHELL,Garnet Leslie	Lt Can 27Bn 20-4-17CR France 68
MITCHELL,Harold Flinders	2Lt Aust 45Inf kia 5-4-18 CR France 197
MITCHELL,James	2Lt Can 5BdeHQ &RFC 18Sqn 26-4-16CR France 32
MITCHELL,Jared Carl	Lt Can16Bn 16-9-17CR France 179
MITCHELL,John Broughton.MC&Bar.	Capt Can 10Bn C'Coy kia 29-9-18 CR France 214
MITCHELL,John Tyler	Lt Aust 41Bn 1-9-18 MR 26
MITCHELL,R.P.	Capt SASAMC 11-11-19 CR EAfrica 36
MITCHELL,Stanley Hall	Lt Can 11Bn ded 8-4-15 CR Canada 119
MITCHELL,Thomas	Lt Aust 59Inf kia 12-5-17 CR France 1486
MITCHELL,William Hamilton	Lt Can 8Bn kia 27-11-16 CR France 81
MITCHENER,John Roy	Lt Can PPCLI dow 27-9-16 CR France 40
MIVILLE DECHENE,Arthur Leon	Capt Can 22Bn 1-10-16CR France 314
MOFFAT,Harvey Peter	Lt Can CFA 3Bde 2-9-18 CR France 155
MOFFAT,Hayward Hugh.MC.	Capt Aust 1Inf dow 21-9-18 CR France 1468
MOFFATT,Herbert William Sargent	LtAust 43Inf31-7-17MR 29
MOFFITT,Harry Lowry	Lt Aust 53Inf kia 19-7-16 MR 7
MOGG,Cyril Knox Barrow	Capt Can 7Bn (BCR) kia 11-11-17 MR 29
MOLLISON,Benjamin.MC.	LtT Capt NZ 25/30 2/3RB kia 21-3-18 CR Belgium 19
MOLLOY,Cyril Henry.MC.	Capt NZ 24318 1OIR kia 12-10-17 CR Belgium 123
MOLLOY,William	Lt Can 1CMR 10-4-17CR France 1321
MOLSON,Percival.MC.	Capt Can PPCLI 5-7-17 CR France 81
MOLTER,Wilfred Michael	Chpn4Cl SA att1SAH ded 24-10-18 CR SAfrica 7
MOLYNEUX,W.H.A.	Col SA HQRecs&CampStaff ded 23-12-17 CR SAfrica 62
MONCKTON-CASE,John	Lt Can CETD 9-11-17CR Kent 15 MOCKTON
MONCREIFF,Norman Halliday	Maj Can 2CMR 18-11-16 CR France 145
MONCRIEFF,John Bain	2Lt Aust MGC 13Coy 3-9-16 MR 26
MONEY,Percy Frederick	Capt Aust AAMC 3AGH ded 22-12-16 CR Dorset 110
MONIE,Bruce Lawson	Lt Aust 18Bn 27-7-16MR 26
MONK,William Mulock Carleton	Capt Can 1HyBty ded 20-2-19 CR Canada 1694
MONKMAN,Herbert Stanley	Capt Can 3CMR 1-12-15CR Belgium 339
MONKS,Albert Merton	Lt Can 29Bn 21-8-17MR 23
MONRO,David Henry Carmichael	Lt Can 29Bn kia 4-5-16 CR Belgium 15
MONSON,Harold Frederic John.MID	2Lt NZ 10/3405 2CIR kia 20-9-16 MR 11
MONTAGNON,Bernhard Coeure.MC.	Lt Can16MGCoy dow 14-11-17 CR France 40
MONTAGUE,Henry Loban	Lt Aust 4Bn 15-4-18MR 26
MONTEITH,Robert Henry	Lt Aust 26Inf kia 2-9-18 CR France 511
MONTGOMERY,Clark Cairnforth Stitzel	LtCan BCRD &RFC 66Sqn kld 14-8-17 CR France 134
MONTGOMERY,Glyde Gregory	Cdt Can RAF CFA 1919
MONTGOMERY,James William	Lt Can 46Bn ded 26-10-18 CR Lancs 34
MONTGOMERY,Neville	Lt Can 29Bn kia 21-8-17 MR 23
MONTGOMERY,William Augustine	Lt Can 1MMGBde kia 5-11-18 CR France 1253
MONTGOMERY-CAMPBELL,Herbert	Lt Can 5CMR 1-10-16MR 23
MOODY,Harold Eric	Lt Aust AFA 3Bde dow 27-8-16 CR France 74
MOOERS,Robert Clayton.MC.	Lt Can 43Bn 29-8-18CR France 1170
MOON,J.E.	Lt SA 2SARif ded 10-4-18 CR Tanzania 1 &EAfrica 15
MOONEY,Robert	2Lt NZ 12/917 AIR kia 8-8-15 MR 5
MOOR,Roland Thomas H.	Lt Can 73Bn 21-11-16 CR France 59
MOORE,Donald MacKenzie	Capt Can 16Bn 22-5-15MR 23

MOORE,Edmund Evelyn W.	Col Can 1InfResBde	6-4-17 CR Canada 1667
MOORE,Edward Cecil Horatio	Maj Can38Bn kia 9-4-17	CR France 81
MOORE,Edmund Fox	Capt Aust 38Inf	4-10-17MR 29
MOORE,Frederick Leslie	Capt Aust 5Inf kia 20-9-17	CR Belgium 72
MOORE,Garnet Westwood	2Lt NZ 33198 2OIR kia 29-11-17	CR Belgium 112
MOORE,Herbert Edward	Lt Can 4CMR	2-10-16MR 23
MOORE,James Anderson	Lt Aust 18Inf kia 22-8-15	MR 6
MOORE,James Joseph	Lt Can 10Bn kia 9-4-17	CR France 68
MOORE,John Charles.MC&Bar.MM.	Lt Aust 60Inf kia 4-7-18	CR France 207
MOORE,Norman John	2Lt Aust 23Inf	3-10-17MR 29
MOORE,Ralph Ingram.MC.DCM.	Capt Aust3Inf C'Coy kia 7-10-17	CR Belgium 88
MOORE,Rupert Cyril	2Lt NZ44943 1/3NZRB kia 12-9-18	CR France 407
MOORE,Samuel Vincent	Lt Aust 8ALH	1-12-17MR 34
MOORE,Stanley Graham.DCM.	Lt Can102Bn kia 27-9-18	CR France 715
MOORE,Stanley.MID.	2Lt NZ16/1329 NZFA 4Bde dow 2-7-16	CR France 285
MOORE,Stuart Aloysius.MC&Bar.	Capt Can 50Bn 2-9-18	CR France 427
MOORE,William Ambrose	Lt Can 58Bn (2COR) kia 26-10-17	MR 29
MOORE,William Henry	2Lt NZ 10/2454 3MGC dow 7-10-17	CR Belgium 11
MOORE,William MacLeod.MC.MIDx3	Capt Can 4DivHQ 7-4-19	CR Belgium 318
MOORE,William Reid	Lt Aust 28Bn	3/6-11-16 MR 26
MOORHEAD,George Oliver	LtCol SA Cmdg1SARif dow 20-5-16	CR EAfrica 78
MOORHOUSE,Edith Ann	Sister AustAANS ded 24-11-18	CR France 1027
MOORHOUSE,Leslie James	Capt Aust 46Inf kia 1-10-16	CR Belgium 37
MOORS,Elphinstone Henry	2Lt Aust16Inf dow 8-8-18	CR France 526
MOORS,William Wellington	Maj Can 19Bn	14-8-16CR France 285
MORAN,Francis	Capt Aust 15Inf dow 20-8-15	MR 6
MORASH,Chesley Clarence	Lt Can25Bn 1922	
MOREAU,Henri Herve	Lt Can 22Bn	4-10-16CR France 1483
MORELL,Throsby.MC.	Maj Aust 3DivHQ	27-2-19CR France 931
MORENCY,Auguste Isaie	Lt Can 22Bn kia 30-9-16	MR 23
MORETON,Letetia Gladys	Sister Aust ANS att2AGH ded 11-11-16	MR 43
MOREY,Howard Victor	Lt Aust 58Bn	2-9-18 MR 26
MORGAN,Albert Norton	Lt Can 10Bn kia 24-5-15	MR 23
MORGAN,Charles Edward Collins.MC.	2Lt NZ 10/1295 AIRdow 5-10-17	
MORGAN,Frederick Hector Edward.MC.	Capt NZ 10/3640 WIR dow 22-7-18	CR Surrey 1
MORGAN,Harry	Lt NZ 12/1075 AIR kia 6/10-5-15	CR Gallipoli 6
MORGAN,Herbert Lewis	2Lt NZ 12/1465 1/3NZRB kia 8-12-17	MR 8
MORGAN,Hugh Philip.MM.	Lt Can 31Bn	7-10-18CR France 274
MORGAN,John	Lt Can 73Bn dow 21-4-17	CR France 64
MORGAN,John Herbert	Lt Can 20Bn	21-2-18CR France 480
MORGAN,Price Jacob	Maj Aust AFA 6Bdedow 4-4-17	CR France 156
MORGAN,Reginald Roy	Lt Aust 3Inf dow 5-5-17	CR France 512
MORGAN,Robert Armstrong	Capt Aust 57Bn	25-4-18MR 26
MORGAN,Samuel John.MID	Capt Aust 26Inf dow 6-11-16	CR France 188
MORGAN,Thomas Henry	Lt Aust 13Bn	11-4-17MR 26
MORGAN,Walter	Lt Aust 9Inf kia 10-8-18	CR France 526
MORIARTY,Daniel Michael	2Lt NZ 6/3224 2CIR kia 8-10-18	CR France 660
MORIN,Joseph Hector Gaston	Capt Can CAMC ded 15-10-18	CR Canada 341
MORISON,Robert William	Lt Can 2Div TMBkia 8-6-16	CR Belgium 127 5 LtTMB
MORKILL,Francis Edward	Capt Can 20Bn	15-9-16CR France 1505
MORLEY,Charles Henry	Lt Aust AAOC ded 13-4-19	CR Surrey 1
MORELY,Charles Reginald	Lt Aust 5ALH dow 8-11-17	CR Palest 1
MORPETH,Allan	2Lt NZ 18899 AIR 1AuklandR kia 2-10-17	CR Belgium 22
MORPHY,Hugh Boulton	Lt Can CFA 2 or 12Bde	16-5-17CR France 12
MORPHY,John Montague	Lt Can 13Bn dow 27-10-17	CR Surrey 1
MORRICE,John.MM&Bar.	Lt Can 1Bn 2-9-18	CR France 687
MORRIS,Basil Menzies	Lt Can Engrs 1TC attRFC kia 17-3-17	CR Belgium 11
MORRIS,Charles	Lt Can 72Bn	1-3-17 CR France 548
MORRIS,Francis Arthur	Capt Aust AIF 23Inf	23-7-19CR Aust 344
MORRIS,Francis William	Lt Can CFA 3Bde	30-9-16CR France 251

MORRIS,George Edward	Lt Can 87Bn (QR) 13-11-17 MR 29
MORRIS,Henry Walter.MC.	Lt Can75Bn 15-8-17CR France 550
MORRIS,John Edward	Lt Can 28Bn kia 9-8-18 CR France 649
MORRIS,William Hugo.MC.	Capt Can PPCLI 1Coy (EOR)kia 30-10-17 MR 29
MORRIS,William John	Lt Can 18Bn 16-9-16CR France 833
MORRISEY,George	Lt Can 4CMR (1COR) kia 3-6-16 MR 29
MORRISON,Charles Sangster McLeod	Lt Can 75Bn 1COR 9-4-17 MR 23
MORRISON,David	Lt Can 2CMR 17-9-16CR France 832
MORRISON,Donald Whitcombe	Lt Can 3Bn 8-8-18 CR France 488
MORRISON,Douglas George	Lt Aust AFC dow 29-10-17 CR France 512
MORRISON,Frederick Charles	Lt Aust 38Inf kia 13-10-17 CR Belgium 125
MORRISON,Herbert Fraser.MC.	Lt Aust 5Inf dow 10-8-18 CR France 71
MORRISON,Malcolm John.MC.	Capt NZ7/2072 2CIR dow 15-8-17 CR France 262
MORRISON,Thomas Edmond	Capt Can CE 1FC 15-6-15CR France 80
MORRISON, William Cameron	Maj NZ 11/625 WMR DivHQ ded 25-11-18 CR NZ 32 Wilson dow
MORROW,Andrew Duncan	Lt Aust 59Inf dow 21-7-16 CR France 285
MORROW,Charles Ernest	Capt Can 10CoyCFC 31-5-17CR Scot 473
MORROW,James Curzon	Lt Can Engrs 3FC kia 26-4-16 CR Belgium 15
MORROW,John D'ole	ChpnH Capt Can ChpnServs att185Inf ded 28-4-21 CR Canada 1691
MORROW,Thomas James	TCapt NZ 44194CanterburyR ded 17-12-23
MORTIMER,Kenneth Malcolm	Capt Aust 29Inf kia 20-7-16 MR 7
MORTON,Alfred Bishop	Capt NZ10/512 InfBdeHQ dow 3-5-15 MR 6
MORTON,Arthur Ernest Bernard	Lt Can 3Bn kia 24-9-16 CR France 1505
MORTON,James MacLaren	Lt Can 31Bn 3-5-17 CR France 557 McLaren
MORTON,Robert	Lt Can 29Bn dow 19-10-18 CR Surrey 2
MORTON,Stanley William	Lt NZ 2/703 NZFA kia 21-10-16 CR France 188
MORWICK,James Hugh.MC.	Lt Can 2MMGBde kld 10-10-18 CR France 147
MOSES,James David	Lt Can MRD &RAF 57Sqn 1-4-18 MR 20
MOSES,Marcus Alwyn	Capt SA 2RhodR 13-9-17CR EAfrica 101
MOSHIER,Heber Havelock	LtCol Can CAMC 11FA29-8-18CR France 81
MOSS,Albert Henry	Lt Aust 15Inf dow 19-6-18 CR France 13
MOSS,Alfred Hubert	Lt Aust AFA 2DAC drd 3-8-18 MR 40
MOSS,Arthur Dudley	2Lt Aust 1Bn 5-5-17 MR 26
MOSS,Charles Alexander	Maj Can 3Bn dow 24-10-16 CR France 145
MOSS,Lionel Tennant	2Lt Aust 20Bn 11-8-18MR 26
MOSS,John	2Lt Aust 11Inf kia 19-7 -18 CR France 28 9-7-18
MOTLEY,Thomas	ChSkipperCan RCN ded 24-12-20 CR Canada 449
MOTT,Arthur Ernest Percival	Lt Aust AFC 1Sqn drd 24-12-17 CR Scot 398
MOTT,John.MC.MID	Lt Can 1CMR 26-8-18MR 23
MOTYER,Arthur John	Lt Can CFA 2Bde 15-9-16CR France 1505
MOULDS,Thomas John.MC&Bar.	Lt Can 3Bn 27-9-18CR France 686
MOULE,Charles Lancelot.MC.	Capt Aust 50Inf dow 19-10-17 CR Belgium 3
MOULE,Frederick Gore	Capt Aust 37Inf dow 8-10-17 CR Belgium 3
MOULSDALE,Frederick William	Capt Aust 7AMGC dow 12-4-18 CR France 44
MOUNTAIN,Arthur Henry Torres	Lt Aust 16Inf kia 27-4-15 MR 6
MOWAT,George	Capt SA 4SAInf A'Coy 12-10-16 CR France 385
MOWAT,Grant Davidson	Capt Can 21Bn 15-8-17MR 23
MOWAT,John McDonald	Maj Can 4Bn 8-10-16MR 23
MOWAT,Oliver Alexander.MC.	Capt Can CFA 16Bde 1919
MOWBRAY,Cyril McLellan	Lt Can 5Bn (SR) kia 10-11-17 MR 29
MOWBRAY,Norma Violet	SNurse Aust AANS ded 21-1-16 CR Egypt 9
MOWDESLEY,S.	Lt SA 2SAInf ded 27-7-19
MOXLEY,William Gowan Watson.MM.	Lt Can5Bn 9-4-17 CR France 68
MOYLAN,John B.MC.	Capt &QM Aust 15ALH ded 28-9-18 CR Palest 8
MUCH,Frank Llewellyn.MC.	Capt Can 2BnCMGC 18-8-18CR France 310
MUCHMORE,Thomas Ernest	Lt Aust FA 4Bde kia 6-10-17 CR Belgium 113
MUCKLE,John Ernest	Lt Can 38Bn kia 15-1-17 CR France 68 Ernie
MUDGE,Charles Edward	2Lt Aust 53Inf kia 19-7-16 CR France 82
MUIL,Robert James	Lt Can 78Bn dow 30-10-17 CR Belgium 3
MUIR,Albert Stanley	Lt Aust 1ALH MGSqn kia 5-11-17 CR Palest 1

MUIR,Alexander Roxburgh.MC.	Lt Aust 45Inf 13-10-17 MR 29
MUIR,Arthur Edward	Lt Can 15Bn 21-5-15MR 23
MUIR,D.A.	4thEngr Can MercMar SS`Pomeranian' 15-4-18MR 24
MUIRHEAD,John Fraser Bryce	Lt Can28Bn ded 6-3-19 CR Canada 1444
MUIRHEAD,William Robert	Capt Can 4CMR (1COR) 26-10-17 MR 29
MULCAHY,Claude Ludovic Hickman	Lt SA 2SAInf dow 11-7-16 CR France 23
MULGAN,William Richard	2Lt NZ 4/499 2AIR kia 29-9-18 MR 12
MULHOLLAND,Duncan Victor	Capt Aust AMGC 1Bn dow 31-5-18 CR France 180
MULHOLLAND,George Buchanan	Lt Can 19Bn kia 21-3-17 CR France 68
MULLANEY,Maurice James	Lt Can 26Bn 9-4-17 CR France 68
MULLARKEY,Niall Joseph	2Lt Aust 1Bn 5-11-16MR 26
MULLETT,Leslie Holmes	2Lt Aust 14Bn 11-4-17MR 26
MULLER-CHATEAU,Leo	Lt Aust RFA Ex1AustInf 27-2-19CR Norfolk 209
MUMMERY,Clarence Tasman.MC&Bar.	Lt Aust 8Inf 20-10-17 MR 29
MUNDELL,David	Lt Can 5Bn dow 26-5-15 CR France 98
MUNDELL,William Twynam.MID	Maj Aust 15Inf dow 19-8-17 CR Belgium 168
MUNDY,Clarence Reginald	Lt Can MRD 16Bn &RAF kld 23-11-18 CR Scot 106
MUNN,Daniel Ellsworth	Capt CanRCR dow 18-4-17 CR France 12
MUNRO.A.D.	Jun4thEngr Can MercMar SS`Missanabie' 9-9-18 MR 24
MUNRO,Freeman	Lt Can 75Bn 15-8-17MR 23
MUNRO,George Edward Buchanan	Lt Aust 24Inf dow 22-5-18 CR France 71
MUNRO,Gertrude Evelyn	Sister Aust AANS ded 10-9-18 CR Greece 9
MUNRO,Gordon Albert.MID	Lt Aust 12Inf kia 25/28-4-15 MR 6
MUNRO,John	Lt Can 44Bn kia 10-4-17 CR France 58
MUNRO,John Mackay	Capt Can 16Bn 1-10-18MR 23
MUNRO,John William	Lt Can 44Wing(Bordon Camp)RAF RCR kldacc 10-8-18 CR Canada 1231
MUNRO,Kenneth	Lt NZ 10/1930 2WIR kia 3-7-16 CR France 922
MUNRO,Mary Frances E.	Nurse Can CAMC 3SH ded 7-9-15 CR Greece 11
MUNRO,Stuart	2Lt Aust 1Bn 22/25-7-16 MR 26
MUNRO,Annie Winniefred	SNurse SA SAMNS GH ded 6-4-17 CR Scot 764
MUNRO,William McClain	Lt Can 15Bn kia 1-5-17 CR France 523
MUNTZ,Herbert Gerard	Capt Can 3Bn dow 30-4-15 CR France 102
MURCHISON,Ninian	Lt Aust 49Inf kia 1-4-18 CR France 196
MURDOCH,Douglas Ray	Lt Can 26Bn dow 15-8-17 CR France 12
MURDOCH,Sydney Richard.DCM.MID	Lt Aust 30Inf kia 3-9-18 CR France 511
MURDOCH,William	Lt Aust 7Aust LtTMB kia 7-6-16 CR France 82
MURPHY,Francis Joseph Patrick	Maj Aust 17Inf ded 11-1-16 CR Greece 11
MURPHY,Francis Michael	Lt Can15Bn 2-9-18 CR France 266
MURPHY,Francis William Joseph	Lt Aust 24Inf kia 4-10-17 CR Belgium 88
MURPHY,James Hector Ross.MC.	Maj Can 16Bn 16-8-17CR France 223
MURPHY,Sterndale Joseph.MC.	Capt Can 3Bn 14-10-18 CR France 273
MURPHY,Vincent Patrick	Capt Can 25Bn &RFC dedacc 12-3-18 CR Surrey 1
MURR,William Henry	Lt Can 85Bn (NSR) 30-10-17 MR 29
MURRAY,A. See McGREGOR,W.C. true name	
MURRAY,Alexander Geddes	Lt SANatLab ded 23-9-18 CR SAfrica 144
MURRAY,Andrew Haldane.MID	Lt SA 7SAH kia 16-9-16 CR EAfrica 24
MURRAY,Anthony Archibald	Lt Can 49Bn attRFC 34Sqn 19-3-17CR France 424
MURRAY,Austin Russell	Lt CanCFA 12Bty 3Bdekia 16-6-16 CR Belgium 15
MURRAY,Edward Aubrey Mutton	Lt Aust 48Inf 12-10-17 MR 29
MURRAY,Harcourt Amory	Maj Can 24Bn kia 1-10-16 MR 23
MURRAY,Harold Gladstone	Lt Can1DAC att RFC kia 16-12-16 CR France 46
MURRAY,James A.	Lt Can `Niobe' 1917
MURRAY,James Cassie	2Lt Aust MGC 7Coy 5-8-16 MR 26
MURRAY,John Thomas	2Lt Aust 9Inf kia 29-10-17 CR Belgium 34
MURRAY,Kenneth William	Lt Can BCRD &RAF 13Sqn 1-7-18 CR France 924
MURRAY,Norman Grant	Lt Capt Can 49Bn kia 8-10-16 CR France 413
MURRAY,Ronald Ernest DSO & Bar.DCM.Col	SABrSAPol ded 29-6-20 CR Hamps 161
MURRAY,Robert Andrew Malcolm.MC.	Lt Aust 45Inf 7-6-17 MR 29
MURRAY,Robert Davis	Capt Aust 2Inf kia 5-9-16 CR Belgium 127
MURRAY,Robert Hunter.MID	Lt Can 8Bn kia 15-8-17 MR 23

MURRAY,Thomas Lockwood	Lt Aust 21Inf kia 25-2-17 CR France 239
MURRAY,Tolford Hamilton	Lt Can CLH 9-4-17 MR 23
MURRAY,Walter James	Lt Can 42Bn dow 7-10-18 CR Scot 713
MURRAY-MACGREGOR,Atholl.MC.MID	Maj SA SAHArty attRGA 172SB 7-12-18CR Italy 11
MURRELL,Sydney Allan	ACapt NZ1/557 2WIR kia 4-11-18 CR France 1077
MUSGROVE,George Henry.DSO.MID	Maj Can20Bn 28-8-18CR France 421
MUSGROVE,Harold Stone	2Lt Can CycCps &RAF 57Sqn 9-8-18 MR 20
MUSGROVE,Herbert Roy	Lt Aust 56Inf kia 2-9-18 CR France 511
MUSSELL,John Clarence	Capt Can27MR 15-9-16MR 23
MUTCH,John Thomas.MC.	Lt Can 72Bn dow 7-11-18 CR France 1252
MUTER,Robert.MC.	Lt Aust 57Inf dow 25-4-18 CR France 119
MUTRIE,Robert John	Maj Can 2CMR kia 5-4-16 CR Belgium 5
MYERS,Jacob Raymond	Lt Can 4CMR ded 17-10-20 CR Canada 1637

N

NAGEL,Harry	Lt Aust FA 11Bde kia 17-10-17 CR Belgium 15
NALDER,Gordon Frederick	Lt Aust 17Bn 3-5-17 MR 26
NANCARROW,Reginald Claude	Lt Aust 31Inf 26-9-17MR 29
NANCARROW,Vincent Fosbery	Lt NZ7/688 CMR ded 4-8-15 CR Europe 1
NAPIER,David George	TCapt NZ23/1906 3/3RB kia 16-9-17 CR Belgium 19
NAPPER,Albert Edward	2Lt Aust 19Inf kia 31-8-18 CR France 511
NARES,Leslie Mowbray	Lt Can 5MGC 29-9-16MR 23
NASH,Allan William	Maj Aust 2ALH kia 29-6-15 CR Gallipoli 31
NASH,Harold Leslie	Capt Aust2Inf kia 6/9-8-15 MR 6
NASH,John Foster Paton.DSO.MIDx2	Capt Can 5Bn23-4-16CR Belgium 127
NASMYTH,Alfred Wylie	Lt Can ARD attRFC 12-10-17 CR Belgium 140
NASMYTH,James Thomas	Lt Can 10Bn (AR) dow 22-4-15 MR 29
NASON,Alexis Painter	Lt Can 13Bn 1918 kia 1-10-18 CR France 597
NATHAN,Lewis Henry	Capt Can 1Bn att 1CanHQ 4-6-17 CR France 12
NATION,George Walter	Lt Can 7Bn kia 25-7-16 CR Belgium 127
NATION,Norman Charles	2Lt Aust 24Inf kia 9-10-17 CR Belgium 125
NAYLOR,Frederick Henry.MID	Capt Aust 1AICC 19-4-17MR 34
NAYLOR,Harry Innott	Lt Aust 11Inf kia 10-8-18 CR France 526
NAYLOR,Samuel Dawson	Lt Can 52Bn (MR) 31-5-16MR 29
NAYLOR,Thomas Christopher	Lt Aust49Inf kia 5-4-18 CR France 177
NEALE,Phillip.MC	Capt Can 44Bn 10-8-18MR 23
NEALE,Stanley Walter.MC.	Capt Aust 59Inf dow 29-9-18 CR France 1495
NEAVERSON,Robert Henry	Lt Aust XXII Cps LtHorse 26-4-18MR 29
NEELANDS,Clifford Abraham	Lt Can 78Bn 11-8-18MR 23
NEELON,Mortimer Arnold.MC.	Capt Can 75Bn kia 28-9-18 CR France 243
NEES,Frederick Arthur	2Lt NZ 36753 1/3NZRB dow 1-9-18 CR France 84
NEETLING, J.M.J.	Lt SA SASC 4-2-15 CR SAfrica 114 J.H.S.
NEIL,Frank Scott	Lt Can 116Bn 23-7-17CR France 68
NEILL,Alexander Guild	Lt Can 72Bn 7-9-18 CR France 95
NEILSON,Alexander Robert	Lt NZ 22690 3\3NZRB dow 28-3-18 CR France 788
NEILSON,Frank Kenny.MM.	Lt Can 14Bn kia 8-8-18 CR France 488
NEILSON,Malcolm Arthur	Maj Can 2Bn 9-4-17 CR France 68
NELSON,Beresford Joseph	2Lt Aust 53Inf kia 19-7-16 MR 7
NELSON,Eric Benjamin	Lt Aust AFC 4Sqn dow 29-1-18 CR France 88
NELSON,Francis Michael	Lt Aust 32Inf kia 26-6-18 CR France 1170
NELSON,Gregory Vincent	Maj Can 18Bn kia 5-3-17 CR France 68
NELSON,Howard Charles Reid	Lt Aust6Inf ded 19-7-19 CR Leics 63
NELSON,Joseph William	Lt Aust15Inf dow 26-9-17 CR Belgium 308
NELSON,Richard Anacletus.MM.	Lt Aust 50Inf dedacc 7-11-17 CR France 177

NELSON,William Thomas	2Lt NZ2/584 FA kia 18-4-18 CR Belgium 11
NETTLETON,Burdett Philip	Lt Aust 1ALH kia 7-8-15 MR 6
NEVILL,Ralph.MC.	Lt Can 78Bn dow 30-9-18 CR France 214
NEVIN,Archibald Remmuth	Lt Aust 15Inf 23-9-16MR 29
NEVITT,Bertram Tschudi	Lt Can 1Bn 22-9-16MR 23
NEW,Ernest Crego	Lt Aust 17Inf 9-10-17MR 29
NEW,John William	Lt Can 38Bn 31-3-17CR France 81
NEWBERRY,J.	2Lt SA 3SAInf kia 20-9-17 MR 29
NEWBY,Arthur Thomas.MC.	Lt Can FGH 10-8-18MR 23
NEWBY,William	Lt SA RAF 1SA Sqn kia 29-10-18 CR France 1272
NEWCOMB,Landell	Lt Can 8Bn (MR)10-11-17 MR 29
NEWELL,L.C.	ChEngr Can MercMar SS'Dunelm' drd 17-10-15 MR 24
NEWHAM,John Drummond	2Lt Aust 5Inf 12-5-15MR 4
NEWITT,Thomas Gordon.MC.MM.	Lt Can 47Bn 1-11-18CR France 1253
NEWLAND,Alfred Lindsay	2Lt Aust 6AMGC kia 9-11-16 CR France 744
NEWLAND,Francis Philip D.MC.	Lt Can 31Bn 9-8-18 CR France 693 8Bn
NEWMAN,Frank Ross	Capt Can 19Bn dow 23-10-16 CR Canada 256
NEWMAN,Harold Arthur	Lt Can 46Bn ded 4-11-18 CR Canada 116
NEWTON,Clarence John Raymond	2Lt Aust 24Inf kia 31-8-18 CR France 511
NEWTON,Denzil Onslow Cochrane.MVO.	Capt Can PPCLI kia 9-1-15 CR Belgium 80 &Belgium187
NICHOLAS,Bryon Fitzgerald.MC.	LtAust 24Inf9-10-17MR 29
NICHOLAS,George Matson.DSO.MID	Maj Aust 24Inf kia 14-11-16 CR France 744
NICHOLAS,James Cornelius	Lt NZ13/278 AMR kia 22-5-15 CR Gallipoli 11
NICHOLAS,James Joachim	LtCol AustAMC 5FA kia 20-9-17 CR Belgium 11
NICHOLAS,Percival Dixon	Capt Aust 12Bn 25-7-16MR 26
NICHOLES,William Pears	Lt Aust 39Inf 12-10-17 MR 29
NICHOLL,Christopher Benoni	Lt Can 5Bn dow 30-7-15 CR France 285
NICHOLLS,Benjamin Ethelbert.MC&Bar.	Capt Can 20Bn 8-5-18 CR France 504
NICHOLLS,William Hardy	Lt Can 235Bn ded 16-2-19 CR Canada 1650
NICHOLLS,William Harold	Capt Aust 15Inf kia 26-1-17 CR France 374
NICHOLS,Lilian Beatrice	Miss AmbDvr Can CASC ded 1-3-19 CR Surrey 1
NICHOLS,Raymond William	Capt Can102/2COR 23-10-16 MR 23
NICHOLSON,Angus	Lt Can 16Bn kia 5-3-18 CR France 161
NICHOLSON,Charles Lorne W.	Lt Can 4CMR 4-11-18CR France 1144
NICHOLSON,Harry Reid	Lt Can 1PnrBn &RFC 20Sqn 24-4-17MR 20
NICHOLSON,Percival Frank	2Lt Aust 57Inf kia 5-4-18 CR France 66
NICKLE,George Moore	Lt Can 44Bn kia 2-1-18 CR France 547
NICKSON,John Reginald	2Lt Can35RFC Ex 2CMR acckld 2-1-18 CR Oxford 74
NICOL,Charles Donald.DCM.MM.	Lt Can 72Bn 20-9-18CR France 597
NICOL,Ewen Cameron	Lt Can 58Bn 13-6-16CR Belgium 127
NICOL,Hector	Lt Aust AFC dedacc 16-10-18 CR Wilts 135
NICOL,Henry Ladds	Lt Can LSH or 8Bn 1-4-18 MR 23
NICOL,John Gordon	Lt Aust 11Bn 22-7-16MR 26
NICOL,Robert Kenneth.MC.	Lt NZ 10/2499 2WIR attDunsterforce kia 5-8-18 MR 61
NICOLSON,Ralph Howison	Capt NZ8/2373 1OIR kia 12-10-17 CR Belgium 123
NISBET,Alexander Goodwin	Lt Can 46Bn !0-4-17CR France 81
NISBET,Pollok Sinclair	LtCan 26Bn 2-6-16 CR Belgium 15
NISBET,Thomas Holmes.MID.	Lt NZ 8/767 OIR kia 7-8-15 CR Gallipoli 20
NIVEN,John Lang	Capt Aust AIF AAMC 1AGH 26-9-16CR Aust 109
NIX,John Edward	Capt Aust 25Bn 5-11-16MR 26
NIXON,Balfour	2Lt NZ 2/119 NZFA ded 7-6-20 CR NZ 194
NIXON,Charles Ashwin	Lt Aust AFA 4Bde dow 24-9-18 CR France 194
NIXON,Stanley	Lt Can 11PPCLI attRAF 55Sqn 1-1-19 CR France 1512
NOBLE,A.R.	Capt SA CapeCps ded 8-10-18 CR SAfrica 121
NOBLE,Francis John Goulbourn	Lt Aust 20Inf kia 31-8-18 CR France 526
NOBLE,Leonard	Lt Can 15Bn 27-9-18CR France 647
NOBLE,William Edward	Lt Aust 53Inf kia 19-7-16 MR 7
NOLAN,Morven Kelynack	2Lt Aust 13Inf dow 26-3-18 CR France 281
NOMMENSEN,Christian Valentine	Lt Aust 47Bn 28-3-18MR 26
NORDHEIMER,Albert Victor Seymour	Lt Can RCD kia 30-3-18 CR France 988

89

NORFOLK,Ernest James	Lt Can 87Bn 30-9-18CR France 240
NORMAN, Augustil Philip	Maj Can 7Bn kia 9-4-17 CR France 1059 Anquetil
NORMAN,Percy	2Lt Aust 52Inf kia 28-3-17 CR France 646
NORRIE,Robert Daniel	2Lt NZ 23/1135 3/3NZRB B'Coy kia 15-9-16 MR 11 24/1152
NORRIS,Armine Frank.MC	Lt Can 1BnCMGC kia 28-9-18 CR France 274
NORRIS,Herbert.DSO.	Capt Can 31Bn dow 25-6-18 CR France 174
NORRIS,Ignatius Bertram	LtCol Aust 53Inf kia 19-7-16 MR 7
NORRIS,Stephen Casimir	Lt CanRNewfndlandR kia 11-10-16 MR 10
NORSWORTHY,Alfred James	Lt Can 73Bn kia 29-3-17 CR France 12
NORSWORTHY,Edward Cuthbert.MID	Maj Can13Bn 22-4-15CR Belgium 125
NORTH,J.G.	2Lt SA 1SAInf dow 22-3-18 CR France 987
NORTH,John Wesley	Lt Can 1CMR kia 29-9-18 CR France 405
NORTHWAY,Francis Louis	Lt SA 1MtdRif kia 26-9-14 CR SAfrica 21
NORTHWOOD,Herbert Braid.MC.	Lt Can 78Bn kia 27-9-18 CR France 714
NORTON,Cory Arthur	Lt Can 116Bn kia 29-9-18 CR France 600
NORTON,Ernest Claude	FtPaymstr AustRAN 18-6-18CR Aust 376
NORTON,Glen	Lt Can 1DivSigCoy 26-9-16CR France 430
NORTON,Rupert Harold Imlay	2Lt NZ 6/2448 1CIR dow 9-5-18 CR France 145
NORTON-TAYLOR,Hugh Wilson	Lt Can21Bn kia 16-9-16 MR 23
NORWOOD,Ernest John	Lt Can 102Bn kia 8-6-17 CR France 81
NOSEDA,Paul Rodolfo	LtT Capt NZ 45897 WellingtonR ded 9-1-21
NOTMAN,Wilfred McKenzie	Lt Can 3Div LtTMB 6-6-16 CR Belgium 72
NOTMAN,William Russell	Lt Can 44Bn 25-10-16 MR 23
NOURSE,Grace E.Boyd	Nurse Can CAMC 1916
NOWLAND,George	Lt Aust AFC kia 22-5-18 CR France 705
NOXON,George Courtland	Lt Can 10Regt 1915
NUGENT,George	Lt Aust 13Inf dow 7-7-18 CR France 29
NUNN,John Reginald	Lt Aust AIF 17Inf9-4-17 CR Aust 112
NUTTER,Edward Roland	2Lt NZ38849 2/3NZRB kia 30-3-18 MR 12

O

OAKES,Charles Elwood	Lt Can 156Bn kldacc 3-10-16 CR Canada 1283
OAKES,Henry Kellett	Capt Can3CMR 8-12-15CR Belgium 138
OAKLEY,Roger Patrick	Lt Can49Bn D'Coy (AR)kia 30-10-17 MR 29
OATLEY,Frederick Dudley Weedon	LtCol Aust AIF 56Inf 28-3-19CR Aust 112
O'BRIEN,Alexander McIntosh	Lt Can 75Bn kia 7-8-17 CR France 81
O'BRIEN,Augustus	Capt Can 1RNcwf'landR dow 18-10-16 CR France 833
O'BRIEN,J.	2Lt Aust 21Inf 22-3-18CR Belgium 339
O'BRIEN,Wilfred John	Lt Can 75Bn 30-9-18CR France 240
O'BRIEN,William	2Lt Aust10Inf kia 9-4-17 CR France 1484
O'CALLAGHAN,Leslie George	Capt NZ 24291 1CIR kia 12-10-17 MR 30
O'CONNELL,John Roy	Lt Aust 35Inf dow 2-6-18 CR France 247
O'CONNOR,Austin James	Lt Aust 7Inf dow 24-9-17 CR Belgium 11
O'CONNOR,Daniel	2Lt NZ24397 2CIR kia 2-5-18 CR France 342
O'CONNOR,Michael Bernard	2Lt NZ 18582 3CIR kia 5-4-18 CR France 35
ODLUM,Stanley Jack	Lt Can 10Bn A'Coy kia 9-4-17 CR France 68
O'DONAGHUE,Charles Kingston	Lt Can 85Bn 27-9-18CR France 714
O'DONAHOE,James Vincent Patrick.DSO.LtCol Can 87Bn att11Bde 8-5-18 CR France 40
O'DONAHUE,John	2Lt Aust 50Inf 10-6-17MR 29
O'DONAHUE,William Charles	Capt Can CAMC ded 9-10-18 CR Canada 1343A
O'DONNELL,Michael	2Lt Aust 14Bn 11-4-17MR 26
O'FARRELL,Patrick John	Lt Aust 5Inf kia 11-8-18 CR France 526
OGILVIE,Thomas Alexander	2Lt Aust 12Inf dow 18-8-15 CR Europe 1
O'GRADY,Amy Veda	Sister Aust ANS 12-8-16MR 65
O'GRADY,John Waller de Courcy	LtCol Can 8Bn 1914
O'HALLORAN,William Eustace	Lt Aust 56Bn 2-4-17 MR 26
O'HEA,Robert Stewart	2Lt Aust 25Bn 29-7-16MR 26

O'KANE,Rosa	SNurse Aust AANS	21-12-18 CR Aust 473
OKEY,Royden Lydiard.MC.	Lt NZ 10/761 1WIR	kia 30-9-18 CR France 407
OLDAKER,Bernard George	Lt Can 8Bn ded	10-6-20 CR Canada 180
OLDERSHAW,Mark	Lt Can 28SasR	15-9-16
OLDFIELD,Herbert Lionel	Maj Can 8Bn dow	6-4-18 CR France 113
OLDFIELD,Laurence	2Lt Aust 22Inf dow	26-6-16 CR France 285
OLDHAM,Edward Castle	Maj Aust 10Inf kia	25-4-15 CR Gallipoli 30
OLDHAM,James Henry	Capt Can 3Bn	24-9-16 CR France 1505
OLDHAM,Walter Herbert.DCM.	Lt Aust 56Inf kia	1-9-18 CR France 692
OLIFENT,Elwin Bruce	2Lt Aust 27Bn	5-11-16 MR 26
OLIFENT,James Harry Smith	Capt Aust AIF AustNaval&MilForce	30-5-20 CR Aust 211A
OLIVE,William	Major Lt Aust Engrs 5FC kia	23-4-16 CR France 275
OLIVER,Albert Henry Boulton	Lt Aust 20Inf kia	11-8-18 CR France 526
OLIVER,Allen.MC.	Lt Can CFA 7Bde	18-11-16 CR France 150
OLIVER,Bernard Elvey	2Lt Aust AFA 101HB 1Bde dow	14-8-16 CR France 51
OLIVER,Cecil Claude	2Lt Aust 9Inf kia	22-9-15 CR Gallipoli 22
OLIVER,Cecil Stanley	Lt Aust 2AMGC dow	31-7-16 CR France 44
OLIVER,Frederick William	Maj Can 28Bn kia	15-9-16 CR France 280
OLIVER,James Donald	Lt Aust 10 LtTMB kia	4-10-17 CR Belgium 125
OLIVER,Moses	Lt Can 44MR	11-5-17
OLIVIER,Adolphe	Lt Can CAMC ded	16-10-18 CR Canada 345
OLIVIER,H.J.	Lt SA MtdCmdos kia	23-12-14 CR SAfrica 107 drd
OLLEY,E.H.	2Lt Aust 26Inf	4-8-16 CR France 1890
O'LOUGHLIN,Henry Herbert George	Capt Aust 5Inf kia	28-2-17 CR France 385
O'MEARA,Bulkeley Ernest Adolphus.DSO.Capt	SA SAIC ded	31-8-16 CR EAfrica 9 ULEA
O'NEILL,James Gordon	2Lt Aust 48Inf kia	8-8-18 CR France 526
O'NEILL,John Irvine	2Lt NZ 16/689 Pnrs kia	3-10-16 MR 11
ONGLEY,Patrick Augustine	2Lt NZ 33169 2OIR kia	27-8-18 CR France 614
OPIE,Elgar Watts	2Lt Aust 6Inf	4-10-17 MR 29
ORCHARD,Geoffrey Duncan	2Lt Aust 16Inf dow	15-10-18 CR France 146
O'REILLY,Fleming Pinkston.MC.	Capt Can 2MMGBde	27-9-18 CR France 214
O'REILLY,Peter Bernard Joseph	Lt Aust FA 10Bde	3-5-17 MR 26
O'REILLY,Richard Hamilton	Lt Can CE 1TC &RAF 62Sqn kia	29-9-18 CR France 1727
ORGAN,Studley	2Lt Aust 27Inf	9-10-17 MR 29
ORLEANS & BRAGAIRZA,A.G.P,Prince of.MC.	Capt Can RCD	1918
ORME,Rupert Austin.MC.	Capt Can 72Bn	10-8-18 CR France 586
ORMSBY,John Anthony Ninian	Lt CanCMMG Bde attRFC	2-8-16 CR France 837
ORR,Henry Noble	Lt Can 2Bn	14-7-17 CR France 32
ORR,John Richard	Lt Can 1CORD 177Bn attRAF 80Sqn kia	9-8-18 CR France 247
ORR,John Percy.MC.	Lt Can 54Bn	8-12-18 CR France 1196
ORR,Robert Wells	Capt Aust 14Bn	11-4-17 MR 26
OSBORNE,Frederick	Lt Aust AIF 43Inf	3-11-18 CR Aust 212
OSBORNE,Hubert Patterson	Capt Can 104Bn attRFC kld	7-7-17 CR Belgium 115
OSGOOD,Giles Dever	Lt Can 26NBR	15-8-17
OSLER,Ralph Featherstone Lake	Lt Can 16Bn	16-6-16 CR Belgium 11
OSTIC,William Clark	Lt Can 4Bn	8-8-18 CR France 29
OSTERHOUT,A.B.	Lt Can 46Bn ded	7-2-20 CR Canada 179
O'SULLIVAN,Alfred	Lt Can 5FldCoy	1916
O'SULLIVAN,Brian More	Capt Aust5Inf dow	23-8-18 CR France 119
O'SULLIVAN,Leo Desmond	2Lt NZ40752 1WIR dow	24-8-18 CR France 84
O'SULLIVAN,Thomas Real	2Lt Aust41Inf kia	17-4-18 CR France 210
OSWALD,Cecil William Orlando	Lt Aust 27Inf kia	31-8-18 CR France 627
OSWALD,George Harry.MC.	Capt Aust43Inf dow	1-9-18 CR France 119
O'TOOLE,Francis	2Lt Can NfndlandR dow	12-10-17 CR Belgium 16
OTT,Franklin Walter.MC.	Capt Can 116Bn kia	17-9-18 CR France 154
OTTAWAY,Bertram Hope	2Lt Aust 48Bn	5-8-16 MR 26
OTTY,Allen.MID	Lt Can 5CMR D'Coy	30-10-17 CR Belgium 126
OTTY,George Nugent Dickson	Lt Can 5CMR D'Coy (QR) kia	3-6-16 MR 29
OUGHTERSON,H.G.	Lt SA4SAInf kia	7-7-16 CR France 630
OUTERBRIDGE,Norman A.	Lt Can 1RNewfndlandR kia	14-4-17 CR France 427

OUTERSON,Joseph	Lt　Can　78Bn　kia　19-11-16　CR France 150
OUTHIT,William Edward	Maj　Can　14Huss HQstaff Mdist13 3-3-18　CR Canada 620
OUTHWAITE,Reginald McR.	Capt&QM　Aust 46Inf　dedacc 16-5-18　CR France 71
OVERTON,Henry Isle	2Lt　NZ2/1329　NZFA　dow 27-9-18　CR France 245
OVERTON,Percy John.MID.	Maj　NZ7/506　CMR　kia 7-8-15　CR Gallipoli 17
OWEN,George Burgoyne	Capt　Aust 3DivHQ　ded 5-11-18　CR France 341
OWEN,Godfrey Felix	Lt　SASAMtdRifs attRIrReg　ded　30-10-18　CR Wilts 115
OWEN,Harold Edward	Capt　NZ 3/3170 NZMC　ded　18-11-20 CR NZ 257
OWEN,Harold Heber	Lt　Can　7Bn　kia　30-1-16　CR Belgium 339
OWEN,Percy Irvine Haylock	2Lt　Aust 3Inf　kia 22-9-17　CR Belgium 125
OWEN,Sidney Smith	Lt　Can　BCRD attRAF 11-12-18　CR France 1142
OWEN-JONES,Frederick	Lt　SA 8SAInf　ded　27-5-21　CR SAfrica 53 25-5-21
OWEN-SMYTHE,Trevor	Lt　Aust 10Inf　kia　16-5-15　CR Gallipoli 30
OWENS,Thomas Sargent	Lt　Can　38Bn　dow　11-8-18　CR France 29
OXENHAM,Gordon Vincent	Lt　Aust　AFC 1Sqn　27-6-18 MR 34

P

PACKMAN,William Lumsden	Lt　Aust　AFA 4Bde　dow　15-11-16　CR France 400
PAE,Peter Richard	Lt　Can 102Bn　1-10-18
PAGE,Frank.MC.MM.	Capt　Aust 9LHorse　dow 29-10-17　CR France 8
PAGE,George Davies	Lt　NZ 12/48　2AIR　dow 6-10-16　CR France 40
PAGE,Harry Routhmell	Lt Can　27Bn　kia　9-6-16　CR Belgium 15 Henry Rauthmell
PAGE,William Charles	Capt　NZ　5/563　ASC　doi 27-5-18　CR Hamps 30
PAINE,A.	Capt　SA　10SAInf　dow 4-9-19　CR Tanzania 1 &EAfrica 4 kia
PAINE,Sydney William	2Lt　NZ 4/429　NZE　kia　19-5-15　CR Gallipoli 8
PALLING,Aubrey	Lt　Aust MGC 6Coy 3-5-17　MR 26
PALLING,John Ferguson	Capt　Can CAMC　ded　31-1-18　CR Canada 1614
PALLISER,Arthur John	Lt　Aust AFC　kia 5-11-18　CR Belgium 413
PALMER,Alan Dexter	Lt　Aust　3ALH MG Sqn 6-8-16　CR Egypt 2
PALMER,Balfour Malcolm	Lt　Can　2CMR A'Coy dow　10-8-18　CR France 360
PALMER,Harry Thomas	Capt　NZ　11/117 WMR MGSect ded　15-7-15　MR 6
PALMER,Henry Arthur.DCM.	Lt　Can75Bn　30-9-18 CR France 148
PALMER,Herbert Leopold	Capt　Aust55Inf　kia 11-3-17　CR France 400
PALMER,L.	2Lt　SA　3SAInf　ded　14-2-18　CR France 699
PALMER,Percy Eric	2Lt　Aust　AImpForce &RFC 29Sqn　kia　17-7-17　CR Belgium 95
PALMER,Percival James	Lt　NZ5/118A　2CIR　dow 7-6-17　MR 9
PALMER,Reginald	Lt　Can　27Bn　kia　9-6-16　CR Belgium 15
PALMER,Reginald Eric Dalton	Lt　Aust　46Inf　ded　4-12-18　CR France 717
PALMER,Reginald Wallis	Lt　Aust 5AustPnrs　dedacc 2-4-18　CR France 76
PALMER,William Arnold	Lt　Can 43Bn (MR) kia　14-11-17　MR 29
PAMMENT,Ernest Frederick Murray	Lt Aust 43Inf　kia 30-3-18　CR France 833
PAPINEAU,Talbot Mercer.MC.	Maj　Can PPCLI (EOR)　kia　30-10-17　MR 29
PARES,Thomas Edward	Lt　Can　47Bn　1917
PARK,Robert	Capt　Aust Engrs 13FC　26-9-17 MR 29
PARK,Victor Herbert	Lt　NZ 22603　2WIR　ded　4-3-19　CR France 85
PARKE,George Reginald	Lt　Can18Bn　24-3-17 MR 23
PARKER,Albert Thomas.MC.	Lt Aust60Inf　kia 25-10-17　CR Belgium 19
PARKER,Arthur Allan.MC.	Capt　Can CAMC 6FA　dow　12-10-18　CR France 214
PARKER,Audley	Lt　Aust FA 1Bde　dow 21-7-17　CR Belgium 15
PARKER,Francis Maitland Wyborn	Maj　AustAFA 3Bde　ded　18-3-15　CR Egypt 9
PARKER,Harold Carlyle	Lt　Aust 37Inf　dow PoW　30-1-17　CR France 525
PARKER,Horace	Lt　Can　44Bn　11-8-18 CR France 879
PARKER,John	2Lt　Aust 30Inf　kia　20-7-16　MR 7

PARKER,Raymond H.	Lt Can 38Bn 18-11-16 CR France 150
PARKER,Thomas Joseph	Lt Aust 4DivSigs kia 12-10-17 CR Belgium 84
PARKER,William	2Lt Aust 27Inf ded 28-2-17 CR France 146
PARKER,William	2Lt Aust AFC dedacc 1-9-18 CR Glouc 172
PARKES,Adrian Wesley	Lt Aust 1DivMedTMBkia 15-7-17 CR Belgium 72
PARKES,Reuben	2Lt Aust 34Bn 30-3-18MR 26
PARKHURST,Arthur Usk	Maj SA SAMC ded 27-11-18 CR Safrica 30
PARR,Alfred John.DCM.	2Lt Aust59Inf dow 1-10-18 CR France 234
PARR,Clayton Bowers	Maj Can 24Bn 3-10-16CR France 59
PARROTT,Henry Joseph	2Lt Aust 9Inf kia 9-4-17 CR France 646
PARRY,Ernest Charles	Capt NZ 12/2904 1AIR 16Coy kia 6-10-17 MR 30
PARRY,Harry Leslie	2Lt Aust 11Inf kia 28-6-15 CR Gallipoli 22
PARRY,Melville Sims	Lt Can 50Bn ded 7-9-20 CR Canada 180
PARSONS,Cecil Braithwaite	Lt SA 1SAInf kia 16-7-16 MR 21
PARSONS,William Henry.MM.	2Lt Aust 22Inf kia 26-3-18 CR Belgium 339
PARTINGTON,Charles Thomas	Maj Can29Bn 26-9-16MR 23
PASCOE,William Henry Eric John	2Lt Aust 6Bn 8-5-17 MR 26
PASCOE-WEBBE,Illaesus Faustus	Lt Aust FA 13Bde kia 19-8-17 CR Belgium 10
PASSMORE,Harold Egbert	Lt Can8Bn kia 22-5-15 CR France 279
PATERSON,A.	Lt Aust 32Inf 20-7-16CR France 566
PATERSON,Bruce	Capt Aust AIF 27Inf10-10-18 CR Aust 287
PATERSON,David	2Lt NZ 11/596 WMR kia 1-4-18 MR 34
PATERSON,Ernest Ellerman.MC.	Lt Aust 22Inf kia 3-10-18 CR France 234
PATERSON,George Irving	Capt Can SRD 152Bn &RAF 82Sqn kia 2-4-18 CR France 425
PATERSON,George M. Sub	Lt Aust RAN attDport Div HMS`Defence'kia 31-5-16 MR 2
PATERSON,Lachlan George	Lt Aust AFA 21Bde dow 6-8-16 CR France 74
PATERSON,M.	2Lt Aust 2Inf 9-4-17 CR France 529
PATERSON,Malcolm Eric	Lt Aust 28Inf kia 8-8-18 CR France 144
PATERSON,Murray Hulme.MC	Capt Can CAMC dedacc 15-9-17 CR Surrey 1
PATERSON,Ogilvie Brown	2Lt/ Lt Aust 26Inf AIF29-7-16MR 26 &CR France 390
PATERSON,William.DCM.	Lt Can 7Bn ded 28-1-19 CR Belgium 267
PATERSON,William Fergus	Capt NZ 3/4277 NZMC ded 14-11-18 CR Surrey 1
PATON,Frederick William	Lt Can 5Bn kia 16-8-17 CR France 550
PATTEN,Edgar William Galbraith	Lt Can 58Bn C'Coy (2COR) kia 26-10-17 MR 29
PATTERSON,Cecil Norman.MC.	2Lt Aust 43Bn 1-9-18 MR 26
PATTERSON,George Holbrook	Maj Aust FA7Bde kia 14-4-17 CR Belgium 53
PATTERSON,Nolan Tweedale	Lt CanCFA 3Bde dow 1-6-16 CR Belgium 11
PATTERSON,Penistan James	Lt Aust 12Inf kia 25/28-4-15 MR 6
PATTERSON,William Roger	Lt Can CASC 3DivMechTransCoy 4-2-19 CR Numb 2
PATTINSON,John Frank	Lt Aust Engrs 2TC kia 14-5-18 CR France 116
PATTISON,Albert Dale	Lt AustAFA 4Bde dow 4-7-18 CR France 102
PATTISON,Charles Joseph	2Lt SA 1SAInf dow 24-10-16 CR France 145
PATTISON,Hugh Macmillan	Lt Can21Bn 12-10-18 CR France 214
PATTISON,Walker Byron James	Lt Aust 9Inf dow 10-5-15 CR Egypt 9
PATTON,Hugh Lindsay.MM.	2Lt NZ 12/3121 1AIR kia 27-8-18 CR France 512
PATTON,John Henry	Lt Can 3Bn 3-5-17 MR 23
PATTRICK,Beresford Septimus Nunn	2Lt Aust 13Bn 29-8-16MR 26
PATTRICK,Kenneth Nunn	Capt Aust 13Inf kia 8-8-18 CR France 1170
PAUL,C.Stewart.DFC.	Lt Aust AFC 1Sqn drd 22-1-19 MR 41
PAUL,John Charles	Lt Aust 8Inf kia 25-4-15 MR 6
PAUL,Sydney Victor	2Lt NZ10/2274 1WIR kia 23-10-17 MR 30
PAULIN,Arthur Hilton	Capt Can 3ResB n ded 13-3-17 CR Canada 1563 133Bn
PAULIN,Harry	Capt Aust 53Inf kia 19-7-16 MR 7
PAULING,Frank William	2Lt NZ 45037 NZRB dow 16-2-19 CR NZ 10
PAWLEY,Norman Howard.MC.	Lt Can 44Bn 1917
PAYNE, C.H .	Lt SA SAEngrs ded 9-4-18 CR EAfrica 92 C.A.
PAYNE,James Humphrey Allen	Capt SA 8SAInf ded 28-7-17 CR Tanzania 1 &EAfrica 38
PAYNE,James Nelson.MIDx2	Lt SA 8SAInf dow 20-7-17 CR Tanzania 1 &EAfrica 38
PAYNE,Lancelot Joseph Wollard.MC.	LtAust 25Inf dow 30-5-18 CR France 71
PAYNE,Richard Norman	Lt Can 93Bn 1916

PAYNE,William Henry	Capt	Aust Engrs CavDiv SigSqn ded 10-12-17 CR Iran 8
PEACH,Percy Walter	Lt Can 52Bn	12-10-16 CR Bucks 6
PEACOP,Edward Layle	Lt Can 43Bn	1921
PEAKER,Cecil Howard	Lt Can 4CMR (1COR)2-6-16 MR 29	
PEARCE,Alfred Alexander	2Lt Aust 10Inf kia 10-8-18 CR France 526	
PEARCE,Charles George	Capt Aust AIF AFA 8Bde 8-8-21 CR Aust 112	
PEARCE,Clyde Bowman	2Lt Aust 52Inf 10-6-17MR 29	
PEARCE,Gordon MacKenzie	Lt Can 124PnrBn 1917	
PEARCE,John Joseph Langley	2Lt NZ 38867 1CIR dow 25-8-18 CR France 84	
PEARCE,Joseph William.MC.	Capt Aust 21Inf 4-10-17MR 29	
PEARCE,Norman Matthew	Capt Aust 6ALH kia 29-7-16 CR Egypt 2	
PEARCE,Sydney Mattinson	Lt Aust 27Bn 4-8-16 MR 26	
PEARCE,Walter King	Lt Can 1CMR A'Coy 15-9-16MR 23	
PEARSON,Ebenezer Ralph	2Lt Aust 58Bn 26-3-17MR 26	
PEARSON,J.E.	1stEngr CanMercMar SS`Pomeranian' 15-4-18MR 24	
PEARSON,Ralph Odell	Lt CanCMGC 2TankBnded 14-10-18 MR 24	
PEARSON,William David	Lt Can15Bn 27-9-18CR France 274	
PEART,William Andrew Reginald	Maj Aust FA 2Bde dow 3-11-17 CR Belgium 11	
PEAT,J.	Capt Aust 44Inf 27-6-17CR Belgium 90	
PECK,E.J.	Lt Aust Engrs 1FC11-12-16 CR Wilts 115	
PEDLEY,Hugh Stowell.MC.	Capt Can 12LTMB 1918	
PEEL,John Clifford	2Lt Aust RFC 19-9-18MR 26	
PEERLESS,Arthur Neville	Lt Can 2Bn 29-4-16CR Belgium 11	
PEERS,Charles Thompson	Lt Can102Bn 8-8-18 CR France 589	
PEIRCE,Arthur Henry Markham	Lt Can46Bn 6-5-17 MR 23	
PELLETIER,Charles Adolphe	Lt Can CETD &RAF 1Sqn 11-5-18MR 20	
PELLETIER,RÇne Archer	Lt Can 14Bn kia 27-9-16 CR France 59	
PELTON,Norman Gilbert	Capt Aust 58Inf kia 12-5-17 CR France 1486	
PEMBERTON,Warren Colclough	Lt Can 48Bn attRFC kld 25-4-16 CR Hamps 4 3Pnrs	
PENDERGAST,Francis Thomas	Lt Can 21Bn 4-11-17CR Belgium 125	
PENNIMAN,Raynond B.MC.	Lt Can RCR 8-10-16MR 23	
PENNY,Bertram Stephens	Lt Aust AIF 16Inf 3-11-19CR Aust 212	
PENNY,Edward Goff Trevor.MC.	Lt Can 14Bn 8-8-18 CR France 488	
PENNY,John A.	StaffSurg Aust RANR 18-4-16CR Aust 187	
PENNYCOOK,William Scott.MID	LtCol NZ 9/1209 2OIR kia 24-8-18 CR France 512	
PEPLER,Stanley James	Lt Can 51Bn &RFC 43Sqn 6-3-17 MR 20	
PEPPERCORN,John Saxon	Lt Aust AIF 1ATC 28-5-19CR Aust 197	
PEPPIATT,Frederick Charles	Lt Can 18Bn 9-5-17 CR France 777	
PERCY,Frank	2Lt NZ 10/1053 1WIR dow 15-8-16 CR France 922	
PERCY,Frederick Leonard.MM.	2Lt Aust 4Bn 14-4-18MR 26	
PERDOMO,S.A.	2Lt Honduras BrHondTerForce 16-7-21CR CentAmerica 1	
PERDUE,Mowbray Macdonell	Lt Can 44Bn 9-5-17 MR 23	
PERKINS, Louis Clarence	Lt Can 27Bn 4-5-17 CR France 95 Lewis	
PERMEZEL,Cedric Holroyd	Capt Aust 7Inf dow 14-7-15 MR 6	
PERRATON,Frederick Arnott	Lt Can 21RBn &RFC1-3-17 CR Devon 237	
PERRAU,Robert Donaldson	2Lt Aust 35Inf 11-6-17MR 29	
PERREM,Charles Henry.MC.	2Lt SA 1SAInf dow 19-10-18 CR France 528	
PERRY,Edgar Seymour	Lt NZ 9/661 OMR kia 21-8-15 MR 14	
PERRY,Gilbert Douglas	2Lt Aust AFC dedacc 29-6-18 CR Glouc 174	
PERRY,Theophilus William	Lt Aust 45Inf kia 5-4-18 CR France 197	
PERTUS, Remi Alphonse	Lt Can CFC &RAF kia 29-8-18 CR France 1170	
PESKETT,Leonard Bertram	Lt Aust 5DivTMB dow 3-6-18 CR France 119	
PESTELL,Joseph Victor	2Lt Aust 3Inf kia 30-8-16 CR Belgium 127	
PETERMANN,Wilfred Ferrier.MID	Maj Can 13Bn 26-9-16CR France 430	
PETERS,A.J.	Cmdr Can MercMar SS`LakeMichigan'15-4-18MR 24	
PETERS,Gerald Hamilton	Lt Can 7Bn (BCR) 3-6-16 MR 29	
PETERSEN,Frederick Theodore.MC.	LtAust Engrs 1FC kia 11-9-18 CR France 446	
PETERSEN,Hans Victor	Lt Aust42Bn 24-8-18MR 26	
PETERSON,Harold Maxmilliam	Lt NZ 2/2700 NZFA DAC dow 4-10-17 CR Belgium 101
PETHEBRIDGE,Samuel Augustus.KCMG.Sir	BrigGen Aust AustNaval&MilForce 25-1-18CR Aust 305

PETRIE,Arnold James	2Lt NZ3/1186 1AIR 6Coy dow 18-4-18 CR France 62
PETTIGREW,Harold James	Lt Aust 9Inf kia 21-8-16 CR France 314
PETTY,Gertrude	Nurse Can CAMC 1919
PFLAUM,Theodore Milton	2Lt Aust MGC 25Coy dow 24-9-17 CR Belgium 11
PFRIMMER,V.Ralph	Lt Can RFC 1DAC1917
PHILBRICK,Bertie Raymond	Capt Can 46Bn 9-9-16 CR Belgium 37
PHILIPPSON,Clarence Lancelot	2Lt Aust 48Inf dow 7-11-16 CR France 64
PHILLIPS,Edward James.MC.	Lt SA 3SAInf dow 16-10-16 CR France 177
PHILLIPS,Eugene Summerville.MC.	Lt Can 46Bn 1-11-18CR France 1258
PHILLIPS,Frederick Stobo.MM.	2Lt Aust 1Inf kia 5-11-16 CR France 277
PHILLIPS,Leslie Moore.DCM.	2Lt Aust 6Inf kia 14-4-18 CR France 200
PHILLIPS,Norman Clive	Lt Aust 51Inf dow 17-5-18 CR France 29
PHILPOT,James Temple	2Lt Aust 3Inf dow 25-7-16 CR France 44
PHINNEY,Henry Havelock.MC.	Lt Can CFA 1Bde 1921
PICARD,Romulus Emanuel	Capt Can 3Bn 3-5-17 MR 23
PICK,Peter Wilson	Capt Can 1Bn kia 15-6-15 CR France 571
PICKBURN,William Henry.MID	Maj SA HArty dow 13-11-16 CR France 40
PICKERING,George	Lt Aust AFC 3Sqn ded 21-11-18 CR Essex 1
PICKERING,Lisle Barrington	Lt SA HQRecs&CampStaff ded 9-10-18 CR SAfrica 119
PICKERING,Howard Vincent	Lt Can4CMR (1COR) kia 26-10-17 MR 29
PICKETT,Reginald James.MC.	Lt Aust 24Inf 9-10-17MR 29
PICKUP,Walter Willett	Capt Can 14Bn 9-4-17 CR France 523
PICOT,Thomas Arthur Essex	Lt Aust 18Inf kia 29-7-16 CR France 832
PICTON-WARD,Espine Montgomery	Lt Can16Bn kia 22-5-15 MR 23
PIDCOCK,John William.MC.	Lt AustAFA 42Bty dow 5-4-18 CR France 62
PIDDINGTON,William Thomas	2Lt Aust 55Inf kia 4-7-18 CR France 209
PIDGEON,Ivan Farquhar William	Lt Aust Engrs 5FC kia 4-5-17 CR France 1484
PIERCE,Benjamin Clifford	Lt Can 4CMR kia 9-4-17 CR France 68
PIERCY,Harold Eustace	Lt Can 13Bn dow 14-10-16 CR France 59
PIERCY,John George.DSO.	LtCol Can CFA 1Bde 18-11-18 CR France 1196
PIESSE,Vernon Frederick	Capt Aust 10ALH kia 7-8-15 MR 6
PIETERS,P.J.C.	Lt SA ProtGarR 25-10-18 CR SAfrica 1
PIGGIN,Frederick P.Loverseed	Lt SA RhodNatR kia 20-12-16 CR EAfrica 15
PIGGOTT,Francis John	Capt Aust 36Inf kia 10-6-17 CR Belgium 110
PIGOU,Arthur Comyn	Lt NZ 7/260 CMR HQ ded 12-12-18 CR Asia 52
PIKE,Arthur William	Lt Can 75Bn 9-8-18 MR 23 Wilson
PIKE,Claude Wellington	Lt Can 3Bn 8-10-16CR France 1505
PILCHER,Norman Campbell	Maj Can 5CMR kia 19-5-16 CR Belgium 5
PILKINGTON,Stanley Howard	2Lt AustAFC 2Sqn dedacc 24-10-17 CR Surrey 1
PILLING,Ewen George	Lt NZ 8/1601 OIR kia 7-6-17 MR 9
PILLOW,Roy Nelson	Cadet14061Aust AFC 7Sqn dedacc 24-8-18 CR Glouc 172
PIMM,Alfred George	Lt Can 2CMR 9-4-17 CR France 573
PINEO,Harold Macdonald	Lt CanRAF 181Bn ded 18-12-18 CR Canada 11
PINEO,Henry Hoyt	Capt Can 5CMR kia 21-7-16 CR Belgium 5
PINKHAM,Ernest Frederick	Capt Can 31Bn kia 15-9-16 MR 23
PIRIE,Gordon Moore	Lt Can 116Bn ded 21-8-20 CR Canada 1663
PITMAN,Talbot Lawrence.MC.	Lt Aust 44Inf 26-10-17 CR Belgium 123
PITT,Eryl Stephens	Capt NZ 19085 2AIR kia 12-10-17 CR Belgium 125
PITT,J.H.	Capt SASASC 16-4-17MR 46
PITTS,Frederick	Capt Can58Bn 28-6-17CR France 12
PITTS,Harry James	Capt Can 5CMR dow 3-6-16 CR Belgium 11
PLACE,Herbert Lancelot.DCM.	Lt Aust 21Inf 9-10-17MR 29
PLANT,Harold Frederick Hood.MID	Capt Aust AAMC 1AGH kia 7-8-16 CR France 515
PLANTE,Louis Alexander	Capt Maj Can 167Bn dedacc 26-6-16 CR Canada 324 Alexandre
PLASKITT,Wilfred Mirfield	2Lt Aust AFA 11Bde kia 31-3-18 CR France 197
PLATT,Edward Cuthbert	Lt Can24Bn (QR) 7-11-17MR 29
PLATT,Edwin	Capt Can 8Bn kia11—4-17917CR France 68
PLATT,Francis Joseph	Lt Aust 15Inf kia 8-8-15 MR 6
PLATT,Henry Errol Beauchamp	Lt Can 3Bn A'Coy dow 5-5-16 CR Belgium 11
PLAYNE,John Morton	2Lt Aust Engrs 2FCkia 7-8-15 MR 6

PLOW,Arthur.MC.MM.	Maj Can 14Bn 19-4-18CR France 184
PLOWMAN,Hugh McDonald	Capt Aust 60Inf kia 19-7-16 MR 7
PLUMMER,John.MC.	Lt Aust 19Inf kia 31-8-18 CR France 511
PLUMMER,R.G.	Lt Aust AMGC 5 Coy ded 14-2-19 CR France 1211
PLUNKETT,Edward Arthur P.	Lt Can CFA 4Bde 1917
POCOCK,A.A.	Maj SA 5Horse ded 16-1-17 CR SAfrica 66
POCKLEY,B.C.A.	Capt Aust AIF AAMC 11-9-14CR PNG 5
POCKLEY,John Graham Antill	Lt Aust 33Bn 30-3-18MR 26
POLE,T.R.M.	Lt SA 5SAH kia 10-8-16 CR Tanzania 1 &EAfrica 9
POLLARD,Walter Henry	Lt Can 7Bn dow 28-9-18 CR France 214
POLLOCK,Martin	Lt Can 27Bn 3-5-17 MR 23
POLLOCK,Robert	Capt Can 58Bn 29-9-18CR France 714
POLLOCK,William Grieve	Lt Aust 7Inf 3-10-17MR 29
POLSON,Cecil	2Lt NZ 38868 2/3NZRB kia 26-8-18 CR France 1484
POLSON,G.	2Lt SA 4SAInf kia 12-10-16 CR France 385
PONTING,Cecil Arthur	Lt SA 10Horse kia 26-11-17 MR 52
PONTON,John Ronald	Lt Can 46Bn A'Coy dow 28-10-16 CR France 40
POOLE,Bernard Routh	Capt Can CAVC att5CRT 3-5-17 CR France 1182
POOLE,W.J.S.G.	Lt Aust 7Inf 9-8-18 CR France 526
POOLEY,John Ellis	2Lt Aust38Bn 1-1-17 MR 26
POPE,Charles.VC.	Lt Aust 11Inf kia 15-4-17 CR France 1496
POPE,Charles Alexander	Lt Can PPCLI kia 7-5-16 CR Belgium 309
POPE,Frank	Lt Can 49Bn kia 26-8-18 CR France 732
POPE,Jerry Gordon	Lt Can 14Bn 16-8-17CR France 219
POPE,Robert Mayes	Lt Can HMCS`Galiano' 30-10-18
POPE-HENNESSY,Brian.MC.	2Lt SA 2SAInf kia 10-4-18 MR 29
POPE-HENNESSY,Hugh	Lt Can 49Bn 30-4-17CR France 924
POPHAM,Clark Hall	Lt Can 8Bn kia 26-9-16 CR France 314
POPPLEWELL,H.B.	Capt SA KAR
PORTEOUS,H.E.	2Lt SA 3SAInf kia 12-4-17 CR France 452
PORTEOUS,John Robert	Lt Aust 20Inf kia 23-5-16 CR France 83
PORTER,Everett Addison	Lt Can 47Bn dow 12-11-16 CR France 59
PORTER,George Basil Lee.MC.MID	Lt NZ 6/122 2CIR Ex 1BrWIndR kia 8-10-18 CR France 660
PORTER,George Reginald.MID	Capt Aust 44Inf dedacc 10-12-17 CR Belgium 138
PORTER,Harvey Ernest Maxwell	Lt Can 3Bn attRFC 13Sqn kia 18-7-17 CR France 113
PORTER,James Herbert	Maj Can 20Bn ded 21-6-19 CR Canada 1608
PORTER,Katherine Agnes Lawrence.RRC.MID	Sister Aust AANS 16-7-19CR Aust 112
PORTER,Roger Morrow	Lt Can 2Bn kia 30-8-18 CR France 310
PORTER,Simon Fahey.MC.	Capt Aust15Inf dow 25-11-18 CR Surrey 1
PORTER,William Ridgeway	Lt Aust 18Bn 3-5-17 MR 26
POSSINGHAM,Alfred Harold	Capt Aust8Inf 8-5-15 MR 4
POSTE,Henry Thomas.MC&Bar.	Lt Can 3Bn dow 9-8-18 CR France 29
POTT,Frank	Capt Can 10Bn (AR) 22-4-15MR 29
POTTER,Frank Hales.MID	Lt Aust 10AMGC dow 3-11-17 CR France 64
POTTON,Leonard Harry	Capt NZ13/120 NZDC ded 14-11-18 CR NZ 271
POTTS,James McComming	Lt Can 21Bn kia 8-8-18 CR France 29
POTTS,James Watson	Lt Can 44Bn kia 3-6-17 CR France 81
POWELL,Alan Torrance.DSO.	Maj Can 14Bn dow 19-4-18 CR France 95
POWELL,Charles Donald	2Lt SA HArty 74 SB dow 4-4-17 CR France 96
POWELL,Harry Cecil Wells	2Lt SA 1SAInf kia 18-10-18 CR France 940
POWELL,George Eyre.MM.	2Lt Aust 28Bn 26-3-17MR 26
POWELL,Haynes Robert	Lt Can 13Bn 21-5-15MR 23
POWELL,Robert B.	Lt Can 16Bn 28-4-17CR France 68
POWELL,Thomas Henry Norman	2Lt Aust 1AustDivHQ dedacc 24-4-17 CR Surrey 1
POWELL,Vernon Harcourt de Butts.MC.	Maj Can CFA 53Bty 13Bde 2-1-18 CR Cambs 32
POWER,Edward Victor	Lt Can 24Bn kia 8-8-18 CR France 652
POWER,Kathleen	Sister Aust AANS 13-8-16MR 65
POWER,Noel P.	Lt Aust 4Inf 4-10-17MR 29
POWER,Walter	Lt SA 1CapeCps kia 6-11-17 CR Tanzania 1 &EAfrica 11
POWER,William Ford	Lt Can 8CRT ded 9-11-18 CR Canada 547

POWIS,Gordon Douglas	Maj Can 31Bn B'Coy (AR) kia 6-11-17 MR 29
POWLEY,Alfred James.MC.	Capt NZ 24/8 4\3NZRB dow 20-9-16 Cr France 833
POZZI,Leonard Lambert	2Lt Aust 6Inf 8-5-15 MR 4
PRATT,Albert Ernest	2Lt Aust53Inf kia 19-7-16 CR France 832
PRATT,Austin Craig.MC	Lt Can 2BnCE ded 11-2-19 CR France 40
PRATT, William John	Lt Can 75Bn dow 10-6-17 CR France 81 J.W.
PRENTICE,George Henry	2Lt NZ6/329 3CanterburyR 12Coy ded 18-11-18 CR NZ 243
PRESCOTT,Joseph Hammill	Lt Can 4CMR 2-10-16MR 23
PRESTON,Alan Hurst.MC.MID.	Lt NZ 10/910 MGC 5Coy kia 7-6-17 CR Belgium 89
PRESTON,Harold Brant.MC.	Lt Can 54Bn kia 27-9-18 CR France 715
PRESTON,Wilfred John.MC&Bar.	Capt Can 116Bn 5-11-18CR Germany 1
PREW,Harold Edward	Lt SA 1SAInf ded 19-10-17 CR Surrey 1
PRICE,Charles H.	Lt Can PPCLI 24-1-15CR Belgium 111
PRICE,Edward Arthur	2Lt NZ32226 2CIR dow 10-10-18 CR France 398
PRICE,Evan Edward.DSO.MC&Bar.	Lt Can RCD ded 11-9-19 CR Canada 1688
PRICE,James Sanford	Lt Can CFA 3Bde 13-9-16CR France 832
PRICE,John Herbert	Lt Can 27Bn kia 11-8-17 CR France 570
PRICE,John Warren	Lt Can RAF CFA ded 9-10-18 CR Canada 1054
PRICE,Richard	Maj NZ 8/1094 OIR kia 2/3-5-15 MR 6
PRICE,Robert Walter Francis.MC.	LtCan 54Bn kia 27-9-18 CR France 715
PRICHARD,Arvan James	Lt Aust MGC 2Bn 18-7-18MR 26
PRICHARD,Edward Owen	Lt Aust 21Inf kia 13-3-17 CR France 512
PRIEST,Arthur Francis Lester	LtNZ 6/1695 CIRdow 8-8-15 MR 5
PRIEST,Roy Simpson	Capt NZ 7/103 ICC kia 19-4-17 MR 34
PRIESTLEY,Alfred John	2Lt NZ 2/158 NZFA kia 1-9-18 CR France 745
PRIESTLEY,Phillip Henry	Maj Aust 8ALH kia 3-5-18 CR Syria 2
PRIMMER,Jacob Hope	Capt NZ 2/282 NZVC kldacc 12-6-17 CR Belgium 42 ded
PRIMROSE,Howard Primrose	Lt Can 4Bn kia 26-5-16 CR Belgium 15
PRIMROSE,Leslie John	Lt Aust AFC 2Sqn 4-6-18 CR France 1421
PRINGLE,Eden Lyal	Nurse Can CANS 3SHkld 30-5-18 CR France 84
PRINGLE,John Percival.MM.	Lt Can 2Bn 3Coy kia 9-9-16 CR France 430
PRINGLE,Thomas Stanley	Lt Can52Bn 22-6-16CR France 102
PRINGLE,W.R.	Lt SA PofWVltrs
PRITCHARD,Leslie Byrt	2Lt Aust 22Inf kia 5-8-16 CR France 280
PROBERT,James Thomas.MC.	Lt Can RCR 30-9-18CR France 243
PROCKTER,Charlton Hogarth	2Lt Aust 11Inf kia 6-8-15 CR Gallipoli 22
PROCTOR,James Thomas Gordon	2Lt Aust 15Bn 11-4-17MR 26
PROCTOR,John Alexander	Lt Can116Bn kldacc 31-3-19 CR Canada 1566
PROFFITT,William Reynolds	Lt NZ 24/548 3MGC kia 4-10-17 MR 30
PROSSER,Arthur Dillwyn	Lt Can 13Bn 13-6-16CR Belgium 112
PROUDFOOT,William.MC.	Lt Can 15Bn kia 27-9-18 CR France 274
PRYCE,Alfred Walter	Lt Can27Bn 1922
PRYCE,Jack Stanley	2Lt NZ8/1820 1OIR TMB kia 6-10-18 MR 12
PRYCE-JONES,Reginald Ernest	Lt Can 50Bn same as below?? 1916
PRYCE-JONES,Rex.MID	Lt Can 50Bn kia 18-11-16 CR France 430
PUCKLE,Charles Edward Murray	2Lt Aust11Inf kia 3-8-15 CR Gallipoli 22
PUE,William Howson	Lt Can 2CMR 15-10-16 CR France 40
PUGH,George Harold	Lt Aust 4Inf kia 5-9-16 CR Belgium 127
PULFORD,Fred Meikle	Capt Can 27Bn kia 1-10-18 CR France 715
PULLING,Charles Willoughby Lee	2Lt Aust 13Inf kia 7-8-15 CR Gallipoli 17
PUNNETT,Hubert Gordon	Lt Can 60Bn 26-11-16 CR France 523
PURBRICK,Rupert Benjamin	Lt Aust 7Inf kia 9-8-18 CR France 526
PURCELL-COHEN,Rupert	Capt Aust AIF AustNaval&MilForce 8-11-17CR Aust 94
PURDY,Robert Gleadow.MC&Bar.	TMaj NZ 23/10 1/3NZRB kia 28-3-18 CR France 62
PURNELL,Francis Ormond	Capt Aust46Inf kia 13-11-16 CR France 307
PURVES,George.MC.	Maj Can 43Bn dow 11-10-16 CR France 52
PURVIS,William George	2Lt Aust34Inf 12-10-17 MR 29
PUTNEY,Frederick William	2Lt Aust 36Inf kia 12-10-17 CR Belgium 125
PYBUS,Raymond Keith	Maj Aust AFA 11Bde kia 15-4-17 CR France 565
PYE,Cecil Robert Arthur.DSO.	LtCol Aust 19Inf kia 4-10-17 CR Belgium 34

PYE,Raymond Elton   Lt   Aust 17Inf   kia   17-5-16 CR France 83
PYMAN,Colin Keith Lee.DSO&Bar.MID Maj   Can   5Bn 10-8-18CR France 1170

Q

QUAIL,James Cooper   Lt   Can   1CMR   1-1-18 CR France 551
QUANBURY,John Henry   Lt   Can   2CMR   dow 14-8-16 CR London 8
QUAY,Frank   Mr   SA   Civilian Ex1SAInf ded 3-8-18   CR France 65
QUILLIAM,Cecil Wilfrid   2Lt NZ 60294   2WIR   kia 4-11-18 CR France 1077
QUINAN,Barrington Chadwick   Capt   Can 3Bn &RAF ded   20-7-18 CR Scot 674 5Bn
QUINLAN,Francis Timothy   Lt   Can   5CRT   29-9-17CR Belgium 10 Frank
QUINN,Hugh.MID   Maj   Aust 15Inf   kia 29-5-15 CR Gallipoli 31
QUINN,Roland Martin   Capt   NZ5/564   ASC   ded 2-2-18   CR NZ 258
QUINTON,Richard John   2Lt   SA 4SAInf B'Coy kia   12-10-16 MR 21

R

RADCLIFFE,Leslie Caldwell   2Lt Aust   49Inf   kia 2-8-18   CR France 486
RADDALL,Thomas Head.DSO.   LtCol   Can 8Bn   kia   9-8-18   CR France 693
RADFORD,Kenneth Coventry   Lt Aust 7FA   kia 1-4-18   CR France 833
RAE,Albert Norman   2Lt Aust 10Inf kia 8-10-17 CR Belgium 125
RAE,Mary Helen   SNurse NZ 22/161 ANS   drd 23-10-15 MR 35
RAE,Thomas Handley   2Lt   NZ 12/3453 2/3NZRB B'Coykia   4-11-18 CR France 1077
RAE,William John   Capt   Aust 3AICC   27-3-17MR 34
RAINBOTH,John   Lt   Can   BDCFC 230Bn ded   5-3-18   CR Canada 261
RAINIER,H.A.   Lt SA 2CaprCps 10-10-18 CR SAfrica 121
RALFE,Henry Douglas Eyre   Capt   Aust AFC 3Sqn   kia 6-5-18   CR France 71
RALLINSHAW,William Morton   2Lt NZ 8/2506 1OIR   kia 30-9-16   MR 11
RALPH,Percy Edgar.MM.   2Lt Aust 53Inf   kia 30-9-18 CR France 446
RALSTON,Ivan Steele.MC.   Maj   Can 85Bn   kia 10-8-18 CR France 586
RAMPF,Austin   2Lt   SA 2SAInf   kia 12-10-18 MR 21
RAMSAY,Allan George   Capt   SASA Forces att3/2KAR   6-1-19 CR Tanzania 1 &EAfrica 8
RAMSAY,Charles John Alexander   Lt Aust 39Inf   kia 1-12-17 CR Belgium 339
RAMSAY,Lisle Craddock   Lt   Can15Bn 9-4-17 CR France 68
RAMSAY,William Thomas   Lt   Can PPCLI   kia 28-9-18 CR France 481
RAND,Edwin Arthur   Lt   Can   8MR   28-4-17MR 23
RANDELL,Edward   Lt   Aust 13Inf   kia 11-6-17 CR Belgium 89
RANDS,Frederick   Chpn4Cl NZ 42884   Chpns att1AIR ded   14-2-19 CR Germany 1
RANIER.H.A.   Lt SA CapeCps ded   10-10-18
RANKIN,Franklin Sharp   Lt CanCE 1FC &RFC 18Sqn 23-10-16 MR 20
RANKIN,William Evelyn Dunsynne   Lt Aust 29Inf   kia 29-7-18   CR France 207
RANNARD,Richard Roland R.   Lt   Aust 2Inf   kia 17-4-18 CR France 193
RANSON,Joseph Robert   Lt   Aust 8   LtTMB   kia 4-7-18   CR France 207
RASON,William H.   Capt   Can CASC 3DivTr 5-11-18CR France 1277
RATHBONE,George Henry   Lt   Can RFC 9ResBn 29-4-17MR 20 AlbertaR & 12RFC
RATTRAY,Lorna Aylmer   SNurse   NZ 22/160   ANS   drd 23-10-15 MR 35

RATZ,John Henry	Maj Can CAMC 11-2-18CR Canada 1214
RAWLINSON,Robert John.MM.	Lt Can 8Bn 30-9-18CR France 214
RAWS,John Alexander	2Lt Aust 23Bn 23-8-16MR 26
RAWS,Robert Goldthorpe	Lt Aust 23Bn 28-7-16MR 26
RAWSON,James Gerald	Lt Aust 59Inf dow 5-7-18 CR France 71
RAY,John.DSO.	Maj Aust AFA 2DAC dedacc 5-10-18 CR France 446
RAYMOND,Archibald Hewland	Capt AustAFA 2Bde kia 3-3-17 CR France 453
RAYMOND,Frederick Courtney	Lt Can CETD ded 31-3-17 CR Surrey 1
RAYMOND,G.V.	2Lt Can CMGC &RAF 24-7-18CR France 1429
RAYNER,Fairburn Andrew	Lt Can 1PnrBn dow 9-6-16 CR Belgium 11
RAYNES,Sidney Herbert	Maj Can 62Bn3ArmyHQ att1BlkW 20-4-18CR France 88
READ,Charles Albert	Lt Aust19Inf kia 22-12-17 CR Belgium 68
READ, Edric Hurdman	Lt Can 16RFC CFC kia 26-12-17 CR France 95 Edrick
READ,T.R.	Lt Aust 17Inf CR France 446
READ,Walter Douglas	Lt Can 21Bn ded 28-1-19 CR Canada 1688
READE,Thomas Harold	Lt Can 29Bn kia 5-4-18 CR France 103
REAUNIE,John Stanley	Lt Can 13Bn dow 1-10-18 CR France 240 REAUME
REDDA,M.A.	Lt SA 8SAInf kia 21-3-16
REDDIHOUGH,Wilfred	Lt Can 16Bn kia 4-3-18 CR France 161
REDDOCK,Samuel Allan	Lt Can 3Bn dow 26-5-15 CR France 102
REDDOCK,William Adam	Lt Can 54Bn kia 1-3-17 CR France 81
REDFORD,Thomas Harold	Maj Aust 8ALH kia 7-8-15 CR Gallipoli 11
REDHEAD,Archibald Frank	2Lt Aust 23Inf kia 6-5-17 CR France 568
REDMOND,John	Capt Aust 41Inf 5-10-17MR 29
REED,Arthur	Lt Can RCR 30-10-17 MR 29
REED,Benjamin Trenholme	Lt CanCFA 11Bty3Bdekia 12-11-17 CR Belgium 165
REED,Clifton Algernon	Lt Can 14Regt CanMilitia ded 6-7-17 CR Canada 1270
REED,Frederick H.	Lt Can 5Bn 2-10-18CR France 273
REED,Percival Francis.MC.	LtAust 12Inf kia 24-4-18 CR France 324
REEDER,George Thomas	Lt&QM Aust 2DivHQ dow 21-2-16 CR Egypt 9
REEDMAN,William Edward	Lt Can 73Bn dow 26-11-16 CR France 40
REES,Reginald William	2Lt Aust 27Inf dow 11-11-16 CR France 833
REEVE,Alan	Lt Can 3Bn &RFC 11Sqn 27-3-18MR 20
REEVE,Llewellyn William Pearce	2Lt NZ 33072 2CIR dow 13-11-17 CR Surrey 1
REEVE,Stanley Thornton Seymour	Lt Can 50Bn kia 22-8-17 CR France 480
REEVE,William Alfred Campbell	2Lt NZ 24/660 2/3NZRB kia 29-3-18 MR 12
REEVE,William Augustus	Lt Can 10AR 24-5-15MR 23
REEVES,Leslie Charles	2Lt Aust 60Inf dow 14-9-18 CR France 145
REEVES,Samuel John.MC	Lt Can 15Bn kia 16-8-17 CR France 223
REHDER,Lorne Henry	Lt Can 54Bn kia 8-8-18 CR France 589
REID,Adam Ernest	Lt Can 54Bn 1916
REID,Albert Sidney	Capt NZ 25/66 OIR kia 29-11-17 CR Belgium 308
REID,Alexander	2Lt Aust 26Bn 28-2-17MR 26
REID,Andrew Lambert	Lt Aust 51Inf 9-6-17 MR 29
REID,Cecil Glenford	FltCadet Can RAF 6Sqn Ex 74CanInf kld 10-1-19 CR Lincs 181
REID,Charles McKillop	Lt Can 50Bn (AR) 26-10-17 CR Belgium 88 &MR29
REID,Edward Ogilvy	Maj Can 52Bn 15-6-21CR USA 170
REID,Francis Walter	2Lt Aust 54Inf dow 24-4-18 CR France 145
REID,George	Lt Can 72Bn 9-4-17 CR France 548
REID,George Alexander	Maj Can 58/2COR 8-10-16MR 23
REID,James Mansfield.MC.	Lt Aust Engrs 2FC dow 30-10-17 CR Belgium 11
REID,James Moffat	Maj Aust 1ALH kia 7-8-15 MR 6
REID,John Cecil Drury.MC.	Lt Aust 4Pnrs dow 10-6-17 CR Belgium 89
REID,John Stuart	Lt NZ 8/1003 OIR kia 3-5-15 MR 6
REID,Lestock Henry	2Lt NZ4/52A Pnrs kia 20-5-16 CR France 922
REID,Mordant Leslie	Lt Aust11Inf kia 25-4-15 MR 6
REID,Ralph Douglas	Lt Can 85Bn 5-5-17 CR France 58
REID,Reginald John	Lt Aust Engrs 5DivSigs kia 31-7-17 CR Belgium 10
REID,Richard	LtCol Can GenList 21-10-18 CR Middx 59
REID,Robert Bruce	2Lt Can RNewfndlandRkia 1-7-16 MR 10

REID,Stuart Graham Templeton	2Lt NZ 12/503 AIR 6Coy kia 8-5-15 CR Gallipoli 1
REINECKE,George Shuttleworth	Lt Aust 52Bn 3-9-16 MR 26
REININGER,Frederick	Lt Aust 49Bn 3-9-16 MR 26 &CR France 1890
RENAUD,Alexander Logie Howard	Maj Can 22Bn 15-9-16 CR France 1505
RENDELL,Clifford	2Lt Can NewfndlandR dow 22-7-16 CR France 40
RENDELL,Herbert.MC.	Capt Can1NewfndlandR kia 29-9-18 CR Belgium 157
RENDER,McKenzie	Maj Can 16Bn 8-8-18 CR France 487
RENNIE,A.	3rdOff Can MercMar SS`Pomeranian' 15-4-18 MR 24
RENNIE,Gordon James	Capt SA 6SAInf dow 12-2-16 CR EAfrica 56 kia
RENNIE,George Ewen	2Lt Aust 2AMGC kia 5-10-18 CR France 446
RENNIE,Samuel Gordon.MM.	Lt Can 2MMGBde 27-9-18 MR 23
RENNIE,John	2Lt Aust 16Inf ded 15-10-15 CR Egypt 9
RENNISON,Lancelot	Lt Can CFA 3Bde 27-9-18 CR France 714
RENOUF,Edward	Lt Can 54Bn 19-10-16 CR France 280
RENTOUL,Dougal Neil.MC.	Lt Aust Engrs 2DivSigs 3-5-17 MR 26
RETCHFORD,Albert Roy.MC.	Lt Aust 11Inf kia 3-6-18 CR France 28
RETCHFORD,Harold Ernest	2Lt Aust 2ndPnrs 5-8-16 MR 26
RETIEF, G .	LtCol SA 1MtdRif ded 9-4-15 CR SAfrica 172 P.H.
REVILL,John Albert	Capt Can RFC ARD kia 11-11-17 CR France 120
REX,Horace Joseph	Lt Aust 1AMGC 7-10-17 MR 29
REYNELL,Carew.MID	LtCol Aust 9ALH kia 28-8-15 CR Gallipoli 16
REYNOLDS,Edgar Kinsey	Lt Can ARD 9ResBn attRFC kld 27-6-17 CR Norfolk 127
REYNOLDS,Ernest Alfred	Lt Can 4/1COR 3-10-16 MR 23
REYNOLDS,Gerald Ellis	Lt Can PPCLI & RAF 102Sqdn kld 27-6-18 CR France 806
REYNOLDS,Herbert John	Lt Can 28Bn (SR)6-11-17 MR 29
REYNOLDS,John Edward	Lt Can 8Bn 23-4-15 CR Belgium 115
REYNOLDS,Phoebe M.	Sister NZ22/87 ANS ded 7-6-23
REYNOLDS,William Rees	2Lt Aust 33Inf 12-10-17 MR 29
RHEAD,Herbert Walter John	Capt Aust 49Inf 7-6-17 MR 29
RHIND,James Morrison	Lt Aust 60Inf kia 19-7-16 MR 7
RHINESMITH,Albert Martin	2Lt NZ 41145 1OIR kia 24-7-18 CR France 204
RHYNEHART,Harold Leslie	2Lt Aust 24Bn 3-5-17 MR 26
RICE,Robert Stacey	Lt Can 1MtdRif SasR Ex 61Bn 15-9-16 MR 23
RICHARD,Lawrence Brown	Lt Can 14Bn 9-4-17 CR France 523
RICHARDS,Earle Gordon	Lt Can 4CMR dow 30-3-17 CR France 68
RICHARDS,Evan Selwyn	Capt Aust 20Inf dow 5-9-16 CR France 74
RICHARDS,George James.MC.	Capt Aust 17Inf dow 23-9-17 CR Belgium 11
RICHARDS,Harry	Capt 422675 Can 8Bn 2-1-17 CR London 8
RICHARDS,Hugh Liddon	Lt NZ8/161 OIR 14Coy kia 3-5-15 MR 6
RICHARDS,Joseph Vanston	Lt Can31Bn 5-7-16 CR Belgium 15
RICHARDS,Joseph Wilfred	Lt Can RAF 67PnrBn 1-4-18 CR Oxford 63
RICHARDS,Philip Charles.MID	LtSA 9SAInf ded 12-2-17 CR SAfrica 84
RICHARDS,Percy John Lester	Capt Can 43Bn 8-8-18 CR France 485
RICHARDS,Robert	Lt NZ 2/197 NZFA dow 23-5-15 CR Egypt 6
RICHARDS,Samuel Jabez	Maj Aust AAMC ded 21-7-15 MR 6
RICHARDS,William Paul	2Lt NZ 24298 AIR 2AuklandR dow 7-10-17 CR Belgium 3
RICHARDSON,Alan Skirving	Lt Can 5Bn dow 25-7-16 CR Belgium 11
RICHARDSON,E.H.	Lt SA5NatLab C'Coydrd 21-2-17 MR 40
RICHARDSON,Edward Henry	Lt Aust 30Inf kia 22-6-18 CR France 207
RICHARDSON,Ernest	Lt Aust 2ndPnrs 2-8-16 MR 26
RICHARDSON,Frank	Lt NZ 8/3843 1CIR kia 15-7-18 CR France 281
RICHARDSON,George	2Lt NZ 8/2710 OIR 1 OtagoR dow 20-7-17 CR Belgium 50
RICHARDSON,George Taylor	Capt Can 2Bn 9-2-16 CR France 285
RICHARDSON,Herbert George	Lt NZ 12/1492 AIR 3Coy kia 25-4-15 MR 6
RICHARDSON,Hugh Douglas	Lt NZ23/2507 AIR 3AuklandR dow 5-10-17 CR Belgium 3 23/2509
RICHARDSON,John Launcelot	2Lt Aust 17Inf kia 31-8-18 CR France 624
RICHARDSON,Joseph.DCM.	Lt Can2Bn dow 5-9-16 CR France 51
RICHARDSON,Osma Voy	Lt Aust 48Bn 7-8-16 MR 26
RICHARDSON,Paul H.	Lt Can 42Bn 2-6-16 CR Belgium 4
RICHARDSON,Rupert Noel	Capt Aust6ALH kia 17-9-15 CR Gallipoli 22

RICHER,Cuno Edward McGill	Lt Can CFA 14Bde 3-9-18 CR France 14
RICHMOND,David	Lt Can 31Bn B'Coy 9-10-18CR France 214
RICHMOND,George Herbert	2Lt Aust 21Bn 26-8-16MR 26
RICHMOND,James Macdonald.DSO.MC.	Maj MIDx4 NZ 2/311 NZFA kia 27-10-18 CR France 288
RICKARD,Thomas Nathaniel	2Lt Aust 53Inf kia 19-7-16 MR 7
RICKETTS,Neville Hamilton	Lt Can 5Bn 31-12-15 CR France 285
RICONO,Martin	Capt SA RAMC att5NatLab ded 5-3-17 CR France 40
RIDDELL,James Ross	Lt Can PPCLI kia 30-10-17 CR Belgium 8
RIDDELL,Robert Burns	Lt Aust38Inf dow 10-9-18 CR Surrey 1
RIDDIFORD,Richard.OBE.MC.MIDx2.	Capt NZ 9/1623 WIR DivHQ ded 10-2-19 CR Surrey 1 11-2-19
RIDER,Charles Geoffrey	Lt SA 6SAInf Ex DurbanLI ded 13-5-16 CR EAfrica 58
RIDGE,F.E.	Lt Aust AFA 12th 26-11-18 CR France 457
RIDGWAY,Francis Leigh.DCM.	Lt Aust 6ALH kia 28-3-18 CR Syria 2
RIDLEY,Henry Quentin	Lt Aust48Inf kia 12-10-17 CR Belgium 123
RIDLEY,Thomas.MC.DCM.	Lt Aust 17Inf dow 10-9-18 CR France 145
RIDLEY,William John	Capt Aust FA 11Bde kia 7-6-17 CR Belgium 42
RIDGWAY,Doris Alice	SNurse Aust AANS 6-1-19 CR Aust 472
RIDGWAY,Isaac Althorp	2Lt Aust6Inf dow 12-5-15 MR 6
RIEGER,Ralph Joseph	Lt Can 38Bn kia 2-9-18 CR France 426
RIETCHEL,Ernest Otto.MC.	Capt Can 16Bn kia 16-8-18 CR France 699
RIGBY,Frank	Lt Aust 21Inf 4-10-17MR 29
RIGBY,John Samuel Thompson.MM.	Lt Aust21Inf 4-10-17MR 29
RIGBY,Percy George.MIDx2	Maj Can 7Bn kia 10-3-15 CR France 347
RIGBY,William John	Lt Aust 9Inf kia 25/28-4-15 MR 6
RIGG,Bernard Leslie	2Lt NZ 2/2250 FA dow 19-3-18 CR Belgium 19
RIGG,Percy Reginald	2Lt Aust 41Bn 1-9-18 MR 26
RIGGALL,Louisa	Nurse Aust ARCS ded 31-8-18 CR France 145
RIGHETTI,Alan Serafino	Lt Aust 2ALH kia 4-8-16 CR Egypt 2
RILEY,Charles	Lt Can CFA 5Bde kia 8-11-17 CR Belgium 10
RILEY,Charles Edward	Lt Can 24Bn B'Coy dow 1-9-18 CR France 52
RILEY,Harry Bolton	Lt NZ 7/1801 2CIR kia 2-10-16 MR 11
RIMMER,Alfred Baldwin	Lt Can 1Bn 9-7-16 CR Belgium 112
RINGWOOD,Thomas Duncan John(Ring)	Maj Can Cmdg CFA 60Bty14Bde kia 10-8-18 CR France 699
RINTEL,Horace Lisle	Lt Aust 8Inf kia 20-9-17 CR Belgium 125
RIPLEY,Alvin	Maj Can CFA 5Bde2-5-17 CR France 268
RISING,Hugh William Orr	Lt Can 46Bn 2-9-18 CR France 427
RISK,William	Lt NZ 11/600 WMR kia 28-8-15 CR Gallipoli 16
RITCHIE,Eric Cecil Howard	2Lt Aust 3Inf kia 20-9-17 CR Belgium 125
RITCHIE,Frank Lane	2Lt Aust 4Inf kia 6/8-8-15 CR Gallipoli 7
RITCHIE,Hubert Sydney	Lt Can 24Bn kia 15-8-17 CR France 480
RITCHIE,Vincent Theodore	2Lt Aust 35Inf kia 12-10-17 CR Belgium 123
ROACH,Eric Mervyn	Lt Aust 1AMGC kia 10-8-18 CR France 526
ROADKNIGHT,James	Lt Aust 37Inf 12-10-17 MR 29
ROADKNIGHT,Walter	Lt Aust 37Inf dow 11-8-18 CR France 119
ROBB,D.B.	2Lt SA 4SAInf kia 15-3-18 CR France 439
ROBB,James Thompson	Lt Can 4Bn 9-4-17 CR France 68
ROBB,John Frederick	2Lt Aust 59Inf kia 23-3-17 CR France 564
ROBBIE,George Alexander	2Lt NZ 24/1306 WIR 2WellingtonR kia 22-7-17 CR Belgium 51
ROBBINS,Charles Arthur Laurence	2Lt Aust 22Inf kia 9-3-18 CR Belgium 339
ROBERTS Charles Hartley	Capt Aust60Inf kia 29-9-18 CR France 365
ROBERTS,Harold.MC.	Lt Aust FA 3Bde kia 17-9-17 CR Belgium 15
ROBERTS,James Gershom	Lt Can 78Bn 10-8-18CR France 586
ROBERTS,Jean O.	Sister Can CAMC ded 3-11-18 CR Canada 487
ROBERTS,John Powe	Lt Aust 9Inf kia 25/28-4-15 CR Gallipoli 11
ROBERTS,Leonard Edmund Wadsworth	Capt Aust AAMC dow 2-9-18 CR France 119
ROBERTS,Leslie	Lt Aust 39Inf kia 30-4-17 CR Belgium 451
ROBERTS,Maurice Cameron.MC.	Capt Can 19Bn A'Coy dow 10-11-18 CR Belgium 202
ROBERTS,R.H.O.	2Lt Aust41Inf 8-8-18 CR France 1170
ROBERTS,Robert James.DCM.	Lt Can RCR ded 24-4-21 CR Canada 256
ROBERTSON,Alex Gordon	Lt Aust AIF 4Pnrs 22-6-19CR Aust 146

101

ROBERTSON,Alexander Carmichael	Maj Can CAMC 2GH ded 12-7-19 CR Canada 547
ROBERTSON,Alexander John	2Lt Aust11Inf kia 6-8-15 CR Gallipoli 22
ROBERTSON,Alexander Maxwell.MC.	Capt Aust 29Inf kia 29-7-18 CR France 207
ROBERTSON,Cecil Ewart G.	Lt Can 19Bn 10-11-18 CR Belgium 202
ROBERTSON,Douglas Leslie	Lt NZ 37054 2WIR kia 27-3-18 CR France 156
ROBERTSON,Geoffrey Ochiltree	Lt Aust 9ALH dow 13-8-16 CR Egypt 2
ROBERTSON,Gregor Gordon	Capt Aust 31Inf kia 20-7-16 CR Belgium 125
ROBERTSON,Henry Alexander	Lt Can 44MR 11-5-17MR 23
ROBERTSON,James Ernest	Lt Can 27Bn 9-3-16 CR Belgium 182
ROBERTSON,John Shirley	Lt Can R1 CMRD 43Bn attRAF kld 16-11-17 CR Lincs 181
ROBERTSON,Lyall Ralston	Lt Can 50Bn 26-10-17 CR Belgium 125
ROBERTSON,Stanley Currie.MC.MID	Lt Can 10Bn 4-5-17 CR France 64
ROBERTSON,Sydney Beresford	Maj Aust 9Inf kia 25/28-4-15 CR Gallipoli 30
ROBERTSON,Thomas	Lt Aust 15Inf kia 27-4-15 MR 6
ROBERTSON,Thomas Gilbert	Lt NZ 39721 3/3NZRB kia 22-8-18 CR France 1327
ROBERTSON,Thomas Jaffray	Lt Can 4Bn 5-11-17CR Belgium 10
ROBERTSON,William Francis	Lt Aust 37Inf kia 7-6-17 CR Belgium 451
ROBIDOUX,J.Emile Joseph	Lt Can 22Bn drd 13-6-17 CR Canada 333
ROBIN,James Keeling.MC.	Lt Aust 4 LtTMB kia 2-2-17 CR France 374
ROBINS,Archibald John	Lt Can PPCLI 28-9-18CR France 481
ROBINS,Victor Wentworth	Lt Aust2Inf kia 9-4-17 CR France 530
ROBINSON,Charles Bryan.MC.	Capt Can 7Bn 2-9-18 CR France 688
ROBINSON,David Alexander	Lt Can 1Bn kia 18-2-18 CR France 1724
ROBINSON,Frank Stanley	Capt NZ 2/833 3NZFA kia 25-9-16 CR France 399
ROBINSON,Frederic Reginald	Lt Can 73Bn kia 19-8-16 CR Belgium 6 Frederick
ROBINSON, Frederic Wilfred	Capt Can 1Bn kia 15-6-15 CR France 571 Frederec Wilfrid
ROBINSON,George.MC.	Capt Can CLH attRAF 19-5-18CR Kent 197
ROBINSON,George Edward	Lt Can R&FDep dedacc 20-3-18 CR Canada 1479
ROBINSON,George Lancaster	FltCadet Can PPCLI &RAF 13TrgDepotStn ded 1-11-18 CR Shrop 145
ROBINSON,George Spinks Hunter	2Lt Aust 41Inf dow 25-4-18 CR France 71
ROBINSON,George Victor	Lt CanCASC 1918
ROBINSON,George Wilfred	Lt Can116Bn ded 11-11-18 CR France 40
ROBINSON,James Edward	Lt Can 1BnCMGC 2-9-18 CR France 687
ROBINSON,Joseph William George	Lt Can 60QuebecR 16-9-16MR 23
ROBINSON,Thomas Carey	Lt Aust 38Inf 12-10-17 MR 29
ROBINSON,Thomas Henry	2Lt SA 1SAInf kia 24-3-18 CR France 1472
ROBITAILLE,Joseph Napoleon.MM.	Lt Can 4Bn 27-9-18CR France 481
ROBSON,Henry	Lt Aust 6ALH kia 24-7-15 CR Gallipoli 22
ROCHE,Basil Joseph	Lt Can 1MtdRif SasR 15-9-16MR 23
ROCHE,Charles Joseph	Lt Can 13Bn 27-6-16CR Belgium 11
ROCHE,George E.MM.	Lt Can 25Bn att5 LtTMBkia 8-6-18 CR France 174
ROCHESTER,Frank	Lt Aust Engrs 1FC kia 23-4-18 CR France 28
ROCHESTER,George Harvey.MC.	Lt Can 54Bn 28.9.18 CR France 1184
ROCK,George McLeod	Lt Can 8Bn 10-11-17 CR Belgium 84
RODDA,Matthias Aitken	Lt SA 8SAInf kia 21-3-16 CR EAfrica 13
RODDA,Errol Edward	2Lt Aust 8Inf kia 18-8-16 CR France 239
RODGER,William Alexander	Lt Can 78Bn &RAF 10-11-18 CR Belgium 226 &Belgium406
RODGERS,Jesse.MC.MM.	2Lt NZ 9/77 2OIR dow 30-7-17 CR France 297
RODGERSON,James Stuart	Lt Can 102Bn 13-5-17CR France 81
RODNIGHT,Eric	Lt Can 15MGCoy 29-10-17 MR 29
RODRIGUEZ,Percy John	2Lt Aust 23Bn 20-3-17MR 26
RODSTED,James Jacob	Capt Aust 10ALH dow 6-11-17 CR Egypt 9
ROEBUCK,James Vernon	2Lt Aust AFA 13Bde dow 10-8-18 CR France 71
ROGER,Alexander	Lt Aust 44Inf kia 22-8-18 CR France 642
ROGERS,Albert George	Lt Can87Bn 18-11-16 CR France 150
ROGERS,Arthur Thomas.MC.	Capt Aust 32Inf kia 29-9-18 CR France 375
ROGERS,Blythe D.	Lt Can 6FldCoy 1920
ROGERS,David Thomson.DSO.	Maj AustFA 3Bde dow 16-9-17 CR Belgium 15
ROGERS,Frederick Arthur	Lt Can 1Bn 11-7-17CR France 178
ROGERS,Garfield Redman	Lt CanCFA 1Bde attRFC 16Sqn 21-4-17CR France 32

ROGERS,George Clarence.MC.	Capt Can 52Sqdn RFC BCRD 30-10-17 CR France 1361
ROGERS,George Thomas	2Lt Aust 13Inf dow 17-8-16 CR France 40
ROGERS,John	2Lt Aust 7Inf kia 1-11-16 CR France 374
ROGERS,Lawrence Browning.MM	Lt Can5CMR (QR) kia 30-10-17 MR 29
ROGERS,Margaret	SNurse NZ 22/175 ANS drd 23-10-15 CR Greece 9
ROGERS,Nellie Grace	Nurse Can CAMC 19-10-18 CR Canada 1200
ROGERS,Ralph Beverly	Lt Can25Bn 10-6-16CR Belgium 127
ROGERS,Roy L.	Lt Can 43Bn ded 12-7-19 CR Canada 388
ROGERS,Victor.DSO.MID.	Maj NZ 2/122 NZFA 5Bty kia 8-2-18 CR Belgium 35
ROGERS,W.R.DCM.MM&Bar	2Lt Aust 16Inf 8-8-18 CR France 526
ROHAN,Martin Driscoll.MID.	TCapt NZ 27692 4\3NZRB kia 22-8-18 CR France 798
ROLLE,Absolom Richard Eng	Capt Aust RAN HMAS`Franklin' 19-9-19CR Aust 94
ROLPH,John William.MM.	Lt Can46Bn 28-9-18CR France 148
ROLSTON,James William	Lt Aust 1MGC dow 27-5-18 CR France 28
ROOKE,James Arthur	Lt Can 87Bn 9-4-17 CR France 81 Alfred
ROOKE,Lester George	Lt Can RCR 9-4-17 CR France 68 ROOKS
ROSAMOND,Alexander George	Lt Can PPCLI EOR15-9-16MR 23
ROSE,Claud Vincent	Lt SA SAF att2/2KAR kia 6-9-18 CR EAfrica 90
ROSE,Edward Leigh	Lt Can 1PnrBn 6-6-16 CR Belgium 127
ROSE,Ernest Clifford	Lt Aust 31Inf 26-9-17MR 29
ROSE,Evelyn Jack	2Lt NZ 25147 1AIR 6Coy kia 4-10-17 MR 30
ROSEBY,Percy Richardson	Lt SA 2SAInf dow 25-7-16 CR France 23
ROSENTHAL,Samuel	Lt Aust 58Inf kia 25-9-17 CR Belgium 112
ROSKAMS,Leopold James Cecil	2Lt Aust 10ALH kia 7-8-15 CR Gallipoli 29
ROSS,Ada Janet	Sister Can CAMC 1GH 12-7-18CR Derbyshire 57
ROSS,Andrew.MC.	Capt Can CAMC 12FA kia 29-9-18 CR France 686
ROSS,Arthur Cecil.MC&Bar.	Capt Can 5Bn 10-8-18CR France 1170
ROSS,Arthur McKay	Maj Can 87Bn 9-4-17 CR France 81
ROSS,Charles Frederick Douglas	LtCan CE 3TC9-5-16 CR Belgium 127
ROSS,David McD.	LtCmdr Aust RNR HMAS`Penguin'24-6-19CR Aust 47
ROSS,Donald	2Lt SA 4SAInf kia 20-7-16 MR 21
ROSS,Douglas Nicol.MM.	Lt Can 7Bn &RFC 24Sqn 17-2-18MR 20
ROSS,Elsie Gertrude	Nurse Can CAMC ded 26-2-16 CR Canada 1207
ROSS,Fleming.MID.	Maj NZ 10/3144 WIR kia 18-9-16 MR 11
ROSS,Frank Gordon	Lt Aust AFA 3Bde dow 6-11-16 CR France 145
ROSS,George Adam Russell	Lt Can 15Bn 3-6-16 CR Belgium 127
ROSS,George H.	Capt Can 16Bn (MR) 24-4-15MR 29
ROSS,Gordon Knox	Lt Can 14Bn 30-4-16CR Belgium 11
ROSS,Harold.MM.	2Lt Aust 8Inf 4-10-17MR 29
ROSS,Harold Osborne	Lt Can 44MR 9-5-17 MR 23
ROSS,Herbert Clive	Lt Aust AIF 11Inf 13-2-19CR Aust 471
ROSS,John McKenzie	2Lt SA 2SAInf kia 12-4-17 MR 20
ROSS,James Stuart Leslie	Lt Aust AFC dedacc 13-11-19 CR Surrey 1
ROSS,John Alexander.DSO.	Maj Can 24QuebecR 19-9-16MR 23
ROSS,John Douglas	Lt Can 2CMR &CASCded 26-2-20 CR Canada 180
ROSS,Joseph	Capt Can 72Bn dow 11-4-17 CR France 12
ROSS,Leslie George King	Lt Aust 33Inf ded 9-11-18 CR France 1170
ROSS,Percy A.	Lt Can 42Bn kia 5-10-16 CR France 430
ROSS,R.Wallace	2Lt Can 1RNewfndlandR kia 1-7-16 CR France 1501
ROSS,Roderick Arthur	Lt Can 27MR 2-10-16MR 23
ROSS,T.H.MC.	Capt SA4SAInf 3-4-17 CR France 1182
ROSS,Thomas John	Lt Aust 7Inf kia 9-8-18 CR France 526
ROSS,Vernon John Wallace	Lt Aust 23Inf kia 23-4-18 CR France 196
ROSS,Walter	Maj Can CAMC 6-2-20 CR Canada 115
ROSS,William George	Lt Can7Bn kia 9-4-17 CR France 1059
ROSSITER,Walter Wrixon.MID	Lt Can 42Bn 12-10-17 CR France 95
ROTH,Louis Carl.MC.	Capt Aust2Pnrs dow 6-10-18 CR France 446
ROTHERY,Elizabeth	SNurse Aust AIF AANS 15-6-18CR Aust 293
ROTHNIE,George	Maj Can 102Bn 1916
ROUGH,Alexander H	Capt Can CASC ded 26-8-16 CR Canada 256

ROUND,Henry Barrington	Capt CanCAPC 49Bn ded 1-7-21 CR Canada 547
ROUNDING,Lewis ArthurH	Capt Can68Bn 16-5-16CR Kent 180
ROUNDS,Herbert Charles	Capt Can 4CMR 26-8-18CR France 1189
ROUS,Frederic William.MC.	Lt Can 4CMR 1921
ROUSSEAU,W.P.	Maj SA MilMagistrate 3-9-18 CR SAfrica 23
ROUTH,William Bissett.MM.	Lt Can CFA 4Bde 1921
ROUTLEDGE,Allan.MID	Lt Can 42Bn dow 23-9-16 CR France 40
ROWAN,Andrew Percival	Capt Aust 10ALH kia 7-8-15 CR Gallipoli 29
ROWAN,Frederick John.MID	Maj Can 13Bn kia 9-10-16 CR France 239
ROWAN,Thomas Kingsley	Lt Aust FA 4Bde 23-8-18MR 26
ROWAN,W.S.	SecretaryAust YMCA attAIF 4Div 14-1-17CR France 177
ROWAT,Thomas Alexander	Lt Can 38Bn kia 28-6-17 CR France 81
ROWBOTHAM,Stanley Edward	2Lt Aust 1Inf kia 6-1-17 CR France 307
ROWDON,,Victor Kirby	WTO Can `Niobe' 1918
ROWE,Arthur Barton	Lt Can 27Bn kia 8-10-18 CR France 715
ROWE,Bernard Alan	Capt Can 123CoyCFC 19-2-19CR Hamps 154
ROWE,Francis Godolphin	Lt Aust AFA 14Bde kia 11-3-17 CR France 374
ROWE,James	Lt Can 5Bn dow 10-8-18 CR France 1170
ROWELL,Edward Leslie Graham.MC.	Lt Aust 25Inf dow 15-11-17 CR France 134
ROWELL,Frank Milton	LtCol Aust 3ALH ded 8-8-15 MR 6
ROWLAND,Albert Edward Mackay	2Lt NZ32540 3NZRB h'Coy kia 23-7-18 CR France 622
ROWLAND,Elmer McLeod	Lt Can CFA 22-5-20CR Canada 1095
ROWLANDS,Verner Stanley	Maj Aust 2Inf kia 30-9-16 CR Belgium 167
ROWLES,Bertie Hamilton	Lt Can 1CMR (SR) 3-6-16 MR 29
ROWLEY,Eric Grahame	Lt Can 2COR attRFC6-7-17 CR France 44
ROWSELL,H.John R.	2Lt Can 1NewfndlandRdow 8-7-16 CR France 51
ROWSELL,Reginald S.MC.	Capt Can RNewfndlandRkia 14-4-17 MR 10
ROY,Adolphe Victor	Maj Can 22Bn 6-10-15CR Belgium 60
ROY,J.Emile	Capt Can CanArty 9-11-18CR Canada 324A
RUDDLE,Charles Henry	Lt Aust 9Inf dow 23-7-16 CR France 703
RUDDOCK,Harold Edwy Colston	Lt Aust28Inf dow 22-11-15 CR Egypt 6
RUDDOCK,Walter David	Capt NZ13/125 3AIR dow 13-6-17 CR France 297
RUGGLES,Ronald Taylor	Capt Can 246 Bn ded 15-2-17 CR Canada 613 24Bn
RUGGLES,Walter Trueman	Capt Can 85Bn ded 4-2-19 CR Canada 617A
RULE,Clarence William	2Lt NZ 26/902 4/3NZRB kia 5-10-18 CR France 911
RULE,Edgar	Lt Can 4CMR 29-9-18CR France 1496
RULE,Esson Thomas James	Lt Aust 50Inf kia 3-4-17 CR France 1488
RULE,John Lindon	2Lt Aust 31Inf dow 2-11-16 CR France 432
RULE,William Bramwell	Lt NZ 39722 1/3NZRB kia 12-10-17 MR 30
RUNDLE,Beaumont	Lt Aust AFA 4DACdow 15-4-17 CR France 251
RUSCONI,Alberto	Lt Can 49Bn (AR) kia 30-10-17 MR 29
RUSH,Arthur Leslie.DCM.	Lt Aust AMGC 15Coy 5Bn kia 25-4-18 CR France 144
RUSH,Bertie Danson.MC.	Lt Aust 30Inf dow 4-9-18 CR France 627
RUSH,Crawford Thomas	Lt Can 102Bn 21-10-16 CR France 430
RUSH,Horace Roy	Capt Aust 20Inf kia 15-11-16 CR France 399
RUSSEL,Hugh.MC.	Lt Aust 3ATC dow 23-1-18 CR France 224
RUSSELL,A.	Capt SA SASC ded 18-3-17 CR Tanzania 1 &EAfrica 8
RUSSELL,Bertram John.MID.	2Lt NZ 2/683 1NZFA kia 2-9-18 CR France 306
RUSSELL,Douglas Clark	Lt Can 49Bn 9-9-18 CR France 310
RUSSELL,James	Lt Can 16Bn dedacc 18-8-16 CR France 102
RUSSELL,James Cosmo.DSO.	LtCol IA 9HodsonsHorse att6CamH31-7-17CR Belgium 7
RUSSELL,Neil Ruffell	2Lt NZ 32542 1AIR kia 26-3-18 CR France 156
RUSSELL,Richard Easton	Capt Can 26Bn (NBR) kia 6-11-17 MR 29
RUSSELL,S.A.	Capt SA 4SAInf dow 11-7-16 CR France 66
RUSSELL,Sidney Henry Ernest.MM.	Lt Aust 9Inf kia 20-7-18 CR France 28
RUSSELL,William Roy	Lt Can2Bn 3-5-17 CR France 777
RUST,Benjamin Henry	Capt Can 13Bn dow 19-7-16 CR Belgium 11
RUTHERFORD,Arthur Henry	Lt SA 1RhodNatR 23-7-17CR EAfrica 40 RUTHERFOORD
RUTHERFORD,Cecil Alphonso	Lt Can 19Bn kia 27-8-18 CR France 162
RUTHERFORD,Thomas George.MID	Lt Can 10Bn dow 12-10-16 CR France 40

RUTHERFORD,Thos Wyville Leonard.MC.Capt NZ 6/718 1CIRded 19-10-18 CR Asia 82
RUTLAND,John Bishop   Lt Aust 14Inf kia 1-5-15 CR Gallipoli 25
RUTLEDGE,Alexander Herbert   Lt Can 12MGCoy 26-10-17 CR Belgium 84
RUTLEDGE,Harry Forster   Lt Aust FA 7Bde kia 9-10-17 CR Belgium 128
RUTLEDGE,Noel Beresford Forster LtAust AFA 3DivHvyTMB kia 3-6-17 CR Belgium 451
RUTLEDGE,Stanley Arthur   Lt Can SRD 28Bn attRFC kldacc 16-11-17 CR Lincs 67
RUTTAN,Arthur Charles   Maj Can GHQ 144Bn ded 2-11-18 CR Canada 116
RYALL,William Thomas   2Lt Can RNewfndlandR kia 1-7-16 MR 10
RYAN,Bliss Wilberforce.MM.   Lt Can Engrs attRFC kia 20-9-17 CR Belgium 18
RYAN,Charles Francis   2Lt Aust 45Inf 7-6-17 MR 29
RYAN,Francis Joseph   Lt Aust FA 4Bde kia 2-10-17 CR Belgium 15
RYAN,Henry Joseph   Lt Aust 25Inf kia 17-7-18 CR France 144
RYAN,Patrick Francis.DCM.   Lt Aust 2Inf kia 18-9-18 CR France 528
RYAN,Thomas Lloyd.MM.   2Lt Aust 17Inf 20-9-17MR 29
RYBURN,Eric Middleton   2Lt NZ 8/1625 2OIR kia 12-10-17 MR 30
RYDER,Frederick Hugh   Lt Can72Bn kia 27-9-18 CR France 714
RYERSON,George Crowther   Capt Can 3Bn (1COR) kia 23-4-15 MR 29
RYERSON,John Egerton   Capt Can 58Bn att 9TMBty 19-9-16CR France 832
RYRIE,Evan   Lt Can 15Bn 19-7-17CR France 224
RYRIE,Harold Stewart.DSO.MID   Maj Aust AIF 6ALH 10-12-19 CR Aust 112

S

SACHS,Roy Tessier Seaver   Lt Can 16Bn 13-6-16CR Belgium 11
SAGE,George   Lt Can 12CRT ded 21-5-18 CR Canada 256
SAILMAN,Robert Thomas   Lt Can 85Bn (NSR) 30-10-17 MR 29
SAKER,Richard   Maj Aust 5Inf kia 25/26-4-15 CR Gallipoli 7
SALE,Charles Edward   Maj Can 18Bn 17-1-16CR France 285
SALE,Gordon Nicholson   Lt Can 13Bn 26-9-16CR France 430
SALE,John Bonwell   Maj NZ 3/4316 TrngUnit ded 11-11-18 CR NZ 257
SALES,George Edward   Lt Can 43B n ded 30-10-18 CR Canada 115 10Bn
SALMON,Dudley Frederick   Lt Aust 47Inf kia 8-6-17 CR Belgium 168
SALMON,Percy William   2Lt Aust 24Inf kia 1-9-18 CR France 1472
SALMOND,William Guthrie A   Capt NZ 66227 1WIR kia 9-7-18 CR France 798
SALSBURY,Harry Edwin.MC&Bar.   Capt Can 4Bn ded 8-2-21 CR Canada 1345
SALTAU,Victor Leslie   2Lt Aust 5Inf dow 10-5-15 CR Gallipoli 1
SALVATOR,   Sister SA Nyasaland NursServ8-9-18 CR EAfrica 77
SAMPLE,Thomas Rodgers   Lt Can 2Bn 29-9-18CR France 214
SAMPSON,May Belle.MID   NSister Can CAMC HS drd 27-6-18 MR 24
SAMPSON,Victor Horatio Buller   Maj Aust 53Inf kia 19-7-16 MR 7
SAMUEL,Claude Montefiore   2Lt NZ 41998 MGC ded 13-9-18 MR 12
SAMUELS,Robert Oswald   Lt Aust 1Inf kia 9-8-18 CR France 144
SANDEMAN,David Richard   Maj Can 5Bn (SR) 24-4-15MR 29
SANDERS,Francis Roy   Lt Aust 26Inf 4-10-17MR 29
SANDERSON,Frederick John   2Lt Aust 6Inf kia 4-5-17 CR France 438
SANDERSON,George Edward   Lt Aust 1AICC 30-3-18MR 34
SANDFORD,Percy Harold   2Lt Aust42Inf dpw 1-9-18 CR France 624
SANDHAM,George   Capt NZ 3/81 NZMC ded 22-8-22
SANDLAND,Arnold Cooper   Lt Aust 10Inf dow 4-8-16 CR France 102
SANDLAND,Morton Reginald   Lt Aust3ALH kia 31-10-17 CR Palest 1
SANDOE,Joseph Henry   2Lt Aust 45Inf kia 18-9-18 CR France 375 served as DIETZE,J.H.
SANDY,James Lionel Montague   Lt Aust Aust Flying Cps kia 17-12-17 CR France 787
SANER,H.E.   Capt SA CapeAuxHorseTrCps ded 18-11-18
SANGSTER,Henry Walker   Capt Can 29Bn A'Coy 26-9-16MR 23

SANSON,Henry Samuel McDougall	Lt NZ 14030 2OIR kia 24-8-18 CR France 512
SAPHIR,Max.MC.	2Lt SA 4SAInf A'Coykia 22-3-18 MR 27
SAPTE,William Travis	Capt Can RCR 8-10-16CR France 314
SARA,John Thomas Leonard	Lt Can 31Bn 5-8-16 CR Belgium 11
SARA,Russell Eric	Lt Aust 7Inf kia 21-9-17 CR Belgium 115
SARA,William Ross	Lt Aust 6Inf dow 10-1-17 CR France 882
SARE,Gladys Irene	NSister Can CAMC HS drd 27-6-18 MR 24
SARE,Harry Frank	Maj Can 87Bn D'Coy kia 9-4-17 CR France 81
SARE,Harry Keith	Capt NZ25/5 3/3NZRB D'Coy dow 16-9-16 CR France 177
SARGENT,Marcus Strong	Lt Aust 32Inf dow 26-5-18 CR France 40
SARGOOD,Cedric Rolfe	Lt NZ 8/1626 OIR kia 9-8-15 MR 5
SAUNDERS,Austin Lyman	Capt Can 52Bn kia 10-7-16 CR Belgium 11
SAUNDERS,Herbert Clement.MM.	Lt Can 47Bn BCR attRAF 46Sqn kia 18-9-18 CR France 1495
SAUNDERS,James Joshua	Capt Aust AIF 25AMGC 13-3-20CR Aust 92
SAUNDERS,Thomas Brebant	Lt Can 13Bn kia 13-6-16 CR Belgium 11 BrÇhaut
SAUNDERSON,G.	Lt SA SASC SARlysded 26-12-18 CR SAfrica 30
SAUNDES,Frederick	Aust RAN 13-8-21CR Aust 94
SAVAGE,E.B.MC.	Capt Can CFA ded 2-3-20 CR Canada 256
SAVAGE,Edwin George	Lt Can 87Bn 9-4-17 CR France 81
SAVAGE,Richard Attlesey	2Lt NZ 8/727 2OIR kia 5-11-18 CR France 521
SAVAGE,Thomas Copeland	Maj NZ 3/719 NZMC 2NZSH ded 13-8-15 CR Egypt 9
SAWER,Edgar Geoffrey.MC.	Maj Aust AIF AMGC 31-5-18CR Aust 307
SAWLE,William Tregerthen	Lt Can 3BnCMGC 3.10.18 CR France 1184
SAWLOR,Ray Haliburton	Lt CanNBRD 26Bn attRFC 11-8-17CR Belgium 173
SAWTELL,Percy Roach.MM&Bar.	Lt Can 50Bn D'Coy dow 21-6-17 CR France 81
SAXBY,Conrad Gordon.DSO.MID.	LtCol NZ 13/2150 Pnrs ded 27-11-18 CR Surrey 1
SAYER,William Samuel	Lt Aust 12Inf kia 23-4-18 CR France 324
SCADDAN,Charles Mansfield	Lt Can 31Bn 7-11-17CR Belgium 11
SCAMMELL,Sidney	Lt Aust 22Bn 3-5-17 MR 26
SCANLAN,William Maunsell.MM.	Lt Can 5Inf 2TC dow 10-4-17 CR France 12
SCANLON,Herbert Douglas	2Lt Aust 22Inf kia 5-8-16 CR France 832
SCARR,Frank Sydney	Lt Aust Egnrs 5FC 6-5-17 MR 26
SCATCHERD,John Labatt.MC&Bar.	Lt Can CFA 3Bde 3-9-18 CR France 421
SCHACHE,Oswald Bernhard	2Lt Aust 8Inf dedacc 25-7-17 CR France 251
SCHAFFER,Harold	Lt Can 7BnCE 30-10-18 CR France 1144
SCHEEPERS,Johannes Christoffel.MC.	Capt MID SA 1SAInf kia 20-7-18 CR France 25
SCHOLES,John Ernest	Capt Aust 7Inf ded 10-10-17 CR France 64
SCHREIBER,William Eric Brymer	Lt Can ASC MT DivAmmPk 4-5-15 CR Belgium 39
SCHULER,Phillip Frederick Edward	Lt Aust AASC 3DivTrn dow 23-6-17 CR France 297
SCHURMAN,Frederick Bulmer	Capt Can260Bn 1922
SCLATER,Arthur Norman.MC.	Lt Can 13Bn 8-8-18 CR France 489
SCLATER,James Loutit	Maj Can 7Bn 15-8-17MR 23
SCOBIE,Robert	LtCol Aust 2Inf kia 6/8-8-15 CR Gallipoli 7
SCOBIE,Walter Farmes	Capt Aust 4Pnrs kia 7-8-16 CR France 832
SCOTT,Alan Humphrey.DSO.	LtCol Aust 56Inf kia 1-10-17 CR Belgium 308
SCOTT,Alexander McKay	Lt Can 21Bn kia 11-10-18 CR France 761
SCOTT,Andrew	Lt Can 58Bn 18-4-17CR France 64
SCOTT,Andrew Anderson	Lt Aust 25Inf 4-10-17MR 29
SCOTT,Arthur Earnshaw	2Lt SA 4SAInf A'Coy Ex C'Coy kia 24-3-18 MR 27
SCOTT,Arthur George	Capt Can 4Bn (1COR) 9-7-16 MR 29
SCOTT,Blaney Edmund.MC.DFC.	Lt Can CFA 2DivTMB &RAF ded 9-10-19 CR Canada 183
SCOTT,Campbell Craig.MM.	Lt Can 27MR 3-5-17 MR 23
SCOTT,Charles Bever	Lt Can 54Bn kia 27-6-17 CR France 81
SCOTT,Charles Douglas.MC.	Lt Aust 47Inf kia 7-6-17 CR Belgium 168
SCOTT,Charles Wiliiam	Lt Aust 58Inf attAFC dedacc 28-8-18 CR Glouc 172
SCOTT,Cleve James.MC.	Lt Aust10Inf kia 22-7-18 CR France 25
SCOTT,Ernest Charles Gordon	Lt Aust 10ALH dow 19-7-15 MR 6
SCOTT,Ernest James	Lt Can 3Bn kia 3-5-17 CR France 68
SCOTT,Frank John.MID	Lt Aust 10Inf 8-10-17MR 29
SCOTT,Frank William	Lt Can 49Bn (AR) 5-6-16 MR 29

SCOTT,Frederick Grundy	Lt Can CFA 8Bde kia 20-4-17 CR France 924
SCOTT,George Herbert.MC.	Lt Can 31Bn 28-9-16CR France 44
SCOTT,George Leslie	2Lt Aust 18Inf dow 8-10-18 CR France 446
SCOTT,George Norman	2Lt Aust 58Inf kia 19-7-16 MR 7
SCOTT,Harold Archibald	Maj Can 4CMR (1COR) kia 26-10-17 MR 29
SCOTT,Harold Anderson	Lt Can 2BnCMGC dow 9-11-18 CR France 1252
SCOTT,Henry Hutton	Capt Can 87Bn kia 21-10-16 CR France 150
SCOTT,Howard Elliott	Lt Can 24Bn kia 16-9-16 CR France 1890
SCOTT,James Nimmo.MC.MID	Lt Can 8Bn 22-5-15MR 23
SCOTT,James Peter H	Capt&QM Can CAMC 16-5-19CR Surrey 1 16Bn
SCOTT,John Burns.MID	Maj Aust 10ALH kia 8-10-15 CR Gallipoli 18
SCOTT,Lloyd James Daniel	Lt Can 38Bn kia 29-9-18 CR France 715
SCOTT,Norman.MM.	Lt Can PPCLI &RAFkld 20-6-18 CR Lancs 78
SCOTT,Quinten Longden	Lt SA 1SAInf dow 14-4-17 CR France 95
SCOTT,Robert Francis Coghill.MID.	Capt NZ 10-2482 2WIR dow 9-6-17 CR France 285
SCOTT,Stanley William.MID	Lt Can 46Bn 11-11-16 MR 23
SCOTT,Stephen William.MM.	Lt Can 3Bn kia 1-10-18 CR France 481
SCOTT,Tom Farrar.MM.	2Lt CanRAF 75Sqn Ex CanAMC kld 21-5-18 CR Norfolk 259
SCOTT,Victor Richard Stanley	Lt NZ 10275 2AIR kia 4-10-17 CR Belgium 125
SCOTT,Walter Frank	Lt Can 47Bn 10-8-18CR France 699
SCOTT,Walter Eric	Lt Aust 7Inf kia 9-8-18 CR France 526
SCOTT,William Norman Eric	Lt Aust AFC 3Sqn kia 2-12-17 CR France 285
SCOTT,William Robert	Lt Aust FA 12Bde kia 29-9-17 CR Belgium 19
SCOUGALL,Frank Burdett	Lt Aust 9Inf 20-9-17MR 29
SCOUGALL,Walter Mowbray	Lt Can 24Bn 15-8-17MR 23
SCOULER,Matthew Allison	Lt AustAMGC 8Coy kia 16-4-18 CR France 144
SCOULLAR,William Arthur	2Lt NZ 24/946 3/3NZRB kia 6-4-18 MR 12
SCOVIL,Earle Markee.MM.	Lt CanRes Depot RAF 1Bn dedacc 21-7-18 CR Canada 961
SCREATON,Thomas Gerald Norman	Lt NZ 12/32 AIR 15NAukCoy kia 8-5-15 MR 13
SCULLY,Creagh Patrick	Lt SA 1SAInf ded 5-11-18 CR Surrey 1
SCULLY,Harold Leo	Lt Can 18Bn 7-6-18 CR France 95
SEABROOK,William Keith	2Lt Aust 17Inf dow 21-9-17 CR Belgium 11
SEARLE,Archibald Henry	2Lt Aust AFC 1Sqn 13-7-17MR 34
SEARS,Archibald Arthur	Capt Can 38Bn 18-11-16 CR France 150
SEATON,William Fallis.MC.	Maj Can 31Bn 28-12-18 CR Hamps 2
SECCOMBE,Harold Clifford	Lt Can 2026 10Bn dow 20-10-15 CR Belgium 339
SECORD,James B.Archibald	Capt Can CAVC 1918
SEDDON,Richard John Spotswood	Capt NZ 57384 3/3NZRB kia 21-8-18 CR France 1327
SEDDON,Thomas Alexander	2Lt Aust 11AMGC dow 28-3-17 CR France 297
SEELENMEYER,Cyril Robert.MC.MID	Maj Aust AAVC dow 8-8-18 CR France 1172
SEELEY,George Norman	Lt Aust AIF 29Inf4-4-19 CR Aust 307
SELBIE,Robert Joseph	Lt Can13Bn 13-6-16CR Belgium 112
SELDON,Richard Thomas Francis	Lt Aust 4Inf kia 6/8-8-15 CR Gallipoli 23
SELKIRK,Ernest	2Lt Aust 51Inf 9-6-17 MR 29
SELL,Cyril Leggatt.MC&Bar	Capt Aust 19Inf dow 7-10-18 CR France 123
SELL,Leslie Simeon John	2Lt Aust AFC 3Sqn dow 25-3-18 CR France 200
SELLARS,Ernest George	2Lt Aust15Inf kia 23-6-18 CR France 23
SELLARS,Robert Clive	2Lt Aust36Inf dow 12-6-17 CR France 102
SELLECK,Horace Ferdinand	Capt Aust 38Inf kia 20-7-18 CR France 1170
SELLERS,George Edward	Lt Can CorpsCycBn 2-9-18 CR France 532
SELTH,Norman William Gilbert	2Lt Aust 27Inf kia 4-8-16 CR France 280
SELWYN-SMITH,Hubert George	Capt Aust 49Inf 7-6-17 MR 29
SEMPLE,Francis Herbert	Lt Aust 18Inf kia 19-5-18 CR France 833
SENIOR,Charles Hastings Alexander.MC.	Capt NZ 12/2905 AuklandR ded 27-10-18 CR NZ 224
SENNITT,Alfred Josiah	2Lt Aust 21Inf kia 1-9-18 CR France 511
SERGEANT,John Edwin.MID	Maj Aust 8Inf kia 25-4-15 CR Gallipoli 22
SERPELL,Samuel Llewellyn.MC.	Capt NZ 3/2874 MC attCanterburyR kia 15-12-17 CR Belgium 72
SERVICE,Albert Niven Parker	Lt Can 52Bn 18-8-16CR Belgium 127
SESSARAGO,Frederick Harold	Lt Aust 42Inf kia 4-7-18 CR France 1170
SETON,Miles Charles Cariston	Maj Aust AAMC 13-1-19CR Surrey 1

SEVERN,Vernon Nicholl	Lt Can 43Bn (MR) kia 26-10-17 MR 29
SEWELL,Philip Beauchamp	Capt Aust AAMC kia 24-4-18 CR France 1170
SEXTON,James Walter	Maj Aust AFA 101HB dow 13-9-18 CR France 145
SHADWICK,John Alfred	Lt Aust 48Bn 11-4-17MR 26
SHALLBERG,John Reginald	2Lt Aust 8Inf dow 7-8-15 MR 6
SHAND,Donald	Lt Can 43Bn 2-11-18CR Scot 881
SHANLY,Coote Nisbit.DSO.	LtCol Can CAPC ded 7-9-16 CR Canada 1694
SHANNON,Ernest	Lt Aust 34Inf kia 1-6-17 CR Belgium 451
SHANNON,Robert	Lt Can 1CMR 26-8-18CR France 1189
SHAPIRA,Francis Cunningham	2Lt Aust AFC 69Sqn dedacc 21-8-17 CR Surrey 1
SHAPPERE,Cyril Solomon	Lt Aust 3Inf dow 29-12-16 CR France 400
SHARLAND,Charles Frederic	Lt Aust 40Inf12-10-17 MR 29
SHARMAN,William Wilson	Lt Can47Bn kia 29-9-18 CR France 715
SHARP,Duncan	Lt Aust 11Inf kia 10-8-18 CR France 526
SHARP,Ivan Victor	Lt NZ12876 NZFA Res ded 12-7-16 CR NZ 238A
SHARP,James Richard	Lt Can 50Bn 11-5-17CR France 81
SHARP,Wylie	Lt Can 14Bn kia 26-9-16 CR France 430
SHARPE,Frederick	2Lt Aust 10Inf kia 23-8-18 CR France 526
SHARPE,Samuel Simpson.DSO.MP.	LtCol Can 116Bn ded 27-10-18 CR Canada 1579
SHARPE,William Frederick	Lt Can RFC 1Bn 1915
SHARPLES,Eric Alfred	Lt Can 31Bn 15-9-16MR 23
SHARPLES,John Wilson	Lt Can 3BdeCGA 30-10-18 CR France 1252
SHAUGHNESSY,Alfred Thomas TheHon.	Capt Can 60Bn kia 31-3-16 CR Belgium 309
SHAW,Alfred Ernest	LtCol Can 1CMR (SR) kia 3-6-16 MR 29
SHAW, Allan Crawford	Maj Can 14Bn 19-5-15MR 23 Alan
SHAW,Bernard Joseph.MM.	Lt Aust 15Inf kia 8-8-18 CR France 699
SHAW,David John	Lt NZ 14023 4/3NZRB kia 30-3-18 MR 12
SHAW,Edward John	Lt Aust 20Bn 3-5-17 MR 26
SHAW,Ervin David	1stLt USAAviationSect attRAF 48Sqn kia 9-7-18 CR France 314
SHAW,Frank	Lt Aust 59Inf 12-10-17 MR 29
SHAW,Frederick John	2Lt NZ24299 2OIR dow 10-6-17 CR France 285
SHAW,Greville Havergal	LtCol Can 12BnCE kia 3-11-18 CR France 1142
SHAW,Harold Baker	2Lt Aust 10Inf kia 19-5-16 CR France 254
SHAW,John	Lt Can 43Bn 1-10-18CR France 241
SHAW,Leonard James	2Lt NZ 7/13232AIR 6Coykia 29-9-18 MR 12
SHEARD,Alfred Edwin	Lt Aust 50Inf dow 29-3-17 CR France 251
SHEARWOOD,Ernest Maxwell	Lt Aust 53Inf kia 1-9-18 CR France 624
SHEATH,Abel Richmond.MC.	Lt Aust 18Inf kia 8-8-18 CR France 1170
SHEEN,Sydney John	Lt Aust 2Inf dow 20-9-18 CR France 446
SHEEN,Walter Roy.MC.	Capt Aust 56Inf kia 22-10-16 CR France 744
SHEFFIELD,Geoffrey	Lt Can 43Bn 12-4-17CR France 102
SHELDON,Walter Claude.MID	Lt Aust 48Inf dow 4-10-18 CR France 146
SHELLEY,Roland Parker	Lt Aust 2AMGC kia 4-7-18 CR France 303
SHELLINGTON,Percy Gordon	2Lt Can RFC Ex CanEngrskld 26-8-17 CR Norfolk 247
SHENNAN,J.E.	Capt SA SASC
SHEPHERD,Edwin Charles	Lt Can 4CMR A'Coy (1COR) 26-10-17 MR 29
SHEPHERD,Ernest Gordon	Lt Can 42Bn 1-10-18CR France 481
SHEPHERD,Martin Louis	Maj Can 21Bn 15-9-16CR France 1505
SHEPHERD,Oscar Dudley	2Lt Aust AFC dedacc 11-8-18 CR Glouc 172
SHEPLEY,Joseph Gore	Lt Can CETD ded 26-10-18 CR Sussex 200
SHEPPARD,Edmund Culver	Capt Can RAF 196Bn1921
SHEPPARD,John Douglas	Lt Can 123PnrBn 7-11-18CR Hamps 2
SHEPPERD,George Joseph.MM.	2Lt Aust 26Inf kia 3-7-18 CR France 144
SHERAR,Roderick Oliver	2Lt Aust AFC dedacc 11-5-18 CR Warwick 89
SHERBON,Ivan Brunker.MC.	Maj Aust 19Inf kia 14-11-16 CR France 389
SHERIDAN,Frank J.	Lt Can 16Bn ded 7-4-21 CR Canada 179
SHERIDAN,George Byford	2Lt NZ 12/4512 2AIR kia 15-9-16 MR 11
SHERIDAN,Thomas Francis	Capt Aust29Inf kia 20-7-16 MR 7
SHERINGHAM,Edward Oswald	Lt Can 1BnCMGC kia 1-10-18 CR France 597
SHERRING,Aubrey John Bickley	Lt Aust AASC 7Coy kia 31-7-15 CR Gallipoli 30

SHERSON,Edward	Maj NZ 278122AIR kia 30-9-18 CR France 911
SHERWIM,Raymond.MC.	Lt Aust 12Bn 8-4-17 MR 26
SHIELD,Hubert Mark	Lt Aust 9Bn 13-4-17MR 26
SHIELD,James Coleman	Capt Can 7Bn 6-5-16 CR Belgium 11
SHIELDS,Donald De Vere	Lt Can RCR 42Bn 10-11-18 CR Belgium 241
SHIERLAW,Norman Craig.MC.	Capt Aust 13Inf dow 11-4-17 CR France 1486
SHIPMAN,Charles Simpson	Maj Can 78Bn 9-4-17 CR France 81
SHIPTON,Bernard.MC.MM.	Lt Can2CMR dow 2-11-17 CR Belgium 11
SHIPWAY,John Cecil	Lt Can 24Bn kia 28-8-18 CR France 310
SHIRRIFF,Francis McKider.MID	Lt Can 25Bn 9-4-17 CR France 522
SHIRTLEY,William Frederick	LtAust 13Bn 11-4-17MR 26
SHORE,Albert	Lt Can 52Bn 1-10-18CR France 599
SHORROCK,J.DSO.	Lt Aust 28Inf 26-11-19 CR Aust 471
SHORT,Aubrey Vincent.MID	Maj NZ 3/183 NZMC ded 15-11-18 CR NZ 32
SHORT,James	Lt NZ 9/1354 Pnrs dow 28-5-16 CR France 285
SHORT,Leslie Ellis	Lt Aust AFA 1Bde kia 28-4-18 CR France 26
SHORTALL,Richard A.	Lt Can 1RNewfndlandR kia 1-7-16 CR France 1490
SHORTER,Claude Lyndon	2Lt Aust 2Inf dow 24-7-16 CR France 44
SHORTT,Allen.MM.or MC.	Lt Can 58Bn 10-12-16 MR 23
SHOUT,Alfred John.VC.MC.	Capt Aust 1Inf dow 11-8-15 MR 6
SHREVE,Charles Dayrell.MC.	Lt Can CFA 9Bde 7-10-18CR France 715
SHRIMPTON,Francis John	Lt Aust2TMB att6Inf dow 15-4-18 ·CR France 200
SHRUB,Alfred Boniface	2Lt Aust15Bn 8-8-16 MR 26
SIBBISON,Horace Hubert	Lt Aust 21Bn 14-4-18MR 26
SIDDALL,Norman	Lt Aust AFA 4Bty 2Bde kia 29-5-15 CR Gallipoli 30
SIEVWRIGHT,George W.	Capt Can 194B n 12-11-16 CR Canada 547 13SSC
SILBERMAN,Boris	Lt Can 14Bn 1917
SILLAR,Roy Allan	Capt Aust AAMC dedacc 30-6-18 CR Wilts 187
SILLS,George Luther	Capt Can CAMC HS drd 27-6-18 MR 24
SILVERA,L G	2Lt WInd 6BrWIndies R 26-4-17CR France 787
SILWELL,Lawrence Hurt	LtCol Can HQMD13 ded 28-1-18 CR Canada 543 SITWELL
SIMMONS,Eric Dowson	Lt Aust 11Bn 15-4-17MR 26
SIMMONS,John Grant	Lt Aust 12Inf dow 19-9-18 CR France 194
SIMMS,Hugh Rutherford	Lt Can 26Bn dow 14-10-18 CR France 686
SIMON,Frank	LtT Capt NZ 66142 OIR 1 OtagoRkia 10-1-18 CR Belgium 19
SIMONDS,Robert Hazelette	Lt Can PPCLI 9-4-17 CR France 58
SIMPSON,Ernest Alroy	Lt Can58Bn 1916 CR France 430
SIMPSON,Frank Richard	2Lt NZ12/3822 1AIR dow 4-12-16 CR France 40
SIMPSON,Fred Irwin	Capt Can RFC 1CMR kia 12-3-17 CR France 105
SIMPSON,Frederick Norman	2Lt Aust 3Pnrs drd 28-12-16 CR France 922
SIMPSON,George	Lt Aust 6Inf kia 23-8-18 CR France 699
SIMPSON,Harold Newman	Lt Can 31Bn 3-10-16CR France 102
SIMPSON,Hector Joseph	Lt SARhodNatR kia 29-1-17 CR EAfrica 40
SIMPSON,Hubert	Lt Aust 13Inf dow 30-3-18 CR France 281
SIMPSON,James Duncan	Lt Can Engrs 1TCkia 24-8-16 CR Belgium 15
SIMPSON,James William Albert.MC.	LtCol Aust 36Inf kia 21-1-17 CR France 922
SIMPSON,John Laurence.MID	Lt Aust 60Inf kia 26-4-18 CR France 424
SIMPSON,Joseph Donaldson.MC.	Maj Can10Bn att44ImpInfBde11-10-18 CR France 106
SIMPSON,Stewart Basil.MID	Lt Can 5CMR 1-10-16MR 23
SIMPSON,William Alexander	Lt Can 8Bn 15-8-17MR 23
SIMPSON,William Stephen	Lt NZ 12/1795 AIR 15Coy kia 31-5-15 MR 6
SIMS, Do uglas Co lin	Lt Can 4CMR (1COR) 26-10-17 MR 29 C.D.
SIMS,Frederick George	Capt Aust 43Inf 4-10-17MR 29
SIMS,Percy James	Lt Aust RFC 4Sqn 29-10-18 MR 26
SIMSON,John	Lt Aust FA 4Bty 2Bde kia 31-7-17 CR Belgium 15
SINCLAIR,Archibald Niven.MC.	Capt Aust 2Pnrs dow 14-10-17 CR Belgium 72
SINCLAIR,Aubrey Clyde	Lt Aust32Inf kia 29-9-18 CR France 375
SINCLAIR,Colin Duncan	Lt Can PPCLI attRFC 17-3-18CR Lincs 100
SINCLAIR,David Harold Maclean	Lt Aust 2ALH kia 20-4-17 CR Palest 1
SINCLAIR,James	Lt Can 87Bn dow 16-4-17 CR France 64

SINCLAIR,John	2Lt NZ 36761 2CIR kia 27-3-18 MR 12
SINCLAIR,Lindsay McNabb	Lt Can 1BnCE 18-8-18CR France 487
SINCLAIR,Robert Christie	2Lt NZ 2/201 NZFA 3Bty kia 5-10-16 CR France 401
SINCLAIR,William Smith	Maj NZ 3/446 NZMC ded 25-1-19 CR NZ 68A
SINGLE,Raymond Vallack	Capt Aust56Inf 26-9-17MR 29
SITWELL,L.H. see SILWELL	
SIVES,John Pauling.MM.	2Lt Aust 4Bn 7-5-17 MR 26
SKEAFF,John Murray	Lt Can 92Bn ded 24-1-16 CR Canada 1688
SKEDDEN,Charles Edwin Lloyd	Lt Can 173Bn &RAF 74Sqn 8-5-18 CR France 180
SKELLY,Percy William.MID.	Capt NZ 41235 NZRB 3BdeHQ dow 9-6-18 CR France 84
SKELTON,Edwin Kerr	Lt Can CFA &RFC 1Sqn 9-1-18 MR 20
SKELTON,George Harry	Lt Aust 31Inf kia 19-7-18 CR France 207 served as ELTON
SKELTON,William Godfray	2Lt NZ 6/1101 CIR 13Coy kia 3-5-15 MR 6
SKENE,Joseph Leo	Lt Aust AFA 3Bde kia 12-12-15 CR Gallipoli 31
SKENE,Stanley Donald.MC.	Capt Can 15Bn IntelOff 10-10-18 CR France 421
SKENE-SMITH,Alexander.MC.	Lt Aust 22Inf kia 9-10-17 CR Belgium 125
SKERTCHLY,Harold Brandon	Lt Aust 14Inf ded 15-5-15 CR Egypt 9
SKEWES,Arthur William	Lt Aust 41Inf 5-10-17MR 29
SKILL,Albert Thomas	Lt Can 58Bn (2COR) kia 26-10-17 MR 29
SKINNER,Alex George Angus	Lt AustFA 13Bde kia 3-11-17 CR Belgium 125
SKINNER,Frank William	Lt Can 7Bn dow 5-5-16 CR Belgium 11
SLACK,W.J.	LtCol Honduras BrHondTerForces 26-1-15CR CentAmerica 1
SLADE,Daniel Gregory	2Lt NZ 12/250 2AIR kia 30-9-18 CR France 918
SLADE,Elliott Darcy	Lt Aust 33Bn 30-3-18MR 26
SLADEN,Reginald Lawrence	Lt CanPPCLI 9-4-17 CR France 1321
SLAGHT,John Onion.MC.	Capt Can 38Bn kia 16-3-18 CR France 81
SLATER,Joseph Henry.MID	Capt Aust22Bn 3-5-17 MR 26
SLATTERY,Edward.DCM.MM&2Bars.	Lt Can 3Bn kia 30-8-18 CR France 313
SLATTERY,Francis William	2Lt Aust 3ALH MGSqn 17-9-16MR 34
SLAUGHTER,Jacob William	Lt Can 5Bn 9-8-18 CR France 693
SLOSS,Bruce	Lt Aust AMGC 10Coy kia 4-1-17 CR France 922
SMALL,Douglas Farquharson	Lt Can 42Bn 9-4-17 CR France 81
SMALL,George.MC.	Lt Aust 17Inf kia 31-8-18 CR France 624
SMEDLEY,Francis John.MC.	Lt Aust7Inf dow 20-8-18 CR Surrey 1
SMITH,Albert David	Lt NZ 14716 1/3NZRB kia 12-10-17 MR 30
SMITH,Albert Edward	Lt Can 1CMR 22-8-17MR 23
SMITH,Alexander Laing	2Lt NZ 24412 1OIR kia 12-10-17 MR 30
SMITH,Anthony	Lt Can 72Bn dow 10-8-18 CR France 1170
SMITH,Arthur Henry	Lt Aust 55Inf kia 19-8-18 CR France 526
SMITH,Arthur Percival	Lt Aust 1ATC kia 29-6-16 CR France 922
SMITH,Bronson Howard	Capt Can RFC 25Bn 1917
SMITH,Cecil Parker	Lt Can24Bn 17-9-16MR 23
SMITH,Charles Harold	2Lt Aust51Bn 3-9-16 MR 26
SMITH,Charles Harold	Lt Can44Bn 2-9-18 MR 23
SMITH,Charles Henry Vernon	Capt Can CAMC 2GH 1-11-18CR Sussex 200
SMITH,Charles John	Maj Can 13Bn kia 27-6-16 CR Belgium 11
SMITH,Charles Morrison.MM.	2Lt Aust 23Inf dow 7-5-17 CR France 512
SMITH,Colin Lawson.MC.	Lt Aust 3Inf kia 24-6-18 CR France 25
SMITH,Colin Macpherson	Lt Aust 10Inf dow 6-10-17 CR Belgium 11
SMITH,Digby Alfred	Lt Can78Bn (MR)1-11-17MR 29
SMITH,Douglas	Lt Can 43Bn kia 28-8-18 CR France 421
SMITH,Edwin Crago	2Lt NZ 22540 1AIR kia 3-6-17 CR France 262
SMITH,Ellis Austin William	2LtAust 28Inf 20-9-17MR 29
SMITH,Eric Summers	2Lt NZ 29702 3/3NZRB C'Coykia 12-10-17 MR 30
SMITH,Eric Wilkes Talbot.MID	LtAust 10Inf dow 30-4-15 CR Egypt 3
SMITH,Frank Peter	2Lt SA1SAInf kia 24-3-18 MR 27
SMITH,Francis Lawrence.MC.MM.	Lt Aust AASC 1DivTrn dow 1-7-18 CR France 134
SMITH,Frank.MC.	Capt Aust 51Inf kia 25-4-18 CR France 144
SMITH,Frederick George	Lt Aust2Inf dow 8-5-15 CR Egypt 9
SMITH,Forbes Tynan Gold	Lt Aust 3Inf dow 2-10-17 CR Belgium 19

SMITH,George	Capt SA 4SAInf mbk 17-4-18 MR 29
SMITH,George Achilles	Capt Aust ImpCamelCps 3AustBn kia 9-1-17 CR Egypt 2
SMITH,George John Lorne	Capt Can 1Bn kia 15-6-15 CR France 571
SMITH,George Lander	Lt Can 5Bn 29-5-16 CR France 102
SMITH,Harold Archibald.MC.	Lt Can 5CMR dow 14-9-18 CR Surrey 1
SMITH,Harold Edward Benjamin	2Lt Aust 19Inf 8-10-17 MR 29
SMITH,Harold Ernest	Capt Aust 22Bn 26-8-16 MR 26
SMITH,Harold George	2Lt Aust 15Inf dow 10-5-15 MR 6
SMITH,Harold Percival	Lt Can CFA 3Bde kia 12-10-16 CR France 430
SMITH,Harry Lawrence	Lt Can CASC 1DivMTCoy 5-2-19 CR Belgium 267
SMITH,Harry Roy	Capt Can CAMC ded 14-1-19 CR Canada 1688
SMITH,Henry Albert.MC.	Lt Can 1CMR 1-10-16 MR 23
SMITH,James Bradford Hales	Lt Aust 20Inf 2-8-18 CR France 29
SMITH,Jeffery Filder	Lt Can 13Bn 29-6-17 MR 23
SMITH,John Cochrane	Lt Can 5Bn (SR) 10-11-17 MR 29
SMITH,John Huntingdon	2Lt Aust 60Inf kia 19-7-16 CR France 348
SMITH,John James	2Lt Aust 26Inf kia 5-11-16 CR France 744
SMITH,John Lyall.MC.	Lt Aust 25Bn 29-7-16 MR 26
SMITH,Keith Glendinning	Lt NZ 5/146 2OIR kia 12-10-17 CR Belgium 125
SMITH,L.L.	Capt Aust 51Inf 2-4-17 CR France 568
SMITH,Leonard.MC.	2Lt NZ 2/15 NZFA 6HB &5Reinf dow 13-6-17 CR France 297
SMITH,Leonard Whitman	Lt Can 1CMR 26-8-18 CR France 1189
SMITH,Leslie Kennedy	Lt Aust 58Inf 25-9-17 MR 29
SMITH,Muir Paul.MID	Lt Aust 4Inf kia 26-4-15 MR 6
SMITH,Murray Turley	Lt Can 3Bn dow 31-10-16 CR France 52
SMITH,Oscar Charles	2Lt NZ 8/3075 MGC kia 26-8-18 CR France 1484
SMITH,Perceval Lascelles.MC.	Capt Aust 39Inf dow 2-9-18 CR France 119
SMITH,Philip James.DSO.	Lt Aust AIF 23Inf 1-7-21 CR Aust 306
SMITH,Quinton Robert	2Lt Aust 14Inf dow 3-5-15 MR 6
SMITH,Reginald George	Capt Can 47Bn 5-5-17 CR France 81
SMITH,Reginald Sidney	Lt Can 9InfB deHQ ded 17-12-18 CR Belgium 241 7Bn
SMITH,Richard Godfrey	Capt Aust 21Inf kia 26-8-16 CR France 832
SMITH,Richard Langford	Lt Can 2BdeCGA 1918
SMITH,Robert James.MC&Bar.	Capt Aust 4DivSigCoy dedacc 22-7-18 CR France 300
SMITH,Robert McLuckie	Lt Aust 26Inf kia 17-7-18 CR France 144
äSMITH,Robert Scott	Capt Can CAMC 22-12-17 CR Surrey 1
SMITH,Roy Alfred Walter	Lt Aust 19Inf dow 15-10-17 CR Belgium 11
SMITH,Samuel R.	2Lt Can RNewfndlandR kia 14-4-17 MR 10
SMITH,Stafford S.	Lt Can 44Bn 3-6-17 MR 23
SMITH,Stanley Brown	2Lt Aust 16Inf 18-4-17 CR France 1142
SMITH,Thomas Clarke	Lt SA 3SAH kia 8-5-16 CR Tanzania 1 &EAfrica 5
SMITH,Teesdale Boake	Lt Aust 2Inf 4-10-17 MR 29
SMITH,Thomas Arthur.MC.	Lt Can 1MMGBde 22-10-18 CR France 147
SMITH,Thomas Oscar	Capt Aust 3Inf kia 7-5-15 CR Gallipoli 24
SMITH,W.	3rdEngr Can MercMar SS`Pomeranian' 15-4-18 MR 24
SMITH,W.R.	Lt SA 1CapeCps ded 22-10-18 CR SAfrica 121
SMITH,Walter Calkin	Lt CanCFA 1Bde 30-9-18 CR France 147
SMITH,Walter Willoughby.MC.	Lt Aust 33Inf ded 28-11-18 CR France 52
SMITH,William Charles Richard	Lt Aust 18Inf 20-9-17 CR Belgium 453 &MR29
SMITH,William Foster	Lt Aust 9Bn 10-8-18 MR 26
SMITH,William Henry Gordon.MC.	Lt Aust 7Inf ded 30-10-18 CR Surrey 1
SMITH REWSE,Meyrick B.W.MID	Lt Can 8Bn 22-5-15 CR France 279
SMITHERS,Kenneth	Lt Aust 30Inf kia 10-10-17 CR Belgium 88
SMYTER,Arnold Edward	Lt Can 1Bn (WOR)kia 6-11-17 MR 29
SMYTH,George Crawford	Lt Can 24Bn B'Coy kia 9-4-17 CR France 68
SMYTHE,Ernest George	2Lt Aust 51Inf kia 3-9-16 CR France 516
SNADDON,Andrew Johnston	Maj Can 4Bn kia 8-10-16 CR France 239
SNAPE,Harold John	2Lt Aust AFA 47Bty 12Bde dow 19-8-18 CR France 145
SNEATH,Thomas D'Arcy.MC.	Maj Can 5CMR kia 15-3-18 CR France 522
SNEATH,Thomas Herbert	Lt Can 3Bn 9-9-16 CR France 59

SNIDER,Arthur Westbrook	Capt CanCAPC 209Bnded 8-7-19 CR Canada 1563
SNOW,Geoffrey Allan	Lt Can 15Bn 1916
SNOWBALL,John Iley	Capt Aust 57Inf dow 14-8-18 CR France 119
SNYDER,Frederick Carl Henry	Lt Can 25RBn &RFC 45Sqn7-7-17 MR 20 Carle
SNYDER,William Hilliard	Lt Can 1MMGBde 24-3-18MR 23
SOLLING,Erick Martin	2Lt Aust 2Inf kia 25-4-15 MR 6
SOLOMON,Alexander	Lt Can 87Bn 15-8-17CR France 557
SOMERS,Ralph Barry Lake	2Lt NZ44955 2AIR A'Coy dow 30-9-18 CR France 1483
SOMERSET,Francis Henry	2Lt SA 3SAInf D'Coy dow 20-7-16 CR France 402
SOMERSET,Wyndham Alan	2Lt Aust 19Bn 14-11-16 MR 26
SOMERVILLE,John Raymond	Lt Aust 27Bn 5-11-16MR 26
SOMERVILLE,Kenneth Ian	Lt Can 5CMR Ex60Bndow 16-3-18 CR France 522
SOMMERVILLE,Charles Leslie	Maj NZ 16038 WMR dow 2-4-18
SOPER,Russell Wright	Lt Can 116Bn 2-4-18 CR France 58
SORBY,Joseph Austin	Lt Aust AFA 8Bde ded 4-4-18 CR Yorks 542
SOULE,Ivan Edgar	Lt Can RCR 26-8-18MR 23
SOULSBY,Robert	Lt Can 9MGCoy 31-5-17CR France 68
SOUTER,Alexander Carr	Lt Can 5CRT 19-5-17CR France 1182
SOUTER,James George.MM.	Lt Can 16Bn 9-10-18CR France 113
SOUTER,James Mitchell	Lt Can59RFC 133Bn 11-4-17CR France 777
SOUTER,John Francis	Capt Aust AIF AAMC 26-2-16CR Aust 212B
SOUTH,Harold	Capt Aust AAMC ded 9-9-19 CR Wilts 167
SOUTHAM,Gordon Hamilton	Maj Can CFA 8Bde 15-10-16 CR France 430
SOUTHBY,Henry	Capt Aust 39Inf 12-10-17 MR 29
SOUTHERN,Harold Alfred	Capt Aust 16Inf kia 2-5-15 MR 6
SOUTHWELL,Leonard Vincent	Lt Can 15ResBn attRAF dow 14-3-18 CR France 134
SOWELL,Herbert Keith	Lt Aust 18Inf kia 3-5-17 CR France 646
SPARGO,Edwin Bennett	Lt Aust 6Inf kia 7-8-15 MR 6
SPARKS, Le titia	NSister Can CAMC 7GH 20-8-17CR Sussex 111 E.
SPARLING,Charles A. H	Capt Can ChpnServs ded 26-10-18 CR Canada 1667
SPARROW,Charles Hutchinson	Lt Can 47Bn kia 31-3-17 CR France 81
SPARROW,Sydney Hubert.MM.	2Lt Aust 5 LtTMB dow 9-5-17 CR France 512
SPEAR,Reginald Gordon.MC.	Lt Can 46Bn 23-10-18 CR France 646
SPEARS,Walter	2Lt Aust AIF 59Inf27-12-17 CR Aust 138A
SPEDDING,Arthur Vivian	Capt NZ 8/1093 OIR kia 2/3-5-15 MR 6
SPEDDING,Eric Claude	2Lt NZ 13845 2OIR dow 7-10-16 CR France 40
SPEEDY,Louisa Ellen	Miss NZ VolWkr ded 11-1-19 CR Surrey 1
SPEERING,K.D.	Lt Aust 39Inf 4-10-17CR Belgium 125
SPEIGHT,Harold Ellison.MC.	2LtNZ 2/1499 NZFA 19-11-18 NZ 232
SPENCE,France Sherlaw	Lt Aust AFA 13Bde kia 10-6-18 CR France 119
SPENCE,Francis Robert	Maj Can2Bn 18-8-17CR France 178
SPENCE,John Clauson	Lt Can 18Bn kia 27-8-18 CR France 310
SPENCE,Lyell Campbell.MC.	Lt Can CFA 6Bde &RAF kia 25-5-18 CR France 10
SPENCE,Robert	2Lt NZ 24413 3/3NZRB kia 12-10-17 MR 30
SPENCE,Robert John	Lt Can 8Bn 26-9-16MR 23
SPENCE,Walter Kennedy	Lt Aust 52Inf dow 2-10-17 CR France 40
SPENCER,Evan David	Lt Can 5CRT att RAFkld 11-6-18 CR France 792
SPENCER,Frederick Temple.DCM.MID	Maj Can 1Bn 4-4-17 MR 23
SPENCER,Harold Innes.MM.	Lt Aust33Inf kia 1-10-18 CR France 212
SPENCER,Kingsley	Lt Can 52Bn dow 8-8-18 CR France 303
SPENCER,William James	Lt Aust 15Inf kia 4-7-18 CR France 1170
SPIERS,Gavin Hume	Lt Can 27Bn 7-6-18 CR France 504
SPINKS,Richard Coupland	Lt Can 2CMR kia 10-4-17 CR France 68
SPLANE,Howard Mylne	Maj Can 31Bn kia 15-9-16 CR France 280
SPOUSE,John	Lt Can 7BnCE kia 21-7-18 CR France 504
SPRADO,Frederick Emerson	Lt Can LSH 8-8-18 MR 23
SPRATT,Stuart Frank	2Lt Aust56Inf dow 18-4-18 CR France 37
SPREADBOROUGH,Ernest William	Lt Aust 31Inf kia 19/20-7-16 MR 7
SPRIGGS,Charles Arnold.DCM.	2Lt NZ 25/69 1/3NZRB kia 8-10-18 CR France 611
SPRINGFIELD,Eric	2Lt Aust 31Inf dow 25-10-16 CR France 389

SPROTT,John.MM.	Lt Aust 10Inf kia 24-4-18 CR France 324
SPROULE,Milton Frederick.MC.	Capt CanCFA 10Bde15-11-17 CR Belgium 11 Lt
SPRUYT de BAY,Michael Hubert Alex	Lt Can PPCLI kia 2-6-16 CR Belgium 111
SPURR,Edgar Smith.MC.	Lt Can25Bn 14-6-18CR France 174
SPYKER,Edward Ross	2Lt SA 1SAInf kia 23-9-17 CR Belgium 84
STABLES,Robert Hugh	2Lt NZ22527 3WIR dow 18-10-17 CR Belgium 167
STACEY,John Randolph	Lt Can RAF Ex 1Bn kld 8-4-18 CR Middx 66
STAFFORD,Alexander Boswell.MID	Maj Can CFA 39Bty10Bde dow 24-6-17 CR France 178
STAFFORD,Louis Norman	Lt Aust 55Bn 4-7-18 MR 26
STAFFORD,Mary Florence	SNurse Aust AIF AANS 1AGH 19-3-19CR Aust 212A
STAIRS,Gavin Lang	Capt Can 14Bn 3Coy7-9-16 MR 23
STAIRS,George William	Lt Can 14Bn (QR) 24-4-15MR 29
STAIRS,John Cuthbert	Lt Can 25Bn C'Coy kia 15-9-16 CR France 430
STAIRS, Kenneth Charles	Lt Can CFA 60Bty14Bde kia 30-9-18 CR France 481
STAIRS,Philip Boyd.DSO.	Lt Can CFA 5DivTMB 21-11-18 CR France 1142
STALKER,Robert Alexander	Lt Can 102Bn 9-4-17 CR France 81
STAMERS,Anna Irene	NSister CanCAMC HS drd 27-6-18 MR 24
STANDISH,Charles Colin.MM.	Lt Can 19Bn 9-5-17 CR France 68
STANDRING,Hubert Eric T	Lt NZ 9/481 NZFA TMB kia 17-8-17 CR France 262
STANFORD,Arnold George	Lt Can 54Bn 25-10-16 MR 23
STANSELL,Lionel Brough	Capt NZ 26/7 4/3NZRB dow 4-6-16 CR France 285
STANTON,Frederick Bertram	Capt Aust 14Bn 11-4-17MR 26
STANTON,R.R.	Lt SA ColdGds Ex 7SAInf 18-10-18 CR Berks 84
STAPLES,Harold Kilburn	Lt Can 75Bn 9-8-18 CR France 589
STAPLES,Herbert Edward Grant.MM.	Lt Aust 54Inf dow 20-4-18 CR France 185
STAPLETON,P.R.MC.	Lt SA 1SAInf kia 8-12-17 CR France 439
STARKINGS,Arthur George	Lt Can 38Bn 27-9-18CR France 714
STARR,Rupert Kelson	Lt Can 4Bn kia 9-4-17 CR France 68
STATHAM,Frank Hadfield.MID.	Maj NZ 8/977A OIR kia 8/9-8-15 MR 5
STAUFFER,Joseph Emmett	Lt Can 50AR kia 10-4-17 MR 23
ST.CLAIR-LIMRICK,Ian	Lt SA 10Inf 17-8-16CR EAfrica 36
STEACIE,Richard	Capt Can14Bn (QR) 22-4-15MR 29
STEACY,William Edward.MC.	Maj Can CFA 7Bty2Bde 25-11-18 CR France 788
STEAD,Oswald Victor	Lt NZ 6/2381 CIR ded 27-8-15 CR Greece 10
STEADMAN,Horace Basten	Lt Can 15Bn 2-9-18 CR France 687
STEADMAN,Noel	Lt NZ 12/4 AIR kia 6/10-5-15 MR 13
STEEL,Arthur Valentine	2Lt Aust 1Inf kia 5-11-16 CR France 512
STEEL,Oswald Leslie Jennings	Capt Aust FA 14Bde kia 6-8-17 CR Belgium 10
STEELE,Alexander.DSO.DCM.	Maj Aust 11Inf 7-10-17MR 29
STEELE,Norman Leslie	2Lt AustAFC 1Sqn 20-4-17MR 34
STEELE,Owen William	Lt Can 1RNewfndlandRdow 8-7-16 CR France 344
STEELE,Philip John Rupert	Lt Aust AFA 4Bde dow 8-1-17 CR France 145
STEER,Charles Pearman	Lt Can2CMR D'Coy 22-5-17CR France 68
STEER,James Hubert	Lt SA FldArty kia 18-12-17 CR Palest 9
STEINKE,I.C.A.	Lt SA SAIC dow 7-10-14
STENHOUSE,John William	2Lt Aust 9Inf 7-10-17MR 29
STENT,G.B.	Lt SA 7SAInf 18-12-19 CR SAfrica 53
STEPHEN,David Robert.MC.	Lt Aust 44Inf kia 28-3-18 CR France 1170
STEPHENS,Francis Chaltan	Lt Capt Can13Bn ded 16-10-18 CR Canada 256
STEPHENS,Frederick Henry	Lt Can CORD 2Bn attRFC 3Sqn 23-11-17 MR 20
STEPHENS,Harry	Capt Aust 30Inf kia 18-11-17 CR Belgium 48
STEPHENS,J.F.	2Lt Aust 3MGC 25-4-18CR France 27
STEPHENS,Laurence de Kalisz	Lt Can 42Bn (QR) kia 2-6-16 MR 29
STEPHENSON,James Lloyd	Lt Can 14Bn 9-4-17 CR France 523 STEVENSON
STEPHENSON,John Sydney	2Lt Can RNewfndlandRkia 14-4-17 MR 10
STEPHENSON,Keith Robert	2Lt Aust 8Inf dow 30-7-16 CR France 74
STEPHENSON,Leonard Armstrong	2Lt Aust 16Bn 30-8-16MR 26
STERLING,John Harold.MC.	2Lt Aust 60Inf kia 19-7-16 MR 7
STERT,G.B.	Lt SA 7SAInf ded 18-12-19
STEVEN,James Thomson	Lt NZ 10716 CycBn dow 17-11-17 CR Belgium 72

STEVENS,Albert Edward.MM.	2Lt Aust45Inf	kia 7-2-18 CR Belgium 131
STEVENS,Edward Toynbee	Lt Aust 37Inf	kia 11-10-17 CR Belgium 125
STEVENS,William Duncan	Lt Can 29Bn	kia 30-5-16 CR Belgium 15
STEVENS,William Ernest	2Lt NZ 26/472 4/3NZRB	kia 15-8-17 CR Belgium 109
STEVENS,William Johnstone	Chpn3Cl Aust att5Inf	dow 15-11-17 CR Surrey 1
STEVENSON,Ernest Grant.MC.	Lt Can 4CRT	2-11-18CR France 52
STEVENSON,Francis Walter	Lt Aust 52Inf	kia 7-6-17 CR Belgium 168
STEVENSON,Augustus Ralph Wickham	Lt Can 15Bn	kia 7-9-16 CR France 430
STEVENSON,Vere Cumming.MM.	2Lt Aust 34Inf	kia 14-7-18 CR France 1170
STEWART,Andrew Rodgie	Lt Can RCHA A'Bty	9-7-17 CR France 725
STEWART,Cedric Alwyn	Maj Aust AMC 1FA	kia 28-4-18 CR France 25
STEWART,Charles James Townshend.DSO&Bar.LtCol	Can PPCLI	28-9-18CR France 481
STEWART,Charles Milton	Lt Can 1CMR	9-4-17 CR France 522
STEWART,Charles Walter	Maj Can10Bn	kia 3-6-16 CR Belgium 127
STEWART,Douglas Macbean.MID.	LtCol NZ 6/1171 CIR	kia 25-4-15 MR 6
STEWART,George Hepburn	LtCol NZ 9/999 OMR	ded 20-11-15 CR Greece 11
STEWART,Harry	2Lt NZ 18429 1/3NZRB	kia 12-10-17 MR 30
STEWART,James Douglas	Lt NZ 16/514 AMR	kia 14-11-17 CR Palest 9
STEWART,John Albert	Lt Can 8Bn	dow 16-11-17 CR France 134
STEWART,John Herchmer	Lt Can PPCLI	17-6-15CR France 1140
STEWART,John Hope Johnstone	2Lt Aust 13Inf	21-10-17 MR 29
STEWART,M.G.	Lt Aust Engrs 13FC	31-7-17MR 26
STEWART,Robert H.	Capt Can 10Bn	22-5-15CR France 260
STEWART,Robert William	Lt Can 42Bn	dow 25-3-17 CR France 95
STEWART,Stanley Peter	Maj Capt Can 10Bn	9-4-17 CR France 68
STEWART,Walter Wilson	LtCol Can 1MMGBde	kia 11-4-17 CR France 68
STEWART,William	Lt Can 13Bn	20-10-18 CR France 1196
STEWART,William Andrew	Lt Can 883571 50Bn	27-9-18CR France 482
STEWART,William Kelvey	Lt Aust2Inf	kia 23-8-18 CR France 526
STEWART,William Morrison	2Lt Aust 19Bn	14-11-16 MR 26
STEYTLER,E.D.	2Lt SA PofWVltrs	
STIBBARD,Sydney	Capt Can 44Bn	3-6-17 MR 23
STILL,Geoffrey	Lt Can 7Bn	dow 11-11-17 CR Belgium 11
STILL,Ormond Montgomery.MC.	Lt Can CE 1ATCoy	16-8-18CR France 1170
STINSON,Charles Russell.MC.MID	Maj Can 27Bn (MR)	kia 6-11-17 MR 29
STIRLING,Frank Malcolm	2Lt Aust 29Bn	7-10-16MR 26
STIRLING,Robert Archibald	Lt Can 2Bn (EOR)	24-4-15MR 29
STIRRETT,Ernest Zavitz Surg	Lt Can RNCVR HMS`Niobe'	23-6-17CR Canada 1690
STITT,O.M.MC. see STILL,O.M.		
STIVER,Claud Franklin	Lt Can 72Bn	10-8-18CR France 586
STIVER,Harry Cecil.MC.	Lt Can 8Bn (MR)	10-11-17 MR 29
St.LIMERICK,I.	Lt SA10SAInf see Limerick,St Ian.	
STOBIE,Gerald Leslie	2Lt NZ 6/4151 3/3NZRB	kia 26-8-18 CR France 560
STOCK,James Robert	Lt Aust 5Inf	20-9-17MR 29
STOCKFELD,G.R.	Capt Aust 59Inf	26-9-17CR Belgium 112
STOCKHAM,Sydney Clezy	Lt Aust 27Inf	dow 18-8-18 CR France 119
STOCKHAUSEN,Frederick Hope	Lt Can 58Bn	kia 1-10-18 CR France 240
STOCKWELL,Thomas Hodges.MM.	Lt Can 7Bn	15-8-17MR 23
STONE, Franklyn George	Lt Can 49Bn (AR)	30-10-17 MR 29 Franklin
STONE,J E	Lt Aust see TAYLOR,H E real name	
STONE,Victor Augustus	Lt Can 8Bn	10-11-17 CR Belgium 10 Augusta
STONE,William John	Capt NZ6/1990 CIR 1CanterburyR	dow 13-10-17 CR Belgium 11
STONEMAN,John Herbert Adams	Lt Can 4CMGC 13MGCoy	29-9-18CR France 274
STONES,Gerald Cunliffe	Lt Aust 4ALH attAFC	kia 30-5-17 CR Egypt 2
STOOKE,Ernest Cecil.DCM.	Lt Aust AFC 1Sqn	kia 19-8-18 CR Palest 9
STORCH,Louis Albert	Lt Aust AFC 4Sqn	kia 22-4-18 CR France 88
STORER,John Henry	Lt Can 8Bn	5-3-17 CR France 68
STORER,William Edgar Harry	Lt Aust 1 2LtTMB	kia 21-2-17 CR France 307
STOREY,Duncan Stewart	Maj Can 162Bn	23-3-17CR Canada 1217
STORRER,Henry Haigh	Capt Aust AFC	kia 2-12-17 CR France 285

St.PINNOCK,Charles Clifford Denham	2LtAust 57Inf kia 19-8-16 CR France 348
STRACHAN,William Leighton	Capt Aust 6Inf kia 25/28-4-15 CR Gallipoli 7
STRACK,Karl Justus	2Lt NZ10/2822 3WIR kia 4-10-17 MR 30
STRANACK,William Garland	Lt SA 2SAInf dow 30-1-16 CR Egypt 3
STRANG,John Donald Kay.MIDx2	Capt NZ 9/781 3/3NZRB kia 15-9-16 CR France 277
STRANGE,Frank	LtCol Can COC 1DivHQded 6-1-15 CR Canada 1270
STRANGMAN,John Gerald	2Lt Aust 54Inf kia 19/20-7-16 MR 7
STRATFORD,George Stacey	Lt Can PPCLI A'Coy (EOR)kia 17-11-17 MR 29
STRATFORD,Joseph Benjamin.MC	Capt Can FGH kia 2-4-18 CR France 987
STRAW,James Holmes	2Lt NZ 3/161 2OIR dow 24-8-18 CR France 84
STREET,Laurence Whistler	Lt Aust 3Inf kia 19-5-15 CR Gallipoli 24
STREETER,Henry	Lt Aust AFC kia 17-2-18 CR France 285
STRICKLAND,Roland D'Arcy	Lt Can 28Bn 20-5-17CR France 68
STRINGER,Alfred Stanley	2Lt Aust 5Inf kia 25-7-16 CR France 832
STRONG,Charles St.Clair	Capt Can 1NfndlandR dow 13-4-18 CR Belgium 11
STRONG,Randolph William	Lt Can 134CoyCFC 26-7-18CR Derby 57 CGA 7SB
STRONG,William	Lt Can 11MGCoy ded 21-12-19 CR USA 234
STROOD,Percy Samson	Lt Can 1CMR kia 8-10-15 CR Belgium 37
STRUBEN,Kenneth Keir	2Lt SA 4SAInf dow 14-1-18 CR France 446
STRUTHERS,James Barr	Lt NZ6/3889 2OIR dow 27-9-16 CR France 145
STUART,Alexander	Lt Aust 25Bn 5-8-16 MR 26
STUART,Cobham Claude A.	Eng Lt AustRAN 17-8-19CR Aust 112
STUART,Henry Cuthbert	Lt Can2Bn 9-9-16 CR France 1506
STUART,Herbert James	Lt Can RCR 3-10-16CR France 314
STUART,Horace Tasman	2Lt Aust 40Inf ded 13-3-17 CR Surrey 1
STUART,James Duff	Maj Can 1PnrBn &RFC 43Sqn 7-3-17 MR 20
STUART,Peter Fitzalan MacDonald	LtAust 49Bn 4-9-16 MR 26
STUART,William Alexander	2Lt NZ 27613 2InfBdeHQ kia 16-8-18 CR France 156
STUART-BAILEY,Charles	Lt Can 44Bn kia 29-10-17 CR Belgium 3
STUART-MASON,Albert Charles	Lt Aust 3Inf kia 25-7-18 CR France 25
STUART-SINCLAIR,John Francis	Lt Aust 28Inf 29-10-17 CR Belgium 11
STUART-SMITH,Philip James	Lt Can LSH &RAF 74Sqn 8-5-18 MR 20
STUBBS,Bartholomew James	2Lt Aust 51Inf 26-9-17MR 29
STUBBS,Eric Guy	Lt NZ 22623 MGC dow 3-10-18 CR France 512
STUBBS,Thomas Ebenezer	2Lt NZ24415 2/3NZRB kia 12-10-17 CR Belgium 126
STUCKEY,Frederick	Maj NZ 12/2 AIR dow 25-4-15 MR 6
STUMKE,John Charles Augustus	Lt SA SAIC dow 29-9-14 CR SAfrica 127
STUPART,Frederic Gustavus	Lt Can 75Bn dow 22-10-16 CR France 59
SULIVAN,Henry Ernest	Capt CanPPCLI 31-10-17 CR Belgium 22
SULLIVAN,Alfred Amory	Capt SA 2SAInf kia 12-10-16 MR 21
SULLIVAN,James.MC&Bar.MM.	Capt Aust 21Inf kia 5-10-18 CR France 375
SULLIVAN,Wilfred Charles Percy	LtCan 25Bn att43Bn C'Coy 8-10-16MR 23
SUMMERS,Eli Charles	2Lt Aust 7Inf kia 11-8-18 CR France 526
SUMMERS,Lionel Logan.MC.	2Lt Aust 11Inf dedacc 12-11-17 CR France 145
SUMMERS,Michael Francis	Capt Can 1RNewfndlandRdow 16-7-16 CR France 169
SUMPTION,John Francis	Maj Can 14Bn dow 22-10-16 CR France 145
SUNLEY,John Maxwell	2Lt NZ 2/1878 NZFA 5Btydow 9-9-16 CR France 188
SURTEES,William	Lt Aust AMGC 11Coy kia 4-4-18 CR France 210
SUTCLIFFE,Charles Elliott	Maj Can 77Bn attRFA 54Sqn kia6-6-17 CR Canada 1430 &CR France1736dow
SUTER,Gordon Wilson	Lt Can 12BnCE 2-9-18 CR France 1182
SUTHERLAND,Alan D'Arcy	2Lt Aust RAF Ex 48AustInf 28-2-17CR Wilts 116
SUTHERLAND,Alexander Reuben	2Lt NZ 10/3752 1OIR kia 25-9-16 CR France 432
SUTHERLAND,Alister Morphett	Lt NZ StaffCps att21Lancers ded 28-8-20 MR 69
SUTHERLAND,Douglas Adamson	Lt Can26Bn 15-10-17 CR France 268
SUTHERLAND,Edwin Boyett	Lt Aust57Inf kia 22-9-16 CR France 348
SUTHERLAND,George Bruce	Lt Can29BCR 21-8-17MR 23
SUTHERLAND,James Watson	Lt Can CGA ded 31-1-21 CR Canada 323A
SUTHERLAND,John.DSO.MID	Maj Can116Bn 27-8-18CR France 154
SUTHERLAND,John Clifton	Lt Can RCR kia 5-4-18 CR France 68
SUTHERLAND,John Elliot	Lt Can 58Bn 29-7-16CR Belgium 5

SUTHERLAND,William   2Lt Aust13Inf   kia 21-8-15 MR 6
SUTTON,Percy Villiers   Lt Can   RCR 8-10-16CR France 314
SWAIN,Leonard Ruben   Lt Can   31Bn   15-9-16MR 23 Reuben
SWAIN,Roy Vivian   2Lt Aust 47Inf   dow 7-8-16   CR France 44
SWAINE,Herbert Miller   Lt Capt Can 21Bn   ded 19-2-18 CR Canada 1270
SWANN,John Nuel   Lt Aust 45Inf   kia 7-6-17   CR Belgium 168
SWANN,Lyell Keith.MM.   Lt Aust AFC   dow 14-11-18 CR France 1030
SWANN,Peter Robert.MM.   Lt Can   20Bn   8-8-18 CR France 29
SWANNELL,Blair Inskip   Maj Aust1Inf   kia 25-4-15   CR Gallipoli 10
SWANNELL,Charles Edgar.MM.   Lt CanRAF 16Bn   19-7-18CR Sussex 178
SWANSON,John W.King   Capt Can   46Bn   dow 13-4-17 CR France 12
SWANTON,Robert   Lt Aust 22Inf   kia 23-7-18 CR France 144
SWANSTON,Walter   2Lt   Aust 2ALH dow 1-11-17 CR Palest 1
SWART,L.J.   Capt   SA 2MtdBdeSctskia 20-3-15 CR SAfrica 17
SWARTS,Jack Bertram.MM.   Lt Can 58Bn   30-9-18CR France 714
SWEENEY,Leo John.MC.   Lt Can 196Bn &RAF 30-4-18CR France 134
SWEENEY,W.P.   2Lt   SA   3SAInf kia 20-9-17
SWEET,John Hales   Maj   Can   72Bn kia 9-4-17   CR France 81
SWENDSON,Harry   Lt   Aust 4Inf   4-10-17MR 29
 served as DAVENPORT
SWIFT,Thomas Lemon   Lt   Can 1Bn   15-6-15MR 23
SWINARD,Nathaniel Charles   2Lt NZ 8/116   2CIR   kia 20-9-16 MR 11
SWINBURNE,Harry Laffer   Lt Aust 29Inf   kia 2-3-17   CR France 307
SWINNERTON,Aysceau F.R.W.   Lt Can 75Bn 1-3-17 MR 23
SWINTON,John   Lt Can 50Bn   13-2-17MR 23
SWITZER,Albert Robert   Lt Can 19Bn   ded   23-4-19 CR Hamps 2
SWORDER,Malcolm   Lt Can LSH attRFC 59Sqn kld 18-3-18 CR France 518
SWORDER,Norman   Lt   Can   RAF LSH 17-4-18CR France 268
SYDDALL,George Baxby   Capt Can   223Bn attRFC 56Sqn   kld 4-1-18 CR France 285
SYDES,Edward John Read   Chpn   Aust att5FldAmbded   15-11-18 CR London 9
SYDIE,Jack.MC.   Lt Can 1CMR   26-8-18CR France 1189
SYLVESTER,George McDonald   Lt Can 14Bn 26-9-16MR 23
SYLVESTRE,Charles Joseph   Maj   Can 22Bn 1-10-16MR 23
SYMINGTON,William Albert   Lt Aust 4Inf   kia 18-4-17 CR France 245
SYMMES,H.C.   Maj   SA   2SAInf 9-4-17 CR France 728
SYMONDS,Herbert Boyd   Lt Can   14Bn   9-4-17 CR France 523
SYMONDS,J.H.MC.   Lt SA SA GL   ded 15-11-18 CR SAfrica 30
SYMONS,John Hannaford   Capt   Can 4CMR (1COR) 2-6-16 MR 29
SYMONS,Parker Whitley   Lt Aust AFC 4Sqn kia 5-11-18 CR Belgium 362
SYNNOTT,Bartle Patrick   Lt Aust 31Inf   kia 24-5-17 CR France 646

T

TAFFT,Paul George   Lt Can 31Bn   1915
TAIT,Eric Fullerton   Lt Aust   AFA 10Bde 20-9-17MR 29
TAIT,James Edward.VC.MC.   Capt   Can 78Bn kia 11-8-18 CR France 692
TAIT,Kenneth James.MC.   Capt   NZ 1/185 AMR   kia 23-3-18 MR 34
TAIT,William Elmer   Lt Can 7Bn 28-9-18CR France 214
TALBOT,Arthur   2Lt NZ 14037 2CIR kia 12-10-17 MR 30
TALLMAN,Stanley Bliss   Lt CanRCD   ded 5-11-18 CR Surrey 1
TANDY,Arthur Elton   Lt Aust1TC kia 25-4-17 CR Belgium 5
TANNANT,William Galbraith   Lt Can LSH1915
TANNER,Arthur William   LtCol Can CAMC 10FA dow 4-6-16 CR Belgium 11

TANSEY,Lionel Matthew	2Lt NZ25/25 MGC ded 12-3-19 CR NZ 291
TAPLIN,Archibald Stevens	Lt Aust 17Inf 3-5-17 CR France 646
TAPNER,Benjamin Stavely	Lt Aust 22Inf dow 29-7-16 CR France 74
TARBUTT,Henry William	Lt SA BrNRhodPol kia 9-8-17 CR EAfrica 40
TARR,Bernard	2Lt Aust 52Inf dow 9-6-17
TARRANT,Francis Joseph	Lt Aust AFC 3Sqn kia 17-2-18 CR France 285
TASKER,Leonard Francis	Lt Can 87Bn kia 2-9-18 CR France 310
TASSIE,Benjamin Bertchael Eager	LtCan 1Bn dow 3-9-18 CR France 103
TATHAM,Errol Victor	2Lt SA 2SAInf B'Coy kia 18-7-16 MR 21
TATHAM,Russell Pears	2Lt SA 2SAInf kia 20-7-16 MR 21
TATLOW,John Garnett.MC.	Maj CanLSH A'Sqdn 23-3-18 MR 23
TATNALL,William Henry	Capt Aust 24Inf kia 7-8-16 CR France 515
TAYLER,George Washington	Lt NZ 10/1681 WIR kia 8-8-15 MR 5
TAYLOR,Adrian Aubrey Charles	Capt RDFus attEgyptPolice 28-6-15 MR 4
TAYLOR,Albert Ernest	Lt Aust Engrs 1FC 23-7-16 MR 26
TAYLOR,Albert Lawrence Deane	Lt AustAFC 3Sqn kia 20-5-18 CR France 71
TAYLOR,Arthur	Lt Can 7Bn 22-9-16 CR France 59
TAYLOR,Benjamin Anderson	Lt Can5CMGC 4-7-17 CR France 178
TAYLOR,Clarence Henry.MC.	Maj Aust 6Inf dow 12-10-17 CR France 40
TAYLOR,Frank William	Lt Aust 3Inf dow 22-6-18 CR France 134
TAYLOR,Geoffrey Barron	Lt Can 15Bn (1COR) kia 24-4-15 MR 29
TAYLOR,George.MM.	2Lt Aust 2Pnrs kia 29-9-17 CR Belgium 72
TAYLOR,George Hayward	2Lt Can RNewfndlandR kia 1-7-16 MR 10
TAYLOR,George Vallance	Capt Can CFA 2DAC 13-11-16 CR France 150
TAYLOR,Gerald Ingram	Lt Can 1Bn 16-10-18 CR France 273
TAYLOR,H.MC.MM.	Lt Aust AFC 18-8-18 CR Warwick 7
TAYLOR,Harold	Capt Aust 54Inf kia 19/20-7-16 CR France 348
TAYLOR,Harry	HCapt&QMCan 2Bn 6-12-18 CR Belgium 287
TAYLOR,Harry Edward	Lt Aust 21Inf served as STONE,J E kia 3-8-16 CR France 832
TAYLOR,Henry Percy	Capt NZ 11/156 WMR kia 29-8-15 MR 14
TAYLOR,Howard T.	Lt Can 5Bn 6-6-16 CR Belgium 132
TAYLOR,James Albert.DCM.	2Lt NZ 23/1213 2AIR kia 31-8-18 CR France 307
TAYLOR,James Edward Sydney.MID	Lt Aust44Inf kia 14-3-17 CR France 922
TAYLOR,Kenneth Churchill Craigie.DSO.	Maj Can 29Bn 12-9-16 CR France 1505
TAYLOR,Leonard	Lt Aust 25Bn 11-6-18 MR 26
TAYLOR,Norman Claude	2Lt Aust AFA 10Bde kia 17-10-18 CR France 1352
TAYLOR,P.MM.	Lt Aust 26Inf 2-9-18 CR France 511
TAYLOR,Robert Bertram	Lt Can 2Bn 26-4-16 CR Belgium 11
TAYLOR,Rupert Warren	Lt Can 87Bn kia 9-4-17 CR France 81
TAYLOR,Thomas George.DCM.	Lt Aust 41Inf dow 5-7-17 CR France 297
TAYLOR,Thomas Joseph	Lt Can 72Bn att12LTMB kia 10-8-18 CR France 586
TAYLOR,Thomas Wardlaw.MC.	Maj Can 43Bn kia 24-10-18 CR France 1144
TAYLOR,William Alfred	2Lt Aust 8Bn 26-7-16 MR 26
TAYLOR,William Massey.MM.	2Lt Aust49Bn 5-4-18 MR 26
TAYLOR,William Wallace.MC.	Lt Can 1Bn 9-4-18 CR France 40
TEAGUE,Harold Oscar.MID	Capt Aust 11Inf kia 14-2-17 CR France 385
TEASDALE,Charles Claude	Lt Aust 5Inf 1-10-17 MR29
TEDDER,Alma Reginald O'Neil	Lt Aust AASC ded 23-2-19 CR France 65
TEED,Daniel Lionel.MC.	Lt Can CFA 9Bde kia 1-9-18 CR France 154
TEED,Hugh Mariner	Lt Can 2Bn dedacc 7-1-17 CR France 32
TEITZEL,Louis Walter	Lt Aust 25Inf kia 29-7-16 CR France 744
TEMPLE,Anthony	Capt Can 2CMR kia 5-4-16 CR Belgium 5
TEMPLE,Claude Castlemaine	Lt Can 2MtdRif BCR 2-10-16 MR 23
TEMPLEMAN,Harry	Lt Aust 25Inf kia 8-8-18 CR France 144
TEMPLEMAN,Jean	NSister Can CAMC HS drd 27-6-18 MR 24
TEMPLETON,Thomas Harvey	Lt Aust 14Inf 24-9-17 MR 29
TENAILLE,Daniel Jean	Maj Can5Bn 24-5-15 CR France 727
TENBOSCH,Christian Peter	2Lt Aust Engrs 8FC kia 19-7-16 CR France 525
TENCH,George Thomas Kellett.MID	Lt Aust 32Inf dow 29-9-18 CR France 375
TENNANT,Thomas	Lt Aust AMGC 5Coy kia 14-11-16 CR France 385

TENNANT,William Galbraith	Lt Can LSH kia 25-5-15 CR France 98
TENNENT,Robert	2Lt NZ 15320 2/3NZRB kia 26-6-17 MR 9
TERRAS,James Sutter	Lt Aust 45Inf kia 28-3-18 CR France 177
TERRY,Eustace Ernest.MM.	Lt Aust12Inf kia 25-8-18 CR France 526
TERRY,Henry Walter Seymer	Lt SA 2SAInf kia 22-3-18 MR 27
TERRY,Sydney Dorsey	Capt Can 102Bn kia 25-8-17 CR France 81
TETT,Arthur Hopkins	Lt Can 5ResBn 26-8-17CR Somerset 68
THAIRS,Edward Fox	Lt Can 3Bn C'Coykia 8-8-18 CR France 488
THOM,Charles Henry Wallace	Lt Aust Engrs 4FC kia 29-10-15 CR Gallipoli 31
THOM,Ernest Colin	Lt Can 31AR 26-9-16MR 23
THOMAS,Cecil William	Lt Aust AIF 13Aust LtTMB 14-2-20CR Aust 94
THOMAS,Charles Ernest	LtCol NZ 3/118A NZMC kia 28-8-15 CR Gallipoli 18
THOMAS,Claude Edward.MID	Lt Aust 4AASC dow 16-12-15 CR Egypt 3
THOMAS,David Evan	Lt Can 8Bn kia 27-4-17 CR France 95
THOMAS,Eric Hamilton	Lt Aust Engrs 4FC dow 2-5-18 CR France 1173
THOMAS,Fred	Capt NZ 12/3843 AIR 2AuklandR HaurakiCoy dow 4-10-17 CR Belgium 3 5-10-17
THOMAS,Henry Robertson	2Lt Aust 38Inf kia 1-2-17 CR France 922
THOMAS,Herbert Richard	2Lt Aust22Inf kia 5-8-16 CR France 832
THOMAS,James Henry	Lt NZ 14903 2CIR kia 4-9-18 CR France 756
THOMAS,Norman James.MM.	Lt Can 425411 28Bn (SR)kia 6-11-17 MR 29
THOMAS,Reginald Norman	2Lt Aust 24Inf kia 27-8-16 CR France 832
THOMAS,Theodore Gauntlett	Lt Can 47Bn 12-8-18CR France 649
THOMAS,William Alfred	Lt NZ 18896 2AIR kia 2-2-17 CR France 276
THOMPDON,Ada Mildred	SNurse Aust AANS 1-1-19 CR Aust 456
THOMPSON,Alfred Charles	Capt Aust 6ALH kia 2-11-17 CR Palest 1
THOMPSON,Alfred Hamilton	Lt Can 5ResBn 1COR &RAF ded 26-9-18 CR France 134
THOMPSON,Andrew Stevenson.MSM.MID.	2Lt NZ 12/886 3AIR kia 4-8-17 CR Belgium 136
THOMPSON,Arthur Oliver	Capt Can 72Bn 29-9-18CR France 597
THOMPSON,Astley John Onslow.VD.MID	LtCol Aust 4Inf kia 26-4-15 CR Gallipoli 24
THOMPSON,Bernard	Lt See WILSON true name
THOMPSON,Campbell Henry	Lt Aust 2Inf 16-9-17MR 29
THOMPSON,Charles Everett	Lt Can CAMC MB ded 3-2-17 CR Canada 1667
THOMPSON,Charles Gordon	Lt Can CFA 11Bde ded 28-1-19 CR London 32 9Bde
THOMPSON,Cyprian Alfred	Lt Can RCR D'Coy 8-4-17 CR France 68
THOMPSON,Edward Payson	Lt Can 16Bn kia 16-8-18 CR France 699
THOMPSON,G.K.	Capt Aust AFA 24Bde 19-7-16CR France 276
THOMPSON,George Robert	Lt Aust AFC dedacc 3-7-18 CR Glouc 172
THOMPSON,Harold Hubert	Lt Aust 18Inf dow 15-4-18 CR France 494
THOMPSON,Harold William.MC.	Lt Aust 14Inf dow 9-8-18 CR France 71
THOMPSON,Harry Nelson	Lt Can 5Bn 9-4-17 CR France 68
THOMPSON,Harry Purdy	Capt Can CADC 2-11-18CR Kent 227
THOMPSON,Henry Aubrey	Capt Can 14Bn 27-9-18CR France 214
THOMPSON,Horace William Blair	2Lt Aust 11Inf kia 3-5-15 CR Gallipoli 25
THOMPSON,Hubert Gordon	Capt Aust 56Inf 26-9-17MR 29
THOMPSON,Ivo Garfield	Lt Aust 58Inf kia 4-7-18 CR France 195
THOMPSON,James Roxburgh	2Lt Aust 6Inf 9-8-16 CR France 40
THOMPSON,John Alexander McKay	Lt Can 10Bn 1915
THOMPSON,John Ernest	2Lt NZ 22678 2OIR kia 4-11-18 CR France 307 2-9-18
THOMPSON,Kenneth Sanders	2Lt Aust 42Inf kia 31-8-18 CR France 511
THOMPSON,Margaret Hepple	SNurse NZ 22/486 AANS 28-2-21CR NZ 53
THOMPSON,Robert John	Capt Aust 26Bn 5-8-16 MR 26
THOMPSON,Stanley Bowerman	2Lt Aust 14Bn 11-4-17MR 26
THOMPSON,William Crang	Lt Can 44Bn attRFC 16-10-17 CR Scot 398
THOMPSON,William Percy	Lt Can5Bn 9-4-17 CR France 68
THOMPSON,William Phillips	Lt NZ 15468 2CIR 12Coy dow 7-6-17 MR 9
THOMPSON,William Theodore	2Lt Aust 38Inf kia 16-1-17 CR France 922
THOMSON,Alexander Thomas.DSO.MC	LtCol Can 10 att4Bn kia 19-11-17 CR France 68 Thomson
THOMSON,Alister McLean	2Lt NZ 10/3808 2WIR B'Coy kia 17-6-17 CR France 922
THOMSON,Andrew James	Lt Can 16Bn 28-4-18CR France 184
THOMSON,Arnold	2Lt NZ 44565 2/3NZRB dow 27-8-18 CR France 84

THOMSON,Bruce Garie	Lt Aust AFC 3Sqn kia 3-10-18 CR France 234
THOMSON,Burns Kerweld	Maj Can 1MtdRif SasR kia 15-9-16 MR 23
THOMSON,Colin Leslie	Lt Aust 35Inf kia 4-4-18 CR France 424
THOMSON,Douglas Cameron	Lt Can 10Bn 3-9-18 CR France 57
THOMSON,Frederick James	Lt Aust 49Inf kia 10-6-18 CR France 1170
THOMSON,Frederick T.	AssPmster Can VR465 RNCVR ded 31-3-18 CR Canada 1245
THOMSON,Henry Richard	Lt Can 58Bn dow 25-10-17 CR Belgium 11
THOMSON,James McAulay	2Lt SA 2SAInf dow 17-10-16 CR France 145
THOMSON,James Douglas	2Lt NZ 12/2572 NZMGC dow 28-8-18 CR France 84
THOMSON,James Elliott	2Lt Can 1RNewfndlandR kia 3-3-17 CR France 216
THOMSON,James Joseph	Lt Aust 57Inf dow 29-9-18 CR France 446
THOMSON,John	Lt Can CE 124Bn &RAF N'Flt 27-10-18 MR 20
THOMSON,John Leslie	Lt Can 21Bn 19-7-16CR Belgium 37
THOMSON,Louis Neil F.	2Lt Aust 4Inf kia 6/8-8-15 CR Gallipoli 7
THOMSON,Robert McDonnell	LtCol Can 43Bn 8-10-16CR France 430
THOMSON,Russell B.	Maj Can 19Bn kia 9-4-17 CR France 68
THOMSON,Sidney Alexander	Lt Aust 6Inf kia 10-8-18 CR France 526
THOMSON,William Davidson	Lt Can PPCLI attRFCkia 5-1-17 CR Belgium 11
THORBURN,R.B.MID	Lt SA 4SAInf kia 20-7-16 CR France 402
THORBY,Charles Frederick	2Lt NZ 11/612 ICC kia 30-3-18 MR 34
THORNE,Alan	Lt Aust 7ALH kia 27-7-15 CR Gallipoli 22
THORNE,Stephen Osborn	Lt Can 17ResBn ded 9-2-16 CR Kent 180
THORNE,Sydney Lodge	Maj Can 60Bn 26-11-16 CR France 523
THORNLEY,James Walter	2Lt Aust 13Bn 11-4-17MR 26
THORNTON,Ernest	Maj Can 5Bn ded 9-11-18 CR Canada 119
THORNTON,Sydney Whitta	HLt Aust RCS AANS ded 19-11-19 CR Oxford 69
THORPE,H.S.MM.	2Lt SA 3SAInf kia 24-12-17 CR France 439
THORPE,James Stokesbury	Lt Can 3MGCoy kia 13-6-16 CR Belgium 11
THRELFELL,I.	LtCol SA 10Horse ded 4-1-18 CR SAfrica 30
THRING,Andrew Henry	Lt Can 260Bn 18-3-19CR Europe 193 &MR 70
THROSSELL,Frank Eric	Lt Aust10ALH kia 19-4-17 CR Palest 8
THURBER,Sydney Welton .MC.	Lt Can 85Bn 14-10-18 CR France 34 Wilton
THURNHILL,Samuel Raymond.MC.	Lt Aust AFA 2Bde kia 5-11-16 CR France 432
THURSTANS,Alfred Charles	2Lt Aust 40Inf kia 5-4-18 CR France 207
THURSTON,Arnold Monroe	Lt Can FA 2DAC att2DivTMB kia 26-6-16 CR Belgium 15
THWAITE,William	Lt Can 38Bn 10-8-18CR France 692
THWAITES,Basil Champion	Lt Can 7Bn (BCR) 10-11-17 MR 29
THYER,Walter Hervey	2Lt Aust 16Inf kia 29-8-15 CR Gallipoli 16
TICKNER,Mervyn Ray.DCM.	2Lt Aust 19Inf 20-9-17MR 29
TIDDY,Alfred James	2Lt NZ8/2521 1OIR kia 7-6-17 CR Belgium 89
TIEGS,Albert Henry	2Lt Aust28Inf kia 26-3-17 CR France 644
TIERNEY,Michael	Lt Can 2Bn 21-5-17CR Canada 1271
TILLETT,John Rowland	Capt Aust AMC 7FA dow 2-10-17 CR Belgium 11
TINGLEY,Frank Harvey.MC.	Capt Can CFA 23Bty5Bde 14-10-18 CR France 34
TINKESS,Ivan Wellington	Lt Can 44Bn dow 13-2-17 CR France 12
TINLING,Charles Burnaby.MID	Lt Can 42Bn dow 15-4-17 CR France 12
TINSON,Garnet Edmund Iles	Lt Aust1ALH dow 9-8-15 MR 6
TIPPET,Harold Freeman	2Lt Aust 24Inf dow 18-9-15 MR 6
TOBIN,Charles Edward O'Hara	Capt NZ 18/4 ChpnsDept 20-3-21NZ 271
TOBIN,James J.	2Lt Can 1RNewfndlandR kia 20-11-17 CR France 911
TODD,Bertram Grieve	Lt Can 87Bn 5-11-16CR France 239
TODD,James Harvey	Maj Can CAMC ded 17-10-18 CR Canada 1688
TODD,Thomas John.CMG.DSO&Bar	LtCol Aust 10ALH ded 23-1-19 CR Egypt 9
TODHUNTER,Gilbert	Lt Can 10Bn kia 20-5-15 CR France 705
TOFFT,P.G.	Lt Can 31Bn (AR)13-10-15 MR 29
TOFT,Cecil George	2Lt Aust 25Inf kia 4-7-18 CR France 424
TOLEMAN,Kenneth	2Lt Aust 16Inf dow 12-10-16 CR Belgium 11
TOLHURST,Alexander Molesworth	Capt NZ 3/746 NZMC att4RB kia 8-5-18 CR France 63
TOLLIS,Thomas William	Capt Aust 33Inf kia 22-8-18 CR France 247
TOMPSETT,Norman	2Lt NZ 12/24952OIR kia 12-10-17 MR 30

TONKIN,William Henry	Lt Aust 4Bn 7-5-17 MR 26
TONKS,H.A.C.	2Lt Aust AFC 21-6-17CR Belgium 140
TOOKE,John Conrad Austin	2Lt SA 2SAInf kia 17-6-17 CR France 40 drd
TOOKE,William Marais Bompas	2Lt SA 2SAInf kia 12-4-17 CR France 604
TOOKER,Noel Longfield	Capt Can 54Bn kia 1-3-17 CR France 81
TOOLE,David Frederick Jack.MC&Bar.	Capt Can 49Bn kia 29-9-18 CR France 481
TOOLE,Edward Thomas	Lt Can 31AR 15-9-16MR 23
TOONE,John Algernon Edmund	Capt Aust3Pnrs kia 6-9-18 CR France 449
TOOTELL,Alfred Ernest	Lt Aust 33Inf kia 30-8-18 CR France 624
TOOTH,John Leslie	2Lt Aust 13AMGC 8-6-17 MR 29
TOOTH,Owen William	Lt Aust 6ALH kia 3-12-17 CR Palest 9
TOPHAM,Albert Alfred.MID	Lt SA GL attRoadCps ded 7-12-18 CR EAfrica 36
TOPP,Samuel James	Lt Aust 58Bn 12-5-17MR 26
TOPPIN,F.	Lt SA SASigs ded 8-12-18 CR SAfrica 69
TORRANCE,Samuel Greenshields	Capt Can 58Bn 13-11-17 CR Belgium 22
TOSTEVIN,George	Maj Aust AMGC 1Coy dow 5-5-17 CR France 1488
TOUGH,William Gordon	Lt Can2BdeCGA 15-9-18CR France 95
TOWERS,Norman Ewart	Capt Can RCR att7LTMB dow 20-9-16 CR France 145
TOWERS,Tom	2Lt Aust 32Inf kia 4-12-17 CR Belgium 168
TOWL,Percy Gilchrist.DSO.MID	Capt Aust 37Inf dow 8-9-18 CR France 526
TOWN,Charles James	2Lt Aust 51Inf kia 25-4-18 CR France 144
TOWNLEY,Max Mingaye	Lt Can 72Bn kia 9-4-17 CR France 81
TOWNSEND,Alan Jarvis Hamilton	Lt Can 4Bn dow 19-9-16 CR France 59
TOWNSHEND,Samuel Edward	Capt Aust 16Inf kia 9-5-15 MR 6
TRACEY,Norbert John	2Lt Aust 5Inf kia 18-8-16 CR France 1505
TRACEY,Thomas Leonard	Lt Can 2PnrBn 12-9-16CR France 1505
TRAINER,James Joseph	Lt NZ 57318 NZRB ded 21-11-21
TRANGMAR,Arthur James	2Lt Aust 39Inf kia 21-2-18 CR Belgium 339
TRANTER,Joseph Lionel	Lt Can 1WOR kia 15-6-15 MR 23
TRAVERS,Oliver.MC.	HCapt &QM Can 49Bn kia 29-10-17 CR Belgium 8
TRAVIS,Clifford Weldon	Lt Can 2BnCMGC 28-8-18CR France 310
TREADWELL,Edward Jabez Cooper	Cadet959 Aust AFC 4Sqn doi 20-9-17 CR Shrop 145
TREBILCOCK,Alsey Joseph	Lt Can 1MGCoy 6-11-17CR Belgium 10
TREES,Christopher Frank	Lt Can 2CMR 29-9-18CR France 715
TREMAIN,Robert Lloyd	2Lt Aust 23Bn 26-8-16MR 26
TREMBLAY,Albert Jaques	Lt Can2PnrBn (WOR) &RAF kldacc 31-8-18 CR Hamps 202 & 65
TREMEWAN,Hugh Spencer	Capt NZ 10/24801WIR dow 16-9-16 CR France 177
TRENDELL,Edwin Alfred.MC&Bar.MM.MID Lt Can 19Bn4-11-17CR Belgium 84
TRETHEWEY,Bertram Donne	2Lt SA4SAInf A'Coykia 20-9-17 CR Belgium 101
TREVELYAN,William John	HLt Can CAMC ded 31-5-18 CR Canada 1691
TRIBE,A.L.	Capt SA2RhodR &3/2KAR 17-11-17 CR EAfrica 11
TRICKETT,James John	Lt Aust 4DivAmmCol AFA ded 12-2-17 CR France 833
TRIGGS,Guy	Lt Can PPCLI 28-9-18CR France 481
TRIMMER,Alfred Syer.MC.	Maj Can10Bn 28-4-17CR France 68
TRIPP,Harlow Victor	Lt CanLSH 1918
TRITTON,George	Lt Can 44MR 19-2-18MR 23
TROTHEWEY,B.D.	2Lt SA4SAInf kia 20-9-17
TROTMAN,George Leopold Sanders	2Lt Aust 7Inf kia 17-4-18 CR France 200
TROTTER,Claud Hendley	Lt Can 10Bn &RAF 44Sqn kld 13-10-18 CR Essex 164
TROTTER,Stuart Fowden	Lt Can209Bn attRFC 6-7-17 CR France 285
TROUT,Roy Cumestree	Lt Aust AFC 69Sqnkld 27-7-17 CR Warwick 50
TRUEMAN,Thomas George	Rev Aust YMCA att5Inf kia 22-3-18 CR Belgium 97
TRUMBELL,Orville Edmond	Lt Can 52Bn B'Coy (MR)kia 12-11-17 MR 29
TRUSDALE,Alice L.	Sister Can CAMC ded 12-9-19 CR Canada 1564
TRYON,Frederick Charles Hilbers	Maj Can 73Bn dow 14-11-16 CR France 59
TUBB,Frederick Harold.VC.	Maj Aust 7Inf dow 20-9-17 CR Belgium 11
TUBMAN,Esther Maude	SNurse NZ 22/517 NZANS ded 18-9-18 CR Wilts 115
TUBMAN,Leslie Watters.MC.MID	Lt Can 2Bn 3.5.17 CR France 96
TUCK,Gilbert Bernard Owen	2Lt Aust54Inf kia 19-2-17 CR France 744
TUCK,William Sinclair.MID	Capt Can CFA 2LTMB30-10-16 CR France 133

TUCKER,Alfred Joseph	2Lt Aust 59Inf dow 29-9-18 CR France 446
TUCKER,Percival George.MC.	Lt Can 24Bn kia 28-8-18 CR France 310
TUCKER,Virgil	Capt Aust 16Bn 11-4-17MR 26
TUCKER,Wilfred Leslie.DCM.	Lt Aust 7Inf dow 25-7-18 CR France 34
TUCKETT,Francis John.MC.	Lt Aust 3DivSigs kia 14-10-17 CR Belgium 84
TUCKETT,Philip	2Lt Aust 49Inf kia 24-11-16 CR France 277
TUFTS,Gordon Harrison.MC.	Capt Can 27MR 21-8-17MR 23
TUNSTALL,George Stanley	Lt Can 16Bn Secnd to RAF 18-5-18CR Lincs 181
TUPPER, Addie Allen.RRC.	Nurse Can CAMC 2CanGH 9-12-16CR Middx 83 Adruenna
TUPPER,James Henry	Maj Can 25Bn 16-9-16CR France 430
TUPPER,Murray Lamont	Capt Can 25NSR 27-8-18MR 23
TUPPER,Victor Gordon.MC.	Capt Can 16Bn OC 3Coy kia 9-4-17 CR France 68
TURGEON,Arthur	Lt Can 22Bn ded 28-8-19 CR Canada 254 41Bn
TURNBULL,Alexander Phipps	2Lt Aust 10ALH kia 7-8-15 CR Gallipoli 29
TURNBULL,Kenneth	Lt Can 73Bn 19-8-16CR Belgium 6
TURNBULL,Richard Leonard	2Lt Aust4Inf kia 23-12-16 CR France 374
TURNBULL,Walter James.MC.	Lt CanCFA 10Bde kia 14-11-16 CR France 150
TURNER,Alexander	Lt Can 44Bn C'Coy kia 10-8-18 CR France 692
TURNER,Charles Horace	Lt Aust 5Pnrs dow 11-4-17 CR France 1484
TURNER,Frank	Lt SA SAFldArty kia 18-10-17 CR Tanzania 1 &EAfrica 11
TURNER,Felix George	Lt AustAFA 3Bde kia 18-9-18 CR France 446
TURNER,Frederick Charles	2Lt Aust AFC 1Sqn dedacc 16-6-18 CR Yorks 361
TURNER,George Harold.MC.	Lt AustEngrs 15FC26-9-17MR 29
TURNER,George James	Lt Can 16Bn (MR) Secnd to RAF 10-4-18CR Palest 9
TURNER,John Lancelot Harcourt.MC.MIDx2	Capt NZ 24882 NZFA kia 14-7-16 CR France 922
TURNER,Reginald Graham Tillyer	LtAust 49Bn 5-4-18 MR 26
TURNER,Samuel	Lt Aust 25Inf B'Coy dow 24-4-17 CR France 512
TURNER,William Vincent.MM.	Lt Aust 2Pnrs dow 5-5-17 CR France 512
TURNER,William Wilson.MID.	Maj NZ 23469 2OIR kia 12-10-17 MR 30
TURNOUR,John Edward.MID	Lt Aust 59Inf dow 28-9-17 CR Belgium 11
TWEED,Thomas McLellan	Capt Can 50Bn 10-8-18CR France 649
TWEEDY,G.H.	Lt SA 4 MR 22-2-15CR SAfrica 65
TWEEDY,R.P.	HLt Aust AustRedCross 15-2-19CR Surrey 1
TWIGDEN,G.W.	Lt Aust Engrs 4FC 7-4-17 CR France 1484
TWINING,Harvey Alexander	2Lt NZ 14040 AuklandR ded 19-11-18 CR NZ 194
TWISLETON,Francis Morphet.MC.MID.	Maj NZ 9/662 AMR dow 15-11-17 CR Palest 9
TWISS,Robert Dudley	Lt Can 43MR 8-10-16MR 23
TWIST,Dorothy Pearson	Nurse Can82/T/118 CanMilitaryVAD 26-9-18CR Hamps 1
TWOMEY,Francis O'Connor	Lt Aust 54Inf dow 29-9-18 CR France 1461
TYE,Archibald John.MC.	2Lt Aust 28Inf 21-9-17MR 29
TYNDALL,Douglas Montagu	Lt SANatLabCps dedacc 18-6-18 CR France 134
TYRRELL,James Thomas	Capt Aust 40Inf kia 10-1-17 CR France 922
TYSON,Fanny Isobel Catherine	Sister Aust AANS ded 20-4-19 CR Wilts 167
TYSON,James Gordon.MC.	Capt Aust 3Inf kia 3-5-17 CR France 1486

U

UATUKU te Irititt	Lt NZ 20701 MaoriPnrs ded 31-8-17 CR NZ 200
UGLOW,Henry Wright	Lt Can 4CMR (1COR) 3-6-16 MR 29
UGLOW,Richard Hubert Louis	Lt Can CE 3DivSigCoydow 16-6-17 CR France 178

UNWIN,Harry Wallace	Lt Can 1Bn B'Coy kia 22-9-16 CR France 430
UPTON,Francis Clive Ramsden.MC.	2Lt NZ 6/854 2CIR kia 2-10-16 MR 11
UPTON,Herbert Marshall	Lt Can 2Bn 30-8-18CR France 568
UPTON,Selwyn Arthur	Lt Aust 20Inf kia 3-5-17 CR France 568
UREN,Harold Frederick	Lt Aust 12Inf dow 9-4-17 CR France 307
UREN,William	Capt Aust 41Inf kia 1-9-18 CR France 511
URQHART,Roderick William	Lt Aust 8ALH 7-8-16 MR 34
UTHER,Gordon Arthvael	Maj Aust 20Inf dow 11-12-15 CR Gallipoli 29
UYS,Jacobus Nicolaas	Lt SA MtdCmdos kia 20-3-15 CR SAfrica 68

V

VAIL,Francis HaddinettSub	Lt Aust RAN 10-7-21CR Aust 307
VAILE,Walter Hugh	2Lt Aust 59Inf dow 24-7-16
VALIQUET,Elzear Augustin	Lt Can 22Bn dow 23-7-17 CR France 201
VALLANCE,Henry Walter	Lt Can 4Bn 13-6-16CR Belgium 126
VALLANCE,William Bertram.MID	Capt SA 11SAInf ded 17-5-17 CR SAfrica 144 VALLANCEY
VALLIS,Thomas James	Lt Aust 3Bn 11-8-18MR 26
Van BUSKIRK,Le Roy E.	Lt Can CCRD FortGarryH &RFC 9-12-17CR Wilts 116
VAN DIGGELEN,Henry Jean	Capt SAHQRecs&CampStaff ded 21-10-17 CR SAfrica 69 21-10-18
Van KLEECK,Stuart Bruce	Maj Can 2CMR 29-9-18CR France 715
VAN NIEKERK,H.J.	Lt SA 11SAInf ded 17-11-16 CR Tanzania 1 &EAfrica 4
Van PETTEN,Emery James	Lt Can 49Bn (AR)30-10-17 MR 29
Van STRAUBENZEE,Charles T.	LtCol Can RCD9-10-18CR France 441
VAN VELDEN,C.J.H.	2Lt SA RAF Ex SARifs 24-2-19CR London 8
VAN ZYL,Gideon Hendrick	LtCol SA SAMC ded 10-10-18 CR SAfrica 144
Van der SMISSEN,William Henry Victor	Capt Can 3Bn C'Coy (1COR) kia 13-6-16 MR 29
VANDERPUMP,Archibald Edward.MC.	Capt Can 52Bn 27-8-18CR France 155
VANSITTART,George Edward.MID	Maj Can CFA 4Bde dow 14-5-16 CR Belgium 11
VASSY,Peter Constantine	Lt AustAASC 9Coy drd 13-10-15 MR 6
VAUGHAN,Ben	Lt Aust 12Inf kia 21-4-18 CR France 28
VAUGHAN,Robert Patrick	2Lt NZ 18021 2/3NZRB kia 12-10-17 MR 30
VAVASOUR,George Marmaduke	2Lt NZ 33106 2/3NZRB kia 12-10-17 MR 30
VEILLEUX,Charles Alfred	Lt Can 22Bn 15-8-18CR France 145
VENABLES,Joseph Kendrick.MC.	Capt NZ 3/1272 NZMC attNZ EntrenchBn dow 9-5-18 CR France 142
VENN,Archie Valentine	Lt Can 58Bn kia 1-10-18 CR France 714
VERCOE-ROGERS,John	Lt Can 78Bn 27-9-18CR France 714
VERGE.Arthur	Capt Aust 6ALH ded 8-9-15 CR Egypt 3
VERNER, John Douglas.MC&Bar.	Capt Can 43Bn 16-2-19CR Sussex 200 Jack
VERNON,Ronald Cecil	Lt SA BaseDepotCoy ded 11-10-18 CR SAfrica 144
VERNON,William.MC.	Capt Can38Bn 29-9-18CR France 715
VERRILLS,Ernest James	2Lt Aust17Inf kia 9-10-17 CR Belgium 123
VERRY,Reginald Herbert	Lt Aust 49Inf kia 5-4-18 CR France 177
VERSFELD,J.M.	Lt SA 4SAH dow 20-5-16 CR Tanzania 1 &EAfrica 5
VERSO,Cyril Linton	Lt Aust AFA 4Bde 19-9-17MR 29
VESSEY,Edward John	Capt Can 60Bn 4-6-16 CR Belgium 72
VIAL,Alan Herbert.MM.	Lt NZ 2/1684 5/2NZFA ded 19-6-19 CR Hamps 11
VIAL,Lorimer James	Lt Aust 8Inf kia 9-8-18 CR France 526
VIBERT,Wilson George	Lt Can44Bn 28-9-18CR France 714
VICCARS,Stanley George	2Lt Aust1Inf kia 21-5-18 CR France 26
VICKER,A.De M.W.	Lt SA 1SAInf
VICKERS,Thomas Newell	Lt Can 78Bn dow 9-4-17 CR France 548
VICKERY,George B.	Lt Can 8MR 28-4-17MR 23

VICKERY,Henry George	Lt Can 10Bn 27-6-17CR France 68
VIDAL,C.H.	Intptr Aust att 41Inf 7-6-17 CR France 285
VIDAL,Maurice Henry	Lt Can 75Bn 29-7-17CR France 81
VIDGEN,Jack Grahame	2Lt Aust 15Inf kia 8-8-15 MR 6
VIEN,Louis Stanislas	Lt Can 22Bn 27-8-18CR France 310
VINCENT,Charles John	Lt Can52MR 22-9-16MR 23
VINCENT,Raymond George	Lt Can 73Bn dow 29-3-17 CR France12
VINE-HALL,Noel	2Lt 13Inf dow 3-6-15 MR 6
VINING,Roy Lindley	Lt Can 1BnCMGC 1918
VIPAN,C.A.	2Lt SA CapeCps kia 20-9-18
VIRGOE,Randall Gordon	2Lt Aust10Inf kia 21-12-17 CR Belgium 109
VIVIAN,Edward Valentine.MC.	Capt SA 3SAInf kia 25-9 -17 MR 29 20-9-17
VOELKER,Charles Richmond	Lt Can50Bn 10-4-18CR France 184
VOGAN,Arthur Henry	2Lt Aust 55Inf dow 4-2-17 CR France 177
VON ZWEIGBERGH,H.E.C.	Lt SA 9Inf 20-10-18 CR SAfrica 144
VOWELS,Philip Edward Michael.MC&Bar	Lt Aust 11Inf kia 11-5-18 CR France 28
VOYCE,Thomas Archibald	Lt Can 1Bn (WOR)9-7-16 MR 29

W

WADDINGHAM,Francis Henry	2Lt Aust AMGC 7Coy dow 10-3-17 CR France 177
WADE,Lionel	Lt NZ 13/246 AuklandR dow 16-7-21 CR NZ 257
WADE,Robert Hunter	2Lt NZ 45263 1OIR dow 26-10-18 CR France 40
WADGE,Ernest	Lt Can CLH 12-11-17 CR Belgium 84
WADGE,Herbert	Lt Aust 4Pnrs kia 20-11-16 CR France 374
WADSLEY,Lennard Lewis	Lt Aust 52Bn 3-9-16 MR 26
WADSWORTH,D'Arcy Rein	Lt Can 75Bn B'Coydow 18-10-16 CR France 59
WAGNER,Archie Frank	Lt Can PPCLI kia 9-4-17 CR France 1321
WAINE,Malcolm Lyle	Capt Can CASC attRFC4-5-17 CR Middx 34
WAINGARTH,Jack Henry	Lt Aust AFC 4Sqn dedacc 4-2-19 CR Glouc 172
WAITE,George Douglas	Lt Can FGH 10-8-18MR 23
WAITE,George Ebington	Lt NZ8/1855 OIR kia 7-8-15 MR 5
WAITE,Hugh Conyers	Lt Can 2/8WYorksR Ex CanInf VancouverBn 6-4-17 CR France 568
WAKE,Gladys Maude Mary	Nurse Can CANS 1GH dow 21-5-18 CR France 40
WAKELIN,William Richard.MID.	Capt NZ 6/2891 CIR ded 5-2-19 CR Wilts 160
WALDIE,Walter Scott	Lt Can 54CoyCFC 1CORdepot ded 19-2-19 CR Canada 1511
WALDRON,Frederick George	Lt Can1MMGBde 24-3-18MR 23
WALDRON,Stanley Mott	Maj Can CFA 15Bty6Bde 4-5-17 CR France 268
WALE,Philip George	2Lt Aust 7Inf 8-5-15 MR 4
WALES,Aylmer Templer	2Lt SA2SAInf C'Coy dow 17-7-16 CR France 141
WALKER,Albert Reginald	2Lt Aust 47Inf 9-6-17 MR 29
WALKER,Alexander Ralph	Lt Aust 10Inf dow 23-8-16 CR France 44
WALKER, Henry Valmond	Lt Can 58/2COR8-10-16MR 23 Harry
WALKER,Arthur	Lt Aust Engrs 1DivSigCoy 31-7-17MR 29
WALKER,Arthur Leslie.DSO.MC.	Maj Can 24Bn att5InfBde HQ 9-8-18 CR France 652
WALKER,Austin Harry	Lt Can 13QuebecR9-10-16MR 23
WALKER,Frank	2Lt Aust 46Bn 11-4-17MR 26
WALKER,James Gilbert	Lt Can 13Bn 13-6-16CR Belgium 11
WALKER,Jean Miles	Matron Aust AANS ded 30-10-18 CR Wilts 167
WALKER, John Gordon	Lt Can 52Bn kia 28-6-17 CR France 268 Jack

WALKER,John Harold	Lt Aust 26Inf kia 29-10-17 CR Belgium 72
WALKER,John Mercer	Lt Aust AFC 1Sqnkia 22-8-18 CR Palest 9
WALKER,John Stuart Dight.MC.	Capt Aust 11Inf kia 21-7-18 CR France 28
WALKER,Joseph Tackaberry	Lt Can 58Bn kia 20-9-16 CR France 280
WALKER,Kenneth Leigh.MID	2Lt Aust 7Inf dow 12-7-15 MR 6
WALKER,Kilian Frederick	2Lt Aust 25Bn 5-8-16 MR 26
WALKER,Lorne Campbell	Capt Can CFA 60Bty2Bde 13-7-17CR Canada 1228
WALKER,Norman Eden	Lt Can 124PnrBn 13-4-17CR France 81
WALKER,Philip Ilderton.MC.	Capt Can 24Bn C'Coy 28-8-18CR France 310
WALKER,Stanley	Capt Can 5SasR 26-9-16MR 23
WALKER,William Earling.MC.	Lt Can 75Bn dow 12-11-18 CR Surrey 91
WALKER,William Hope	Capt Can SRD attRFC 18-8-17CR France 1295
WALKLATE,Harold Vernon	Capt Aust 14Inf 22-10-17 MR 29
WALL,Harry Melbourne Moir.MC.	Lt Aust22Inf kia 27-8-18 CR France 692
WALLACE,Ernest Donald	Lt Can MMG Bde attRFC kld 27-3-17 CR Oxford 74
WALLACE,Henry Atholl Charles	Capt Can 10Bn (AR) kia 22-4-15 MR 29
WALLACE,Henry Norman	Lt Aust AIF 43Inf1-7-20 CR Aust 240
WALLACE,James Hutton	Lt Can 25Bn 28-4-17CR France 777
WALLACE,James Miller	Lt Can 43Bn 27-8-18CR France 155
WALLACE,John George	Lt Can 38Bn dow 18-11-16 CR France 314
WALLACE,Matthew Maurice.MC.	Lt Can 54Bn 2-9-18 CR France 426
WALLACE,R.C.	Lt SA 10SAInf kia 31-5-16 CR Tanzania 1 &EAfrica 31
WALLACE,Robert Eugene	Maj Can 15Bn 9-4-17 CR France 523
WALLACE,Thomas Albert	2Lt Aust AMGC 2Bn dow 17-8-18 CR France 1170
WALLACH,Clarence.MC.	Capt Aust 19Inf dow 22-4-18 CR France 122
WALLACH,Neville.MC.	Capt Aust 13Inf kia 1-5-18 CR France 1170
WALLACK,Gordon Townshend	Capt Aust 2Inf kia 19-5-15 CR Gallipoli 7
WALLER,John Charles	Lt Can 4Bn kia 3-5-17 CR France 68
WALLER,Philip Dudley	2Lt SA HArty 71SB kia 14-12-17 CR France 381
WALMSLEY,Arthur George	Lt Aust 21Inf 9-10-17MR 29
WALSH,Charles Gavan	2Lt Aust 28Inf kia 19-9-17 CR Belgium 96
WALSH,D'Arcy Stuart	2Lt Aust 43Inf 4-10-17MR 29
WALSH,Douglas John.MC.	Lt Aust AIF 10Inf 12-8-18CR Aust 212
WALSH,John Douglas	Capt SA 2SAInf kia 23-1-16 CR Egypt 3
WALSH,John Edward Steele	2Lt Aust 9A LtTMB kia 23-12-16 CR France 922
WALSH,John Francis	Maj Aust 15Inf kia 28-4-15 MR 6
WALSH,John Parnell.MID	Capt CanCAMC att2CanInf 17-8-16CR London 9
WALSH,Michael Francis	2Lt NZ 24/1923 3/3NZRB kia 23-12-16 CR France 923
WALSH,Patrick George	Lt Aust AFC dedacc 30-9-18 CR Glouc 172
WALSH,Richard Edward	Lt Aust 44Inf kia 8-6-17 CR Belgium 108
WALSH,Thomas Morrow	Lt Can RCR 8-10-16MR 23
WALSH,Thomas Patrick	2Lt NZ 4/1482 NZRB kia 4-5-18 CR France 643
WALSH,William Thomas	2Lt Aust 51Inf dow 13-10-17 CR Belgium 11
WALTER,Royland Allin.MC.	Lt Can 49Bn dow 29-9-18 CR France 214
WALTER,William Guy Ardagh	2Lt Aust48Bn 5-8-16 MR 26
WALTERS,Arthur George Allan	Lt Aust 18Inf kia 19-5-18 CR France 833
WALTERS,George Robert Stewart	Lt Aust11Inf kia 22/25-7-16 CR France 280
WALTERS,Joseph John	Lt Can 20Bn kia 10-5-17 CR France 557
WALTHER,Bernhardt Hermann	Capt Aust AMGC 3Coydow 25-7-16 CR France 74
WALTON,Ernest Bowe	Lt SA SASC 27-10-18 CR SAfrica 23
WAND,W.	2Lt Aust 36Inf 13-10-17 CR Belgium 3
WANDEN,Eric Win	2Lt NZ 7/566 CMR kia 25-9-18 CR Syria 2
WANKLYN,Andrew Angus	Lt Can PPCLI (EOR) kia 2-6-16 CR Belgium 453 &MR 29
WANLISS,Harold Boyd.DSO.	Capt Aust 14Inf 26-9-17MR 29
WANSBROUGH,Charles Vivian	Maj Can47Bn 3-4-17 CR France 88
WARBURTON,George	Lt Can 46Bn kia 27-9-18 CR France 714
WARD,A.E.MC&Bar.	Capt SA 1SAInf kia 10-4-18 MR 29
WARD,Charles Kay	Capt NZ 3/71 NZDC believed ded 18-1-18 CR Surrey 156
WARD,Cyril Cutcliffe.MC.	Lt Aust 26Inf dow 8-3-17 CR France 177
WARD,Frederick Henry	Capt Aust 23Inf dow 2-8-16 CR France 44

WARD,James.MC&2Bars.DCM.	Capt Can CFA 3Bde 23-2-19CR Belgium 265
WARD,John Simeon	Maj Can PPCLI dow 13-3-15 CR France 102
WARD,John William	Lt Can 26NBR kia 17-9-16 MR 23
WARD,Leslie Arnold	2Lt Aust 26Inf kia 14-11-16 CR France 385
WARD,Leslie Norman.MC.	Lt Aust 48Inf kia 19-9-18 CR France 366
WARD,Sidney	2Lt Aust 1Inf 21-9-17MR 29
WARDEN,Bruce Wynter	2Lt Aust 56Inf dow 27-9-17 CR Belgium 11
WARDLE,Ida	SNurse SA SAMNS 13-10-18 CR SAfrica 144
WARDROP,Charles Lawrence	Capt NZ 23/121/3NZRB kia 12-10-17 CR Belgium 126 Laurence
WAREHAM,Edward Graham	Lt Aust 15Inf kia 10-5-15 MR 6
WARK,Joseph	Capt Can CAMC 1GH ded 16-12-19 CR Canada 474
WARMINGTON,John Nicol	Maj Can 14Bn kia 19-5-15 CR France 727
WARN,Archibald Herbert	2Lt SA SASC ded 30-3-18 CR EAfrica 77 29-3-18
WARN,Lancelot Rodney	Capt Can 16Bn 4-2-19 CR Hamps 57
WARNEMINDE,Claude James	Lt Aust 9Inf dow 13-3-18 CR France 193
WARNE-SMITH,Waldo Esmond.MC.	Lt Aust 6Inf dow 20-9-18 CR France 146
WARNER,Leslie William Roy	Lt Aust34Inf dow 8-6-17 CR France 285
WARREN,Arthur	Capt Aust 9Inf kia 18-6-16 CR France 348
WARREN,Ernest Albert	Capt Aust 27Bn 5-11-16MR 26
WARREN,Ralph William	Lt NZ18437 MGC ded 26-11-18 CR Lincs 61
WARREN,Robert	Lt Aust 14Inf kia 8-8-15 MR 6
WARREN,Trumbull	Capt Can 15Bn 20-4-15CR Belgium 84
WARREN,William Henry Farrington.DSO.	Cmdr Aust RAN HM TBD`Parramatta' 13-4-18CR Italy 17
WARRY,Victor Thomas Symes	Lt Aust 25Bn 29-7-16MR 26
WARWICK,Rowland	2Lt Aust 42Inf kia 31-8-18 CR France 624
WASHBURN,Robert Grant	Lt Can 19Bn 1917
WASHINGTON,Hubert Howells	Lt Can 4Bn 1915
WATERFIELD,Horace Clare	Lt Can 72Bn dow 5-5-18 CR France 40
WATERHOUSE,Leslie.MM.	Lt Aust 43Inf dow 22-7-18 CR Surrey 1
WATERS,Leslie John	Lt Aust 15Inf kia 27-4-15 CR Gallipoli 8
WATERSTON,Douglas	Capt Can CAMC 9FA att43Bn kia 22-5-16 CR Belgium 15
WATKINS,Harold Thomas	Lt Aust 13Inf kia 25-4-15 CR Gallipoli 25
WATKINS, J.R.	SNurse SA SAMNS 21-10-18 CR SAfrica 144 J.K.
WATKINS,John Melvyn.MC.	2Lt NZ2/376 NZFA kia 1-9-18 CR France 745
WATSON,A.B.	5thEngr Can MercMar SS`Pomeranian' 15-4-18MR 24
WATSON,Albert B.MM.	Capt Can 29Bn 9-8-18 CR France 649
WATSON,Alfred Edward	2Lt Aust 3Inf dow 13-10-17 CR Belgium 3
WATSON,Basil Morris	Lt Can14Bn dow 3-3-18 CR France 223
WATSON,Beatrice Middleton	SNurse Aust AANS att1AustStatHosp ded 2-6-16 CR Egypt 8
WATSON,Charles Harold	Lt CanCFA 4Bde 11-8-18CR France 649
WATSON,Cyril Austin	2Lt Aust38Inf kia 23-2-17 CR France 922
WATSON,Edward Baker	2Lt Aust 3Inf dow 27-6-16 CR France 254
WATSON,Frederick Johnston	Lt Can 43Bn 10-6-16CR Belgium 134
WATSON,Frederick William.DCM.	2Lt NZ 12/1020 3MGC kia 7-6-17 CR Belgium 42
WATSON,George Williamson	Lt Aust 58Inf kia 19-8-16 CR France 348
WATSON,Herbert Henry	Lt Aust 48Bn 11-4-17MR 26
WATSON,Hugh Jarman	Lt Can 124PnrBn dow 29-11-17 CR Canada 1688
WATSON,Humphrey John Fletcher	Lt Aust3Inf 4-10-17MR 29
WATSON,J.C.	Capt Can MercMar SS`Armonia' ded 15-3-18 MR 24
WATSON,James Cameron	Lt Can 75Bn 30-9-18CR France 148
WATSON,John Edward	Lt NZ 37059 2OIR kia 24-8-18 CR France 512
WATSON,John Malcolm	Capt Aust 15Bn 11-4-17MR 26
WATSON,Joseph Longstaff	Lt Can16Bn 8-11-17CR Belgium 125
WATSON,Kenneth Robert	2Lt NZ 2/1116 NZFA dow 5-10-16
WATSON,Norman Forrester	2Lt NZ9/96 Pnrs kia 12-10-17 MR 30 1OIR
WATSON,Robert Morgan	2Lt NZ 9/499 OMR kia 22-8-15 MR 14
WATSON,Stafford Brierley	2Lt Aust 2Inf dow 10-4-17 CR France 564
WATSON,Thomas Henry	Lt NZ 12/26051MGC dow 2-10-16 CR France 833
WATSON,William Robert	Lt SA 7SAInf ded 28-6-17 CR SAfrica 42
WATSON,William.MC.	Lt Aust 48Inf dow 28-4-17 CR France 145

WATT,Alfred	Lt Aust 8ALH kia 3-11-17 CR Palest 1
WATT,Charles	2Lt NZ 11/165 WMR 6Coy kia 30-5-15 MR 6
WATT,Charles	Lt Can 42Bn dow 11-7-17 CR France 40
WATT,Edmund	Lt Aust 1AMGC 20-9-17MR 29
WATT,J.MBE.	Capt SA SASigs PostalCps ded 22-12-18 MR 52
WATT,John Robertson	Maj SA NatalHorse kia 27-4-15 CR SAfrica 3
WATT,William Francis	2Lt NZ 24119 2CIR kia 1/2-10-16 MR 11
WATTAM,Richard John	Lt Can 42Bn kia 9-4-17 CR France 81
WATTERS,James Campbell	2Lt SAHArty 71SB dow 19-10-17 CR Belgium 3
WATTS,Bertram Alexander Gordon.DSO.	LtCol Aust AFA 4Bde kia 10-4-17 CR France 1484
WATTS,Cecil Thomas	Cadet Aust 31928 AFC kld 3-9-18 CR Essex 7
WATTS,Ellis James	2Lt NZ26/21 1/3NZRB kia 3-12-17 MR 8
WATTS,George Gordon	2Lt Aust 28Inf kia 20-9-17 CR Belgium 308
WATTS,Raymond Thomas	Capt Aust 6Inf dow 10-5-15 MR 6
WATTS,Richard	Lt Aust AIF AMGC 25-11-17 CR Aust 171
WATTS,Robert Edward	Lt Can 84Bn ded 9-6-16 CR Canada 1468
WATTS,Wilfred John	Capt Can 4Bn RAF 44Wing ded 21-10-18 CR Canada 1688
WAUD,Edward Wilkes	Capt Can 13Bn 6-4-18 CR France 113
WAUDE,Sydney	Lt Can 50Bn kia 31-5-17 CR France 81
WAUGH,Alexander Logan	Lt Can MGSqd 1-12-17MR 23
WAUGH,George Noel	Capt NZ 10/86 NZVC dow 26-5-17 CR France 769
WAY,John Hatherly	Lt Can 58Bn D'Coy kia 27-8-18 CR France 421
WEAR,James Symington.MID	Capt Can 20/1COR kia 15-9-16 MR 23
WEARE,Cecil.MC.	Capt Can 25Bn 31-10-17 CR Belgium 11
WEAVER,Ralph Lincoln	Lt Can24Bn kia 2-10-18 CR France 147
WEBB,Ernest Charles	Lt Aust 1Bn 5-5-17 MR 26
WEBB,Ernest John Herbert	Lt NZ 10/1021 NZMC doi 17-11-14 CR Asia 9
WEBB,Matthew	2Lt SA 1SAInfkia 22-3-18 MR 27
WEBBER,Harry	Capt Aust 12Inf kia 10-3-18 CR Belgium 131
WEBER,George Roy	Lt Can 116/2COR 23-7-17MR 23
WEBSTER,George	2Lt NZ 33087 2AIR 15Coy kia 24-8-18 MR 12
WEBSTER,J.B.	Lt SA 1SAInf
WEBSTER,Lawrence Fitzgerald	Lt Can 5CMR (QR) 30-10-17 MR 29
WEBSTER,Les ter Olney	Maj Can 50Bnkia 19-8-16 CR Belgium 15 Lister
WEBSTER,Tom	Lt Aust 5ALH dow 8-11-17 CR Palest 1
WEBSTER,William Wellington	Lt Can 13LRlyOC ded 29-3-20 CR Canada 116
WEEKS,Clarence Gladstone.MC.	Lt Can 75Bn 22-8-18CR France 29
WEIR,Douglas	Capt Can 55Dist CFC 12-11-18 CR Scot 235
WEIR,Frank Joseph	Lt Aust 58Inf kia 29-9-18 CR France 375
WEIR,Frederick James	Lt NZ 13/428 AMR dow 2-6-15 MR 6
WEIR,John	Lt Can 50Bn 1917
WEIR,Norman McLeod	HCapt Can CADC ded 11-2-19 CR Canada 1245
WEIR,Richard Lewis.MC.DCM.	2Lt Aust 21Inf kia 26-7-18 CR France 1170
WEIS,Michael.MID	Lt Aust 23Inf dow 18-8-18 CR France 119
WELCH,Ernest Havelock	Lt Can 26NBR 30-9-16MR 23
WELCH,Leslie Barnard	Maj Aust 28Bn 29-7-16MR 26
WELLAND,Joseph Frank	Lt Can 1Bn (WOR) kia 6-11-17 MR 29 Flanklin
WELLINGS,Leonard	Lt Aust 41Inf dow 3-6-17 CR France 285
WELLS,Charles Walter	Lt Aust AIF AFA 25Bde 14-6-21CR Aust 469
WELLS,Clifford Almon	Lt Can8Bn 28-4-17CR France 777
WELLS,Ewart Linley	2Lt NZ10/2029 WIR kia 8-8-15 MR 5
WELLS,Geoffrey Erskine.MID	Capt Aust FA 11Bde dow 6-10-17 CR Belgium 15
WELLS,Gerald Edwin	Lt Can 46SasR 25-10-16 MR 23
WELLS,John Clarence	Maj Aust AAMC dow 10-8-18 CR France 71
WELLS,Richard William	Maj Aust6Inf dow 11-5-15 CR Gallipoli 1
WELLWOOD,John Alexander	Capt Can CAMC 20-12-20 CR Canada11 40
WELSH,Leonard Alfred.MC.	Lt Can LSH kia 9-10-18 CR France1 395
WELSH,T.MC.	Capt SA SAMC 1FA att2SAInf kia 12-4-17 CR France 451
WENDT,Kenneth Koeppen	2Lt Aust 10Inf kia 6-5-17 CR France 1485
WERDEN,Frederick Asa	Lt Can 75Bn dow 1-10-18 CR France 214

WERTHEIMER,Arnold Talbot	Lt Aust 12Inf kia 4-6-18 CR France 193
WESSELS,P.R.	Capt SA 2MilConst 24-10-18 CR SAfrica 8
WEST,Albert Smethurst	Lt Aust 17Inf dow 17-7-18 CR France 29
WEST,Caspar de Freitaz	Lt Can 102Bn kia 12-5-17 CR France 81
WEST,Charles Eric	Capt Can 4BnCE 23-10-18 CR Surrey 1
WEST,Claude Bertie	2Lt Aust 1Inf dow 16-5-17 CR France 40
WEST,Leslie James.DCM.	Lt Aust 35Bn 4-4-18 MR 26
WEST,Percy d'Evereux	Lt SA SASC Supplies ded 21-12-17 CR EAfrica 39
WEST,Randolph Hadden Arnold	Lt Can 1MMGBde (Borden's MMGBty) 24-3-18 MR 23
WEST,Thomas	Lt Can 42Bn 29-9-18CR France 481
WESTAWAY,Harold Windsor	Lt Aust 22Inf kia 18-8-18 CR France 1472
WESTBROOK,Thomas Kennedy	Capt Aust 2Bn 7-5-17 MR 26
WESTGARTH,Mervyn	Lt Aust 12ALH ded 19-2-18 CR Egypt 7
WESTON,Whitford Wells	Lt Can3Bn kia 13-6-16 CR Belgium 123
WETMORE,Hastings De Blais	Lt Can 4Bn 27-9-18CR France 481 Blois
WETMORE,Norman Howard.MID	Capt&Adjt Can 25Bn kia 8-8-18 CR France 1170
WEYNAND,Norman Leslie	Lt Aust 9Bn 23-7-16MR 26
WHEATLEY,Arthur Wilfred	Lt Aust9Inf kia 25-4-18 CR France 324
WHEATLEY,Leslie Albert	Lt Can SRD 19ResBn attRFC 9Sqn kia 2-7-17 CR France 446
WHEATON,George	2Lt Aust 32Inf dedacc 7-11-17 CR France 177
WHEELER,William Arthur	Capt NZ 3/1258 NZMC ded 16-12-18 CR NZ 208
WHELAN,M.E.	Lt SA 2SAInf 18-10-18 CR France 528 WHEELAN
WHIDBORNE,Charles Hobson	2Lt Aust 4Inf kia 6/9-8-15 CR Gallipoli 7
WHIGHAM-TEASDALE,Richard William	Lt Can CLH 10-11-18 CR France 1277
WHISHAW,Mabel Helen	SNurse NZ 22/371 NZANS ded 10-11-18 CR NZ 243
WHITAKER,Frederick Charles	2Lt NZ 8/504 1OIR dow 25-3-17 CR Belgium 138
WHITAKER,Herbert Atherton	Lt Can 9MGC dow 25-10-16 CR France 64
WHITE,Albert Edward.MC.	Lt Can 52Bn 28-9-18CR France 714
WHITE,Alexander Denchar Hudson	Lt Aust 10Inf dow 18-9-18 CR France 1468
WHITE,Alexander Henry.MID	LtCol Aust 8ALH kia 7-8-15 MR 6
WHITE,Basil	2Lt Aust 39Inf 6-12-16CR France 285
WHITE,Bertram Edward	Capt Aust 25Inf A'Coy dow 26-11-16 CR France 145
WHITE,Charles Harold Ophir	2Lt Aust 3Inf kia 8-8-15 MR 6
WHITE,Charles Herbert	Lt Can 20Bn 17-8-17CR France 480
WHITE,Charles Oscar	Lt Aust 2Inf 4-10-17MR 29
WHITE,Eric Edward	Lt Can BCR attRFC 7-8-17 CR Belgium 140
served as MACFARLANE,James Lennox	
WHITE,G.C.	Lt SA CapeCps dow 17-10-18
WHITE,Hedley Hastings	Lt Can74Regt 1917
WHITE,John Stanley	Lt Can 7Bn dow 24-8-16 CR London 8
WHITE,Kenneth Robert	2Lt NZ 14726 1AIR kia 4-10-17 MR 30
WHITE,Louis Clerville.MM.	2Lt Aust 8Bn 23-8-18MR 26
WHITE,P.R.	Capt Can 39Bn 24-7-21CR Canada 1245
WHITE,Ronald John S	Lt Can RFC & 78Bn 27-10-17 CR France 787 Manitoba R
WHITEFORD,Clarence George	Lt Aust 10Inf kia 25-2-17 CR France 385
WHITEHEAD,Edward Ashworth	Capt Can 14Bn 3-6-16 CR Belgium 127
WHITEHEAD,Eric	2Lt Aust 8ALH kia 7-8-15 MR 6
WHITEHEAD,Herbert Howard	Lt Can 31Bn attRFC 2Sqn 20-8-16CR France 924
WHITEHEAD,Lionel Ward	Capt Can13Bn (QR) kia 22-4-15 MR 29
WHITEHEAD,Robert Whitworth	2Lt Aust21Bn 3-5-17 MR 26
WHITEHEAD,William Duncan	Capt Can CASC 4DivTr dow 27-9-18 CR France 686
WHITEHOUSE,Norman Clyde	2Lt Aust 15Inf kia 16-8-17 CR Belgium 168
WHITELAW,Frederick Francis.MC.	LtAust 29Inf dow 10-8-18 CR France 69
WHITELY,Anna Elizabeth	Nurse Can CANS 10SH 21-4-18CR France 64
WHITEMAN,Harry	Capt Can 10Bn 1-4-16 CR France 285
WHITESIDE,Alexander Forrester	Capt Can 3PnrBn kia 28-3-16 CR Belgium 5
WHITFIELD,Wesley Frank	Capt Aust11ALH kia 25-9-18 CR Palest 11
WHITFORD,S.H.	2Lt SA 2SA Infdow 21-3-18 CR France 987 3SAInf
WHITFORD,Walter Lyon	Capt Can 25Bn ded 21-3-19 CR Canada 803
WHITING,Ernest	Capt&Adjt SA 1SAInf dow 16-10-16 CR France 385

WHITING,Norman Alexander	2Lt NZ7/274A CMR ded 16-4-19 CR NZ 117
WHITLOCK,Arthur Sidney	Capt Aust 34Inf 8-6-17 MR 29
WHITLOW,Francis Milthorp.MID	Capt Can 2CMR 10-8-18CR France 360
WHITMORE,Thomas Hazell	Capt Can CAMC att5Bn 8-8-18 CR France 29
WHITSIDE,James Le Roy	Lt Can 46Bn dow 11-11-16 CR France 59
WHITSON, C.B.R .MC.	Capt SA 1SAInf 16-10-18 CR France 1394 C.R.R.
WHITTAKER,Charles Kenneth.MC.	Lt Can CFA 10Bde 26-4-17CR France 68
WHITTLE,John	Lt Aust 48Inf kia 29-3-18 CR France 196
WHYBORN,Benjamin	Lt Aust 27Bn 5-11-16MR 26
WHYTE,Charles William Millar	LtAust 3ATC kia 22-7-16 CR France 285
WHYTE,Wilfred.MC.	Capt Can 31Bn 21-10-18 CR France 34
WICKENS,Herbert Gourlay	Maj Can 3Bn 20-9-17CR France 570
WICKHAM,Lindsay Claude.MM.	2Lt Aust 10Bn 25-7-16MR 26
WICKHAM,Mema	2Lt NZ 16/858 Pnrs doi 31-12-18 CR France 1359
WICKS,George Viner	2Lt Aust AFC dedacc 13-10-18 CR Berks 86
WICKSON,Edward Arthur	Capt Can 84Bn attRFC kia 16-6-17 CR Belgium 6 51Bn
WIDEMAN,Maurice Edwin	Maj Can 26Bn dow 9-5-17 CR Surrey 1
WIDMEYER,Stuart Robertson.MM.	Lt Can 16Bn kia 1-10-18 CR France 421
WIGHT,John Henry	Lt Can 52Bn 3-10-18CR France 214
WIGHTON,Charles	Capt Can 1RNewfndlandR kia 25-11-15 CR Gallipoli 4
WILCOCK,Arthur	Lt Aust 24Inf 4-10-17MR 29
WIILLIAMS,Maldwyn Leslie.MID	LtCol Aust AAMC 1FA dow 3-3-17 CR France 177
WILDGOOSE,Richard.DCM.	Lt Can CFA 14Bde 1922
WILEY,Francis Hill	2Lt SA 2SAInf kld 3-7-18 CR Surrey 1
WILGRESS,Geo Kesteven Kortright.MID	Lt Can 21Bn 27-11-15 CR Belgium 37
WILKES,Charles Frederick.MID.	2Lt NZ 8/2181 1OIR D'Coy dow 7-6-17 CR France 285
WILKES,Maurice Fisken	Lt Can 19/1COR 15-9-16MR 23
WILKES,Norman William	Lt Aust 2Inf dow 4-10-17 CR Belgium 72
WILKINS,C.	Capt SA MtdCmdos kia 16-1-15 CR SAfrica 107 WILKENS
WILKINS,John Fox	Lt Can 24QuebecR 15-8-17MR 23
WILKINS,Reginald Prinsep	Lt Can 44Bn 27-9-18CR France 714
WILKINSON,Albert Edward	Capt NZ13/988 AMR dow 28-8-15 MR 6
WILKINSON,George	Lt Aust 18Inf dow 19-5-18 CR France 196
WILKINSON,John Taylor	Lt Can 78Bn 4-4-17 CR France 81
WILKINSON,Norman Robson	Lt Aust Engrs 4FC26-9-17MR 29
WILKINSON,Thomas	2Lt Aust 49Inf kia 3-9-16 CR France 393
WILKINSON,William Henry	Lt Aust37Inf kia 30-9-18 CR France 212
WILKINSON,Rogers William	Capt NZ 8/810 OIR dow 22-9-15 CR London 1
WILL,F.G.	Lt SA MtdCmdos kia 18-1-15 CR SAfrica 128
WILLANS,Richard Hart Keatings	Capt Can 2Bn dow 12-9-16 CR France 51 Harte Keatinge
WILLARD,William Hartley	Lt Can 18WOR 15-9-16MR 23
WILLENBROCK,John Henry	Capt Aust 49Bn 5-4-18 MR 26
WILLIAMS,Alfred John.MID.	Lt NZ 6/775 2WIR kia 1-10-18 CR France 1483
WILLIAMS, Allan Gordon	Lt Can 43Bn 27-8-18CR France 419 Alan
WILLIAMS,Allen Douglas	2Lt NZ 32555 CIR kia 27-3-18 MR 12
WILLIAMS,Alman Clare	Maj Can 5Bn kia 26-9-16 CR France 430
WILLIAMS,Arthur James	Maj Can RCR 15-8-16CR Belgium 72
WILLIAMS,Arthur Stuart	Lt Aust Engrs 3FC 22-7-16MR 26
WILLIAMS,Blodwyn Elizabeth	Sister Aust AIF AANS 24-5-20CR Aust 288
WILLIAMS,Charles Morrice.MC.	Capt Aust 24Inf kia 9-10-17 CR Belgium 125
WILLIAMS,Clarence Earl	Capt Can 26NBR 15-9-16MR 23
WILLIAMS,D.A.	2Lt SA 3SAInf mbk 18-9-17 MR 29
WILLIAMS,Frank Bernard	2Lt NZ23/955 4/3NZRB kia 17-9-16 CR France 277
WILLIAMS,Frank Hill	Lt Aust 1Inf dow 10-7-18 CR France 134
WILLIAMS,George Edward James	Lt Aust Engrs 2FC dow 25-10-17 CR Belgium 11
WILLIAMS,Hugh	2Lt SA 4SAInf dow 17-4-17 CR France 40
WILLIAMS,H.E.	Lt Aust 1AMGC 21-9-18CR France 446
WILLIAMS,Herbert Edwin	Lt Aust 1Inf kia 25-4-15 MR 6
WILLIAMS,Howard de Nytt	Capt Aust 51Bn 3-9-16 MR 26
WILLIAMS,John Howard	Lt SA RhodNatRdow 19-8-17 CR EAfrica 40

WILLIAMS,James William	Lt Can 87Bn kia 18-11-16 CR France 150
WILLIAMS,John Anthony	2Lt Aust 12Inf kia 7-8-15 MR 6
WILLIAMS,Kenneth Fenwick A.	Capt Can CASC 3FldBkyded 4-8-18 CR Canada 1271
WILLIAMS,Kenneth Struthers	Lt NZ 7/1689 CMR ded 25-3-20 CR NZ 10
WILLIAMS,M.L. see WIILIAMS.M.L.	
WILLIAMS,Mark Webber	Lt Can PPCLI (EOR) 2Coy kia 30-10-17 MR 29
WILLIAMS,Philip Edward	Lt Can43Wing RAF 124Bn ded 22-10-18 CR Canada 1688
WILLIAMS,Russell	Lt Can 19Bn 9-5-17 CR France 68
WILLIAMS,Thomas Lewis Owen.MC	Capt Can 28Bn 1918
WILLIAMS,Welland Grange	Lt Can 7MGC 49Bnkia 24-4-17 CR France 68
WILLIAMS,William	2Lt NZ 23/323 1/3NZRB kia 5-10-18 CR France 256
WILLIAMS,William Keith Gaster	2Lt NZ 23/649 MGC 2Coy kia 9-6-17 CR Belgium 89 8-6-17
WILLIAMSON,Adam Miller	Capt Can 1Bn D'Coy 30-8-18CR France 688
WILLIAMSON,Alexander David	Lt CanRCHA kia 10-8-17 CR France 161
WILLIAMSON,Alfred	Capt Aust 14Bn 11-4-17MR 26
WILLIAMSON,George Massey	Lt Can 14Bn (QR)23-4-15MR 29
WILLIAMSON,John Cedrick	Lt Aust AFA 4Bde 5-10-17MR 29
WILLIS,Henry John	Lt Aust 37Bn 30-8-18MR 26
WILLIS,Philip.MM.	2Lt Can31Bn &RAF 107Sqn 9-8-18 MR 20
WILLIS,William Organ	Capt Aust 15Inf kia 3-5-15 MR 6
WILLISON,Willianm Taylor	Lt Can 5CMR 15-9-16CR France 280
WILLOUGHBY,Frederick.MM.	Lt Can 19Bn 19-8-19CR Yorks 547
WILLOUGHBY,Samuel Thomas	Lt Can 2TankBn 23-10-18 CR Glouc 9
WILLOX,George Martin	Lt SAMilLabCps8-12-18CR EAfrica 36
WILLSHIRE,William Stanley.MC.	Capt Aust 27Inf kia 29-8-18 CR France 692
WILLSON,	Major Percy Lt Can 5Bn dow 30-9-16 CR France 40
WILMOT,Percy Charles	Lt Can 25Bn ded 26-12-19 CR Canada 658 WILLMOT
WILMOTT,William Frederick	Capt Aust 52Inf dow 25-4-18 CR France 300
WILSDON,Walter Henry.DCM.	2Lt Aust10Inf 8-10-17MR 29
WILSHIRE,Lionel Ernest Osborne	2Lt Aust 35Inf kia 31-5-17 CR Belgium 451
WILSHIRE,Sydney Harold Osborne	Lt Aust FA 13Bde kia 31-7-17 CR Belgium 10
WILSON,Ancotts Cracroft	Lt NZ 15448 2CIR 1Coy dow 12-6-17 CR France 200
WILSON,Arthur Patrick.MC.	Lt Can 1Bn 1-9-18 CR France 145
WILSON,Calvin P.	Lt Can RCGA 20-10-18 CR Canada 1247B
WILSON,Cecil Sturt	2Lt Aust 8ALH dow 11-8-15 MR 6
WILSON,Charles Arthur	Lt Can 49Bn (AR) 5-6-16 MR 29
WILSON,Charles Blair.MID	Maj Can 42Bn kia 15-9-16 CR France 430
WILSON,E.	2Lt SA 3SAInf kld 2-5-16 CR France 1091
WILSON,E.F.B.	Maj SA SAMC 1SAGHdedacc 17-8-17 CR France 52
WILSON,Edmund Robinson.MID.	Lt NZ 10/75 WIR MGSect kia 27-4-15 MR 6
WILSON,Edward Henry	Lt Aust 8ALH ded 18-3-16 CR Egypt 8
WILSON,Eliot Gratton.MID	Lt Aust 8ALH kia 7-8-15 MR 6
WILSON,Ernest Leslie Claude	Lt Aust FA 11Bde dow 9-10-17 CR Belgium 11
served as THOMPSON	
WILSON,Frank John	2Lt Aust 36Inf 21-7-17MR 29
WILSON,Frank Reginald	2Lt NZ 12/2616 1AIR dow 19-9-16 CR France 177
WILSON,Frederick Gladstone	Lt Aust 13Inf kia 26-4-15 CR Gallipoli 25
WILSON,George Colin Campbell	Lt Aust 41Inf dow 7-7-17 CR Belgium 42
WILSON,George Robert	Lt Can 5SasR 16-8-17MR 23
WILSON,Harold MacKenzie	Lt Can 15Bn kldacc 9-6-16 CR Belgium 11
WILSON,Harold Stinson	Lt Can20Bn 11-10-18 CR France 761
WILSON,James Brazil	Lt Aust 52Bn 3-9-16 MR 26 & CR France 785
WILSON,James Maitland	Lt Aust 1Pnrs kia 20-9-17 CR Belgium 34
WILSON,John	2Lt NZ 24/1234 4/3NZRB kia 12-9-18 CR France 662
WILSON,John Carandini.MID	Capt Aust3Inf dow 21-5-15 CR Egypt 6
WILSON,John Harold	2Lt Aust 37Inf kia 21-7-17 CR Belgium 42
WILSON,John James	Lt SA MilLabCps ded 3-1-19 CR EAfrica 36
WILSON,John Leslie	Lt NZ7/149 CMR dow 23-7-17 CR Egypt 2
WILSON,John Sidney	Capt Aust AAMC 15FA dow 9-8-18 CR France 1170
WILSON,Joseph Harold	Lt Can 102Bn 11-4-17CR France 81

WILSON,L.H.	Capt SA 8SAInf kia 19-7-17 CR Tanzania 1 &EAfrica 38	
WILSON,Leslie McLean	Lt Can 8Bn 12-11-17 CR Belgium 3	
WILSON,Louis Geldart.MIDx2.	Capt NZ 8/992 2OIR kia 2-10-16 MR 11	
WILSON,Matthew Maurice	Lt Can 18Bn 10-10-18 CR France 214	
WILSON,Maurice	Lt Aust 5Pnrs 8-10-17MR 29	
WILSON,Robert	LtCol Can DGMS Staff 1GHded 1-11-19 CR Canada 256	
WILSON,Robert Garrick	LtCol Aust ImpForcesCanteensded 9-2-16 CR Egypt 9	
WILSON,Robert Harold	Lt Can CAVC 21-10-17 CR Canada 1688	
WILSON,Robert Johnston	Lt Can 43Bn 16-8-18CR France 987	
WILSON, Sydney Harold	Capt Can 27Bn (MR) kia 7-11-17 MR 29	
WILSON,William Bell	Lt Can47Bn kia 9/10-8-18 CR France 585	
WILSON,William George.MC.	Capt Aust 53Inf kia 30-9-18 CR France 446	
WILSON,William James	Capt Can 2CMR dow 31-12-17 CR France 223	
WILSON,William Robert	Lt Can44Bn 25-10-16 CR France 239	
WILSON,William Tully	Lt Can CFA 6Bde 1-11-17CR Belgium 10	
WILSON,William Webster	HCapt Can1DivSigCoy9-10-16MR 23	
WILSON,Winter Muir	2Lt Aust Engrs 1DivSigs kia 16-9-17 CR Belgium 115	
WILTHEW,Harold William	2Lt Aust31Inf kia 4-11-16 CR France 744	
WILTON,Arthur.MC.	Capt Can 27Bn dow 4-5-17 CR France 12	
WILTON,Walter Barron	Lt Can 27Bn 21-8-17CR France 480 Baron	
WINCHESTER,Murray MacKay	Lt Can 75/1COR 9-4-17 MR 23	
WINDER,Holloway Elliott	Lt NZ 13/758 AMR kia 8-8-15 MR 5	
WINDEYER,Charles Robert	2Lt Aust 49Inf 12-10-17 MR 29	
WINER,P.	Lt SA 7Horse kia 15-9-16 CR EAfrica 39	
WINGOOD,Allan Charles	Capt Can8MR 26-9-16MR 23	
WINNIFRITH,Gordon Stevenson.MC.	Capt Can 15Bn 27-9-18CR France 272	
WINSLOW,Jasper Andrew	Capt Can CFA 3DACded 22-3-17 CR France 32	
WINSLOW,Rainsford Hannay	Maj Can 1TrangCoy Engrs dow 9-9-18 CR France 14	
WINSTONE,Ernest Charles	Maj NZ 3/2259 HomeServSection 21-4-18CR NZ 225	
WINTER,Edward Arthur	Lt Aust 23Inf dow 6-5-17 CR France 512	
WINTER,Francis Bussell.MC.	Capt Can26NBR C'Coy kia 15-8-17 MR 23 Bassell	
WINTER,W.C.P.	Surg Lt Honduras BrHondTerForces 3-12-18CR CentAmerica 1	
WINTER-EVANS,Alfred.DSO.MIDx2.	LtCol NZ 26/11 3/3NZRB kia 12-10-17 MR 30	
WINTERFORD,Alfred Edwin	Lt Aust 25Inf kia 10-6-18 CR France 247	
WINTERS,Arthur Nicholas	Lt Can 28Bn 23-6-18CR France 504	
WITHROW,William James	Lt Can 2PnrBn D'Coy 4-5-17 CR France 68	
WOLFENDEN,Clarence William	Lt Aust AFA4Bty2Bde kia 11-5-15 CR Gallipoli 30	
WOLFENDEN,Francis Cooley	Maj Can CFC BD 22-6-17CR Surrey 78	
WOLSTENHOLME,Albert Edward	Maj NZ 26/1 4/3NZRB kia 3-7-16 CR France 922	
WOOD,Alan Carruthers	2Lt NZ4/178A 2/3NZRB kia 4-11-18 CR France 1077	
WOOD,Albert Frederick	Lt Aust27Inf dow 11-6-18 CR France 209	
WOOD,Arthur Vincent.MC.	Maj Can72Bn kia 2-9-18 CR France 162	
WOOD,Frank Abbott	Lt Can 3ResBn Secnd toRAF kld 4-1-18 CR Norfolk 259	
WOOD,George	Lt Aust 58Inf dow 26-10-17 CR France 40	
WOOD,George Huntly.MID.	Capt NZ 3/2053 NZMC MFA dow 11-8-16 CR Egypt 9	
WOOD,Gordon Thomas	Lt Aust 34Inf kia 27-1-17 CR France 922	
WOOD,Harry Vasey	Lt Aust 29Inf kia 2-3-17 CR France 374	
WOOD,John Butler	Capt Aust AFA 6Bde kia 15-3-17 CR France 385	
WOOD,John Reginald.DCM.	Lt AustAMGC 2Bn dow 20-8-18 CR France 119	
WOOD,Lowell Wallace	Lt Can 4Bn dow 17-10-18 CR France 40	
WOOD,Ramsay	Lt Aust 14Inf kia 4-7-18 CR France 424	
WOOD,Simon McGregor	Lt Aust 11Bn 24-4-18MR 26	
WOOD,Stanley Willis	Capt Can 16Bn kia 13-6-16 CR Belgium 11	
WOODBURN,William John	2Lt Aust 23Inf dow 2-10-17 CR Belgium 11	
WOODCOCK,Frank Fremont	Lt Can EatonsMMGC3-11-17CR Belgium 125	
WOODCOCK,Frank Sydney	Lt Can 46SasR 25-10-16 MR 23	
WOODFORD,John Edward	Lt Aust 41Inf kia 12-8-18 CR France 526	
WOODFORDE,Philip Sydney Soane.MID	Maj Aust 1Inf dow 6-5-17 CR France 512	
WOODHEAD,Harry.MID	Maj SA 1SAInf A'Coymbk 19-10-16 MR 21	
WOODHILL,Geofrey Guy	2Lt Aust 20Inf kia 1-8-16 CR France 267	

WOODHOUSE,Thomas John	2Lt Aust 12Inf kia 9-8-15 MR 6	
WOODLAND,Brinley Pearce	Capt Aust 18Inf kia 9-10-17 CR Belgium 115	
WOODRIFF,Geoffrey Besant	Lt Aust 18Bn 19-5-18 MR 26	
WOODROW,Sydney	Lt Aust AFC dedacc 23-9-16 CR Warwick 67	
WOODRUFF,Samuel DeVeaux	Lt Can 116Bn 13-7-18 CR France 174	
WOODS,Augustus Oliver.MC.	Maj Aust 26Inf kia 2-9-18 CR France 511	
WOODS,Cecil Talbot	Lt Aust8ALH kia 7-8-15 MR 6	
WOODS,Charles Halkett Carson	Lt Can 20RFC & CASC 21-9-17 MR 20	
WOODS,Frederick Frank	Capt Aust16Inf dow 4-7-18 CR France 119	
WOODS,John Robinson.MID	Capt Can 4CMR kia 24-10-17 CR Belgium 101	
WOODS,Selwyn Gorton	LtT Capt NZ12337 RB dow 5-12-17 CR Belgium 11	
WOODS,Thomas Zachary	Capt Can CAVC att2CanInfBdeHQ dow 9-4-16 CR Belgium 11	
WOODYATT,Percy Severn Roy	Lt Aust 2ALH kia 4-8-16 CR Egypt 2	
WOOLER,George Richard D.	Lt Can5Bn 15-8-17 CR France 550	
WOOLHOUSE,Fred Smith	Lt Aust AFC kia 10-4-18 CR France 705	
WOOLLEY,Charles Russell	2Lt Aust 55Inf dow 4-4-17 CR France 832	
WORKMAN,Marvin J.	Lt Can 75Bn 9-4-17 CR France 1896	
WORLAND,Edward John.MC.	Lt Aust 35Inf dow 30-8-18 CR France 119	
WORRALL,Dick.DSO&Bar.MC&Bar.MID	LtCol Can 14Bn ded 15-2-20 CR Canada 256	
WORRALL,Edgar Sydney	2Lt Aust 24Inf kia 4-10-17 CR Belgium 88	
WORSEY,Thomas Arthur	Lt Can 7BCR 8-9-16 MR 23	
WORSLEY,Harold James	2Lt NZ 24/1548 3MGC dow 14-10-16 CR London 29	
WORSLEY,J.A.	Capt SA SAVC 21-8-14 CR SAfrica 148	
WORSLEY,Reginald Eric Milne	2Lt Can AlbertR &GL attRFC 12Sqn 8-3-18 CR France 214	
WRATHALL,Henry Stephen	Lt Aust 60Inf 15-10-17 MR 29	
WRIGHT,Benson	Lt Can 75Bn 18-11-16 CR France 239	
WRIGHT,Clifford	Lt Can 49Bn ded 18-3-19 CR Canada 545	
WRIGHT,Cuthbert Pittman	Lt Can RCR 2-10-18 CR France 214	
WRIGHT,Daniel Utley	Lt Can 75Bn 9-8-18 CR France 589	
WRIGHT,Douglas Archibald	Lt Can PPCLI dow 12-8-18 CR France 360	
WRIGHT,Douglas Christie	Lt Can 18Bn attRFC 28Sqn kia 20-2-18 CR Italy 9	
WRIGHT,Edwin Bunce	HCapt Can 169Bn ded 2-1-19 CR Canada 1691 84Bn	
WRIGHT,Ernest Edward	Lt Aust 60Inf kia 19-7-16 MR 7	
WRIGHT,George Henry	Lt Can Cps of Guides ded 15-9-17 CR Canada 740	
WRIGHT,Gordon Brooks.DSO.	Maj Can 3FldCoy 21-5-15 CR France 410	
WRIGHT,Harry Marshall	Lt NZ 6/2016 CIR kia 7-8-15 MR 5	
WRIGHT,Henry Robert Lindsay	Lt Can 1DivTMB kia 28-8-18 CR France 419	
WRIGHT,John Christie	2Lt Aust20Bn 2-5-17 MR 26	
WRIGHT,John Robert.MID	2Lt Aust 1ALH kia 3-11-17 CR Palest 1	
WRIGHT,Joshua Stanley	Maj Can 50AR 18-11-16 MR 23	
WRIGHT,Lovell Lawrence	2Lt Aust23Inf dow 27-2-17 CR France 430	
WRIGHT,Percy	Lt Can 4CMR dow 1-9-18 CR France 14	
WRIGHT, R.J.J .	Capt SA SAMC ded 9-2-15 CR SAfrica 172 R.J.T.	
WRIGHT,William	Lt Can RAF 31Bn ded 20-11-18 CR Scot 592	
WRIGHT,William Henry	2Lt NZ12/3881 3/3NZRB kia 7-10-18 CR France 1483	
WRIGHT,William Jonathan	Lt Can19Bn 18-8-17 CR France 570	
WRIGHT,William Richard	Lt Can 18Bn 13-5-17 CR France 68	
WRY,Arthur Howard	Skipper Can RCN HMCS`Niobe' ded 3-12-17 CR Canada 1060	
WYATT,Sydney Joseph	2Lt NZ 40172 3/3NZRB kia 18-3-18 MR 8	
WYLIE,James Archibald	Lt Can 15/1COR 16-8-17 MR 23	
WYMOND,Lindsay.MID	Lt Aust AIF 22Inf 7-5-19 CR Aust 307	
WYNDHAM,Heathcote	Lt Aust 38Inf kia 17-7-17 CR Belgium 42	

Y

YALDWYN,H.	Lt Aust AIF 5ALH 17-7-16 CR Aust 146
YATES,Albert Edward	Capt Aust 35Inf kia 8-8-18 CR France 1170
YATES,Arthur William	2Lt Aust 22Inf dow 8-8-16 CR France 74
YATES,Henry Brydges	LtCol Can 3GenHosp 1916
YATES,Thomas	Lt Can 28Bn (SR) 6-11-17 MR 29
YEADON,Charles Frederick.MC.	2Lt Aust 22Bn 5-8-16 MR 26 &CR France 1890
YEATS,William	Lt Aust 2Bn 4-5-17 MR 26
YELLOWLEES,Norman James L.	CaptCan CAMC 4GH 5-5-16 CR Greece 7
YEOMANS,Geoffrey Heron	Lt Aust 1Bn 22-7-16 MR 26
YERXA,Guy Randolph.MC.	Lt Can 50AR 10-4-17 MR 23
YOUDEN,Frederick Charles	2Lt Aust 15Inf kia 8-8-15 MR 6
YOUL,John Beresford	2Lt Aust 12Bn 5-5-17 MR 26
YOUKLES,Isador Benjamin	Lt Can 87QuebecR 15-8-17 MR 23
YOUNG,Albert Victor	2Lt NZ 1/11 WIR 2WellingtonR kia 1-5-17 CR Belgium 43
YOUNG,Alexander.VC.	Lt SA 4SAInf kia 19-10-16 MR 21
YOUNG,Alexander	MajCan 52Bn (MR) kia 3-6-16 MR 29
YOUNG,Alexander Stewart	2Lt Aust 17Inf dow 2-3-17 CR France 177
YOUNG,Arthur Hamilton	Capt Can CAPC att7BdeHQ 7-9-18 CR France 1182
YOUNG,Charles Edward	Lt SA MilLabCps ded 17-12-18 CR EAfrica 36
YOUNG,Charles Le Fanu	CaptNZ 16/1328Pnrs ded 10-2-21 CR NZ 61
YOUNG,Ernest Herbert	Maj Can 10SH ded 8-8-21 CR Canada 1228 M.
YOUNG,James Christian Lawrence	Maj Can 1DivHQ 1Bn 13-10-18 CR France 155
YOUNG,James McStay	Lt Can 70Bn 7-5-19 CR Canada 1175
YOUNG,John	Capt Aust 44Inf 10-10-17 MR 92
YOUNG,Reginald	Lt Can LSH 1-12-17 CR France 407
YOUNG,Robert Percy	Capt Aust AAMC 3FA kia 18-9-18 CR France 366
YOUNG,Roland McDonald	Lt Aust 6Inf kia 25-4-15 MR 6
YOUNG,Samuel Leslie	Lt Can 46SasR 11-11-16 MR 23
YOUNG,William Lancelot.MC.	Capt Aust 45Inf kia 7-6-17 CR Belgium 74
YOUNGER,Frank Lawrence.MM.	Lt Can 8LTMB 1919
YOUNGER,John James A.	Lt Aust 10Inf kia 10-8-18 CR France 526
YOUNGS,John Lant.MC.	Lt Can 1Bn kia 9-4-17 CR France 68

Z

ZIEGLER,Eric Hallman	Lt Can 7MGC dow 7-6-16 CR Belgium 11
ZIMMERMAN,Adam Leonard	Capt Can CFA 4Bde 1918
ZOLLER,Edward Daniel	Lt Can 19/1COR kia 8-5-17 MR 23 Ezra
ZOUCH,Essington Lowther	Lt Aust 7ALH dow 17-11-17 CR Palest 2

APPENDIX 1

A list of the memorials and cemeteries mentioned in the list of officers.

MEMORIALS.

MR1   Naval Memorial,Chatham.
MR2   Naval Memorial,Plymouth.
MR3   Naval Memorial,Portsmouth.
MR4   Helles Memorial,Gallipoli.
MR5   The Chunuk Bair Memorial,Gallipoli.
MR6   The Lone Pine Memorial,Gallipoil.
MR7   VC Corner Australian Cemetery,Fromelles.
MR8   The Buttes New British Cemetery (NZ) Memorial.
MR9   Messines Ridge (NZ) Memorial.
MR10 Beaumont Hamel (Newfoundland) Memorial.
MR11 Caterpillar Valley (NZ) Memorial.
MR12 Grevillers (NZ) Memorial.
MR13 Twelve Tree Copse (NZ) Memorial.
MR14 Hill 60 (NZ) Memorial.
MR15 La Ferte-Sous-Jouarre Memorial,France.
MR16 Vis-En-Artois Memorial,France.
MR17 Cambrai Memorial,France.
MR18 Soissons Memorial,France.
MR19 Loos Memorial,France.
MR20 Arras Memorial,France.
MR21 Theipval Memorial,France.
MR22 Le Touret Memorial,France.
MR23 Vimy Memorial,France.
MR24 Halifax Memorial,Nova Scotia,Canada.
MR25 Victoria Memorial,British Columbia,Canada.
MR26 Villers-Brettonneux Memorial,France.
MR27 Pozieres Memorial,France.
MR28 Neuve-Chapelle Indian Memorial,France.
MR29 Ypres (Menin Gate) Memorial,Belgium.
MR30 Tyne Cot Memorial,Belgium.
MR31 Nieuport Memorial,Belgium.
MR32 Ploegsteert Memorial,Belgium.
MR33 Heliopolis (Port Tewfik) Memorial,Egypt.
MR34 Jerusalem Memorial,Israel.
MR35 Mikra Memorial,Salonica,Greece.
MR36 Hong Kong Memorial.
MR37 Dorian Memorial,Greece.
MR38 Basra Memorial,Iraq.
MR39 Tower Hill Memorial,London.
MR40 Hollybrook Memorial,Southampton,England.
MR41 Chatby Memorial,Egypt.
MR42 Kantara Memorial,Egypt.
MR43 Delhi Memorial,India.
MR44 Shillong Memorial,India.
MR45 Mombasa African Memorial,East Africa.
MR46 Mombasa British Memorial,East Africa.
MR47 Tanga British Memorial Cemetery,East Africa.
MR49 Nairobi African Memorial,East Africa.
MR50 Nairobi British and Indian Memorial,East Africa.
MR51 Dar Es Salaam African Memorial,East Africa.
MR52 Dar Es Salaam British and Indian Memorial, EastAfrica.
MR53 Aden Memorial,Arabia
MR54 Abercorn Memorial,N.Rhodesia.
MR55 Ikawa Memorial,N.Rhodesia.
MR56 Livingstone Camp Memorial,N.Rhodesia.
MR57 Salisbury Park Memorial,S.Rhodesia.
MR58 Mont-Fleuri Memorial,Seychelles.
MR59 Bardera Fort Memorial,Somaliland.
MR60 Berbera Memorial,Somaliland.
MR61 Tehran Memorial,Iran.
MR63 Bombay Memorial,India.
MR64 Bombay (St Thomas) Cathedral Memorial,India.
MR65 Kirkee Memorial,India.
MR66 Madras Memorial,India.
MR67 Karachi Memorial,Pakistan.
MR68 Taukkyan Memorial,Burma.
MR69 Delhi 1914-1918 War Memorial,India.
MR70 Brookwood (Russia) Memorial,England.

CEMETERIES.

EAST AFRICA.
2   Handeni Cemetery.
6   Korogwe Churchyard.
7   Korogwe Military Cemetery.
8   Lindi Cemetery.
9   Mhonda Mission Cemetery.
10   Mingoyo Cemetery.
11   Mtama Cemetery.
12   Mwanza Cemetery.
13   New Moshi British Cemetery.
15   Songea European Cemetery.
19   Tanga Main Cemetery.
22   Bweho Chini Military Graves.
23   Chogowali Military Grave.
24   Dakawa (Mgeta River and Wami River) Military Graves.
28   Longido Cemetery.
29   Luchomo Military Grave.
30   Mahiwa Military Graves.
32   Mikese Military Grave.
33   Mkwera Military Graves.
35   Dar Es Salaam (Sea View) Cemetery.
36   Dar Es Salaam (Upanga Street) Cemetery.
38   Kilwa Kivinje Cemetery.
39   Morogoro Cemetery.
40   Iringa Cemetery.
42   Kajiado Cemetery.
43   Kisii Boma Military Grave.
44   Kisumu Cemetery.
46   Molo Military Grave.
47   Mombasa Protestant Cemetery.
49   Mumias European Cemetery.
50   Mwele Ndogo Military Grave.
51   Nairobi Forest Cemetery.
52   Nairobi South Cemetery.
53   Naivasha Cemetery.
54   Nakuru Cemetery.
56   Taveta Military Cemetery.
58   Voi Cemetery.
59   Wajir Cemetery.
60   Hargeisa War Cemetery.
61   Mogadishu African War Cemetery.

66	Port Louis Western Cemetery.	48	Nsanakang Cemetery Enclosure.
67	Port Louis (Roche-Bois) Eastern Cemetery.	49	Nsanakang European Cemetery.
77	Mangochi Town Cemetery.	50	Udi Military Grave.
78	Karonga Church of Central Africa Presbyterian Cemetery.	52	Yola Station Cemetery.
80	Karonga New War Cemetery.	53	Zaria European Cemetery.
86	Zomba Town Cemetery.	54	Zungeru Cemetery.
87	Beira Christian Cemetery.	55	Calabar Memorial.
89	Maputo Cemetery.	56	Ibadan Memorial.
90	Lumbo British Cemetery.	57	Lokoja Memorial.
92	Pemba Cemetery.	58	Zaria Memorial.
101	Harare (Pioneer)Cemetery.	61	Duala Cemetery.
116	Khartoum War Cemetery.		
124	Entebbe European Cemetery.	ASIA.	
125	Jinja Roman Catholic Churchyard.	9	Colombo (Kanatte) General Cemetery,Sri Lanka.
126	Kabarole Mission Cemetery.	20	Sai Wan Bay Memorial (UMA & UMB),Hong Kong.
127	Kampala (Jinja Road) European Cemetery.	33	Hong Kong Cemetery,Hong Kong.
128	Mbarara (St James) Churchyard.	40	Yokohama War Cemetery,Japan.
		45	Kranji War Cemetery,Singapore.
SOUTH AFRICA.		51	Haidar Pasha Cemetery,Istanbul.
18	Trekkopjes Cemetery.	52	Chanak Consular Cemetery,Asiatic side of the Dardanelles.
26	Durban (Ordnance Road) Military Cemetery.	53	Famagusta Military Cemetery,Cyprus.
30	Durban (Stellawood) Cemetery.	60	Maala Cemetery,Aden.
42	Benoni Cemetery.	61	Perim Cemetery,Aden.
52	Johannesburg (Braamfontein) Cemetery.	62	Sheikh Othman Cemetery,Aden.
53	Johannesburg (Brixton New) Cemetery.	64	Horth Point Christian Cemetery,Kamaran Island.
63	Potchefstroom European Cemetery.	66	Muscat Old Cemetery,Oman.
69	Roberts Heights Military Cemetery,Pretoria.	81	Haidar Pasha Memorial.
72	Tzaneen Estate Cemetery,Selati Valley.	82	Tehran War Cemetery,Iran.
81	Rooidam Military Cemetery,Tempe.		
130	Mafeking Cemetery.	AUSTRALIA.	
136	Muizenberg Cemetery,Cape Town.	35	Deniliquin General Cemetery.
144	Plumstead Cemetery,Cape Town.	40	Field of Mars Cemetery,Ryde.
158	Simonstown (Dido Valley) Cemetery.	47	Gore Hill Cemetery.
171	Woltemade Cemetery,Cape Town.	85	Orange Cemetery.
172	Wynberg (Church Street) Cemetery,Cape Town.	92	Randwick General Cemetery,Sydney.
		94	Rookwood Necropolis,Sydney.
WEST AFRICA.		109	South Head General Cemetery,Watson's Bay.
1	Christiansborg Civil Cemetery.	112	Sydney (Waverley) General Cemetery.
2	Gambaga European Cemetery.	138A	New South Wales Garden of Rememberance.
3	Kumasi European Cemetery.	146	Brisbane General Cemetery.
4	Sekondi (Shama Road) European Cemetery now Takoradi European Cemetery,Ghana.	171	Gladstone Cemetery.
5	Chra Village Cemetery now Whala Cemetery.	197	Roma Cemetery.
6	Kumasi Memorial.	206	Toowoomba Cemetery.
8	Elisabethville Cemetery.	211A	Queensland Garden of Remembrance.
12	Bougie Communal Cemetery,Algeria.	212	Adelaide (West Terrace) Cemetery.
17	Relizane Communal Cemetery.	212A	Adelaide (West Terrace) A.I.F. Cemetery.
23	Bathurst Memorial.	212B	Adelaide (West Terrace) Roman Catholic Cemetery.
24	Funchal British Cemetery,Maderia.	240	Stirling District Cemetery.
28	Freetown Memorial.	245	Willaston General Cemetery.
30	Freetown (King Tom) Cemetery.	252	Carr Villa General Cemetery,Launceston.
33	Bakundi Military Grave.	262	Hobart (Cornelian Bay) Public Cemetery.
35	Bauchi European Cemetery.	287	Bairnsdale Public Cemetery.
39	Enugu Military Grave.	288	Ballarat (New) General Cemetery.
40	Ibadan Mission Church Cemetery.	293	Beechworth Cemetery.
41	Lkoyi New Cemetery,Lagos.	296	Bendigo Civil Cemetery.
42	Kaduna Cemetery.	304	Boroondara General Cemetery,Kew.
45	Lokoja Town Cemetery.	305	Box Hill General Cemetery.
46	Mamfe European Cemetery.	306	Bright Cemetery.
47	Maio Kalei Military Grave.	307	Brighton General Cemetery.
		322	Cobram Cemetery.

323	Coburg General Cemetery.	44	Potijze Burial Ground.
325	Corryong Cemetery.	45	Potijze Chateau Grounds Cemetery.
328	Creswick Public Cemetery.	46	Potijze Chateau Lawn Cemetery.
344	Fawkner Memorial Park Cemetery,Melbourne.	47	Potijze Chateau Wood Cemetery.
375	Maryborough Public Cemetery.	48	La Plus Douve Farm Cemetery,Ploegsteert.
376	Melbourne Gemeral Cemetery.	49	Ration Farm (La Plus Douve) Annexe,Ploegsteert.
377	Merbein Public Cemetery.	50	Underhill Farm Cemetery,Ploegsteert.
410	Seymour General Cemetery.	52	Prowse Point Military Cemetery,Warneton.
421	Swanwater West General Cemetery.	53	Hyde Park Corner (Royal Berks) Cemetery,Ploegsteert.
430	Violet Town Public Cemetery.	54	Berks Cemetery Extension,Ploegsteert.
456	Freemantle Cemetery.	56	Chester Farm Cemetery,Zillebeke.
459	Ivanhoe Station Private Burial Ground,Wyndham.	57	Ypres Town Cemetery,Menin Gate.
469	Northam Cemetery.	58	Ypres Town Cemetery Extension,Menin Gate.
471	Perth (Karrakatta) General Cemetery.	59	Ramparts Cemetery,Lille Gate,Ypres.
472	Perth War Cemetery.	60	La Laiterie Military Cemetery,Kemmel.
473	Quarantine Station,Woodmans Point.	61	Spanbroekmolen British Cemetery,Wytschaete.
481	Duntroon Military College Grounds.	62	Lone Tree Cemetery,Spanbroekmolen,Wytschaete.
		63	St Julien Dressing Station Cemetery,Langemarck.
BELGIUM.		64	Minty Farm Cemetery,St Jan.
1	Ferme-Olivier Cemetery,Elverdinghe.	65	No Man's Cot Cemetery,Boezinge.
2	Hop Store Cemetery,Vlamertinghe.	66	Welsh Cemetery (Caesar's Nose),Boezinge.
3	Nine Elms British Cemetery,Poperinghe.	67	Colne Valley Cemetery,Boezinge.
4	Vlamertinghe Military Cemetery.	68	Lancashire Cottage Cemetery,Ploegsteert
5	Poperinghe New Military Cemetery.	69	Ploegsteert Churchyard.
6	Brandhoek Military Cemetery,Vlamertinghe.	70	Ploegsteert Wood Military Cemetery,Warneton.
7	Brandhoek New Military Cemetery,Vlamertinghe.	71	Rifle House Cemetery,Warneton.
8	Brandhoek New Military Cemetery No.3,Vlamertinghe.	72	Menin Road South Military Cemetery,Ypres.
9	Hospital Farm Cemetery,Elverdinghe.	73	Essex Farm Cemetery,Boesinghe.
10	Vlamertinghe New Military Cemetery.	74	Wytschaete Military Cemetery.
11	Lijssenthoek Military Cemetery.	75	Derry House Cemetery No.2,Wytschaete.
12	Canada Farm Cemetery,Elverdinghe.	76	Torreken Farm Cemetery No.1,Wytschaete.
13	Bleuet Farm Cemetery,Elverdinghe.	77	Somer Farm Cemetery,Wytschaete.
15	Reninghelst New Military Cemetery.	78	Cabin Hill Cemetery,Wytschaete.
16	Dozinghem Military Cemetery,Westvleteren.	79	Lindenhoek Chalet Military Cemetery,Kemmel.
17	Kemmel Chateau Military Cemetery.	80	Dickebusch Old Military Cemetery.
18	Mendinghem Military Cemetery,Proven.	81	Reninghelst Churchyard.
19	Huts Cemetery,Dickebusch.	82	Reninghelst Churchyard Extension.
20	Duhallow A.D.S. Cemetery,Ypres.	83	Clement House Cemetery,Langemarck.
21	La Clytte Military Cemetery,Reninghelst.	84	Ypres Reservoir Cemetery.
22	Oxford Road Cemetery,Ieper.	85	Talana Farm Cemetery,Boesinghe.
23	Bard Cottage Cemetery,Boezinge.	86	Dragoon Camp Cemetery,Boesinghe.
24	Coxyde Military Cemetery.	87	Ruisseau Farm Cemetery,Langemarck.
25	Solferino Farm Cemetery,Brielen.	88	Aeroplane Cemetery,Ypres.
26	Divisional Collecting Post Cemetery,Boesinghe.	89	Wulverghem-Lindenhoek Road Military Cemetery.
27	Track "X" Cemetery,St Jean-Les-Ypres.	90	Westhof Farm Cemetery,Neuve-Eglise.
28	Dickebusch New Military Cemetery.	91	La Brique Military Cemetery No.1,St Jean-Les-Ypres.
29	Dickebusch New Military Cemetery Extension.	92	La Brique Military Cemetery No.2,St Jean-Les-Ypres.
30	Gunners Farm Cemetery,Ploegsteert.	93	Wieltje Farm Cemetery,St Jean-Les-Ypres.
31	Motor Car Corner Cemetery,Ploegsteert.	94	Buffs Road Cemetery,St Jean-Les-Ypres.
32	Le Touquet Railway Crossing Cemetery,Ploegsteert.	96	New Irish Farm Cemetery,St Jean-Les-Ypres.
33	Calvaire (Essex) Military Cemetery,Ploegsteert.	97	Dranoutre Military Cemetery.
34	Belgian Battery Corner Cemetery,Ypres.	98	Dranoutre Churchyard.
35	Divisional Cemetery,Dickebusch Road,Vlamertinghe.	99	Packhorse Farm Shrine Cemetery,Wulverghem.
36	Gwalia Cemetery,Poperinghe.	100	Pond Farm Cemetery,Wulverghem.
37	Ridge Wood Military Cemetery,Voormezeele.	101	White House Cemetery,St Jean-Les-Ypres.
38	Haringhe (Bandaghem) Military Cemetery.	102	Klein-Vierstraat British Cemetery,Kemmel.
40	Abeele Aerodrome Military Cemetery,Watou.	103	Suffolk Cemetery,Vierstraat,Kemmel.
41	Watou Churchyard.	104	Godezonne Farm Cemetery,Kemmel.
42	Kandahar Farm Cemetery,Neuve-Eglise.	105	Elzenwalle Brasserie Cemetery,Voormezeele.
43	St Quentin Cabaret Military Cemetery,Ploegsteert.	106	Artillery Wood Cemetery,Boesinghe.

107	R.E. Farm Cemetery, Wytschaete.	178	Breedene Churchyard.
111	Voormezeele Enclosure No.3.	182	Locre Churchyard.
112	Hooge Crater Cemetery, Zillebeke.	183	Locre Hospice Cemetery.
113	Birr Cross Roads Cemetery, Zillebeke.	184	Locre No.10 Cemetery.
114	R.E. Grave, Railway Wood, Zillebeke.	185	Grootebeek British Cemetery, Reninghelst.
115	Perth Cemetery (China Wall), Zillebeke.	186	Kemmel Churchyard.
116	Zantvoorde British Cemetery.	187	Dickebusch Churchyard.
117	Zantvoorde Churchyard.	188	Hagle Dump Cemetery, Elverdinghe.
118	Oak Dump Cemetery, Voormezeele.	191	Westoutre Churchyard Extension.
120	Woods Cemetery, Zillebeke.	192	Westoutre British Cemetery.
121	1/D.C.L.I. Cemetery, The Bluff, Zillebeke.	193	Boesinghe Churchyard.
122	Hedge Row Trench Cemetery, Zillebeke.	195	Angreau Communal Cemetery.
123	Passchendaele New British Cemetery.	197	Audregnies Churchyard.
124	Voormezeele Enclosures No.1 & No.2.	198	Elouges Communal Cemetery.
125	Tyne Cot Cemetery, Passchendaele.	199	Erquelinnes Communal Cemetery.
126	Poelcapelle British Cemetery.	201	Hautrage Military Cemetery.
127	Railway Dugouts Burial Ground (Transport Farm), Zillebeke.	202	Frameries Communal Cemetery.
128	Dochy Farm New British Cemetery, Langemarck.	203	Quievrain Communal Cemetery.
129	Seaforth Cemetery, Cheddar Villa, Langemarck.	204	Roisin Communal Cemetery.
130	Bridge House Cemetery, Langemarck.	205	Thulin New Communal Cemetery.
131	Spoilbank Cemetery, Zillebeke.	206	Flenu Communal Cemetery.
132	Larch Wood (Railway Cutting) Cemetery, Zillebeke.	214	Jemappes Communal Cemetery.
133	Tuileries British Cemetery, Zillebeke.	216	Wiheries Communal Cemetery.
134	Zillebeke Churchyard.	218	Blaugies Communal Cemetery.
135	Railway Chateau Cemetery, Vlamertinghe.	219	Boussu Communal Cemetery.
136	London Rifle Brigade Cemetery, Ploegsteert.	221	Boussu-lez-Walcourt Communal Cemetery.
137	Tancrez Farm Cemetery, Ploegsteert.	226	Froidchapelle Communal Cemetery.
138	Maple Leaf Cemetery, Romarin, Neuve-Eglise.	229	Harchies Communal Cemetery.
140	Harlebeke New British Cemetery.	231	Jurbise Churchyard.
141	Staceghem Communal Cemetery, Harlebeke.	234	Monbliart Communal Cemetery, Beaumont.
143	Vichte Military Cemetery.	236	Quevy-Le-Petit Communal Cemetery.
147	Hulste Communal Cemetery.	241	Mons Communal Cemetery.
149	Wielsbeke Churchyard.	242	St Symphorien Military Cemetery.
150	Poperinghe Communal Cemetery.	243	La Louviere Communal Cemetery.
151	Poperinghe Old Military Cemetery.	244	Maisieres Communal Cemetery.
152	Oosttaverne Wood Cemetery, Wyschaete.	246	Asquillies Churchyard.
153	Croonaert Chapel Cemetery, Wyschaete.	256	Harveng Churchyard.
154	Bus House Cemetery, Voormezeele.	261	Nouvelles Communal Cemetery.
155	Irish House Cemetery, Kemmel.	262	Rouveroy Communal Cemetery.
156	Dadizeele Communal Cemetery.	265	Belgrade Cemetery, Namur.
157	Dadizeele New British Cemetery.	266	Liege (Robermont) Cemetery.
158	Moorseele Military Cemetery.	267	Huy (La Sarte) Communal Cemetery.
159	Kezelberg Military Cemetery, Moorseele.	268	Houyet Churchyard.
160	Ledeghem Churchyard.	269	Theux Communal Cemetery.
161	Ledeghem Military Cemetery.	275	Gougnies Communal Cemetery.
162	Moorslede Communal Cemetery.	302	Malonne Communal Cemetery.
163	Slypskappelle Churchyard, Moorslede.	307	Polygon Wood Cemetery, Zonnebeke.
165	Bedford House Cemetery, Enclosure No.2, Zillebeke.	308	Buttes New British Cemetery, Polygon Wood, Zonnebeke.
166	Bedford House Cemetery Enclosure No.3, Zillebeke.	310	Divisional Collecting Post Cemetery Extension, Boesinghe.
167	Bedford House Cemetery Enclosure No.4, Zillebeke.	316	Halle Communal Cemetery.
167a	Bedford House Cemetery Enclosure No.6, Zillebeke.	320	Louvain Communal Cemetery.
168	Messines Ridge British Cemetery.	321	Nivelles (Nijvel) Communal Cemetery.
169	Wulverghem Churchyard.	330	Charleroi Communal Cemetery.
170	Neuve-Eglise Churchyard.	332	Gosselies Comunal Cemetery.
171	Adinkerke Churchyard Extension.	336	Marcinelle New Communal Cemetery.
172	Adinkerke Military Cemetery, Furnes.	337	Soumoy Communal Cemetery.
173	Ramscappelle Road Military Cemetery, St Georges.	339	Berks Cemetery Extension (Rosenberg Chateau Plots), Ploegsteert.
174	Nieuport Communal Cemetery.	342	Schoonselhof Cemetery, Antwerp.
175	Ostende New Communal Cemetery.	344	Audenarde Communal Cemetery.
176	Steenkerke Belgian Military Cemetery.		

348	Bottelaere Churchyard,East Flanders.		
349	Bouchaute Churchyard.		

348 Bottelaere Churchyard,East Flanders.
349 Bouchaute Churchyard.
353 Ghent City Cemetery.
354 Gysenzelle Churchyard,East Flanders.
355 Landeghem Churchyard,East Flanders.
357 Meerendre Churchyard,East Flanders.
358 Mooregem Churchyard.
359 Nazareth Churchyard,East Flanders.
364 Scheldewindeke Churchyard,East Flanders.
365 Termonde Communal Cemetery Extension,East Flanders.
367 Escanaffles Communal Cemetery,Hainault.
370 Beveren-Sur-Yser Churchyard.
371 Blankenberghe Communal Cemetery.
375 Hoogstaede Belgian Military Cemetery.
376 Houttabe Churchyard,West Flanders.
378 Knocke Churchyard,West Flanders.
379 Oostcamp Churchyard.
380 Oostnieuwkerke Churchyard.
381 Oostrosbeke Communal Cemetery.
383 Roulers Communal Cemetery.
384 Ruddervoorde Communal Cemetery.
385 Stalhille Churchyard,West Flanders.
388 Wenduyne Churchyard,West Flanders.
390 Zeeburugge Churchyard,Bruges.
391 Zeeburugge Memorial,West Flanders.
392 Courtrai (La Madeleine) Cemetery.
393 Courtrai (St Jean) Cemetery.
396 Ath Communal Cemetery.
400 Lessines Communal Cemetery.
402 Bisseghem Communal Cemetery.
405 Winkel-St Eloi Churchyard.
406 Tournai Communal Cemetery Allied Extension.
408 Hecstert Military Cemetery.
409 Leuze Communal Cemetery.
410 Menin Communal Cemetery.
413 Anbaing Churchyard.
414 Bleharies Communal Cemetery.
417 Esplechin Churchyard.
420 Froidmont Communal Cemetery.
423 La Glanerie Churchyard.
428 Orcq Communal Cemetery.
432 Rumillies Churchyard.
435 Taintegnies Communal Cemetery.
438 Warcoing Churchyard.
441 Coyghem Churchyard.
442 Dottignies Communal Cemetery.
443 Espierres Churchyard.
448 Rolleghen Churchyard.
449 St Genois Churchyard.
450 Wevelghem Communal Cemetery.
451 Strand Military Cemetery,Ploegsteert.
452 Kemmel Cemetery.
453 Sanctuary Wood Cemetery, Zillebeke.
454 Voormezele Churchyard.

BERMUDA.
1 Bermuda Royal Naval Cemetery,Ireland Island.

BURMA.
122a Rangoon War Cemetery.
129a Taukkyan War Cemetery.

CANADA.
10 Souris (Glenwood) Cemetery.
11 Virden Cemetery.
17 Glencross Burying Ground.
32 Basswood Cemetery,Marquette.
35 Clanwilliam Presbyterian Cemetery,Marquette.
50 MacGregor Cemetery,Neepawa.
78 Arborg (Ardal) Lutheran Cemetery.
99 Deloraine Cemetery,Souris,Manitoba.
109 St Boniface (Belgian Sacred Heart) Church Cemetery.
110 Springfield (Sunnyside) Cemetery,Springfield.
112 Kildonan Cemetery,Winnipeg.
114 West Kildonan Jewish Cemetery,Winnipeg.
115 Winnipeg (Brookside) Cemetery,Winnipeg.
116 Winnipeg (Elmwood) Cemetery.
119 Winnipeg (St John's) Cemetery.
132 Sandwick Anglican Cemetery.
146 Nelson Memorial Park.
151 Trail (Mountain View) Cemetery,Kootenay.
152 Cobble Hill (St John the Baptist) Anglican Church Cemetery,Nanaimo.
154 Esquimalt Veterans' Cemetery,Nanaimo.
155 Gabriola Island Graveyard,Nanaimo,British Columbia.
166 South Saanich (Mount Newton) Roman Catholic Cemetery.
171 New Westminster (Fraser) Cemetery.
174 New Westminster (Fraser) Cemetery,St Peter's Romam Catholic Sect.
177 Prince Rupert (Fairview) Cemetery.
179 Burnaby (Ocean View) Burial Park.
180 Vancouver (Mountain View) Cemetery,Vancouver.
183 Victoria (Ross Bay) Cemetery,Victoria.
254 Montreal (Notre Dame des Neiges) Cemetery,Hochelaga.
256 Montreal (Mount Royal) Cemetery,Hochelaga,Quebec.
257 Montreal (Shaar Hashomayin) Cemetery,Hochelaga.
261 Aylmer (St Paul's) Roman Catholic Cemetery,Hull,Quebec.
274 Joliette Cemetery.
300 Notre Dame de Stanbridge Roman Catholic Cemetery,Missiquoi.
302 Rawdon (United Church) Cemetery.
323A Quebec City (Mount Hermon) Cemetery,Quebec.
324 Quebec City (St Charles) Cemetery.
324A Quebec City (Ste Foye) Cemetery.
333 Sorel (Sts Anges) Cemetery.
341 St Hyacinthe (Notre Dame de Rosaire) Cemetery.
342 St John's Roman Catholic Cemetery.
345 Three Rivers (St Louis) Cemetery.
354 Sherbrooke (St Peter's) Protestant Cemetery.
360 Stanstead (Crystal Lake) Cemetery.
372 St Eustache Cemetery.
388 Oxbow Cemetery.
392 Battleford Municipal Cemetery.
423 Preeceville Cemetery,Mackenzie,Saskatchewan.
440 Moose Jaw Cemetery,Moose Jaw.
449 North Battleford Cemetery,North Battleford.
457 Prince Albert (South Hill) Cemetery.
465 Broadview Cemetery.
469 Grenfell Cemetery,Qu'Appelle.
474 Moosomin South Cemetery

487 Regina Cemetery.
506 Saskatoon (Woodlawn) Cemetery,Saskatoon.
542 Calgary Roman Catholic Cemetery.
543 Calgary Union Cemetery.
545A Edmonton (Mount Pleasant) Cemetery.
547 Edmonton Cemetery,East Edmonton,Alberta.
562 Fort Macleod Union Cemetery.
576 Red Deer Cemetery.
609 Annapolis Royal (St Alban's) Anglican Cemetery.
613 Bridgetown (Riverside) Cemetery.
617A Lawrencetown (Valley West Whitman) Cemetery.
620 Melvern Square (Church Grove) Cemetery.
622 Paradise Public Cemetery.
637 Tracadie Roman Catholic Cemetery.
644 Donkin (St Luke's) Cemetery.
653 North Sydney (St Joseph's) Roman Catholic Cemetery.
657A Sydney (Calvary)Roman Catholic Cemetery.
658 Sydney (HardwoodHill) Cemetery.
674 Truro Cemetery.
694 Paarsboro (Baptist) Church Cemetery.
699 Springhill (Hillside) Cemetery.
731 Bedford (Brookside) Cemetery.
740 Halifax (Camp Hill) Cemetery,Nova Scotia.
742 Halifax (Fort Massey) Cemetery.
745 Halifax (Mount Olivet) Cemetery.
745A Halifax (St John's) Cemetery.
777 Hillsborough (Elmwood) Protestant Cemetery.
793 Kentville (Oak Grove) Cemetery.
803 Chester (St Stephen's) Cemetery.
811 New Germany (St John's-in-the-Wilderness Church)Cemetery.
818 New Glasgow (Riverside) Cemetery.
832 Westville (Auburn) Cemetery.
835 Brooklyn (Ocean View) Cemetery.
869 Iona (St Columba's) Cemetery.
887 Yarmouth (Mountain) Cemetery.
911 Summerside People's Cemetery.
912 Summerside (St Paul's) Cemetery.
954 Grand Manan Church of England Cemetery.
961 St Stephen Rural Cemetery.
993 Sussex Corner (Church of England) Cemetery.
1019 Campbellton Rural Cemetery.
1028 St John (Fernhill) Cemetery,New Brunswick.
1054 Moncton (Elmwood) Cemetery.
1055 Moncton (Shediac Road) Roman Catholic Cemetery.
1060 Sackville Rural Cemetery.
1087 Kincardine Cemetery,Bruce,Ontario.
1091 Port Elgin (Sanctuary Park) Cemetery,Bruce.
1094 Teeswater Cemetery,Bruce.
1095 Walkerton Cemetery.
1097 Aylmer Cemetery.
1100 Corinth Baptist Cemetery.
1105 St Thomas Cemetery.
1113 Cottam (Trinity) Anglican Churchyard.
1114 Kingsville (Greenhill) Cemetery,Essex,Ontario.
1119 Sandwich (St John's) Anglican Churchyard.
1121 Walkerville (St Mary's) Anglican Cemetery Essex.
1125 Bayfield Cemetery,Huron.
1132 Goderich (Maitland) Cemetery.
1134 Hensall Union Cemetery.

1140 Wingham Cemetery.
1143 Chatham (Maple Leaf) Cemetery,Kent,Ontario.
1154A Forest (Beechwood) Cemetery,Lambton.
1156 Sarnia (Lake View) Cemetery,Lambton.
1166 Wyoming Cemetery,Lambton.
1175 London (Mount Pleasant) Cemetery,Middlesex.
1177 London (St Pater's) Roman Catholic Cemetery.
1178 London (Woodland) Cemetery,Middlesex.
1181 Lucan (St Patrick's) Roman Catholic Cemetery,Middlesex.
1183 Strathroy Cemetery,Middlesex.
1192 Norwich Cemetery,Oxford.
1197 Woodstock (Hillview) United Cemetery,Oxford.
1200 Listowel (Fairview) Cemetery,Perth.
1206 St Mary's Cemetery,Perth.
1207 Stratford (Avondale) Cemetery.
1208 Ayr Cemetery.
1214 Elmira Union Cemetery.
1217 Kitchener (Mount Hope) Roman Catholic Cemetery,Waterloo.
1219 Preston Public Cemetery.
1224 Erin Cemetery,Wellington.
1228 Guelph (Woodlawn) Cemetery.
1231 Morristown (Crown) Cemetery,Wellington.
1232 Mount Forest Cemetery.
1245 Ottawa (Beechwood) Cemetery,Carleton,Ontario.
1246 Ottawa (Notre Dame) Roman Catholic Cemetery,Carleton.
1247B South March (St John's) Cemetery.
1255 Williamsburg (Colquhoun) Presbyterian Cemetery.
1268 Godfrey (Piccadilly) Cemetery,Frontenae.
1270 Kingston (Cataraqui) Cemetery.
1271 Kingston (St Mary's) Cemetery.
1282A South Lancaster (St Andrew's) Presbyterian Cemetery.
1283 Bishop's Mills (Alexander) Cemetery.
1287 Oxford Mills Union Central Burial ground.
1297 Albury Cemetery,Hastings.
1298 Bancroft (Mount Pleasant) Cemetery.
1300 Belleville Cemetery,Hastings.
1303 Deseronto Cemetery,Hastings.
1304/1305 Deseronto (St Vincent de Paul) Cemetery,Hastings.
1322 Beckwith (St Fillan's) Cemetery,Lanark.
1325 Carleton Place (St Mary's) Cemetery.
1337 Brockville (Oakland) Cemetery.
1343A Westport (St Edward's) Cemetery.
1345 Camden East Anglican Cemetery.
1357 Campbellford (Christ Church) Cemetery.
1379 Norwood Protestant Cemetery,Peterborough.
1380 Peterborough (Little Lake) Cemetery,Peterborough,Ontario.
1386 L'Original (Cassburn) Cemetery.
1387A Vanleek Hill Roman Catholic Cemetery,Prescott.
1391 Picton (Mount Olivet) Cemetery,Prince Edward.
1409 Renfrew (Thompson Ville) Cemetery.
1430 Lindsay (Riverside) Cemetery,Victoria,Ontario.
1431 Lindsay (St Mary's) Catholic Cemetery.
1438 Kenora (Lake of the Woods) Cemetery,Kenora.
1440 Fort Frances Cemetery,Rainy River.

1444 Fort William (Mountain View) Cemetery,Thunder Bay.
1448 Port Arthur (St Andrew's) Roman Catholic Cemetery.
1456 Sault Ste Marie (Greenwood) Cemetery.
1464 Brantford (Greenwood) Cemetery,Brant,Ontario.
1468 Farringdon Cemetery.
1479 Orangeville (Greenwood) Cemetery.
1484 Durham Cemetery,Grey.
1488 Harkaway Cemetery.
1494 Thornbury Cemetery,Grey.
1497 Cayuga Riverside Cemetery.
1498 Dunnville (Riverside) Cemetery,Haldimand.
1511 Burlington (Greenwood) Cemetery.
1517 Oakville (St Jude's) Cemetery.
1518 Beansville (Mount Osborne) Cemetery,Lincoln.
1522 Grimsby (St Andrew's) Anglican Cemetery,Lincoln.
1531 St Catharines (Victoria Lawn) Cemetery,Lincoln,Ontario.
1536 Bracebridge (United Church) Cemetery.
1558 Delhi Cemetery,Norfolk.
1563 Simcoe (Oakwood) Cemetery.
1564 Waterford (Greenwood) Cemetery.
1566 Beaverton (Stone Church) United Church Cemetery.
1570 Oshawa union Cemetery,Ontario.
1575 Sunderland Cemetery,Ontario.
1579 Uxbridge Cemetery.
1582 Whitevale Cemetery.
1595 Brampton Cemetery.
1597 Dixie (Union) Cemetery.
1598 Mono Mills (Mitchell's) Cemetery,Peel.
1600 Alliston Union Cemetery,Simcoe.
1607 Collingwood (St Mary's) Roman Catholic Cemetery,Simcoe.
1608 Collingwood United Cemetery,Simcoe.
1612 Elmvale Presbyterian Cemetery,Simcoe.
1614 Innisfil (St Paul's) Cemetery.
1637 Haileybury (Mount Pleasant) Cemetery.
1650 Niagara Falls (Fairview) Cemetery.
1660 Welland (Woodlawn) Cemetery,Welland.
1663 Dundas (Grove) Cemetery.
1667 Hamilton Cemetery,Wentworth,Ontario.
1668A Hamilton (Woodland) Cemetery.
1679 Mount Albert Cemetery.
1686 Toronto (Forest Lawn) Mausoleum.
1687 Toronto (Mount Hope) Cemetery,York.
1688 Toronto (Mount Pleasant) Cemetery,York,Ontario.
1689 Toronto Necropolis,York.
1690 Toronto (Park Lawn) Cemetery.
1691 Toronto (Prospect) Cemetery,York,Ontario.
1692 Toronto Roselawn) Hebrew Cemetery.
1694 Toronto (St James's) Cemetery,York,Ontario.
1695 Toronto St John's,Norway)Cemetery,York.

CENTRAL AMERICA.
6 Quirigua Hospital Cemetery,Guatemala.

EGYPT.
1 Alexandria (Hadra) War Memorial Cemetery.
2 Kantara War Memorial Cemetery
3 Chatby Military Cemetery.
6 Chatby War Memorial Cemetery.
7 Port Said War Memorial Cemetery.

8 Ismailia War Memorial Cemetery.
9 Cairo War Memorial Cemetery.
10 Cairo New British Protestant Cemetery.
13 Cairo Civil International Cemetery.
15 Suez War Memorial Cemetery.
19 Mersa Matruh Military Cemetery.

EUROPE.
1 Pieta Military Cemetery,Malta.
3 Ta Braxia Cemetery,Malta.
4 Addolorata Cemetery,Malta.
5 Rinella Military Cemetery,Malta.
6 Malta Naval Cemetery.
7 Pembroke Military Cemetery,Malta.
9 Marsa Jewish Cemetery,Malta.
17 Plovdiv Central Cemetery,Bulgaria.
20 Sofia War Cemetery,Bulgaria.
23 Gibraltar (North Front) Cemetery,Gibraltar.
26A Rakoskeresztur Hungarian National Cemetery,Hungary.
28 Lisbon (St George) British Churchyard,Portugal.
30 Bucharest War Cemetery,Romania.
34 Bilbao British Cemetery,Lujua,Spain.
42 Madrid British Cemetery,Spain.
46 Villagarcia British Naval Cemetery,Spain.
51 Vevey (St Martin's) Cemetery,Switzerland.
56 Belgrade New Cemetery,Yugoslavia.
57 Chela Kula Military Cemetery,Nish,Yugoslavia.
58 Skoplje (Uskub) British Cemetery,Yugoslavia.
58a Kuzala Cemetery,Rijeka,Yugoslavia.
64 Skagen Cemetery,Denmark.
66 Copenhagen Western Cemetery,Denmark.
67 Borsmose Churchyard,Aal,Denmark.
72 Haurvig Churchyard,Denmark.
74 Vederso Churchyard,Denmark.
86A Bergen-Op-Zoom War Cemetery,Holland.
90 Flushing Vlissingen Northern Cemetery,Holland.
96 Noordwijk General Cemetery,Holland.
97 Orthen Protestant Cemetery,Hertogenbosch,Holland.
99 Rotterdam (Crooswijk) General Cemetery,Holland.
100 'S Hertogenbosch General Cemetery,Holland.
110 Kragero Cemetery,Norway.
131 Narvik Cemetery,Norway.
135 Faberg Churchyard,Norway.
136 Lillehammer Churchyard,Norway.
146 Fredrikstad Military Cemetery,Norway.
148 Tonsberg Old Cemetery,Norway.
149 Poznan Old Garrison Cemetery,Poland.
150a Malbork Commonwealth War Cemetery,Poland.
178A Kviberg Cemetery,Sweden.
179 Archangel Allied Cemetery,Russia.
180 Archangel Memorial,Russia.
193 Churkin Russian Naval Cemetery,Vladivostok,Siberia.
195 Vladivostok Memorial,Siberia.

FRANCE.
1 Le Treport Military Cemetery.
2 Forceville Communal Cemetery Extension.
3 Louvencourt Military Cemetery.
4 Acheux British Cemetery.
5 Bertrancourt Military Cemetery.

#	Cemetery	#	Cemetery
8	Calais Southern Cemetery.	84	Bagneux British Cemetery,Gezaincourt.
10	Pernes British Cemetery.	85	Ste Marie Cemetery,Le Havre.
12	Barlin Communal Cemetery Extension.	87	Sanvic Communal Cemetery.
13	Mont Huon Military Cemetery,Le Treport.	88	Lapugnoy Military Cemetery.
14	Ligny-St Flochel British Cemetery,Averdoingt.	94	Marles-Les-Mines Communal Cemetery.
15	Maroeuil British Cemetery.	95	Aubigny Communal Cemetery Extension.
16	BoisGuillaume Communal Cemetery.	96	Ste Catherine British Cemetery.
18	Morbecque British Cemetery.	97	St Nicholas British Cemetery.
19	Le Grand Hasard Military Cemetery,Morbecque.	98	Chocques Military Cemetery.
20	Thiennes British Cemetery.	100	Arneke British Cemetery.
21	Tannay British Cemetery,Thiennes.	102	Boulogne Eastern Cemetery.
22	Corbie Communal Cemetery.	103	Bac-Du-Sud British Cemetery,Bailleulval.
23	Corbie Communal Cemetery Extension.	104	Gouy-En-Artois Communal Cemetery Extension.
24	Cinq Rues British Cemetery,Hazebrouck.	105	Grove Town Cemetery,Meaulte.
25	La Kreule Military Cemetery,Hazebrouck.	106	Houchin British Cemetery.
26	Le Peuplier Military Cemetery,Caestre.	107	Houchin Communal Cemetery.
27	Caestre Military Cemetery.	108	Fouquieres Churchyard.
28	Borre British Cemetery.	109	Fouquieres Churchyard Extension.
29	Crouy British Cemetery,Crouy-Sur-Somme.	112	Gosnay Communal Cemetery.
30	Crouy Communal Cemetery,Crouy-Sur-Somme.	113	Duisans British Cemetery,Etrun.
31	Aire Communal Cemetery.	114	Cambrin Churchyard Extension.
32	Bruay Communal Cemetery Extension.	115	Philosophe British Cemetery,Mazingarbe.
33	Sandpits British Cemetery,Labeuvriere.	116	Querrieu British Cemetery.
34	Terlincthun British Cemetery,Wimille.	119	Daours Communal Cemetery Extension.
35	Auchonvillers Military Cemetery.	120	Warlincourt Halte British Cemetery,Saulty.
37	Picquigny British Cemetery.	121	Etretat Churchyard.
39	Longpre-Les-Corps Saints British Cemetery.	122	Etretat Churchyard Extension.
40	Etaples Military Cemetery.	123	Tourgeville Military Cemetery.
41	Varennes Military Cemetery.	131	Mailly Wood Cemetery.
43	Warloy-Baillon Communal Cemetery.	133	Courcelles-Au-Bois Communal Cemetery Extension.
44	Warloy-Baillon Communal Cemetery Extension.	134	Longuenesse (St Omer) Souvenir Cemetery.
46	Avesnes-Le-Comte Communal Cemetery Extension.	139	Godewaersvelde British Cemetery.
49	Izel-Les-Hameau Communal Cemetery.	140	Godewaersvelde Churchyard.
51	Abbeville Communal Cemetery.	141	Dive Copse British Cemetery,Sailly-Le-Sec.
52	Abbeville Communal Cemetery Extension.	142	Esquelbecq Military Cemetery.
53	Haute-Avesnes British Cemetery.	144	Adelaide Cemetery,Villers-Bretonneux.
54	Dainville British Cemetery.	145	St Sever Cemetery,Rouen.
55	Dainville Communal Cemetery.	146	St Sever Cemetery Extension,Rouen.
57	Wanquetin Communal Cemetery Extension.	147	Haynecourt British Cemetery.
58	La Chaudiere Military Cemetery,Vimy.	149	Maroc British Cemetery,Grenay.
59	Contay British Cemetery.	150	Bapaume Post Military Cemetery,Albert.
60	Harponville Communal Cemetery.	151	Peake Wood Cemetery,Fricourt.
61	Harponville Communal Cemetery Extension.	152	Munich Trench British Cemetery,Beaumont-Hamel.
62	Doullens Communal Cemetery Extension No.1.	153	Waggon Road Cemetery,Beaumont-Hamel.
63	Doullens Communal Cemetery Extension No.2.	154	Monchy British Cemetery,Monchy-Le-Preux.
64	Wimereux Communal Cemetery.	155	Windmill British Cemetery,Monchy-Le_Preux.
65	Les Baraques Military Cemetery,Sangatte.	156	Euston Road Cemetery,Colincamps.
66	La Neuville British Cemetery,Corbie.	157	Louez Military Cemetery,Duisans.
67	La Neuville Communal Cemetery,Corbie.	158	Habarcq Communal Cemetery Extension.
68	Ecoivres Military Cemetery,Mont-St Eloy.	160	Bully-Grenay Communal Cemetery French Extension.
69	Pernois British Cemetery,Halloy-Les-Pernois.	161	Bully-Grenay Communal Cemetery British Extension.
71	Vignacourt British Cemetery.	162	Wancourt British Cemetery.
74	Puchevillers British Cemetery.	163	Cambrin Military Cemetery.
76	Toutencourt Communal Cemetery.	164	Bray Military Cemetery.
77	Herissart Communal Cemetery.	166	Bray-Sur-Somme Communal Cemetery.
79	Molliens-Au-Bois Communal Cemetery.	167	Beauval Communal Cemetery.
80	Bethune Town Cemetery.	169	Gezaincourt Communal Cemetery Extension.
81	Villers Station Cemetery,Villers-Au-Bois.	172	Beauquesne Communal Cemetery.
82	Ration Farm Military Cemetery,La Chapelle-D'Armentieres.	174	Wailly Orchard Cemetery.
83	Brewery Orchard Cemetery,Bois-Grenier.	175	Fermont Military Cemetery,Riviere.

176 Dernancourt Communal Cemetery.	249 Gonnehem Churchyard.
177 Dernancourt Communal Cemetery Extension.	250 Gonnehem British Cemetery.
178 Noeux-Les-Mines Communal Cemetery.	251 Aveluy Communal Cemetery Extension.
179 Noeux-Les-Mines Communal Cemetery Extension.	252 Aveluy Wood Cemetery (Lancashire Dump),Mesnil-Martinsart.
180 Ebblinghem Military Cemetery.	
184 Roclincourt Military Cemetery.	253 Sailly-Sur-La-Lys Churchyard.
185 Namps-Au-Val British Cemetery.	254 Sailly-Sur-La-Lys Canadian Cemetery.
188 Dartmoor Cemetery,Becordel-Becourt.	255 Anzac Cemetery,Sailly-Sur-La-Lys.
189 Norfolk Cemetery,Becordel-Becourt.	256 Anneux British Cemetery.
190 Highland Cemetery,Le Cateau.	257 Sailly-Labourse Communal Cemetery.
192 Neuvilly Communal Cemetery Extension.	258 Sailly-Labourse Communal Cemetery Extension.
193 Outersteene Communal Cemetery Extension,Bailleul.	259 Labourse Communal Cemetery.
194 Doingt Communal Cemetery Extension.	260 Brown's Road Military Cemetery,Festubert.
196 Ribemont Communal Cemetery Extension.	261 Post Office Rifles Cemetery,Festubert.
197 Millencourt Communal Cemetery Extension.	262 Pont-D'Achelles Military Cemetery,Nieppe.
198 Buire-Sur-L'Ancre Communal Cemetery.	263 Pont-De-Nieppe Communal Cemetery.
200 Hazebrouck Communal Cemetery.	264 Nieppe Communal Cemetery.
201 Lillers Communal Cemetery.	265 Roclincourt Valley Cemetery.
202 Lillers Communal Cemetery Extension.	266 Anzin-St Aubin British Cemetery.
203 Couin British Cemetery.	267 Gordon Dump Cemetery,Ovillers-La Boisselle.
204 Couin New British Cemetery.	268 La Targette British Cemetery (Aux-Rietz),Neuville-St Vaast.
206 Romeries Communal Cemetery Extension.	
207 Mericourt-L'Abbe Communal Cemetery Extension.	269 Petit-Vimy British Cemetery,Vimy.
208 Franvillers Communal Cemetery.	270 St Aubert British Cemetery.
209 Franvillers Communal Cemetery Extension.	271 Avesnes-Le-Sec Communal Cemetery Extension.
210 Bonnay Communal Cemetery Extension.	272 Quarry Cemetery,Marquion.
212 Unicorn Cemetery,Vend'Huile.	273 Chapel Corner Cemetery,Sauchy-Lestree.
214 Bucquoy Road Cemetery,Ficheux.	274 Sains-Les-Marquion British Cemetery.
215 Connaught Cemetery,Thiepval.	275 Erquinghem-Lys Churchyard Extension.
216 Sailly-Saillisel British Cemetery.	276 "Y" Farm Military Cemetery,Bois-Grenier.
217 Morval British Cemetery.	277 Bulls Road Cemetery,Flers.
218 Rancourt Military Cemetery.	278 Thilloy Road Cemetery,Beaulencourt.
219 Dud Corner Cemetery,Loos.	279 Guards Cemetery,Windy Corner,Cuinchy.
220 Knightsbridge Cemetery,Mesnil-Martinsart.	280 Courcelette British Cemetery.
221 Beaumont-Hamel British Cemetery.	281 Foncquevillers Military Cemetery.
222 Mazingarbe Communal Cemetery.	283 Hannescamps New Military Cemetery.
223 Mazingarbe Communal Cemetery Extension.	284 Bailleul Communal Cemetery.
224 Hersin Communal Cemetery Extension.	285 Bailleul Communal Cemetery Extension.
225 St Hilaire Cemetery,Frevent.	286 Briastre Communal Cemetery.
226 St Hilaire Cemetery Extension,Frevent.	287 Belle Vue British Cemetery,Briastre.
228 Montay Communal Cemetery.	288 Solesmes Communal Cemetery.
229 Montay British Cemetery.	289 Solesmes British Cemetery.
230 Montay-Neuvilly Road Cemetery,Montay.	290 Crucifix Cemetery,Vendegies-Sur-Ecaillon.
231 Pommereuil British Cemetery.	292 Vertain Communal Cemetery Extension.
232 Martinsart British Cemetery.	293 Lonsdale Cemetery,Aveluy and Authuile.
233 Mesnil Communal Cemetery Extension.	294 Guillemont Road Cemetery,Guillemont.
234 Prospect Hill Cemetery,Gouy.	295 Bouzincourt Communal Cemetery.
235 Ramicourt British Cemetery.	296 Bouzincourt Communal Cemetery Extension.
236 Joncourt British Cemetery.	297 Trois-Arbres Cemetery,Steenwerck.
237 Joncourt East British Cemetery.	298 Le Grand Beaumart British Cemetery,Steenwerck.
238 Joncourt Communal Cemetery.	299 St Acheul French National Cemetery,Amiens.
239 Adanac Military Cemetery,Miraumont and Pys.	300 St Pierre Cemetery,Amiens.
241 Ramillies British Cemetery.	303 Longueau British Cemetery.
242 Proville British Cemetery.	304 Camon Communal Cemetery.
244 Neuville-St Remy Churchyard.	306 Bancourt Communal Cemetery.
245 Lebucquiere Communal Cemetery Extension.	307 Bancourt British Cemetery.
246 Blighty Valley Cemetery,Authuile Wood,Authuile and Aveluy.	308 Manchester Cemetery,Riencourt-Les-Bapaume.
	309 Sun Quarry Cemetery,Cherisy.
247 Beacon Cemetery,Sailly-Laurette.	311 Orange Trench Cemetery,Monchy-Le-Preux.
248 St Venant-Robecq Road British Cemetery,Robecq.	312 Happy Valley British Cemetery,Fampoux.

314	Regina Trench Cemetery,Grandcourt.	386	Bazentin-Le-Petit Communal Cemetery.
315	Haspres Coppice Cemetery,Haspres.	387	Bazentin-Le-Petit Communal Cemetery Extension.
316	York Cemetery,Haspres.	388	Bazentin-Le-Petit Military Cemetery.
319	Quievy Communal Cemetery Extension.	389	Thistle Dump Cemetery,High Wood,Longueval.
320	St Hilaire-Les Cambrai British Cemetery.	390	London Cemetery and Extension,High Wood,Longueval.
321	Canonne Farm British Cemetery,Sommaing.	392	Martinpuich British Cemetery.
323	Montrecourt Churchyard.	393	Ovillers Military Cemetery.
324	Meteren Military Cemetery.	394	Citadel New Military Cemetery,Fricourt.
327	Brie British Cemetery.	395	Bray Hill British Cemetery,Bray-Sur-Somme.
328	Ennemain Communal Cemetery Extension.	396	Bray Vale British Cemetery,Bray-Sur-Somme.
329	Bronfay Farm Military Cemetery,Bray-Sur-Somme.	397	Dantzig Alley British Cemetery,Mametz.
330	Devonshire Cemetery,Mametz.	398	Rocquigny-Equancourt Road British Cemetery,Manancourt.
331	Gordon Cemetery,Mametz.	399	Quarry Cemetery,Montauban.
332	Awoingt British Cemetery.	400	Bernafay Wood British Cemetery,Montauban.
333	Awoingt Churchyard.	401	Longueval Road Cemetery.
336	Estourmel Churchyard.	402	Delville Wood Cemetery,Longueval.
337	Carnieres Communal Cemetery Extension.	403	Cambrai East Military Cemetery.
338	Forenville Military Cemetery.	404	Drummond Cemetery,Raillencourt.
339	Ancre British Cemetery,Beaumont-Hamel.	406	Sucrerie Cemetery,Epinoy.
340	Busigny Communal Cemetery.	407	Villers Hill British Cemetery,Villers-Guislain.
341	Busigny Communal Cemetery Extension.	410	Hinges Military Cemetery.
342	Sailly-Au-Bois Military Cemetery.	411	Le Vertannoy British Cemetery,Hinges.
343	Hedauville Communal Cemetery Extension.	412	Mont-Bernenchon British Cemetery,Gonnehem.
344	Mailly-Maillet Communal Cemetery Extension.	413	Mont-Bernenchon Churchyard.
345	Merville Communal Cemetery.	414	Annezin Communal Cemetery.
346	Merville Communal Cemetery Extension.	415	Gouzeaucourt New British Cemetery.
347	Rue-David Military Cemetery,Fleurbaix.	417	Heudicourt Communal Cemetery Extension.
348	Rue-Du-Bois Military Cemetery,Fleurbaix.	418	Beaurains Road Cemetery,Beaurains.
349	White City Cemetery,Bois-Grenier.	419	Achicourt Road Cemetery,Achicourt.
350	Vieux-Berquin Communal Cemetery.	420	Agny Military Cemetery.
352	Aval Wood Military Cemetery,Vieux-Berquin.	421	Vis-En-Artois British Cemetery,Haucourt.
353	Nieppe-Bois (Rue-Du-Bois) British Cemetery,Vieux-Berquin.	423	Vermelles British Cemetery.
		424	Crucifix Corner Cemetery,Villers-Bretonneux.
354	La Gorgue Communal Cemetery.	425	Hangard Communal Cemetery Extension.
355	Lestrem Communal Cemetery.	426	Dury Mill British Cemetery.
356	Calonne-Sur-La-Lys Communal Cemetery.	427	Dury Crucifix Cemetery.
357	Lowrie Cemetery,Havrincourt.	429	Sauchy-Cauchy Communal Cemetery Extension.
358	Grand Ravine British Cemetery,Havrincourt.	430	Albert Communal Cemetery Extension.
359	Ribecourt Railway Cemetery.	432	Caterpillar Valley Cemetery,Longueval.
360	Bouchoir New British Cemetery.	433	Ecoust-St Mein British Cemetery.
363	Villers-Faucon Communal Cemetery.	434	Heninel-Croisilles Road Cemetery.
364	Villeers-Faucon Communal Cemetery Extension.	435	Lagnicourt Hedge Cemetery.
365	Ste Emilie Valley Cemetery,Villers-Faucon.	437	Morchies Australian Cemetery.
366	Jeancourt Communal Cemetery Extension.	438	Morchies Military Cemetery.
368	Epehy Communal Cemetery.	439	Fins New British Cemetery,Sorel-Le-Grand.
369	Epehy Wood Farm Cemetery,Epehy.	441	Premont British Cemetery.
370	Meaulte Military Cemetery.	443	Montbrehain British Cemetery.
372	Fricourt British Cemetery (Bray Road).	444	Calvaire Cemetery,Montbrehain.
373	Fricourt New Military Cemetery.	445	High Tree Cemetery,Montbrehain.
374	Guards' Cemetery,Lesboeufs.	446	Tincourt New British Cemetery.
375	Bellicourt British Cemetery.	448	Aizecourt-Le-Bas Churchyard.
376	Uplands Cemetery,Magny-La-Fosse.	451	Athies Communal Cemetery Extension.
377	Janval Cemetery,Dieppe.	452	Point-Du-Jour Military Cemetery,Athies.
379	Fifteen Ravine British Cemetery,Villers-Plouich.	453	Flatiron Copse Cemetery,Mametz.
380	Delsaux Farm Cemetery,Beugny.	457	City of Paris Cemetery,Pantin.
381	Red Cross Corner Cemetery,Beugny.	461	Levallois-Perret Communal Cemetery.
382	Haplincourt Communal Cemetery.	462	Neuilly-Sur-Seine New Communal Cemetery.
383	Mill Road Cemetery,Thiepval.	473	Les Gonards Cemetery,Versailles.
384	Grandcourt Road Cemetery,Grandcourt.	477	St Germain-En-Laye Old Communal Cemetery.
385	Warlencourt British Cemetery.	480	Aix-Noulette Communal Cemetery Extension.

481 Ontario Cemetery,Sains-Les-Marquion.
482 Triangle Cemetery,Inchy-En-Artois.
484 Moeuvres British Cemetery.
485 Hourges Orchard Cemetery,Domart-Sur-La-Luce.
487 Demuin British Cemetery.
489 Hangard Wood British Cemetery.
490 Gentelles Communal Cemetery.
495 St Venant Communal Cemetery.
496 St Venant Communal Cemetery Extension.
498 Berguette Churchyard.
500 Busnes Communal Cemetery.
501 Berles-Au-Bois Churchyard Extension.
502 Berles New Military Cemetery.
503 Berles Position Military Cemetery.
504 Bellacourt Military Cemetery,Riviere.
505 De Cuisine Ravine British Cemetery,Basseux.
506 Beaumetz-Les-Loges Communal Cemetery.
511 Peronne Communal Cemetery Extension,Ste Radegonde.
512 Grevillers British Cemetery.
513 Carnoy Military Cemetery.
514 Queens Cemetery,Bucquoy.
515 Becourt Military Cemetery,Becordel-Becourt.
516 Bouzincourt Ridge Cemetery,Albert.
517 Achiet-Le-Grand Communal Cemetery.
518 Achiet-Le-Grand Communal Cemetery Extension.
521 Cross Roads Cemetery,Fontaine-Au-Bois.
522 Thelus Military Cemetery.
523 Nine Elms Military Cemetery,Thelus.
524 Raperie British Cemetery,Villemontoire.
525 Rue-Petillon Military Cemetery.
526 Heath Cemetery,Harbonnieres.
527 Roisel Communal Cemetery.
528 Roisel Communal Cemetery Extension.
529 Hermies British Cemetery.
530 Hermies Hill British Cemetery.
531 Feuchy Chapel British Cemetery,Wancourt.
532 Tigris Lane Cemetery,Wancourt.
533 Frankfurt Trench British Cemetery,Beaumont-Hamel.
534 New Munich Trench British Cemetery,Beaumont-Hamel.
535 Stump Road Cemetery,Grandcourt.
536 Guemappe British Cemetery,Wancourt.
537 Tank Cemetery,Guemappe.
538 Heninel Communal Cemetery Extension.
539 Bootham Cemetery,Heninel.
540 Cherisy Road East Cemetery,Heninel.
541 Rookery British Cemetery,Heninel.
543 Vis-En-Artois Communal Cemetery.
544 Fampoux British Cemetery.
545 Level Crossing Cemetery,Fampoux.
546 Crump Trench British Cemetery,Fampoux.
547 Sucrerie Cemetery,Ablain-St Nazaire.
548 Givenchy-En-Gohelle Canadian Cemetery,Souchez.
549 Zouave Valley Cemetery,Souchez.
550 Loos British Cemetery.
551 St Patrick's Cemetery,Loos.
552 Bois-Carre Military Cemetery,Haisnes.
553 Ninth Avenue Cemetery,Haisnes.
554 Fosse 7 Military Cemetery (Quality Street),Mazingarbe.
557 Lievin Communal Cemetery Extension.
558 Bois-De-Noulette British Cemetery,Aix-Noulette.
559 Tranchee De Mecknes Cemetery,Aix-Noulette.
560 Beaulencourt British Cemetery,Ligny-Thilloy.
561 Beugnatre Communal Cemetery.
562 Barastre Communal Cemetery.
563 Favreuil British Cemetery.
564 Bapaume Australian Cemetery.
566 Le Trou Aid Post Cemetery,Fleurbaix.
567 Aubers Ridge British Cemetery,Aubers.
568 H.A.C. Cemetery,Ecoust-St Mein.
570 Fosse No.10 Communal Cemetery Extension,Sains-En-Gohelle.
571 Beuvry Communal Cemetery.
572 Beuvry Communal Cemetery Extension.
573 Quatre-Vents Military Cemetery,Estree-Cauchy.
576 Gommecourt Wood New Cemetery,Foncquevillers.
577 Bucquoy Communal Cemetery.
578 Bucquoy Communal Cemetery Extension.
579 Shrine Cemetery,Bucquoy.
580 Owl Trench Cemetery,Hebuterne.
581 Tilloy British Cemetery,Tilloy-Les-Mofflaines.
582 Cayeux Communal Cemetery.
583 Cayeux Military Cemetery.
585 Le Quesnel Communal Cemetery Extension.
586 Hillside Cemetery,Le Quesnel.
587 Mezieres Communal Cemetery Extension.
588 Beaucourt-En-Santerre Churchyard.
589 Beaucourt British Cemetery.
591 Cojeul British Cemetery,St Martin-Sur-Cojeul.
592 St Martin Calvaire British Cemetery,St Martin-Sur-Cojeul.
593 Boyelles Communal Cemetery Extension.
594 Hibers Trench Cemetery,Wancourt.
595 Neuville-Vitasse Road Cemetery,Neuville-Vitasse.
596 Henin Crucifix Cemetery.
597 Sancourt British Cemetery.
598 Porte-De-Paris Cemetery,Cambrai.
602 Cantaing British Cemetery.
604 Brown's Copse Cemetery,Roeux.
605 Pargny British Cemetery.
609 Voyennes Communal Cemetery.
610 Nesle Communal Cemetery.
611 Naves Communal Cemetery Extension.
612 Wellington Cemetery,Rieux-En-Cambresis.
613 Villers-En-Cauchies Communal Cemetery.
614 Mory Abbey Military Cemetery,Mory.
615 Mory Street Military Cemetery,St Leger.
616 St Leger British Cemetery.
617 Gomiecourt South Cemetery.
618 Railway Cutting Cemetery,Courcelles-Le-Comte.
619 Warry Copse Cemetery,Courcelles-Le-Comte.
620 Ervillers Military Cemetery.
622 Marfaux British Cemetery.
624 Hem Farm Military Cemetery,Hem-Monacu.
625 Suzanne Communal Cemetery Extension.
626 Suzanne Military Cemetery No.3
629 Frise Communal Cemetery.
630 Peronne Road Cemetery,Maricourt.
631 St Vaast Post Military Cemetery, Richebourg-L'Avoue.
632 Rue-Des-Berceaux Military Cemetery, Richebourg-L'Avoue.
633 Morlancourt British Cemetery No.1

634	Morlancourt British Cemetery No.2,Ville-Sur-Ancre.
636	Ville-Sur-Ancre Communal Cemetery Extension.
637	Point 110 Old Military Cemetery,Fricourt.
638	Point 110 New Military Cemetery,Fricourt.
639	Chipilly Communal Cemetery.
643	Sucrerie Military Cemetery,Colincamps.
644	Bailleul Road East Cemetery,St Laurent-Blangy.
645	Bailleul Road West Cemetery,St Laurent-Blangy.
646	Queant Road Cemetery,Buissy.
647	Cagnicourt British Cemetery.
648	Rosieres Communal Cemetery.
649	Rosieres Communal Cemetery Extension.
650	Rosieres British Cemetery,Vauvillers.
651	Caix Communal Cemetery.
652	Caix British Cemetery.
657	Caudry Old Communal Cemetery.
658	Caudry British Cemetery.
660	Honnechy British Cemetery.
661	Inchy Communal Cemetery Extension.
662	Metz-En-Couture Communal Cemetery British Extension.
663	Targelle Ravine British Cemetery,Villers-Guislain.
664	Villers-Guislain Communal Cemetery.
665	Pigeon Ravine Cemetery,Epehy.
666	Domino British Cemetery,Epehy.
667	Villers-Plouich Communal Cemetery.
668	Sunken Road Cemetery,Villers-Plouich.
669	Saulcourt Churchyard Extension,Guyencourt-Saulcourt.
672	Savy British Cemetery.
673	Marteville Communal Cemetery,Attilly.
674	Vermand Communal Cemetery.
675	Roupy Communal Cemetery.
680	"X" Farm Cemetery,La Chapelle-D'Armentieres.
681	Chapelle-D'Armentieres Old Military Cemetery.
682	Chapelle-D'Armentieres New Military Cemetery.
683	La Chapelle-D'Armentieres Communal Cemetery.
684	Bois-Grenier Communal Cemetery.
685	Suffolk Cemetery,La Rolanderie Farm,Erquinghem-Lys.
686	Queant Communal Cemetery British Extension.
687	Dominion Cemetery,Hendecourt-Les-Cagnicourt.
689	Croisilles Railway Cemetery.
690	Ecoust Military Cemetery,Ecoust-St Mein.
692	Fouquescourt British Cemetery.
694	Vrely Communal Cemetery Extension.
699	Cerisy-Gailly Military Cemetery.
700	Cerisy-Gailly French National Cemetery.
701	Hamel Military Cemetery,Beaumont-Hamel.
702	Authuile Military Cemetery.
703	Contalmaison Chateau Cemetery.
704	Senlis Communal Cemetery Extension.
705	Pont-Du-Hem Military Cemetery,La Gorgue.
706	Royal Irish Rifles Graveyard,Laventie.
707	Rue-Du-Bacquerot (13th London) Graveyard,Laventie.
708	Euston Post Cemetery,Laventie.
709	Neuve-Chapelle British Cemetery.
710	Neuve-Chapelle Farm Cemetery.
711	Ribecourt British Cemetery.
712	Ribecourt Road Cemetery,Trescault.
713	Trescault Communal Cemetery.
714	Quarry Wood Cemetery,Sains-Les-Marquion.
716	Le Cateau Military Cemetery.
717	Le Cateau Communal Cemetery.
718	Selridge British Cemetery,Montay.
720	Cuinchy Communal Cemetery.
721	Woburn Abbey Cemetery,Cuinchy.
725	Vadencourt British Cemetery,Maissemy.
727	Le Touret Military Cemetery,Richebourg-L'Avoue.
728	Highland Cemetery,Roclincourt.
729	Mindel Trench British Cemetery,St Laurent-Blangy.
730	Hervin Farm British Cemetery,St Laurent-Blangy.
731	Bunyans Cemetery,Tilloy-Les-Mofflaines.
733	Ghissignies British Cemetery.
734	Englefontaine Churchyard.
735	Englefontaine British Cemetery.
737	Poix-Du-Nord Communal Cemetery Extension.
738	Preux-Au-Bois Communal Cemetery.
739	Bermerain Communal Cemetery.
742	Serre Road Cemetery No.1,Beaumont-Hamel,Hebuterne and Puisieux.
743	Serre Road Cemetery No.3,Puisieux.
744	A.I.F. Burial Ground,Grass Lane,Flers.
745	Bienvillers Military Cemetery.
747	Humbercamps Communal Cemetery Extension.
748	Bailleulmont Communal Cemetery.
749	Barly French Military Cemetery.
755	Ruyaulcourt Military Cemetery.
756	Beaumetz Cross Roads Cemetery,Beaumetz-Les-Cambrai.
757	Beaumetz-Les-Cambrai Military Cemetery No.1
758	Bertincourt Chateau British Cemetery.
759	Louverval Military Cemetery,Doignies.
760	Iwuy Communal Cemetery.
761	Niagara Cemetery,Iwuy.
765	Gorre British Cemetery,Beuvry.
768	Estaires Communal Cemetery.
769	Estaires Communal Cemetery Extension.
770	Blargies Communal Cemetery Extension.
772	Forges-Les-Eaux Communal Cemetery.
777	Orchard Dump Cemetery,Arleux-En-Gohelle.
779	Lens Communal Cemetery,Sallaumines.
782	Billy-Montigny Communal Cemetery.
783	Izel-Les-Equerchin Communal Cemetery.
785	Combles Communal Cemetery Extension.
786	Guards' Cemetery,Combles.
787	St Pol Communal Cemetery Extension.
788	St Pol British Cemetery,St Pol-Sur-Ternoise.
790	Hesdin Communal Cemetery.
792	Huby-St Leu British Cemetery.
795	St Georges Churchyard.
798	Gommecourt British Cemetery No.2,Hebuterne.
800	Rossignol Wood Cemetery,Hebuterne.
801	Luke Copse British Cemetery,Puisieux.
802	Queens Cemetery,Puisieux.
803	Ten Tree Alley Cemetery,Puisieux.
804	Quesnoy Farm Military Cemetery,Bucquoy.
805	Fienvillers British Cemetery.
806	Pont-Remy British Cemetery.
808	St Ouen Communal Cemetery.
813	Bonneville Communal Cemetery.
816	Conde-Folie Communal Cemetery.
817	Coulonvillers Communal Cemetery.
818	Cramont Communal Cemetery.

832	Pozieres British Cemetery,Ovillers-La Boisselle.	932	Landrecies Communal Cemetery.
833	Heilly Station Cemetery,Mericourt-L'Abbe.	933	Landrecies British Cemetery.
834	Caulaincourt Communal Cemetery.	934	Hautmont Communal Cemetery.
835	Trefcon British Cemetery,Caulaincourt.	935	Berlaimont Communal Cemetery.
836	Hancourt British Cemetery.	936	Berlaimont Communal Cemetery Extension.
837	Beaumetz Communal Cemetery.	937	Pont-Sur-Sambre Communal Cemetery.
839	Mons-En-Chaussee Communal Cemetery.	938	Sebourg British Cemetery.
840	Tertry Communal Cemetery.	939	Sebourg Communal Cemetery.
841	Vraignes Communal Cemetery.	940	Ors British Cemetery.
844	Beaurevoir British Cemetery.	941	Aulnoye Communal Cemetery.
845	Guizancourt Farm Cemetery,Gouy.	943	Grand-Fyat Communal Cemetery.
846	Serain Communal Cemetery Extension.	944	Maroilles Communal Cemetery.
847	Fresnoy-Le-Grand Communal Cemetery Extension.	948	Bermeries Communal Cemetery.
848	Brancourt-Le-Grand Communal Cemetery.	949	Brttrechies Communal Cemetery.
849	Brancourt-Le-Grand Military Cemetery.	952	Ecuelin Churchyard.
855	Bertenacre Military Cemetery,Fletre.	953	Eth Communal Cemetery.
856	Mont-Noir Military Cemetery,St Jans-Cappel.	954	Feignies Communal Cemetery.
857	Borre Churchyard.	955	Gommegnies Communal Cemetery.
858	Caestre Communal Cemetery.	957	Hargnies Communal Cemetery.
860	Hondeghem Churchyard.	963	Leval Communal Cemetery.
861	La Creche Communal Cemetery,Bailleul.	965	Malplaquet Communal Cemetery,Taisnieres-Sur-Hon.
864	Vauxbuin French National Cemetery.	968	Monceau-St Waast Communal Cemetery.
865	Buzancy Military Cemetery.	978	St Remy-Chaussee Communal Cemetery.
866	Oulchy-Le-Chateau Churchyard Extension.	979	St Waast-La-Vallee Communal Cemetery.
867	Crouy-Vauxrot French National Cemetery,Crouy.	981	Semousies Churchyard.
870	Chacrise Communal Cemetery.	982	Taisnieres-En-Thierache Communal Cemetery.
874	Ste Marguerite Churchyard.	984	Wargnies-Le-Grand Churchyard.
878	Villemontoire Communal Cemetery.	985	Wargnies-Le-Petit Communal Cemetery.
879	Boves East Communal Cemetery.	987	Roye New British Cemetery.
880	Boves West Communal Cemetery.	988	Moreuil Communal Cemetery Allied Extension.
881	Boves West Communal Cemetery Extension.	1003	Hailles Communal Cemetery.
882	Allonville Communal Cemetery.	1008	Rouvrel Communal Cemetery.
885	Frechencourt Communal Cemetery.	1012	Englebelmer Communal Cemetery.
886	Bavelincourt Communal Cemetery.	1013	Englebelmer Communal Cemetery Extension.
887	Montigny Communal Cemetery (Somme).	1014	St Amand British Cemetery.
888	Montigny Communal Cemetery Extension (Somme).	1016	Henu Churchyard.
889	Blangy-Tronville Communal Cemetery.	1017	Mondicourt Communal Cemetery.
891	Bertangles Communal Cemetery.	1022	Ignaucourt Churchyard.
904	Neuville-Bourjonval Communal Cemetery.	1027	Lille Southern Cemetery.
905	Neuville-Bourjonval British Cemetery.	1028	St Andre Communal Cemetery.
906	Five Points Cemetery,Lechelle.	1029	Tourcoing (Pont-Neuville) Communal Cemetery.
907	Ytres Communal Cemetery.	1030	Ascq Communal Cemetery.
908	Manancourt Communal Cemetery.	1031	Halluin Communal Cemetery.
910	Marcoing Communal Cemetery.	1032	Linselles Communal Cemetery.
911	Marcoing British Cemetery.	1033	Fretin Communal Cemetery.
912	Masnieres British Cemetery,Marcoing.	1034	Cretinier Cemetery,Wattrelos.
913	Noyelles-Sur-L'Escaut Communal Cemetery.	1039	Bousbecques Communal Cemetery.
914	Noyelles-Sur-L'Escaut Communal Cemetery Extension.	1040	Camphin-en-Pevele Communal Cemetery.
915	Rumilly Communal Cemetery Extension.	1041	Criox Communal Cemetery.
916	Cagnoncles Communal Cemetery.	1042	Genech Communal Cemetery.
920	Niergnies Communal Cemetery.	1044	hem Communal Cemetery.
921	Le Bizet Cemetery,Armentieres.	1049	Mouvaux New Comunal Cemetery.
922	Cite Bonjean Military Cemetery,Armentieres.	1050	Neuville-En-Ferrain Communal Cemetery.
924	Cabaret-Rouge British Cemetery.Souchez.	1054	Sailly-Les-Lannoy Churchyard.
925	Ayette British Cemetery.	1056	Templeuve Communal Cemetery.
927	Douchy-Les-Ayette British Cemetery.	1058	Willems Communal Cemetery.
928	Avesnes-Sur-Helpe Communal Cemetery.	1059	Arras Road Cemetery,Roclincourt.
929	Fontaine-Au-Bois Communal Cemetery.	1061	Grand-Seraucourt British Cemetery.
930	Dourlers Communal Cemetery Extension.	1063	Noyon New British Cemetery.
931	Maubeuge (Sous-Le-Bois) Cemetery.	1065	Thiescourt French National Cemetery.

1066 Montescourt-Lizerolles Communal Cemetery.	1201 Villers-au-Tertre Communal Cemetery.
1071 Blerancourt Communal Cemetery.	1202 Ham Communal Cemetery.
1074 Jussy Communal Cemetery.	1203 Ham British Cematery, Muille-Villette.
1076 Le Quesnoy Communal Cemetery.	1204 Foreste Communal Cemetery.
1078 Preseau Communal Cemetery.	1205 Douilly Communal Cemetery.
1079 Preseau Communal Cemetery Extension.	1206 Eppeville Churchyard.
1080 Villers-Pol Communal Cemetery Extension.	1211 Maubeuge-Centre Cemetery.
1081 Ruesnes Communal Cemetery.	1216 Sains-Du-Nord Communal Cemetery.
1082 Capelle-Beaudignies Road Cemetery, Capelle.	1219 Floursies Churchyard.
1084 Artres Communal Cemetery.	1223 Solre-Le-Chateau Communal Cemetery.
1085 Curgies Communal Cemetery.	1225 Senlis French National Cemetery.
1087 Maresches Communal Cemetery.	1227 Compiegne South Communal Cemetery.
1091 Steenwerck Communal Cemetery.	1228 Royallieu French National Cemetery, Compiegne.
1092 Croix-Du-Bac British Cemetery, Steenwerck.	1230 Verberie French National Cemetery.
1094 Haverskerque British Cemetery.	1231 Nery Communal Cemetery.
1095 Laventie Communal Cemetery.	1232 Beauvais Communal Cemetery.
1100 Steenbecque Churchyard.	1233 Marissel French National Cemetery.
1106 Vieille-Chapelle New Military Cemetery, Lacouture.	1234 Dompierre French National Cemetery.
1107 Vailly British Cemetery.	1235 Vignemont French National Cemetery.
1108 Guards' Grave, Villers-Cotterets Forest.	1236 Annel Communal Cemetery, Longueil-Annel.
1110 Braine Communal Cemetery.	1242 Hardivillers Communal Cemetery.
1111 Soupir Churchyard.	1252 Denain Communal Cemetery.
1112 Soupir Communal Cemetery.	1254 Famars Communal Cemetery Extension.
1113 Montreuil-Aux-Lions British Cemetery.	1256 Maing Communal Cemetery extension.
1117 Bezu-Le-Guery Communal Cemetery.	1257 Qucrenaing Communal Cemetery.
1128 Gandelu Communal Cemetery.	1258 Thiant Communal Cemetery.
1129 Haramont Communal Cemetery.	1259 Vendegies Cross Roads British Cemetery, Bermerain.
1134 Priez Communal Cemetery.	1260 Verchain British Cemetery, Verchain-Maugre.
1139 Vieil-Arcy Communal Cemetery.	1266 St Souplet British Cemetery.
1140 Houplines Communal Cemetery Extension.	1268 Vaux-Andigny British Cemetery.
1141 Ferme Buterne Military Cemetery, Houplines.	1269 La Vallee-Mulatre Communal Cemetery.
1142 Valenciennes (St Roch) Communal Cemetery.	1270 La Vallee-Mulatre Communal Cemetery Extension.
1144 Raismes Communal Cemetery.	1271 Wassigny Communal Cemetery.
1147 Bruille-St Amand Churchyard.	1272 Le Rejet-De-Beaulieu Communal Cemetery.
1154 Thivencelle Churchyard.	1274 St Benin Communal Cemetery (Nord).
1157 Rue-Du-Bacquerot No.1 Military Cemetery, Laventie.	1276 Douai Communal Cemetery.
1158 Fauquissart Military Cemetery, Laventie.	1277 Douai British Cemetery, Cuincy.
1159 Quesnoy-Sur-Deule Communal Cemetery.	1278 Brebieres British Cemetery.
1160 Quesnoy-Sur-Deule Communal Cemetery, German Extension.	1279 Annoeullin Communal Cemetery German Extension.
1161 Isbergues Communal Cemetery.	1280 Abscon Communal Cemetery.
1169 St Hilaire-Cottes Churchyard.	1281 Arleux-Du-Nord Communal Cemetery.
1170 Villers-Bretonneux Military Cemetery, Fouilloy.	1284 Auby Communal Cemetery.
1172 Fouilloy Communal Cemetery.	1285 Auchy Churchyard.
1173 Aubigny British Cemetery (Somme).	1287 Brillon Communal Cemetery.
1180 Neufchatel Churchyard.	1290 Flers-en-Escrebieux Communal Cemetery.
1182 Faubourg-D'Amiens Cemetery, Arras.	1293 Hem-Lenglet Communal Cemetery.
1183 Boisleux-Au-Mont Communal Cemetery.	1295 Lallaing Communal Cemetery.
1184 Sunken Road Cemetery, Boisleux St Marc.	1296 Lecelles Churchyard.
1185 London Cemetery, Neuville-Vitasse.	1301 Paillencourt Churchyard.
1186 Henin Communal Cemetery Extension.	1307 Sin-le-Noble Communal Cemetery.
1187 Summit Trench Cemetery, Croisilles.	1308 Somain Communal Cemetery.
1188 Feuchy British Cemetery.	1310 Beaumont Communal Cemetery.
1190 Sunken Road Cemetery, Fampoux.	1311 Corbehem Communal Cemetery.
1191 Albuera Cemetery, Bailleul-Sire-Berthoult.	1312 Courrieres Communal Cemetery.
1192 Naval Trench Cemetery, Gavrelle.	1314 Noyelles-Godault Communal Cemetery.
1193 Chili Trench Cemetery, Gavrelle.	1316 Quiery-La-Motte Communal Cemetery.
1194 Roeux British Cemetery.	1321 Bois-Carre British Cemetery, Thelus.
1196 Auberchicourt British Cemetery.	1325 Vimy Communal Cemetery, Farbus.
1198 Masny Churchyard.	1326 Hebuterne Communal Cemetery.
	1327 Hebuterne Military Cemetery.

1328 Vendresse Churchyard.
1329 Vendresse British Cemetery.
1331 hermonville Military Cemetery.
1332 Jonchery-Sur-Vesle British Cemetery.
1333 Beaurepaire French National Cemetery,Pontavert.
1334 Berry-au-Bac French National Cemetery.
1337 Longueval Communal Cemetery.
1339 Bourg-Et-Comin Communal Cemetery.
1340 Moulins Churchyard.
1341 Moulins New Communal Cemetery.
1342 Paissy Churchyard.
1345 Bois-Des-Angles British Cemetery,Crevecoeur-Sur-L'Escaut.
1346 Moulin-De-Pierre British Cemetery,Villeers-Outreau.
1347 Esnes Communal Cemetery.
1348 Fontaine-Au-Pire Communal Cemetery.
1349 Ligny-En-Cambresis Communal Cemetery.
1350 Haucourt Communal Cemetery.
1351 Becquigny Communal Cemetery.
1352 Escaufort Communal Cemetery.
1354 Selvigny Communal Cemetery.
1355 Wambaix Communal Cemetery.
1357 Bleue-Maison Military Cemetery,Eperlecques.
1358 Croix-Rouge Military Cemetery,Quaedypre.
1359 Dunkerque Town Cemetery.
1360 Malo-Les-Bains Communal Cemetery.
1361 Zuydcoote Military Cemetery.
1364 Buysscheure Churchyard.
1366 Houtkerque Churchyard.
1367 Ledeerzeele Churchyard.
1369 Steenvorde Communal Cemetery.
1372 Wormhoudt Communal Cemetery.
1374 Audruicq Churchyard.
1386 Quietiste Military Cemetery,Le Cateau.
1387 Beauvois-En-Cambresis Communal Cemetery.
1388 Bethencourt Communal Cemetery.
1390 Bevillers Communal Cemetery.
1391 Bertry Communal Cemetery.
1392 Maurois Communal Cemetery.
1393 Montigny Communal Cemetery (Nord).
1394 Reumont Churchyard.
1395 Troisvilles Communal Cemetery.
1396 Viesly Communal Cemetery.
1402 Nesles-La-Gilberde Communal Cemetery.
1404 Mailly-Le-Camp French Cemetery.
1410 Dormans French National Cemetery.
1415 Sezanne Communal Cemetery.
1416 Soulieres Churchyard.
1420 Baron Communal Cemetery.
1421 Catenoy French National Cemetery.
1422 Creil Communal Cemetery.
1425 Bassevelle Churchyard.
1426 Bellot Communal Cemetery.
1429 Coulommieers Communal Cemetery.
1432 Fretoy Communal Cemetery.
1436 La Haute-Maison,Ferme Des Arceries.
1438 Meaux Communal Cemetery.
1439 Melun North Cemetery.
1440 Montereau Communal Cemetery.
1441 Nangis Communal Cemetery.

1443 Orly-Sur-Morin Communal Cemetery.
1445 Perreuse Chateau French National Cemetery,Signy-Signets.
1451 Sablonnieres New Communal Cemetery.
1461 Hargicourt British Cemetery.
1462 Hargicourt Communal Cemetery Extension.
1463 Ronssoy Communal Cemetery.
1464 Villeret Churchyard.
1465 Hesbecourt Communal Cemetery.
1467 Somme American Cemetery,Bony.
1468 La Chapelette British Cemetery,Peronne.
1472 Assevillers New British Cemetery.
1473 Foucaucourt Communal Cemetery.
1475 Vendegies-Au-Bois British Cemetery.
1476 Amerval Communal Cemetery Extension,Solesmes.
1477 Ovillers New Communal Cemetery,Solesmes.
1478 Forest Communal Cemetery (Nord).
1479 Ors Communal Cemetery.
1480 Beaurain British Cemetery.
1482 Bousies Communal Cemetery.
1483 Flesquieres Hill British Cemetery.
1484 Vaulx Hill Cemetery,Vaulx-Vraucourt.
1485 Vaux Australian Field Ambulance Cemetery,Vaulx-Vraucourt.
1486 Vraucourt Copse Cemetery,Vaulx-Vraucourt.
1487 L'Homme Mort British Cemetery,Ecoust-St Mein.
1488 Noreuil Australian Cemetery.
1489 Croisilles British Cemetery.
1490 "Y" Ravine Cemetery,Beaumont-Hamel.
1491 Redan Ridge Cemetery No.1,Beaumont-Hamel.
1492 Redan Ridge Cemetery No.2,Beaumont-Hamel.
1494 Templeux-Le-Guerard Communal Cemetery Extension.
1495 Templeux-Le-Guerard British Cemetery.
1496 Moeuvres Communal Cemetery Extension.
1497 Sanders Keep Military Cemetery,Graincourt-Les-Havrincourt.
1498 Orival Wood Cemetery,Flesquieres.
1499 Demicourt Communal Cemetery,Boursies.
1500 Hawthorn Ridge Cemetery No.1,Auchon-Villers.
1501 Hawthorn Ridge Cemetery No.2,Auchon-Villers.
1502 Hunter's Cemetery,Beaumont-Hamel.
1504 Miraumont Communal Cemetery.
1512 Fillievres British Cemetery.
1525 Wavans British Cemetery.
1545 Doudelainville Communal Cemetery.
1553 Le Crotoy Communal Cemetery.
1564 Quend Communal Cemetery.
1568 Vaux-En-Amienois Communal Cemetery.
1571 Mazargues Cemetery Extension.
1586 Fruges Communal Cemetery.
1597 Rimboval Churchyard.
1615 Rethel French National Cemetery.
1630 Ingwiller Communal Cemetery.
1632 Plaine French National Cemetery.
1633 Roppenheim Communal Cemetery.
1643 Neuf-Brisach Communal Cemetery.
1644 Arnaville Churchyard.
1649 Joeuf Communal Cemetery.
1658 Commercy French National Cemetery.
1660 Latour-en-Woevre Communal Cemetery.

1662 Antilly Churchyard.
1664 Ars-sur-Moselle Churchyard.
1667 Chambieres French National (Mixed) Cemetery,Metz.
1671 Moulin-les-Metz Communal Cemetery.
1672 Rechicourt-le-Chateau Communal Cemetery.
1674 Ste Ruffine Communal Cemetery.
1675 Sarralbe Military Cemetery.
1678 Charmes Military Cemetery,Essegny.
1689 Chambrecy British Cemetery.
1690 Courmas British Cemetery.
1693 Epernay French National Cemetery.
1695 La Neuville-Aux-Larris Military Cemetery.
1697 St Imoge Churchyard.
1699 Vandieres Churchyard.
1700 Berthaucouer Communal Cemetery,Pontru.
1701 Chapelle British Cemetery,Holnon.
1703 Guise (La Desolation) French National Cemetery,Flavigny-Le-Petit.
1704 La Baraque British Cemetery,Bellenglise.
1706 Levergies Communal Cemetery.
1707 Ribemont Communal Cemetery.
1710 Sequehart British Cemetery No.1
1712 Brissay-Choigny Churchyard.
1715 Moy-De-L'Aisne Communal Cemetery.
1717 Sery-Les-Mezieres Communal Cemetery.
1723 St Mary's A.D.S. Cemetery,Haisnes.
1724 Carvin Communal Cemetery.
1725 Don Communal Cemetery.Annoeullin.
1726 Phalempin Communal Cemetery.
1727 Rumaucourt Communal Cemetery.
1730 Wicres Churchyard.
1732 Santes Churchyard.
1737 Estevelles Communal Cemetery.
1744 Monchy-Breton Churchyard.
1745 Nedonchel Churchyard.
1749 Sauchy-Lestree Communal Cemetery.
1751 Etreux British Cemetery.
1752 Etreux Communal Cemetery.
1753 La Ville-Aux-Bois British Cemetery.
1754 St Erme Communal Cemetery Extension.
1755 Sissonne British Cemetery.
1760 Esqueheries Communal Cemetery.
1766 Etroeungt Communal Cemetery.
1775 Nice (Caucade) British Civil Cemetery.
1776 Nice (Caucade) Communal Cemetery.
1778 Troyes Town Cemetery.
1779 Gruissan Communal Cemetery.
1783 Senas Communal Cemetery.
1787 Courban RAF Cemetery.
1788 Dijon (Les Pejoces) Cemetery.
1798 Conches-En-Ouche Communal Cemetery.
1799 Evreux Communal Cemetery.
1805 Maintenon Communal Cemetery.
1808 Guilvinec Communal Cemetery.
1822 Talence Communal Cemetery.
1826 Luxeuil Communal Cemetery.
1830 Champagnole Communal Cemetery.
1839 St Nazaire (Toutes-Aides) Cemetery.
1841 Orleans Main Cemetery.
1844 Vendome Town Cemetery.

1845 Angers West Cemetery.
1848 Tourlaville Communal Cemetery.
1849 Tourlaville Communal Cemetery Extension.
1856 Lyon (La Guillotiere) Old Communal Cemetery.
1858 St Germain-Au-Mont-D'Or Communal Cemetery Extension.
1862 Le Mans West Cemetery.
1866 Asnieres-Sur-Oise Communal Cemetery.
1868 Louvres Communal Cemetery.
1886 Monaco Principality Cemetery,La Condamine.
1887 Laventie Military Cemetery.
1888 Haubourdin Communal Cemetery.
1890 Serre Road Cemetery No.2,Beaumont-Hamel and Hebuterne.
1891 Thiepval Anglo-French Cemetery,Authuile.
1893 Chauny Communal Cemetery British Extension.
1894 Montcornet Military Cemetery.
1896 Canadian Cemetery No.2,Neuville-St Vaast.

GALLIPOLI.
1   Lancashire Landing Cemetery,Helles.
2   Redoubt Cemetery,Helles.
3   Pink Farm Cemetery,Helles.
4   Azmak Cemetery,Sulva.
5   Green Hill Cemetery,Sulva.
6   Twelve Tree Copse Cemetery,Helles.
7   Lone Pine Cemetery,Anzac.
13 The Farm Cemetery,Anzac.
14 Skew Bridge Cemetery,Helles.
15 "V" Beach Cemetery,Helles.
17 7th Field Ambulance Cemetery,Anzac.
18 Embarkation Pier Cemetery,Anzac.
19 No.2 Outpost Cemetery,Anzac.
20 New Zealand No.2 Outpost Cemetery,Anzac.
26 Lala Baba Cemetery,Sulva.
27 Hill 10 Cemetery,Sulva.
29 Ari Burnu Cemetery,Anzac.
30 Beach Cemetery,Anzac.
31 Shrapnel Valley Cemetery,Anzac.

GERMANY.
1   Cologne Southern Cemetery.
2   Hamburg Cemetery,Ohlsdorf.
3   Niederzwehren Cemetery,Cassel.
4   Berlin South-Western Cemetery,Stahnsdorf.
5   Aachen Military Cemetery.
9   Coblenz Jewish Cemetery.

GREECE.
1   Sarigol Military Cemetery.
2   Kirechkoi-Hortakoi Military Cemetery.
3   Struma Military Cemetery.
4   Lahana Military Cemetery.
5   Doiran Military Cemetery.
6   Karasouli Military Cemetery.
7   Salonika Anglo-French Military Cemetery, Lembet Road.
8   Salonika Protestant Cemetery.
9   Mikra British Cemetery,Salonika.

10 East Mudros Military Cemetery, Lemnos.
11 Portianos Military Cemetery, West Mudros, Lemnos.
14 Syra New British Cemetery.
16 Suda Bay War Cemetery, Crete.
17 Corfu British Cemetery.
18 Bralo British Cemetery.
19 Dedeagatch British Cemetery.
21 Athens New Protestant Cemetery.
23 Volo Municipal Cemetery.

INDIA.
48 Delhi War Cemetery.
97a Calcutta (Bhowanipore) Cemetery.
164 Madras (St Mary's) Cemetery.

IRAQ.
1 Kut War Cemetery.
5 Amara War Cemetery.
6 Basra War Cemetery.
8 Baghdad (North Gate) War Cemetery.
9 Baghdad East Jewish Cemetery.

ITALY.
1 Barenthal Military Cemetery.
2 Boscon British Cemetery.
3 Magnaboschi British Cemetery.
4 Granezza British Cemetery.
5 Cavalletto British Cemetery.
6 Taranto Town Cemetery Extension.
7 Giavera British Cemetery.
8 Memorial to the Missing, Giavera British Cemetery.
9 Tezze British Cemetery, Vazzola.
10 Dueville Communal Cemetery Extension.
11 Montecchio Precalcino Communal Cemetery Extension.
12 Staglieno Cemetery, Genoa.
13 Savona Town Cemetery.
14 Savona Memorial.
15 Arquata Scrivia Communal Cemetery Extension.
16 Bordighera British Cemetery.
17 Bari War Cemetery.
19 Faenza Communal Cemetery.
24 Carloforte Communal Cemetery.
29 Foggia Communal Cemetery.
35 Porto Empedocle Communal Cemetery.
37 Otranto Town Cemetery.
42 Messine Town Cemetery.
45 Carmignano Di Brenta Communal Cemetery.
48 Padua Main Cemetery.
56 Oneglia Town Cemetery.
57 San Remo Town Cemetery.
59 Testaccio Protestant Cemetery, Rome.
61 Syracuse Communal Cemetery.
65 Turin Town Cemetery.
71 Mattarello Communal Cemetery.
72 Romagnano Communal Cemetery.
74 Altivole Communal Cemetery.
75 Conegliano (San Giuseppe) Communal Cemetery.
76 Falze Communal Cemetery, Trevignano.
80 Corva Cemetery.
81 Fontanafredda Communal Cemetery.
83 Venice (San Michele) Cemetery.

LEBANON.
1 Beirut British War Cemetery.

NEW ZEALAND.
1 Addington Cemetery.
8 Blenheim (Omaka) Public Cemetery.
10 Bromley General Cemetery.
32 Linwood Cemetery.
40 Nelson Cemetery.
53 Sydenham Cemetery.
61 Waimairi Cemetery.
68A The Canterbury Memorial.
77 Dunedin Eastern Necropolis Public Cemetery.
78 Dunedin Eastern Necropolis Soldiers' Cemetery.
79 Dunedin Northern Cemetery.
80 Dunedin Southern Cemetery.
88 Invercargill Eastern Soldiers' Cemetery.
117 Warrington Cemetery.
134 Epsom (St Andrew) Churchyard.
184 Otahuhu Public Cemetery.
194 Purewa Cemetery.
200 Ruatoki North (Otenuku) Native Burial Ground.
209 Te Awamutu Cemetery.
224 Waikaraka Cemetery.
225 Waikumete Public Cemetery, Glen Eden.
226 Waikumete Soldiers' Cemetery, Glen Eden.
232 Whakatane Cemetery.
238A The Auckland Memorial.
239 Aramoho Public Cemetery.
242 Eltham Cemetery.
243 Featherston Soldiers' Cemetery.
245 Foxton Cemetery.
251 Hastings Cemetery.
253 Hawera Cemetery.
257 Karori Great War Memorial Cemetery.
258 Karori Public Cemetery.
265 Mangatera Cemetery.
271 Masterton Cemetery.
275 Napier (Park Island) Cemetery.
291 Raetihi Cemetery.
320 Suva Cemetery, Fiji.

NEWFOUNDLAND.
59 St John's Church of England Cemetery.

PAKISTAN.
50a Rawalpindi War Cemetery.

PALESTINE or ISRAEL.
1 Beersheba War Cemetery.
2 Deir El Belah War Cemetery.
3 Jerusalem War Cemetery.
5 Jerusalem Protestant Cemetery, Mount Zion.
8 Gaza War Cemetery.
9 Ramleh War Cemetery.
11 Haifa War Cemetery.
14 Richon-Le-Zion Jewish Cemetery.

PAPUA NEW GUINEA.
1   Kavieng European Cemetery,New Ireland.
5   Rabaul (Bita Paka) War Cemetery,New Britain.

SOUTH AMERICA.
6   The Timehri Memorial (U.M.A.),Guyana.
12 Guayacan Protestant Cemetery,Chile.

SYRIA.
2   Damascus Commonwealth War Cemetery.

TANZANIA.
1   Dar Es Salaam War Cemetery,Bagamoyo Road.

U.S.A.
11 San Diego (Greenwoood) Cemetery,California.
12 San Diego Masonic Cemetery,California.
13 San Francisco (Cypress Lawn) Cemetery,California.
51 Covington (Mount Hope) Cemetery,Indiana.
52 Indianapolis (Crown Hill) Cemetery,Indiana.
77 Avon (St Michael's) Cemetery (Norfolk),Massachusetts.
79 Brookline (Holy Hood) Cemetery,Massachusetts.
92 Mount Auburn Cemetery,Cambridge & Watertown,Massachusetts.
97 Weston (Linwood) Cemetery,Massachusetts.
107 Detroit (Mount Olivet) Cemetery,Michigan.
121 St Louis (Bellefontaine) Public Cemetery,Missouri.
132 Asbury First Presbyterian Church Cemetery,New Jersey.
137 Rosedale Cemetery,Montclair & Orange,New Jersey.
143 Amityville Cemetery,NewYork.
147 Bronx (St Raymond's) Cemetery,New York.
149 Brooklyn (Greenwood) Cemetery,New York.
155 Cape Vincent (Riverside) Cemetery,New York.
169 New York (Woodlawn) Cemetery,New York.
184 Akron (Glendale) Cemetery (Summit),Ohio.
187 Chillicothe (Grandview) Cemetery (Ross),Ohio.
228 Fort Worth (Greenwood) Cemetery (Tarrant),Texas.
230 Memphis (Fairview) Cemetery,Texas.
234 Arlington National Cemetery (Arlington),Virginia.
234a Newport News (Green Lawn) Cemetery (Warwick),Virginia.
238 Colville (Highland) Cemetery,Washington.
246 Nuuanu Cemetery,Honolulu,Hawaii.

WEST INDIES.
29 Port of Spain Memorial (U.M.A.),Trinadad & Tobago.
36 Kingstown (St George) Cathedral Close,St Vincent.

ENGLISH, IRISH, SCOTTISH and WELSH COUNTIES.

BEDFORD & HUNTINGDON.
8   Higham Gobion (St Mary) Churchyard,Beds.
22 Ampthill (St Andrew) Churchyard,Beds.
23 Bedford Cemetery,Beds.
34 Pavenham (St Peter) Churchyard,Beds.
48 Campton and Shefford Cemetery,Beds.
65 Biggleswade Cemetery,Beds.
66 Dunstable Cemetery,Beds.
70 Eaton Socon Churchyard,Beds.
74 Luton Church Burial Ground,Beds.
75 Luton General Cemetery,Beds.
78 Houghton Regis (All Saints) Churchyard,Beds.
83 Huntingdon Cemetery,Hunts.
90 Upwood Cemetery,Hunts.
102 Ramsey (St Thomas a Becket) Churchyard,Hunts.
104 St Ives Public Cemetery,Hunts.
111 Somersham (St John the Baptist) Churchyard,Hunts.
113 Wyton (All Saints) Churchyard,Hunts.
124 St Neots Cemetery,Hunts.
125 Molesworth (St Peter) Churchyard,Hunts.

BERKSHIRE.
1   Abingdon Cemetery.
2   Abingdon (SS Mary & Edmund) Roman Catholic Churchyard,St Helen Without.
6   Kennington Cemetery,Radley.
15 Wootton (St Peter) Churchyard.
19 Bradfield (St Andrew) Churchyard.
23 Stratfield Mortimer (St Mary) Churchyard.
27 Yattendon (SS Peter & Paul) Churchyard.
28 Bisham (All Saints) Churchyard.
29 Boyne Hill (All Saints) Chhurchyard,Bray.
31 Cookham Cemetery.
33 Hurley (St Mary) Churchyard.
37 Stubbings (St James the Less) Churchyard,Bisham.
39 Ascot (All Saints) Churchyard Extension,Winkfield.
42 Cranbourne (St Peter) Churchyard,Winkfield.
43 Crowthorne (St John the Baptist) Churchyard.
45 Sandhurst Royal Military College Cemetery.
47 Warfield (St Michael) Churchyard Extension.
56 Hinton Waldrist (St Margaret) Churchyard.
66 Hungerford Church Cemetery.
71 Maidenhead Cemetery.
72 Newbury Old Cemetery.
73 Chieveley (St Mary) Churchyard.
83 Clewer (St Andrew)Churchyard.
84 Windsor Cemetery.
85 Reading (Caversham) Cemetery.
86 Reading Cemetery.
93 Long Wittenham (St Mary) Churchyard.
94 Sotwell (St James) Churchyard.
112 Wokingham (All Saints) Churchyard.
113 Wokingham (St Paul) Churchyard.
116 Bearwood (St Catherine) Churchyard,Hurst St Nicholas.
117 Earley (St Peter) Churchyard.
119 Hurst (St Nicholas) Churchyard Extension.
121 Sonning (St Andrew) Churchyard.
124 Wargrave (St Mary) Churchyard.
125 Wokingham (St Sebastian) Churchyard,Wokingham Without.

BUCKINGHAMSHIRE.
12 Penn Street (Holy Trinity) Churchyard,Penn.
32 Weston Turville (St Mary) Churchyard.
36 Beaconsfield Cemetery.
37 Bletchley (St Mary) Churchyard.
39 Buckingham Cemetery.
50 Twyford (The Assumption) Churchyard.
51 High Wycombe Cemetery.

54	Cliveden War Cemetery, Taplow.
55	Datchet Cemetery.
57	Dorney Burial Ground.
69	Wyrardisbury (St Andrew) Churchyard.
76	Long Crendon (St Mary) Churchyard.
80	Marlow Cemetery.
82	Marlow (St Peter) Roman Catholic Churchyard.
86	Moulsoe (St Mary) Churchyard.
91	Wavendon (St Mary) Churchyard.
96	Upton-Cum-Chalvey (St Mary) Churchyard.
116	Great Hampden (St Mary Magdalene) Churchyard, Great & Little Hampden.
120	Monks Risborough (St Dunstan) Churchyard.
123	Tylers Green (St Margaret) Churchyard, Chepping Wycombe Rural.

CAMBRIDGESHIRE.
1 Cambridge General Cemetery.
2 Cambridge (Mill Road) Cemetery.
3 Cambridge (SS Gile's & Peter's) Cemetery.
16 Cambridge Borough Cemetery, Fen Ditton.
19 Cottenham (All Saints) Churchyard.
21 Dry Drayton (SS Peter & Paul) Churchyard.
25 Great Shelford (St Mary) Churchyard.
31 Horningsea (St Peter) Churchyard.
37 Stapleford (St Andrew) Churchyard.
39 Trumpington (SS Mary & Michael) New Churchyard.
51 Weston Colville (St Mary) Churchyard.
74 Newmarket Cemetery, Wood Ditton
82 Boxworth (St Peter) Churchyard.
84 Chatteris General Cemertery.
91 Wilburton (St Peter) Church.
97 Doddington (St Mary) Churchyard.
103 Wisbech Borough Cemetery.

CHESHIRE.
1 Alsager (Christ Church) Churchyard.
2 Ashton-Upon-Mersey (St Martin) Churchyard.
3 Bebington Cemetery.
4 Bebington (St Andrew) Churchyard.
6 Higher Bebington (Christ Church) Churchyard.
8 Birkenhead (Flaybrick Hill) Cemetery.
11 Bowdon (St Mary) Churchyard.
18 Northenden (St Wilfrid) Churchyard.
19 Over Peover (St Lawrence) Churchyard, Peover Superior.
22 Rostherne (St Mary) Churchyard.
26 Cheadle and Gatley Cemetery.
28 Chester General Cemetery.
30 Christleton (St James) Churchyard.
31 Eccleston (St Mary) Churchyard.
32 Great Saughall (All Saints) Churchyard.
35 Shotwick (St Michael) Churchyard.
44 Church Lawton (All Saints) Churchyard.
51 Crewe Cemetery.
53 Ashton-Under-Lyne and Dunkinfield Joint Cemetery.
56 Altrincham Cemetery.
59 Norbury (St Thomas) Churchyard.
61 Hoylake (Holy Trinity) Churchyard.
62 West Kirby (St Bridget) Churchyard.
72 Macclesfield Cemetery.

74 Alderley Edge Cemetery.
84 Prestbury (St Peter) Churchyard.
86 Siddington (All Saints) Churchyard.
97 Middlewich Cemetery.
98 Mottram-In-Longdendale Cemetery.
111 Wybunbury (St Chad) Churchyard.
113 Nantwich (All Saints) Church Cemetery.
114 Nantwich General Cemetery.
117 Neston-Cum-Parkgate Cemetery.
119 Davenham (St Wilfred) Churchyard.
123 Lostock Gralam (St John) Churchyard.
127 Northwich Cemetery.
128 Northwich (St Helen) Churchyard.
131 Appleton Thorn (St Cross) Churchyard, Appleton.
133 Daresbury (All Saints) Churchyard.
137 Halton Cemetery.
142 Stockton Heath (St Thomas) Churchyard.
143 Stretton (St Matthew) Churchyard.
146 Runcorn Cemetery.
147 Sale Cemetery.
153 Stalybridge (St Paul) Churchyard.
154 Heaton Mersey Congregational Churchyard.
158 Stockport Borough Cemetery.
160 Stockport (Willow Grove) Cemetery.
175 Waverton (St Peter) Churchyard.
178 Egremont (St John) Churchyard.
181 Woodchurch (Holy Cross) Churchyard.
182 Wallasey (Rake Lane) Cemetery.
183 Lindow (St John) Churchyard.
184 Wilmslow Cemetery.
186 Over (St Chad) Churchyard.
190 Bidston (St Oswald) Churchyard.
192 Eastham (St Mary) Churchyard.
193 Heswall (St Peter) Churchyard.
194 hooton (St Mary of the Angels) Roman Catholic Cemetery.
197 Thurstaton (St Bartholomew) Churchyard.
198 Willaston (Christ Church) Churchyard.

CORNWALL.
1 Bodmin Cemetery.
4 Egloshayle Church Cemetery.
13 St Mabyn Churchyard.
17 Callington Cemetery.
20 Calstock Cemetery.
23 Camborne (St Martin) Churchyard.
29 Forrabury (St Symphorian) Churchyard, Forrabury and Minster.
36 Mawnan (SS Mawnan and Stephen) Churchyard.
37 Mylor (St Mylor) Churchyard.
40 Falmouth Cemetery.
48 Grade (St Grade and Holy Cross) Churchyard.
49 Gunwalloe (St Winwaloe) Churchyard.
55 Porthleven Cemetery, Sithney.
56 Ruan Minor (St Ruan) Churchyard.
61 St Martin's Churchyard.
64 Launceston Cemetery.
68 North Hill (St Torney) Churchyard.
79 Morval Church Cemetery.
96 Penzance Cemetery.

151

106 St Day (Holy Trinity) Churchyard.
109 Redruth Cemetery.
111 Biscovey (St Mary) Churchyard, St Blazey.
123 St Austell Cemetery.
128 St Columb Major Cemetery.
132 Antony Cemetery.
135 Maker (SS Macra, Mary and Julia) Churchyard.
136 Millbrook Church Cemetery.
138 Rame (St Germanus) Churchyard.
140 St Stephens-By-Saltash (St Stephen) Churchyard.
142 St Ives Cemetery.
148 Launcells (St Swithin) Churchyard.
161 Feock Church Cemetery.
163 Kenwyn (St Kenwyn) Churchyard, Kenwyn Rural.
172 Gulval (St Gulval) Churchyard.
175 Perranuthnoe (SS Piran and Nicholas) Churchyard.
177 St Erth (St Ercus) Churchyard, St Erth Rural.

CUMBERLAND AND WESTMORLAND.
6 Aspatria (St Kentigern) Churchyard, Cumberland.
11 Muncaster (St Michael) Churchyard, Cumberland.
13 Brampton (St Martin) Old Churchyard, Cumberland.
17 Carlisle (Dalston Road) Cemetery, Cumberland.
18 Carlisle (Upperby) Cemetery, Cumberland.
25 Wetheral Cemetery, Cumberland.
40 Cockermouth Cemetery, Cumberland.
44 Silloth (St Paul) Churchyard, Cumberland.
45 Crosthwaite (St Kentigern) Churchyard, Cumberland.
46 Keswick (St John) Churchyard, Cumberland.
50 Maryport Cemetery, Cumberland.
54 Great Salkeld (St Cuthbert) Churchyard, Cumberland.
59 Penrith Cemetery, Cumberland.
60 Whitehaven Cemetery, Cumberland.
68 Allonby (Christ Church) Churchyard, Cumberland.
74 Wigton Cemetery, Cumberland.
78 Kirkby Stephen Cemetery, Westmoreland.
82 Kendal (Parkside) Cemetery, Westmorland.
83 Kirkby Lonsdale (St Mary) Churchyard, Westmorland.
85 Arnside Cemetery, Westmorland.
86 Barbon (St Bartholomew) Churchyard, Westmorland.
89 Burton (St James) Churchyard, Westmoreland.
91 Heversham (St Mary) Churchyard, Westmorland.
98 Selside (St Thomas) Churchyard, Whitwell and Selside, Westmorland.
100 Troutbeck (Jesus) Churchyard, Westmorland.
107 Bowness-On-Windermere Cemetery, Westmorland.
108 Windermere (St Mary's) Cemetery, Westmorland.

DERBYSHIRE.
2 Alfreton (Lea Brooks) Cemetery.
3 Alfreton (St Martin) Churchyard.
26 Tideswell (St John the Baptist) Churchyard.
29 Bakewell Cemetery.
30 Baslow (St Anne) Churchyard.
32 Crich (St Mary) Churchyard.
34 Denby (St Mary) Churchyard.
39 Mackworth (All Saints) Churchyard.
42 South Wingfield (Park) Burial Ground.
47 Shirebrook Cemetery.
51 Bolsover (St Mary) Old Churchyard.
57 Buxton Cemetery.
58 Fairfield (St Peter) Churchyard.
61 Castleton (St Edmund) Churchyard.
66 Edale (Holy Trinity) Churchyard.
76 Whittington (St Bartholomew) Churchyard.
97 Derby (Normanton) Cemetery.
98 Derby (Nottingham Road) Cemetery.
99 Derby (Uttoxeter Road) Cemetery.
117 Heanor Cemetery.
120 Long Eaton Cemetery.
122 Cromford (St Mary) Churchyard.
127 Dore (Christ Church) Churchyard.
129 Church Broughton (St Michael) Churchyard.
135 Newton Solney (St Mary) Churchyard.
145 Ockbrook (All Saints) Churchyard.
146 Risley (All Saints) Churchyard.

DEVONSHIRE.
1 Plymouth Old Cemetery.
2 Efford Cemetery, Plymouth.
3 Weston Mill Cemetery, Plymouth.
6 Beer Church Cemetery.
10 Hawkchurch (St John the Baptist) Churchyard.
11 Kilmington (St Giles) Churchyard.
12 Musbury (St Michael) Churchyard.
15 Axminster Cemetery.
17 Barnstaple Cemetery.
21 Braunton (St Brannock) Churchyard.
29 Horwood Churchyard.
33 Morte Hoe Cemetery.
36 Westleigh (St Peter) Churchyard.
37 Bideford Church Cemetery.
38 Bideford Public Cemetery.
39 Abbotsham Churchyard.
40 Alwington (St Andrew) Churchyard.
41 Bucks Mills Church Cemetery, Woolfardisworthy.
46 Brixham Noncomformist Cemetery.
47 Brixham (St Mary) Churchyard.
50 Budleigh Salterton Cemetery.
67 Townstall (St Clement) Churchyard.
68 Dawlish Cemetery.
69 Exeter Higher Cemetery.
70 Exeter (Exwick) Cemetery.
71 Heavitree (St Michael) Churchyard Extension.
72 Littleham (SS Margaret and Andrew) Churchyard.
73 Withycombe Raleigh (St John in the Wilderness) Churchyard.
74 Great Torrington Cemetery.
76 Bradworthy (St John the Baptist) Churchyard.
86 Feniton (St Andrew) Churchyard.
87 Gittisham (St Michael) Churchyard.
91 Ilfracombe (Holy Trinity) Churchyard.
92 Ilfracombe (St Brannock's Road) Cemetery.
96 Chivelstone (St Silvester) Churchyard.
100 Loddiswell (St Michael) Churchyard.
102 Modbury (St George) Churchyard.
107 Thurlestone (All Saints) Churchyard.
128 Highweek (All Saints) Churchyard Extension.
130 Wolborough (St Mary) Churchyard.
132 Northam (St Margaret) Churchyard.

138 Hatherleigh (St John the Baptist) Churchyard.
152 Collaton (St Mary) Churchyard.
153 Paignton Cemetery.
158 Plympton St Maurice Churchyard.
172 Pennycross (St Pancras) Churchyard,Weston Peverell.
185 Exminster (St Martin) Churchyard.
200 Topsham Cemetery.
206 Seaton (St Gregory) Churchyard.
207 Sidmouth Cemetery.
230 Marystow (St Mary) Churchyard.
233 Sheepstor Churchyard.
236 Whitchurch (St Andrew) Churchyard.
237 Tavistock New Cemetery.
238 Shaldon (St Nicholas) Churchyard.
239 Teignmouth Cemetery.
243 Bradfield (All Saints) Churchyard.
246 Cullompton Cemetery.
247 Halberton (St Andrew) Churchyard.
248 Huntsham (All Saints) Churchyard.
258 Torquay Extramural Cemetery.
266 Bridgetown and Berry Pomeroy Cemetery.
267 Totnes Cemetery.
274 Kingswear Cemetery.
276 Marldon (St John the Baptist) Churchyard.

DORSET AND CHANNEL ISLANDS.
6 Parnham Private Cemetery,Beaminster,Dorset.
9 Blandford Cemetery.
18 Winterborne Stickland (St Mary) Churchyard.
20 Bridport Cemetery,Dorset.
22 Burton Bradstock Cemetery,Dorset.
27 Whitchurch Canonicorum (St Candida and Holy Cross) Churchyard.
28 Cattistock (SS Peter and Paul) Churchyard,Dorset.
33 Dorchester Cemetery,Dorset.
42 Stratton (St Mary) Churchyard,Dorset.
46 Branksome Park (All Saints) Churchyard,Dorset.
48 Longfleet (St Mary) Churchyard,Dorset.
49 Poole (Branksome) Cemetery,Dorset.
50 Poole Cemetery,Dorset.
51 Poole (Parkstone) Cemetery,Dorset.
52 Broadstone Cemetery,Canford Magna,Dorset.
53 Kinson (St Andrew) Churchyard,Dorset.
57 Portland Royal Naval Cemetery,Dorset.
58 Portland (St George) Churchyard,Dorset.
60 Shaftesbury (Holy Trinity) Churchyard.
67 Gillingham New Cemetery,Dorset.
70 Milton-on-Stour (SS Simon and Jude) Churchyard,Gillingham,Dorset.
73 Sutton Waldron (St Bartholomew) Churchyard.
85 Yetminster (St Andrew) Churchyard,Dorset.
87 Sherborne Cemetery,Dorset.
93 Swanage Old Cemetery,Dorset.
94 Wareham Cemetery,Dorset.
95 Affpuddle (St Laurence) Churchyard,Dorset.
102 Kimmeridge Churchyard,Dorset.
103 Langton Matravers Church Cemetery.
109 Wool (Holy Rood) Churchyard,Dorset.
110 Melcombe Regis Cemetery,Dorset.
111 Weymouth Cemetery,Dorset.

115 Owermoigne (St Michael) Churchyard,Dorset.
133 Witchampton (All Saints) Churchyard,Dorset.
135 Wimborne Minster Cemetery,Dorset.
139 Fort George Military Cemetery,St Peter Port,Guernsey.
141 St Martins New Cemetery,Guernsey.
144 St Peter Port (St John) Churchyard,Guernsey.
149 St Brelade Churchyard,Jersey.
151 St Helier (Almorah) Cemetery,Jersey.
152 St Helier (Mont-A-L'Abbe) New Cemetery,Jersey.
156 St Lawrence Churchyard,Jersey.
160 St Peter Churchyard,Jersey.
162 St Saviour Churchyard,Jersey.

DURHAM.
1 Blaydon (St Cuthbert,Stella) Cemetery.
8 Gateshead East Cemetery.
9 Gateshead (Saltwell) Cemetery.
12 Hebburn Cemetery.
13 Jarrow Cemetery.
15 Ryton Cemetery.
17 Seaham Harbour Cemetery.
18 Harton (St Peter) Churchyard.
19 South Shields (Harton) Cemetery.
23 Boldon Cemetery.
25 Whitburn (St Mary) Churchyard.
26 Sunderland (Bishopwearmouth) Cemetery.
27 Sunderland (Mere Knolls) Cemetery.
28 Sunderland (Ryhope Road) Cemetery.
39 Annfield Plain (Harelaw) Cemetery.
42 Auckland St Andrew Old Churchyard.
55 New Shildon (All Saints) Churchyard,Middridge Grange.
56 West Auckland Cemetery.
59 Gainford (St Mary) Churchyard.
62 Barnard Castle Roman Catholic Cemetery.
64 Benfieldside Cemetery.
81 West Pelton (St Paul) Churchyard,Urpeth.
88 Darlington West Cemetery.
97 Durham (St Oswald's) Burial Ground.
102 Pittington Burial Ground.
106 Shincliffe (St Mary) Churchyard.
108 Castle Eden (St James) Churchyard.
109 Dalton-Le-Dale (Holy Trinity) Churchyard.
115 Monk Hesleden Cemetery.
121 Wingate (Holy Trinity) Churchyard.
124 Hartlepool (Hart Road) New Cemetery.
140 Lanchester (All Saints) Churchyard.
162 Stanley New Cemetery.
164 Egglescliffe (St Mary) Churchyard.
165 Norton (St Mary) Churchyard.
167 Stockton-on-Tees (Durham Road) Cemetery.
173 Edmondbyers (St Edmund) Churchyard.
180 Seaton Carew (Holy Trinity) Churchyard.
181 West Hartlepool North Cemetery.
182 West Hartlepool (Stranton) Cemetery.

EIRE or IRELAND.
2 Chapelizod (St Lawrence) Church of Ireland Churchyard,Dublin City.
3 Clondalkin (St John) Church of Ireland Churchyard.

153

5 Dean's Grange Cemetery,Monkstown.
11 Dublin Friends' Burial Ground,Blackrock.
12 Glasnevin Cemetery,Dublin City.
14 Grangegorman Military Cemetery,Dublin City.
17 Kilgobbin Old Church Cemetery.
24 Mont Jerome Cemetery,Harold's Cross,Dublin City.
27 Royal Hospital Cemetery,Kilmainham,Dublin City.
30 Ballynacally (Kilchreest) Cemetery,County Clare.
34 Ennis (Drumcliff) Cemetery.
45 Scattery Island Graveyard.
48 Ardnagashel Private Burial Ground,County Cork.
49 Ballincollig Military Cemetery,County Cork.
57 Ballynakilla Churchyard,Bere Island,County Cork.
58 Baltimore (Tullagh) Graveyard,County Cork.
63 Blackrock (St Michael) Church of Ireland Churchyard,County Cork.
70 Castlehyde Church of Ireland Churchyard,County Cork.
71 Castlelyons Churchyard,County Cork.
75 Cloyne (St Coleman) Cathedral Churchyard,County Cork.
76 Cobh Old Church Cemetery,County Cork.
77 Cork Military Cemetery,County Cork.
78 Cork (St Finbarr's) Cemetery,County Cork.
81 Corkbeg Church of Ireland Churchyard,County Cork.
84 Currykippane Jewish Cemetery,County Cork.
86 Donoughmore Catholic Churchyard,County Cork.
88 Douglas (St Luke) Church of Ireland Churchyard,County Cork.
90 Drinagh Old Graveyard.
94 Fermoy Military Cemetery,County Cork.
95 Fort Carlisle Military Cemetery,County Cork.
109 Kilnamartyra Catholic Churchyard.
114 Kinsale (St Multose) Church of Ireland Churchyard,County Cork.
122 Millstreet Churchyard,County Cork.
132 Skibbereen (Chapel) Graveyard.
138 Timoleague Church of Ireland Churchyard,County Cork.
143 Youghal (St Mary's) Collegiate Churchyard,County Cork.
148 Dromod Church fo Ireland Churchyard,Waterville, County Kerry.
159 Tralee New Cemetery,County Kerry.
160 Tralee (Ratass) Cemetery,County Kerry.
161 Ardcanny Churchyard,Mellon,County Limerick.
163 Bruree Church of Ireland Churchyard,County Limerick.
166 Limerick (King's Island) Military Cemetery,County Limerick.
167 Limerick (St Lawrence's) Catholic Cemetery,County Limerick.
168 Limerick (St Mary) Cathedral Churchyard,County Limerick.
185 Clonmel Friends' Burial Ground,County Tipperary.
186 Clonmel (St Patrick's) Cemetery,County Tipperary.
194 Lorrha Old Graveyard,County Tipperary.
205 Terryglass (St Columba) Catholic Churchyard,County Tipperary.
215 Ballynakill House Private Burial Ground,County Waterford.
216 Ballynaneashagh (St Otteran's) Catholic Cemetery.
234 Stradbally Church of Ireland Churchyard,County Waterford.
237 Tramore (Holy Cross) Catholic Churchyard,County Waterford.
238 Waterford Protestant Cemetery,County Waterford.
251 Ballymachugh (St Paul) Church of Ireland Churchyard,County Cavan.
260 Kilmore Church of Ireland Cemetery,County Cavan.
267 Clonmany Catholic Churchyard,County Donegal.
270 Cockhill Catholic Cemetery,County Donegal.
286 Lower Fahan (Christ Church) Churchyard,County Donegal.
292 Rathmullan (Old Abbey) Graveyard,County Donegal.
295 Upper Fahan Church of Ireland Churchyard,County Donegal.
301 Galway (Bohermore) New Cemetery,County Galway.
309 Omey (Christ Church) Church of Ireland Churchyard,Clifden,County Galway.
313 Athy (St John's) Old Cemetery,County Kildare.
319 Clane (St Michael) Church of Ireland Churchyard,County Kildare.
322 Curragh Military Cemetery,County Kildare.
336 Nass (Maudlings Or St Magdalen's) Protestant Cemetery,County Kildare.
350 Foulkstown Catholic Churchyard,County Kilkenny.
355 Kilkenny (St Canice) Church of Ireland Cathedral Cemetery,County Kilkenny.
356 Kilkenny (St John) Church of Ireland Churchyard,County Kilkenny.
362 Knocktopher (St David) Church of Ireland Churchyard,County Kilkenny.
381 Durrow Catholic Churchyard,County Leix.
394 Ballymacormick Church of Ireland Churchyard,County Longford.
398 Longford (Ballymacormick) Cemetery,County Longford.
401 Newtown Forbes (St Ann) Church of Ireland Churchyard,County Longford.
406 Drogheda (St Mary) Church of Ireland Churchyard,County Louth.
408 Dromin Old Graveyard,County Louth.
411 Dundalk (St Patrick's) Cemetery,County Louth.
422 Ballina Catholic Cathedral Churchyard,County Mayo.
432 Kilmaine (Holy Trinity) Church of Ireland Churchyard,County Mayo.
434 Newport Presbyterian Churchyard,County Mayo.
437 Ardcath Graveyard,County Meath.
440 Bective (St Mary) Church of Ireland Churchyard,County Meath.
446 Julianstown (St Mary) Church of Ireland Churchyard,County Meath.
451 Loughcrew Church of Ireland Churchyard,County Meath.
459 Slane (St Patrick) Church of Ireland Churchyard,County Meath.
468 Currin Church of Ireland Churchyard,County Monaghan.
475 Ballyburley Church of Ireland Churchyard,Offaly.
476 Ballycumber (Liss) Churchyard,Offaly.

480 Bir Old Graveyard,Offaly.
487 Killoughy Church of Ireland Churchyard,Offaly.
492 Ardcarn (St Beaidh) Church of Ireland Churchyard,County Roscommon.
499 Killaraght Church of Ireland Churchyard,County Sligo.
505 Ballyglass Cemetery,Mullingar,County Westmeath.
506 Cornamagh Cemetery,Athlone,County Westmeath.
510 Rathconnell Church of Ireland Churchyard,County Westmeath.
512 Toberclare Catholic Churchyard,County Westmeath.
522 Kilscoran Church of Ireland Churchyard,County Wexford.
528 Arklow Cemetery,County Wicklow.
531 Delgany (Christ Church) Church of Ireland Churchyard,County Wicklow.
532 Dunlavin (St Nicholas) Churchyard,County Wicklow.
533 Glenealy Church of Ireland Churchyard,County Wicklow.
534 Greystones (Redford) Cemetery,County Wicklow.
537 Kilcommon Church of Ireland Churchyard,County Wicklow.
539 Killiskey Church of Ireland Churchyard,County Wicklow.
541 Powerscourt (St Patrick) Church Of Ireland Churchyard,County Wicklow.

ESSEX.
1   The City of London Cemetery,Manor Park.
5   Manor Park Cemetery.
7   Woodgrange Park Cemetery.
9   Leytonstone (St Patrick's) Roman Catholic Cemetery.
10 Walthamstow (Queen's Road) Cemetery.
11 Walthamstow (St Mary) Churchyard.
12 Walthamstow (St Peter-on-the-Forest) Churchyard.
13 East London Cemetery,Plaistow.
14 West Ham Cemetery.
16 Barking (Rippleside) Cemetery.
29 Shenfield (St Mary) Churchyard.
36 Thorndon Hall (Our Lady & St Lawrence) Chapel.
37 Buckhurst Hill (St John the Baptist) Churchyard.
40 Chingford Mount Cemetery.
43 Grays New Cemetery.
45 Hornchurch (St Andrew) Churchyard.
48 Ilford Cemetery.
50 Loughton Burial Ground.
56 North Ockenden (St Mary Magdalene) Churchyard.
69 Hockley (St Peter) Churchyard.
73 Rochford (St Andrew) Churchyard.
75 Great Warley (Christchurch) Cemetery.
80 Romford Cemetery.
81 Shoeburyness (St Andrew) Churchyard.
83 Southend on Sea (Leigh on Sea) Cemetery.
84 Southend on Sea (North Road) Cemetery.
86 Southend on Sea (Sutton Road) Cemetery.
88 Wanstead (St Mary) Churchyard.
95 Great Henny (St Mary) Churchyard.
96 Liston Churchyard.
102 Fairsted (SS Mary and Peter) Churchyard.
105 Coggeshall Burial Ground.
106 Hatfield Peverel (St Andrew) Churchyard.
107 Kelvedon (St Mary) Churchyard Extension.
110 Wethersfield (St Mary Magdalene) Churchyard.
112 Brightlingsea (All Saints) Churchyard.
118 Chelmsford (Rectory Lane) Cemetery.
119 Chelmsford (Writtle Road) Cemetery.
120 Springfield (Holy Trinity) Churchyard.
122 Broomfield (St Mary) Churchyard.
123 Danbury (St John the Baptist) Churchyard.
124 East Hanningfield (All Saints) Churchyard.
128 Great Waltham (SS Mary and Lawrence) Churchyard.
130 Ingatestone and Fryerning Cemetery.
132 Little Waltham (St Martin) Churchyard.
137 Sandon (St Andrew) Churchyard.
141 Widford (St mary) Churchyard.
145 Berechurch (St Michael) Churchyard.
146 Colchester Cemetery.
149 Lexden (St Leonard) Churchyard.
158 Little Dunmow (St Mary) Churchyard.
164 Chigwell Row (All Saints) Churchyard,Chigwell.
167 Harlow (St Mary) Churchyard.
172 North Weald Bassett (St Andrew) Churchyard.
175 Coopersale (St Alban) Churchyard.
176 Frinton-on-Sea (St Mary) Churchyard.
185 Dovercourt (All Saints) Churchyard.
186 Harwich Cemetery.
193 East Donyland (St lawrence) Churchyard.
196 Great Horkesley (All Saints) Churchyard.
208 Maldon Cemetery.
209 Maldon (St Mary) Churchyard.
210 Bradwell-near-the-Sea (St Thomas the Apostle) Church Cemetery.
211 Goldhanger (St Peter) Churchyard.
212 Great Braxted (All Saints) Churchyard.
213 Heybridge Cemetery.
221 Southminster (St Leonard) Churchyard.
222 Stow Maries (SS Mary and Margaret) Churchyard.
231 Woodham Walter (St Michael) Churchyard.
234 Chipping Ongar Cemetery,Ongar.
242 Stapleford Abbots (St Mary) Churchyard.
246 Saffron Walden Friends' Burial Ground.
254 Littlebury (Holy Trinity) Churchyard.
255 Newport (Sr Mary) Churchyard.
256 Quendon Churchyard,Quendon and Rickling.
258 Rickling (All Saints) Churchyard,Quendon and Rickling.
261 Birchanger (St Mary) Churchyard.
267 Alresford (St Peter) Churchyard.
268 Ardleigh Cemetery.
270 Bradfield (St Lawrence) Churchyard.
274 Kirby-Le-Soken (St Michael) Churchyard.
275 Little Bentley (St Mary) Churchyard.
285 Witham (All Saints) Churchyard.
287 Wivenhoe (Bellevue Road) Cemetery.

GLOUCESTERSHIRE.
5   Bristol (Arno's Vale) Cemetery.
6   Bristol (Holy Souls) Roman Catholic Cemetery.
9   Bristol (Canford) Cemetery.
10 Bristol Cathedral Burial Ground.
11 Bristol (Greenbank) Cemetery.
15 Bristol (Shirehampton) Cemetery.
19 Westbury-on-Trym (Holy Trinity) Church
24 Charlton Kings Cemetery.

27	Cheltenham Cemetery,Prestbury.	60	Botley (All Saints) Churchyard.
30	Great Witcombe (St Mary) Churchyard.	62	Hound (St Mary) Churchyard Extension.
31	Leckhampton (St Peter) Churchyard.	64	Netley Military Cemetery,Hound.
32	Prestbury (St Mary) Churchyard,Dowdeswell.	65	West End (St James's) Cemetery.
38	Frenchay (St John the Baptist) Churchyard,Winterbourne.	67	Aldershot Jewish Cemetery.
40	Little Badminton Churchyard,Hawkesbury.	70	Cheriton (St Michael) Churchyard.
51	Brimpsfield (St Michael) Churchyard.	76	Bentley (St Mary) Churchyard.
61	Quenington Cemetery.	83	Grayshott (St Luke) Churchyard.
67	Cirencester Cemetery.	85	Headley (All Saints) Churchyard Extension.
69	Lower Cam (St Bartholomew) Churchyard,Cam.	87	Kingsley (St Nicholas) Old Churchyard.
72	Slimbridge (St John) Churchyard.	90	Andover Cemetery.
86	Gloucester Cemetery.	98	Penton Mewsey (Holy Trinity) Churchyard.
88	Barnwood (St Lawrence) Churchyard.	106	Basingstoke (South View) Cemetery.
92	Hempsted (St Swithun) Churchyard.	115	Newnham (St Nicholas) Churchyard.
102	Wotton Congregational Church Cemetery,Wotton St Mary With-Out.	117	Preston Candover (St Mary) Old Churchyard.
109	Lydney (St Mary) Churchyard.	119	Sherfield-Upon-Loddon (St Leonard) churchyard.
124	Newnham (St Peter) Churchyard.	122	Upton Grey (St Mary) Churchyard.
126	Chedworth (St Andrew) Churchyard.	130	Shedfield (St John the Baptist) Churchyard.
133	Whittington Cemetery.	132	Swanmore (St Barnabas) Churchyard.
138	Great Barrington Cemetery.	136	Crofton (Holy Rood) Old Churchyard.
143	Amberley Church Cemetery,Minchinhampton.	138	Porchester (St Mary) Churchyard.
159	Rodborough (St Mary Magdalene) Churchyard.	139	Sarisbury (St Paul's) Burial Ground.
164	Stonehouse (St Cyr) Churchyard Extension.	144	Farnborough Abbey Roman Catholic Churchyard.
168	Stroud Cemetery.	145	Farnborough Burial Ground.
176	Ashchurch (St Nicholas) Churchyard.	146	Fleet (All Saints) Churchyard.
178	Kemerton (St Nicholas) Churchyard.	150	Eversley (St Mary) Churchyard Extension.
182	Berkeley Cemetery.	151	Ewshott (St Mary) Churchyard,Crookham.
190	Thornbury Cemetery.	153	Hartley Wintney (St Mary) Old Churchyard.
203	Eastington (St Michael) Churchyard.	157	Odiham Cemetery.
214	Stanton (St Michael) Churchyard.	159	Yateley (St Peter) Churchyard.
		160	Bedhampton (St Thomas) Churchyard.
		161	North Hayling (St Peter) Churchyard.

HAMPSHIRE.

1	Aldershot Military Cemetery.	173	Highclere Cemetery.
4	Gosport (Ann's Hill) Cemetery.	176	Buriton (St Mary) Churchyard.
5	Haslar Royal Naval Cemetery.	179	Steep (All Saints) Churchyard.
6	Alverstoke (Sr Mark) Churchyard.	180	Petersfield Cemetery.
7	Eastney Cemetery,Portsmouth.	182	Braishfield (All Saints) Churchyard,Michelmersh.
8	Milton Cemetery,Portsmouth.	186	Rownhams (St John) Churchyard.
9	Portsea Cemetery,Portsmouth.	191	Nether Wallop (St Andrew) Churchyard.
10	Portsdown (Christ Church) Cemetery,Portsmouth.	192	Stockbridge Cemetery.
11	Portsdown (Christ Church) Military Cemetery,Portsmouth.	202	Winchester (West Hill) Old Cemetery.
12	Wymering (SS Peter and Paul) Churchyard,Portsmouth.	205	Compton (All Saints) Churchyard.
13	Bournemouth East Cemetery.	214	Ryde Borough Cemetery,Isle of Wight.
15	Bournemouth (Wimborne Road) Cemetery.	216	East Cowes Cemetery,Isle of Wight.
17	Christchurch Cemetery.	217	Oakfield (St John's) Cemetery,Isle of Wight.
19	Highcliffe (St Mark) Churchyard.	218	St Helens Churchyard,Isle of Wight.
22	Throop Congregational Churchyard,Holdenhurst.	219	Sandown (Christ Church) Churchyard,Isle of Wight.
23	Fordingbridge Cemetery.	220	Shanklin Cemetery,Isle of Wight.
28	Lymington Cemetery.	221	Ventnor Cemetery,Isle of Wight.
30	Brockenhurst (St Nicholas) Cemetery.	232	Carisbrooke Cemetery,Isle of Wight.
31	East Boldre (St Paul) Churchyard.	234	Freshwater (All Saints) Churchyard,Isle Of Wight.
34	Milton (St Mary Magdalene) Churchyard.	240	Parkhurst Military Cemetery,Carisbrooke,Isle of Wight.
36	Beaulieu Cemetery.	241	Shalfleet Churchyard,Isle of Wight.
41	Eling (St Mary) Churchyard Extension.	242	Shorwell (St Peter) New Churchyard,Isle of Wight.
43	Exbury (St Catherine) Church.	245	Wippingham (St Mildred) Churchyard,Isle of Wight.
53	North Stoneham (St Nicholas) Churchyard.	246	Whitwell New Burial Ground,Isle of Wight.
56	Southampton (Hollybrook) Cemetery.		
57	Southampton Old Cemetery.		
58	Southampton (St Mary Extra) Cemetery.		

HEREFORD AND WORCESTER.
9   Whitbourne (St John the Baptist) Churchyard Extension,Hereford.
18   Hereford Cemetery,Hereford.
51   Bosbury (Holy Trinity(Churchyard,Hereford.
54   Colwall (St James the Great) Churchyard,Hereford.
56   Much Marcle (St Bartholomew) Churchyard,Hereford.
59   Ledbury Cemetery,Hereford.
96   Mansell Gamage (St Giles) Churchyard,Hereford.
110 Bromsgrove Cemetery,Worcester.
116 Martin Hussingtree (St Michael) Churchyard,Worcester.
129 Broadway (St Eadburgh) Churchyard,Worcester.
144 Kidderminster (St John the Baptist) Churchyard,Worcester.
154 Great Malvern Cemetery,Worcester.
162 Harpley (St Bartholomew) Churchyard,Lower Sapey,Worcester.
166 Martley (St Peter) Churchyard,Worcester.
182 Blockley Church Cemetery,Worcester.
186 Stourbridge Cemetery,Worcester.
189 Lower Mitton (St Michael) Churchyard,Worcester.
191 Tenbury (St Mary) Churchyard,Worcester.
201 Kempsey (St Mary) Churchyard,Worcester.
208 Worcester (Astwood) Cemetery,Worcester.

HERTFORD.
10   Shenley (St Botolph) Churchyard.
12   Chipping Barnet Church Burial Ground.
24   Layston Churchyard.
29   Chorley Wood (Christ Church) Churchyard.
30   Great Northern London Cemetery.
31   Great Birkhamsted (St Peter) Churchyard.
37   Harpenden (St Nicholas) Churchyard.
38   Bishop's Hatfield (St Etheldreda) Church Cemetery.
60   Tewin (St Peter) Churchyard.
72   Knebworth (St Mary) Churchyard.
81   Hitchin Cemetery.
84   Rickmansworth Cemetery.
87   St Albans Cemetery.
91   Redbourn (St Mary) Churchyard.
108 Wareside (Holy Trinity) Churchyard,Ware Rural.
110 Watford Cemetery.
115 Radlett (Christ Church) Churchyard,Aldenham.
116 Welwyn Cemetery.

HUNTINGDON. see BEDFORDSHIRE & HUNTINGDON

KENT.
2   Deal Cemetery.
5   Charlton Cemetery.
7   Dover (St James's) Cemetery.
8   Dover (St Mary's) New Cemetery.
14   River (St Peter) Churchyard.
15   St Margaret's-at-Cliffe (St Margaret) Churchyard.
24   Birchington (All Saints) Churchyard.
25   Minster Cemetery.
27   Margate Cemetery.
28   Ramsgate Cemetery.
29   Ramsgate (St Augustine) Roman Catholic Churchyard.
30   St Lawrence Cemetery.
34   Walmer (St Mary) Old Churchyard.
37   Hackington (St Stephen) Churchyard.
38   Herne Bay Cemetery,Herne.
42   Chatham Cemetery.
44   Luton (Christ Church) Churchyard.
46   Gillingham New Cemetery.
47   Rainham (St Margaret) Churchyard.
61   Fort Pitt Military Cemetery.
62   Frindsbury (All Saints) Churchyard.
63   Rochester (St Margaret's) Cemetery.
64   Rochester (St Nicholas) Cemetery.
65   Eastchurch (All Saints) Churchyard.
67   Isle of Sheppey General Cemetery,Minster-in-Sheppey.
68   Leysdown (St Clemeny) Churchyard.
71   Sittingbourne Cemetery.
82   Beckenham (St George) Churchyard.
83   Crystal Palace District Cemetery.
85   Bexley Heath Cemetery.
86   East Wickham (St Michael) Churchyard.
89   Bromley Hill Cemetery.
90   Bromley (London Road) Cemetery.
91   Plaistow (St Mary's) Cemetery.
95   Hayes Churchyard.
96   Keston Churchyard.
97   Knockholt (St Katharine) Churchyard.
99   Orpington (All Saints) Churchyard.
100 St Paul's Cray (St Paulinus) Churchyard.
102 Chislehurst Cemetery.
103 Chislehurst (St Nicholas) Churchyard.
105 Crayford (St Paulinus) Churchyard.
109 Darenth (St Margaret) Churchyard.
122 Wilmington (St Michael) Churchyard.
124 Dartford (East Hill) Cemetery.
125 Dartford (Watling Street) Cemetery.
127 Erith (Brook Street) Cemetery.
129 Gravesend Cemetery.
130 Northfleet Cemetery.
141 Fordcombe (St Peter) Churchyard,Penshurst.
147 Riverhead (St Mary) Churchyard.
153 Sevenoaks (Greatness Park) Cemetery.
154 Sevenoaks (St Nicholas) Churchyard.
156 Foots Cray Baptist Chapelyard.
157 Sidcup Cemetery.
160 Ashford Cemetery.
164 Bridge (St Peter) Churchyard.
175 Canterbury Cemetery.
177 Canterbury (St Martin) Churchyard.
179 Cheriton (St Martin) Churchyard.
180 Shorncliffe Military Cemetery.
182 Cranbrook Cemetery.
191 Chilham (St Mary) Churchyard.
197 Wye (SS Gregory and Martin) Churchyard.
200 Hawkinge (St Michael) Churchyard.
201 Lyminge (SS Mary & Eadburg) Churchyard.
203 Saltwood (SS Peter and Paul) Churchyard.
205 Faversham Cemetery.
212 Osprine (SS Peter and Paul) Churchyard.
216 Throwley (St Michael) Churchyard.
217 Folkestone Old Cemetery.
221 Detling (St Martin) Churchyard.

224 Harrietsham (St John the Baptist) Churchyard.
225 Hollingbourne (All Saints) Churchyard.
230 Hythe Cemetery.
231 Lydd (All Saints) Churchyard Extension.
232 Maidstone Cemetery.
234 Bearstead (Holy Cross) Churchyard Extension.
235 Boughton Monchelsea (St Peter) Churchyard.
239 Linton (St Nicholas) Churchyard.
243 Staplehurst (All Saints) Churchyard.
252 East Peckham (St Michael) Churchyard.
259 West Malling (St Mary) Churchyard.
261 New Romney (St Nicholas) Churchyard.
267 Rusthall (St Paul) Churchyard.
268 Tunbridge Wells Cemetery.
269 Southborough Cemetery.
272 Tenterden (St Mildred's) Cemetery.
279 Brenchley (All Saints) Churchyard.
280 Groombridge (St John) Churchyard,Speldhurst.
281 Hildenborough (St John the Devine) Churchyard.
282 Horsmonden (St Margaret) Churchyard.
284 Matfield (St Luke) Churchyard,Brenchley.
285 Paddock Wood (St Andrew) Churchyard,Brenchley.
287 Speldhurst (St Mary) Churchyard.
289 Tonbridge Cemetery.
296 Kingsnorth Churchyard.
298 Westwell Burial Ground.
301 Wrotham (St George) Churchyard Extension.

LANCASHIRE.
1 Allerton Cemetery,Liverpool.
2 Anfield Cemetery,Liverpool.
4 Everton Cemetery,Liverpool.
7 Kirkdale Cemetery,Liverpool.
8 Knotty Ash (St John the Evangelist) Churchyard.
9 Lingfield Road (Broad Green) Jewish Cemetery,Liverpool.
10 Much Woolton (St Mary's) Roman Catholic Cemetery,Liverpool.
12 St Jame's Cemetery,Liverpool.
14 Toxteth Park Cemetery,Liverpool.
18 Wavertree (Holy Trinity) Churchyard,Liverpool.
19 Birch-in-Rusholme (St James) Churchyard,Manchester.
23 Cheetham Hill (St Luke) Churchyard.
24 Cheetham Hill Wesleyan Cemetery,Manchester.
30 Manchester Crematorium.
32 Manchester (Gorton) Cemetery.
33 Manchester (Philips Park) Cemetery.
34 Manchester Southern Cemetery.
35 Moston (St Joseph's) Roman Catholic Cemetery,Manchester.
37 Newton Heath (All Saints) Churchyard,Manchester.
39 Withington (St Paul) Churchyard.
40 Barrow-in-Furness Cemetery.
42 Bispham (All Hallows) Churchyard.
43 Blackpool Cemetery.
46 Fleetwood Protestant Dissenters' Cemetery.
48 Fleetwood (St Peter) Churchyard Extension.
52 Lund (St John) Churchyard,Clifton-with-Salwick.
71 Grange-Over-Sands Cemetery.
76 Lancaster Cemetery.
77 Lancaster (Scotforth) Cemetery.

80 Bolton-le-Sands (Holy Trinity) Churchyard.
86 Warton (St Oswald) Churchyard,Warton-with-Lundeth.
92 Lytham (St Cuthbert) Churchyard.
95 St Anne's-on-Sea Churchyard.
96 Heysham (St Peter) Churchyard.
98 Morecombe (Torrisholme) Cemetery.
101 Ashton-on-Ribble (St Andrew) Churchyard.
102 Preston (New Hall Lane) Cemetery.
103 Broughton (St John the Baptist) Churchyard.
104 Cottam (St Andrew) Churchyard,Lea Ashton,Ingol and Cottam.
108 Grimsargh (St Michael) Churchyard,Grimsargh-with-Brockholes.
111 Longton (St Andrew) Churchyard.
112 Longton (St Oswald) Roman Catholic Churchyard.
114 Penwortham (St Mary) Churchyard.
143 Walton-Le-Dale (St Leonard) Churchyard.
146 Bootle Cemetery.
149 Great Crosby (St Luke) Churchyard.
150 Great Crosby (SS Peter and Paul) Roman Catholic Churchyard.
152 Huyton (St Agnes) Roman Catholic Churchyard.
154 Roby (St Bartholomew) Churchyard.
155 Liverpool (West Derby) Cemetery.
156 Liverpool (Yew Tree) Roman Catholic Cemetery.
157 Newton-in-Makerfield Cemetery.
160 Prescot (St Mary) Churchyard.
164 St Helens Cemetery.
168 Ince Blundell Roman Catholic Cemetery.
169 Liverpool (Ford) Roman Catholic Cemetery.
170 Sefton (St Helen) Churchyard.
171 Warrington Cemetery.
176 Hollinfare Cemetery,Rixton-with-Glazebrook.
179 Eccleston (Christ Church) Churchyard.
181 Halewood (St Nicholas) Churchyard.
186 Farnworth (St Luke) Churchyard.
189 Accrington Cemetery.
193 Blackburn Cemetery.
198 Mellor (St Mary) Churchyard.
199 Mellor Wesleyan Methodist Chapelyard.
205 Burnley Cemetery.
206 Habergham (All Saints) Churchyard.
209 Briercliffe (St James) Churchyard.
210 Foulridge (St Michael) Churchyard.
211 Haggate Baptist Chapelyard,Briercliffe.
216 Newchurch-in-Pendle (St Mary) Churchyard,Goldshaw Booth.
217 Read (St John) Churchyard.
219 Wheatley Lane Inghamite Chapelyard,Wheatley Carr Booth.
222 Church and Clayton-le-Moors Joint Cemetery.
226 Clitheroe (St Mary's) Burial Ground.
233 Whalley (Queen Mary's Hospital) Military Cemetery.
235 Colne Cemetery.
237 Great Harwood Cemetery.
243 Nelson Cemetery.
246 Padiham Cemetery.
255 Bolton (Astley Bridge) Cemetery.
256 Bolton (Heaton) Cemetery.
257 Bolton (Tonge) Cemetery.

261 Halliwell (St Peter) Churchyard.
263 Bury Cemetery.
266 Bury (St Paul) Churchyard.
267 Elton (All Saints) Churchyard.
277 Darwen Cemetery.
278 Hoddlesden (St Paul) Churchyard.
283 Haslingden Holden Hall) Cemetery.
284 Haslingden (St James the Great) Churchyard.
313 Rawtenstall (Longholme) Wesleyan Chapelyard.
317 Rochdale Cemetery.
321 Tottington (St Anne) Churchyard.
322 Tottington (St John) Free Church of England Churchyard.
327 Harwood (Christ Church) Churchyard.
336 Whitworth Cemetery.
342 Ashton-in-Makerfield (St Thomas) Churchyard.
343 Ashton-in-Makerfield (St Thomas) Churchyard, Heath Lane Extension.
346 Chorley Cemetery.
366 Formby (St Peter) Churchyard.
368 Wigan Cemetery.
380 Southport (Birkdale) Cemetery.
381 Southport (Duke Street) Cemetery.
383 Southport (St Cuthbert) Churchyard.
386 Aughton (Christ Church) Churchyard.
387 Aughton (St Michael) Churchyard.
391 Maghull (St Andrew) Churchyard.
401 Douglas Cemetery, Isle of Man.
403 Kirk Braddan (St Brendan) New Churchyard, Isle of Man.
405 Kirk Christ Lezayre (Holy Trinity) Churchyard, Isle of Man.
410 Kirk Malew (St Malew) Churchyard, Isle of Man.
413 Kirk Maughold (St Machut) Churchyard, Isle of Man.
416 Ashton-under-Lyne (Hurst) Cemetery.
420 Audenshaw Cemetery.
421 Audenshaw (St Stephen) Churchyard.
427 Oldham (Chadderton) Cemetery.
434 Eccles (Peel Green) Cemetery.
436 Monton Unitarian Churchyard.
438 Hindley (All Saints) Churchyard.
441 Hey (St John the Baptist) Churchyard Extension.
443 Leigh Cemetery.
450 Middleton New Cemetery.
463 Prestwich (St Margaret) Churchyard.
464 Prestwich (St Mary) Churchyard.
471 Higher Broughton (St John) Churchyard.
472 Kersal (St Paul) Churchyard.
474 Salford (Weaste) Cemetery.
475 Stretford Cemetery.
478 Pendlebury (St Augustine of Canterbury) Churchyard.
481 Swinton Cemetery.
483 Tyldesley Cemetery.
487 Urmston Cemetery.
489 Whitefield British Jews' Cemetery.
491 Worsley (St Mark) Churchyard.

LEICESTERSHIRE.
13 Barrow-upon-Soar Cemetery.
15 Leicester (Gilroes) Cemetery, Gilroes.
24 Woodhouse Eaves (St Paul) Churchyard Extension, Woodhouse.
25 Bottesford (St Mary) Churchyard.
55 Burbage (St Catherine) Churchyard.
63 Leicester (Welford Road) Cemetery.
64 Loughborough (Leicester Road) Cemetery.
70 Lutterworth (St Mary) Churchyard.
87 Shenton (St John) Churchyard.
97 Market Harborough (Northampton Road) Cemetery.
117 Sysonby Churchyard.
119 Quorn (St Bartholomew) Churchyard.
120 Shepshed Cemetery.

LINCOLNSHIRE.
1 Boston Cemetery.
6 Freiston (St James) Churchyard.
10 Skirbeck Quarter (St Thomas) Churchyard.
14 Fleet (St Mary Magdalene) Churchyard.
25 Gosberton Cemetery.
29 Spalding Cemetery.
34 Folkingham (St Andrew) Churchyard.
38 Market Deeping Cemetery.
44 Bourne Cemetery.
53 Waddington (St Michael) Churchyard.
57 Fulbeck (St Nicholas) Churchyard.
60 Stubton (St Martin) Churchyard.
61 Grantham Cemetery.
67 Harlaxton (SS Mary and Peter) Churchyard.
69 Londonthorpe (St John the Baptist) Churchyard.
76 Billinghay Cemetery.
78 Cranwell (St Andrew) Churchyard.
86 Leasingham (St Andrew) Churchyard.
98 Quarrington (St Botolph) Churchyard.
100 Stamford Cemetery.
115 Middle Rasen (St Peter) Churchyard.
123 Cleethorpes Cemetery.
136 Gainsborough General Cemetery.
142 Broughton Cemetery.
152 Scawby (St Hibald) Churchyard.
156 Grimsby (Scartho Road) Cemetery.
158 Scartho (St Giles) Churchyard.
159 Great Coates (St Nicholas) Churchyard.
160 Immingham (St Andrew) Churchyard.
162 Stallingborough (SS Peter and Paul) Churchyard.
179 Lincoln (Canwick Road) Cemetery.
181 Lincoln (Newport) Cemetery.
183 Louth Cemetery.
202 Mablethorpe (St Mary) Churchyard.
220 Hogsthorpe (St Mary) Churchyard.
225 Spilsby Cemetery.
236 Goltho (St George) Churchyard.
239 Nettleham (All Saints) New Churchyard.

LONDON.
1 Wandsworth Cemetery.
2 Nunhead (All Saints) Cemetery.
3 Camberwell (Forest Hill Road) Cemetery.
4 Brompton Cemetery, Kensington.
5 Fulham Old Cemetery.
6 Fulham (St Thomas of Canterbury) Roman Catholic Cemetery.
7 Hammersmith Cemetery.
8 Kensal Green (All Souls) Cemetery, Kensington and Hammersmith.

9   Kensal Green (St Mary's) Roman Catholic Cemetery,Hammersmith.
10 Abney Park Cemetery,Stoke Newington.
11 City of London and Tower Hamlets Cemetery,Stepney.
12 Hampstead Cemetery.
13 Hampstead (St John) Additional Burial Ground.
14 Highgate Cemetery,St Pancras.
15 St Paul's Cathedral.
16 Savoy Chapel.
18 Battersea (St Mary's,Battersea Rise) Cemetery.
19 Deptford Cemetery,Brockley.
20 Lambeth Cemetery,Tooting.
22 Lewisham (Ladywell) Cemetery.
23 Norwood Cemetery.
24 Putney Cemetery.
25 Putney Vale Cemetery.
26 Streatham Cemetery (Garratt lane).
27 Tooting (St Nicholas) Churchyard.
28 Charlton Cemetery,Greenwich.
29 Greenwich Cemetery.
30 Greenwich Royal Naval Cemetery.
32 Eltham (St John the Baptist) Churchyard,Woolwich.
33 Plumstead Cemetery,Woolwich.
35 Woolwich Cemetery.

MIDDLESEX.
1   Edmonton Cemetery.
5   Enfield Chase Cemetery.
6   Enfield Highway Cemetery.
7   Enfield Highway (St James) Churchyard.
9   Southgate Cemetery.
12 South Mimms (St Giles) Churchyard.
13 Tottenham and Wood Green Cemetery.
15 Islington Cemetery.
16 St Marylebone Cemetery.
17 St Pancras Cemetery.
18 Harrow on the Hill (St Mary) Lower Churchyard.
19 Harrow on the Hill Cemetery.
21 Edgware (St Margaret) Churchyard.
23 Harrow Waeld (All Saints) Churchyard Extension.
25 Pinner Cemetery.
26 Golders Green Crematorium.
27 Golders Green Jewish Cemetery.
28 Hampstead Garden Suburb (St Jude) Church.
29 Hendon Park Cemetery.
30 Hendon (St Mary) Churchyard.
34 Ruislip (St Martin) Churchyard Extension.
35 Wealdstone Cemetery.
37 Wembley Old Burial Ground.
38 Wembley (St John the Evangelist) Churchyard.
39 Paddington Cemetery.
40 Willesden Jewish Cemetery.
41 Willesden Liberal Jewish Cemetery.
42 Willesden New Cemetery.
43 Willesden Old Cemetery.
44 Acton Cemetery.
46 Chiswick Cemetery.
47 New Brentford (St Lawrence) Churchyard.
48 Ealing and Old Brentford Cemetery.
49 Greenford (Holy Cross) Churchyard.
51 Kensington (Hanwell) Cemetery.
52 Perivale Cemetery.
53 Westminster City Cemetery.
56 Feltham Cemetery.
58 Hampton Burial Ground.
62 Harlington (SS Peter and Paul) Churchyard.
64 Hayes (St Mary) Churchyard.
66 Heston (St Leonard) Churchyard.
68 New Brentford Cemetery.
69 Southall Cemetery.
70 Ashford Cemetery.
74 Littleton (St Mary Magdalene) Churchyard.
76 Sunbury New Cemetery.
77 Teddington Cemetery.
78 Hounslow Cemetery.
80 Twickenham Parochial Cemetery.
83 Hillingdon Cemetery.
84 Uxbridge Cemetery.
85 Harmondsworth (St Mary) Churchyard.

MONMOUTHSHIRE.
4   Abergavenny New Cemetery,Llanfoist.
9   Llanfoist (St Faith) Churchyard.
11 Llanover (St Bartholomew) Churchyard.
19 Trevethin (St Cadoc) Churchyard.
34 Caldicot (St Mary) Churchyard.
52 Newport (Christchurch) Cemetery,Christchurch.
67 Newport (St Woollos) Cemetery.
69 Panteg Cemetery.
76 Graig Congregational Chapelyard.
81 Malpas (St Mary) Churchyard.
82 Marshfield (St Mary) Churchyard.
83 Rogerstone (Bethesda) Baptist Chapelyard.
89 Usk (St Mary Magdalene) Churchyard.

NORFOLK.
11 Heydon (SS Peter and Paul) Churchyard.
15 Stratton Strawless (St Margaret) Churchyard.
21 Cantley (St Margaret) Churchyard.
24 Redenhall (The Assumption) Churchyard,Redwnhall-with-Harleston.
26 Thorpe-Next-Norwich (St Andrew) Church Cemetery.
30 Cromer No.2 Burial Ground.
43 Pulham St Mary the Virgin Churchyard.
58 Docking (St Mary) Churchyard.
60 Heacham (St Mary) Churchyard.
61 Hunstanton (St Mary) Churchyard.
67 Stanhoe (All Saints) Churchyard.
73 Marham (Holy Trinity) Churchyard.
74 Runcton Holme (St James) Churchyard,South Runcton.
77 Stradsett (St Mary) Churchyard.
85 Great Yarmouth (Caister) Cemetery,East Caister.
88 Ormesby St Margaret Churchyard,Ormsby.
94 Aldborough (St Mary) Churchyard.
96 Beeston Regis (All Saints) Churchyard.
101 Mundesley (All Saints) Churchyard.
103 Overstrand (St Martin) Churchyard.
109 Upper Sheringham (All Saints) Churchyard.
110 West Runton (Holy Trinity) Churchyard,Runton.

111 Weybourne (All Saints) Churchyard.
118 Kimberley (St Peter) Churchyard.
127 Hillington (St Mary) Churchyard.
128 Little Massingham (St Andrew) Churchyard.
131 Great Yarmouth (Gorleston) Cemetery.
132 Great Yarmouth New Cemetery.
133 Great Yarmouth Old Cemetery.
137 Colney (St Andrew) Churchyard.
138 Cringleford (St Peter) Churchyard.
139 East Carleton (St Mary) Churchyard.
151 King's Lynn Cemetery.
162 Hedenham (St Peter) Churchyard.
172 Woodton (All Saints) Churchyard.
179 Upwell (St Peter) Churchyard.
184 East Bilney (St Mary) Churchyard,Beetley.
195 Mileham (St John the Baptist) Churchyard.
207 Eaton (St Andrew) New Churchyard,Norwich.
209 Norwich Cemetery.
210 Norwich (The Rosary) Cemetery.
231 Hoveton St John Churchyard,Hoveton.
235 Sloley (St Bartholomew) Churchyard.
247 Narborough (All Saints) Churchyard.
254 Swaffham (SS Peter and Paul) Churchyard.
255 Thetford Cemetery.
256 Blo'Norton (St Andrew) Churchyard.
259 East Harling Cemetery,Harling.
261 Feltwell (St Nicholas) Churchyard.
285 Attleborough Cemetery.
288 Breckles (St Margaret) Churchyard,Stow Bedon.
301 Watton Nonconformist Burial Ground.

NORTHAMPTON.
1 Brackley (St Peter) Churchyard.
6 Helmdon (St Mary Magdalene) Churchyard.
13 Church Brampton (St Botolph) Churchyard.
27 Barby (St Mary) Churchyard.
31 Yelvertoft (All Saints) Churchyard.
32 Daventry (Holy Cross) Churchyard.
38 Newnham (St Michael) Churchyard.
55 Castle Ashby (St Mary Magdalene) Churchyard.
60 Northampton (Towcester Road) Cemetery,Hardingstone.
67 Cottingham (St Mary Magdalene) Churchyard.
74 Kettering Cemetery.
76 Middleton Cheney (All Saints) Churchyard.
78 Abington (SS Peter and Paul) Churchyard.
79 Northampton General Cemetery.
80 Dallington Cemetery.
82 Great Billing (St Andrew) Churchyard Roman Catholic Extension.
107 Raunds Wesleyan Methodist Chapelyard.
143 Wellingborough (Doddington Road) Cemetery.
144 Wellingborough (London Road) Cemetery.
146 Barnack Cemetery,Soke of Peterborough.
151 Peterborough Old Cemetery,Soke of Peterborough.
161 Hambleton (St Andrew) Churchyard,Rutland.
164 Oakham Cemetery,Rutland.

NORTHERN IRELAND.
14 Layde Church of Ireland Churchyard,Cushendall,County Antrim.
33 Belfast City Cemetery,County Antrim.
37 Carnmoney Cemetery,County Antrim.
40 Carrickfergus (Victoria) Cemetery,County Antrim.
42 Ballylinney Presbyterian Cemetery,County Antrim.
45 Glenarm New Cemetery,County Antrim.
52 Larne New Cemetery,County Antrim.
56 Drumbeg (St Patrick) Church of Ireland Churchyard,County Antrim.
57 Dundrod Presbyterian Churchyard,County Antrim.
68 Kilmore (St Aidnan) Church of Ireland Churchyard,County Armagh.
71 Armagh (St Mark) Church of Ireland Churchyard,County Armagh.
74 Derrytrasna Roman Catholic Churchyard,County Armagh.
79 Seagoe Cemetery,County Armagh.
80 Lurgan (Dougher) Roman Catholic Cemetery,County Armagh.
85 Bessbrook (Christ Church) Church of Ireland Churchyard Extension,County Armagh.
102 Tullylish (All Saints) Church of Ireland Churchyard,County Down.
105 Banbridge Roman Catholic Cemetery,County Down.
106 Banbridge Town Cemetery,County Down.
107 Bangor New Cemetery,County Down.
110 Belfast (Dundonald) Cemetery,County Down.
124 Down Cathedral New Cemetery,County Down.
136 Hillsborough (St Malachi) Church of Ireland Churchyard,County Down.
137 Knockbreda Church of Ireland Churchyard,Newtownbreda,County Down.
138 Holywood Cemetery,County Down.
145 Newcastle (St John's) Cemetery,County Down.
146 Colonallan Church of Ireland Churchyard,County Down.
165 Kinawley Church of Ireland Churchyard,Derrylin,County Fermanagh.
168 Enniskillen New Cemetery,County Fermanagh.
181 Coleraine Cemetery,County Londonderry.
183 Killowen (St John) Church of Ireland Churchyard,County Londonderry.
188 Kilrea (St Patrick) Church of Ireland Churchyard,County Londonderry.
196 Londonderry City Cemetery,County Londonderry.
201 Glendermot Church of Ireland Churchyard,County Londonderry.
222 Killeeshil (St Paul) Church of Ireland Churchyard,County Tyrone.
229 Dungannon Borough Cemetery,County Tyrone.
231 Cappagh (St Eugenius) Church of Ireland Churchyard,East Mountjoy,County Tyrone.
239 Kilskeery Church of Ireland Churchyard,County Tyrone.
242 Omagh New Cemetery,County Tyrone.
248 Strabane Cemetery,County Tyrone.

NORTHUMBERLAND.
1   Newcastle-upon-Tyne (All Saints) Cemetery.
2   Newcastle-upon-Tyne (Byker and Heaton) Cemetery.
3   Newcastle-upon-Tyne (Old Jesmond) General Cemetery.
4   Newcastle-upon-Tyne (St Andrew's and Jesmond) Cemetery.
5   Newcastle-upon-Tyne (St John's, Westgate and Elswick) Cemetery.
7   Newcastle-upon-Tyne (St Nicholas) Cemetery.
11 Alnwick Cemetery.
11a Bolton Churchyard.
19 South Charlton (St James) Churchyard.
20 Warkworth (St laurence) Church Burial Ground.
26 Bedlington (St Cuthbert) Churchyard.
34 Berwick-upon-Tweed Cemetery.
36 Blyth Cemetery.
39 Horton (St Mary) Churchyard, Blyth.
43 North Gosforth Joint Burial Ground.
49 Earsdon (St Alban) Churchyard, Seaton Valley.
56 Old Bewick (Holy Trinity) Churchyard.
58 Wooler (St Mary) Church Burial Ground.
60 Gosforth (St Nicholas) Churchyard.
74 Longbenton (Benton) Cemetery.
75 Morpeth (SS Mary and James) Churchyard.
78 Cresswell (St Bartholomew) Churchyard.
83 Newburn (Lemington) Cemetery.
86 Ancroft (St Anne) Churchyard.
87 Norham (St Cuthbert) Churchyard.
96 Tynemouth (Preston) Cemetery.
97 Wallsend (Church Bank) Cemetery.
99 Whitley Bay (Hartley South) Cemetery.

NOTTINGHAMSHIRE.
2   Annesley and Felley Cemetery, Annesley.
32 Plumtree (St Mary) Churchyard.
39 East Retford Cemetery.
60 Hucknall Cemetery.
66 East Leake (St Mary the Virgin) Churchyard.
68 Mansfield (Nottingham Road) Cemetery.
70 Forest Town (St Alban) Churchyard.
84 Nottingham Church Cemetery.
85 Nottingham General Cemetery.
96 Halam (St Michael) Churchyard.
106 Southwell Minster (St Mary) Churchyard.
112 Sutton-in-Ashfield Cemetery.
121 Worksop (Retford Road) Cemetery.

OXFORDSHIRE.
1   Banbury Cemetery.
3   Alkerton (St Michael) churchyard.
24 Bicester Cemetery.
32 Spelsbury (All Saints) Churchyard.
36 Dorchester Cemetery.
44 Goring (St Thomas of Canterbury) Churchyard.
45 Mapledurham (St Margaret) Churchyard.
51 Henley-on-Thames Cemetery.
69 Oxford (Botley) Cemetery.
71 Oxford (Holy Cross) Cemetery.
73 Oxford (Rose Hill) Cemetery.
74 Oxford (Wolvercote) Cemetery.

85 Brize Norton (St Brice) Churchyard Extension.
97 Witney Burial Ground.

SCOTLAND.
1   Applin Old Churchyard, Lismore and Applin, Argyll.
2   Applin (St Cross) Episcopalian Churchyard, Lismore and Applin, Argyll.
4   Ardmarnoch House Burial Ground, Filfinan, Argyll.
9   Campbeltown (Kilkerrean) Cemetery, Argyll.
14 Dunoon Cemetery, Dunoon and Kilmun, Argyll.
15 Dunoon (Holy Trinity) Episcopalian Churchyard, Dunoon and Kilmun, Argyll.
22 Kiells Old Churchyard, Jara, Argyll.
26 Kilbride Parish Churchyard, Kilfinan, Argyll.
31 Kilchoman New Cemetery, Argyll.
41 Kilmhoiri Old Churchyard, Craignish, Argyll.
44 Kilmory Castle Burial Ground, Glassary, Argyll.
45 Kilmun Cemetery, Dunoon and Kilmun, Argyll.
50 Kilvickeon Old Churchyard, Kilfinichen and Kilvickeon, Argyll.
52 Lochgoilhead Parish Churchyard, Lochgoilhead and Kilmorich, Argyll.
54 Oban (Pennyfuir) Cemetery, Kilmore and kilbride, Argyll.
60 Tarbert Burial Ground, Kilcalmonell, Argyll.
64 Alloa (Sunnyside) Cemetery, Clackmannan.
69 Tillicoultry Cemetery, Clackmannan.
76 Boturich Castle Private Cemetery, Kilmaronock, Dumbarton.
77 Cardross Parish Churchyard, Dumbarton.
80 Dumbarton Cemetery, Dumbarton.
81 Faslane Cemetery, Row, Dumbarton.
82 Helensburgh Cemetery, Row, Dumbarton.
84 Kirkintilloch (Auld Aisle) Cemetery, Dumbarton.
86 New Patrick Cemetery, Dumbarton.
87 New Kilpatrick Parish Churchyard, Dumbarton.
92 Abercrombie Old Chapelyard, Fife.
97 Ballingry Cemetery, Fife.
105 Cowdenbeath Cemetery, Beath, Fife.
109 Cupar New Cemetery, Fife.
112 Dunfermline Cemetery, Fife.
115 East Wemyss Cemetery, Wemyss, Fife.
118 Forgan (Vicarsford) Cemetery, Fife.
119 Inverkeithing Cemetery, Fife.
122 Kilconquhar Parish Churchyard, Fife.
127 Kirkcaldy Cemetery, Kirkcaldy and Dysart, Fife.
136 Newburgh Cemetery, Fife.
141 St Andrews Eastern Cemetery, Fife.
142 St Andrews Western Cemetery, Fife.
151 Kinross East Burying Ground, Kinross.
153 Orwell Parish Churchyard, Kinross.
167 Callander Cemetery, Perth.
169 Comrie Cemetery, Perth.
171 Crieff Cemetery, Perth.
180 Innerwick-in-Glenlyon Parish Churchyard, Fortingall, Perth.
187 Kinfauns Parish Churchyard, Perth.
199 Perth (Wellshill) Cemetery, Perth.
200 Pitlochry New Cemetery, Moulin, Perth.
203 St Madoes Parish Churchyard, Perth.

204 Scone Cemetery,Perth.
208 Trossachs Parish Churchyard,Callander,Perth.
211 Denny Cemetery,Stirling.
212 Falkirk Cemetery,Stirling.
214 Grangemouth Burial Ground,Stirling.
226 Stirling (Ballengeich) Cemetery,Stirling.
228 Stirling (Mar Place) Cemetery,Stirling.
229 Stirling (Valley) Cemetery,Stirling.
231 Colinton Parish Churchyard,Edinburgh.
232 Corstorphine Parish Churchyard,Edinburgh.
235 Edinburgh (Comely Bank) Cemetery.
236 Edinburgh (Dalry) Cemetery.
237 Edinburgh (Dean,Western) Cemetery.
238 Edinburgh Eastern Cemetery.
239 Edinburgh (Grange) Cemetery.
240 Edinburgh (Liberton) Cemetery.
241 Edinburgh (Morningside) Cemetery.
242 Edinburgh (New Calton) Burial Ground.
244 Edinburgh (Newington) Cemetery.
245 Edinburgh (North Merchiston) Cemetery.
246 Edinburgh (Piershill) Cemetery.
247 Edinburgh (Portobello) Cemetery.
248 Edinburgh Roman Catholic Cemetery.
249 Edinburgh (Rosebank) Cemetery.
252 Edinburgh (Seafield) Cemetery.
253 Edinburgh (Warriston) Cemetery.
258 Cockpen Old Churchyard,Edinburgh.
259 Cranston Parish Churchyard,Midlothian.
262 Dalkeith (Eskbank) Cemetery,Midlothian.
263 Dalmahoy (Sr Mary) Episcopalian Churchyard,Ratho,Midlothian.
267 Inveresk Parish Churchyard,Midlothian.
269 Lasswade Old Churchyard,Midlothian.
270 Loanhead Cemetery,Lasswade,Midlothian.
274 Penicuik Cemetery,Midlothian.
275 Penicuik Parish Churchyard,Midlothian.
277 Roslin Cemetery,Lasswade,Midlothian.
279 West Calder Cemetry,Midlothian.
280 Aberdeen (Allenvale) Cemetery.
281 Aberdeen (Grove) Cemetery.
283 Aberdeen (Nellfield) Cemetery.
286 Aberdeen (St Peter's) Cemetery.
287 Aberdeen (Springbank) Cemetery.
288 Aberdeen (Trinity) Cemetery.
294 Belhelvie Old Cemetery,Aberdeen.
308 Ellon Cemetery,Aberdeen.
310 Folla-Rule (Sr George) Episcopalian Churchyard,Fyvie,Aberdeen.
313 Fraserburgh (Kirkton) Cemetery,Aberdeen.
319 Huntly Cemetery,Aberdeen.
329 Kincardine O'Neil (Christ Church) Episcopalian Churchyard,Aberdeen.
330 Kincardine O'Neil Old Churchyard,Aberdeen.
333 Kintore Parish Churchyard,Aberdeen.
339 Longside New Parish Churchyard,Aberdeen.
341 Lonmay Parish Churchyard,Aberdeen.
353 New Pitsligo Parish Churchyard,Tyrie,Aberdeen.
357 Old Machar Cathedral Churchyard,Aberdeen.
358 Peterculter Parish Churchyard,Aberdeen.
359 Peterculter New Burial Ground,Aberdeen.
360 Peterhead New Cemetery,Aberdeen.
378 Turriff Cemetery,Aberdeen.
380 Arbroath Eastern Cemetery,Arbroath and St Vigeans,Angus.
381 Arbroath western Cemetery,Arbroath and St Vigeans,Angus.
383 Brechin Cemetery,Angus.
385 Dundee Eastern Necropolis,Angus.
386 Dundee Western Cemetery,Angus.
387 Dundee Western Necropolis,Angus.
395 Monifieth Cemetery,Angus.
396 Montrose (Rosehill) Cemetery,Angus.
398 Montrose (Sleepyhillock) Cemetery,Angus.
422 Cuier Churchyard,Barra,Inverness.
424 Daviot Parish Churchyard,Daviot and Dunlichity,Inverness.
430 Fort William (St Andrew) Episcopalian Churchyard,Kilmallie,Inverness.
435 Heisker Island Graves,North Uist,Inverness.
438 Insh (St Eunan) Churchyard,Kingussie,Inverness.
442 Inverness (Tomnahurich) Cemetery.
447 Kilmallie Old Churchyard,Inverness.
455 Kilmuir Old Churchyard,Duirinish,Inverness.
458 Kingussie Parish Churchyard,Kingussie and Insh,Inverness.
484 Banchory Ternan Parish Churchyard,Kincardine.
495 Laurencekirk Cemetery,Kincardine.
497 Nigg New Parish Churchyard,Kincardine.
500 St Cyrus Upper (Parish) Churchyard,Kincardine.
501 Ardrossan Cemetery,Ayr.
503 Ayr Cemetery.
508 Colmonell Parish Churchyard,Ayr.
510 Cumnock New Cemetery,Old Cumnock,Ayr.
514 Darvel Cemetery,Ayr.
517 Dundonald (Troon) Cemetery,Ayr.
520 Girvan (Doune) Cemetery,Ayr.
522 Irvine Cemetery,Ayr.
523 Irvine Parish Churchyard,Ayr.
525 Kilmarnock Cemetery,Ayr.
528 Kirkmichael Parish Churchyard,Ayr.
530 Largs Cemetery,Ayr.
531 Mauchline Cemetery,Ayr.
533 Monkton and Prestwick Cemetery,Ayr.
546 Symington Parish Churchyard,Ayr.
547 Tarbolton Parish Churchyard,Ayr.
549 West Kilbride Cemetery,Ayr.
556 Earlston Parish Churchyard,Berwick.
558 Eyemouth Cemetery,Berwick.
561 Greenlaw Parish Churchyard,Berwick.
563 Hutton Parish Churchyard,Berwick.
566 Lennel Old Churchyard,Berwick.
567 Longformacus New Burial Ground,Berwick.
569 Mordington Burial Ground,Berwick.
579 Rothesay Cemetery,Bute.
581 Annan Cemetery,Dumfries.
582 Applrgarth Parish Churchyard,Dumfries.
591 Dryfesdale Cemetery,Dunfries.
596 Dunfries (St Michael's) New Cemetery,Dumfries.
608 Kirkpartick-Juxta Parish Churchyard,Dumfries.

612 Moffat Cemetery,Kirkpatrick-Juxta,Dumfries.
613 Morton New Cemetery,Dumfries.
617 St Mungo Old Parish Churchyard,Dumfries.
621 Troqueer New Burial Ground,Dumfries.
625 Aberlady Parish Churchyard,East Lothian.
626 Athelstaneford Parish Churchyard,East Lothian.
627 Dirleton Parish Churchyard,East Lothian.
632 Haddington Cemetery,East Lothian.
639 Prestonkirk Parish Churchyard,East Lothian.
640 Prestonpans New Cemetery,East Lothian.
644 Tynninghame Burial Ground,East Lothian.
660 Kirkbean Parish Churchyard,Kirkcudbright.
669 Innerleithen Cemetery,Peebles.
671 Peebles Cemetery.
674 Cathcart Cemetery,Renfrew.
675 Eastwood Cemetery,Renfrew.
677 Greenock Cemetery,Renfrew.
679 Kilbarchan Cemetery,Renfrew.
680 Kilmacolm Cemetery,Renfrew.
682 Neilston Cemetery,Renfrew.
683 Paisley Abbey Cemetery,Renfrew.
684 Paisley (Hawkhead) Cemetery,Renfrew.
685 Piasley (Woodside) Cemetery,Renfrew.
686 Port Glasgow Cemetery,Renfrew.
687 Renfrew (Arkleston) Cemetery,Renfrew.
696 Kelso Cemetery,Roxburgh.
711 Ashkirk Parish Church,Selkirk.
713 Galashiels (Eastlands) Cemetery,Selkirk.
717 Selkirk Parish Churchyard.
718 Selkirk (shawfield) Cemetery,Selkirk.
721 Bo'ness Cemetery,Bo'ness and Carriden,West Lothian.
722 Dalmeny Cemetery,West Lothian.
723 Ecclesmachan Cemetery,West Lothian.
725 Kirkliston Burial Ground,West Lothian.
726 Linlithgow Cemetery,West Lothian.
728 Polkemmet Private Burying Ground,Whitburn,West Lothian.
729 Uphall Cemetery,West Lothian.
730 Whitburn Cemetery,West Lothian.
742 Portpatrick Cemetery,Wigtown.
746 Stoneykirk Parish Churchyard,Wigtown.
752 Glasgow (Craigton) Cemetery.
754 Glasgow Eastern Necropolis.
755 Glasgow (Lambhill) Cemetery.
756 Glasgow Necropolis.
757 Glasgow (Riddrie Park) Cemetery.
758 Glasgow (St Kentigern's) Roman Catholic Cemetery.
760 Glasgow (Sandymount) Cemetery.
761 Glasgow (Sighthill) Cemetery.
762 Glasgow Southern Necropolis (Central Division).
764 Glasgow Western Necropolis.
766 Tollcross (Central) United Free Churchyard,Glasgow.
774 Cadder Cemetery,Lanark.
775 Cambuslang (Westburn) Cemetery,Lanark.
776 Cambusnethan Cemetery,Lanark.
780 Carluke (Wilton) Cemetery,Lanark.
783 Carnwath New Cemetery,Lanark.
789 Culter Parish Churchyard,Lanark.
790 Dalziel (Airbles) Cemetery,Lanark.
792 Dalziel (Old Manse Road) Burial Ground,Lanark.

795 East Kilbride Cemetery,Lanark.
798 Hamilton (Bent) Cemetery,Lanark.
799 Hamilton Parish Cemetery,Lanark.
803 Lanark (St Leonard's) Cemetery.
805 Lanark (St Nicholas) Cemetery.
807 Lesmahagow Cemetery,Lanark.
808 New Monkland Cemetery,Lanark.
810 Old Monkland Cemetery,Lanark.
811 Pettinain Parish Churchyard,Lanark.
812 Rutherglen Cemetery,Lanark.
816 Strathaven New Cemetery,Avondale,Lanark.
820 Banff Cemetery,Banff.
827 Cullen Cemetery,Banff.
832 Gamrie Old Churchyard,Banff.
835 Keith (Broomhill) Cemetery,Banff.
838 Macduff Parish Churchyard,Banff.
840 Martlach Parish Churchyard,Banff.
843 Rathven (Hillhead) Cemetery,Banff.
854 Halkirk Parish Churchyard,Caithness.
858 Olrig New Cemetery,Caithness.
862 Thurso Cemetery,Caithness.
871 Duffus Cemetery,Moray.
874 Elgin New Cemetery,Moray.
876 Forres (Cluny Hill) Cemetery,Moray.
877 Grantown-on-Spey New Burial Ground,Cromdale,Moray.
879 Kinloss Abbey Churchyard,Moray.
881 Knockando Parish Churchyard,Moray.
886 Nairn Cemetery,Nairn.
893 Evie Cemetery,Evie and Rendall,Orkney.
899 Kirkwall (St Olaf's) Cemetery,Kirkwall and St Olaf,Orkney.
900 Lyness Naval Cemetery,Hoy and Graemsay,Orkney.
902 Osmondwall Cemetery,Walls and Flotta,Orkney.
909 Stenness Parish Churchyard,Orkney.
926 Cromarty Parish Cemetery,Ross and Cromarty.
935 Fodderty Old Churchyard,Ross and Cromarty.
936 Foich Burial Ground,Lochbroom,Ross and Cromarty.
956 Londubh Old Churchyard,Gairloch,Ross and Cromarty.
963 Rosskeen Parish Churchyard Extension,Ross and Cromarty.
965 Sandwick Cemetery,Stornoway,Ross and Cromarty.
966 Suddie Old Churchyard,Knockbain,Ross and Cromarty.
967 Tain (St Duthus) Cemetery,Ross and Cromarty.
968 Tarbat Parish Churchyard,Ross and Cromarty.
975 Brora Cemetery,Clyne,Sutherland.
990 Melness Cemetery,Tongue,Sutherland.
1014 Lerwick New Cemetery,Zetland.
1030 Voe Old Churchyard,Delting,Zetland.

SHROPSHIRE.
11 Dorrington (St Edward the Confessor) Churchyard,Condover.
19 Shrewsbury General Cemetery,Meole Brace.
37 Church Stretton (St Lawrence) Churchyard Extension.
48 Dawley Magna (Holy Trinity) Churchyard.
52 Stoke-upon-Tern (St Peter) Churchyard Extension.
60 Little Ness (St Martin) Churchyard.
63 Petton Churchyard.
67 Ludlow New Cemetery.
70 Ashford Bowdler (St Andrew) Churchyard.

74	Caynham (St Mary) Churchyard.
81	Little Drayton (Christ Church) Churchyard.
82	Market Drayton Cemetery.
89	Newport Cemetery.
93	Oswestry General Cemetery.
95	Haughton (St Chad) Churchyard, West Felton.
97	Knockin (St Mary) Churchyard.
100	Moreton (SS Philip and James) Churchyard, Llanyblodwel.
101	Nantmawr Congregational Chapelyard, Oswestry Rural.
104	St Martin's Churchyard.
111	Donington (St Cuthbert) Churchyard.
114	Shifnal (St Andrew) Churchyard.
120	Hadley General Cemetery.
125	Clive (All Saints) Churchyard.
129	Prees (St Chad) Churchyard.
130	Shawbury (St Mary) Churchyard.
138	Broseley Cemetery.
143	Willey (St John the Devine) Churchyard.
145	Tilstock (Christ Church) Churchyard, Whitchurch Rural.
147	Whitchurch Cemetery.

SOMERSET.
- 10 Burrington (Holy Trinity) Churchyard.
- 17 Uphill (St Nicholas) Churchyard.
- 19 Wedmore (St Mary Magdalene) Churchyard.
- 25 Bath (Locksbrook) Cemetery.
- 26 Bath (St James's) Cemetery.
- 30 Bathwick Church Cemetery.
- 31 Bathampton (St Nicholas) Churchyard.
- 33 Bathford (St Swithun) Churchyard.
- 35 Charlcombe (St Mary) Churchyard.
- 37 Lansdown Cemetery, Charlcombe.
- 40 Wellow Cemetery.
- 42 Bridgwater (Wembdon Road) Cemetery (Chapel Portion).
- 43 Bridgwater (Wembdon Road) Cemetery (Church Portion).
- 49 Middlezoy (Holy Cross) Churchyard.
- 67 Hinton St George (St George) Churchyard.
- 71 Clevedon (St Andrew) Churchyard.
- 96 Frome (St John the Baptist) Churchyard.
- 99 Highbridge Cemetery.
- 101 Corston (All Saints) Church.
- 103 Keynsham Cemetery.
- 118 Kingweston (All Saints) Churchyard.
- 126 Easton-in-Gordano (St George) Churchyard.
- 139 Minehead Cemetery.
- 141 Radstock (St Nicholas) Churchyard.
- 153 Shepton Mallet Burial Ground.
- 157 Taunton (St Mary's) Cemetery.
- 161 Churchstanton (St Paul) Churchyard.
- 172 Staple Fitzpaine (St Peter) Churchyard.
- 173 Staplegrove (St John) Churchyard.
- 176 West Monkton (St Augustine) Churchyard.
- 183 Sampford Arundel (Holy Cross) Churchyard.
- 185 Wells Cathedral Cemetery.
- 186 Wells Cemetery.
- 196 Wookey (St Matthew) Churchyard Extension.
- 197 Weston-Super-Mare Cemetery.
- 198 Carhampton (St John the Baptist) Churchyard.
- 199 Crowcombe (Holy Ghost) Churchyard.
- 210 Holford (St Mary) Churchyard.
- 219 Redlynch (St Peter) Church, Bruton.
- 222 South Cadbury (St Thomas A Becket) Churchyard.

STAFFORDSHIRE.
- 4 Brierley Hill (South Street) Baptist Churchyard.
- 6 Ogley Hay (St James) Churchyard.
- 21 Coseley (Christ Church) Churchyard.
- 33 Cradley Heath (St Luke) Churchyard.
- 35 Rowley Regis (St Giles) Churchyard.
- 41 Codsall (St Nicholas) Churchyard Extensions.
- 45 Pattingham (St Chad) Churchyard.
- 47 Pennfields (St Philip) Churchyard, Trysull and Seisdon.
- 49 Wombourn (St Benedict) churchyard.
- 52 Smethwick (Uplands) Cemetery.
- 57 Tetenhall Regis (St Michael) Churchyard.
- 60 Walsall (Bloxwich) Cemetery.
- 61 Walsall (Ryecroft) Cemetery.
- 65 Pelsall (St Michael) Churchyard.
- 67 Rushall (St Michael) Churchyard.
- 70 Wednesbury Cemetery.
- 71 Wednesfield (St Thomas) Churchyard Extension.
- 73 West Bromwich Cemetery.
- 78 Wolverhampton General Cemetery.
- 82 Biddulph (St Lawrence) Churchyard.
- 84 Burton-upon-Trent Cemetery.
- 85 Horninglow (St John) Churchyard.
- 87 Alton (St John) Roman Catholic Churchyard.
- 91 Cheddleton (St Edward the Confessor) Churchyard.
- 93 Kingsley (St Werburgh) Churchyard.
- 94 Upper Tean (Christ Church) Churchyard, Checkley.
- 105 Norton-in-the-Moors (St Bartholomew) Churchyard.
- 108 Lichfield (St Chad) Churchyard.
- 109 Lichfield (St Michael) Churchyard.
- 114 Cannock Chase Military Burial Ground, Brereton.
- 125 Whittington (St Giles) Churchyard.
- 134 Castle Church (St Mary) Chuhrchyard.
- 135 Stafford Cemetery.
- 140 Great Haywood (St Stephen) Churchyard, Colwick.
- 143 Ingestre (St Mary) Churchyard.
- 152 Normacot (Holy Evangelists) Churchyard.
- 153 Stoke-on-Trent (Burslem) Cemetery.
- 156 Stoke-on-Trent (Hartshill) Cemetery.
- 170 Rangemore (All Saints) Churchyard, Tatenhill.
- 176 Blithfield (St Leonard) Churchyard.
- 177 Denstone (All Saints) Churchyard.
- 180 Newborough (All Saints) Churchyard.
- 183 Uttoxeter Cemetery.

SUFFOLK.
- 1 Aldeburgh (SS Peter and Paul) Churchyard.
- 2 Beccles Cemetery.
- 3 Aldringham (St Andrew) Churchyard.
- 9 Dunwich (St James) Churchyard.
- 23 Wenhaston (St Peter) Churchyard.
- 45 Bungay Cemetery.
- 54 Felixstowe New Cemetery.
- 55 Felixstowe (SS Peter and Paul) Churchyard.
- 64 Redgrave (St Botolph) Churchyard.
- 69 Badingham (St John the Baptist) Churchyard.
- 83 Ipswich Cemetery.

85	Lowestoft (Beccles Road) Cemetery.	72	Ockley Cemetery.
86	Lowestoft (Kirkley) Cemetery.	75	Dorking Cemetery.
91	Burgh Castle (St Peter) Churchyard.	76	East Molesey Cemetery.
92	Carlton Colville Additional Churchyard.	78	Egham (St Jude's) Cemetery.
93	Carlton Colville (St Peter) Churchyard.	80	Ashtead (St Giles) Churchyard.
98	Oulton (St Michael) Churchyard.	83	Cobham Cemetery.
106	Earl Soham Cemetery.	84	Ewell (St Mary) Churchyard.
113	Orford (St Bartholomew) Churchyard.	86	Hatchford (St Matthew) Churchyard, Cobham.
121	Brantham (St Michael) Churchyard.	88	Little Bookahm Churchyard.
126	East Bergholt Cemetery.	91	Epsom Cemetery.
128	Holbrook (All Saints) Churchyard.	93	Claygate (Holy Trinity) Churchyard.
130	Shotley (St Mary) Churchyard.	94	Esher (Christ Church) Churchyard.
133	Stutton (St Peter) Churchyard.	95	Long Ditton (St Mary) Churchyard.
137	Southwold (St Edmund) Churchyard.	96	Thames Ditton (St Nicholas) Churchyard.
138	Stowmarket Cemetery.	97	Ash Cemetery, Ash and Normandy.
173	Euston (St Genevieve) Churchyard.	99	Frensham (St Mary) Churchyard.
176	Bury St Edmunds Cemetery.	102	Shottermill (St Stephen) Churchyard.
207	Nayland Cemetery, Nayland-with-Wissington.	103	Tilford (All Saints) Churchyard, Farnham Rural.
215	Icklingham (St James) Churchyard.	104	Wyke (St Mark) Churchyard, Ash and Normandy.
224	Exning Cemetery.	106	Farnham Civil Cemetery.
225	Sudbury Cemetery.	110	Wrecclesham (St Peter) Churchyard Extension.
240	Flempton (St Catherine) Churchyard.	112	Frimley (St Peter) Churchyard.
242	Great Livermere (St Peter) Churchyard.	113	York Town (St Michael) Churchyard.
		114	Busbridge (St John the Baptist) Churchyard.
SURREY.		115	Godalming New Cemetery.
1	Brookwood Military Cemetery.	118	Guildford (Stoke) Cemetery.
2	Barnes (East Sheen) Cemetery.	126	Send (St Mary) Churchyard, Send and Ripley.
3	Barnes Old Cemetery.	128	Shere (St James) Churchyard.
4	Mortlake Burial Ground.	131	Worplesdon (St Mary) Churchyard.
6	Bandon Hill Cemetery, Beddington.	132	Ham (St Andrew) Churchyard.
8	Carshalton (All Saints) Churchyard.	134	Bramley Cemetery.
9	Caterham Burial Ground.	135	Chiddingfold (St Mary) Churchyard.
10	Warlingham (All Saints) Churchyard.	136	Cranleigh Cemetery.
11	Whyteleafe (St Luke) Churchyard.	138	Grayswood (All Saints) Churchyard, Witley.
13	Sanderstead (All Saints) Churchyard.	142	Shamley Green (Christ Church) Churchyard, Wonersh.
15	Croydon (Mitcham Road) Cemetery.	143	Thursley (St Michael) Churchyard.
16	Croydon (Queen's Road) Cemetery.	148	Kingston-on-Thames Cemetery.
18	Shirley (St John) Churchyard.	150	Fulham New Cemetery, North Sheen.
21	Chelsham (St Leonard) Churchyard.	151	Petersham (St Peter) Churchyard.
27	Godstone (St Nicholas) Churchyard.	152	Richmond Cemetery.
29	Limpsfield (St Peter) Churchyard.	153	Surbiton Cemetery.
32	Tandridge (St Peter) Churchyard.	154	Malden (St John the Baptist) Churchyard.
34	Battersea Cemetery, Morden.	156	Walton-on-Thames Cemetery.
35	Merton (St Mary) Churchyard.	157	Weybridge Cemetery.
36	Morden (St Laurence) Churchyard.	158	Windlesham Additional Burial Ground.
37	Mitcham Burial Ground.	159	Windlesham (Bagshot) Burial Ground.
38	Streatham Park Cemetery.	160	Brookwood Cemetery (The London Necropolis).
41	Reigate Cemetery.	161	Horsell (St Mary) churchyard.
42	Betchworth (St Michael) Churchyard.	162	Woking Crematorium.
43	Buckland (St Mary) Churchyard.		
45	Chipstaed (St Margaret) Churchyard.	SUSSEX.	
47	Kingswood (St Andrew) Churchyard.	2	Arundel Roman Catholic Cemetery.
52	Walton-on-the-Hill (St Peter) Churchyard.	4	Bognor Regis Cemetery.
55	Sutton Cemetery.	5	Chichester Cemetery.
57	Wimbledon (Gap Road) Cemetery.	9	Lyminster (St Mary Magdalene) Churchyard.
58	Wimbledon (St Mary-on-the-Hill) Churchyard.	13	Coolhurst Churchyard, Lower Beeding.
60	Byfleet (St Mary) Churchyard.	15	Crawley Monastery Burial Ground.
62	Valley End (St Saviour) Churchyard, Chobham.	17	Ifield (St Margaret) Churchyard.
64	Addlestone Burial Ground.	19	Nuthurst (St Andrew) Churchyard.
70	Holmwood (St Mary Magdalene) Churchyard, Capel.	23	Slinfold (St Peter) Churchyard.

24	Warnham (St Margaret) Churchyard.		**WALES.**
27	Horsham (Hills) Cemetery.	1	Aberdare Cemetery, Glamorgan.
30	Easebourne (St Mary) Churchyard.	3	Barry (Merthyr Dyfan) Cemetery, Glamorgan.
52	Stopham (St Mary) Churchyard.	4	Bridgend Cemetery, Glamorgan.
55	Old Shoreham Cemetery.	7	Nolton (St Mary) Churchyard, Glamorgan.
57	Southwick (St Michael) Churchyard.	9	Caerphilly (St Martin) Churchyard.
58	Henfield Cemetery.	12	Llanfabon (St Mabon) Churchyard, Glamorgan.
64	Pulborough (St Mary) Churchyard.	13	Llanfaban (St Mabon) Churchyard Extension, Glamorgan.
72	West Dean Cemetery.	16	Ystrad Mynach (Holy Trinity) Churchyard, Glamorgan.
83	Oving (St Andrew) Churchyard Extension.	17	Cardiff Cemetery, Glamorgan.
85	Selsey Cemetery.	19	Cardiff (Llandaff) Cemetery, Glamorgan.
88	Westhampnett (St Peter) Churchyard.	20	Llanishen (St Isan) Churchyard, Glamorgan.
89	West Stoke (St Andrew) Churchyard.	26	Radyr (St John the Baptist) Old Churchyard, Glamorgan.
93	Heene (St Botolph) Churchyard Extension.	29	St Fagans (St Fagan) Churchyard, Glamorgan.
95	Worthing (Broadwater) Cemetery.	30	St George-super-Ely (St George) Churchyard, Glamorgan.
102	Sedlescombe (St John the Baptist) Churchyard.	31	St Nicholas Churchyard, Glamorgan.
107	Bexhill Cemetery.	35	Whitchurch (St Mary) Churchyard, Glamorgan.
109	Little Common (St Mark) Churchyard.	37	Llanblethian (St John the Baptist) Churchyard, Glamorgan.
110	Brighton and Preston Cemetery.	54	Reynoldston (St George) Churchyard, Glamorgan.
111	Brighton Borough Cemetery.	77	Merthyr Tydfil (Ffrwd) Cemetery, Glamorgan.
112	Brighton Extramural Cemetery.	78	Merthyr Tydfil (Pant) Cemetery, Glamorgan.
114	Rottingdean (St Margaret) Churchyard.	83	Mountain Ash (Maesyrarian) Cemetery, Glamorgan.
124	Glynde Churchyard.	85	Neath (Ynysmaerdy) Cemetery, Glamorgan.
125	Hamsey (St Peter) Churchyard.	86	Aberpergwm (St Cattwg) Churchyard Private Extension, Neath Higher, Glamorgan.
128	Ringmer (St Mary) Churchyard.	95	Pontrhydyfen (Jerusalem) Calvinistic Methodist Chapelyard, Michaelston Higher, Glamorgan.
134	Hurstpierpoint (Holy Trinity) Churchyard.	107	Penarth Cemetery, Glamorgan.
135	Hurstpierpoint New Cemetery.	108	Penarth (St Augustine of Canterbury) Churchyard.
136	Hurstpierpoint Old Cemetery.	118	Pyle (St James) Churchyard, Glamorgan.
138	Lindfield (Walstead) Cemetery.	119	St Bride's Major (St Bridget) Churchyard, Glamorgan.
139	Newtimber (St John) Churchyard.	135	Pontypridd (Glyntaff) Cemetery, Glamorgan.
143	Cuckfield Cemetery.	137	Newton Nottage (St John the Baptist) Churchyard, Glamorgan.
144	Eastbourne (Ocklynge) Cemetery.	149	Rhondda (Treorchy) Cemetery, Glamorgan.
151	Pevensey (St Nicholas) Churchyard.	152	Cockett (St Peter) Churchyard, Glamorgan.
156	Coleman's Hatch (Holy Trinity) Churchyard, Hartfield.	163	Morriston (Horeb) Congregational Chapelyard, Glamorgan.
159	Forest Row Cemetery.	165	Sketty (Bethel) Welsh Congregational Chapelyard, Glamorgan.
163	Withyham (St Michael) Churchyard.	166	Sketty (St Paul) Churchyard, Glamorgan.
164	Worth (St Nicholas) Churchyard.	167	Swansea (Cwmgelly) Cemetery, Glamorgan.
165	East Grinstead (Mount Noddy) Cemetery.	168	Swansea (Danygraig) Cemetery, Glamorgan.
176	Fairlight (St Andrew) Churchyard.	171	Swansea (Oystermouth) Cemetery. Glamorgan.
177	Guestling (St Lawrence) Churchyard.	174	Brecon (St David) Churchyard, Brecknock.
178	Hastings Cemetery, Ore.	177	Cwmswyg Congregational Chapelyard, Traianglas, Brecknock.
182	Aldrington (St Leonard) Churchyard.	178	Devynnock (St Cynog) Churchyard, Maescar, Brecknock.
183	Hove Cemetery.	195	Penderyn (St Cynog) Churchyard, Brecknock.
184	Hove (St Andrew) Churchayrd.	199	Ystradgynlais (St Cynog) Churchyard, Ystradgynlais Lower, Brecknock.
185	Lewes Cemetery.	201	Llanfihangel Ystrad (St Michael) Churchyard, Cardigan.
187	Lewes (St John the Baptist-Subcastro) Churchyard.	203	Aberystwyth Cemetery, Cardigan.
189	Southover (St John the Baptist) Churchyard.	212	Cardigan Cemetery.
190	Kingston-near-Lewes (St Pancras) Churchyard.	214	Llandygwydd (St Tygwydd) Churchyard, Cardigan.
191	Newhaven Cemetery.	219	lampeter (St Peter) Churchyard, Cardigan.
197	Rye Cemetery, Rye Foreign.	231	Llangranog (St David) Churchyard, Cardigan.
199	Winchelsea (St Thomas) Churchyard.	238	Llangeitho (St Ceitho) Churchyard, Cardigan.
200	Seaford Cemetery.		
201	Burwash (St Bartholomew) Churchyard.		
203	Eridge Green (Holy Trinity) Churchyard, Frant.		
204	Frant (St Alban) Churchyard.		
216	Framfield (St Thomas Becket) Churchyard.		
219	High Hurstwood (Holy Trinity) Churchyard, Buxted.		
220	Isfield (St Margaret) Churchyard.		
225	Waldron (All Saints) Churchyard.		
226	Uckfield Cemetery.		

240 Tregaron (Bwlchgwynt) Calvinistic Methodist Chapelyard,Caron Township,Cardigan
241 Tredaron (Sr Caron) Churchyard Extension,Caron Township,Cardigan.
245 Carmarthen Cemetery.
251 Llanllwch (St Luke) Churchyard,Carmarthen.
278 Llanegwad (St Egwad) Churchyard,Carmarthen.
289 Llanelly Church Cemetery,Carmarthen.
306 Llanfihangel Ar Arth (St Michael) Churchyard,Carmarthen.
335 Cemmaes Calvinistic Methodist Chapelyard,Montgomery.
358 Welshpool (Christ Church) Churchyard,Montgomery.
361 Fishguard Church Cemetery,Pembroke.
367 Haverfordwest St Mary Church Cemetery,Pembroke.
368 Haverfordwest (St Thomas of Canterbury) Churchyard,Pembroke.
372 Herbrandston (St Mary) Churchyard,Pembroke.
383 Treffgarne (St Michael) Churchyard,Pembroke.
389 Milford Haven Cemetery,Pembroke.
393 Llawhaden (St Aidan) Churchyard,Pembroke.
402 Pembroke Dock (Llanion) Cemetery,Pembroke.
404 Pembroke (St Daniel) Churchyard,Pembroke.
416 Stackpole Elidor (SS Elidyr and James) Churchyard,Pembroke.
429 Llandrindod Wells Cemetery,Radnor.
439 Llansantffraid Cwmdeuddr (St Winifred) Churchyard,Radnor.
440 Llanyre (St LLyr) Churchyard,Radnor.
447 Llanedwen (St Edwen) Churchyard,Anglesey.
454 Amlwch Cemetery,Anglesey.
460 Holyhead (St Mary) Roman Catholic Churchyard,Anglesey.
461 Holyhead (St Seiriol) Churchyard,Anglesey.
462 Llangefni Cemetery,Anglesey.
463 Llandysilio (St Tyssilio) Churchyard,Anglesey.
480 Four Mile Bridge Wesleyan Chapelyard,Rhoscolyn,Anglesey.
491 Bangor (Glanadda) Cemetery,Caernarvon.
497 Llanbeblig (St Peblig) Churchayrd,Caernarvon.
498 Conway (St Agnes) Churchyard,Caernarvon.
506 Llysfaen (St Cynfran) Churchyard,Caernarvon.
518 Clynnog Fawr (St Beuno) Churchyard,Clynnog,Caernarvon.
531 Llanwnda (St Gwyndaf) Churchyard,Caernarvon.
535 Llandudno (Great Orme's Head) Cemetery,Caernarvon.
536 Llandudno (St Tudno) Churchyard,Caernarvon.
537 Llanrhos (SS Eleri and Mary) Churchyard,Caernarvon.
546 Llanbedrog Cemetery,Caernarvon.
550 Llangybi (Capel Helyg) Independent Chapelyard,Caernarvon.
564 Penmaenmawr (Dwygyfylchi) Cemetery,Caernarvon.
568 Abergele Cemetery,Denbigh.
571 Colwyn Bay (Bronynant) Cemetery,Denbigh.
597 Llanbedr Dyffryn Clwyd (St Peter) Churchyard,Denbigh.
603 Rhewl Calvinistic Methodist Chapelyard,Llanynys Rural,Denbigh.
609 St George (St George) Churchyard,Denbigh.
613 Wrexham Cemetery,Denbigh.
619 Gresford (All Saints) Churchyard,Denbigh.
629 Ruabon Cemetery,Denbigh.
637 Hawarden (St Deiniol) Churchyard,Flint.
646 Caerfallwch (St Paul) Churchyard,Northop,Flint.
648 Gwernafield (Holy Trinity) Churchyard,Mold Rural,Flint.
651 Holywell (Zion) Congregational Chapelyard,Holywell Rural,Flint.
658 Pontblyddyn (Christ Church) Churchyard,Mold Rural,Flint.
659 Whitford (SS Beuno and Mary) Churchyard,Flint.
664 Bangor Monachorum (St Dunawd) Churchyard,Flint.
671 Rhyl Church Cemetery,Flint.
672 Rhyl Town Cemetery,Flint.
673 Bodelwyddan (St Margaret) Churchyard,Flint.
677 St Asaph Cathedral Churchyard,Flint.
681 Harlech (St Tanwg) Churchyard,Merioneth.
684 Llanfair (St Mary) Churchyard,Marioneth.
690 Trawsfynydd (Penycefn) Cemetery,Merioneth.
692 Brithdir (St Mark) Churchyard,Brithdir and Islaw'roreth,Merioneth.
693 Llanaber (St Mary) Churchyard,Merioneth.
706 Corwen (SS Mael and Sulien) Churchyard,Merioneth.
713 Festiniog (Llan) Cemetery,Merioneth.
714 Festiniog (Newborough) Burial Ground,Merioneth.
725 Aberdovey Cemetery,Merioneth.

WARWICKSHIRE.
1 Acock's Green (St Mary) Churchyard.
3 Birmingham (Brandwood End) Cemetery.
4 Birmingham Crematorium.
5 Birmingham General Cemetery.
6 Birmingham (Handsworth) Cemetery.
7 Birmingham (Lodge Hill) Cemetery.
9 Birmingham (Witton) Cemetery.
10 Birmingham (Yardley) Cemetery.
12 Edgbaston (St Bartholomew) Churchyard.
14 Erdington (St Barnabas) Churchyard.
16 Handsworth (St Mary) Churchyard.
19 King's Norton (St Nicholas) Churchyard.
22 Northfield (St Laurence) Churchyard Extension.
23 Perry Barr (St John) Churchyard.
30 Coughton Church Cemetery.
32 Studley (St Mary) Churchyard.
37 Atherstone Cemetery.
40 Polesworth (St Editha) Churchyard.
47 Long Compton (SS Peter and Paul) Churchyard.
50 Coventry (London Road) Cemetery.
55 Radford (St Nicholas) Churchyard.
57 Farnborough (St Botolph) Churchyard.
60 Wyken (St Mary Magdalene) Churchyard.
63 Kenilworth (St Nicholas) Churchyard.
65 Castle Bromwich (SS Mary and Margaret) Churchyard.
66 Coleshill Cemetery.
67 Curdworth (St Peter) Churchyard.
69 Hampton-in-Arden (SS Mary and Bartholomew) Churchyard.
70 Maxstoke (St Michael) Churchyard.
74 Monks Kirby (St Edith) Churchyard.

75	Chilvers Coton (All Saints) Churchyard.	2	Hull Western Cemetery.
81	Astley (St Mary) Churchyard.	3	Hull Northern Cemetery.
82	Wolvey Cemetery.	5	Hull General Cemetery.
83	Leamington (Milverton) Cemetery.	6	Hull (Holy Trinity, Hessle Road) Cemetery.
84	Leamington (Whitnash Road) Cemetery.	11	Beverley (St Martin's) Cemetery.
88	Brinklow Cemetery.	12	Beverley (St Mary's) Cemetery.
89	Clifton-on-Dunsmore (St Mary) Additional Churchyard.	22	Bridlington Cemetery.
96	Wolston Cemetery.	35	Sledmere (St Mary) Churchyard.
97	Rugby (Clifton Road) Cemetery.	38	Fulford Water Burial Ground.
98	Rugby (St Marie) Roman Catholic Churchyard.	42	Filey (St Oswald) Churchyard.
100	Knowle (SS John the Baptist and Ann) Churchyard.	43	Great Driffield Cemetery.
101	Olton Franciscan Cemetery, Solihull.	45	Hessle Cemetery.
102	Salter Street (St Patrick) Churchyard, Tanworth.	46	Hornsea Cemetery.
106	Temple Balsall (St Mary) Churchyard, Balsall.	62	Burstwick (All Saints) Churchyard.
112	Napton-on-the-Hill Cemetery.	63	Easington Cemetery.
115	Southam (St James) Churchyard.	79	Wilberfoss (St John the Baptist) Churchyard.
117	Stratford-on-Avon Cemetery.	81	Barlby (All Saints) Churchyard.
129	Wellesbourne (St Peter) Churchyard, Wellesbourne Hastings.	83	Kirk Ella Church Cemetery.
134	Hill (St James the Great) Churchyard.	93	Sigglesthorne (St Laurence) Churchyard.
135	Sutton Coldfield Cemetery.	96	Withernsea Cemetery.
143	Budbrooke (St Michael) Churchyard.	97	Withernsea (St Nicholas) Churchyard.
151	Warwick Cemetery, Budbrooke.	98	York Cemetery.
152	Wasperton (St John the Baptist) Churchyard.	100	Aysgarth (St Andrew) Churchyard, Gould.
		104	Fencote (St Andrew) Churchyard, Kirkby Fleetham.
		106	Thornton Watlass (St Mary) Churchyard.

WILTSHIRE.

1	Amesbury Cemetery.	110	Eryholme (St Mary) Churchyard.
2	Bulford Church Cemetery.	114	Coxwold (St Michael) Churchyard.
3	Durrington Cemetery.	119	Eston Cemetery.
4	Figheldean (St Michael) Churchyard.	123	Huntington (All Saints) Churchyard.
12	Wilsford (St Michael) Churchyard.	126	Guisborough Cemetery.
14	Winterbourne Gunner (St Mary) Churchyard.	127	Marske-in-Cleveland (St Germain) Churchyard.
16	Atworth (St Michael) Churchyard.	138	Finghall (St Andrew) Churchyard.
18	Holt Cemetery.	154	Middlesbrough (Linthorpe) Cemetery.
25	East Tytherton Moravian Burial Ground, Bremhill.	156	North Ormesby (St Joseph's) Roman Catholic Cemetery.
28	Yatesbury (All Saints) Churchyard.	159	Northallerton Cemetery.
29	Chippenham Cemetery.	171	Thornton Dale (All Saints) Churchyard.
56	Devizes Cemetery, Roundway.	172	Coatham (Christ Church) Churchyard.
64	Chisledon Cemetery.	173	Redcar Cemetery.
86	Sopworth (St Mary) Churchyard.	175	Grinton (St Andrew) Churchyard.
100	Melksham Cemetery.	176	Richmond Cemetery.
115	Tidworth Military Cemetery, North Tidworth.	178	Catterick Cemetery.
116	Upavon Cemetery.	181	Hipswell (St John) Churchyard.
121	Chilton Foliat (St Mary) Churchyard.	183	Saltburn-by-the-Sea Cemetery.
128	East Harnham (All Saints) Churchyard.	185	Scarborough Cemetery.
129	Salisbury (London Road) Cemetery.	186	Brompton (All Saints) Churchyard.
142	Swindon (Radnor Street) Cemetery.	192	Seamer (St Martin) Churchyard.
145	Chicklade (All Saints) Churchyard.	194	Boosbeck (St Aidan) Churchyard.
153	Swallowcliffe (St Peter) Churchyard.	195	Brotton Church Cemetery.
157	Bishopstrow (St Aldhelm) Churchyard.	208	Kirk Leavington (St Martin) Churchyard.
167	Sutton Veny (St John) Churchyard.	222	Whitby Cemetery.
176	Keevil (St Leonard) Churchyard.	228	Lythe (St Oswald) Churchyard.
179	Wilton Cemetery.	230	Bishopthorpe (St Andrew) Churchyard.
180	Barford St Martin Cemetery.	244	Goole Cemetery.
186	Burcombe (St John the Baptist) Churchyard, Burcombe Without.	245	Acomb (St Stephen) Churchyard.
194	Salisbury (Devizes Road) Cemetery, Bemerton.	249	Little Ouseburn (Holy Trinity) Churchyard.
		250	Moor Monkton (All Saints) Churchyard.
		253	Guiseley Primitive Methodist Chapelyard.
		256	Harrowgate (Grove Road) Cemetery.
		264	Skelbrooke (St Michael) Churchyard.

YORKSHIRE.

1	Hull (Hedon Road) Cemetery.	267	Horsforth Cemetery.

274	Knaresborough Cemetery.
275	Knottingley Cemetery.
276	Normanton Cemetery.
283	Pontefract Cemetery.
292	Rawdon (St Peter) Churchyard.
294	Ripon Cemetery.
303	Selby Cemetery.
305	Acaster Selby (St John) Churchyard.
308	Healaugh (St John the Baptist) Churchyard.
311	Kirkby Wharfe (St John the Baptist) Churchyard Extension, Kirkby Wharfe and North Milford.
319	Tadcaster Cemetery, Tadcaster West.
321	Sandal Magna (St Helen) Churchyard.
323	Wakefield Cemetery.
328	Wath-upon-Dearne Cemetery.
335	Spofforth (All Saints) Churchyard, Spofforth-with-Stockeld.
338	Wetherby Cemetery.
344	Calverley (St Wilfred) Churchyard.
346	Farsley (St John) Churchyard.
354	Beeston Burial Ground.
357	Chapel Allerton (St Matthew) Old Churchyard.
361	Lawnswood Cemetery.
362	Leeds (Burmantofts) Cemetery.
363	Leeds (Gelderd Road) English Hebrew Cemetery.
368	Leeds (Hunslet Old) Cemetery.
372	Meanwood (Holy Trinity) Churchyard.
373	Moor Allerton (St John) Churchyard.
375	Roundhay (St John) Churchyard.
381	Methley (St Oswald) Churchyard.
383	Pudsey Cemetery.
388	Pool (St Wilfrid) Churchyard.
396	Bingley Cemetery.
406	Bradford (Bowling) Cemetery.
408	Bradford (Scholemoor) Cemetery.
410	Bradford (Undercliffe) Cemetery.
411	Buttershaw (St Paul) Churchyard.
417	Idle (Holy Trinity) Churchyard.
418	Idle Upper Chapel (Congregational) Cemetery.
425	Wibsey (Holy Trinity) Churchyard.
428	Burley-in-Wharfedale Church Cemetery.
436	Haworth (St Michael) Churchyard.
438	Ilkley Cemetery.
439	Keighley (Utley) Cemetery.
447	Otley, Newall-with-Clifton and Lindley Cemetery.
448	Oxenhope Cemetery.
462	Kirkby Malham (St Michael) Churchyard.
467	Shelf Wesleyan Chapelyard.
468	Shipley (Hirst Wood) Church Burial Ground.
469	Shipley (Nab Wood) Cemetery.
474	Addingham (St Peter) Churchyard.
475	Bolton Abbey (SS Mary and Cuthbert) Churchyard.
481	Gargrave (St Andrew) Churchyard.
482	Kettlewell (St Mary) Churchyard, Kettlewell-with-Starbotton.
483	Kildwick (St Andrew) Churchyard.
485	Rylstone (St Peter) Churchyard.
487	Thornton-in-Craven (St Oswald) Churchyard, Thornton.
500	Doncaster Cemetery.
501	Doncaster (Christ Church) Churchyard.
504	Campsall Old Cemetery.
528	Rotherham (Masbrough) Cemetery.
529	Rotherham (Moorgate) Cemetery.
537	Thrybergh (St Leonard) Old Cemetery.
542	Ecclesall (All Saints) Churchyard.
543	Ecclesall (All Saints) Churchyard.
546	Sheffield (Abbey Lane) Cemetery.
547	Sheffield (Burngreave) Cemetery.
548	Sheffield (City Road) Cemetery.
551	Sheffield General Cemetery.
557	Sheffield (St Michael's) Roman Catholic Cemetery.
561	Wadsley Churchyard.
569	Tickhill (St Mary) Churchyard.
570	Altofts Cemetery.
574	Ardsley (Christ Church) Churchyard.
575	Barnsley Cemetery.
583	Brighouse Cemetery.
588	Dewsbury Cemetery.
590	Dewsbury Moor (St John) Churchyard.
591	Lower Whitley (SS Mary and Michael) Churchyard.
595	Drighlington (St Paul) Churchyard.
597	Elland-cum-Greetland Cemetery.
606	Halifax (Lister Lane) Cemetery.
607	Halifax (Stoney Royd) Cemetery.
612	King Cross Wesleyan Chapelyard.
613	Luddenden Cemetery.
619	Salterhebble (All Saints) Churchyard.
620	Warley Congregational Cemetery.
631	Holmfirth Wesleyan Burial Ground.
635	Brockholes (St George) Churchyard.
639	Armitage Bridge (St Paul) Churchyard.
642	Huddersfield (Almondbury) Cemetery.
643	Huddersfield (Edgerton) Cemetery.
644	Huddersfield (Lockwood) Cemetery.
645	Lindley (St Stephen) Churchyard.
652	Salendine Nook Baptist Chapelyard.
677	Ossett (Holy Trinity) Churchyard.
686	Friezland (Christ Church) Churchyard.
701	Sowerby (St Mary) Churchyard.
705	Cleckheaton (St John) Churchyard.
707	Cleckheaton (Whitechapel Lane) Cemetery.
715	Outland (Bethel) United Methodist Chapelyard.
717	Stainland (St Andrew) Churchyard.
719	Outwood Cemetery.
730	Shore General Baptist Chapelyard.
737	Heptonstall Slack Baptist Cemetery.
738	Wadsworth (Wainsgate) Baptist Chapelyard.
740	Bradfield (St Nicholas) Churchyard.

Appendix 2

This is a list of abreviations used in the list of officers. The majority not mentioned as they are self evident. Others are a combination of the abreviations listed below.

ACapt,ALt,etc	Acting Captain,Acting Lieutenant,etc
A/A Bde	Anti Aircraft Brigade
acc	Accidentally
AICC	Australian Imp. Camel Corps
AIR	Auckland Infantry Regt
AMR	Auckland Mounted Rifles
Att	Attached
Aust	Australian/Australia
Bde	Brigade
Bn	Battalion
Can	Canadian/Canada
CIR	Canterbury Infantry Regt
CMR (if NZ)	Canterbury Mounted Rifles
CMR (if Can)	Canadian Mounted Rifles
Cmdg	Commanding
Cps	Corps
CR	Cemetery Register
Ded	Died
Dow	Died of Wounds
Drd	Drowned
Ex	Formerly
FGH	Fort Gary Horse
HQ	Headquarters
kia	Killed in action
kld	Killed
MID	Mentioned in Despatches
MR	Memorial Register
NZ	New Zealand
OIR	Otago Infantry Regt
OMR	Otago Mounted Rifles
PPCLI	Princess Patrica's Can. Light Inf.
RAF	Royal Air Force
Res	Reserve
RoO	Reserve of Officers
SA	South African/South Africa
Sqdn or Sqn	Squadron
TCapt,TLt,etc	Temporary Captain,Temporary Lieutenant,Etc
TMB	Trench Mortar Battery
WIR	Wellington Infantry Regt
WMR	Wellington Mountrd Rifles